Insiders' Guide®

to

Portland, Oregon

Help Us Keep This Guide Up to Date

Every effort has been made by the authors and editors to make this guide as accurate and useful as possible. However, many things can change after a guide is published—establishments close, phone numbers change, hiking trails are rerouted, facilities come under new management, etc.

We would love to hear from you concerning your experiences with this guide and how you feel it could be improved and be kept up to date. While we may not be able to respond to all comments and suggestions, we'll take them to heart and we'll also make certain to share them with the author. Please send your comments and suggestions to the following address:

The Globe Pequot Press
Reader Response/Editorial Department
P. O. Box 480
Guilford, CT 06437

Or you may e-mail us at:

editorial@globe-pequot.com

Thanks for your input, and happy travels!

Insiders' Guide® Series

Insiders' Guide®
to Portland, Oregon

Including the Metro Area and Vancouver, Washington

Second Edition

By Dave Johnson and Rachel Dresbeck

Guilford, Connecticut
An imprint of The Globe Pequot Press

The prices and rates in this guidebook were confirmed at press time. We recommend, however, that you call establishments before traveling to obtain current information.

Cover photos: front: courtesy of OMSI; back (from left): storefront, Rachel Dresbeck; golf course, Ron Thurston; art gallery, courtesy of the Portland Art Museum; pagoda garden, Roger Leudtke; building, Rachel Dresbeck; gyroscope, Dave Johnson.

Maps by Trapper Badovinac

ISSN: 1534-2689
ISBN: 0-7627-1046-2

Manufactured in the United States of America
Second Edition/First Printing

Publications from the Insiders' Guide® series are available at special discounts for bulk purchases for sales promotions, premiums, or fund-raisings. Special editions, including personalized covers, can be created in large quantities for special needs. For more information, please contact The Globe Pequot Press at (800) 962-0973.

Contents

Directory of Maps

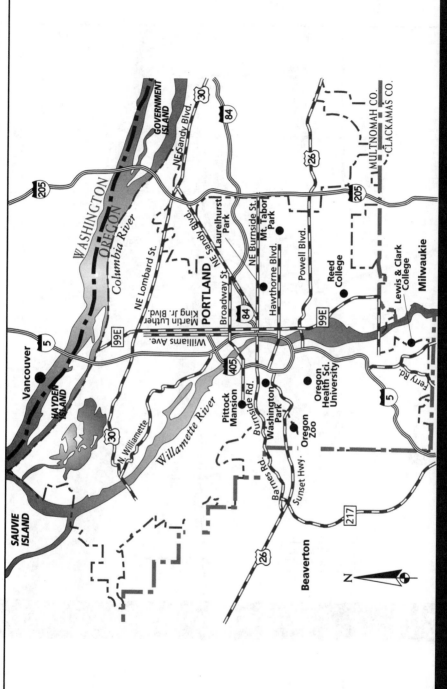

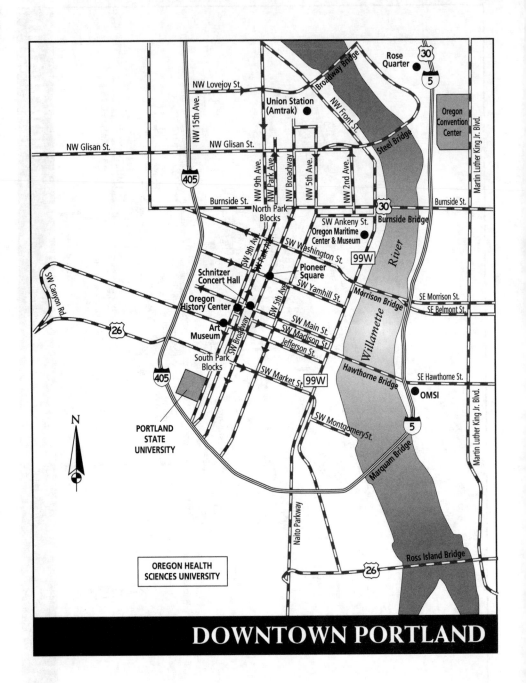

DOWNTOWN PORTLAND

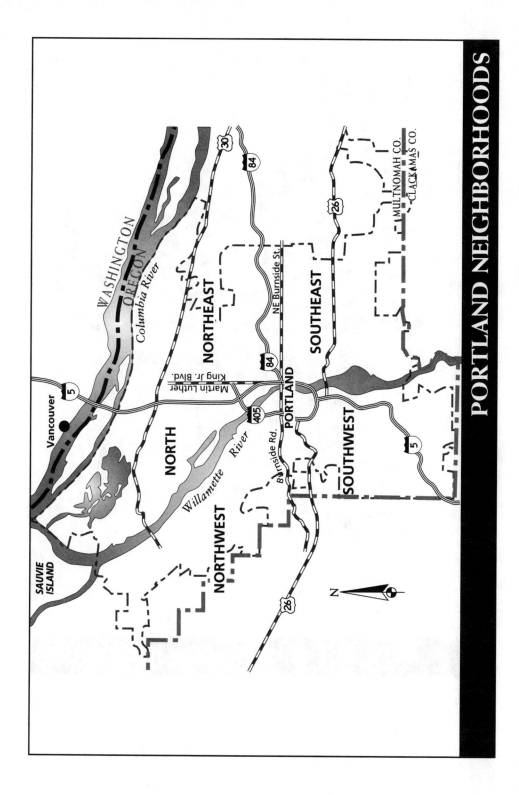

PORTLAND NEIGHBORHOODS

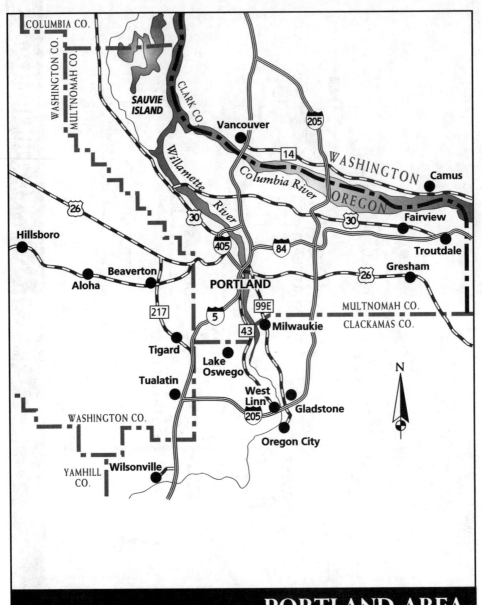

PORTLAND AREA

Acknowledgments

Rachel Dresbeck

Portland is a city of neighborhoods, so first I would like to thank my neighbors for their insight and sustenance, as well as their photos. The Banchero, Frost, and Forrest families deserve special mention for their hospitality and witticisms. Mary Allison was especially generous, and Malu Wilkinson was especially wise. In addition to these lovely people, I would also like to thank my other "neighbors" throughout the city, including Cynthia and David Dixon, Cara and Houston Bolles, Linda Colwell and Sam Averett, Shari Sirkin, Anne Williams, Mary Johnson, Sharon Lewis, Annabelle Domenighini, Laurie Lopez, Heidi Carr, Patty Romaine-Moody, Ellen McFarland, and Patricia Taylor. Each one of these persons has made an immeasurable contribution to the animus of this book.

Many other people throughout Portland and beyond contributed to my research, and I deeply appreciate their willingness to share information and advice. Thanks especially to Ron Thurston, Katherine Hart, and Greg Higgins for being good sports. I would also like to thank my editors, Erin Turner and Erika Serviss, for their guidance.

Thanks to Monna Powers for keeping me and my house together. As always, my husband Tom and my daughters Flannery and Cleo demonstrated uncomplaining patience as I researched and wrote this book, and I am deeply grateful for their company. My brother Brian introduced me to the true Portland many years ago, and it is to him that I dedicate this book.

Dave Johnson

If I ever had any doubts about the oft-celebrated friendliness here in Portland, they were quickly dissipated when I started working on the Insiders' Guide. Whenever I made a phone call or visit to a bed and breakfast, nightclub, airfield, ski lodge, swimming pool, or public school, I had a pleasant time talking to a courteous, helpful, cheerful Portlander. That alone made writing my portion of this book much easier. Particular thanks should go to the librarians at the Multnomah County Library for directing me toward obscure facts, the staff at the Oregon Department of Highways for their help with the historic Columbia Gorge Highway, and Portland Parks and Recreation for not responding, "It's that guy again!"

Also included on my list of thanks should be Stewart Warren, author of *The Oregon Handbook*, whose collegial generosity is greatly appreciated. Also, Ted Brewer and Nancy Tannler, publishers of *The Southeast Examiner*, for giving me slack when it came to newspaper deadlines and for their photos of the Columbia Gorge and Mount Hood. Then there's John Rumler, my friend who invited me to tackle the task of co-authoring the guidebook with him. I remember when we used to sit on a picnic table in one of Portland's neighborhood parks and talk about our craft and visions for the future. Hardly did we realize that we would be yoked together like two journalistic oxen for all the months it has taken to assemble the information in this guide. It's been fun working with Rachel.

Lastly, my thanks to my wife, Josephine Bridges, who helped gather data as well as offering encouragement during those days when it was hard to start that familiar engine of completion.

In Portland, the fire department will still come to your block party. CREDIT: CHRIS FROST

How to Use This Book

For a big city, Portland is small. For a city that has contributed much to cyberspace, Portland is concerned with human space. It is the home of groundbreaking biomedical research, one of the largest and best independent bookstores in the world, important museums, theaters, and colleges, world-class firms for animation, advertising, and athletic wear. Yet it is also renowned for its amiable, everyday civility, for its sidewalk cafes, transportation system, charming neighborhoods, and strong ethic of planning. The parks contain more forest than any city in the nation. People ride their bikes or walk to work. The library serves coffee. Portland is a city where the fire department will still come to your block party.

This lovely mixture of nature and culture, of sophistication and friendliness, draws people from all over the world to visit, and sometimes when they have visited, they want to stay. The *Insiders' Guide to Portland* is designed to allow you to make the best use of your time here, however long it is. Thus, this book is not meant for display on your coffee table at home. Think of it as a workbook. Pack it in your carry-on bag, keep it in your glove compartment, use your highlighter, annotate it, fold the corners of the pages—use it well and often.

Our guide is organized into thematic chapters that cover everything from accommodations to well-being, both physical and spiritual. The internal organization of chapters will vary depending on their content. For example, the Annual Events chapter is sorted chronologically, but the Recreation chapter is set up alphabetically by topic. Many chapters, such as Accommodations, Restaurants, or Attractions may be additionally organized into geographic areas for easier navigation. Portland is divided into eastern and western halves by the Willamette River. It is further divided by Burnside Street, which runs east and west, into four quadrants: Southwest, Northwest, Southeast, and Northeast. A fifth "quadrant," North Portland, the portion west of Williams Avenue, extends from the Broadway Bridge to the Columbia River; however, for the purposes of this book, listings in North Portland and Northeast Portland have been kept together. Vancouver, which is immediately north of Portland just across the Columbia River in the state of Washington, is also mentioned frequently in our book, as are the towns that surround the city. Thus you will also find sections for Vancouver and for Outlying Areas, for a total of six basic geographical divisions.

The first chapters are designed to help you orient yourself to the Portland Metro area by giving you information about transportation and history. The next several chapters concern the exigencies of daily living—where to eat and sleep. Then we devote a large number of chapters to various forms of recreation; these range from telling you how to find a nearby brewpub, antique shop, or climbing park to securing Blazers tickets. We also include a chapter on Daytrips, should you want to go exploring the innumerable attractions of the region beyond the city limits. And after exploring all that the region has to offer, many people who visit Portland find they would like to live here. The final seven chapters are devoted to the concerns of potential and actual relocaters, from finding a house and school to figuring out which newspapers to read. Within all chapters, you will find frequent cross-references, and even, for the sake of convenience, some cross-listings.

Portland is a big city but it's accessible via all modes of transportation. CREDIT: COURTESY OF THE BICYCLE TRANSPORTATION ALLIANCE

A few basic maps are included in the guide, but you may also want to purchase a more detailed map of the city and surrounding areas in order to prevent those interesting discussions between driver and navigator about which way to turn.

The Greater Portland Metro area comprises Multnomah, Washington, and Clackamas Counties. You won't notice when you cross from one county into another, but you will need to know which county you are dealing with for the sake of real estate, schools, and government. In some critical chapters, then, we will point out these distinctions.

Area Codes and Ten-Digit Dialing

Due to a proliferation of telephone numbers, Portland, like most metropolitan areas, has added area codes in the past couple of years. The area codes that serve Portland are (503) and (971). These are also codes for Salem and northern coastal towns. Area code (541) will give you access to southern, central, and eastern Oregon, including the central and southern coasts. Area code (360) serves Vancouver, Washington, and other parts of Clark County, which are considered part of the Portland Metro area. When you use the telephone, you will need to dial the area code first—all ten digits. (It won't be a long-distance call unless you dial a "1" first, which would make eleven digits.) To make everything simple, we have included area codes with all phone numbers.

Looking Ahead

Don't just take our word for it: use this guide to help you explore for yourself the charms of Portland. Our dynamic city is always changing, adding new attractions and business, and closing others down. You may discover some of these changes in your own travels. Let us know about those that ought to be reported in future editions. If, in your journey to becoming an Insider, you find you have something to tell us, please write to us in care of the Insiders' Guides, P. O. Box 480, Guilford, Connecticut 06437-0480, or visit us on-line at www.insiders.com.

Insiders' Tip

Planning to start a business in Oregon and need to know about licensing? Want to find out the average price for an apartment rental in Clackamas? Want information on state parks and campgrounds? Go to Oregon On Line, the Web site for the state of Oregon, and an exhaustive resource for information on all things Oregon. You can find it at www.state.or.us/.

Area Overview

Portland, Oregon's largest city, sits tucked beneath a forested ridge near the banks of the Willamette River a few miles from its confluence with the Columbia River. The hub of a metropolitan area, it's home to one and 1.5 million Oregonians and Washingtonians.

As its name implies, Portland is a port city connecting with the Pacific via 110 miles of the Columbia River. Its busy shipping schedule makes it the third leading commercial maritime center on the West Coast. A significant portion of its freight is eastern Oregon grain, barged down the Columbia, loaded into huge grain elevators, and poured into freighters heading for Asia. On the receiving end, Portland is the third largest West Coast port for ships bringing Japanese cars into the United States.

Portland's role as a shipping city is an old one. From its earliest days, Portland was filling the mercantile needs of homesteaders in the fertile Willamette Valley and miners in the gold-laced hills of southern Oregon. In fact, this pioneer municipality played that role so successfully that it soon was doubling and tripling in size. Trees were felled everywhere to build homes and businesses in the expanding burg originally called Stumptown, a name derived from the hundreds of fir stumps left in its streets by hasty builders. As a safety measure, city officials painted them white for wagoneers out after dark.

The city continued to grow, changing its name to Portland with the toss of a coin in 1845 (see History). Designated as the terminus of the Northern Pacific Railroad in 1883, the thriving port began to play a major role in the shipment of lumber, produce, and livestock from the Pacific Northwest to San Francisco and other West Coast ports as well as eastern cities. But it was the Lewis and Clark Centennial Exposition held in 1905 that truly put the town on the map. After the commercial success and national notoriety of the exposition, Portland, with a population of 90,000, became a true commercial hub.

During the Victorian era, Portland strove for a genteel façade as it shifted from rowdy pioneer village to civilized metropolis. It never projected a glamorous presence, but it did achieve a more refined image than other new cities. As local historian Terence O'Donnell quipped, "San Francisco grew up as the debutante, Seattle the tart, and Portland the spinster." Later on, Portland would attain a different sort of image. During World War I Portland became a shipbuilding center, helping the war effort by building ships for the navy. During World War II, small freighters called Liberty Ships, which carried troops and supplies across sub-infested waters, were made and launched here in Portland.

After the world wars, Portland thrived, but by the late '60s the city was faced with serious economic problems. Due to environmental concerns and international competition, its economy, dependent on timber and Pacific fisheries, spiraled downward. The decline of these two major industries affected secondary service and retail businesses. But the Portland spirit rose to the challenge: In 1973, the city council and planners came up with the Downtown Plan, a vision that reinvigorated local retail, housing, entertainment, and government. A westside freeway was torn down and redirected around town and the Tom McCall Waterfront Park, named after a popular Oregon governor, was built along the edge of the Willamette River. Other major changes that dynamically rearranged Portland were a downtown transit mall along 5th and 6th Streets, light rail connecting to the outer Eastside and Pioneer Square, and a central open space for community events.

When the economy bounced back, suburban sprawl ensued. So an urban-growth boundary was designed as an outer edge for housing developments within the city limits of Portland and its neighboring towns. This strategy, combined with tax breaks and grants for low-income housing, encouraged contractors to "in-fill" within the growth boundary. It worked! Instead of a decaying downtown district surrounded by precious farmland-turned-suburbs, Portland proper became a vibrant city filled with high-density vertical shops, apartments, and other mercantile and living spaces.

In the 1980s and '90s, the Portland economy got another big boost with the sprouting of the Silicon Forest. Attracted by cheap electricity generated by dams on the Columbia River, lots of clean water, and tax incentives offered by city and county governments, chip makers flocked to the area. Portland soon became the leading city in the world for the manufacture of silicon wafer chips. By 1995, almost a third of U.S. high-tech investment was pouring into Portland's cyber-scene. According to recent statistics, the Portland-Vancouver metropolitan area has five times the concentration of chip companies and suppliers as the national average.

By then, Nike was also making an impact on the local economy with its global market for footgear and other athletic apparel. It is estimated that this swooshy outfit a few miles southwest of Portland currently brings in $16 billion a year.

But there is more to living in a city than making a living. Also known as the "City of Roses," (a more gentle appellation than "Stumptown"), our town celebrates a terrific climate in which to grow these lovely flowers, which are celebrated each June with a party called the Rose Festival, a splendiferous blowout that includes three parades, a carnival, a crowning of a queen, and a visit from a dozen ships from the U.S. Navy, U.S. Coast Guard, and the Canadian Navy and Coast Guard. As most sailors will agree, the festival days make Portland the best liberty town in the world.

Part of what makes those roses grow, of course, is rain. While Portland has eighty-two days per year when the sky is blue and the sun is shining, it also has, on the average, eighty-two partly cloudy days and 220 cloudy days per year, with 165 of those coming with at least some precipitation. Thus, we have another moniker for Portland: Puddletown. The designation for the nearby international airport, PDX, is yet another nickname. But call it what you may, this vest-pocket metropolis has a solid reputation as a "liveable community," to use a buzzword snatched by campaigning national politicians. *Money Magazine* agreed, labeling it in 2000 as the most liveable city in the United States. It is also a "city that works" as proudly proclaimed on Portland public-works vehicles.

Insiders' Tip

Wondering where to park your car without losing your shirt, or how to get to a certain restaurant? If you're downtown, and spot a pair of friendly Portlanders in Kelly green jackets, the answers may be near. The Association for Portland Progress trains "Portland Guides" to answer these questions and more. If you don't spot these helpers you can also just call (503) 224-8684.

There are a few planned communities mostly in Washington County to the south-west of town, that could be inserted anywhere in the U.S.A., but there are also a lively handful of towns with their own personalities surrounding Portland. They include Troutdale, Fairview, Gresham, Oregon City, and Milwaukie and Wilsonville on the east side of the Willamette; Lake Oswego, Tigard, Beaverton, Tualatin, West Linn, and Hills-boro on the west. And just across the Columbia, the booming town of Vancouver, fourth-largest city in Washington, is also part of the Portland Metro region.

So what's going on in this population node in the Pacific Northwest, a low-key region known to most Americans for its trees and fish, wild-eyed radicals, and vociferous gree-nies? The answer is simply that those who live here fiercely defend their quality of life. Portland's charmingly eclectic, European-style skyline and its numerous greenways sug-gest that this laid-back community values art and nature along with commerce. Also, it has more movie theaters, restaurants, microbreweries, and bookstores per capita than any other U.S. city.

Despite the Greater Portland area's population boom and its current economic pros-perity, Portlanders are still continuing with the 1973 plan mentioned above. The result is a revitalized downtown-in-progress, with building cranes standing about like gigantic erector sets. There are dozens of public fountains, and a scattering of public art, from large abstract sculpture to cavorting brass ducks, bears, and beavers. The Westside MAX lightrail continuing from Gresham through downtown to Hillsboro has whimsical, award-winning sculptures and murals. The queen of all this public art is a hammered-copper sculpture, *Portlandia*, by Raymond Kaskey. Second in size to the nation's other hammered-copper damsel, the Statue of Liberty, it looms above the entrance of the Port-land Building, a quirky candy box filled with white-collar city workers at Southwest Fifth and Main Streets. These two works of art—civic architecture and statue—seem to meld together to personify the Portland spirit.

Another element that defines the essence of Portland is the 40-mile Willamette River Greenway, a network of pedestrian and bike trails on both sides of the Willamette that will eventually stretch into a 140-mile-long system connecting thirty parks. Currently it is a paved trail that can take you from the Oregon Museum of Science and Industry on the East Side, across the Burnside Bridge to the industrial northwest, and then south through Tom McCall Park to Willamette Park off Macadam Avenue. The new Eastside Esplande runs from the steel bridge south to the Hawthorne Bridge.

And then there are the wonders of nature surrounding the city: the stunningly scenic Columbia Gorge; Mount Hood, one of the crown jewels of the Oregon Cascades; and the North Coast, with beaches, jutting capes, and art colonies. (Read more about these in our Daytrips chapter.) And Portland's big sister, Seattle, is just a few miles farther, 173 miles to the north.

Besides these well-known places within easy reach of Portland there are hundreds of smaller ones. The woods and the rivers beckon Portlanders, who enjoy the out-of-doors. We like to go camping, hiking, fishing, skiing, and rafting and kayaking down white-water rapids or canoeing more tranquil waters. Which is not to say that we don't appre-ciate city life with all its amenities. One of the most enjoyable examples of the new Portland are five modern streetcars and two vintage trolleys built in the Czech Republic. This mode of genteel transportation, reminiscent of San Francisco, runs from Portland State University in Southwest downtown, through the Pearl District to 23rd Avenue in the Northwest, and back to PSU. Hop on board! Or to feel like a real Portlander while commuting to your job by streetcar, auto, foot, or MAX, stop by a coffeehouse for a dou-ble latte, and after work enjoy a few microbrews.

The walkway along Tom McCall Waterfront Park will lead you to the Portland, *a floating maritime history museum.* CREDIT: DAVID JOHNSON

Lest you get the idea we're all alike, we have to admit to differences of style and opinion; we aren't a batch of clones with a standardized "Portland" look or style. A way to understand our town's diversity, as well as our shared world view, is to consider the places that together form the city. With the Willamette River as a vertical boundary and Burnside Street as the horizontal line, the city is quartered like a compass, with the Northwest portion being the smallest, since the river veers west. The remaining northern portion is usually called North and Northeast, though here we'll combine the two. To the south of Burnside Street are the roughly equal Southeast and Southwest portions of the city. We'll briefly examine these divisions, starting with the latter, and also take a brief look at other parts of the complete Portland Metro area: Vancouver and Outlying Areas. (And if you'd like more information than you find here, turn to our Neighborhoods and Real Estate chapter.)

Southwest Portland

This quadrant encompasses downtown Portland and the west hills that rise above the business district. The result is an urban village cradled by a friendly wilderness. A walk about this section is not as strenuous or overwhelming as hiking along those lengthy blocks in Manhattan, Chicago, or other major cities. Rather, this smaller metropolis has short blocks, platted in the nineteenth century to contain lots of little stores, and lots of cross-streets, thus limiting the size and height of new construction.

Built on the hills above downtown are affluent neighborhoods with lovely homes lining winding hillside streets. Originally dubbed "Nob Hill" on both sloping sides of

Burnside, its southwestern residential zone is called the "West End." Down on the plains of the Willamette River, homes still standing are more modest.

A good place to start a tour of the Southwest is Pioneer Square, the town's front porch, which is bordered by Yamhill Street, Morrison Street, 6th Avenue, and Broadway Street. This post-modern plaza is populated with every variety of city folk from sidewalk preachers to hacky-sack kickers to lunch munchers snatching a burrito or chicken sandwich from nearby fast-food stands.

Depending on the time of year, it's also the site of sandcastle contests, winter beer-tasting galas, flower gardens, a huge Christmas tree, and a summer barbecue with free chili and hot dogs. Pioneer Square is also a mecca for information. Located here is Powell's Travel Store, the Tri-Met bus information and tickets office, and the POVA Information Center. Here, Portland Oregon Visitor Information offers info and tickets to special events to Portland's 125,000 annual visitors.

Also located in the Southwest is Tom McCall Waterfront Park. Along this esplanade are the Salmon Springs Fountain, children's play areas, a monument to the Battleship Oregon, and a sculpture garden dedicated to the World War II relocation trauma of Oregon's Japanese-American community (see Parks). You can also get a riverside view of the city's eight bridges.

If you show up on the right day you can peruse hundreds of craft and food booths at another neighborhood attraction: the Saturday Market, 108 W. Burnside Street. On the western side of the downtown district, Southwest Broadway is our version of the "Great White Way," with cinemas and performing arts centers. The most recent addition to Broadway and the city's upthrusting skyline is the Fox Tower built on the site of the old Fox Theater. The tower has seven cinemas at street level and upper floors of techno-wired office space. A few blocks south is the Oregon Historical Center filled with ongoing exhibits and new shows that combine to tell the story of the state, from ancient epochs to the golden days of the Portland Trailblazers basketball team. Across the shady South Park blocks is the Portland Art Museum with a lovely Monet and other European paintings, an exciting new Native American wing and blockbuster touring exhibits, including historical Russian, Chinese, and Ottoman art.

The Southwest is also home to one of Portland's most famous haunts—Powell's City of Books, 1005 W. Burnside Street, reportedly the largest new-and-used bookshop in the world. Another popular edifice is the recently rehabilitated stadium on the westside at the base of the hills. First called Multnomah Field as a site for carnivals and pageants, it is now PGE Park, home to baseball and soccer teams. Other highlights of Southwest Portland are Washington Park, nestled on the east side of the long ridge called Forest Park, the International Rose Test Gardens, impeccably lovely Japanese Garden, and the Washington Park Zoo.

Northwest Portland

Old Town on the north side of Burnside Street includes Chinatown and the Skidmore District, both recently enhanced by renovated streets, brick sidewalks, and old-fashioned lampposts. Chinatown, with its entrance at 4th Avenue and Burnside Street, is an Asian-American neighborhood with grocery stores, restaurants, and art galleries. This small neighborhood was once home to the West Coast's largest population of Chinese Americans, immigrants who mined for gold here and built the railroad. A Chinese garden at the entrance to the district is one of the few authentic classic gardens in the United States.

Nearby is the Skidmore Historic District, north of W. Burnside Street and between Front and 4th Avenues. Once the hangout of unemployed loggers and sailors, this riverside cluster of streets helped coin the term "Skid Row," borrowed from "Skid Road," a muddy path of logs leading down from the forests to the river. You may still see a few transients and folks down on their luck lining up for a Salvation Army lunch here. But this sad reality aside, Skidmore is worth a visit for its charming old buildings and its colorful history as the riverside district that was once most of what was called Portland.

Heading west and just north of Powell's bookstore and the historic Blitz-Weinhard Brewery currently under renovation as a mini-mall, is the Pearl District. This gem of a neighborhood nestled in the oyster of downtown Portland, was originally an industrial zone. The Pearl is now a thriving arts scene with revamped warehouses morphed into art galleries, artists' lofts, antique stores, and classic furnishings shops. First-Thursday gallery walks turn the neighborhood into one big open house.

The literary scene is also alive and well in this quadrant (and all over town) where cheap rent gives writers a chance to do the "real work." One spot that attracts talent is the Northwest Neighborhood Cultural Center, 1819 N.W. Everett Street, where writers compete in the "Great Northwest Salmon Slam," a variation on the trendy poetry slam.

The Pearl also hosts the Weiden & Kennedy Advertising Agency (they do ads for Nike and Coca-Cola) and Will Vinton and his team of claymation artists (creators of the Singing California Raisins commercial and "P.J.'s" and "Gary and Mike" animated TV shows). Other film, video, mixed-media companies and recording studios dot this art-slanted neighborhood, from which top talent is always emerging (Portland native Matt Groening of *The Simpsons* fame relocated to Southern Cal, but who know what hometown artist will have the next big idea?)

Tucked to the Northeast of the Pearl District is Riverfront, a district still in its formative stage. With a stretch of apartment buildings already along the Willamette, plans call for industrial sections to be replaced with shops, boutiques, restaurants, and other urban attractions.

The Northwest also has another reputation as the place to have fun shopping. West of Pearl and across U.S. Highway 405 is a shopping district nicknamed Trendy-Third. Here, along 21st and 23rd Avenues, you'll find charmingly unique boutiques, antique shops, and bookstores in delightfully renovated Victorians with names like Nostalgic Nomad, Paint the Sky Kites, Why Not, and La Battega di Mamma Ro. The district is also home to some of the city's best restaurants. A popular dessert stop is Papa Haydn's, 701 N.W. 23rd Avenue (see our Restaurants chapter). After the rigors of retail therapy, it's fun to head up to the Pittock Mansion and its forty-six-acre site, 3229 N.W. Pittock Drive to view the city below and take a meander through the French-style château built by a local newspaper mogul.

Southeast Portland

From the funky shops on Foster Road, to stately Reed College, to seven quirky eateries clustered along Clinton Street, the neighborhoods of Southeast Portland offer a wealth of variety. The Hawthorne and nearby Belmont Districts are filled with single-family homes and apartment buildings mixed with a hopping row of earthy shops, music and bookstores, coffeehouses, microbrew pubs, and restaurants geared to every palate. It's a delightful area for shopping and browsing or for lunch, dinner, and weekend brunches. Don't leave town without a visit to the "Hip Strip," a section of Hawthorne Boulevard from 30th to 50th Avenues that's a Pacific Northwest version of Greenwich Village.

Sellwood, a historic district annexed to Portland in 1893, features "Antique Row," more than fifty antique stores tucked into the neighborhood of Victorian homes and turn-of-the-century architecture (see Shopping). The area where Sellwood meets the river, Oaks Bottom, is home to the Oaks Bottom Wildlife Sanctuary (see our Recreation chapter), a refuge for herons, beavers, ducks, and other marsh animals and birds. Here, the neighborhood floats in houseboats along the river's edge. Westmoreland, north of Sellwood, is graced with its share of fine restaurants and unique shops as well one of the city's most beautiful parks, a haven for picnickers, joggers, basketball players, and duck feeders. Across McLoughlin Avenue, Eastmoreland's residential neighborhood is quiet and tranquil, bordered by the public Eastmoreland Golf Course, the resplendently brick-ish campus of Reed College, and Crystal Springs Rhododendron Garden exploding in a riot of color each spring with its seven acres of rhododendrons, azaleas, and hybrids, At the gateway to inner Southeast is the tranquil, historic neighborhood of Brooklyn. Once home to East Coast immigrants working at the nearby rail yard, it is now a pleasant and closed-in sanctuary, away from chain stores and suburban blight.

North/Northeast Portland

The majority of Portland's residents live on the east side of the Willamette River. Beautiful older homes line tree-shaded streets in neighborhoods such as Eastmoreland, Laurelhurst, Irvington, and Alameda. Attractive shopping areas draw people from around the region who come to find specialty clothing, gifts, and home accessories. The popular Lloyd Center is the largest single shopping destination in the area (see Shopping). By light rail, Lloyd Center is just minutes from downtown. Around Lloyd Center, the Northeast Broadway Business District is blossoming and just to the east, the delightful Hollywood District offers a tasty blend of affordable housing and retail businesses and small shops. New businesses, specialty shops, bookstores, and markets have joined the neighborhood and opened their doors all along Northeast Broadway and Weidler Streets, and on many sections of Sandy Boulevard.

Insiders' Tip

When it gets too hot, many Portlanders head for the coast; others just hop in a MAX car and head for the Oregon Zoo. After entering a tunnel, MAX stops deep inside the massive ridge that looms to the west of downtown. Once off the train and in a climate that is always 50 degrees Fahrenheit, you descend even deeper (260 feet) to a station that is the farthest underground station in North America. Then you take an elevator up to ground level and the zoo. But if you want to stick around in the station, you can enjoy looking at core sample timelines, and other delightfully presented art and information about the geology, botany, and biology of the ridge.

Portland's bustling Convention District lies between the Lloyd District and the river, uniting the form and function of a huge meeting center with true artistic flair. The 150-foot high twin spires stamp the center's bold profile on the city's distinctive skyline. The center's walls, lamps, and tiles display whimsical and stunning artistic detail. Fascinating plaques displayed in the lobby carry insightful quotes about Oregon. A Chinese dragon boat is suspended at the airy base of the center's south spire, while a dramatic bronze pendulum sways below the north spire. Large murals by Lucinda Parker and Bill Hoppe celebrate Oregon's natural bounty and, outside, temple bells from Portland's sister cities Sapporo, Japan, and Ulsan, South Korea, offer friendly greetings to visitors. Light rail stops outside the center's north entrance and also serves the adjacent Rose Quarter, a forty-three-acre complex, featuring the Memorial Coliseum arena, the Rose Garden arena, One Center Court entertainment complex, and four parking garages. The Rose Quarter hosts a variety of sports events, including those of the Portland Trailblazers, the Portland Fire, the Portland Winter Hawks, and college basketball and indoor-soccer teams (for more on these, see Spectator Sports). The arenas are also booked with rodeos, circuses, concerts, ice shows, gymnastic events, and they are linked to the nearby Convention Center to accommodate the numerous trade shows and conventions that Portland hosts. Other neighborhoods further north, such as Hayden Island, St. Johns, and Kenton, offer their own distinctive charms. These areas, rich in history and blessed with many well-maintained parks and green spaces, hold some of the city's best-kept secrets. Many of the city's treasures are off this beaten path.

Vancouver

Located across the Columbia River from Portland via Interstate 5 or the Interstate 205 bridge, Vancouver is one of Washington's fastest growing communities with a population of 132,000. This richly historic city, named after British explorer George Vancouver, has fifty-five parks and playgrounds inside city limits, the Columbia Way Promenade stretching for over a mile along the river's edge, the Burnt Bridge Creek Greenway, and Discovery Trail. Vancouver is both a modern metropolis and a natural setting for the scenic Pacific Northwest outdoors.

But it's the history of this settlement that really puts it on the map. Once the Northwestern headquarters for the Hudson's Bay Company and the oldest settlement in the region, Fort Vancouver—now just Vancouver—was the center of all fur trading in the West. After the United States claimed the Pacific Northwest, the fort at Vancouver became a barracks for U.S. soldiers including Generals Ulysses Grant, Philip Sheridan, and most recently, George Marshall. In 1996, Congress passed the Vancouver National Historic Reserve, which established a partnership for the management of historic sites at Fort Vancouver, Columbia Park, and Pearson Field where the Russian transpolar flight set down in 1947.

Vancouver is currently working to revitalize a downtown hit hard by suburban flight. Plans are in the works to build a special events center downtown to hold concerts, conferences, and other major events. Meanwhile, Vancouver is known for tossing parties. Its biggest bash is held on the Fourth of July when it stages the largest fireworks show west of the Mississippi. Other parties include Fort Vancouver Days, a hot-air balloon festival, the Sturgeon Festival celebrating those huge prehistoric fish still cruising in the Columbia, and the Buffalo Soldiers Reunion Parade. The last event celebrates those African American soldiers who served in the U.S. Army Cavalry and were dubbed Buffalo Soldiers by Native Americans impressed with their prowess on the battlefield. Admittedly in the cultural and economic shadow of the big town across the river, Vancouver is reinventing itself as a modern metropolis proud of its vivid heritage.

Outlying Areas

Beaverton

Beaverton, just seven miles southwest of downtown Portland, has a population of 68,000. With a few cybernetic campuses producing electronic and computer-based products, a charming little downtown area, a grid of strip malls, and lots of planned communities, Beaverton is blossoming into a healthy place to live and raise kids. It has 25 miles of bike paths and two of the nation's top-rated golf courses—Pumpkin Ridge and the Reserve (see our Golf chapter). Every year, the town shares its appetite with visitors at the "Taste of Beaverton," a weekend festival with food booths and lots of music (see our Festivals and Annual Events chapter). Keep an eye out for the brick watchtower.

Fairview

Fairview, a small town of 6,000, is located 8 miles from Portland on Interstate 84. Inside its modest borders is Blue Lake (see our chapter on Recreation), a popular recreational spot. Long a shopping center for workers at nearby mills and along the docks of the Columbia River, Fairview is also home to the Columbia Gorge Factory Stores with more than forty manufacturer's outlets (see our Shopping chapter) and of Edgefield, a cheerfully eccentric inn, restaurant, and movie theater (see our Bed and Breakfast Inns and Attractions) that was once the county poor house. This McMenamin brothers' hotspot is located between Fairview and Troutdale, both havens for those who want to get away from the big city.

Gladstone

Across the Clackamas River from Oregon City, Gladstone is a stubbornly independent little burg of 12,000, just 12 miles from Portland. Definitely a country town, it's sited just north of the confluence of the Willamette and Clackamas Rivers. There is a swimming and fishing spot called High Rocks nearby, 2 miles of frontage along the Willamette, which includes a boat launch for fisherfolk at the Meldrum Park Recreational Area.

Founded in 1911, Gladstone became nationally known as the site of one of the largest Chautauqua Centers in the country. Chautauqua festivals, popular events that reached their highpoint at the turn of the century, featured singers, storytellers, musicians, and philosophers who entertained audiences under huge tents pitched in broad meadows. Now a sleepy village, Gladstone is more known as auto row where local automobile dealers compete for consumer attention with a barrage of their photos along McLaughlin Boulevard.

Gresham

A bustling town at the eastern terminus of the MAX light rail line, Gresham is changing from a farm town into one of Portland's fastest growing communities. Recently, a new city hall, conference center, and plaza were built at the last light rail station as part of a downtown plan to reinvigorate the city. Gresham is known for the Mount Hood Jazz and Blues Festivals produced by Mount Hood Community College, located in Gresham (see our Festivals and Annual Events Chapter).

Hillsboro

Hillsboro, 18 miles from Portland, is a classic small American city with a population of 70,000. Besides being home to Nike, it's also the state's ground zero for computer chip and other electronic-product design and manufacturing. In addition, it is also the western terminus of the MAX light rail line and the shopping center for migrant and well-established workers who toil in the fields west of town. Just off U.S. Highway 26 is the

A pair of brass otters cavort in public at a water tank/sculpture in downtown Portland. CREDIT: DAVID JOHNSON

Hillsboro Airport, a busy facility serving the Silicon Forest execs. Hillsboro is also the site of the Rose Festival Air Show.

Lake Oswego

Nestled against a natural lake with a population of 35,000, the prim city of Lake Oswego is eight miles from Portland. It was once the living quarters for workers at a flourmill down by the Willamette River. Now it's a tidy little town with upscale shops and restaurants and expensive homes circling the lake and set along the slopes above it. A city trail system inviting hikers and bikers to meander about has made Lake Oswego a popular place with the outdoor crowd.

Milwaukie

No, it's not the town made famous by beer, but instead it's the place where the Bing cherry was developed. Seems the city fathers and mothers spelled it differently than the larger Wisconsin burg so folks wouldn't be confused. Located on the east bank of the Willamette across from Lake Oswego, it was once a farming community and now welcomes shoppers from around the metro area who flock to the adjacent Clackamas Town Center, one of the largest malls in the country. In mid-June, Milwaukie tosses a bash called Festival Daze with lots of festivities, including a parade.

Oregon City

The oldest city in Oregon, this bustling paper mill town of 20,000 just downstream from Willamette Falls and 15 miles from Portland, is also home to the End of the Oregon Trail Interpretive Center (see our Close-up in the History chapter). It was here at Oregon City that thousands of pioneers traveled to get a new start in life in the fertile Willamette Valley. This historic town is also where Dr. John McLoughlin, the famous chief of Hudson's Bay Company's Fort Vancouver, retired after many years of service. And even earlier, it was a gathering spot for Native Americans who used nearby Willamette Falls to fish for salmon spawning up the river. Archeological evidence suggests that the Clackamas tribe lived here since 500 B.C. Visitors to Oregon City also enjoy using the Municipal Elevator, which ascends to the bluff above the river. Located at 300 Seventh Street, it is the only municipal elevator in North America.

Insiders' Tip

If you'd like to spend the day exploring Portland without the hassle of driving, try taking the bus. You can buy an all-day pass for $3.50 at the Tri-Met Office in Pioneer Square, on Broadway between Morrison Street and Yamhill Street or at Albertsons, Fred Meyer, and Safeway stores. You can also order passes and tickets by mail. For information on this option, call (503) 238-RIDE.

Tigard

Tucked between Beaverton and Tualatin and split down the center by U.S. Highway 99, Tigard is 10 miles from downtown Portland and has a population of 37,000 with an estimated growth to 47,000 by 2005. Before construction of U.S. Highway 5, Tigard hosted a bounty of travelers, as U.S. Highway 99 once was the major connector for towns in the Willamette Valley. Now it is home to thousands of professionals and technicians working in the Silicon Forest or in Portland. A highlight of Tigard is Fanno Creek Park, located behind city hall between Hall Boulevard and Main Street. This grassy, wooded wetland is a popular refuge for locals and visitors alike.

Troutdale

With a population of 14,000 and a distance of 12 miles from Portland east on Interstate 84, Troutdale has been targeted for expanded suburbia. Meanwhile the little burg up on the windy gorge has touched up its main street to give it the appearance of a historically chic little village. First settled in the mid-nineteenth century by John Harlow, a sea captain from Maine who had trout in his farm ponds, Troutdale first profited from the opening of the Columbia River Highway in 1916 and then became the Celery Capital of the World in the 1920s. Since then it has served as the gateway to the Columbia River Gorge Scenic Area. In 1998, its Main Street became a stretch of the Historic Columbia River Highway, part of an "All-American Road," one of nine in the country so designated by the U.S. Department of Transportation.

Tualatin

Down at the southern boundary of the Portland Metro area, 10 miles from downtown, Tualatin, a small city of 20,000, is fueled by the Silicon Forest economy. It has reshaped its downtown area into a European-style plaza with restaurants, shops, and living spaces all circling a placid pond. To celebrate both its urban renaissance and its long-standing local pastime of catching crayfish in the Tualatin River, the town invites folks to its yearly Crawdad Festival every June.

West Linn

A historic village just across the Willamette from Oregon City and eight miles from Portland, West Linn has 19,000 citizens who call their town the City of Hills, Trees, and Rivers. Started as a 1,000-acre land claim with flour and lumber mills located along the river for power, it has slowly grown into a popular place to build a fine home. One of its distinctive items is the locks, still in use, constructed in 1868 to ease vessels around Willamette Falls.

Wilsonville

Located 17 miles south of Portland at the southern gateway to the metro area, Wilsonville has 13,000 residents, many of whom work at Nike's nearest satellite plant and at Tektronix, a huge company that manufactures computer printers and other high-tech products. It is also a horticultural center, the hub of a blooming greenbelt, producing flowers, garden plants, hazelnuts, and other fruits and vegetables. When its citizens relax, they head for one of its three golf courses or launch their fishing boat or pleasure craft from one of the docks along the Willamette River, which winds through their city.

Close-up

How to Talk Like a Native

While Oregonians, especially natives, don't have any revealing regional accent per se, there is a vernacular. To aid you in communicating effectively here in Portland, we offer the following list of local phrases and pronunciations.

The Banfield: Interstate 84, which runs east from Portland to eastern Oregon and beyond. A major commute route and parking lot.

The Big O: *The Oregonian*, Portland's daily newspaper. (Often referred to by critics as *The Boregonian* and *The Snoregonian*.)

City of Roses: While it sounds like a cemetery, this is another self-created name for the city of Portland.

The Coast: The beaches along the Pacific Ocean anywhere between Astoria, Oregon, and the California border.

Couch Street: No matter how it is spelled, Oregonians pronounce it "kooch."

Fareless Square: The 300-block area of downtown, including the transit mall and The Lloyd Center on the Eastside where rides on buses and light rail vehicles are free (hence, fare-less).

Freddy's: Any Fred Meyer store.

Glisan Street: It doesn't make any sense, but locals pronounce it "Gliss-an."

MAX: More formally, the Metropolitan Area Express (except that there are no express trains), this is the light rail system operated by Tri-Met. The system runs from Hillsboro to Gresham. Do not get caught riding MAX (outside Fareless Square) without a ticket or valid transfer.

Nordie's: The Nordstrom department store.

OMSI: Oregon Museum of Science and Industry.

Oregon: Correctly pronounced "OR-uh-gun," never "OR-uh-gone."

PAM: Portland Art Museum

PDX: The international baggage handlers and airline code for Portland International Airport. Less frequently used as shorthand for Portland.

PICA: Portland Institute of Contemporary Art

Pill Hill: The complex of hospitals and medical facilities, including the U.S. Veterans Administration Hospital and the hospitals and clinics of the Oregon Health Sciences University.

The Mountain: Mount Hood. If you looking directly at Mount Hood, you are facing east.

Reedies: Students at Reed College in southeast Portland. The people Portlanders love to make fun of because they are so, so . . . different. The connotation is that if you are bright enough (and wealthy enough) to attend Reed, you are smart and more than a little offbeat. Some of the best minds in the state are at Reed.

The Schnitz: The Arlene Schnitzer Concert Hall, named after the grande dame of one of Portland's most prominent—and richest—families. The name was worth an estimated $2 million or so.

The Sunset: Oregon Highway 26, which runs west from Portland to the Oregon Coast. Another major commute route, parking lot, and perpetual construction zone.

Trendy-Third: Somewhat archaic and now rarely used, the term refers to the trendy (spendy and self-consciously hip for Portland) shops, people, and restaurants on N.W. 23rd Avenue.

Willamette: The Willamette River. This river divides Portland into east and west neighborhoods before flowing into the Columbia at Kelly Point. Residents on each side have strongly held opinions about the other's attitudes, political perspectives, lifestyles, and personalities. Don't ask, don't tell. The correct pronunciation is "Wil-Lám-et," not "Will-a-met."

Willie Week: *Willamette Week*. The area's major weekly newspaper.

Last Impressions

Well, that's a sampler of the history, current sites, sounds, feel, and flavor of Stumptown, Puddletown, PDX, and the Rose City—an overlay of four cities, a grid of four quadrants. Here, to polish off our profile, are a few more images:

At the hectic corner of Sandy Boulevard and 12th Avenue, the fresh smell of baked bread from Franz Bakery floats above the rush of traffic. It's Thursday morning, so garbage trucks creeping along side streets and tree-lined avenues, slow down for yellow bins filled with cans, bottles, and newspapers. We are serious about recycling here in our world of no styrofoam and the first place in the country to have a bottle bill. A few streets away, a van pulls up to a small house and a delivery person from Loaves and Fishes takes a "meal on wheels" to a happy, hungry senior. Just east of the Ross Island Bridge above a steady stream of traffic on Powell Boulevard, a bicyclist sheathed in lycra stops on the bike bridge to gaze at sunrise-tinted glacial Wy'East in the native tongue, or Mount Hood as christened by Lewis and Clark. Out on the Willamette near the RiverPlace docks, a skiff with a multicolored popsicle sail cruises by a dragonboat with an earnest crew practicing for races held during the Rose Festival. Further down river in a nest high in the girders of the Fremont Bridge, a Peregrine falcon tends to her chicks and far south on Ross Island, a pair of bald eagles soar above the sand and gravel quarry.

These raptors hang around here because it's a good place to live. We agree. We have some of the purest drinking water in the world, trickling down from Bull Run Reservoir high in the Cascade Mountains east of town. We are vigilantly keeping an eye on the purity of that water and the quality of our lifestyles all the while leaving as gentle a collective footprint as we can on the land beneath us. It is, as some would say, *trés* Portland.

Getting Here, Getting Around

Bordered by mountains, flanked by rivers, surrounded by fertile farmland, the Portland Metro area is well known for its beautiful setting. But don't let those high mountains fool you: Portland accommodates many modes of transportation and allows easy travel once you arrive. The territory is well served by trains, planes, and buses. Portland International Airport, or PDX, is the regional airport for all of Oregon and much of southwestern Washington. From here, in addition to its national and international service, commercial air service provides flights to Eugene, Salem, and Medford. Feeder and regional airlines also serve Pendleton and Klamath Falls in eastern and southern Oregon, in addition to providing flights to Newport and North Bend on the Oregon coast. Flights to the airport in Redmond, Oregon, will take you to the popular resorts and natural attractions of Bend and the rest of central Oregon.

Portland's Amtrak station operates trains to and from Seattle, Los Angeles, and Chicago, as well as nearby towns such as Corvallis and Eugene. Greyhound buses provide ground transportation in all directions, and buses run regularly to and from Seattle, Tacoma, and Olympia in Washington; Boise, Idaho; Denver; Salt Lake City; and major cities in California.

Two interstate highways intersect Portland. Interstate 84 runs east and west through the Columbia Gorge from Portland to Idaho and beyond. And Interstate 5 is the superslab that runs through Portland on its way from Canada to Mexico. Often you'll hear references to the 1–5 Corridor, the stretch of freeway from Wilsonville, down to Salem, then Albany south to Eugene.

From 1–5 there are routes west across the Coastal Range to the Pacific Ocean and U.S. Highway 101, and east through several mountain passes, across the Cascade Mountains to central and eastern Oregon. During the winter, some of the passes through the Cascades are closed. Those that remain open year-round may be subject to periodic closures due to weather, despite the near-heroic efforts of the Oregon Department of Transportation. Traction devices (chains and studded tires) are often required for winter travel through the Cascades (and at times, through the Coast Range). The Oregon State Police strictly enforce laws requiring motorists to carry traction devices.

This is the Great American West, so travel distances are greater than in other parts of the country; for instance, Seattle, the closest large city, is a three to four hours' drive north. However, one of the most prized features of the Portland Metro area is its nearness to so many beautiful areas of recreation, nature, and culture. Year-round skiing at Timberline on Mount Hood is a ninety-minute drive from the city center. A loop around Mount Hood to Hood River and then back down the Columbia Gorge is a pleasant way to spend the day, as is a trip to the Johnson Ridge Observatory at Mount St. Helens. The spectacular Oregon Coast is less than two hours from Portland, and the heart of Oregon's wine country is no more than forty-five minutes from downtown. (See Daytrips for more information on these outings.)

You will find that Portland is not difficult to navigate once you understand its idiosyncrasies. As we described in "How to Use This Book," the city is divided into east and west by the Willamette River, and north and south by Burnside Street. These serve as your orientation marks. Addresses and street numbers are organized around these two starting points. If you're on S.W. 10th Avenue downtown, you'll know that you're ten blocks west of the Willamette River. Similarly, Burnside Street is ground zero for street addresses, and they rise in number the further north or south that you travel from Burnside. So if your S.W. 10th Avenue address happens to be 423, you'll know that you're about four blocks south of Burnside.

Traveling by Air

Portland International Airport
7000 N. E. Airport Wy.
(503) 460–4234, (800) 815–4636,
TDD (877) 739–4636
www.portlandairportpdx.com

Each year, nearly 14 million passengers arrive at or depart from Portland International Airport, otherwise known as PDX (its aeronautical code). New records for numbers of passengers have been set each quarter for the past several years. To meet the demands of these numbers, the Port of Portland, which operates the airport, has embarked on a huge, expensive, multiyear expansion program. The construction includes expanded terminal space and passenger services, new passenger boarding gates, a new control tower, and an improved drainage system to prevent toxic chemicals, such as de-icing fluids, from draining into the Columbia River. The regional light rail system, MAX, is building a line to the airport. And, of course, the parking garage is being expanded. PDX parking usually follows one of Murphy's immutable laws, which states, "the number of cars will expand to fill all available and planned parking spaces, requiring another garage expansion whose construction will reduce the number of parking spaces available." However, in spite of the inconvenience of construction, you'll find PDX a notably clean and pleasant airport.

Getting to and from PDX by car is easy. There are clear directions to the freeways from the airport access roads. Likewise, airport exits are very well marked on Interstates 84, 405, and 5. Airport traffic is funneled onto Interstate 205. The freeway exit leads directly to the airport terminal, the car rental lots, and hotels on the airport's property (see our Accommodations chapter for those hotels near the airport). A cadre of easily identified helpers is on site to provide directions to travelers. They cannot help with the parking situation or the amount of traffic, but they can point you to your gate, the correct baggage carousel, or any other location within the airport complex. Travelers arriving at or departing from PDX should expect to pass through a metal detector and send their hand luggage through the customary airport security X-ray screening. Also be prepared to show photo identification, such as a driver's license, when you check in at the airline's ticket counter. Although there isn't a viewing area to watch planes arrive and depart, the airport's large glass windows do offer views of the aircraft ramps and taxiways, and limited views of the active runways.

Nearly twenty different cargo airlines serve PDX, so there is a good mix of aircraft types, ranging from DC–3s and aging Convairs to modern jets. The occasional Russian aircraft also shows up, so there is a chance to catch a glimpse of something novel, such as a civilian IL–76

Insiders' Tip

To get to the airport, stay on the freeways. You can reach the airport via city streets, but the freeways will get you there much more directly—and quickly.

with unusual markings. There is very limited helicopter traffic in and out of the airport, but the Air Force Reserve flies HH-60 Blackhawks. Military traffic, which shares the airport's runways with commercial and general aviation traffic, includes F-15s, C-1-30s, C-1-41s and C-5A/Bs, F-16s, and the occasional U.S. Navy P-3.

PDX is a safe airport. There has not been a major civil airline crash at the airport since 1978, when a United Airlines DC-8 ran out of fuel and landed about a mile short of the runway. The airport's crews are experienced in responding to the Oregon winters, and the airport is rarely closed. Bad weather in other parts of the country, especially in Denver, Chicago, Los Angeles, and San Francisco, can cause delays in flights heading for Portland. At certain times of the year, particularly in the fall, early morning fog can wreak havoc with departure times at PDX, and some regional flights are affected by local weather at their intended destinations.

Once you've arrived at PDX, you'll find the airport has many services for the weary and rushed traveler. Airport service workers offer transportation to or from the passenger gates in electric carts. Baggage carts are available for rent at a nominal fee ($2). In addition to now-expected amenities—telephones, express package drop-offs, fax machines, stamp machines, and ATMs—PDX offers several play areas to help divert the children. A children's Flight Deck area with a child-sized model aircraft fuselage and control tower allows the kids enough amusement to sustain them through their upcoming flights. (We sometimes visit this attraction on a rainy afternoon even when we have no other business at the airport.) And children and their parents will both enjoy eavesdropping on conversations between pilots and the tower as well as on the weather reports. You'll also find several Lego tables scattered around the airport.

While waiting for a flight, you might catch a glimpse of the military planes that travel in and out of the airport. You can also shop at some of the area's best stores. You can buy reading material at Powell's books, sportswear at Norm Thompson's, great woolens at Pendleton, athletic footwear and apparel at Nike, and souvenirs from our state at Made in Oregon. You may choose to dine or snack at one of the food courts located throughout the airport. Local and regional craft beers at several pubs or delicious pastries from Marsee Baking may comfort you before your flight. And, unsurprisingly, there are several places to get a latte or espresso.

Parking at the airport is getting easier. There are three main areas: the economy lot, the long-term lot, and the parking garage. If you plan to leave your car at the airport while you are gone, use the economy lot, which lies two miles east of the airport terminal. Rates are $8 per day, $48 per week maximum. Free PDX shuttles run from the lot to the terminal every fifteen to twenty minutes; remember to allow extra time to get to the terminal. (Be sure to remember whether you parked in the red or blue section). This lot can fill up during peak holiday traveling times. Use the long-term lot for shorter stays exceeding four hours. Rates are $3 per hour and $12 per day maximum, and shuttles are also available from this lot. (You can also walk to the airport through the garage tunnels, which are carpeted, well lit, and spacious.) The parking garage rate is also $3 per hour, but will cost you $16 per day. For updated parking information, call (877) 739-4636 before leaving for the airport.

Ground transportation from the airport is available by taxi and other ride services. The Ground Transportation Center is across the first roadway on the lower level of the airport, just outside of the baggage claim area; that is, it is just east of the main terminal, in the direction of the parking garage. Posted signs will tell you whether you are in the right section for your chosen mode of transport; you can also ask the airport service personnel who are always in attendance to direct you. Taxi service is provided by Broadway Cab (503) 227-1234, Green Cab (503) 234-1414, New Rose City Cab (503) 282-7707, Portland Taxi (503) 256-5400, and Radio Cab (503) 227-1212. Taxis to downtown Portland usually cost from $22 to $28; the trip downtown takes from 20 to 40 minutes. The Grayline Airporter Shuttle, (503) 285-9845, runs every 45 minutes from 5 A.M. to midnight; it stops at Union Station and a number of hotels throughout the city. The one-way fare is $15 and a round-trip ticket (required for the discount) is $22. A number of hotels provide their own free shuttle services; these are usually hotels outside the downtown area. You can find out which hotels offer this service by checking the Reservation Board in the baggage claim area. Some of these courtesy shuttles run regularly at scheduled times while others need to be summoned.

You will also find a number of other shuttle and towncar services in the Ground Transportation Center. The prices for these will vary depending on the number of passengers, the distance you will travel, and the luxuriousness of the vehicle. Be sure to clarify the price before you begin your journey. Willamette Express has starting airport rates of $15 to $35; they cover a wide radius in the Willamette Valley, including Portland. They may be reached at (503) 280-9883. Pacific Executive Services can provide towncars; call ahead at (888) TOWNCAR or (503) 234-2400. The Beaverton Airporter Shuttle may be reached at (503) 760-6565, and Coachman Towncar may be contacted on-line at www.ETowncar.com or by phone at (503) 761-1986.

For car rentals at the airport, go to the Parking Garage's first floor where there is a suite of counters. The agencies with offices in the garage include Avis Rent-A-Car (503) 249-4950, Budget Rent-A-Car (503) 249-6500, Dollar Rent-A-Car (503) 249-4792, Hertz Rent-A-Car (503) 249-8216, and National Car Rental (503) 249-4900. Some car rental agencies have kiosks just outside the car rental center in the parking garage; these include Enterprise Rent-A-Car, (503) 252-1500, Thrifty Car Rental, (503) 254-6563, and Alamo, (800) 327-9633. Thrifty also has a nearby off-site location; shuttles to this agency, as well as to Alamo, may be found on the Ground Transportation road closest to the rental car center. For more information, see the section on renting a car, below.

Insiders' Tip

If you have rented a car that must be returned at the airport, remember to fill the gas tank before you leave for PDX, preferably in town, where you won't have to wander through unknown neighborhoods in search of a station and you'll have a choice of what to pay for fuel. There are no gas stations on the airport's grounds. Once you are on I-205 or I-84 en route to the airport, you will need to leave the freeway to get gas.

Perhaps the best deal at PDX is to take a Tri-Met bus from downtown, the railroad station, and bus station to the airport. Tri-Met's No. 12 bus stops in front of the Ground Transportation Center west of the parking garage. The trip costs $1.20. Tri-Met may, however, discontinue bus service to the airport once the MAX line (see below) is firmly established.

An extension of the area's light rail system, MAX, is now under construction and scheduled to begin service to the airport in September 2001. This will get air passengers out to the airport more quickly, easily and affordably than any other option. Contact Tri-Met (see below) for more information.

Other Airfields

Beside PDX, the Port of Portland owns and operates three other airfields that are open for general aviation: Portland-Hillsboro, Portland-Mulino and Portland-Troutdale Airports, all of which can be reached at (503) 944–7000.

Pearson Field
1115 E. Reserve St., Vancouver
(360) 696–8446
(360) 735–9441 (FBO)

Pearson Field, snug against Fort Vancouver Historic Site within walking distance of downtown Vancouver, is the oldest continually operating airfield in the United States. Still open for general aviation, it has a 3,300-foot lighted runway and a Fixed Base Operator to help with refueling and other pilot needs. Antique aircraft and other memorabilia are on display on the grounds of the airfield at the Pearson Field Museum, (360) 694–7026. Throughout the year the museum hosts several events, including Big Band dance concerts, fly-ins, and parachute jumps. (See our Attractions chapter for more information on Pearson Field.)

Traveling by Train

Amtrak at Union Station
800 N.W. 6th Ave.
(503) 273–4865 (station information)
(503) 273–4866 (daily arrival and departure information)
(800) 872–7245 (reservations and schedule information)

One of Portland's most charming postcard views is a glance at Union Station with its brick clock tower that actually keeps good time. Our town's classic train depot, built in the 1890s, is the second oldest operating train terminal in the U.S. Its well-preserved appeal is evident in its high ceilings and marble floor, and its historic photographs add to the adventure of traveling by rail. This surviving relic of the days before air service and RVs also serves as what transportation planners call a "multimodal transportation center." This means you can, with relative ease, arrive in Portland by train or intercity bus and have immediate access to local bus and cab service (see Attractions for more information on this Portland landmark). In fact, because Union Station is part of the downtown Portland transit mall and falls within the Fareless Square boundaries, you can take a bus from the train station to downtown Portland for free.

Portland's Union Station is an important stop on several major rail routes. The Empire Builder, a passenger train that originates in Chicago, stops here, as does another classic train, the Coast Starlight, which runs daily from Los Angeles to and Seattle. Amtrak's Mt. Adams, partially funded by the states of Washington and Oregon, connects Seattle and Portland (as well as Eugene) with a number of intermediate stops that include Salem and Albany in Oregon and Vancouver, Olympia, and Tacoma in Washington.

This train features the state-of-the-art, Spanish-built, high-speed Talgo, an ultra-modern "tilt" train on an extended test-run in Oregon and Washington. If you're a train fan, consider a daytrip north to Seat-tle or Olympia on the Talgo. If you tire of the scenery, you can make use of the films, videos, and computer jacks that the train includes as part of its conveniences.

Traveling by Bus

Greyhound Lines
550 N.W. 6th Ave.
(503) 243–2357, (800) 231–2222

The Greyhound Lines bus station is a remarkably clean and modern terminal located on the far northern end of the city's recently remodeled transit mall adjacent to Amtrak's Union Station, both of which are a short walk from down-town. The station has plenty of seating, a concession wall, and a small pleasant cafe. Greyhound is the only transcontinental bus line serving Portland and Vancouver. The bus also stops in Tigard, at 12555 S.W. Main, (503) 620–6638.

The Green Tortoise Adventure Travel Line
494 Broadway, San Francisco, CA 94133
(800) 867–8647
www.64.70.148.149 (really)

Looking for a comfy and cool way to travel up to Seattle or south all the way to Los Angeles? How about a laid-back bus trip on the Green Tortoise? This green bus offers cheap transportation to free-spirited, usually younger, folk. You will always meet interesting people on the Green Tortoise, whether your fellow pas-sengers are students heading back to the University of Oregon in Eugene, foreign visitors traveling on a budget, or wander-ers seeking adventure on the open road. Passengers often find new friends and off-the-road adventures as the old turtle meanders down the highway.

You can pick up the Green Tortoise in Portland in front of Union Station at N.W. 6th Avenue and N.W. Irving Street just below the clock tower. Trips north to Seattle cost $15 with no reservation (just pay the driver) and leave at 4 P.M. on Tues-days and Saturdays. Trips to San Fran-cisco ($59) and L.A. ($79) leave Sunday and Thursday at 12:30 P.M. You will need a reservation to travel south of Eugene; tickets are $15.

Traveling by Car

As the Portland Metro region has grown, so has the amount of traffic and congestion. During rush hours, 7 to 8:30 A.M. and again from 3:30 to 6 P.M., car and bus traffic pours into downtown from all directions. Commuters going to high-tech jobs in Washington County have a reverse commute, but their mushrooming numbers create rush-hour traf-fic in both directions on freeways, the region's main arterials, downtown streets, and often on secondary streets.

You will want to bear in mind a few things as you travel the city. The downtown area is laid on a grid of one-way streets, so look carefully before making a turn lest you find your-self heading straight into traffic. The major southbound street is Broadway; the major northbound street is 4th Avenue. Tenth and Eleventh Avenues are also important north- and south-bound streets, and Naito Parkway (recently called Front Avenue) runs along the Willamette River; it permits both north- and south-bound traffic. Important east-bound streets are Market, Alder, and Columbia; westbound arterials include Clay, Washington, and Jefferson. Burnside allows both east- and west-bound traffic, but the places where you are allowed to make a left turn off Burnside are rare in the downtown area.

Cyclists celebrate Earth Day in Portland. CREDIT: COURTESY OF THE BICYCLE TRANSPORTATION ALLIANCE

Two major streets, 6th Avenue and 5th Avenue, are the arterials for the bus system downtown, making up a large component of the transit mall. This is helpful to know if you are planning to ride the bus, but you also need to know it if you're driving downtown because you must be alert to the traffic markings. Some blocks along these streets are for buses only, some blocks allow cars, and some blocks funnel cars right into "turn only" lanes. Car drivers should also pay attention to the "No Turn on Red" signs downtown, since they will prevent cars from being hit by MAX trains. Furthermore, you must allow buses the right of way if you are driving behind them and they are signalling to pull into traffic. A flashing red YIELD sign on the bus will let you know if you are hogging the road illegally.

You should know a few other important streets and highways in the area. Interstate 205, the freeway that takes you to the airport, will also take you south around the eastern edge of the city of Portland to communities such as Oregon City and West Linn before it connects back up with I-5 just south of Lake Oswego. To the north, I-205 takes you across the Columbia River into Washington State, hooking up with I-5 north of Vancouver. U.S. Highways 99E and 99W are also critical roads. They are the eastern and western sides of U.S. Highway 99, the principal thoroughfare of Oregon before I-5 was built, which splits in two just north of Eugene. The directions "W" and "E" designate which side of the Willamette River you are on. South of Portland, 99W is also called the West Pacific Highway, but in the city limits it has several names. In order, from south to north, they are Barbour Boulevard, Naito Parkway, and, when it finally crosses the Willamette again, N. Interstate Avenue. Similarly, the East Pacific Highway, 99E, is also called McLoughlin Boulevard from Oregon City north until just north of the Ross Island Bridge. At that point, 99E splits into a north-bound arterial called Grand Avenue, and a south-bound arterial called Martin Luther King Jr. Boulevard (or MLK). These two rejoin north of Broadway to form Martin Luther King Jr. Boulevard. Both 99W and 99E merge into I-5 immediately south of the Columbia River.

Unfortunately, driving east and west over the hills that divide the city from the western suburbs like Tigard and Beaverton can present some difficulties. The main route, U.S. Highway 26, is responsible for some of the worst traffic in the city just west of downtown, where it is called the Sunset Highway. This is the main route of travel between downtown Portland and the west side of the Metro region, and it gets backed up in the Sunset Tunnel, which takes cars under the west side of the hills, backed up again as it climbs the Sylvan Pass, and backed up yet again at the interchange with State Highway 217. To travel east and west, you might try a couple of alternate routes. Burnside will take you over the hill into Beaverton from downtown; when it splits in two, follow S.W. Barnes Road to 217. The Beaverton-Hillsdale Highway, or State Highway 10, can be a good choice; you can also take I-5 to U.S. Highway 99W or to 217. But all of these routes will present the driver with substantial amounts of traffic, and they might take you out of your way. Consult your map carefully.

Another caveat: U.S. 26 turns into a business route when it hits downtown Portland's west side. To follow it east through town, on your way to Mt. Hood, for instance, you must be attentive to the signs that direct you toward the Ross Island Bridge, where the highway turns into Powell Boulevard for miles until it passes through the eastern Multnomah town of Sandy and becomes a proper highway again.

Broadway can also be confusing because it extends from Northeast Portland (where it is called "Northeast Broadway") across the Broadway Bridge to downtown Portland, where it is technically named "Southwest Broadway." But nobody calls it that—downtowners call it just plain "Broadway." While Broadway passes through downtown, it takes the place of 7th Avenue, so you will find it between 6th and 8th Avenues. And after it passes through downtown, it turns into Broadway Drive. If you're unsure which Broadway is meant, check the exact street address.

Cars, buses, streetcars, lightrail, bikes, pedestrians, and the occasional horse all share the streets of Portland. The freeways have additional factors to consider. Traffic not only consists of cars, motorcycles, vans, and the ubiquitous sport-utility vehicles, but also heavy trucks. It is not uncommon to find triple-trailers (legal on some Oregon freeways) and muddy, heavily loaded log trucks bumper to bumper with shiny new BMWs and battered VW bugs covered with Grateful Dead decals.

Driving on the freeways through the heavy Oregon mist requires particular attention. At higher speeds, hydroplaning on a sheet of water can occur, and stopping distances stretch when roads get wet. Spray from passing cars, buses, and trucks can muddy windshields, blocking a driver's vision before the windshield wipers can clear the water. Sudden entry into unseen pools of standing water, especially in the fall when leaves clog drains, can cause a driver to momentarily lose control. In winter, freezing rain and invisible black ice can make driving difficult for everyone, but especially for those who exceed speed limits.

Please don't drink and drive. Driving under the influence of intoxicating drinks or drugs is a serious offense in Oregon. If your trip calls for a visit to the wine country and a tasting of the vintages, take along a designated driver or limit your imbibing. It is also illegal to have an open container of an alcoholic beverage in your vehicle. Oregon's public safety officers are professionals who take their responsibilities seriously. Meeting one practicing his or her profession might save your life, but it also could ruin your travel plans.

Distractions should also be kept to a minimum. Radar detectors are permitted, but it is illegal to have a television in a motor vehicle located in such a position where the driver can watch it. And be especially careful when you are talking on the phone!

In rural areas, herds of livestock have the right of way when crossing a road. Bicyclists have an equal legal right to the road, and drivers of motorized vehicles are required to stay out of marked bicycle lanes. Special blue pavement markings alert drivers to places where they must be particularly watchful of bicycle right-of-way; areas where bike lanes cross auto turn lanes are notorious for accidents and the city is trying to make them safer for everyone. Also, you should know that it is legal for motorized wheelchairs to travel in bike lanes.

Some of Oregon's more traditional rules of the road follow:

Moving violation fines can double in school and construction zones.

At most intersections, and the exceptions are well marked, drivers can make a right turn through a red light after making a complete stop, as long as the turn does not cross other lanes of traffic.

Car insurance is mandatory in Oregon, and drivers must carry proof of insurance.

Oregon law requires the driver and all passengers to wear seat belts. Children four and younger or weighing less than forty pounds are required to ride in a secured car seat. Failure to wear a seat belt is cause for a police officer to stop a vehicle and issue a warning or citation. The law applies to both Oregonians and out-of-state drivers. (Noted for their common sense approach to things, 82 percent of Oregonians regularly wear seat belts when driving or riding in a car.) Motorcyclists and bicyclists as well as their passengers must wear helmets.

Speed limits are usually well posted. For cars, the speed limit is 55 mph on open highways, 65 mph on freeways outside metropolitan areas, 25 mph on residential streets, and 20 mph in business districts and school zones. Photo radar will occasionally enforce these limits, but signs will warn you if the area is patrolled by this system. Driving in Oregon is governed by the basic rule that a driver must always drive at a speed that is reasonable under existing conditions on all roadways at all times. To obey this basic rule, you may have to drive at a slower speed than the legal posted speed limit if conditions warrant it.

Insiders' Tip

Like other cities, Portland sometimes changes the name of a major street to honor an individual. Martin Luther King Jr. Boulevard was once Union Avenue. The most recent street to change its identity is S.W. Naito Parkway, formerly known as S.W. Front. It was renamed in honor of the late Bill Naito, a driving force in Portland's downtown revival. Some mapmakers have not yet caught up with this change, but S.W. Front Avenue and S.W. Naito Parkway are, in fact, the same street.

Parking

Parking on downtown streets during business hours takes some patience, especially given downtown Portland's grid of one-way streets. Meters cost $1 per hour and allow parking for periods of time between fifteen minutes and three hours. Meters accept nickels, dimes, and quarters. No pennies, half-dollars, silver dollars, or Canadian or other foreign coins, please. And don't try to stay past the time allotted: car tires are frequently chalked to make sure drivers refrain from plugging their meters. Once a parking patrol member has started to write you a citation, it is yours.

If you do get a ticket, fines begin at $12 and go upwards depending on the severity of your violation. Meters are enforced Monday through Saturday from 8 A.M. to 6 P.M. Parking after 6 P.M. is free, but if you pull into an empty space at 5:55 P.M., plug the meter. Sunday parking is free. Special parking zones for trucks, motorcycles, compact cars, theaters, hotels, churches, and carpools abound and are usually well marked with violations well enforced.

You may see a few streets with special "Pay to Park" stations along them. These central pay station machines work by issuing paper stubs that are placed on the dashboards or by simply allowing you to pay for the space that your car occupies. The rates are the same as regular meters. Portland is in the process of determining which of these systems works the best and trying to work out the inevitable bugs; the city hopes to have the system in place sometime within the next year. A couple of warnings: the machines don't take dollar bills. And while in the future the pay stations will be designed to accommodate Smart Card technology, in the meantime make sure you have exact change. And we mean exact. Say, for instance, that you are at a ninety-minute meter. If you don't have the right blend of coins and must put in $1.55, the machine will refund your money without giving you a parking stub. You'll either have to move your car or park for less time. The city is trying to resolve this particular issue, and indeed by the time you read this, they may have. But consider yourself forewarned.

Municipal and private parking garages are an alternative to on-street meters. There are six clearly marked Smart Park garages in downtown Portland, where parking is 95 cents an hour for the first four hours. On the weekend you can park at Smart Park for $2 for the whole evening when entering after 6 P.M. or all day on weekends for only $3. Many downtown merchants will validate your Smart Park ticket for two hours of free parking if you spend $25 or more in their stores. Private garages and parking lots charge anywhere from $1.75 an hour to $4 an hour, with daily rates as high as $17.

Insiders' Tip

Oregon is one of two states in the country that prohibits self-serve gas stations. Don't try to fill your tank yourself, or you will be descended upon by irate attendants. Unfortunately, our laws do not mandate oil checks or cleaning of windshields; these you may have to do yourself.

Construction and special events such as the Rose Festival Parade and the Portland Marathon affect on-street driving and parking, though the city's parking division makes a good effort to post warning signs about temporary restrictions. But if you ignore the signs and don't move your car, they will "move" it for you—right down to the city towing lot.

Outside of downtown Portland and popular shopping and eating districts such as N.W. 23rd Avenue and N.E. Broadway, parking is easier. At the large malls and shopping centers and popular attractions, such as the Oregon Zoo, you can expect the usual automobile anarchy as drivers search for the most desirable parking spaces. As expected, this competition heats up when it rains and during the annual Christmas shopping frenzy.

Rental Cars

Most major rental-car agencies are represented in Portland and Vancouver, and there are several local rental-car providers as well. Of note, however, is a priority service and discounted rates provided by the Oregon-Idaho Automobile Association with Hertz. This service for members can be reached at (800) 654–3080. For car rentals at Portland International Airport, see the PDX entry. Downtown and airport rental agencies are included in the following listings; they can lead you to branch offices throughout the city.

Avis
330 S.W. Washington
(503) 227–0220, (800) 831–2847

Bee Rent-a-Car
84 N.E. Weidler
(503) 233–7368 (Eastside),
(503) 292–3545 (Westside)

Budget
2323 N.E. Columbia Blvd.
(800) 249–6500 (airport)

2033 S.W. 4th St.
(800) 527–7000 (downtown)

Enterprise Rent-a-Car
445 S.W. Pine St.
(503) 275–5359 (downtown),

10947 N.E. Holman St.
(503) 252–1500 (airport)

Enterprise has twenty-one rental stations throughout the region.

Hertz Rent-A-Car
9445 N.E. Airport Wy.
(800) 654–1313, (503) 249–8216 (airport)

330 S.W. Pine
(503) 249–5727 (downtown)

National Car Rental
9225 N.E. Airport Wy.
(503) 249–4900, (800) 227–7368

Mass Transportation

Tri-Met
4012 S.E. 17th Ave.
(503) 238–RIDE (trip information)
www.tri-met.org

Tri-Met is Portland's award-winning mass transit system. Tri-Met comprises both the bus system and the region's light rail system, MAX, and the system is noted for its efficiency, comprehensiveness, and accommodation—as displayed, for example, in its modernized low-level vehicles for easier boarding and unloading. Operating in three counties (Multnomah, Washington, and Clackamas), Tri-Met's buses are scheduled on 101 different routes that cover more than 600 square miles. Downtown Portland's Fareless Square, bordered by the Willamette River, N.W. Irving Street, and I-405, provides free rides within its boundaries and along the transit mall, where riders can transfer to MAX. The downtown transit mall extends all the way to Union Station for connections to Amtrak and the intercity bus service. Smaller conventional buses and vans now provide service on less traveled suburban routes, and there is a wheelchair-accessible special service. MAX extends from the eastern suburb of Gresham all the way to Hillsboro in Washington County, with trains scheduled every fifteen minutes during the day to all of downtown, Old Town, the Oregon Zoo, the Lloyd Center, and the Rose Quarter. Fares, based on a geographic zone system, run $1.20 and $1.50 for a one-way trip, with discounts for senior citizens and youth. Children six and younger ride for free. Bus drivers will not give you change, though dollar bills are accepted on the bus. A day ticket ($4) can be used on both buses and light rail, traveling to all zones, and you can also get discounted fares if you buy books of tickets or monthly passes. These books and passes are widely available throughout the city at many drug, grocery, and bookstores. The Tri-Met Web site has a comprehensive list of outlets.

Bus routes vary in frequency and how early and how long each bus travels its route. Schedules for individual bus lines and the light rail lines are free and commonly available at banks, stores, post offices, bookstores, and dozens of other locations, or accessible on the Web at www.tri-met.org.

Tri-Met has an excellent safety record, but don't leave your common sense at home. All stops are marked by blue and white signs displaying the route numbers of the buses serving that line, and many are well lit, with covered bus shelters to protect you from the rain and wind, but not all stops are so well equipped. On the transit mall, a stretch of 5th and 6th Avenues is used only by buses, and there are more elaborate shelters with route maps and video screens displaying information and arrival times for the next bus. The system is divided into regions, designated by regional symbols; these symbols mark service to specific areas from the transit mall.

After 8 P.M., you can ask the driver to let you off the bus any place that he or she can stop safely; many drivers will also stop at night if you wave the bus down between established stops. Be observant when boarding buses: those marked with an "X" are express buses that most commonly run during commute hours. After leaving the transit mall, they will stop only at major stops until they reach a

Insiders' Tip

Wondering whether it's too icy to drive? Want to know in advance how many orange signs will interfere with your commute? The Oregon Department of Transportation (ODOT) has two fine resources to alert you to road conditions in Portland and elsewhere in Oregon. You can call (800) 977-6368 to check the latest road conditions, and you can visit their Web site at www.tripcheck.com/ for a comprehensive guide to road work, traffic delays, road closures, and other helpful information. They will also be able to tell you whether any mountain passes you are planning to ascend will require you to use traction devices—a requirement that is strictly enforced.

local transit center. Most drivers are very careful to announce that they are driving an express route. If in doubt, ask. Tri-Met's drivers, with rare exception, are courteous and knowledgeable and recognize the long-term value of being helpful to all riders.

All Tri-Met tickets and transfers are good on any Tri-Met route. Fares are paid upon boarding the bus, and passengers receive a time-sensitive transfer that also serves as a receipt. Tickets, which are stamped with the date and time of purchase, are required for travel on the light rail lines and are available from machines at every station. Make sure to insert your MAX ticket into the validator machine before you board. MAX tickets and bus transfers can be used interchangeably; they are good for an hour or so past the time they are validated or handed to you. Hold onto your ticket or transfer! Tri-Met inspectors can ask for proof of fare payment, and there is a hefty fine of $89 if you don't have proof that you are riding legally.

C-Tran
8700 N.E. Vancouver Mall Dr., Vancouver
(360) 695–0123, (503) 283–8054
www.c-tran.com

C-Tran is the bus service for Vancouver and Clark County, Washington. By arrangement with Tri-Met, C-Tran also offers service across the Columbia River to downtown Portland. Unlike the Tri-Met, there isn't a time-transfer receipt. To get from Vancouver to Portland the ticket price is $1.40. An All-Zone ticket for Tri-Met will be honored on C-Tran.

Streetcars

For the first half of the twentieth century, Portlanders used streetcars to get around town. Now, after a fifty-year absence, Portland is bringing the streetcar back in order to connect the major westside business districts. Beginning in July 2001, the streetcar will once again carry passengers through the city. The 2-mile route extends from Portland State University north to Good Samaritan Hospital (between N.W. Lovejoy and N.W. Northrup at N.W. 23rd), travelling through the Pearl District and along 10th and 11th Avenues. This means you can drive downtown for shopping, then hop on a streetcar to visit Powell's City of Books at 10th and Burnside before your lunch reservation in the Pearl District, all without having to move your car. Like the bus, streetcars will stop every 2 or 3 blocks, and they are scheduled to run from 6 A.M. to midnight every day, every ten minutes during the day, and a little less frequently at night. Fares will follow the same schedule as the MAX and the bus, and their tickets and transfers will be honored. And riding in the Fareless Square is still free. While the streetcar may be an old form of transportation, these are thoroughly modern, with air-conditioning, low-floor center sections, and full wheelchair access.

Those with a nostalgic bent can still ride an old-fashioned streetcar. The Vintage Trolley, a trolley operation using replicas of the streetcars that once served the city, runs on Sundays from the Lloyd Center MAX Station through downtown and back. For more information, you can contact Vintage Trolley Inc. at 115 N.W. First Avenue, Suite 200, Portland, OR 97209, or telephone them at (503) 323–7363. You can also check Tri-Met's useful Web site at www.tri-met.org, which includes an itinerary of historic buildings that the Trolley passes as it travels along.

Taxis and Other Modes of Transportation

Portland, Oregon, isn't New York City or Washington, D.C., where taxis are a way of urban life. Good luck trying to flag one from the corner: they will rarely, if ever, stop. However, you can telephone for one. If you're walking around town, the best cab-finding solution is to head to a hotel and have the doorperson call a cab. If you're at a restaurant, the maitre d' will usually call one for you. If you know your plans for a specific trip or destination, phone ahead and schedule a cab. Fares start at $2.50 and go up $1.50 per mile. A good rule of thumb for tipping is to tip the same as you would in a restaurant—10 percent to 20 percent depending on the quality of service. Cab fare from the airport to downtown for two passengers and their luggage should run between $25 and $35. Portland cab companies include the following; also see the Traveling by Air section for more information on taxi and towncar services:

Broadway Cab
1734 N.W. 15th Ave.
(503) 227–1234

Radio Cab
1613 N.W. Kearney St.
(503) 227–1212

Portland Taxi
12624 N.E. Halsey St.
(503) 256–5400

Sharing a Car

Portland is a great city for those who like to walk, bike, or use mass transit. Yet even if you have liberated yourself from car ownership, you may find yourself needing to use one occasionally. CarSharing Portland is an unusual co-operative that distributes the cost of owning a car among its members. Cars, a few trucks, a minivan, and even a couple of gas-electric hybrid cars are available all day, every day, at specific locations around town. Members are charged for the number of hours they use the cars and the number of miles they drive them, portioning the fees for insurance, gas, repair, and cleaning among everybody. To use a car, you call ahead to make a reservation, pick up the car at the designated spot, and return it to the same location at the time you have arranged. For more information, contact CarSharing Portland, 620 S.W. Main Street, Suite 228, Portland, OR 97205, or call them at (503) 872–9882. Visiting their Web site, www.carsharing-pdx.com, is an education in itself.

Biking

More and more people are riding their bikes in Portland. The city estimates that more than 2,400 people cross the Hawthorne Bridge on bike each day, compared with 200 in 1975. The city has established nearly 200 miles of bikeways that include both off-street paths and bike lanes along streets. Special blue zones warn motorists that cyclists have the right of way in these lanes, and that cars must yield to bikes when cars are attempting to turn a corner or into a right-turn lane. Such attention to bicycle riding has earned Portland accolades across the nation. Every year, it is at or near the top of accoladed bicycle cities. *Bicycling Magazine* named Portland the most bike-friendly big city in the U.S.A. in 1995, 1998, and 1999.

Portland's reputation as a bike-friendly city is in part due to the efforts of the Bicycle Transportation Alliance (BTA), founded in 1990. This award-winning advocacy outfit has been tireless in its efforts to establish more bike lanes, encourage local developers to meet their legal requirements for bike and pedestrian access, and develop other initiatives

Portland is friendly to cyclists of every size. CREDIT: COURTESY OF THE BICYCLE TRANSPORTATION ALLIANCE

to promote two-wheeled travel. They work with employers to promote bike commuting, which saves firms the steep cost of providing downtown parking. They initiated the campaign to allow bike access to the mass transit system and have been successful at creating bike access to most of the bridges that span the Willamette River—both measures have dramatically increased the number of bike commuters. And their insistence that streets should include people as well as cars has been great for the local economy: the successful redevelopment of the N.E. Broadway area around the Lloyd Center, with its bike lanes, wide sidewalks, and mellower traffic speeds, can be directly linked to the efforts of the BTA.

BTA organizes bike parking at festivals and other community events, carries out bicycle safety programs in the schools, and helps to sponsor the annual Bridge Pedal (see our Festivals and Annual Events and Recreation chapters). Proceeds from the event not only benefit Providence Hospital but also help sponsor more bike programs. BTA may be reached at (503) 226-0676, or at their website, www.bta4bikes.org.

Portland also has a vigorous city-sponsored bicycle office, which can be found at 1120 S.W. 5th Avenue, Room 170, (503) 823-7671. This office can provide maps and other information about bike routes, bike parking, and other crucial information. With state and local funds, the City of Portland Bicycle Program continues to expand and improve the region's network of bike paths. Cyclists are allowed on six of Portland's downtown bridges. Bike storage lockers may be found in many parts of the city, and all of Tri-Met's buses and MAX light rail trains are equipped with bike racks. With a $5 permit and a video-lesson, bicyclists are issued a permit that allows them to mount their bikes on the racks on a first-come, first-serve basis. For more information, visit their Web site at www.trans.ci.portland.or.us/Traffic_Management/Bicycle_Program. To learn more about biking in the Portland area, see the biking section in the Recreation chapter.

Walking

Walking in Portland is one of its chief pleasures. Miles of paths line the waterfront, inviting pedestrians to ramble. Not only is the downtown area clean and well maintained, but the little villagelike neighborhoods that make up the city encourage residents to walk to

Insiders' Tip

If you see a one-speed, unlocked yellow bike parked in downtown Portland, go ahead and ride it. No, really—the Community Cycling Center maintains these yellow bikes, which are donated and fixed up by volunteers, and anyone can use them. Just be sure to put the bike in a bike rack when your journey is finished, so someone else can use it too. For more information, call the Community Cycling Center at (503) 288-8864.

Portland neighborhoods make alternative transportation popular with everyone. CREDIT: RACHEL DRESBECK

the store, the bank, the library, dinner, even work. The city has several redevelopment projects underway. These include increasing the size of the sidewalks in these neighborhoods, as they have found that promoting foot traffic is a smart business move. And moving your legs to get to your business can also be a smart move; on any given morning, you will find pedestrians strolling across downtown bridges, taking advantage of their commute time to exercise their legs, minds, and souls as they prepare for their day. If you're thinking of relocating, you might consider the walking potential of any prospective neighborhoods. And you might even find a great job in your own neighborhood and be able to walk to work. See the hiking section in the Recreation chapter and the Portland's Parks chapter for more excellent walks in the area.

Portland's Bridges

Portland is a city of bridges: More than ten span the Willamette River, from the St. Johns Bridge on the north end to the Sellwood Bridge on the south. Because Portland is a deep-water port, all five bridges in the heart of downtown are drawbridges that raise to let large ships pass through. Each bridge has singular characteristics. The Hawthorne Bridge, for example, is the oldest operating vertical-lift bridge in the nation, while the Steel Bridge is a rare example of a bridge with twin decks capable of independent movement. Besides being useful, Portland's bridges are beautiful: They add charm to the cityscape, especially when viewed from the new Eastbank Esplanade, a pedestrian and bike path along the Willamette that stretches 1.5 miles from the Steel Bridge to the Hawthorne Bridge. This path, which includes the longest floating walkway in the United States, can be reached from the east side of any downtown bridge. (All entrances are wheelchair-accessible, except for the one at the Morrison Bridge.) For more information, visit the Esplanade Web site at www.parks.ci. portland.or.us/Eastbank/esplanade.htm. For bridge fanatics, the Oregon Department of Transportation (ODOT) maintains a meticulous Web site that features the engineering and historical details of our bridges: www.odot.state.or.us/eshtm. As an introduction, here is a survey of our Willamette River bridges.

The Broadway Bridge

The Broadway Bridge began carrying traffic in 1913. This 1,736-foot drawbridge with an unusual bascule span was designed by Ralph Modjeski. Unlike the Morrison and Burnside Bridges, which have their counterweights hidden inside their piers, the counterweights that open this bridge are above the deck. To allow maximum clearance, they roll back and forth on giant bull wheels. This rare, rolling lift mechanism is called a Rall, and the Broadway Bridge is the largest Rall bridge in the world. The middle of the bridge affords great views of the Fremont Bridge and the Willamette River to the north, and of Union Station and five other bridges to the south.

Burnside Bridge

Burnside Street is Portland's aorta, and the Burnside Bridge its beating heart. That's because Portland is divided into north-south sectors by Burnside Street—one of the city's longest and busiest streets—while the Willamette River defines the east-west sides, and the Burnside Bridge is at the center of it all. It is only fitting, then, that this bridge was designed by Joseph B. Straus, who also designed the Golden Gate Bridge. The Burnside Bridge, completed in 1926, is a 2,308-foot drawbridge with a double-leaf bascule. In addition to good city views, the subtle aesthetic design of details such as turrets on the operator's house make this bridge worth a stroll. The Burnside Bridge is one of the heaviest bascule highway bridges in the nation, though its massive piers are supported by timber pilings.

Fremont Bridge

The Fremont Bridge, the most recent addition to the Willamette River's "bridge club" in Portland, was completed in 1973 but its beautiful arches have shaped the cityscape as profoundly as older bridges on the Willamette. (Planners made sure this bridge would be attractive after the hue and cry stirred up by the uninspired design of the Marquam Bridge, below.) It's the longest bridge in Oregon, and at 902 feet, the longest tied-arch bridge in the entire world. This double-decker bridge carries traffic from northbound Interstate 405 and westbound U.S. Highway 30 to Interstate 5.

Hawthorne Bridge

The Hawthorne Bridge replaced the earlier Madison Street Bridge, but nonetheless is the oldest bridge across the Willamette in Portland. It was finished in 1910 and remodeled in 1998–99; it now includes beautifully wide sidewalks and bike paths, making it a favorite for pedestrians and cyclists. The Hawthorne Bridge, lovely as it is, demands more patience than some bridges in town because it has the lowest clearance, 53 feet at low water. In the spring when water is high, the Hawthorne Bridge raises even for small river traffic such as tourist steamer ships and floating restaurants—and, joke the residents, kayaks and canoes. Just so you know, on the east side of the river, the Hawthorne Bridge leads to Hawthorne Boulevard, but on the west side, Hawthorne turns into Main and Madison Streets.

Marquam Bridge

One of two newer bridges built in the 1960s to accommodate the city's increased traffic, the multilane, double-deck Marquam Bridge opened in 1966. The eastward-bound upper deck of the Marquam provides a panoramic view of the Willamette River, Tom McCall Waterfront Park, and downtown Portland that is unrivaled, but the bridge itself is no beauty. After it was built, critics reviled Marquam and demanded that Portland's next bridge be more appealing. (It is therefore ironic that the bridge is named after P. A. Marquam, a state legislator, county judge, and land baron who owned the Marquam Grand Opera House, one of the finest examples of architecture in the state.) Homeliness aside, this massive structure, also known as the I–5 bridge, is quite a workhorse. Connecting Interstate 5 to Interstate 84 East on the east side and Interstate 405 North on the west side, with major traffic arteries merging and dividing at both ends of it, it carries large volumes of busy traffic that attempt to travel at high speeds. Traffic is usually forced to slow down because of the balletic movements of entering, merging, and exiting drivers who are simultaneously trying to see the view.

Morrison Bridge

When first built in 1887 by the Willamette Iron Bridge Company, the Morrison Bridge was the largest span west of the Mississippi. It was rebuilt in 1905 and again in 1958, as a drawbridge. The Morrison Bridge is between the Hawthorne and Burnside Bridges and it provides entrances to and exits from I–5. Leaving I–5 southbound at the City Center exit, which takes you to the Morrison Bridge, provides one of the loveliest views of downtown Portland, especially at night when the river and bridge are illuminated. The Morrison Bridge, needless to say, is another hard worker. Carrying more than 55,000 cars daily, it is the largest mechanical structure in the entire state of Oregon with incredibly powerful gears hidden under its deck.

Ross Island Bridge

Designed by Gustav Lindenthal, the 3,700-foot Ross Island Bridge opened in 1926. This bridge is not a drawbridge, but a cantilever deck truss that sits high above the river. The bridge has pretty balustrades and an expansive view, but its aesthetic appeal is diminished by a high volume of speeding traffic. The Ross Island Bridge carries U.S. Hwy. 26 over the Willemette, connecting to Arthur Street on the west side and to Powell Boulevard on the east. Besides the volume of traffic, its other drawback is that the westward approach, which connects Barbour Boulevard, Oregon Hwy. 43, and Arthur Street, is confusing and awkward. A two-year renovation project that started in 2000 should improve things, but in the meantime, the Ross Island Bridge is more difficult than usual. Travelers should note that two lanes of the bridge are closed to traffic during the day, and the entire bridge is closed from 8 P.M. to 5 A.M. Monday through Friday, for the duration of the repairs.

Sellwood Bridge

The Sellwood Bridge, finished in 1925, was the first bridge in Portland that didn't move. Its design is called a "Warren deck truss," and this lofty, narrow span allows just two lanes of traffic to flow from Oregon Highway 43 on the west side to the Portland neighborhood of Sellwood on the east side. It is the busiest two-lane bridge in Oregon, though because it is so high, the views (for passengers, anyway) are impressive. A good portion of the Sellwood is more than one hundred years old, since it includes sections of the original Burnside Bridge, which was torn down in 1925. The steel girder approaches from the Burnside were reused at each side of the Sellwood. The Sellwood is one of three local bridges designed by renowned engineer Gustav Lindenthal.

St. Johns Bridge

The St. Johns Bridge was *not* designed by Joseph Straus, in spite of its being the only steel bridge in Portland. It was completed in 1931 to gasps of appreciation from local citizens who admired its Gothic arches and graceful towers. When it was built, it was the longest suspension bridge west of Detroit, at 1, 207 feet. And its 400-foot towers made it impressively tall, as well. Today, other bridges are larger, but none are as distinctive as the St. Johns Bridge, which is now a historical landmark. Underneath its majestic arches lies Cathedral Park, one of the most scenic recreation areas in the city.

Steel Bridge

The Steel Bridge was completed in 1912 and immediately hailed as an exemplar of imaginative engineering. This unusual bridge is one of the only known dual-lift bridges in the world: the lower deck, accommodating Amtrak and freight trains, lifts independently from the upper deck, which carries light rail and vehicles. Engineers claim that this bridge, properly lubricated, could function forever. The new Steel Bridge RiverWalk allows bikes and pedestrians to cross the churning Willamette River waters just 30 feet above them.

Portland is a good city for walking. CREDIT: RACHEL DRESBECK

History

After paddling a canoe on the backwaters of the Willamette River, Asa Lovejoy and a Tennessee drifter named William Overton put in at a point referred to only as "the clearing." The two men agreed that the mountain-ringed, timber-rich land looked like an excellent location to site a town. But Overton lacked the twenty-five cents needed to file a land claim, so he struck a deal with Lovejoy: In return for a quarter, Overton would share his claim to the 640-acre site. The two partners filed a claim in 1842; Overton, however, soon became bored with clearing trees and building roads, and sold his half to Francis W. Pettygrove.

This unlikely series of events set the stage in 1845, for "the clearing" to be named in an odd way. Pettygrove, a native of Maine and a shopkeeper, wanted to name the site "Portland," in honor of his state's largest city. But Lovejoy, a lawyer hailing from Massachusetts, preferred to name the upstart "Boston." The two men agreed to let the debate be settled by the flip of a copper penny. As everyone knows, Pettygrove and the name of Portland, won out that day. The original "Portland Penny" is on permanent display at the Oregon History Center where it serves as a reminder of how the city came to be named.

Early History

Of course, the story of Portland and the surrounding area begins thousands of years before these nineteenth-century events, and well before White men ever touched Oregon's shores. The first migration to Oregon occurred during the Ice Age when sea levels fell exposing a narrow strip of land across the Bering Sea. The game animals that traveled across in search of warmer lands were followed by small bands of nomadic Asian hunters as early as 30,000 years ago. Historians believe that the first Native Americans, including the Klamath, Modock, Bannock, Nez Perce, and Chinook tribes came to Oregon between 10,000 to 12,000 years ago. The coastal tribes relied heavily on abundant salmon, shellfish, seals, and the occasional stranded whale. The tribes farther inland lived on game, and altered the landscape drastically, as they burned forests and grasslands to attract their prey. This last group, the nomadic hunters and gatherers, were the ones to first greet the early European fur traders who reached the Oregon territory even before Lewis and Clark. At first they welcomed these strange visitors, and accepted their gifts, including guns, whiskey, trinkets, and tools. But in time, due to broken promises, land greed, and accusations of thievery, many conflicts broke out.

The first European to see the Oregon coast was probably Juan Rodriguez Cabrillo, a Spanish sea captain who attempted to map the Pacific coast in 1543; however, he did not set foot on land. Sir Francis Drake is said to have had that honor in 1579 when he claimed the area for England in the name of Queen Elizabeth. That claim, however, was hollow, as it would be another 200 years before the next English vessel reached Oregon.

Numerous European ships landed on the Oregon coast in the late sixteenth century and the early seventeenth century; however those expeditions revealed little about the inland regions. By 1750, Russian trappers had worked their way down through Alaska and Canada to the Oregon shoreline in search of otter, but for some reason they did not establish a colony or permanent community, choosing instead to build Fort Ross along the northern California coast in 1812. In fact, no less than four nations laid claim to Oregon: Spain, Russia, Britain, and the United States, but not one built a single settlement to signify a legal presence.

In 1788, John Meares blundered past the mouth of the Columbia River, and Captain George Vancouver also missed it in 1792, leaving the second largest river in the United States to be discovered by Captain Robert Gray of Boston, who named it after his vessel, the USS *Columbia*.

Inland Oregon also took a while to be discovered. In the early 1800s, Oregon (and the American West in general) was still very much an unknown and uncharted place devoid of cities, railroads, and cattle ranches. The region was quiet, pristine, and wild. Easterners heard tall tales about the western mountains and desert swarming with fierce savages, but very few White men had been there.

The Lewis and Clark Expedition

President Thomas Jefferson planned a secretive mission in 1803: to send a small party of men overland to the Pacific—a bold venture that no one before had even attempted. Congress covertly approved the trip, along with its budget of $2,500, because this "Corps of Discovery" would be venturing outside U.S. jurisdiction onto British territory. What Jefferson hoped to find was an expeditious water route to the Pacific via the Missouri River, its tributaries, and a legendary River of the West that flowed down from the Rockies to the Pacific, in hope that the distance between the east- and west-flowing rivers would be a one-day portage. It would be a simple route west for traders, emigrants, and adventurers. Aware of the momentous opportunity, Jefferson also charged the group with collecting scientific information about the region's interior.

President Jefferson chose his neighbor, longtime friend, and personal secretary, Meriwether Lewis to lead the leather-fringed contingent across the Louisiana Purchase and to the Pacific Coast. Lewis in turn, wisely selected sinewy frontiersman and mapmaker William Clark to be his co-leader.

In the spring of 1804, Lewis and Clark, along with a few dozen other hardy men, left St. Louis and started up the Missouri River heading west. Over the next two years the group—eventually christened "The Corps of Discovery"—would traverse Missouri,

Insiders' Tip

Some historians believe that the name "Oregon" is derived from the French "ouragan," meaning "storm" or "hurricane," since early French-Canadian trappers called the Columbia River the River of Storms.

Nebraska, the Dakotas, Montana, Wyoming, Washington, and Oregon. The journey took so long that the few insiders who knew about it feared that the members of the expedition had perished. But on December 5, 1805, Lewis and Clark reached the Pacific Ocean and Clark wrote in his diary, "We now discover that we have found the most practicable and navigable passage across the continent of North America." In reality, he couldn't have been further from the truth.

The route discovered by Lewis and Clark was far too difficult for others to follow. Indeed, no pioneer wagon ever did follow their trail. In fact, Lolo Pass, where their expedition crossed the most difficult section of the Rocky Mountains, is a rough haul even today—almost 300 years later. But because their detailed maps and notes provided a wealth of solid scientific data, the West was no longer an uncharted mystery and their expedition was celebrated as an outrageous success. Although they examined only a small portion of the Northwest Coast and the Columbia River, they gathered much valuable and accurate information about the rest of the Northwest from friendly native peoples. Their reports stirred excitement in the East; their vivid descriptions of a land of bounty created an "Oregon fever" among fur traders who had previously trapped and traded in the Rocky Mountains.

The Astorians

The second major westward expedition was not funded by a government or spurred by religious zeal to convert, but rather it was backed by one of the world's richest men—John Jacob Astor, who whetted his appetite for adventure by reading about Lewis and Clark's great journey. By 1810 Astor saw an opportunity to make a new fortune: a fur-trading enterprise at the mouth of the Columbia River. But one dilemma stood in his way: How could he get his men safely across the uncharted American West? He had a couple of ideas.

In 1811, he dispatched an overland party to follow the trail of the early explorers and to establish trading posts. He also sent another party there by sea, in a ship traveling around Cape Horn. The ship arrived safely, but was destroyed afterwards in a skirmish with Native Americans.

The land expedition also had problems. At a particularly dangerous spot on the Snake River known as Caldron Linn, one of the canoes capsized, drowning at least one man and losing a large portion of much-needed staples and supplies. The party soon discovered that the river did not become more placid downstream and that the Snake River was too treacherous to navigate. They came to the conclusion that there was no quick and easy water route to the Pacific, an assessment that would stymie pioneers for the next hundred years.

In the end, Astor's overland party finally did make it to Oregon but the enterprise was in deep trouble. Their only hope was to send a few men back East to get help from Astor. Robert Stuart led the mission back to St. Louis—an arduous journey that took nearly a year. Fortunately, Stuart made an incredible discovery along the way. In what is now the state of Wyoming, he discovered a 20-mile-wide gap in the Rocky Mountains where wagons could pass. Named South Pass, the only way over the mountains would unlock the door to western migration and more than a half-million emigrants would eventually ride their conestoga wagons through to the other side. Where Lewis and Clark had valiantly failed, Robert Stuart succeeded through a twist of fate.

Despite Stuart's fortuitous discovery, it would take several more decades before the huge western migration began due largely to Lt. Zebulon Pike.

In 1806, Pike journeyed west to explore the Great Plains and Rocky Mountains. Unfortunately, in his avidly read and distributed reports, Pike referred to the plains as "the Great American Desert," a name that stuck. Even though much of the region is nothing like a desert, easterners conjured images of inhospitable sand dunes, rattlesnakes, and cactus. No emigrant dared to cross such a severe wasteland—so the big move west was delayed.

If Pike's influence didn't cast a large enough shadow of doubt about the merits of traveling west, his opinion that the West was a vast desert was confirmed by Major Steven Long, who led an expedition west in 1819. Long and his men passed through what is now Oklahoma, Nebraska, Colorado, Kansas, and Oklahoma. He concluded that the entire region was unfit for human habitation. Potential settlers stayed away, believing the West was uninhabitable wasteland, and so the West remained largely untouched, allowing the Native American tribes a few extra years of peace.

Fur Trappers and Adventurers

Native Americans were not the only inhabitants of the West during this period. While potential settlers stayed away, a vigorous bunch of adventurous entrepreneurs meandered throughout the western mountains. These "mountain men," were solitary fur trappers who lived thousands of miles from civilization. Most had no home, no money, and no possessions—except what they wore and carried on their backs. They lived completely off the land, on a diet of buffalo, elk, and mountain goat. Many trappers roamed constantly in search of beaver pelts; many married Native American women and earned the respect and fondness of various tribes.

Even before Lewis and Clark finished their epic journey to the Pacific, mountain men were traveling up and down the Missouri River, exploring new uncharted territory such as the Oregon paradise.

One of the most famous mountain men, Jim Bridger, sailed down the Bear River in Utah until he found a huge body of salt water in 1824. He thought he had reached the Pacific Ocean, but actually, Bridger had discovered the Great Salt Lake. Later in the 1840s, Bridger built a fort in what is now Wyoming near South Pass. His goal was to sell supplies to the flood of emigrants then heading for Oregon. But the fort tied him down, and so within a few years, Bridger sold his fort and returned to the only lifestyle he knew—adventure.

Perhaps the greatest mountain man of them all was Jedediah Smith. Incredibly tough, he once sewed on a huge chunk of his scalp after an angry bear clawed it off. In 1825, Smith rediscovered South Pass—the key passageway through the treacherous Rocky Mountains. South Pass had been visited by an earlier explorer (remember Robert Stuart?), but the location had been kept secret. Smith made sure everyone knew about this important corridor. Later, after reportedly treating natives callously, Smith was ambushed by angry Umpqua along the Oregon coast at the mouth of Smith River near Reedsport. After surviving that skirmish, Smith was killed by Comanches in 1831.

The Legacy of the Fur Trade

A ruthless entrepreneur named Manuel Lisa was one of the first to organize the scattered mountain men into a large fur-trading company. In 1807, he efficiently built a chain of forts along the Missouri River allowing his men to fan out in all directions to harvest the abundant beaver. Hoping to duplicate Lisa's success, William Ashley put an ad in a St. Louis newspaper in 1822, recruiting able-bodied men for his new enterprise, and there was no shortage of applicants.

Ashley sent his men out alone and made arrangements to meet them all at a centrally located place a year later. At the predetermined time, Ashley stocked his wagons with supplies to replenish his men and then headed off to meet them. Ashley's yearly journey began in St. Louis and took him deep into the heart of the Rockies. His wagons were the first vehicles to penetrate the West and although he wasn't aware of it, he was blazing a wagon road for the settlers who would follow a decade later.

Each year, when Ashley finally reached his men, it was cause for celebration—a wild party they called "the rendezvous." Every year throughout the 1820s and '30s it was a raucous occasion: gambling, fist fighting, drinking, storytelling, and general hell-raising that went into the early hours of the morning for more than a week.

Age of Pioneers

By the late 1830s, beaver hats were going out of style in New York and London, and so pelts were no longer in demand. As a result, many mountain men were forced to find a new livelihood. Some became farmers, others led the pioneer wagons trains that were streaming west. A few French-Canadian trappers retired from a dominant outfit, the Hudson's Bay Company, and settled in lush valleys southwest of what would soon become Portland. The sun had finally set on the era of the mountain man and the age of the pioneers was dawning. At the vanguard of this shift was explorer John Frémont and his guide, Kit Carson. Frémont became known as one of America's biggest heroes because of his pioneering journeys west along the Oregon Trail in 1842 and 1843. He got the job largely because his wife's father was the powerful Missouri senator Thomas Hart Benton who believed America had an innate right to all the lands of the West, an idea loftily called "Manifest Destiny." And so Frémont was ordered by the powers-that-be to make the West seem attractive and worth settling, even if it meant stretching a few facts.

Frémont's reports on his journeys were so positive and upbeat they made the trip West seem easy and enjoyable, which it definitely was not. Yet the pioneers, armed with faith and hope, came to this promised land of milk and honey in unprecedented numbers.

Oregon Trail

Driving this great movement was more than just positive reports. In 1843, the federal government allotted 640 acres of land to every adult homesteader and 160 acres to every child, with hopes of anchoring the United States claims to the Northwest Territories. Most of those who came as far west as Oregon made the land trip that John Frémont publicized. However, some came by water, and did so even before a land route was established. The sea route never was a popular choice, though. The fare was prohibitive, and most westward-bound pioneers came from central states far from seaports. Also, the sea journey often took up to full year compared to between five to eight months by wagon.

Those who did come by land took the route that came to be known as the Oregon Trail (although in fact it actually forks in southern Idaho, with a lower extension ending in California). Legend enjoyed by Oregonians to this day has it that those who were greedy for gold headed south at the fork to California and those who wanted a better life headed north to the Oregon Territory. Nearly 2,000 miles long, the main route west stretched from Independence, Missouri, to Oregon City, Oregon. Portions of it followed the Platte River for 540 miles through Nebraska to Fort Laramie in present-day Wyoming. The trail wound along the North Platte and Sweetwater Rivers to South Pass in the Wind River Range of the Rocky Mountains. From there the main trail went south to Fort Bridger, Wyoming, before turning into the Bear River Valley and north to Fort Hall in present-day Idaho. The Oregon Trail then followed the Snake River to the Salmon Falls and then went north past Fort Boise. The route entered what is now Oregon, passed through the Grande Ronde River Valley, crossed the Blue Mountains, and followed the Umatilla River to the Columbia River. Shorter and more direct routes were developed along some parts of the trail, but they were often more difficult.

Like many other main routes in the United States, sections of the Oregon Trail had been used by the Native Americans and trappers. As early as 1742, part of the trail in Wyoming had been blazed by previous explorers, but Lewis and Clark made it better known. Later, mountain men, including James Bridger, who founded Fort Bridger in 1843, often served as trail guides. The difficult and dangerous journey, often complicated by poor planning and shoddy equipment, disease, and less frequently by attacks from Native Americans, took early pioneers an average of five months. The increasing number of pioneers on the trail was soon a growing menace to the tribes that were at first quite friendly.

The Missouri River heads due west from St. Louis; so the journey for a good many emigrants started right here, where they loaded their wagons onto steamships for the upstream journey. The first part of the trip was easy, but 200 miles from St. Louis, the Missouri takes a cruel turn to the north. There the pioneers unloaded their wagons and began the hard journey by land at any one of several small towns called "jumping off" places. Independence, Missouri, was the first option; further upstream were the cities of Westport, St. Joseph, Omaha, and Council Bluffs. The economies of these frontier towns grew so dependent on emigrants passing through that many of these cities hired agents to go east and badmouth the competing villages.

The first organized party of emigrants to actually reach the Oregon Territory came with the American pioneer physician Elijah White. Under the leadership of John Bidwell, an Ohio schoolteacher, this group loaded their wagons and left Missouri in 1841 and in 1842 reached Oregon. Although the terminus of their journey was Oregon City, later settlers would head for the verdant Willamette Valley. During the 1840s thousands of pioneers settled there, where wheat, fruits, and vegetables thrived. Others were attracted to other parts of the state, for gold prospecting and to harvest Oregon's bountiful supply of Douglas-fir trees.

The Oregon Trail directed the flow of westward expansion and was of paramount importance to the settlement and development of the Pacific Northwest. Before the completion of the first transcontinental railroad in 1870, an estimated 350,000 pioneers followed the Oregon Trail westward, more than all the other routes combined.

In Oregon, the trail's route (generally along today's Interstate 84) has remained a principal course of east-west travel to the present day. The road crosses a diverse range of

Close-up

Oregon Trail Memorial

The Oregon Trail, including the Barlow Road, its most western segment, is a 2,000-mile monument that honors the determination of the human spirit. Between 1841 and the turn of the century, Americans from all walks of life sold most of their worldly possessions, piled a few cherished and needed items in a wagon, and set off on an epic journey. The four-to-eight-month odyssey covered some of the harshest and most impassable territory in the world. One in ten travelers fell victim to disease or injury along the way and many were buried under the trail itself to protect their graves from scavenging animals.

In 1978, Congress memorialized the vital role that the Oregon Trail played in our nation's history by naming it a National Historic Trail, designating it the primary route of the early pioneers, including its full length between Independence, Missouri, and Oregon City, Oregon. This route is based on the travel that occurred during the period from 1841 to 1848 and includes the 100-mile Barlow Road, developed in 1846 between The Dalles and Oregon City.

Three years later, the National Park Service issued a three-volume document identifying Oregon City in Clackamas County as the true and correct End of the Oregon National Historic Trail. The significance of Abernethy Green is its historic designation as the official end of the Oregon Trail. It served as the main arrival area for emigrants and the land grant of Oregon's first provisional governor, George Abernethy.

The End of the Oregon Trail Interpretive Center opened on Abernethy Green in Oregon City in 1995. (For more detailed information about the Interpretive Center, see Attractions.) The site is bounded by the confluence of the Willamette and Clackamas Rivers on the west, and wooded bluffs along the east and south. Abernethy Creek is also located at the southern edge, at the foot of a bluff.

The center is housed in three giant covered-wagon-shaped buildings. One of them houses a multimedia theater where the story of the pioneers crossing the trail unfolds in great detail, beginning in a provisions store in St. Louis. The Oregon Trail Pageant also brings the history to the stage for thousands of visitors to enjoy each year.

terrain and historical interest—the rugged Blue Mountains crossover in northeastern Oregon, the dry plateaus located between Pendleton and The Dalles, the rugged and awesome Cascade Mountains and Columbia Gorge section, and even the geographic end of the trail in Oregon City, where the Willamette Valley settlements all began.

Native Americans

The first section of this well-traveled route bisected the territories of two major Native American tribes—the Cheyenne to the north and the Pawnee to the south. Although the emigrants worried about both tribes, the expected attacks did not come. Most of the accounts in the first few years are of friendly Native Americans being quite sociable. Many journals record instances of Native Americans helping the settlers pull out stuck wagons, rescuing drowning children, and even rounding up lost cattle.

One interesting diary of a widowed woman who headed west reveals how sympathetic some tribal people were. When the woman and her children reached Wyoming, a Sioux war party suddenly came down from the hills. The Native Americans admired her pluck—and stayed with her for four days to guard against the predation of their enemies, the Cheyenne. After escorting her through the dangerous area of Wyoming, they killed an antelope for her family, waved goodbye, and rode off.

In reality, most of the encounters with Native Americans were simple business transactions. The settlers offered clothes, tobacco, or rifles in exchange for Native American horses or food. The Native Americans looked upon the emigrants as just another source of trade, but once they started seeing more and more of them, they became alarmed. By then it was too late. Within a few years, the pioneers had overgrazed the prairie grasses, burned all the available firewood, and thousands of buffalo were massacred for fun by visitors on a lark, leaving a trail of rotting carcasses littering the landscape. As a result, many tribes along the Platte River became impoverished.

Portland's Early Days

As the Native American's way of life was disappearing, the new settlers were busy creating a new one. Gradually the Oregon Territory began to acquire the sheen of civilization. A dozen years after the first wagon trains arrived at the end of the Oregon Trail, the hamlets and burgs along the Willamette began sprouting business districts with general stores, blacksmith shops, tanneries, well-furnished hotels, and white-steepled churches. In Portland, the crude log cabins of the frontiersmen were gradually giving way to tidy frame houses with glass windows, ornamental woodwork, and papered walls. A virtually pristine tract of forestland in 1844, Portland boasted 821 residents by 1850, making it the region's most populous community. Mail still arrived by steamship, which took the route around Cape Horn and was distributed to the forty post offices in the area. And thanks to the vision of New England sailor Captain John Couch who picked Portland over Oregon City as a deep-water harbor for his shipping, the city soon became known as a port deserving its name.

As proper civilization took hold in Portland, the city also attracted a few lawless individuals who've served to provide color for our local history. One such person was Portland's "Sweet Mary" who created a floating brothel. Another was Joseph "Bunco" Kelly, a hotelier known for shanghaiing young men and selling them to ship captains short of crew members. Kelly carted them off when they were drunk. Upon waking, the young men had bigger problems than a hangover! Eventually, however, the wilder side of

Portland with its teeming saloons and shady houses of ill-repute was tamed by an indignant citizenry. The prospering economy was turning Stumptown into a real city, complete with officials intent upon creating a structure of law and order. Rules of decorum came to Portland in the 1870s when it was illegal to fire a pistol downtown or drive your carriage faster than six miles per hour. The town gained its most notable nickname in 1889 when local artist, writer, and bon vivant, C.E.S. Woods called for an annual rose show. With an agreeable climate and zealous boosterism at work, the Portland Rose Festival was launched in what would soon be known as the "City of Roses." Since the replacement of the downtown wharves in 1929 with a seawall stretching along most of the city's shoreline on the Willamette River, it has become a tradition to welcome a fleet of U.S. and Canadian warships to dock during the festival.

Part of the early growing economy was agriculture. In 1847 Henry Lewelling brought the first of 700 apple, cherry, peach, plum, and pear saplings into the Willamette Valley, beginning a new agricultural venture. In 1849, the California gold rush created a huge demand for these crops and other staples, thus boosting Portland's economy. The first crop of 100 apples was sent to California mining camps where there was such a scarcity of fresh fruit that scurvy (caused by a vitamin C deficiency) was a leading cause of death. For a time the apples sold for the astronomical sum of $5 apiece, the going rate for a week's room and board! Other Oregon goods ranging from lumber to eggs remained in constant demand, which in turn fueled a new rush of men and women anxious to farm in the Willamette Valley. In 1851, the decidedly unglamorous name of Stumptown was dropped and the city of Portland was officially incorporated. (For more details about Portland's early history, see the Neighborhoods and Real Estate chapter, especially the Linnton and Oregon City sections, and the Area Overview chapter.)

In 1853, Washington split from the Oregon Territory, claiming land north of the Columbia River, which continues to form part of the interstate boundary. The next year Oregon voters rejected statehood because they were split on whether or not to enter the United States as a slave state or as a free state. Although slavery was voted down, 7,277 to 2,645, only 1,081 men voted to let free Black men settle in Oregon compared to 8,640 who were opposed to their presence. Statehood initiatives were also rejected in 1855 and 1856. However on Valentine's Day, 1859, Oregon became a state, with Oregon City, the largest city in the territory, becoming the capital and regional center for all the Oregon Territories.

Insiders' Tip

South Pass, a relatively easy crossing through the Rocky Mountains and a major landmark of the Old West, represents the halfway point on the Oregon Trail and is located in what is now Wyoming.

The Skidmore Foundation in Old Town, named after a city commissioner who visited Paris in the 1870s, was first used as a drinking trough for horses, men, and dogs. CREDIT: DAVID JOHNSON

Indian Treaties Ignored

In the1860s prosperity continued for Portland's 821 residents as the Oregon Steam Navigation Company secured a monopoly on all shipping on the Columbia River. By 1870, Portland boasted the largest population (9,565) in the Pacific Northwest until the Alaska gold rush of 1897 fueled Seattle's rise. In 1883, the transcontinental railroad arrived in Portland with ex-President U.S. Grant on board. This linkage by rail enabled export of lumber, beef, salmon, and other goods to the major eastern cities, triggering the biggest economic and population growth spurt in the state's history.

Sadly, this led to the further subjugation and maltreatment of the state's indigenous peoples. Impatient settlers and loggers repeatedly trampled Indian treaties by taking land reserved for tribal peoples. Private property was a foreign concept to Native Americans who believed the forests and fields were community properties for the general welfare of all. The friction intensified as miners stampeded into areas where silver or gold were found. Native Americans, who were neither taxpayers nor voters, protested the violations in vain. Battles and hostilities sporadically broke out throughout the West. In Oregon, Chief Joseph and the Nez Perce were routed from their homes in the Wallowas to eventually surrender in southern Canada. The Modoc tribe was forced off their land and herded across the California border where they held 1,500 troops at bay in the lava beds for six months. These conflicts were repeated around the western states until the last organized tribal resistance died out in the 1890s.

Logging

Logging continued to be the cornerstone of the economy, and the timber industry was king in Oregon, pressuring Congress to repeal the Forest Preservation Act of 1891, opening up millions of acres of public land in Oregon and other northwestern states for huge clear cuts. Theodore Roosevelt responded by setting aside large forest reserves where timber operations were prohibited. These reserves eventually grew into the USDA Forest Service, which later compromised his intent by allowing timber sales. Recently Forest Service administrators have made significant moves to return federal forests to a protected status.

Back in town in 1905, the huge Forestry Building with its classic logs conjoined, helped celebrate the history of logging in Oregon and the centennial of the Lewis and Clark Expedition. Along with bandstands, exhibit buildings, and other architectural oddities, the big party took place in the northwest part of Portland, which is now an industrial zone. Unfortunately, the forestry building burned in the 1980s.

The War Years

Wartime Workers and Population Growth

During World War I, thousands of unskilled workers swarmed to Portland to work on Swan Island, a bustling center of shipbuilding and repair. But the war to end all wars caused only a ripple in Oregon, compared to World War II, which forever altered the human and physical shape of the Portland area.

Henry J. Kaiser's Oregon Shipbuilding Corporation began building freighters of the famous Liberty Ship class when World War II was less than a month old. The first Kaiser shipyard in the Portland area was the St. Johns Yard. At the end of one year, it launched 36 ships. By war's end, the yard built 141 vessels, including Liberty Ships and their successor, the Victory Ship.

During World War II, the demand for wartime workers and the passage of tens of thousands of enlisted men and women through Oregon swelled the state's population from less than 1.1 million in 1940, to more than 1.5 million in 1950. The City of Portland's 1940 population of 305,000 jumped to 374,000 residents in just three years.

Minority Groups

The Rise and Fall of Vanport

These new members of the populace included large numbers of emigrants from the deep South: They arrived by the trainload, lured from the poverty and oppression of the deep South. Between 1940 and 1945, Portland's African-American population surged from 2,100 to 15,000. Hispanics and Asians also came to Portland to find work in the war industry.

The sudden increase in population strained the city's ability to meet even the most basic needs of these war workers. The state was not always hospitable to minorities, and during the war era, Portland created the instant town of Vanport, largely to insulate itself from these newcomers. Nearly 70,000 workers and their families passed through this city of temporary homes built on a flat floodplain between North Portland and the Columbia River.

The main mast of the U.S.S. Oregon, *a battleship that served in the Spanish American War, World War I, and World War II. Now the mast is at Tom McCall Waterfront Park.* CREDIT: DAVID JOHNSON

Almost overnight Vanport became the state's second-largest city. Three years after the war, about 19,000 people still lived in Vanport. Swollen by rain and melting snow, the Columbia River flooded, breaking the dikes protecting Vanport. On Memorial Day, 1948, the waters swept the town away, killing eighteen residents. The city's entire population, then about one-fourth African American, became homeless.

Some of the flood victims were denied shelter in hotel rooms allegedly reserved for the Rose Festival. The Portland Salvation Army and the Red Cross refused to provide aid to some of the needy, both Black and White. Vanport was never rebuilt and today West Delta Park stands on the site of this former community.

This sad chapter in Portland's history stands next to that of Oregon's Ku Klux Klan, which once boasted a membership of 25,000 and even elected a leader, Grand Dragon Walter Pierce, as governor of the state. Pierce sponsored legislation in 1922 that barred all Catholic schools in the state and also attempted to deny Oregon's Black citizens of their right to vote.

Relocation Camps

African Americans were not the only minority group to suffer maltreatment. The Pearl Harbor bombing created widespread fear of espionage, sabotage, and an invasion aided by Japanese-American citizens. Under Executive Order 9066, issued in February 1942, Japanese-American citizens in certain sensitive areas were forced to relocate.

When the U.S. Army declared Oregon, California, and Washington "strategic areas," they forced more than 110,000 Japanese Americans to relocate to ten relocation centers. More than 4,000 Oregonians of Japanese descent were moved to the Portland Assembly Center, formerly the Portland International Livestock Center. Between May and September of 1942, they lived in former animal stalls and barns, guarded by military police, while permanent relocation camps were built further inland. Several years later, the Executive Order was rescinded, but the Japanese-American population lost their homes, businesses, cars, and farms.

World War II in Portland

The "real" war was closer to Portland than many people imagined. In June of 1942, a submarine of the Imperial Japanese Navy surfaced a few miles off the Oregon coast. Pointing her stern toward a suspected U.S. submarine base, the ship fired on Fort Stevens. In order to preserve the exact location of their coastal defense guns, the frustrated defenders were forbidden to return fire. Fort Stevens thus became the only military installation

Insiders' Tip

Liberty Ship Park, on N.W. Front Street, north of the Broadway Bridge, contains the buried, concrete-filled bow sections of discarded and dismantled Liberty Ships as well as the funnels from the battleship *Oregon* and other maritime artifacts.

in the continental United States to come under direct enemy fire during the war. This was the first attack on the U.S. mainland since the War of 1812. But it was not to be the only Japanese attack here. Many ships were torpedoed off the Oregon coast. For years after the war, rusting mines drifted onto shore. Even today, fishing boats still pull up their nets and find a World War II-era bomb, torpedo, or mine.

Also, in September of 1943, the Japanese launched a single-engine float plane that dropped phosphorus bombs in the Oregon forest northwest of Brookings and on other parts of the West Coast. The only bombs that fell on American soil during the war, their primary purpose was to start forest fires that would divert troops away from the war effort. Of the hundreds of balloon bombs launched by the Japanese, forty-five landed in Oregon. Fortunately, most of these fire starters fizzled in the Oregon rain. But one landed near Bly, a town of 750 people in southeastern Oregon, killing one adult and five children. These were the only civilian deaths from enemy action in the continental U.S. during the war.

One long-range target for these bombs may have been the U.S. Army base at Camp Pendleton. Here Gen. Jimmy Doolittle trained B-17 bomber crews heading for England and for the famous attack on Tokyo. It was after Doolittle's highly symbolic raid that the bombs were dropped in the west.

Post-War Prosperity

War's end brought more changes to Portland and Oregon. Returning veterans enrolled in large numbers at colleges, started families, and bought houses. During the postwar years, prosperity flourished throughout the nation and in Portland. But nature harshly stepped in again in December, 1964. Called the "Worst Flood in the History of Oregon," torrential rain closed all highways in western Oregon and forced 1,500 to evacuate their homes.

In the late 1960s and early 1970s, Governor Tom McCall, a "radical Republican" and visionary, guided the state through a challenging phase by making controlled growth and environmental protection state government's top priorities. As the economy was bolstered by the booming agriculture, timber, fishing, and tourism, many Oregonians enjoyed a period of economic growth and security. Then, in keeping with a national trend, residents and businesses began leaving the inner city in favor of the 'burbs. Not all urban shops and homes were replaced with new ownership, and certain areas began to slide downhill. Gradually, islands of neglect began to appear in Portland's inner city. In the 1980s, many huge projects of the Portland Development Commission focused on areas such as the riverfront and the downtown square area and neglected neighborhoods in Southeast, North, and Northeast Portland. A prime example is Pioneer Square, a central plaza used for festivals, concerts, and lunches away from the office.

By the 1990s the timber industry, while still critical to Oregon's economy, was waning as old growth stands of trees were terribly diminished by decades of uncontrolled over-cutting and poor resource management. The fishing and salmon industry were, likewise, crippled by years of heavy gill netting and drift netting. Meanwhile, manufacturing was growing, fueled by telecommunications and computer technology industries in the Willamette Valley. From the late 1970s and mid-1980s, Portland's suburbs, particularly the Silicon Forest in Washington County, made huge strides and manufacturing and high technology companies began moving to the area, attracted by cheap water, utilities, space, and a high standard of living.

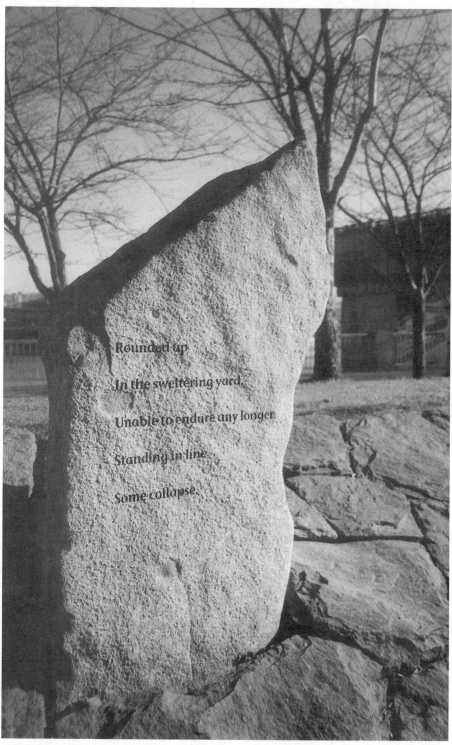

Rounded up

In the sweltering yard.

Unable to endure any longer

Standing in line

Some collapse.

A haiku engraved on a rock in the Japanese American Historical Plaza at Tom McCall Waterfront Park. The plaza honors and remembers Japanese Americans who were interred at western camps during World War II. CREDIT: DAVID JOHNSON

More recently, Portland's economy, while remaining generally healthy and diversified, has suffered several jolts. The slumping economies of many Asian trade partners, especially Japan and Korea, have hurt many Oregon companies around the state. At the same time, large and unanticipated cutbacks in several giant semiconductor plants have added more Oregonians to the unemployment rolls. The construction industry, a generally reliable barometer of the overall business climate in the state, is cooling down substantially from the torrid periods of the early and middle 1990s, but analysts say the market is too diversified and interest rates are too low to lead to a "deep freeze" type of recession that builders experienced in the 1980s.

Fortunately, the long-term prognosis for the state's financial health is good. In the Portland Metro area, numerous high-technology firms, particularly in the fields of telecommunications, medical technology, computer hardware, and software development are experiencing rapid growth.

Demographic experts predict that Oregon's population, which grew at a rate of nearly double the national average during the 1990s, will continue to increase at an impressive rate. Oregon's position, between the states of Washington and California, and connecting to the Pacific Rim nations, puts it in a large economic sphere that is going to continue to generate income and growth. But the growth is not without controversy. As both Oregon and Portland continue to expand, arguments about how much to grow and where to grow will become more heated and intense. Mixed-use development, housing, apartments, and business continue to spring up along light rail in accordance with planner's objectives of higher density. The city's huge and splashy mega-projects of the 1980s are now replaced by smaller, more community-driven developments in such places as Alberta Street, scene of a popular artwalk in Northeast Portland, and the Lents neighborhood in outer Southeast Portland. While the trend in the 1970s and 1980s was flight from the urban areas to the suburbs, many people returned to the inner city in the 1990s and new millenium, starting businesses and fixing up the old homes as well as developing new properties. The results are increased jobs, housing, and livability for all Portlanders.

Bed and Breakfast Inns

Bed and breakfasts offer visitors not only an adventuresome alternative to generic hotel rooms, but also a chance to explore the individual neighborhoods that make up the city. These sojourns, in spots that are usually only seen from the freeway, offer guests a chance to see why people have chosen to live here and how the region's history, climate, geography, diversity, and growth have shaped their lives.

There are trade-offs, such as the occasional shared bath, lack of 24-hour room service, and the rarity of indoor swimming pools and computer ports, but more and more visitors are opting for the less harried atmosphere and the definite sense of place and hospitality that bed and breakfasts provide. Toss in convenient perks, such as fewer parking hassles and lower costs than the average hotel or motel, and it's easy to see the appeal of these homey accommodations.

To choose a bed and breakfast, narrow it down to a half-dozen and give them a call. Inquire about parking, bath facilities, food choices, and nearby attractions. If you decide to stay there, ask for directions from the airport, freeway, or bus or train station. It's not uncommon for a bed and breakfast to mail, fax, or e-mail a confirmation for your stay, information about payment, and a map of how to get there. Tell them what you are interested in, what you want to see, and where you want to go. You may be surprised at how much they know as well as how interested they are in you, your interests, and your comfort.

The bed and breakfasts included here have no-smoking, no-children, and no-pet policies unless mentioned otherwise. All the inns listed are wheelchair accessible.

Price Code

For each bed and breakfast listing we include the following price code, which reflects the cost of double occupancy on a weekend. A 9 percent room tax is reflected in the price code.

$	$50–$75
$$	$75–$100
$$$	$100–$150
$$$$	$150–$200

Southwest Portland

General Hooker's Bed & Breakfast $$-$$$
125 S.W. Hooker St.
(503) 222–4435, (800) 745–4135
www.generalhookers.com

Close to downtown, this charming bed and breakfast is in a mid-sized Victorian building on a tree-lined street in the Lair Hill Historical Conservation District (the district doesn't have a hill as the name implies but rather was named after a chap named Lair Hill). The district boasts a number of older homes, a small park, and tree-lined streets.

The neighborhood's streets were all named for Civil War generals; Hooker Street was named for General Joseph "Fighting Joe" Hooker, a Union general from Massachusetts. In keeping with the historical theme, the house cat is named "Happy Hooker." Though very friendly and well behaved, she's banned from the kitchen and guest rooms.

Fourth-generation Portlander Lori Hall says she's good at giving directions. She adds that her bed and breakfast offers four spacious comfortable rooms, some with private baths and private entrances. The Iris and Daisy rooms can be combined as a suite with a private bath. This inn also has a reference library for travelers. The bed and breakfast does not permit children younger than ten. Smoking is allowed only on the deck.

MacMaster House $$-$$$
1041 S.W. Vista Ave.
(503) 223-7362, (800) 774-9523
www.macmaster.com

Many, if not most, of the of thousands of Portland residents who drive past this bed and breakfast on their way into Washington Park probably don't know it exists. That's good news for tourists, because if Portlanders realized what they were missing, the five rooms in this white Colonial-style mansion would be filled by local residents, not visitors.

Just 2 blocks from Portland's Washington Park-Forest Park complex, MacMaster House is distinguished by its Greek columns, seven fireplaces, and leaded-glass windows. The house and guest rooms are decorated and furnished in a style that owner Cecilia Murphy calls Parisian salon. Rooms have queen-size beds, fireplaces, cable TV, VCRs, and a large film selection. A few have private baths while others share a hallway bath.

Guests gather in the dining room for a hearty gourmet international breakfast that includes croissants, crepes, and omelets prepared by a creative kitchen staff. Breakfast is also offered on the patio and verandah June through October. Besides great food and conversation, guests are treated to views of the city's skyline, Mount Hood, and Mount St. Helens, which can be glimpsed through the trees outside the spacious rooms' windows. The MacMaster House sits in one of Portland's oldest and nicest neighborhoods, and the other large and immaculately kept homes in the neighborhood reflect a variety of architectural styles. The gallery of the Portland Society of Artists; Washington Park with its ponds,

Insiders' Tip

Resources that provide listings of bed and breakfasts in the Portland area and throughout the state include the Oregon Bed and Breakfast Guild, P.O. Box 3187, Ashland, Oregon 97520, (800) 944-6196; LC's Bed and Breakfast Registry, P.O. Box 5214, Portland, Oregon 97208, (503) 261-0804 or (800) 261-0904; and Northwest Bed and Breakfast Reservation Service, 610 S.W. Broadway, Suite 606, Portland, Oregon 97205, (503) 243-7616.

rose gardens, picnic areas, and tennis courts; the lively shopping district along 23rd Avenue; and "Restaurant Row," along 21st Avenue are all just a short walk away. There is convenient access to freeways as well as public transportation, including Westside Max light rail system.

Terwilliger Vista Bed & Breakfast $$-$$$
515 S.W. Westwood Dr.
(503) 244–0602, (503) 293–8042 (fax)
www.terwilligervista.com

Originally built for a prominent Portland family in 1941, the Terwilliger Vista is a large Georgian-style Colonial home in the city's west hills. Large bay windows in the 6,000-square-foot home offer seasonal views of the city's skyline, Mount Hood, the Willamette River, and, even on those darker days of winter, fill the home with light. Located on a half-acre site colored by rose gardens, camellias, and rhododendrons, the bed and breakfast is just six minutes from downtown Portland but a world away from the usual urban irritants of traffic, noise, and crowds.

All five guest rooms are air-conditioned and offer either king- or queen-size beds, private baths, guest refrigerators, cable television, and fireplaces. A two-room suite is also available. Guests can enjoy a continental breakfast, which is served from 7:30 to 8:30 A.M. and a full breakfast from 8:30 to 9:30 A.M. in a spacious dining room. As well as fruits, special breads, and coffeecakes, the meals include soufflés, eggs benedict, and other light and low-cal entrees. A "Romance Package" is also available. It includes a $25 bottle of champagne or sparkling cider, fresh flowers, special sheets, and towels. There is also a common room, where complimentary sodas are made available. The library's relaxing diversions include a collection of books, cards, and games.

Terwilliger Vista is a gracious retreat from a day's activities, offering the convenience of a close-in lodging with the privacy, quiet, and welcome comforts of a fine home.

Northwest Portland

Gedney Garden $
2651 N.W. Cornell Rd.
(503) 226–6514
www.gedneygardens.com

Originally built in 1907, the three guest rooms in this home offer impressive views of the city's skyline, the rivers, and the Cascade Mountains. All the rooms have period furniture circa 1920, and two of the rooms have fireplaces. Due to the building's turn-of-the-century design, guests share a bath. Gedney Garden provides a full breakfast, with cinnamon Dutch apple babies acclaimed as the most popular treat. This B&B is in one of Portland's most desirable neighborhoods, providing downtown convenience with the privacy and calm of an established community.

Heron Haus Bed & Breakfast $$$-$$$$
2545 N.W. Westover Rd.
(503) 274–1846
www.heronhaus.com

Perched on Knob Hill, one the city's poshest neighborhoods near trendy 23rd Avenue, Heron Haus is a turn-of-the-century English Tudor home that offers six guest rooms (all with private baths) on the second floor. With king- or queen-size beds, telephones, and TVs, each room also has a defined sitting area. The Kulia Room includes an elevated spa providing its occupants a view of the city, Mount St. Helens, and Mount Hood. Guests are served a continental breakfast with fresh fruit and a pastry basket. There is an outdoor pool, a mahogany-paneled library, and a sunroom filled with teak furniture.

Century Garden Bed & Breakfast $$
1960 S.E. Larch
(503) 235–6846
www.centurygarden.com

Nestled in Portland's serene Ladd's Addition, this small inn has two rooms with a shared bath that can be rented as a suite with a private bath. The Century Room is decorated as a country farmhouse complete with a tractor seat and the Garden Room is a Victorian parlor with linens and furniture from the era and a balcony overlooking one of the garden circles that highlight this little residential district. One feature not to miss is a large garden basket in the rear of the inn, made from woven reeds and branches. Rates are $69 for double occupancy of one room and $99 for the complete suite. Breakfasts are served any time with an All-American cafe menu that includes eggs cooked any way you like them and gingerbread muffins as a special treat.

North/Northeast Portland

The Clinkerbrick House $-$$
2311 N.E. Schuyler St.
(503) 281–2533

A well-established and popular Portland bed and breakfast, The Clinkerbrick House, a turn-of-the-century Dutch Colonial, has three guest rooms, all with private baths. The rooms are spacious and comfortable, come with queen-size beds, and are decorated with quilts and antiques. Gourmet breakfasts include smoked salmon hash topped with poached eggs, fresh fruit, rhubarb muffins, and in the winter, gingerbread waffles. Located In Portland's charming Irvington neighborhood, this bed and breakfast is close to the Lloyd District and Rose Quarter. It is also a ten-minute drive to downtown or to the city's Pearl District and Northwest neighborhood. Public transportation, a number of bus lines, and light rail are also close by. Rates range from $55 for double occupancy with a shared hall bath and $70 for a room with a private bath.

Insiders' Tip

A great idea for those looking for a wedding anniversary surprise is an overnight stay at one of Portland's cozy bed and breakfast inns. Innkeepers say that lots of couples surprise each other with a stay away from home even if they live in the same city.

The Clinkerbrick House is a turn-of-the-century Dutch Colonial. CREDIT: DAVID JOHNSON

Georgian House Bed & Breakfast   **$$**
1828 N.E. Siskiyou
(503) 281–2250, (888) 282–2250
www.thegeorgianhouse.com

A stay here reveals why Portland prides itself as a city of distinct neighborhoods and one of the nation's most livable cities. A winding staircase, stained-glass windows, and antique furnishings create the mood at this urban bed and breakfast that quietly provides comfortable, air-conditioned lodging for visitors seeking relaxed accommodations. The surrounding neighborhood retains its residential character while being near public transit, shopping, and downtown. The Rose Quarter with the Oregon Convention Center and the covered Lloyd Center with its mix of department stores, movie theaters, and restaurants is also close by.

This classic, immaculately maintained Georgian Colonial home was built in 1922 and has been featured in *Better Homes & Gardens*. The magazine noted that the bed and breakfast has created an atmosphere of an English country home. A breakfast of tea and pastries also reflects this authentic flavor.

Guest rooms have either a private or shared bath and are furnished with antiques. The lower-level spacious and very private Captain Irving Room includes a gas-log fireplace; the Victorian Eastlake Room overlooks the deck, gazebo, and English-style gardens, which feature roses and boxwoods and also provide a variety of berries, grapes, and kiwi for the guests' breakfasts. The Lovejoy Suite, which has the feel of a bridal suite, has a queen-size brass canopy bed and a private bath with clawfoot tub. In the heart of Irvington, this bed and breakfast has rates ranging from $65 to $100. There is ample parking.

The Lion and The Rose   **$$$**
1810 N.E. 15th Ave.
(503) 287–9245, (800) 955–1647
www.lionrose.com

This rambling but immaculately restored Victorian in the well-established Northeast Portland Irvington neighborhood could serve as a postcard image of a past era, offering guests a classic bed-and-breakfast experience.

Convenient to all of Portland and the entire region, this inn is close to the popular shopping, restaurant, and latte-slurping district along N.E. Broadway. The nation's first enclosed mall, The Lloyd Center (which has been remodeled several times in its three-decade history), the Oregon Convention Center, the Rose Garden, the Coliseum, and the Oregon Nature Information Center are also nearby.

Listed on the National Register of Historic Places, the inn's decor and atmosphere create a sense of relaxed elegance. In addition to breakfasts of south-of-the-border quiche, mushroom-and-onion herb quiche, strawberry banana streusel-topped baked French toast or hazelnut bread pudding, guests are served an afternoon dessert tea. The grounds include English-style gardens, a gazebo, fountains, and brick pathways.

Most rooms have private baths, and the Rose Room features a queen-size bed and a Jacuzzi. Other rooms offer guests the chance to sleep in an antique Edwardian bed, a flat-top canopy bed, or a traditional four-poster bed.

McMenamins Kennedy School $$-$$$
5736 N.E. 33rd Ave.
(503) 249-3983
www.mcmenamins.com

Write this address on the blackboard 100 times. This is a student's dream—or a teacher's nightmare—come true. Portland's brewpub kings and urban revivalists, the brothers McMenamin, have converted a derelict former elementary school into a bed and breakfast extraordinaire.

Wherever they learned to do this, they learned their lessons well. Former classrooms have been converted into thirty-five guest rooms, all with queen-size beds and private baths (and no, you don't have to raise your hand or get permission to go).

Set in a traditional Portland neighborhood that actually welcomed the conversion, this unique inn has a very good restaurant, a garden soaking pool, free parking, a collection of artwork and murals by local artists (some of which colorfully document the local history), and a functional gym in case you want to shoot a few hoops. There is also a brewery (what else would be expected from two of the earliest brewpub pioneers), a movie theater, and meeting rooms.

And, with tongue firmly planted in its cheek, the inn has two bars: the Honors

Insiders' Tip

Parents of Portland's college students often opt to stay at a bed and breakfast while visiting their children. It beats sleeping in a dorm room or on a couch and also provides privacy and a chance to savor the town.

Bar and the Detention Bar, though neither carry Teacher's Scotch. There is live music on Thursdays inside and in the courtyard with fine weather.

If you have ever really wanted to sleep in class, this is your chance. You will pay for it, but not dearly. The modest room rate includes a full breakfast at the resident restaurant at no extra charge. Occasionally this bed and breakfast offers $99 packages, which also include free admission to the movie theater, use of the soaking pool and gym, and a $7 credit in the restaurant for an evening meal. You may want to inquire about current offers when you call.

Portland Guest House $-$$$
1720 N.E. 15th Ave.
(503) 282-1402
www.teleport.com/~pgh

A Victorian home in Portland's Irvington neighborhood, this inn offers guests an excellent value and elegant comfortable surroundings. Rooms and suites have high ceilings, lush white carpets, vintage linens, and private baths. They also come with a rarity for bed and breakfasts—private telephones. As for the morning meal, scones, basil omelettes, and fresh fruit are on the menu. Those who choose this charming bed and breakfast will enjoy its close location, brick patio, flower and herb gardens, and walks in the tree-lined neighborhood streets. The innkeeper says there is lots of variety to choose from along with a key to the front door and your room.

Portland White House $$$-$$$$
1914 N.E. 22nd Ave.
(503) 287-7131, (800) 272-7131
www.portlandswhitehouse.com

Completely restored to the grand splendor of 1911, Portland White House was built of Honduran mahogany by early Portland timber magnate Robert Lyle. It has eight guest rooms, all with private baths and featuring period furnishings and decor. The Garden Room sports a private terrace, and the Canopy Room has, of course, a canopied bed. With a circular drive, classic Greek columns, fountains, a carriage house, and Japanese maples, this inn bears some resemblance to its Washington, D.C., namesake, though on a smaller scale. Guests can visit the parlor for sherry or board games. The inn is a local landmark featured in *Sunset Magazine*, close to attractions on the city's East Side and convenient to downtown. This remarkable inn serves a chef's breakfast that may include Gorgonzola Pears Fritatta and sautéed apple custard French toast.

Vancouver

The Vintage Inn $$
310 W. 11th St.
(360) 693-6635, (888) 693-6635
www.vintage-inn.com

In downtown Vancouver, this Victorian home (built in 1903) offers an authentic turn-of-the-century experience. Four guest rooms feature queen-size beds, and since there are shared baths, robes are provided. The inn is furnished with elegant antiques, antique china, and often decorated with fresh-cut flowers. The full breakfast includes dishes such as almond-crusted French toast with fresh strawberries and cheese blintz soufflé. The signature dish is edible morning glory flowers with eggs and fresh herbs from the herb garden.

The downtown location lets guests walk to restaurants, shopping, coffeeshops, galleries, and some of Vancouver's historic attractions, including Fort Vancouver National Historic Reserve. There is also a small meeting space for eight to ten people. C-Trans, the county's bus service, boasts a fleet of newer and well-maintained buses, and a mini-transit mall in downtown eliminates the need for

The Lion and The Rose is a restored Victorian in the historic Irvington District. CREDIT: DAVID JOHNSON

a car to reach many destinations, including downtown Portland.

Convenient to local freeways, the inn can serve as a base for daytrips to the Columbia Gorge, Mount St. Helens, the Oregon and Washington coasts, and downtown Portland. Lastly, the inn is only fifteen minutes from Portland International Airport.

Outlying Areas

Broetje House $$
3101 S.E. Courtney Rd., Milwaukie
(503) 659–8860
www.broetjekouse.citysearch.com

On an acre of scenic grounds with century-old shrubs, flowers and redwoods, this Queen Anne-style home, complete with four-story water tower, was built by noted Oregon horticulturist John F. Broetje in 1899. The building's history includes a role as a winery before its career as a bed and breakfast and a location for weddings, receptions, and other gatherings. This countrylike retreat is still very convenient to all of the area's attractions and is fifteen to twenty minutes from downtown Portland. Guests are served a full country breakfast with signature dishes of oven pancakes topped with fresh fruit and coffeecake muffins. After a night in one of three Victorian rooms furnished in Queen Anne style, guests can relax in the gazebo, the sitting room, or even in the inn's country kitchen. The hostess reports that the bridal suite with its private bath is their most popular selection.

McMenamins Edgefield Bed & Breakfast Resort $$-$$$
2126 S.W. Halsey St., Troutdale
(503) 669–8610, (800) 669–8610
www.mcmenamins.com

Originally built in 1911 as the Mult-nomah County Poor Farm, the Edgefield has been transformed into a unique and spirited place to enjoy the tranquil pleasures of life. This unusual village includes a 104-room bed and breakfast, vineyard and winery, brewery and pub, beer garden, movie theater, eighteen-hole golf course, fine dining at the Black Rabbit Restaurant, and meeting and catering facilities. There is beer, wine, and spirits and a distillery on-site. A highlight of any visit to Edgefield is a tour of the hallways with their amazing array of original art, including portraits of those who lived here when it was the poor farm. Along with the amenities in the bed and breakfast, the Edgefield grounds feature a masseuse, a glassblower's shop, herb and wildflower gardens, year-round events, and outdoor concerts in the summer. Overnight retreats are very popular at Edgefield, especially the midweek retreat package, which is designed specifically for smaller meetings and board retreats. Day or evening excursions are made to Edgefield to taste the beers and wines, sample regional cuisine, attend a historical tour, or simply stroll through scenic gardens. McMenamins Edgefield is located twenty minutes east of downtown Portland and is fifteen minutes from Portland International Airport. Multnomah Falls and the Columbia Gorge National Scenic Area are nearby, as are an incredible array of recreational activities, including skiing, wind surfing, golfing, fishing, hiking, greyhound racing, and bargain shopping at the Columbia Gorge Factory Stores.

Sauvie Island Bed and Breakfast $$
26504 N.W. Reeder Rd., Sauvie Island
(503) 621–3216
www.moriah.com/sauvie

Sauvie Island is a large, flat, fertile island in the far reaches of Northwest Portland, off U.S. Highway 30, the road paralleling the Columbia River and ending at Astoria, where the Columbia meets the Pacific Ocean. With only a single bridge linking the island to the mainland, Sauvie Island includes a large wildlife sanctuary, preserved and protected wetlands, and some of the richest farmland in the nation. While the lowest parts of the island are protected by levees, there are long strips of sandy beaches facing

Insiders' Tip

If you plan to stay in Portland for more than a day or so, how about staying at a bed and breakfast inn in each quadrant of the city? That will give you a sense of the distinctive physical and cultural differences in the various districts. Chatting with innkeepers—most of whom are walking guidebooks—will give you some local lore as well as directions to dinner spots and other attractions.

the river. Though some of the riverfront land is private, much of the shoreline is open to the public.

This two-room bed and breakfast is a retreat on this wondrous isle offering guests an unusual view and perspective of the region. On a clear day, the sun rises over Mount Hood and three snowcapped mountains (Mt. Helens, Mt. Adams, and Mt. Rainier) can be seen north of the Columbia River. Freighters, tankers, container ships, and, in June, American and Canadian Navy vessels heading for the Rose Festival can be seen gliding across the horizon as they head toward the Pacific or to Portland docks.

American bald eagles, great blue herons, osprey, red foxes, wood ducks, and beavers live year-round in the island's wildlife preserves and sanctuaries. Between 2 and 3 million migratory birds and waterfowl, including tundra swans and sand hill cranes, can darken the sky in the fall and spring with their flocks, filling the air with the sound of beating wings.

Both rooms have private baths, and guests can enjoy an outdoor spa and a view of the river and mountains from the deck. In fall and winter, a stone fireplace offers warmth and a sense of comfort against the damp seasonal chill.

Westlund's River's Edge Bed & Breakfast
$$
22502 N.W. Gillihan Rd.,
Sauvie Island
(503) 621–9856
www.riversedge-bb.com

Offering just two guest rooms, each with private entrances, the River's Edge ensures guests a quiet stay in a pastoral setting with many of the conveniences of a large hotel. Though there is a shared bath, the two rooms have queen-size beds, and a guest kitchenette with microwave oven and small refrigerator. A large sitting room is warmed by a wood stove and gives guests the choice of a television, books from the bed and breakfast's library, and a collection of videos. Just 150 feet from the Columbia River, the beach and grassy picnic area (complete with brick fireplace) are perfect places to watch the river traffic or view stunning sunsets and sunrises with Mount Hood and Mount St. Helens providing snowcapped accents. The inn offers a choice of a full breakfast of eggs, pancakes, waffles, and bacon served family style or a continental breakfast replete with pastries and espresso.

Hotels and Motels

All year long, but especially during the summer months, Portland attracts tourists from throughout the United States and all over the world. Visitors come to see the area's natural beauty, which ranges from the snowcapped peaks of the Cascade Mountains to the unrivaled spectacular beauty of the Oregon coast and the Columbia Gorge. Once here, they find a region rich in local and national history and an area that's home to a large community of talented artists, writers, and crafters. It is a region blessed with a mild, if somewhat damp, climate and rich soil that nourishes everything from roses, tulips, and irises to Christmas trees, mint, truffles, and hazelnuts.

Visitors will find more than 20,000 hotel rooms of all types and price ranges in the Portland metropolitan area. Whether you are traveling alone, as a couple, or in a small group, you should be able to find a place to stay that will meet your style and your price range. The greater Portland area has one of the nation's highest hotel occupancy rates, about 75 percent. This testifies to the region's growing population, the development of the visitor and tourism industry, and the area's commercial and business expansion.

While the primary concentrations of lodgings are found downtown, at the Lloyd Center, the Oregon Convention Center, and near Portland International Airport, there are facilities located in almost every part of the region. Several hotels are strung along I-5 north and south of both Portland and Vancouver, in Gresham and Troutdale along I-84 east of the city proper, and near U.S. Highway 26 as it heads through the city of Sandy, Oregon, and up the Mount Hood Corridor. More accommodations are off I-205, which serves as a regional ring road, allowing motorists to bypass Portland's center. Other popular locations for lodging include exits off I-405 and near Oregon Highway 217 and U.S. Highway 26 (often called the Sunset Highway or simply the Sunset) south and west of Portland, where much of the Silicon Forest, Oregon's high-tech zone, is found. Across the Columbia River in Vancouver and Clark County are clusters of hotels and motels (and shopping, restaurants, and other attractions) downtown, north along I-5, and near the Vancouver Mall just off I-205 after it crosses the river into Washington State.

We've included hotels of all sizes. As most of the area's accommodations are downtown or near the airport, that is what we have listed here. But we've included some options for other parts of town as well as for the Outlying Areas—and we've included some inexpensive choices for those weary travelers who just want a hot shower and a soft bed. Traditional hotels are being supplemented by urban bed and breakfasts and hotels offering extended-stay services, which are now found both in the suburbs and in more urban neighborhoods. (You'll find our bed-and-breakfast listings in a separate chapter.) The expansion of the region's lodging options is good news for visitors, because it increases their choices. However, the market for rooms may still be very tight during certain times of the year.

Customer service has become a key marketing strategy. Hotels recognize the value of being agreeable, and they provide a range of services, amenities, and information to guests. Many hotels offer free telephones at Portland International Airport for arriving guests to make reservations or receive directions. Some hotels offer free airport shuttles; others are served by a privately run airport shuttle service.

Most hotels commonly offer smoke-free rooms and rooms for those who smoke, so guests can state their preference when making reservations. Likewise, some hotels accept pets. Others provide free lodging for children staying in the same room as their parents or even grandparents. Compliance with the Americans with Disabilities Act (ADA) means hotel rooms are easier to use for travelers with physical challenges and for older adults.

Not surprisingly, in some areas, particularly downtown, parking is at a premium, though some hotels do offer free parking for guests. Some provide valet parking at their own facilities or nearby garages; others offer their guests discounted parking at local garages.

Keep in mind, the market for rooms may be very tight during certain times of the year, especially during Portland's annual Rose Festival celebration in June. The Portland Art Museum's newly introduced series of "blockbuster" exhibits also draws art patrons from throughout the western United States and Canada, increasing the demand for rooms.

While we have attempted to make this list a comprehensive one, we can't include every hotel in the region, so we strive to provide a variety of locations and price ranges. We figure you know about the reliable national chains like Best Western, Holiday Inn, Radisson Hotels, Ramada, the various incarnations of the Marriott, etc., and you will find these chains citywide and into the Outlying Areas. We list them only when they are especially remarkable. When available, we list toll-free numbers for your convenience and savings.

Price Code

The following price code is based on an average room rate for double occupancy during high season. While there is no sales tax in Oregon, many counties, including Multnomah, Washington, and Clackamas, have a room tax that varies from 7 to 10 percent. Washington State has a 7.25 percent sales tax.

$	$50 and less
$$	$51–$100
$$$	$100–$150
$$$$	$150 and above

Please note that many hotels and motels change their room rates at least twice a year so the ranges we have quoted in this chapter are meant simply as a guide to point you in the right direction, not as the final word on the cost of your stay.

The Benson Hotel $$$$
309 S.W. Broadway
(503) 228–2000, (800) 426–0670

A grand and historic Portland hotel, The Benson was built in 1912 by Portland lumber baron Simon Benson. The elegant lobby exudes warmth and comfort with dark Circassian walnut paneling, stunning Austrian crystal chandeliers, Italian marble floors, and plush oriental carpeting. Plants, lamps, and comfortable chairs and sofas establish well-defined spaces for a sense of privacy. The hotel's huge, glowing fireplace is graced with a delicate metal sculpture of Portland's favorite flower, the rose. Guest rooms are smartly decorated with comfortable, traditional furnishings. The hotel's attention to detail is superb and legendary. For years the Benson has been the hotel of choice for visiting U.S. Presidents (beginning with FDR), movie stars, rock singers, and all manner of dignitaries visiting Portland. Doormen in traditional cloaks and top hats of black and vermilion greet guests and visitors to the Benson. (Even if you don't stay here, drop by the lobby bar for a drink.) The Benson's London Grill restaurant has been a Portland favorite for generations and the adjoining restaurant Piatti, featuring Northern Italian cuisine, is newer and already very popular. On the transit mall in downtown, The Benson is close to galleries, theaters, restaurants, and shopping.

The Clyde Hotel $$
1022 S.W. Stark St.
(503) 224–8000
www.clydehotel.com

Built in 1912, The Clyde Hotel is one of Portland's oldest, but suffered decades of neglect until the present owners began their ambitious, ongoing renovation of the grand old building. The Clyde reopened in October 2000, and there's nothing quite like it in the city. Its vintage charm extends from the funky little rooms to the elegant mezzanine overlooking the beautiful, wood-paneled lobby where patrons can sit and have coffee or read the paper. Bathrooms have claw-foot tubs and tile floors, and all the rooms have small sinks. Rooms are simply furnished, in keeping with the deliberately old-fashioned character of the hotel. There are televisions, but no telephones, in the rooms themselves, though there is a separate room devoted to telephones, vending machines, and Internet hook-up. But the Clyde's proximity to Powell's—just one block away—might make you glad that there's no phone in the room to disturb you. The Clyde is right on the border of the Pearl District, right off the new streetcar line, and thus ideally situated. This hotel might not be for everyone, but for the adventuresome person in search of good value and a little time travel, the Clyde might be just the place.

Days Inn City Center $$
1414 S.W. 6th Ave.
(503) 221–1611, (800) 899–0248

This is a bustling, popular hotel within walking distance of Portland State University, Keller Auditorium and the Performing Arts Center, the business and financial districts, downtown theaters and galleries, and shopping. The hotel is on the airport shuttle route and it also offers free covered parking. There is a full-service family restaurant attracting a loyal clientele of downtown shoppers and office workers as well as guests. There are non-smoking and barrier-free guest rooms and all rooms have computer ports. A heated outdoor swimming pool is available during the appropriate seasons.

DoubleTree Hotel-Portland Downtown $$$
310 S.W. Lincoln St.
(503) 221–0450, (800) 222–TREE

Just 7 blocks from the city's central district, the DoubleTree is within walking distance of Portland State University and Keller Auditorium. It is also conveniently near the off and on ramps to all of the area's major freeways. Within the borders of Tri-Met's Fareless Square, downtown's attractions are a short, free bus ride away. In case of rain, sometimes referred to locally as "Oregon mist," the hotel offers guests the use of umbrellas. Some guest rooms have interior entrances and there is free parking. This two-level hotel has an exercise center and an indoor swimming pool as well as a restaurant, the Cityside, and a lounge, Club Max. Recently remodeled, the hotel's rooms are well appointed, quiet, and comfortable.

Embassy Suites Portland Downtown $$$$
319 S.W. Pine St.
(503) 279–9000 (800)–EMBASSY

The downtown Embassy Suites is one of downtown Portland's newer luxury hotels; its underpinning is the extensive restoration and remodeling of a piece of Portland's history, the Multnomah Hotel. As part of the 1912 Rose Festival, Silas Christopherson flew his Curtiss pusher bi-plane off the hotel's roof. *The Oregonian* wrote that the flight would probably never be done again. They were wrong. In September 1995, Tom Murphy, a pilot from Hood River, Oregon, with approvals from more than two dozen government agencies, duplicated the flight during the building's remodeling.

This sophisticated hotel offers guests well-furnished, two-room suites done in a pleasing and restful contemporary decor. The east facing rooms afford views of Mount Hood, 60 miles distant. A cooked-to-order breakfast and a nightly hosted manager's reception are included in the room rate. In terms of amenities, little is missing. There is 24-hour room service, a heated indoor pool, a sauna and whirlpool, and well-equipped athletic center. Guest rooms include voice mail service, wall jacks for computers, 25-inch color televisions, and a Nintendo system.

Insiders' Tip

If you're traveling with children, room service in the morning may allow you a more relaxed start to your day.

The Fifth Avenue Suites $$$$
506 S.W. Washington St.
(503) 222–0001 (800) 711–2971

Guests at Portland's Fifth Avenue Suites will not recognize it, but this upscale hotel now occupies a building constructed in 1910 that originally housed one of Portland's classic department stores, Lipman Wolfe's. In the heart of Portland's downtown, this is one of the city's newest hotels and occupies a building listed in the National Registry of Historic Places. Guests are just a block from Pioneer Square and Meier & Frank, Portland's other traditional downtown department store. Stations for light rail trains going both east and west are also very close. The shops of Pioneer Place, as well as Nordstrom and Niketown, are an easy 3-block walk from the hotel. Downtown theaters, the art museum, Performing Arts Center, the Oregon History Center, and a host of excellent restaurants are all within a short walk. An evening wine tasting in the comfortable and well-furnished fireside lobby that displays a well-chosen selection of contemporary Northwest art is provided for guests, as well as morning coffee, tea, juice, and newspapers. The adjoining Red Star Tavern & Roast House (see Restaurants) offers a fine menu and is one of the city's most popular restaurants and bars. And don't miss the Aveda Lifestyle Store and

Spa on the ground floor—not only do they sell luscious oils, shampoos, and other products, but they also offer massages, body scrubs, and a number of equally delightful services.

Four Points Hotel—Downtown Portland
$$
50 S.W. Morrison St.
(503) 221–0711, (800) 325–3535

Describing itself as providing contemporary accommodations with a European flair, this Four Points Hotel, which is owned by the Sheraton chain, offers guests a hotel just across from the Willamette River and Portland's Waterfront Park. Guests will also appreciate the hotel's free parking. Some rooms have a view of the Willamette River. The hotel offers immediate access to the city's light rail system. The Morrison Bridge, carrying traffic to Portland's Eastside, is very close, allowing easy access to (and from) all the city's freeways. The Four Points is also close to the large downtown Borders Books & Music and to the city's downtown shopping core. Guests have access to an adjoining fitness club and runners can cross Front Avenue to the Tom McCall Waterfront Park. The hotel also has a small library, twenty-four-hour coffee, a lobby fireplace, and a restaurant.

The Governor Hotel   **$$$$**
611 S.W. 10th at S.W. Alder St.
(503) 224–3400 (800) 554–3456
www.governorhotel.citysearch.com

A complete and historically accurate renovation transformed the Governor into an inviting luxury hotel reminiscent of the past, but with contemporary conveniences. Turn-of-the-century murals depicting the travels of Lewis and Clark, as well as mahogany woodwork, deep leather chairs, and a fireplace make the lobby a comfortable retreat. The beautiful stained-glass dome in the adjacent restaurant captures the grandeur of the building, which is a National Historic Landmark. The well-executed historic restoration extends throughout the hotel,

including the guest rooms. Guests can take advantage of the Princeton Athletic Club, which shares the building with the hotel. The Governor is close to the light rail system as well as downtown shops, galleries, and restaurants. Jake's Bar and Grill, a younger sibling of the original Jake's, one of Portland's oldest restaurants, is adjacent to the Governor.

The Heathman Hotel   **$$$$**
1001 S.W. Broadway at
S.W. Salmon St.
(503) 241–4100, (800) 551–0011
www.heathmanhotel.com

This popular and elegant downtown hotel is next to Portland's Performing Arts Center and within a few blocks of the Portland Art Museum and the Park Blocks. Known for its attention to detail and its superb restaurant, the Heathman Hotel is also distinguished for its collection of work by local and regional artists and by such contemporary American artists as Andy Warhol. The rooms are cozy and conservative but modern and well appointed, and the mini-bars are stocked with snacks from Pacific Northwest companies.

The Heathman Restaurant has long been one of Portland's best; the adjacent Marble Bar is a beautiful place for an evening cocktail. Tea is served every afternoon (reservations strongly suggested) in the Tea Court Lounge. This lounge, with 25-foot ceilings, a handsome fireplace, and a grand staircase to the mezzanine, is an original part of the hotel, and it's a favorite spot to read, relax, or just people-watch. Evenings in the lounge feature light jazz or piano performances by some of the area's best musicians. Guests can take advantage of the hotel's 400-film video collection and a lending library. There is twenty-four-hour room service and guests can arrange sessions with personal trainers in the fitness suite. The mezzanine library displays signed editions of books by authors (including Tom Wolfe, John Updike, and Alice Walker) who have been guests at the hotel. Finally, the Heathman has an outstanding concierge staff who will find you tickets to local shows, make your dinner reservations, hook you up with sightseeing tours, and fulfill other special requests.

The Hilton—Portland $$$$
921 S.W. 6th Ave.
(503) 226–1611, (800) 445–8667

In the center of Portland's vibrant downtown, the Portland Hilton has been recently and gracefully remodeled, rescuing it from its former "bunker" image and creating a well-lit, contemporary facility. The airy rooms, some with views of Mount Hood and the Cascade Mountains, include computer dataports, personalized voice mail, and free cable television. The nicely furnished lobby features a two-story atrium, entrances on both S.W. Broadway and S.W. 6th Avenue, and well-defined spaces with couches, chairs, and tables providing privacy and quiet. There is an attractive display of works by regional artists, and just off the lobby there is a warm, dark-paneled bar and restaurant. The Portland Hilton Athletic Club includes a large indoor pool, a Jacuzzi, sauna and steam rooms, aerobic classes, and exercise equipment as well as the services of fitness trainers and a massage therapist. Serving an international clientele, the Hilton offers foreign currency exchange and a multilingual staff. Here too, the concierge staff is remarkably attentive and knowledgeable; they will help you arrange your dinner and your entertainment, as well as help you find your way around the city.

Hotel Vintage Plaza $$$
422 S.W. Broadway
(503) 228–1212, (800) 243–0555

Featuring a wine country theme that extends to the names of most rooms, to the interior color scheme, and to a nightly complimentary tasting of Oregon wines at the lobby fireplace, the Hotel Vintage Plaza is an intimate downtown hotel with an atmosphere and style that cushions guests from the fatigue of travel, touring, or business. The Vintage Plaza has every-

thing a guest would want. The rooms are private, warm, comfortable, and tasteful. All aspects of the hotel's service are personal and highly polished. There are "starlight rooms" with conservatory windows that let natural light flow into the room and some two-story townhouse suites. Pazzo Ristorante occupies the ground floor; its Northern Italian cuisine touched by Northwest influences is popular with locals too. The hotel, on the north end of downtown, is close to major shopping, cultural, and business districts.

The Imperial Hotel $$
400 S.W. Broadway
(503) 228–7221, (800) 452–2323

Opened in 1908 and now carefully restored, the Imperial is one of Portland's best-kept secrets, offering excellent value. The rooms are large, quiet, and light. The staff is courteous, helpful, resourceful, and knowledgeable about where to go, what to see, and how to get there. The 2 P.M. checkout time adds a morning for last-minute shopping or sightseeing and eliminates the usual stressful rush to leave before 11 A.M. The hotel includes a well-furnished, family-oriented restaurant with good food at moderate prices. A popular bar is just off the lobby. The lobby is attractive, comfortable, and filled with light, and once out the door and past the doormen, you are right downtown. Portland's Old Town and Saturday Market are within easy walking distance.

Mallory Hotel $$-$$$
729 S.W. 15th Ave.
(503) 223–6311, (800) 228–8657

The Mallory (as well as several other Portland hotels) was built in 1912 as part of Portland's growth after the Lewis and Clark Centennial Exposition. Like its sister hotel, the Imperial, the Mallory is one of the best hotel values in the city. The hotel has been owned by the same family for more than fifty years and has recently redecorated all of its 136 guest rooms. While uptown from the downtown core, the Mallory is still very convenient to downtown, to PGE Park, to Washington Park, and to the ever-changing mélange of shops, restaurants, and galleries of the city's vibrant Northwest and Pearl Districts. The hotel is on the city's new Westside light rail line, near I–405, and offers free parking. The 1 P.M. checkout time allows an extra morning of sightseeing, shopping, or relaxation. The hotel's suites have televisions sets in both rooms, eliminating any conflict about who wants to watch what. There is a small bar and the hotel's dining room offers good food at reasonable prices; its German pancakes are a local favorite.

The Mark Spencer Hotel $$
409 S.W. 11th Ave.
(503) 224–3293, (800) 548–3934

Offering both standard guest rooms and one-bedroom suites, the Mark Spencer's rooms also have fully equipped kitchens. The hotel's clientele includes business travelers, visitors, and new residents relocating to the area; many clients stay for extended periods. Perhaps more modest and conservative than some of the newer and trendier downtown hotels, the Mark Spencer's location offers convenience and value. In the same block as Portland's renowned Jake's Famous Crawfish restaurant, the Mark Spencer is just across Burnside Street from Powell's City of Books and close to MAX, the light rail system. The main part of downtown is a short walk away as is Water-front Park, the Portland Art Museum, the Oregon History Center, the newly restored Central Branch of the Multnomah County Library, and the Galleria.

The Marriott Hotel-City Center $$$$
520 S.W. Broadway
(503) 226–6300, (800) 228–9290

The renowned Marriott service and the plentiful amenities you have come to expect are here presented in a boutique hotel setting. This brand-new hotel features nearly 250 rooms and ten suites on twenty floors; it's got a cocktail lounge and a restaurant on the premises; it's in the heart of downtown but close to the Pearl District, the Chinese Garden, and the river. It's a good hotel for the business traveler since the rooms have two-line speaker phones and dataports, and the hotel provides a generous amount of meeting space. It's also a good choice for family travel; not only will the Marriott furnish childcare services, but Rover can stay too, provided he is good. The paneled lobby is quite lovely, with a big chandelier and a sweeping staircase just right for making a spectacular entrance.

The Marriott Hotel-Downtown Portland $$$$
401 S.W. Naito Pkwy.
(503) 226–7600, (800) 228–9290

Across Southwest Front Avenue from the Willamette River and the Tom McCall

Insiders' Tip

Traveling with Fido? The big chain hotels like the Marriott are usually reliable about allowing pets. The Governor Hotel and the Embassy Suites, both downtown, have also been known to accept well-bred dogs. For a list of dog-friendly hotels in Oregon, visit Joey's Dog House at www.home.earthlink.net/~adelsheim/petfriendly.html

Riverfront Park, the uppermost of the Marriott's 503-rooms perch fourteen stories above street-level, offering, weather permitting of course, superb views of Mount Hood. A popular choice for business travelers and meeting and convention attendees, the hotel also attracts its share of tourists. The Marriott includes two restaurants, two bars, an indoor pool, and a twenty-four-hour athletic club. This is a full-service hotel in the broadest sense of the word, with some barrier-free rooms. Arrangements for pets are available. The Marriott is also a scheduled stop on the airport shuttle. The hotel is convenient to Portland's financial district and government buildings and to all of the downtown attractions. Champions, the hotel's sports bar, is a popular and lively lounge and casual restaurant. Champions, and the Marriott as a whole, is popular with NBA teams visiting Portland to take on the Trailblazers at the nearby Rose Garden, so diners may see a favorite basketball player coming in for a snack or meal. The bar's high-tech television system lets it broadcast every NBA game simultaneously (unless the game is blacked out).

The Paramount Hotel $$$$
808 S.W. Taylor
(503) 223–9900
www.portlandparamount.com

The chic Paramount Hotel opened in 2000 and visitors to Portland have been rejoicing. This European-style hotel offers plenty of amenities for travelers, from same-day laundry services to video games. The rooms are lovely, bigger than what you'll find in most hotels, with added luxuries such as granite bathrooms. Some rooms come with terraces and jetted tubs, and two delightful suites are available—these have excellent views of the city, as well as fireplaces and whirlpools. All rooms come with dual-line phones and dataports; two large meeting rooms are also available. The stylish restaurant and bar, the Dragonfish Asian Cafe, also provides room service and catering for business functions. The downtown location could not be more

central; the hotel is a heartbeat away from the Schnitzer, the Portland Art Museum, some of the best downtown shopping, and fabulous restaurants. The Paramount also offers a beautiful fitness center, if you haven't gotten enough exercise walking around downtown. The service, by the way, is excellent—friendly, helpful, and understated.

The RiverPlace Hotel $$$
1510 S.W. Harbor Wy.
(503) 228–3233, (800) 426–0670

On the bank of the Willamette River, the RiverPlace Hotel offers rooms and suites facing the river or offering a north view of the city's skyline. A gazebo offers views of the river, Portland's eastside skyline, and Mount Hood. During the summer, the hotel's patio is a good spot from which to view the frequent displays of fireworks, not to mention a seemingly unending colorful stream of runners, roller-bladers, skateboarders, dog-walkers, cyclists, and people out for a stroll. The river hosts a twenty-four-hour parade of tour boats, sailboats, jet-skis, barges and log-tows, dragon-boats, yachts, kayaks, and the occasional windsurfer.

While separated from the core of the downtown by busy S.W. Naito Parkway, guests can walk along the Tom McCall Waterfront Park to reach downtown's stores, galleries, and other attractions. There also is a small group of shops and stores along the esplanade, facing the river. The lobby is elegant and usually filled with large, artistic displays of fresh flowers. The staff is well trained, polite, and attentive. Some of the rooms feature river views, and all of them are comfortable with large baths and contemporary decor. Guests are given breakfast and have access to the adjacent and trendy RiverPlace Athletic Club for a small fee. The Esplanade, the hotel's restaurant, specializes in Northwest cuisine. The Pilsner Room is a comfortable, casual, and popular high-end brewpub serving a wide range of Oregon and Northwest beers and ales and features an excellent bar menu.

Sumptuous rooms at the Paramount Hotel will refresh the weariest traveler. CREDIT: COURTESY OF THE PARA-
MOUNT HOTEL

Sixth Avenue Motel $$
2221 S.W. 6th Ave.
(503) 226–2979

Situated between Portland State University and downtown proper, this is a small, locally owned motel. The motel takes advantage of its size and location by offering special rates to commercial travelers, older adults, students, and families with members being treated at any of the area's hospitals. Downtown is a short walk and the hotel is within Fareless Square, so guests can take free bus rides to get to and from downtown. A variety of restaurants, lounges, movie theaters, coffeehouses, and the Portland State University Bookstore are nearby. The motel's location also means easy access to and from local freeways.

The Westin Portland $$$$
750 S.W. Alder St.
(503) 294–9000

One of the newest downtown luxury hotels, the Westin imparts the feeling that its guests are the most important creatures in the world with the lushness of its surroundings and the attentiveness of its service. The rooms are elegant, with cozy down blankets and duvets on the beds, and oversized, walk-in showers in the bathrooms. (They also provide CD players and CDs, which are useful because you might not ever leave the room.) Like all state-of-the-art hotels, the Westin's rooms come equipped with two-line phones and dataports, and it also offers high-speed Internet access. For events, the hotel has a number of different-sized meeting rooms, as well as a ballroom; each of these is well appointed. The Westin is able to make use of its corporate resources to provide desirable services like the Westin Kids Club and the Guest Office, but the service is also remarkably thoughtful and charming. Oritalia, the Westin's Asian-Italian-inspired restaurant, has rapidly earned a solid reputation.

Northwest Portland

Silver Cloud Inn $$$
2426 N.W. Vaughn St.
(503) 242–2400, (800) 205–6939

Visitors choosing this Silver Cloud Inn (there is another near the airport) shouldn't be concerned about this hotel's Northwest Portland location, which puts it on the edge of an industrial area. The hotel is tidy, quiet, and within walking distance of good restaurants, an eclectic mix of small shops, a brewpub, and coffeehouses. Close to the intersection of the area's main freeways, the hotel is also near the trendy and *trés* chic shopping districts on N.W. 23rd and N.W. 21st Avenues.

The hotel offers covered parking, a fitness center and spa, a video library, a complimentary breakfast, and cable TV in all the rooms. Pets are also welcome. The hotel's location allows easy access to the highways following the Columbia River to the Oregon coast and to those leading east to Mount Hood and the Columbia Gorge.

Insiders' Tip

If you're yearning for luxury but watching your budget, try the Embassy Suites packages that include Aveda treatments at the adjacent Salon Nyla.

Best Value Inn $
3310 S.E. 82nd Ave.
(503) 777–4786, (800) 358–5066

A safe and affordable port for those watching expenses, the very decent single rooms at Best Value Inn go for $39 and the double-bed rooms accommodate up to four people for $49. This includes cable TV and telephones but no complimentary coffee or other perks. The rooms are big and kept well, and the managers are gracious. The bathrooms are clean and well supplied. Check in after 11 A.M. and you can check out anytime before 4 P.M. The sign says NO PETS, but the proprietors are willing to grant exceptions for small and friendly cats and dogs. This inn is near many restaurants and stores, including a large Food-4-Less, which is less than a block away.

Chestnut Tree Inn $
9699 S.E. Stark St.
(503) 255–4444

Another option for cost conscious travelers seeking a clean, well-lighted place, the Chestnut offers fifty-eight comfortable units equipped with phones, TVs, and small refrigerators. The bathrooms are surprisingly nice, with spacious tubs/showers. This inn is located right off of Interstate 205 and is just one-half mile away from MAX, Portland's light rail, and a host of shopping opportunities. The managers keep the place very clean, run off any rabble-rousers, and will receive your fax at any hour of the day or night. You won't get a continental breakfast, but coffee, tea, cider, and a community microwave are available in the lobby. Single rooms for one or two persons go for about $50 and doubles are around $55.

Monarch Hotel & Conference Center $$$
12566 S.E. 93rd Ave.
(503) 652–1515, (800) 492–8700

The Monarch Hotel & Conference Center is off Interstate 205 with easy access to Interstates 5 and 84; it's close to Clackamas Town Center—one of Oregon's largest enclosed shopping malls. The Monarch, one of the nicest hotels in the area, offers free shuttle service to and from the airport and nearby shopping complexes. Most of the 20,000 square feet of meeting and convention space is situated around a lovely garden courtyard. The 200-room hotel accommodates groups from 10 to 1,000, and offers free parking.

Guests are invited to enjoy the open courtyard swimming pool (in season), which is adjoined by a year-round whirlpool spa and a nearby 20-mile jogging and biking path. Other amenities include Sam's Restaurant, which has built a good reputation, a multilevel lounge featuring live entertainment Wednesday through Saturday, and valet service.

Portland Travelodge Suites $$
7740 S.E. Powell Blvd.
(503) 788–9394

This respected chain's Powell Boulevard facility offers a solid value with double rooms going for around $82 and singles for $70. There aren't any Jacuzzis or luxury suites, but the forty clean, spacious, and comfortable air-conditioned rooms are equipped with cable TV, phones, fax service, and in-room mini-refrigerators and microwave ovens. The friendly and accessible management offers a continental breakfast and fine overall service.

Inner North/Northeast Portland

DoubleTree Hotel Lloyd Center $$-$$$$
1000 N.E. Multnomah St.
(503) 281–6111, (800) 222–8733

A local standard by virtue of its size (476 rooms) and location, this DoubleTree attracts business travelers and visitors, meetings, and conventions as well as dinners and ceremonies that bring out the black-tie and slinky-dress crowd. The lobby, restaurants, and parking garage bustle with swirls of activity, but this continual scene of organized frenzy is easily left behind when you get to your room. Some of the rooms have views of the city skyline, the West Hills, and the Willamette River; others look out over Mount Hood. The hotel's location makes it a good choice for tourists. The Lloyd Center shopping mall is just 3 blocks to the east; the Oregon Convention Center is just 3 blocks to the west. There is a light rail stop across the street, and the hotel offers free parking, so guests can go carless and careless in downtown Portland. The new Westside light rail extension can deliver guests to the Oregon Zoo, PGE Park, or the Goose Hollow neighborhood and the eternally popular Goose Hollow Inn, a tavern owned and managed by Portland's former bicycle-riding mayor, Bud Clark. Guests can choose standard rooms or master suites complete with in-room spas. All rooms have a refrigerator. The hotel's restaurant and lounge, Windows, is on the top floor and offers a panoramic view of the city's skyline and bridges, the West Hills, the Willamette River, and Mount St. Helens.

The hotel is served by the airport shuttle and has a swimming pool and a fitness center, covered parking, a popular restaurant and lounge with entertainment, and a gift shop. Pets are welcome. One of the region's largest shopping centers, the Lloyd Center, with a Nordstrom, a Meier & Frank, and dozens of other stores, a food court, and a covered ice-skating rink, is a very short walk away (see our Shopping chapter for more details).

DoubleTree Hotel Portland—
Columbia River $$
1401 N. Hayden Island Dr.
(503) 283–2111, (800) 222–8733

Just off Interstate 5 on the banks of the mighty Columbia River, the DoubleTree Hotel Portland—Columbia River offers a great value, especially on weekends. The hotel's 351 guest rooms include private balconies, color TV, direct dial phones, irons and ironing boards, coffeemakers, and no telephone credit card access fees. Another plus is the free parking and transportation to Portland International Airport. The DoubleTree also offers Brickstones Restaurant overlooking the Columbia River, the Coffee Garden, the Quiet Bar—featuring a martini-cigar bar—a hair salon, a gift shop, a swimming pool, and a boat dock.

Holiday Inn—Portland at the Oregon
Convention Center $$$
1021 N.E. Grand Ave.
(503) 235–2100, (800) 465–4329

This Holiday Inn is conveniently situated for business or pleasure: The Memorial Coliseum and Rose Quarter complex are 3 blocks to the west, the Oregon Convention Center is across the street, and the Lloyd Center shopping mall and cinema are just 3 blocks to the east. If you need to travel across town, Portland's MAX light rail line stops across the street. The 166 comfortably decorated, air-conditioned guest rooms (including master suites with spas) are each furnished with a mini-refrigerator and two telephones. Free coffee and parking are provided to all guests.

Windows Restaurant & Terrace is located on the top floor of the Holiday Inn, offering a panoramic view of the city and an excellent selection of Northwest cuisine. Health-conscious guests appreciate the state-of-the-art fitness center, which features Universal weight equipment and a sauna.

The entry to the hotel's 4,000-square-foot ballroom affords a terrific view of downtown Portland and the Oregon Convention Center. It's a good idea to call ahead and make reservations well in advance, because this place books up fast, depending on what conventions are in town.

Radisson Hotel Portland $$$
1441 N.E. 2nd Ave.
(503) 233-2401

In the midst of the Lloyd Center Business District, the Radisson Hotel is one of the most convenient locations for events at either the Oregon Convention Center or the Rose Garden area, since both are within a 4-block radius. Recently renovated, the hotel's 238 rooms are equipped with coffeemakers, hair dryers, full-sized ironing boards, cable TV, and pay-per-view movies. A secured executive floor with a lounge offers a relaxed atmosphere for casual meetings. In the morning you can get your jolt of caffeine in your room, in the afternoon sip a drink in the lounge, and later on have dinner in Three Forks, the hotel's restaurant. Or there is room service twenty-four hours a day. For fitness-minded guests, a state-of-the-art exercise facility includes step machines, Lifecycles, treadmills, and weights, all overlooking an outdoor heated pool. Free parking and airport shuttles are provided.

Travelodge—Convention Center $$
1506 N.E. 2nd Ave.
(503) 231-7665

Located in the Lloyd Center Business District, Portland Travelodge Hotel is a convenient base of operations for events at the Oregon Convention Center and the Rose Garden arena—both within 4 blocks. Portland Travelodge Hotel has 236 rooms, including a secured executive floor. All rooms have coffeemakers, hair dryers, cable television, pay-per-view movies, and Showtime I and II.

You can grab a gourmet coffee drink from the lobby espresso cart or a cold beverage in the Encore Lounge. For the fitness-minded, an exercise facility offers step machines, Lifecycles, treadmills, and weights—all overlooking an outdoor heated pool. Free parking and a complimentary airport shuttle is provided, and Bee Rent-A-Car is conveniently located on-site. Their banquet facilities are some of the finest and most reasonable in the city.

Viking Motel $
6701 N. Interstate Ave.
(503) 285-6687

The Viking Motel is a little off the beaten path, but it's an option for those traveling on a tight budget since it offers out-of-towners a decent, very clean room for well

Insiders' Tip

Even if you're not staying in them, Portland's beautiful downtown hotels are good places to visit. The Marble Bar at the Heathman, the lounge at the Benson, and the bars in the Paramount and Westin Hotels are but a few of the agreeable spots to idle for an hour before dinner.

under $50. Located just off Interstate 5, it is only a five-minute drive from downtown Portland. The Viking isn't big, offering only twenty-five rooms, but its staff is well trained and eager to please. Rooms are furnished with refrigerators, telephones, cable television, and several units are equipped with kitchenettes. Free morning coffee, fax service, and laundry facilities are included, and microwave ovens are provided for patrons' use. The Viking Motel is near several restaurants and is also on a city bus line.

Outer North/Northeast Portland (near the airport)

Courtyard by Marriott—Portland Airport
$$-$$$
11550 N.E. Airport Wy.
(503) 252–3200, (800) 321–2211

Less than 3 miles east of the Portland International Airport, this facility offers plenty of user-friendly accommodations for business road warriors and leisure travelers alike. Besides providing free, twenty-four-hour airport transportation, the 150 rooms include AM/FM clock radios, remote color televisions with cable, in-room coffee service, hair dryers, and irons and ironing boards. Each of the ten suites has a VCR, microwave, mini-refrigerator, small bar sink, and two color televisions, and there are also ten wheelchair-accessible rooms. After dining in the Courtyard Cafe (if you prefer, a room service dinner), you may unwind in the cozy lounge watching the 32-inch television or soak your stresses away in the outdoor pool and whirlpool.

DoubleTree Hotel Jantzen Beach $$$-$$$$
909 N. Hayden Island Dr.
(503) 283–4466, (800) 222–8733

With 320 units, the Jantzen Beach arm of this hotel seems to attract more meetings and conventions, though the nearby Columbia River DoubleTree has its share of banquets and galas. The Jantzen Beach area has developed into a huge shopping area, attracting Washington state residents who can avoid their state's sales tax by making purchases in Oregon. Portland Meadows, a horse-racing track, the Expo Center, Portland International Raceway, several golf courses and marinas and Delta Park, a huge mix of soccer and softball fields and open green space are all nearby. A large selection of restaurants, mostly national franchises, are close, as is Waddles, a large restaurant and coffee shop that has been easing hunger pangs since the 1930s. This DoubleTree is a full-service hotel with swimming pools, exercise facilities, restaurants and lounges, a pet-friendly policy, wheelchair-accessible rooms, and free parking. While traffic on Interstate 5 and the Interstate Bridge can be brisk at all hours of the day, this location offers excellent access to Vancouver and Clark County, Washington, and is about a twenty-minute drive, depending on traffic and weather, from downtown Portland.

Hampton Inn Portland Airport $$
8633 N.E. Airport Wy.
(503) 288–2423, (800) 426–7866

Next door to the Sheraton, the Hampton Inn is a newer and lower-cost alternative to its neighbor but offers nearly the same range of amenities. There is a free twenty-four-hour airport shuttle, a continental breakfast buffet, an outdoor swimming pool and hot tub, a hospitality suite, and a small gift shop. Guests at the Hampton Inn can also use the Sheraton's indoor fitness center. The hotel's rooms, of which 75 percent are nonsmoking, are neat, modern, and comfortable and come with a free in-room movie channel as well as a pay-per-view channel. Nintendo video games are also available without charge. There are two telephones in each room, as well as personalized voice mail and dataports for computers. Wheelchair-accessible rooms and special services for hearing-impaired guests are available. Children eighteen and younger or a third or fourth adult can share a room with a paying guest at no extra cost.

The Westin Portland is a touch of luxury in Portland's downtown hotel scene. CREDIT: COURTESY OF THE WESTIN PORTLAND

Holiday Inn Portland Airport $$$
8439 N.E. Columbia Blvd.
(503) 256–5000, (800) 465–4329

Just minutes from the airport (yes, 24-hour free shuttle service is provided) and fifteen minutes from downtown Portland, this hotel is quite attractive and comfortable thanks to a recent $3 million renovation. The 286 sparkling guest rooms feature keyless entry systems, state-of-the-art fire sprinklers, new furniture, irons/boards, hair dryers, and coffeemakers. Guests can take advantage of the on-site newsstand, gift shop, one-day laundry, and dry cleaning services as well as car rental service and free parking. This inn offers an indoor swimming pool, saunas, a Jacuzzi, video games, and exercise equipment. After working up an appetite, the dining options include fine dining at the Northwest Grill, casual breakfasts, lunch, and dinners at the Peppertree, and dancing and other nighttime fun at Flirts Lounge.

Sheraton Portland Airport Hotel $$, $$$
8235 N.E. Airport Wy.
(503) 281–2500, (800) 325–3535

A full-service hotel located on Portland International Airport grounds, this Sheraton is friendly as well as functional. All rooms feature a full-size working desk, lounge chair, two telephones, and a mini bar. Guest services include a business center, an in-house travel agency, a gift shop, exercise facility, heated pool, therapy

pool, saunas, and free parking. Two restaurants are open for breakfast, lunch, and dinner. The hotel offers twenty-four-hour room service, a lobby bar, and Harold's Lounge.

Silver Cloud Inn, Portland Airport
$$-$$$ • 11518 N.E. Glenn Widing Dr.
(503) 252–2222, (800) 205–7892

Seasoned travelers rave about the personalized, friendly service at this two-year-old hotel featuring one hundred lakefront view rooms. Located 3 miles east of Portland International Airport, this Silver Cloud Inn offers all the amenities (except on-site dining), including a heated indoor swimming pool and Jacuzzi, fitness center, meeting facilities, and lots of free goodies such as local and long distance access calls, free laundry service, coffee and tea, and a healthy continental breakfast. The comfortable lobby, warmed by a huge fireplace during the cooler months, sets the tone for this modern but cozy inn. The large glass windows afford a view of migrating ducks and geese, and a small library invites guests to curl up with a book between dashes about town. Rooms are furnished with refrigerators and microwaves; movies and Nintendo games are available. Business-minded travelers appreciate the large work desks and the PC dataports. Free parking and the courtesy airport shuttle make for easy access, and several restaurants are within walking distance.

Vancouver

The Heathman Lodge $$$
7801 N.E. Greenwood Dr., Vancouver
(360) 254–3100, (888) 475–3100

A doorman dressed like a member of the Northwest Canadian Mounted Police and a bronze statue of a Native American holding high a gas-lit torch welcome the delighted visitors to the brand-new Heathman Lodge. Brimming with old-fashioned charm and modern conven-

iences, this hotel is lovely, with a reputation for world-class service and attention. The lobby and other common areas are done in rustic pine, accented by the color and classic designs of Pendleton blankets and pillows and the 121 oversize guest rooms have Pendleton bedspreads and most come with desks and fireplaces. All have a refrigerator, coffeemaker, and microwave, as well as irons, ironing boards, and hair dryers. Business travelers appreciate the two-line telephones, dataports, and voice mail. Feeling guilty about not working out while away from home? This hotel comes equipped with an enclosed swimming pool, sauna and whirlpool, and complete fitness center. The twenty-four-hour room service, laundry facilities, free parking, free morning newspaper, and delicious continental breakfast will also add to your comfort. The Heathman's restaurant, Hudson's Bar and Grill, offers excellent cuisine. Across from Vancouver Mall and a host of restaurants and other services, the Heathman Lodge is fifteen minutes from the Portland Airport.

Red Lion at the Quay $$$
100 Columbia St., Vancouver
(360) 694–8341, (800) 222–8733

On the banks of the Columbia River in downtown Vancouver, this 160-room hotel recently underwent a major remodeling. Just off Interstate 5 after it crosses the Columbia River, this wired hotel is a popular site for meetings, seminars, and banquets, and it offers both standard rooms (smoking and nonsmoking) and suites, some that include hot tubs. The Red Lion at the Quay is close to golf courses, maintains an outdoor pool, and is right off a 3-K jogging path, if the fitness center isn't enough for you. The attached restaurant, the Pacific Grill and Chowder House, offers casual dining with a sweeping view of the Columbia River.

Outlying Areas

The Best Western Hillsboro $$$
3500 N.E. Cornell Rd., Hillsboro
(503) 648–3500

In the center of Oregon's high-tech industry in sprawling and fast-growing Washington County, this Best Western hotel is near Intel, Tektronix, the Oregon Graduate Institute, and Nike, as well as close to the region's vineyards and wineries. It is also across from Hillsboro Airport—which does not have commercial airline service but is an important destination for corporate and other private aircraft. For visitors heading to Astoria, Seaside, Cannon Beach, and other locations on Oregon's North Coast, the hotel is close to U. S. Highway 26, also known as Sunset Highway, the main route between the Portland Metro area and the coast. The hotel suites include in-room spas and mini-refrigerators, large desks, and working spaces. Guest laundry facilities, a fitness room, and fax and copy service are available.

Crowne Plaza $$$
14811 Kruse Oaks Blvd.,
Lake Oswego
(503) 624–8400, (800) 2CROWNE

The Crowne Plaza beckons guests and travelers with its contemporary appearance and soaring glass atrium. The hotel offers free parking and shuttle service to destinations in a 5-mile radius of the hotel. Located at the intersection of Interstate 5 and Oregon Highway 217, the Crowne Plaza is on the edge of the fast-growing Kruse Way business area in Lake Oswego, one of Portland's toniest suburbs, and the newest high-status business address. The hotel is also close to Portland's soaring Mormon Temple, the huge shopping center at Washington Square, and Lewis & Clark College. A small, nearby shopping center includes a deli with specialty coffee drinks and a Chinese restaurant offering Bento and other Asian-style entrees.

The 161 rooms have computer and fax connections. The Crowne Plaza Club, a formal restaurant, offers a complementary breakfast and evening hors d'oeuvres and cocktails. Guests can also get passes to a nearby athletic club. The on-site restaurant, Regions, open from 6 A.M. until 10 P.M., features Northwest cuisine and an appealing selection of local and regional microbrews and Oregon wines.

Fairfield Inn $$
15583 N.W. Gateway Ct., Beaverton
(503) 972–0048, (800) 228–2800

In the heart of Silicon Forest, it is no surprise that each of the 106 rooms at the Marriott-run Fairfield Inn has a dataport for laptop computers and modems as well a desk and other work space. Intel, Fujitsu, Epson, NEC, Tektronix, and Nike are all within a 4-mile radius of the hotel. A heated indoor pool, a whirlpool, and fitness center will help wake you up and get you ready for your day, which begins with a complimentary and healthy continental breakfast. There is no hotel restaurant, but a good eatery, Sweet Tomatoes, is just a brisk walk away.

The Greenwood Inn $$$
10700 S.W. Allen Blvd., Beaverton
(503) 643–7444, (800) 289–1300

This 253-room inn has earned a reputation as one of the most desirable suburban facilities in the Portland region. Offering a range of rooms and suites, some with Jacuzzis and kitchens and some reserved for guests traveling with their four-footed companions, the facility was recently remodeled with the new decor featuring art works by Northwest artists. An elegant courtyard and pool soothe the nerves of those on demanding schedules, and the Pavilion Bar and Grill consistently appears on the various lists of the area's best eateries. The Greenwood Inn's west suburban location allows quick access to the all of Washington County, including Hillsboro Airport, and to the Oregon coast as well as to the regional shopping centers at Washington Square and the Beaverton Mall. It's owned and run by the same folks who run the Heathman Lodge, and it shows.

Residence Inn by Marriott
Portland South $$$
15200 S.W. Bangy Rd., Lake Oswego
(503) 684–2603, (800) 331–3131

Looking more like an apartment complex or condominiums than a hotel, the Residence Inn offers a range of suites and rooms for guests planning an extended stay in the area. This is one of two Residence Inns in the area. It's close to Interstates 5 and 205 and Oregon Highway 217, offering easy access to Washington County and Beaverton, Oregon's Silicon

Insiders' Tip

If you're staying somewhere other than downtown, you might try parking at one of the MAX light rail stations and taking the MAX to your sightseeing destinations. The MAX will take you to the Rose Quarter, the Lloyd Center, the Convention Center, and the Oregon Zoo, in addition to city-center attractions.

Forest. Busy Oregon Highway 217 merges with U.S. Highway 26, the most direct route from the Portland area to the Oregon coast. The Residence Inn is close to Lake Oswego and the Kruse Way business corridor and is convenient to a number of restaurants and specialty shops. There's a complimentary breakfast and late afternoon/early evening snacks and beverages.

The Sweetbrier Inn $$-$$$
7125 S.W. Nyberg Rd., Tualatin
(503) 692–5800, (800) 551–9167

Approximately twenty minutes south of Portland, just off Interstate 5 and close to both the Interstate 205/Interstate 5 and Interstate 5/Oregon Highway 217 interchanges, the Sweetbrier Inn is conveniently accessed. The heated outdoor swimming pool is surrounded by a wooded area and landscaped with seasonal shrubs and flowers. A grove of fir trees borders one side of the hotel. A children's play area is nearby as well as a running track, exercise facilities, and several local golf courses. The Sweetbrier offers smoke-free and wheelchair-accessible rooms. The lobby, lounge, and restaurant all have been recently remodeled and attract a mix of people attending meetings and special events at the hotel as well as business and leisure travelers and local residents. The attractive bar and Sweetbrier Restaurant offer friendly, casual service, very good food, moderate prices, and a relaxing atmosphere. In addition to the standard rooms, The Sweetbrier offers thirty-two new 450-square-foot, luxury suites in a separate building.

Jake's Famous Crawfish is a landmark eatery with great seafood. CREDIT: DAVID JOHNSON

Restaurants

Thanks to two decades of flowering culinary revolution in the birthplace of cookbook author James Beard, Portlanders have a bounty of down-home, ethnic, and upscale eateries to choose from on that special night, work-a-day lunch break, or Sunday brunch. Beard, acclaimed as the expert on American cuisine, would be proud of the chefs, sous-chefs, and griddle-pilots who have combined Pacific Northwest produce, fish, and meats with talents honed in cooking schools and cosmopolitan restaurants in New York, California, and Europe.

Like many other creative artists, chefs and cooks are flocking here because of the quality of life, and by doing so are adding to it by providing Portlanders with a greater array of excellent dining options. The result is that Portland is now internationally regarded, along with New Orleans and San Francisco, as a town with colorfully superb restaurants. The word is out that we are sampling new and innovative ways to prepare Copper River salmon, Dungeness crab, Olympia oysters, Oregon blueberries, Marionberries, raspberries, peaches, and pears. Let's not forget those wild creatures that poke up through the duff of our ancient forests—chanterelles, lobster mushrooms, morels, and shitakes, or our state nut, the filbert (or hazelnut as it is officially designated).

Adding to this abundance of regional foods are those brought by an influx of Asian Americans migrating across the ocean to what is increasingly known as the Pacific Rim. As well as distinctively Pacific Northwestern dining experiences, we now have Vietnamese and Thai restaurants in just about every neighborhood in Portland. These have opened alongside well-established Chinese eateries operated by families whose ancestors worked on Northwest railroads and in gold mines back in the nineteenth century. The Chinese and these new kids on the culinary block add to a multitude of dining choices. Long for Lebanese? Interested in Italian or Ethiopian? Craving Cajun or Mexican? Seeking authentic Southwestern or tangy barbecue? In the mood for a South or Central American dinner? Or do you just want a burger, shake, and fries at a diner adorned with hubcaps on its walls? Take your pick. Portland has it all.

Below you'll find the restaurants grouped according to our usual geographic divisions; within those, we list the entries alphabetically, for quick reference. Unless noted, all the restaurants listed take credit cards and have a no-smoking policy.

Price Code

The price code below reflects the cost of a single meal excluding tips and drinks. As with other Portland purchases, there is no sales tax.

$	$10 and under
$$	$11–$20
$$$	$21–$30
$$$$	$31 and higher

Abou Karim $$
221 S.W. Pine St.
(503) 223–5058

One of Portland's most popular Lebanese restaurants, Abou Karim is charmingly authentic. Here, in a tranquil setting with high ceiling and brick walls, tasty hummus, piquant tabbouleh, and your choice of a stew or kebab will transport you to the far Mideast for a pleasant evening. Try the *ful*, a Mediterranean bean dip, or the *baba ghanouj*, a charcoal-broiled eggplant. The restaurant is open for lunch and dinner.

Al-Amir $-$$
223 S.W. Stark St.
(503) 274–0010

Located at the Bishop's House, Al-Amir is an architectural jewel in Old Town close to jazz clubs and concert halls. You can meander into this Lebanese restaurant for a meal before the nightlife gets lively. Stroll past a long bar into a dimly lit dining room for your exotic culinary treats. Try the spit-roasted lamb and lamb shanks the chefs claim are the best in town. Or if you crave a vegetarian entree, how about Maza Al-Amir, a veritable roundup of tangy tastes, including hummus, tabbouleh, falafel, basmati rice, and a vegetable kabob. Lunch and dinner are served all day.

Bijou Cafe $-$$
132 S.W. 3rd Ave.
(503) 222–3187

With over twenty years of experience as a diner that dishes out the best organic food in town, Bijou Cafe maintains its edge as a leader in its class. In this classic eatery that has the feel of a rustic European cafe, business folk and visitors mingle at the counter, in booths, or at small, intimate tables. Here guests might read the paper while enjoying a hearty breakfast of pancakes, eggs, and corn muffins, or chat over a tofu scramble for lunch.

Dinner favorites are seared filet of salmon snug against a heap of basmati rice pilaf, roast monkfish with asparagus risotto, or guinea hen as you've never savored the exotic bird. The Bijou is open for breakfast and lunch every day and for dinner Tuesday through Saturday.

British Tea Garden $
725 S.W. 10th Ave.
(503) 221–7817
www.citysearch.com

Anglophiles now have a sanctuary where they can sip proper tea and choose from a menu of British edibles, each with a lovely personality. If it is time for tea, pop over for a cup of Russian Caravan, Fortmason, Darjeeling, or Ceylon. While sipping, try your choice of one finger sandwich, a scone with jam and Devonshire clotted cream, or perhaps steak and kidney pie. Sound familiar, chaps? The Tea Garden is open for breakfast and lunch.

Bush Garden $$
900 S.W. Morrison St.
(503) 226–7181
www.citysearch.com

A charming surprise at Bush Garden, which is open for both lunch and dinner, is that dining in a traditional tatami room is easy, due to comfy space for your legs beneath the table. This Japanese restaurant, open since 1969, also has Western-style dining tables where you can sample its sushi, sukiyaki, or sashimi. Here in this tranquil atmosphere, diners can also try the lightly battered chicken or prawn tempura, vegetarian *bento*, or Kaki Furai (local oysters lightly breaded and gently deep-fried).

Chart House $$-$$$
5700 S.W. Terwilliger
(503) 246-6963

101 E. Columbia Way, Vancouver
(360) 693-9211
www.portlandchart-house.com

Both locations for this popular wayside restaurant serve lunch and dinner and have great views of riverside real estate as well as a full menu of hearty fare, including robust entrees such as Orange Basil Salmon, Coconut Crunch Shrimp, and herb-crusted chicken. For a savory side, try the Rock Salt Russet, a russet potato rolled in garlic butter and rock salt and cracked black pepper, served with butter, sour cream, and freshly cut chives. Now that's an impressive evolution of an old favorite.

Couvron $$$
1126 S.W. 18th Ave.
(503) 225-1844

Named after the village where chef Tony Demes' family lives, Couvron is a classic French restaurant, but don't expect quaint, rural dishes. Rather, the haute cuisine at this sophisticated eatery, which serves dinner only, is exquisitely complex. A choice of an appetizer might be roasted wild Scottish woodcock with wild Oregon mushrooms in a roasted garlic butter and bourguignonne sauce or fricassee of sweetbreads and Texas frog legs. Main courses include sautéed Oregon rabbit loin served with pearled barley stew, or Atlantic salmon mignon on a chiffonade potato cake with stewed leeks and red wine sauce.

Dragonfish $$$
808 S.W. Taylor St.
(503) 223-9900.

A delightful new addition to Portland's impressive list of Pan-Asian Restaurants, Dragonfish is centrally located downtown in the lodging boutique, the Paramount Hotel. Both the bar and restaurant (on each side of the lobby) are a quick stop after a film, concert, or play. Before or after an evening of entertainment or simply relaxing after work, the Dragonfish

offers Sushi Hour every night from 4 to 6 P.M. and 10 P.M. to 1 A.M. with sushi at $1. On the restaurant side, the clever and tasty dishes are presented deftly by a staff that is obviously having a good time. A recommended entree is the 4 Onion Beef and the Rock Shrimp Spring Roll appetizer is terrific. The California sushi roll, a good indicator of sushi quality easily passes the test. On the sipping side, there are hot sakes, a wine list, and Asian and American beer. As well as pleasing cuisine, the spot has a understated decor with chopsticks resting on polished black pebbles, black napkins, and bamboo walls. It is not quite over-the-top Kon Tiki, but rather a lively Eastern Hemispheric motif. Check out the wall of pachinko machines flashing and glittering in the bar. Bottom line: Dragonfish is fun!

Fat City Cafe $
7820 S.W. Capitol Hwy.,
Multnomah Village
(503) 245-5457

At a busy corner in a small town that got swallowed up by a bigger city, Fat City Cafe is the famous Multnomah Village diner known for terrific breakfasts. Get there early and get in line. Once you score a seat, order ham and eggs, flapjacks, or your choice of a number of traditional morning meals. While you're waiting, enjoy the lively signage on its walls: In a quirky way it gives a history not only of the village but also of an era when America had diners like this all along every highway. If you're in the neighborhood later in the day—perhaps browsing in Multnomah Village's string of antique shops or one of its trendy gift shops— remember that Fat City Cafe is open all day. You might want to take a break and stop for one of their old-fashioned milkshakes.

Good Dog, Bad Dog $
708 S.W. Alder
(503) 222-3410

A sidewalk sign will alert you that you are closing in on one of the most popular lunch stops in town. This tiny nook (which also serves dinner) is festooned with canine memorabilia: stuffed and ceramic mutts and one notable poster showing a cartoon poodle with a mohawk. The small menu features another kind of dog—sausage. And that's about it. You can munch on a one-third-pound sausage sandwich on a French roll. The list includes bratwurst, kielbasa, a British banger, sweet Italian sausage, or a Magma Dog that counterfolk here claim will melt your face. There is also a garden sausage for wimpier clientele. To round out your lunch you can try the homemade chili, maple-and-bacon beans, or potato salad. And to wash all this outrageous grub down, get yourself a Widmer Hefewiezen or Bud.

Hamburger Mary's $
239 S.W. Broadway
(503) 223–0900

A riotously decorated, nostalgic burger joint, Hamburger Mary's is a Portland institution that serves up great lunches and dinners. This diner/bar combo is outlandishly cluttered with antique signs, bikes and trikes dangling from the ceiling, pinup calendars from the '40s, dollhouses, and a collage of postcards, notes, matchbooks, and other flat memorabilia. In its new location across the street from the Benson Hotel, it offers weary conventioneers a relaxed, informal setting as well as a famous hamburger selection. The burgers come cushioned in homemade buns (you name it—they probably have it). This not-to-miss time capsule also offers Banger Spaghetti, grilled halibut, and a teriyaki chicken stir-fry.

Heathman Restaurant $$$-$$$$
1001 S.W. Broadway
(503) 241–4100
www.citysearch.com

Acclaimed as the premier power lunch spot in town, the Heathman Restaurant is a trendy, spendy eatery. Serving as the house restaurant for the Heathman Hotel, this multilevel dining room filled with leather banquettes and linen-draped tables is usually humming with those who favor French cuisine while mulling over business deals. Samples are a seafood salad of marinated sea bass for lunch and salmon hash for breakfast. Dinners include a Matelote of Trout with crayfish and glazed pearl onions and a Columbia River Farms braised duck. As you might guess, the chef insists on using fresh Pacific Northwest ingredients to render his imaginative entrees.

Higgins Restaurant and Bar $$$
1239 S.W. Broadway
(503) 222–9070

The inventive ways in which chef Greg Higgins uses seasonal, organic food from nearby farms, forests, and streams have won this handsome downtown restaurant the highest marks from critics—as well as from the customers that fill the restaurant every night. Higgins is discerning and unpretentious in its combinations of textures and flavors, relying on traditional means of cooking adapted to contemporary eating habits. Because the menu is seasonal, it changes all the time; however, diners can always count on at least one vegan dish on the menu in addition to the beef, duck, fish, and other entrees. The bar menu carries some notable staples, among them an incredibly savory hamburger and a luscious pastrami sandwich (Greg Higgins makes the pastrami himself). Higgins has an excellent wine list that emphasizes Northwest wines, and a beer list that features about 150 different brews from the world over. A striking union of textures, colors, and light, the tri-level restaurant looks as good as the food does. The downstairs dining room, with its mahogany paneling and dark carpet, is both romantic and elegant; the middle dining room is vibrant with burnished floors and two-toned walls. And the bar, a local favorite, is at once comfortable and urbane. Higgins is open for lunch Monday through Friday and dinner daily. See the Close-up on Greg Higgins in this chapter.

Chef Greg Higgins, left, speaks with a local farmer. CREDIT: COURTESY OF HIGGINS RESTAURANT

Huber's $-$$
411 S.W. 3rd Ave.
(503) 228–5686

Self-described as Portland's oldest restaurant, Huber's opened its doors in 1879 as the Bureau Saloon. In 1884, the bartender, Frank Huber, became a partner and the rest is culinary history. One tale tells of the time during the flood of 1894 when chef Jim Louie stood in a rowboat behind the counter serving steamed clams and turkey sandwiches to customers who rowed in from the other side. Still known for its roast young tom turkey and flaming Spanish coffee, Huber's attracts a steady clientele who also enjoy the Philippine mahogany paneling, stained-glass skylights, and a big brass cash register. A Happy Hour (6 to 8 P.M.) features $1.95 appetizers with well drinks at the usual price.

Jake's Famous Crawfish $$$
401 S.W. 12th Ave.
(503) 226–1419
www.mccormickandschmicks.com

Every large city has its landmark restaurant where locals take visitors to give them a taste of the town. Here in Portland it's Jake's Famous Crawfish serving those little red squigglers and other tasty seafood. Founded in 1892 by Jacob (Jake) Lewis Freiman, the old Stumptown restaurant has changed very little—its maze of booths still snug against brick walls adorned with antique oil paintings. Try the Stark Street Sturgeon with basil dijon, Goose Point oysters, half-pound king crab legs or go for broke with a live Maine lobster. To put it all in perspective, a small plaque announces that on January 24, 1999, at 7 P.M., Jake's served its 3-millionth oyster. That's a lot of shucking! Jakes's serves lunch and dinner.

Marco's $-$$
7910 S.W. 35th Ave.
(503) 245–0199

3449 N.E. 24th Ave.
(503) 287–8011
www.marcoscafe.com

Certainly the most posh spot to dine in Multnomah Village, this often-crowded eatery in a restored 1914 storefront offers creatively zestful omelettes, home fries, and various muffins for breakfast. Pick up the *New York Times* and stop by for an endless, classic brunch! Marco's is open for breakfast, lunch, and dinner. Now diners can stop by a new Marcos in the Northeast.

Martinotti's $
404 S.W. 10th Ave.
(503) 224–9028

This family-run combination of cafe, del-icatessen, and coffeehouse has been in operation for over twenty years, and is popular with the downtown workforce for its great food and excellent brew. One steady customer claims that Portland's "numero uno Italian deli" makes the best cappuccino in town. The lunch-only menu also includes cold and hot sand-wiches, fruit, vegetable and pasta salads, and a generous selection of pastries, can-dies, and other treats.

Mayas Tacqueria $
1000 S.W. Morrison
(503) 226–1946

Here's a Mexican restaurant that's an independent operation minus cute dog or plastic giveaways. Its expansive menu of fresh, homemade lunches and dinners include burritos, quesadillas, tamales, and enchiladas. The interior is reminis-cent of small hole-in-the-wall cafes south of the border that serve filling, tasty food. A popular choice is ceviche (a cold stew of fish and seafood), veggie taco salad, and the enchilada/relleno combination plate. After waiting in line at the cafeteria counter, take your selection upstairs for a quiet meal or climb on a stool and watch pedestrians stroll by on 10th Avenue.

McCormick & Schmick's Seafood Restaurant
$$-$$$
235 S.W. 1st Ave.
(503) 224–7522
www.mccormickandschmicks.com

The original site of what is now a national chain, McCormick & Schmick's Seafood Restaurant has made its reputation through an insistence on fresh seafood served with creative flair. Good bets are the seared ahi tuna, crab cakes, alder-smoked salmon, and shellfish in a coconut, ginger, and lemongrass broth. Lunch is served Monday through Friday; dinner is served every evening.

Ming's Dynasty $
510 S.W. 3rd Ave.
(503) 222–0978

Located in the historic Postal Building, this serenely pleasant Szechwan restaurant with its low ceilings and a subtle decor is a good hideaway from the urban clamor outside on downtown streets and avenues. Sushi fans are quick to claim that its spicy tuna roll with jalapeño wasabi is the best in three counties. The sizzling rice shrimp is also tasty as is the General Tso's Chicken. For dessert, try the chilled loquats. Lunch is served Monday through Thursday; din-ner is served Monday through Saturday.

Mother's Bistro and Bar $-$$
409 S.W. 2nd Ave.
(503) 464–1122

The theme of this warm, cozy, and sedate bistro is the sort of comfort you seek by going home to Mom. On the bistro side in a relaxed atmosphere are photos and portraits of Madonna and child or at least, somebody's mother. The decor includes antique chairs and tables rather than the trendy sleek and chic found else-where. On the bar side, Mother's has an old-world flavor with over-stuffed chairs and sofas and mirrored walls. The service is crisp, presenting Greek omelettes, salmon hash, and crunchy French toast dipped in corn flakes for breakfast. Lunch features an all natural "Painted Hills" beef burger, Mom's Meatloaf, and Italian chopped salad. And dinner offers the ultimate comfort food, chicken and dumplings. For the vegetarian, the menu includes grilled seasonal vegetables.

Newport Bay Restaurant   **$$**
(Mall 205) 9722 S.E. Washington St.
(503) 255–2722

(Jantzen Beach) 11950 N Center St.
(503) 283–3474
0425 S.W. Montgomery St.
(floating restaurant)
(503) 227–3474

2757 S.E. Burnside Rd., Gresham
(503) 661–2722

(Tanasbourne Mall) 2865 N.W. Town Center, Beaverton
(503) 645–2526

(Washington Square)
9699 S.W. Washington Square Rd., Tigard
(503) 245–3474

For all outlets: www.newportbay.com

If you want very good seafood, excellent service, and an upbeat, casual environment, you can't go wrong at a Newport Bay. There are six Newport Bays in the Portland area, and they all stay close to the same formula. Their clam chowder is creamy and thick, the flame-broiled Alaskan salmon is mouthwatering, and the halibut and chips are tried and true favorites. But there's also plenty of chicken, pastas, salads, and daily specials to choose from. All the Newport Bays host a Sunday brunch beginning at 9 A.M. with fresh fruits, pastries, and made-to-order entrees served at your table. Make sure you visit the Riverplace Marina Newport Bay—Portland's only floating restaurant with a 360-degree view of the city—and if you are with someone special, the outdoor patio makes for a memorable dining experience. All Newport Bays offer a full bar and a good selection of wines. Newport Bays are open seven days a week from 11 A.M. until 10 P.M., except on Fridays and Saturdays when they close at 11 P.M.. On Sundays they open at 9 A.M. for a special brunch.

Pazzo   **$$–$$$**
627 S.W. Washington St.
(503) 228–1515
www.pazzorestorantecitysearch.com

Serving breakfast lunch and dinner daily as the resident restaurant at the Hotel Vintage Plaza, Pazzo is a courtly formal dining scene with fine linen, chic surroundings, and surprisingly affordable prices. A great choice for antipasti would be its calamari alla Luciana, featuring sautéed squid with spinach, garlic, chile flakes, and bread crumbs. Then try the garlic ricotta mashed potatoes. Entrees of note: Ravioli di Samone Affumicato with the smoked salmon and mascarpone ravioli drenched in a lemon asparagus cream sauce, and Ossobuco di Agnello (braised local lamb shank served on saffron).

Portland Steak and Chop House   **$–$$$**
121 S.W. 3rd Ave.
(503) 223–6200

Serving as the house restaurant for the historic Embassy Suites Hotel, the Portland Steak and Chop House is self-explanatory. For meat-eaters, this is the spot! Items include a home-style meatloaf, oven-roasted prime rib, seared flank sandwich, or a pepperjack cheeseburger. There are also seafood appetizers, halibut fish and chips, pan-fried oysters, Thai chicken, and, for those who don't prefer the mammal meals, shitake mushrooms. One tasty mix is their chicken gumbo with andouille sausage.

Red Star Tavern & Roast House   **$$–$$$**
503 S.W. Washington St.
(503) 222–0005
www.redstartavern.com

It's hard to miss this comfy, family-style restaurant and bar: It wraps around half a block and has sizeable picture windows, giving diners a view of busy downtown from their wood booths. Once inside, there is an ample menu to consider; it includes wood-grilled baby back ribs, spit-roasted pork loin, oak-roasted vegetables with caramelized garlic, and sweet potato hash. Particularly cozy on those rainy nights after work, the Red Star seems to be a club where anyone can stop by for a congenial evening foray into semi-haute cuisine. The Red Star serves lunch and dinner daily.

Saucebox $-$$
214 S.W. Broadway
(503) 241–3393
www.citysearch.com

Saucebox started as a venue for late-night cocktails and then quickly evolved into a hip bistro with a totally cool decor combined with cheap eats. A restaurant with a Pan-Asian flair until 10 P.M., Saucebox later shifts into a DJ-driven nightclub packed with a young crowd sipping house-infused spirits, including pineapple rum, watermelon or cucumber vodka, or apple-cinnamon brandy. But before the music starts, the menu is in full bloom with treats like an asparagus and prawn salad, roast Javanese salmon, Thai green curry chicken, Malaysian lamb stew, or house-made sweet potato chips. Lunch is served Tuesday through Friday; dinner is served Tuesday through Saturday.

Southpark $-$$
901 S.W. Salmon St.
(503) 326–1300
www.southpark.com

This restaurant is located at the edge of Portland's park blocks, a greenway with sidewalks and statuary stretching from S.W. Market Street to S.W. Salmon Street between S.W. Park Avenue and 9th Avenue. Southpark is not only affordable but it also has a delightful atmosphere. Tall windows offer diners a view of the greenway and passersby, a huge wood-fired oven crackles as it bakes crusty bread and cooks savory meats, and a rotisserie grills chicken with Moroccan spices and smoke-roasted pork.

In the kitchen, chefs prepare marvelous fish dishes such as salmon wrapped in grilled grape leaves, roasted clams with garlic and parsley, and the restaurant's signature appetizer, the Seafood Tower for Two. This edible edifice contains cherrystone clams, oysters, prawns, and Dungeness crab. Vegetarians happily tackle the artichoke and herb ravioli with fresh tomato sauce. For those with a light appetite there are small plates, including roast squash, hummus spread with marinated olives, and pizza cooked in that wood-fired oven. For dessert, try the popular chocolate hazelnut crostata served with roasted banana ice cream. Breakfast, lunch, and dinner are served daily.

Typhoon! $-$$
2310 N.W. Everett St.
(503) 243–7557

400 S.W. Broadway
(503) 224–8285

Located downtown and at the gateway to the trendy northwest shopping district, Typhoon! offers a stormily delicious menu of Thai cuisine in an often-crowded room adorned with Thai motifs. This cheerfully ethnic flavor also extends to the gorgeous "Bopla" plates that carry a generous selection of entrees delivered by a prompt and attentive crew. The Pad Thai Noodles are deftly rendered with fine texture and delicate flavor; the Parang Curry compliments the Pad Thai, and a Gulf of Siam Seafood Platter is plenty to handle on its own. Or you could "Call Me Ginger," a salmon filet basking in a black-bean ginger sauce. Try the curries, sip a Singha beer, hang out on the patio on a balmy summer day and it's easy to imagine you're transported to a folkloric Thailand for an hour or two. The restaurant is open for lunch every day but Sunday and dinner daily.

Alexis $-$$
215 W. Burnside St.
(503) 224–8577

If you can see beyond its tattered neighborhood out on West Burnside, Alexis is a great spot to sample authentic Greek fare and enjoy the graceful gyrations of the house belly dancers. The menu includes the usual Greek fare, including lamb souvlaki (skewered meat), *kalamarakia* (squid), moussaka (eggplant casserole) and spanakopita (layers of filo dough with spinach, rice, and feta cheese). It's all hearty and it's all inexpensive. Alexis serves lunch and dinner.

Bluehour $$$-$$$$
250 N.W. 13th Ave.
(503) 226–3394

Upon the demise of cosmopolitan Zefiro's—considered the poshest of the posh during its sumptuous rein in the N.W.—restaurateur Bruce Carey tinkered with his formula and launched Bluehour, an elegant eatery that has urbane folk lining up to see what the buzz is all about. Inside, the decor is high ceilings and a raucously hip bar. The cuisine is primarily Italian with chocolate pudding and beet terrine as lively outsiders.

Brazen Bean $-$$
2075 N.W. Glisan St.
(503) 294–0636

The three small rooms that combine to make the Brazen Bean have club chairs, a velvet couch, and a swank bar with wrought-iron backed, cushioned stools. The effect is a dramatically stylish setting for drinks and Euro-snacks after 6 P.M. On the list you'll find fennel and sun-dried tomato crackers, chicken liver pâté, and a selection of imported cheeses. A warning to nonsmokers: Get here early before the cigar smokers show up to puff as well as sip and nosh. The Brazen Bean serves dinner daily.

Cafe Azul $-$$
112 N.W. 9th Ave.
(503) 525–4422
www.citysearch.com

Cafe Azul is one of the culinary wonders that have recently opened in the Pearl District to feed folks who are buying condos and lofts, and strollers browsing art galleries, antique stores, and furniture shops in this hip neighborhood. Once inside its mustard- and chile-colored walls, diners can enjoy the Mexican art and be pampered by a convivial, unpretentious crew. Patrons enjoy the zesty margaritas, a smooth pumpkin and garlic soup, a terrific beet salad, in-house tortillas with green pumpkin seed salsa, and a mole Oaxaqueño that blends nuts, seeds, and chiles in a rich, dark chocolate sauce served on poached free-range chicken. After dispatching these robust dishes, there might be room for an Azul banana split, buckwheat crepes, or Manchego y Ate (smooth quince candy and Spanish Manchego cheese served with apples and walnuts). Cafe Azul serves dinner nightly. Cafe Azul serves dinner nightly.

Cafe Des Amis $$$-$$$$
1987 N.W. Kearney St.
(503) 295–6487
www.citysearch.com

Cafe Des Amis easily earns its awards and eminence with a menu that remains the same through trends, drifts, and fickle clientele. Here in this tranquil atmosphere in Northwest Portland amidst brick apartment buildings and sedate Victorian houses, you can treat yourself to Salmon Troisgros (a filet poached in a crème fraiche, white wine, and shallots) or duck with blackberry sauce. Another marvel is a rack of lamb Assyrian marinated in pomegranate juice, red wine, basil, and lemon. Perhaps the signature dish of this wondrous cafe is Poussin with "40 Cloves of Garlic," a small free-range chicken oven roasted with a handful of garlic and then finished with a reduction of white wine, chicken stock, and butter. The Cafe Des Amis serves dinner only.

Caffe Mingo $-$$
807 N.W. 21st Ave.
(503) 226–4646
www.citysearch.com

A cheerfully noisy neighborhood cafe with rustic wooden tables, Caffe Mingo is a not-well-kept secret offering simple Italian dinners for astoundingly affordable prices. The only downside is an expected wait to get to the Polenta con Salsiccia (polenta with mushrooms, served with fresh Italian sausage), Raviolini al Forno (Gorgonzola and walnut raviolini baked in cream with prosciutto, green onions, and red pepper flakes) or Penne al Sugo di Carne (pasta and braised beef infused with Chianti and espresso).

Il Fornaio $$-$$$
115 N.W. 22nd Ave.
(503) 248–9400
www.ilfornaio.com

Originally a bakeshop (Il Fornaio means "The Baker,"), this popular chain restaurant serves food, bread, and wine from Umbra, Toscana, Abruzzo, and other Italian regions, changing its geographic focus twice a month. Il Fornaio is worth a visit not only for its hearty fare focused on a particular region but for the friendly service, which heightens the pleasure of your evening out. If you make it a regular dinner spot, you can get on a mailing list and learn about the regions that are highlighted each month. Of course, you can also choose from the regular menu, featuring wood-fired pizza, rotisserie meats, and mesquite-grilled local fish. If you can't live without the bread served with dinner, take home a loaf from a retail bakery inside the restaurant. Il Fornaio serves lunch and dinner only.

Jo Bar & Rotisserie $$
701 N.W. 23rd Ave.
(503) 222–0048
www.citysearch.com

A sleek little bistro adjacent to and started in 1994 by the Papa Haydn Restaurant (see the entry for both Papa Haydns in the Southeast Portland section), Jo Bar & Rotisserie was named for the composer, Franz Joseph Haydn. Here amidst original art, maple stools and tables, and a wood-burning oven, you can nuzzle a pear cactus margarita or a Bellini (champagne with red peach purée) while waiting for your Oregon crab and shrimp cakes, fingerling potatoes roasted in the oven with raclette cheese, or roasted tuna filet. Vegetarians can choose a risotto with asparagus, snap peas, and artichoke hearts or house-made mozzarella and olive tapenade grilled in a rosemary baguette. Lunch and dinner are served here daily.

Kornblatt's $
628 N.W. 23rd Ave.
(503) 242-0055

Is this a deli or what? Definitely! Ever since 1991 when Josh Kornblatt—a restaurateur who grew up noshing in New York delis—started his own in Portland's Northwest District, people have been flocking from all over town to order the whitefish salad, smoked sturgeon, and other fish flown in fresh from the Big Apple. There are also plenty of "Empire State Sandwiches," including corned beef and chopped liver. Don't forget the chicken broth with matzo balls. Lastly, the bagels have been pronounced almost as good as those in New York by visitors from that particular and picky burg. Breakfast, lunch, and dinner are served all day although who would want a corned beef sandwich at 7 A.M.?

Laslow's $$-$$$
2327 N.W. Kearney St.
(503) 241–8092

One of the town's newer restaurants, Laslow's offers an ambitious and adventuresome menu, so this is a great place to take someone that you want to impress, such as a boss, potential spouse, or editor. However, you may want to call chef and owner Eric Laslow ahead of time to double check the pronunciation of some of the entrees. Dinner selections include: prosciutto-wrapped cod with mushroom risotto, hibiscus-rubbed duck breast with chèvre mashed potatoes, portobello mushrooms, wilted arugula, and parmesan. The lunch menu ranges from grilled swordfish and salmon to a bacon and cheddar cheeseburger. Dinners—currently offered Wednesdays through Sundays—also offer tantalizing appetizers such as home-cured pepper salmon and seared foie gras. The Sunday brunches, featuring Baily's Irish Cream French toast, are becoming quite popular. Desserts here are excellent and the wine list is extensive. Laslow's is open at 7 P.M. for dinner.

L'Auberge $$
2601 N.W. Vaughn
(503) 223–3302

This French restaurant has been around so long that it is the first choice for seasoned gourmands who live here or are in town for a visit. A classic setting of candlelight and fireplaces—or a garden deck in summer—offers locals or visitors a romantic ambience in which to enjoy Chilean sea bass, duck confit, seared duck breast, or grilled salmon cured with Lapsang souchong tea on an a la carte menu. A prix fixe dinner menu includes pork tenderloin with savoy cabbage, crusted cod brandade medaillon with lobster sauce, and mesclun salad with roasted spiced pecans, cherry tomatoes, and mango vinegar.

Lucy's Table $$-$$$
706 N.W. 21st Ave.
(503) 226–6126
www.lucystable.com

A recent arrival on Restaurant Row, Lucy's Table was immediately occupied by folks in search of an aesthetically as well as gastronomically satisfying meal. If the cheerful crowds at this sleek little bistro are an indication, the search was successful. After an understandable wait and perhaps a visit to the triangular bar, you are seated and handed a menu that melds Asian and Mediterranean cuisine with tough choices of small and large plates. If you're not so hungry but having fun, try the caramelized wild boar back ribs, baby spinach salad, or potato-wrapped yellowfin tuna. If you are starved, go for the truffle-scented duck risotto, roasted tandoori chicken, or seared Chilean sea bass. Lucy's serves dinners Monday through Saturday.

Marrakesh $$
1201 N.W. 21st Ave.
(503) 248–9442

Strolling by this corner cafe it is virtually impossible to avoid being enticed by the savory smells drifting outward. Inside this Moroccan oasis, diners can choose from an a la carte menu or fixed price dinners for $16.50, including braised hare, couscous Marrakesh, and chicken with honey and prunes. Or for groups, the chefs will cook a Royale Feast Dinner. An example is Mechoui in which a whole sheep is cooked in a spit over a charcoal fire. Then the Mechoui is delivered piping hot to be spiced with cumin and salt. This particular meal requires eight hungry participants. Marrakesh is open for dinner every evening.

¡OBA! $$$
555 N.W. 12th Ave.
(503) 228–6161
www.oba.com

A first bite into a coconut-encrusted prawn slathered with a jalapeño dipping sauce is a big hint as to why ¡OBA! was named Portland's 1998 Restaurant of the Year by *Northwest Palate* magazine and 1998-99 Restaurant of the Year by *Willamette Week*, our town's largest weekly tabloid. This upscale eatery in "The Pearl" has also won interior designer architectural awards: Its lean and vibrant elegance is apparent in the three distinct dining rooms and stylish bar with high ceilings, pomegranate and squash gold walls, Spanish grillwork, and delicate, shell-like sconces. As well as those signature prawn appetizers, the restaurant serves a small plate of rare ahi tuna with a bright salsa, smoky-flavored tamales stuffed with roasted peppers, seafood empanadas, and chili-corn fritters. Or you may choose to try their remarkable game hen, well marinated in chili sauce, then roasted over a mesquite fire. ¡OBA! serves dinner only.

Paley's Place $$$-$$$$
1204 N.W. 21st Ave.
(503) 243-2403

The Oregonian's 1999 restaurant of the year, Paley's Place is set in a gracious old home at the northern edge of Restaurant Row in the Northwest and is reminiscent of a French country inn. Along with a festive bar side, two dining rooms are so intimate and placid that a convivial spirit inspires between-tables conversations. The alchemy of chef Vitaly Paley's culinary imagination, Kimberley Paley's charming and gregarious command of the dining rooms, and the poised, professional wait staff provide the context for a lovely, sophisticated, innovative meal. And then it arrives: maple glazed chicken with Granny Smith apples, sour cherries, and smoky bacon, an amazingly fresh fish of the day (cod, halibut, Arctic char) served with lentils, fennel and fiddlehead ferns, or sautéed sweetbreads with leek potato gratin and pomegranate sauce. Paley's also has a good selection of vegetarian entrees such as risotto galette with parsley and cilantro. Diners here comment that portions are not only charmingly presented and delicious but just the

right amount. Of course, they could probably find room for more dessert. One of the stars in that firmament is the gingerbread with caramelized pears and molasses ice cream. Dinner is served seven nights a week for dinner only.

Ringside $$-$$$
2165 W. Burnside St.
(503) 223-1513

14021 N.E. Glisan St.
(503) 255-0750
www.ringsidesteakhouse.com

Step in to the Ringside and enter an old-world style where fine cuts of beef still reign supreme. Tom Horan, a nationally known restaurant critic ranked this restaurant as one of the top ten steak houses in the nation. Ringside also has great ambience—the Burnside location has a dark and intimate atmosphere, while the Glisan restaurant is bright and wide open. Whichever you choose, both are big favorites with meat eaters. Sure, they've got darn good appetizers and salads, and plenty of tasty chicken, seafood, and light dinners to choose from. But in Portland, Ringside is synonymous with steaks and chops. Over the last fifty years and three generations of owners, not much has changed at the Ringside. The prime and choice aged beef, fresh seafood, and excellent wine and service have helped Ringside garner more than forty regional and national awards. Go and see for yourself what all the fuss is about. If you're a rib connoisseur, try the ten-ounce Ringside Prime Rib served with au jus and creamed horseradish sauce. Also, don't leave without ordering the huge, luscious onion rings. The desserts, such as the chocolate raspberry torte (made locally by JaCiva's), an exquisite Swiss-chocolate layer cake with raspberry filling, are a terrific way to finish off your feast. Ringside is open weekdays for lunch from 11 A.M. until 2:30 P.M., and for dinner from 5 P.M. until midnight. Saturday hours are from 5 P.M. until midnight and Sundays from 4:30 until 10:30 P.M.

Tapeo $-$$
2764 N.W. Thurman St.
(503) 226–0409

Have you ever wanted to just nibble on lots of small appetizers rather than face the usual single dish? Try a selection of tapas at Tapeo, a Spanish restaurant in the quietly blossoming far northwest section of Portland. These little dishes are served in an intimate setting at small tables just for two while other diners wait and chat amiably on a bench lining one of the muted green walls. The tapas are just the thing for a palate with a wandering spirit. The tapas frías (cold tapas) include marinated fillet of trout, roasted and marinated eggplant, and toasted bread topped with tomato, Spanish Serrano ham, and Manchego cheese. A few tapas calientes (hot tapas) are steamed clams and mussels in a Romesco sauce, seared sea scallops cooked in white wine and saffron, and boneless quail with a bittersweet chocolate sauce. Tapeo is open for dinner only Tuesday through Saturday.

Wildwood $$$-$$$$
1221 N.W. 21st Ave.
(503) 248–9663
www.wildwoodrestaurant.citysearch.com

Out at the far north end of Restaurant Row in the Northwest, Wildwood gracefully, casually lives up to its reputation as the zenith of fine dining with impeccable cuisine and a polished ambience. Original etchings and paintings grace the sponge-painted walls. But as you cozy into an alcove, you'll probably be focused on the outstanding menu, the star of which is Wildwood's signature dish: skillet-roasted Kamilche mussels with garlic, tomato, saffron, and grilled bread. Don't miss that one! Another hit is a piquant Manila clam chowder. Moving on to entrees, you'll find a small but enticing selection, including wild mushroom and asparagus ragout, grilled salmon with leek and potato purée, and Muscovy duck breast with golden potato and mushroom sauté. Lunch and dinner are served daily. Wildwood also offers a brunch on Sunday.

Southeast Portland

Adobe Rose Cafe $
1634 S.E. Bybee Blvd.
(503) 235–9114

If you appreciate high-quality Southwestern food you'll like the Adobe Rose Cafe, which is small—just nine tables—but offers a great value on meals featuring the taste of New Mexico. The highest-priced dinner is $9, and you can grab a zesty lunch for around $6. The atmosphere is casual: Southwestern desert scenes adorn the walls and cactus plants sit in the windows. There's a full-service bar where you can grab a Margarita, your favorite beer, or a mixed drink. The menu isn't the most extensive in town, but everything is very well prepared and the service aims to please. The burritos and enchiladas are superior, especially the *carne adovada* enchilada, a cubed pork tenderloin marinated in red chili sauce and slow cooked

to perfection. Adobe Rose is open Tuesdays through Saturdays from 11:30 A.M. until 2 P.M. for lunch and 5 P.M. until 9 P.M. for dinner. They are closed Sundays and Mondays.

Annie's $
17440 S.E. Stark St.
(503) 252–6760

This little 1950s-style eatery isn't long on atmosphere but it offers a good selection of hot dogs, hamburgers, and ice cream treats. If you like Coney dogs, Annie's is a must stop as the 11-inch-long Coney smothered in their delicious homemade sauce is as good as any in town. They use superior wieners, very fresh buns, and never skimp on the toppings. The burgers are also quite tasty, extremely affordable, and relatively grease-free, and a gargantuan basket of fries can be had for a mere $2. Annie's shakes,

Martinotti's is a downtown Italian-style cafe and deli with great food, wine, and pasta for sale. CREDIT: DAVID JOHNSON

malts, cones, and sundaes are also a nice value. This is a good place to take the little ones and shoot the works or to secretly indulge in your passion for—pardon our oxymoron—high-quality junk food. Annie's is open Mondays through Saturdays from 11 A.M. until 8:30 P.M.

Assaggio $$-$$$
7742 S.E. 13th Ave.
(503) 232–6151

With very good and authentic Italian food, friendly, competent service, and moderate prices, this fine-dining establishment has built a legion of loyal followers. It's often packed with a boisterous and buoyant crowd, and with the wonderful pasta dishes and scrumptious appetizers and desserts, many Portlander's consider Assaggio to be the city's best Italian restaurant. The dark, ivy-covered walls are soothing, and the aroma of rich Italian food will make you eager for your appetizers to arrive. The menu, which respects the traditional pastas, changes with the seasons and honors special events in the old country—during truffle season they feature a Piedmont menu, during Carnival, a Venetian menu, etc. All year around, the spaghetti puttanesca—rich with olives and capers—is a favorite. Assaggio is open Tuesday through Saturday from 5 until 10 P.M. Reservations for only six or more.

Bangkok Kitchen $-$$
2534 S.E. Belmont St.
(503) 236–7349

People come here for hot, delicious, reasonably-priced Thai food, not trendy atmosphere. The spicy noodle dishes, soups, and fried fish basted in chili paste may blister the inside of your mouth but it all tastes so yummy you won't even stop to notice. This is a family restaurant in the truest sense, and all the employees treat guests almost like visitors in their own home. Bangkok Kitchen is open every day from 11 A.M. until 10 P.M.

Caprial's Bistro and Wines
7019 S.E. Woodstock Blvd.
(503) 236–6457
www.caprial.com

If this restaurant critic and I suspect most other reviewers were asked, which is the best restaurant in Portland, they would say Caprial's in a heartbeat. Owned and lovingly operated by John and Caprial Pence for almost a decade, this swank bistro has a gentle blend of European and Northwest flair in both design and flavor. Seating twenty-six, this cozy eatery exudes confidence rather than stretching too hard to impress. The pork loin is almost too exquisite to wrap words around. A cornmeal-crusted sturgeon is well worth the attention of fish lovers. Not only is Caprial a wonder in her own bistro, she also is hostess of two cooking shows on PBS and the author of six cookbooks.

Casablanca $$-$$$
2221 S.E. Hawthorne Blvd.
(503) 233–4400
www.casablanca.pdxguide.com

If you're seeking genuine Moroccan cuisine, this elegant and low-key establishment is sure to delight—and you will be pampered like an honored guest in the sultan's private tent. Everything—from the lamb, honey, and prunes to the tagine of veal and eggplant—is prepared fresh each day. Ask your waiter about The Royal Feast Dinner, a wonderful five-course meal that costs just under $20 and is a great value. Chef Omar Fekhar knows his stuff: He was born in Casablanca, trained in Paris where he owned a restaurant, and once served as Brigitte Bardot's private cook. The menu offers a wide variety of specialties mainly centered around lamb, chicken, seafood, beef, and vegetarian dishes. Dessert here is a unique experience with Moroccan pastries, fruit salad, and crème caramel. The interior is decorated with hand-stenciled trim, rich tap-

estries, and many imported art objects. Here's looking at you, kid. Casablanca is open daily from 5 until 10 P.M.

Café Castagna $-$$
1758 S .E. Hawthorne Blvd.
(503) 231–7373

If you want to sample upscale cuisine at moderate prices, stop by this charming if lean bistro located along mega-trendy Hawthorne. Simple fair includes pizza, braised short ribs, Caesar salad, and roast chicken. According to co-owner Kevin Gibson the menu will change seasonally.

Caswell's $$
533 S.E. Grand
(503) 232–6512

Caswell's used to be a coffeehouse, but just when it got successful, the landlord got greedy and raised the rent. So they found new digs and used the move as a chance to remodel their whole menu. The reasonably priced, Mediterranean-inspired offerings include many vegetarian dishes, but whether you're an herbivore or an omnivore, you can count on deliciously prepared food served in a wonderful ambience. Caswell's has a beautiful marble bar, the perfect place to sip a bourbon and observe the combination of elements—brick, brushed metal, and chrome—that blend to make Caswell's both industrial and homey. Caswell's serves dinner Monday through Friday, from 5 P.M. to 1:30 A.M.

Chez Grill $$
2229 S.E. Hawthorne Blvd.
(503) 239–4002
www.citysearch.com

Hip, fun, and elegant in an unassuming way, Chez Grill is winning lots of fans with its inventive Southwestern brand of cuisine. Every dish on the menu is consistently good, but the oven-roasted game hen, marinated in adobo sauce and served with banana-pepper chutney, coconut rice, and a grilled banana is a knockout. We like to start out with the tortilla soup and the Mexican fruit salad, and the cornmeal-crusted oysters served with a red-chili horseradish sauce are also a treat. The service is competent, friendly, and efficient. Inside, diners may choose between the lounge or the more formal dining area; outside tables are available too. Chez Grill also has a full bar that prepares superb daiquiris. Hours are 4 P.M. until 1 A.M. Monday through Thursday, 4 P.M. until 2 A.M. Friday and Saturday, and 4 P.M. to midnight Sundays.

Compass World Bistro $$
4741 S.E. Hawthorne Blvd.
(503) 231–4840
www.compadworldbistro.com

Compass World Bistro has only been open for a few years, but they are already racking up some impressive awards. This place is so appealing from the moment you walk in the door that it heightens your anticipation for the meal to follow, and chefs Mike Siegel and Chris Migdol won't disappoint you. There's a limited selection of appetizers, but they are all superb. The house smoked-salmon wontons are so scrumptious you may want to make a meal of them. The menu changes monthly as well as seasonally. And the entrees—the hazelnut-crusted chicken with Oregon mixed wild mushrooms or the house-smoked lamb rack served with honey ginger barbecue sauce are works of art. Some exquisite desserts wait in the wings, including freshly baked lemon tarts or dark-chocolate mousse served with white-chocolate curls. Siegel and Migdol sample a new regional cuisine each month, so things never get routine. Garden seating is available, but goes fast in summer months. Compass World Bistro offers monthly wine-tasting dinners. The vast majority of the entrees are under $20. Compass World Bistro is open Tuesdays through Saturdays from 5:30 P.M. until 9:30 P.M. and is also open for brunches on Saturdays and Sundays from 9 A.M. until 2 P.M.

Delta Café
4607 S.E. Woodstock Blvd.
(503) 771–3101

The Southern-roots rock playing on the jukebox hints that this lively eatery offers downhome, "suthrin" cuisine in an unpretentious setting where you needn't worry about which fork to use. Located in the burgeoning Woodstock neighborhood, Delta smells like barbeque and tidy bleach, has Spanish beaded curtains, and a bowl of Rice Krispies treats those who find themselves waiting for a seat. Once you've landed in this slice of the Deep South, try the Cajun meatballs, fried okra, or biscuits and gravy. For sipping we recommend "The Alamo," a shot of Southern Comfort, vodka, triple sec, fresh lemonade, and cola.

DeNicola's Restaurant $-$$
3520 S.E. Powell Blvd.
(503) 239–5220

This well-established family restaurant offers all the Italian favorites you'd expect and prepares them with skill and grace. The eggplant parmigiana, lasagna, and fresh veal entrees are all recommended. Most people would never think of ordering spaghetti and meatballs at an Italian restaurant, but DeNicola's version is awesome. The interior of the restaurant is warm, spacious, and inviting, not crowded or frantic. Classic meals include the linguine, rigatoni, gnocchi, fettucine, and a host of chicken dishes. A children's menu with soups, salads, and pizza is available for the little ones. It's worth mentioning that this place makes one of the best pizzas in town. DeNicola's is open Thursdays through Sundays from 4 until 10 P.M. and on Fridays and Saturdays it stays open an hour later.

Esparza's Tex-Mex Cafe $$
2725 S.E. Ankeny St.
(503) 234–7909

Portlanders have known about the terrific and unique food at this place for ages. Don't be deceived by the humble appearance, as Esparza's is truly a one-of-a-kind eatery. The menu boldly proclaims: "Joe Esparza's own brand of Tex-Mex cooking," and many of the specialties sound like they're straight from a roadhouse on a lonely stretch of highway in the middle of the Lone Star State. From the house-smoked meats and cactus to the barbecued buffalo, this joint will have you licking your chops. The food is honest, authentic, spicy, and tantalizingly aromatic. The prices are reasonable, the portions are generous, and everything we've tried is a winner. Don't miss the fried cactus and buffalo briskets, and be sure to try the daily specials in this 1950s Texas soda-shop style eatery. The food is as spicy and hearty as you'd hope, plus you get to mop up the tasty red-eye gravy with fresh tortillas or homemade mashed potatoes. No reservations means getting a table isn't always a given, but if there is a wait, take comfort in knowing that it's well worth it. Esparza's is open Tuesdays through Thursdays from 11:30 A.M. until 10 P.M. and on Fridays and Saturdays they stay open a half-hour later.

Flying Pie Pizzeria $-$$
7804 S.E. Stark St.
(503) 254–2016

Half the fun of writing this guide is being able to share delightful places like this. For our money, Flying Pie is the best pizza joint in town, no apologies to the competition. The crusts are so good that people who ordinarily won't give pizza a second look find themselves raving about them. The toppings are generously applied, but unlike most pizzas, they're not blended together, so the vegetables, cheese, sausage, and salami all retain their original flavor. The Italian sausage, pastrami, pepperoni, and salami here are excep-

tional. The prices aren't the lowest in town, but Flying Pie makes and hand-rolls their pizza dough each day and uses whole milk in their mozzarella, provolone, and romano cheeses. The pizzas come nice and hot, are moist but not greasy, and are placed over small candle holders to keep them warm. Flying Pie also does four kinds of stuffed, baked old-world pizzas that are so good it's hard to single out just one. Let's just say that the Roma, with spiced beef, black olives, onions, fresh mushrooms, and topped with mozzarella cheese and fresh tomato marinade is our current favorite. The super casual, T-shirt and cutoffs atmosphere is ideal for hunkering down with a great pizza. A half-dozen microbrews and a limited wine selection are available. Flying Pie is open from 11 A.M. until 10 P.M. except on Fridays and Saturdays when they close at 11 P.M.

Genoa $$$$
2832 S.E. Belmont St.
(503) 238–1464
www.genoarestaurant.com

If you want to create some wonderful memories, this place won't let you down. Genoa, on modest little Belmont Street, is truly a fine dining establishment and rates as one of the city's top restaurants. If you order the seven-course dinner, be prepared to relax and enjoy for about two hours. Prices for dinners range from $35 to $50, and the menu, which features Northern Italian cuisine, changes several times a month. During season look for the Umbrian-style homemade egg pasta with fresh black truffle sauce. The romantic and elegant dining room adds immeasurably to the overall experience. The menu features the market's freshest buys of the day, served with superb Italian, Oregon, and California wines, and the desserts are sinfully sumptuous. Genoa opens every day—except Sundays when it is closed—at 5:30 P.M. and schedules its last reservation at 9 P.M.

Henry's Cafe $
2508 S.E. Clinton
(503) 236–8707

Michelle Wong, owner of Common Grounds (see the Coffeehouses chapter), opened this small cafe on 26th and Clinton in 1999, and the neighborhood has been grateful ever since because it offers some of the best breakfasts and lunches in town—or anywhere. Choose from the especially delicious grilled polenta, the blueberry pancakes (made with real pancake batter), and the heavenly meat and potato omelette, which has bits of browned potato, crispy bacon, and savory sausage tucked in its eggy wrapper. If you never liked tuna melts before, it's because you never had one with capers, apple, and white cheddar on rustic Italian bread. Henry's also serves dinner, and has a really decent wine list too. Have a cider-glazed pork chop with a glass of Château Paradis Casseuil, and you will forget all your troubles. Henry's is open from 7 A.M. to 9 P.M. Tuesday through Sunday.

Hollyhurst Neighborhood Grill $-$$
4515 S.E. 41st Ave.
(503) 774–1822

Good old-fashioned American food—such as the Yankee Pot Roast—will never go out of style at this place—nor will great ambience. The Hollyhurst Neighborhood Grill has been pleasing palates for upwards of forty years and is going stronger than ever under its new ownership. There's a nice variety of entrees—ranging from pasta dishes to rosemary chicken sautée, to Southwestern beef tips, to lobster Thermador—but it clearly isn't nouvelle cuisine. This is also a nice place to stop for lunch as the burgers, soups, and salads are winners and the sandwiches are exceptional—especially the triple-decker grilled reuben, which is $7.25 and worth every penny. Soups, stews, desserts, and even salad dressings are all made from scratch. The Hollyhurst—which has its own bakery on-site—offers four separate dining rooms, each very comfortable and equipped with a

fireplace. They have a terrific bar downstairs and a good selection of wines. Ask the proprietor and raconteur Glen Cartwright to tell you about the elaborate mahogany woodcarvings or the ghosts that are said to inhabit the place. The Hollyhurst is open every day from 11:30 A.M. until 9 P.M.

Horse Brass Pub $-$$
4534 S.E. Belmont St.
(503) 232–2202
www.horsebrasspub.com

This neighborhood pub specializes in English food and great American and British beers and microbrews. Filled with British atmosphere, this place is as close to a real old-fashioned pub as you can get. There are always crusty, colorful blokes socializing at the bar, so don't come here if a wee bit o' cigar smoke and loud banter offend you. The menu offers nearly twenty different dishes, such as Bridie (a meat and onion popover smothered in gravy), the traditional steak and kidney pie, a beef and mushroom pie, fish and chips, and, of course, the Banger Dinner—English sausages served with sweet hot mustard, salad, bread, and butter. The Horse Brass Pub is proud of its huge selection of single malt scotches and more than forty-five Northwest microbrews and imported beers. For more detailed information about the alcoholic beverages, see our chapter on microbrew pubs. The Horse Brass is open seven days a week from 11 until 2 A.M.

Il Piatto $$
2348 S.E. Ankeny St.
(503) 236–4997
www.ilpiatto.citysearch.com

A small, family-owned Italian restaurant that oozes warmth and old-world ambience, Il Piatto offers wonderful appetizers and salads, and features such tempting entrees as Coniglio Salmi—marinated rabbit cooked slowly in a sauce of red wine, raisins, and prosciutto. The Ossobucco d' Agnello, another heavenly concoction, is lamb braised in red wine and tomatoes, served with stewed vegetables and polenta. These and other entrees are priced between $9.50 and $19.50 and the pasta and risotti dishes are superb. Il Piatto offers an extensive list of Italian wines. If you like intimate dining you will enjoy this romantic little place. Il Piato is open every day for lunch between 11:30 A.M. and 2 P.M. Sunday through Thursday they are open for dinner from 5:30 until 10 P.M., and on Friday and Saturday they stay open until 11 P.M.

It's a Beautiful Pizza $
3341 S.E. Belmont St.
(503) 233–5444

Great gourmet pizza is served here the way you like it in a funky 1950s atmosphere. There is a huge selection of toppings to choose from, and you can buy pizza whole or by the slice. Beer and wine are available. Hours are Monday through Thursday from 11 A.M. until 10 P.M. and on Fridays and Saturdays from 11 A.M. until 11:30 P.M.

Jarra's Ethiopian Restaurant $-$$
1435 S.E. Hawthorne Blvd.
(503) 230–8990

This family-run Ethiopian diner offers savory native dishes featuring an ethnic bread known as Enjera that is like a spongy and chewy pancake. Topped off with the exotic and spicy sauces, it is the perfect compliment to the fiery African vegetables and spicy and tangy lamb and chicken dishes. Jarra's specialties all come in mild or spicy varieties, and when they say spicy, they mean it—so ask for a large glass of ice water. The bright interior is decorated with Ethiopian arts and crafts and a large tiled fireplace sits near the entrance. Jarra's, which is equipped with a full bar, offers four combination plates—including an awesome vegetable combo—that are popular with adventurous diners. Jarra's is open Tuesdays through Saturdays from 5 until 10 P.M.

La Catalana $$
2821 S.E. Stark St.
(503) 232–0948

This intimate and charming restaurant—and the fine meals it prepares—might make you believe that you are back in the little Spanish village where Ernest Hemingway wrote "A Clean, Well Lighted Place." La Catalana specializes in food from the region of Catalonia and its capital, Barcelona. Seafood is a prime focus, but beef and poultry options are also available and change seasonally. Paella, which is made from an assortment of seafood, house-made chorizo sausage, and chicken is offered each day, year-round. Beer, sangría, and a good selection of Spanish wines, ports, and sherries are available. If you initially have a little trouble deciphering the exotic menu, don't be dismayed. The friendly servers will make you totally at ease, as will the prices, with the entrees all under $20.

La Catalana opens at 6 P.M. and closes at 10 P.M. on Tuesdays through Thursdays, at 10:30 P.M. on Fridays and Saturdays, and at 9 P.M. Sundays. The restaurant is closed Mondays.

Lanai Cafe $
3145 S.E. Hawthorne Blvd.
(503) 239–4857

There isn't one single thing upscale or trendy about this Vietnamese diner, which offers good, low-priced lunch and dinner specials. People don't come here to be seen, but to chow down on tasty healthy fare. Situated in a little, yellow house, Lanai Cafe offers different vegetarian specials each week for around $4. The tofu sour soup that accompanies the meal is hot and spicy, as is the tofu curry, which is served with rice and piled high with fresh vegetables and peanut sauce. The owners of Lanai Cafe are never too busy to make you feel at home. Lanai Cafe is open Mondays through Saturdays from 11 A.M. until 9:30 P.M.

Le Bistro Montage $-$$
301 S.E Morrison St.
(503) 234–1324

Buried deep in the city's bowels under the Morrison Street Bridge, this one-of-a-kind place attracts a colorful crowd and serves wonderfully satisfying Cajun-style seafood. You can't go wrong with the smoked mussels and crayfish, fiery omelettes, thick and tasty macaroni and cheese, or homemade breads and desserts. The cartoon mural of the *Last Supper* is as antiestablishment as most of the tattooed and nose-ringed crowd. If you are in a big hurry or get uptight easily, don't bother coming here. Otherwise, ditch that necktie, c'mon in, and scarf down some of the tastiest Southern-style food in the city. Open seven days a week, lunch hours are 11 A.M. until 2 P.M. and dinner is served from 6 P.M. until 2 A.M. on weekdays and on Friday and Saturdays from 6 P.M. until 4 A.M.

Michael's Italian Beef & Sausage Co. $
1111 S.E. Sandy Blvd.
(503) 230–1899

Yearning for a taste of the Windy City? Michael's is as close as you'll get in this neck of the woods. Go to this place and sink your chops into an authentic Chicago-style meatball sandwich, one of the kosher hot dogs, or tasty beef sausages. Deep-dish Sicilian pizza is another house specialty. But Michael's beef sandwich is the most popular item and it easy to see why—the top rounds are seasoned and roasted, thinly sliced, and marinated in a delicious secret house gravy, while the fresh rolls are stuffed with onions and/or peppers. Michael's is open Mondays through Saturdays from 10:30 A.M. until 9 P.M.

Nature's Deli & Juice Bar $
3016 S.E. Division St.
(Inside Nature's Grocery)
(503) 233–7374
www.wildoats.com

If you think healthy food can't be delicious, try this organic gourmet juice bar turned restaurant of the year, located inside Nature's Northwest Grocery (see Shopping). Whether you prefer to enjoy lunch on the bustling outside patio or eat inside amidst the happy din of health-conscious shoppers, you may be surprised and amused to find that your nutritious, healthy, and politically correct meal tastes darn good. Located inside Nature's Northwest Grocery, this eatery offers a host of sandwiches featuring nitrite-free meats and organic lettuce, onions, and tomatoes. The Gardenburger, topped with mushrooms, red onion, and melted cheddar cheese on a whole wheat roll is our favorite. Entrees vary daily, but include lasagna Raphael, focaccia, chicken pot pie, or a Greek pie or a quiche of the day. Bakery items—scones, croissants, bagels, pies, and tarts are available to round out your meal. Nature's Deli is open seven days a week, from 9 A.M. until 10 P.M.

Nicholas Restaurant $
318 S.E. Grand Ave.
(503) 235–5123

This is a one-of-a kind place that offers wonderful Lebanese and Mediterranean food at user-friendly prices. Nicholas Restaurant is a fun, casual, come-as-you-are and eat-hearty place that serves giant pitas and heaping portions of ethnic food to the accompaniment of lusty music. We like everything about this place—the Mediterranean pizzas, the zesty calzones, and all of the seafood dishes. Stop in and ask for the Vegetarian Mezza Plate. Supposedly for one person, it includes tabbouleh, two falafel balls, yogurt sauce, spinach pie, hummus, and all the fresh, hot pizza bread you can eat. With a side dish it is more than enough for a couple. This place is popular so arrive early to get a table. Nicholas is open Mondays through Saturdays from 10 A.M. until 9 P.M. and Sundays from 11 A.M. until 7 P.M.

Noho's Hawaiian Cafe $
2525 S.E. Clinton St.
(503) 233–5301

Got the rainy-day blues? Come to Noho's, a super-cheery and easy-on-the-budget ethnic cafe that offers tasty Hawaiian fare in a very fun, tropical island-style atmosphere. Don't be confused—many locals still call this place by its former name, Local Boyz. There's no bar here, just plenty of scrumptious and affordable food. Dishes are served in small, medium, and large sizes and the large is easily enough for two normal human beings. The *yakisoba* noodles—served with veggies and a tangy sauce—is a favorite, but the menu offers a selection of exotic meals ranging from Korean short-ribs to seafood entrees and yummy marinated chicken dishes. Everything is served with white rice and macaroni or green salad on the side and—for those who like to swap and share different foods—family-style meals are always available. Noho's is open Sundays through Thursdays from 11 A.M. until 9 P.M., and on Fridays and Saturdays they stay open until 11 P.M.

Oasis Cafe $
3701 S.E. Hawthorne Blvd.
(503) 231–0901

This laid-back and unpretentious cafe knows how to make a good pizza. Quality and variety is a focus at the Oasis, and pizzas—whole or by the slice—can be customized at the patron's request. With thirty different types of pizza toppings, Momma mia! The salads and calzones are also made to specs, and the Oasis offers up some great Greek, spinach, chef, and taco salads too. Oasis makes a different soup each day from scratch, and indeed they taste fresh and homemade. The pizzas are served with a rich, spicy sauce and a thick, garlicky crust that borders on perfection. The best part of the pizza is the toppings, and they don't cut any corners there either. The Oasis Cafe is open from 11 A.M. until 10 P.M. Monday through Thursday; on Fridays and Saturdays they stay open until midnight, and on Sundays they are open from noon until 11 P.M.

Old Wives' Tales $-$$
1300 E. Burnside St.
(503) 238–0470

The consciousness of the 1960s and 1970s live on at this multiethnic, healthy, family-friendly restaurant.

The signature dish here is the famous Hungarian Mushroom Soup, but the menu offers much adventurous fare, including East Indian, West African, and Pan-Asian vegetarian, chicken, and seafood dishes. Old Wives' Tales also has an extensive salad bar and a nice variety of soups and sandwiches. This is also a terrific place for breakfast with a wide assortment of omelettes and delicious poppyseed pancakes.

The Old Wives' Tales has been a favored meeting place for nearly two decades and owner Holly Hunt still does a great deal of work for nonprofit organizations. The restaurant has a bulletin board for meetings and notices and carries many alternative publications. Still, most people come here for the food, especially the Hungarian soup. Some folks who stop in for breakfast ask the waiter to ladle some leftover Hungarian soup across their toast and/or eggs. Old Wives' Tales is opens at 8 A.M. every day and closes at 9 P.M., except Fridays and Saturdays when it closes at 10 P.M.

Otto's Sausage & Meat Market $
4138 S.E. Woodstock St.
(503) 771–6714

Otto's, a third-generation German butcher shop and deli, has the best smoked sausages around. This is the place to go for frankfurters, Swedish potato sausage, smoked German sausage, British bangers, bratwurst, ham hocks, and stuffed chicken breast. You will never get potato salad at a deli that even remotely compares with Otto's tasty homemade concoction. As you would expect, dining is casual at Otto's—there are just eight small tables—but if you are a sausage connoisseur and love ethnic foods you will enjoy your stop here. Otto's is open every day except Sunday from 9:30 A.M. until 6 P.M.

Papa Haydn $$
5829 S.E. Milwaukie Blvd.
(503) 232–9440

701 N.W. 23rd Ave.
(503) 228–7317
www.citysearch.com

This is a no-brainer. In Portland, this is the place to go for desserts—tortes, tarts, cheesecakes, cookies, ice cream bombes—and gelatos and sorbets, and that's just for starters. Papa Haydn's tempting pastry case shows off no less than twenty-five mouthwatering dessert selections, including the outrageously delicious Georgian peanut butter-mousse torte. But they also feature excellent pastas, salads, and several knockout grilled chicken and steak dishes that are slow cooked over a blend of Oregon apple and pear hardwood. Named by *Gourmet Magazine* as one of America's Top Tables in 1996, Papa Haydn also provides full catering service and is known for creating spectacular wedding cakes. Papa Haydn is open from 11:30 A.M. until 10 P.M. Monday through Thursday and until 12 A.M. on Friday and Saturday. On Sunday they are open for brunch from 10 A.M. until 3 P.M.

Produce Row Cafe $
204 S.E. Oak St.
(503) 232–8355

This place is a Portland institution and has served great micros for more than a dozen years.

Wedged between Grand Avenue and Martin Luther King Jr. Boulevard, the funky and fun Produce Row Cafe features an eclectic American-style menu with hearty soups, extra-thick sandwiches, and garden-fresh salads, and a great selection of imported beers and microbrews. The homemade Red-Eye Chili is tangy and fresh, and they don't skimp on the meat.

Produce Row offers more than thirty draughts and the largest selection of bottled beers in Portland. The very nice outdoor beer garden is the place to hang during the summer months. This is basically a wholesome, family-type place where anyone can have a great time. Produce Row is open Monday through Saturday from 11 A.M. until midnight; Fridays from 11 to 1 A.M.; and Sundays from noon until 11 P.M.

Roscoe's $
8105 S.E. Stark St.
(503) 261–9535

This little Montavilla neighborhood restaurant and pub does just about everything right. Open every day for breakfast, lunch, and dinner, they use quality ingredients like fresh-baked skinless chicken breast and they roast their own roast beef. The soups, salsas, dips, and dinner rolls are all made in-house.

Besides offering home-cooked food at an honest price, the owners are usually working behind the counter with their sleeves rolled up, and they're fun to talk to. Roscoe's offers a wide variety of burgers and they're all worthy of mention, none more so than the Montavilla Burger, which is served with cheddar cheese, grilled onions, and mushrooms. The humble hamburger is treated with great respect here—and served with lettuce, tomato, onion, and special house sauce on a sesame bun with chips and a pickle. The onions are sautéed on request, and Roscoe's will also throw in an order of fries for a buck and—speaking of a buck—on Mondays, all burgers are $1 off. Roscoe's also prepares nearly thirty-five different varieties of hot and cold sandwiches, offers vegetarian fare, and has a decent selection of beer, wine, and microbrews to choose from. Ask about their dessert specials, late-night menu, and daily happy hour, which features some great discounts on appetizers and brews. Roscoes serves breakfast, lunch, and dinner every day of the week.

Saigon Kitchen $
835 N.E. Broadway
(503) 281–3669

3829 S.E. Division St.
(503) 236–2312

14280 S.W. Allen Blvd., Beaverton
(503) 646–4611

The cheery and appealing Saigon Kitchens are very popular Vietnamese/Thai restaurants. Go visit a Saigon Kitchen and you'll see why. The menu features a wide range of choices and you can't go wrong because everything is delicious and low priced. The service is pleasant and fast, but not rushed.

The Spicy Shrimp Rice Stick Noodle Soup, which includes shrimp, rice noodles, jalapeños, cilantro, and lime, and comes in a bowl big enough to feed two people is a particular standout. All Saigon Kitchens are open every day of the week, from 11 A.M. until 10 P.M.

Sweetwater's Jam House $$
3350 S.E. Morrison St.
(503) 233–0333

Soul-stirring, lip-smacking, finger-licking good Caribbean-style food and barbecue are the house specialties here. Sweetwater's doesn't take itself seriously, but it is serious about putting on a great feed. If you want to cut loose and have a great meal and a few drinks, this is the place to go. Entrees such as the Jamaican pepper shrimp and stewed oxtail (no fooling) will wake up even the dullest taste buds. Except for a killer Sunday brunch served between 10 A.M. and 2 P.M., this friendly place doesn't mess around with breakfast and lunch, but then look out! If your waiter tells you the food is hot, it is HOT! We recommend everything, especially the Gator Snacks—spicy, deep-fried nuggets of alligator tenderloin served with tropical habanero-tartar sauce and fresh lime wedges. The food here will have you dreamin' of the Caribbean, and almost everything on the menu is well under $15. Like rum? You'll find thirty-one premium

varieties here, as well as pints on tap, microbrews, imports, and a good selection of red and white wines. A late-night happy hour runs daily from 10 P.M. until closing with $2 well drinks and pints. In addition to the Sunday brunch, Sweetwaters is open every day from 5 P.M. until 2:30 A.M.

Tabor Hill Cafe $
3766 S.E. Hawthorne Blvd.
(503) 230–1231

This quintessential Southeast Hawthorne Boulevard neighborhood spot is a popular hangout for the local hipsters as well as more serious-minded business folks who enjoy the fresh, healthy food and congenial atmosphere. This cafe has a flavor all its own and the prices won't give you sticker shock. This isn't an espresso joint, and it isn't fast food. Most of the patrons are regulars who find the superbly prepared breakfasts well worth waiting for. Tabor Hill's soup, sandwich, and pasta selections, while not overly inventive, are nevertheless solid values and very satisfying. Tabor Hill Cafe serves breakfast, lunch, and dinner every day except Monday when it is closed.

Thai Thai Restaurant $
4604 S.E. Hawthorne Blvd.
(503) 236–1466

This is a fun place to treat yourself to a low-cost exotic meal. Thai Thai goes far beyond the standard spring rolls and pad Thai noodles as their menu offers a wide selection of stir-fry dishes with beef, pork, seafood, or tofu and vegetarian alternatives. The atmosphere is bright and inviting and the waiters and waitresses are not too busy to smile, or to keep refilling your water glass—as Thai Thai uses curry and hot peppers generously. Beer is available, but you may find you actually prefer drinking the ginger or jasmine tea. Thai Thai is open for lunch Tuesday through Fridays only, from 11 A.M. until 1 P.M. and they are open for dinner every day except Monday, from 3 until 10 P.M.

Thanh Thao $-$$
4005 S.E. Hawthorne Blvd.
(503) 238–6232

Thanh Thao II $-$$
8355 S.E. Powell Blvd.
(503) 775–0306

A Thai-Vietnamese restaurant at the eastern edge of the Hawthorne District, Thanh Thao serves superb and original rice, vegetarian, meat, and seafood dishes. The prices are quite low in proportion to the large servings of high-quality food. Although we've been back many times, it's hard to pick a favorite dish, because everything is good. The pepper-salted shrimp is a standout, as is the crab and asparagus soup and the cucumber salad. The appetizers and noodle dishes are all excellent, the atmosphere is comfortable, and the service is attentive and courteous. Thanh Thao II features the same menu and is similar in other regards. Thanh Thao is open Monday through Saturday for lunch between 11 A.M. and 3 P.M., and for dinner between 5 and 10 P.M. On Sunday, hours are 4 until 10 P.M.

3 Doors Down $$-$$$
1429 S.E. 37th St.
(503) 236–6886

This is an absolutely delightful neighborhood-style restaurant that's all too easy to miss. 3 Doors Down offers generous portions of high-quality American-Mediterranean fare and pays attention to all the fine details that add to the enjoyment of a meal. The cozy and comfortable setting is a great place to enjoy the restaurant's wide range of pastas. The risottos and Caesar salads are exceptional as is the pan-roasted halibut, the baked steamer clams, and the seafood stew. The prices are surprisingly reasonable, the servers are knowledgeable and pleasant, and although 3 Doors Down does not accept reservations, they will gladly find you if you go window shopping next door to tell you when your table is ready. 3 Doors Down is open Tuesdays through Saturdays from 5 until 10 P.M.

Zell's $
1300 S.E. Morrison St.
(503) 239–0196

This is one of the city's most popular spots for a hearty breakfast. Zell's is known for making very good omelettes and great German pancakes served with fresh fruit and/or berries. If you like spicy omelettes, try the Chorizo De Venus Arana—spicy sausage scrambled in eggs with Anaheim peppers, cheddar cheese, and sour cream. Breakfasts are served with scones, toast, or English muffins, quick bread, or potatoes. For folks who work or do business downtown, this is a bustling place that serves good coffee and quality breakfasts and lunches. The soups are great, and the Fisherman's Stew is a must. Zell's offers outside dining, daily specials, and a full bar. This is a very upbeat place, great for either meeting friends or having a business lunch. The highest-priced item on the menu is under $8. Zell's is open every day of the week for breakfast and lunch.

North/Northeast Portland

Abyssinia Ethiopian Cuisine $-$$
801 N.E. Broadway
(503) 281–1975

Here's an elegant little spot that will lend an exotic touch to a lunch or dinner engagement while not taking a big bite out of your billfold. The atmosphere of the Abyssinia is classic yet comfy with linen tablecloths, flowers, and candles on the tables, and attractive paintings adorning the walls. The food—a variety of genuine (and very spicy) Ethiopian vegetarian, poultry, beef, and lamb dishes, will wake up your taste buds while not setting your mouth on fire. We recommend the Beyaynetu, a combination platter including stewed beef, Ethiopian-style chicken with onions, red-pepper, and a special sauce, and the fresh vegetable dish of the day. All meals are served with Enjera, a tropical bread that looks somewhat like a pancake. It's customary to eat most Ethiopian dishes with the fingers, but you may opt to use a fork, especially if the dinner engagement is a first date. The Abyssinia is open for lunch Monday through Friday from 11:30 A.M. until 2 P.M. and for dinner every evening from 5 until 10 P.M.

Alameda Brewing Co. $
4765 N.E. Fremont St.
(503) 460–9025

This cheery, upscale microbrewery offers great appetizers, creative pasta dishes, and a variety of tempting entrees. For more information see our chapter on brewpubs.

The Alameda Cafe $-$$
4641 N.E. Fremont St.
(503) 284–5314

No relation to the above-mentioned brewhouse, the Alameda Cafe is a fine choice for a quiet, relaxing meal. The tastefully decorated Alameda serves breakfast, lunch, and dinner, and you can't go wrong with any of them. Their cooks gladly prepare your favorite omelette to specs, with a wide choice of cheese, vegetables, and meats, and serve it with home-style potatoes and toast—all for under $7. The lunch menu includes a nice variety of soups, salads, and sandwiches. The Village Greek salad is something special, consisting of Calamata olives with feta, tomatoes, cucumbers, green peppers, onions, and celery tossed in a Greek vinaigrette dressing. For dinner, entrees lean towards seafood, pasta, steaks, and chicken. The New York steak is chargrilled and topped with a Pinot Noir butter. Their oven-roasted mussels, served in a garlic herb broth, are a must. The Alameda has a nice wine selection, a handful of microbrews, and offers many teas and Italian sodas. The Alameda Cafe

is open Monday through Thursday from 7 A.M. until 9 P.M., Saturdays from 8 A.M. until 9 P.M., and Sundays from 8 A.M. until 2 P.M.

Beaterville Cafe $
2201 N. Killingsworth
(503) 735–4652

This place is a refreshing change of pace with its homage to "beaters," otherwise knows as "work cars." But besides the unusual and funky atmosphere—hubcaps, framed pictures of weird cars, and old fenders decorate the walls of this eatery—it is a great place to indulge in a cheap and very tasty breakfast or lunch.

The cooks here have a healthy respect for the humble egg, hence the omelettes are exceptionally well done, with ingredients ranging from the predictable yet tasty mushrooms and cheddar cheese to the sublime smoked salmon concoctions. The chunky red potatoes and homemade croissants are the ideal companions to their legion of omelettes. Outside seating is available. Beaterville is open weekdays from 6 A.M. until 3 P.M., Saturdays 8 A.M. until 2 P.M., and Sundays 9 A.M. until 2 P.M. No lunch on Sunday.

Bernie's Southern Bistro $$
2904 N.E. Alberta St.
(503) 282–9864

This upscale, down-home place, a truly rare find in Portland, serves up delicious helpings of low-country Southern cuisine. Open for dinners only, Bernie's cornmeal-crusted oysters are scrumptious, and the shrimp—sautéed in brandy butter sauce—will have you dreaming of the South. Where else in the city can you feast on fried green tomatoes with smoked tomato coulis, hearty gumbo, fresh cornbread, and green-onion grit cakes? Bernie's serves a catfish dinner that will make you forget all about our Pacific salmon, and the brunches—with sweet potato pancakes, bread pudding French toast with bourbon praline sauce, oysters, and gorgeous poached eggs drenched in béarnaise sauce—are out of this world.

Forget about calories at this place, and by all means, try the brandied shrimp served over green onion cakes. Bernie's, which is open Tuesdays through Saturdays from 5 P.M. until 10 P.M., offers intimate dining indoors and a few outside sidewalk tables during pleasant weather.

Bridges Café and Catering $
2716 N.E. Martin Luther King Jr. Blvd.
(503) 288–4169

As one might surmise, this neighborhood cafe pays tribute to Portland's many bridges (see the Close-up on Portland's bridges in our Getting Here, Getting Around chapter) by naming their delicious sandwiches after the bridges and hanging photos of them on the cheery, yellow walls. There's even a stained-glass rendition of a drawbridge opening its arches. This place also celebrates food, especially breakfasts with top-notch ingredients. The cheese biscuits and omelettes are very good, as are the fresh-baked scones, cookies, and desserts. The lunches are almost all priced under $5 and there are plenty of dishes to satisfy vegetarians and meat-eaters alike. Some of the dishes are unusual, such as the corned beef, cabbage, and beer soup, and the Sellwood Caponata—a mix of roasted eggplant, green and red bell peppers, red onions, capers, garlic, and Provolone served in a warm pita with potato chips and a pickle. Bridges serves beer and wine and is open Monday through Fridays from 7 A.M. until 2 P.M. and Saturdays and Sundays from 8 A.M. until 4 P.M.

El Burrito Loco $
1942 N. Portland Blvd.
(503) 735–9505

18238 S.E. Division St., Gresham
(503) 669–1253

3126 N.E. 82nd Ave.
(503) 252–1343

El Burrito Loco's three locations serve up very good burritos and Mexican food for a price that's hard if not impossible to beat. The best bet is the restaurant's flagship burrito, the hefty El Loco, a flour tortilla stuffed with a chili relleno, shredded steak *picado*, refried beans, and homemade avocado sauce. This is a huge burrito and they don't skimp on ingredients by jamming it full of refried beans. It's hard to find burritos priced at more than $3.50 here, and the soft tacos—double-wrapped in warm corn tortillas and bulging with shredded beef, lettuce, tomatoes, and cheese—are priced so low they are almost a steal. El Burrito Loco is open seven days a week, from 10 A.M. until 10 P.M.

The Fishwife Seafood Restaurant $-$$
5328 N. Lombard St.
(503) 285–7150

People come from all around to feast on the grilled oysters served at this super-friendly, clean, neighborhood seafood restaurant. There's a lot to like—from the homemade fruit cobblers and cheesecakes (and a chocolate mousse cake that would give Martha Stewart a run for her money) to the house's tasty custom coleslaw and salad dressings. The Fishwife is a humble-appearing place, with linoleum floors and many fascinating pictures of ships adorning the walls, along with an assortment of old boating equipment and antique fishing gear. The big attraction, though, is the fish and seafood dishes. The menu boasts standbys such as Northwest cioppino, Alaskan halibut fillet, which is seasoned with lemon and pepper and grilled (or if you prefer, poached with a splash of lemon and wine), and good pasta dishes including shrimp Alfredo and bay scallops Florentine. There's plenty more to choose from on the menu, for big or small appetites. Save room for dessert!

Jim Dandy $
9626 N.E. Sandy Blvd.
(503) 253–2126

Cruise to Jim Dandy, one of Oregon's oldest drive-in restaurants for good, cheap food and a 1950s atmosphere. First opened in 1937, this place even has a vintage jukebox that will bring back memories of your favorite malt shop. The owner has made a few concessions to progress, however, such as offering a basic espresso selection and cholesterol-free eggs. Jim Dandy is much larger on the inside than it looks from the outside; there's plenty of room to sit down, but you can also carry out one of their many breakfasts and lunches. Morning selections, obviously not Cordon Bleu material, are surprisingly extensive, with a wide range of muffins, omelettes, griddlecakes, and biscuits n' gravy. The cinnamon rolls are huge and a steal for $1.25. The lunches include such fare as deli sandwiches, burgers, hot dogs, and fried chicken. You can also order a darn good chef salad, with ham, turkey, tomato, onion, cheese, and bacon for $4.95. The foot-long Coney-Island dogs are a mere $2.40, and the side orders include French fries, tater sticks, spicy fries, onion rings, zucchini slices, battered mushrooms, cheese sticks, mashed potatoes and gravy, and sautéed mushrooms. If you're hungry for ice cream, Jim Dandy has nearly sixty flavor combinations. The milkshakes are very good, and the small ice cream cones are incredibly huge for just 75 cents. This is a terrific place to take the little ones for a fun and inexpensive meal. Jim Dandy's is open Monday through Thursday from 5:30 A.M. until 8 P.M. and Saturday and Sunday 5:30 A.M. until 9 P.M.

Kim Hong $-$$
4239 N.E. Fremont St.
(503) 282–0456

Want to eat like a prince (or princess) without paying a king's ransom? This place is a treasure if you appreciate wonderfully prepared authentic Vietnamese food. Like variety? Come to Kim Hong every other day for a year, and still order something different with every visit. From calamari dishes, to stir-fried frog legs, to clams with ginger or oyster sauce, variety is the word with 160 selections on the menu. The value is incredible—at least thirty lunch specials are priced well under $5. On top of that, the servers here are gracious, friendly, and efficient, adding much enjoyment to the meal. You will find many true ethnic dishes available that you don't see in most Vietnamese restaurants, and they make seven different varieties of *pho*, all of them excellent. A large bowl of *pho* costs just $4.35 and is served with fresh bean sprouts, basil leaf, jalapeño pepper, and a wedge of lime. Kim Hong also boasts an extensive wine list and a nice selection of domestic and imported beers. It's a very charming restaurant, with red linen tablecloths covering all the little tables and Vietnamese music gently playing in the background. Kim Hong is open every day except Monday from 11 A.M. to 3 P.M. for lunch, and 5 until 10 P.M. for dinner.

La Sirenita $-$$
2817 N.E. Alberta St.
(503) 335–8283

Seems everyone on the Eastside knows about the good food and low prices at this small but ambitious northeast *taquería*. The cooks take pride in all they create here, and it shows. Especially good dishes are the chicken and *carne asada*, and the *lengua* (it sounds romantic, but it's a beef tongue). The ridiculously low-priced burritos are colossal and stuffed with shredded beef, chicken, cheese, and fresh veggies. The atmosphere is extremely pleasant with Mexican knickknacks and pictures on the walls. La Sirenita also has a large selection of Mexican sodas. La Sirenita is open every day from 10 A.M. until 10 P.M.

Mama Gianetta's $
5264 N. Lombard St.
(503) 285–8863

This dark hole-in-the-wall serves up generous portions of very good Southern Italian food. Part bar lounge, part restaurant, Mama Gianetta's pastas and spaghetti and meatballs are good choices, as the spices are zesty and the meatballs tender. For lunch, the meatball sandwich is a wonderful value and includes a small salad, all for under $5—and no, that is not a misprint or an error. The manicotti is excellent and so is the cannelloni—a tasty combination of meat-stuffed tubes double-sauced with cream and marinara sauce. Seafood, chicken, and veal dishes are also available. The pasta, however, is the attraction here, and a dozen or so sauces are available for the five styles of noodles. Mama's is open Monday and Tuesday with lunch in the bar from 11 A.M. until 9 P.M., Fridays from 11 A.M. until 10 P.M., Saturdays from 4:30 until 9 P.M., and Sundays from 4:30 until 10 P.M.

My Canh $
1801 N.E. 39th Ave.
(503) 281–0594

This is a terrific little Chinese and Vietnamese restaurant that is tucked away in a corner of the Hollywood District. The outstanding dish here is the bun—steaming vermicelli noodles layered over lettuce and covered with prawns or meat, aromatic cilantro, and mouthwatering peanuts and sweet-and-sour sauce. All of the entrees, particularly the seafood dishes, are quite good at My Canh, but our favorite meal is the vermicelli noodle bun, which is served in a large bowl filled to the brim and served with a fried spring roll and roasted pork and shrimp. My Canh's servers are gracious and efficient and it doesn't take long to enjoy a wonderful lunch here. My Canh is open from 10 A.M. until 10 P.M. Mondays through Saturdays, and Sundays from 4 P.M. until 10 P.M.

Nicola's Pizza $-$$
4826 N. Lombard Ave.
(503) 285–1119

The three Cortese brothers have been preparing great pizzas for twelve years from their little takeout pizza shop in North Portland. This is the real, made-from-scratch stuff, prepared with all fresh vegetables and quality ingredients. The New York-style crusts are slightly crunchy on the outside and warm and chewy on the inside. Nicola's will make your crust anyway you like it—extra thick or thin, and they are generous with the toppings. Most large pizzas (16 inches) are priced in

the $13 to $14 range, and the Kitchen Sink, which is a combo with everything, goes for $18.25. Nicola's was previously all carryout or delivery, but the brothers are currently changing to a full Italian menu and recently built a large and comfortable dining room that accommodates seventy people. In addition, an outdoor patio complete with fountains and hanging plants adds a romantic touch. Hours are 11:30 A.M. until 9 P.M. Tuesday through Thursdays and 11:30 A.M. until 10 P.M. on Fridays and Saturdays. Nicola's is closed on Sundays.

Overlook Restaurant $
1332 N. Skidmore St.
(503) 288–0880

This charmingly down-to-earth restaurant is a great breakfast stop, especially for lovers of biscuits n' gravy. The generous-sized, homemade biscuits are served up piping hot and swimming in spicy and thick sausage gravy. The meal is so huge that you can ask for two plates and share it with a partner. The food at the Overlook isn't creative or exotic, but it is solid, filling, and reliably good. This is a great place to chow down on bacon and eggs with pork chops on the side. There's lots of meat on the lunch and dinner menu, especially steaks, prime rib, and fried chicken. Overlook is open 5 A.M. until 9 P.M. Mondays through Saturdays and Sundays from 6 A.M. until 9 P.M.

Paparazzi Pastaficio $-$$
2015 N.E. Broadway
(503) 281–7701

This friendly neighborhood eatery specializes in Northern Italian dishes such as pasta with scallops, prawn and Dungeness crab, and sweet potato and Parmesan pasta. The soups and salads are satisfying and their small, one-person pizzas are quite good, especially the four-cheese and mushroom varieties. Paparazzi Pastificio serves beer and wine and has a small selection of microbrews. Paparizzi Pastaficio opens at 5 P.M. and closes at 9:30 P.M. Sunday through Thursday, at 10 P.M. on Fridays and Saturdays, and at 9 P.M. on Sundays.

The Refectory $$-$$$
1618 N.E. 122nd Ave.
(503) 255–8545

With its solid and comforting wood-and-brick interior and beamed ceilings accentuated by soft lighting, The Refectory is a relaxing and charming place to savor one of the city's best prime ribs—slow roasted for more than twenty hours and served with creamed horseradish, au jus, and Yorkshire pudding. The menu includes a good variety of beef, chicken, and seafood entrees, and the superior service, excellent desserts, full bar, and extensive wine list add immeasurably to the enjoyment of one's meal. Dinners come with a choice of unlimited refills of either the homemade soups or house garden salads. The adjoining cocktail lounge is a great place to begin working off that prime rib (see the Nightlife chapter). The Refectory opens Monday through Friday at 11:30 A.M. to 9:30 P.M. and Saturdays and Sundays from 5 until 9:30 P.M.

Der Rheinlander/Gustav's
Bier Stube $$-$$$
5035 N.E. Sandy Blvd.
(503) 288–5503

If you are around Portland very long, you'll hear about Horst Mager, a local chef, restaurateur, and celebrity who opened this establishment in 1963 with the aim of serving up authentic Bavarian and German cuisine. This is the hearty brand of food that European peasants might have enjoyed at a big wedding feast. Horst is semi-retired and his capable daughter Suzeanne is now running the businesses and thanks to an extensive remodeling of the Der Rheinlander, the place looks like a big, fabulous dollhouse. Hungry for genuine old-world food and ready to have some old-fashioned fun? The beaming waitresses adorned in milkmaid outfits stop to sing Edelweiss and waiters wearing Bavarian shorts, hats, knee-high socks, and suspenders often serenade the diners, and musicians adorned in similar garb play the accordion. This place is a delightful fun if you enjoy such schtick. The restaurant serves ample portions of strudels, sauerbraten (roast beef marinated in red wine and spices), schnitzel (a breaded cutlet) and spaetzle (small noodles), roast duck, and other ethnic fare. We recommend the Hasenpfeffer, or marinated roast rabbit, which is infused with molasses, Tabasco, and exotic spices turning it dark and rich with a woodsy flavor. Also, the Gustav's Party Feast, for $8.50, includes smoked beer sausage, bratwurst, skinless chicken schnitzel, a mouthwatering slice of rotisserie-roasted pork, and much more. If you have room after all that, this is one of the best spots in town to savor a fresh apple strudel or a sinfully rich cheesecake. The menu offers seasonal specials, so dining options are always changing. Der Rheinlander is open for dinner every day of the week.

Rib Express $-$$
3328 N.E. Killingsworth St.
(503) 288–3836

A splendid choice for takeout soul food, the Rib Express prepares lip-smackin' barbecued ribs and chicken and all the fixin's, including sweet potato pie and peach cobbler. This is a place to get carryout, not to eat in, but don't let that stop you from sampling their famous barbecue sauce—sweet and tangy hickory-flavored stuff that magically turns pork ribs into little pieces of ambrosia. The first time you go to the Rib Express, it may be a bit of a surprise. It isn't a big or impressive place to look at, but just taste the food! It's open every day of the week for lunch and dinner.

Ringside $$-$$$
2165 W. Burnside St.
(503) 223–1513

14021 N.E. Glisan St.
(503) 255–0750

One of Portland's most famous establishments, Ringside has been finding the beef for its customers for over fifty years. In a dimly lit, traditional-steak house setting of red banquette booths and glowing fireplace, diners are offered a traditional menu of various cuts of meat from lamb chops to sirloin to peppered New York steak. This eatery, now on both sides of the river, keeps alive a tradition that has garnered awards and national acclaim. The famed chef James Beard once announced that the onion rings in this emporium of sizzle were "the best I've ever had." Take his word for it and order a batch of these deep-fried monsters. It'll change your life. Ringside serves dinner daily.

Shawdon's Restaurant & Lounge $
2731 N. Killingsworth
(503) 285–4144

This place bills itself as North Portland's best kept secret and we agree. Shawdon's offers wonderful old-fashioned breakfasts with grits, homemade biscuits n' gravy, pancakes, waffles, and eggs and omelettes fixed anyway you can imagine. Lunch isn't highly creative, but the hearty and thick burgers and sandwiches and homemade fish and chicken specials keep regulars happy. The catfish dinners, barbecue ribs, and rib-eye steaks have made Shawdon's a good choice for North Portlanders. There is also a full bar, separate from the lounge, and an all-you-can-eat buffet on Mondays and Tuesdays for $6.75. Shawdon's is open every day of the week from 6 until 2 A.M.

Shenanigan's Restaurant and Lounge
$$-$$$
4575 N. Channel Dr.
(503) 289–0966
www.shenanigansrestaurant.com

This is one of the best on-the-river restaurants in Portland, especially for steak and seafood lovers. Combine the pleasure of fine dining with a festive, but mellow atmosphere and you have Shenanigans. If you are not yet a fan of their Sunday champagne brunches, go once and you will be. Among the brunch choices are smoked salmon, shrimp, Dungeness crab, fresh omelettes and waffles, tempting slices of beef and ham, and a wide assortment of fresh fruit, salads, and desserts. This place is a little out of the way—on Swan Island—but is easy to find and well worth the effort. Shenanigan's full bar is known for making great drinks: From simple Bloody Marys to sublime rum and ice-cream drinks, they do it all. Shenanigans is open seven days a week for lunch and dinner and has a huge banquet room for special occasions.

Stanford's Restaurant & Bar $$
913 Lloyd Center
(503) 335–0811

1440 N. Jantzen Beach Center
(503) 285–2005

1831 S.W. River Dr.
(503) 242–5051

14801 SW Kruse Oaks Blvd., Lake Oswego
(503) 620–3541

2770 NW 188th Ave., Hillsboro
(503) 645–8000
www.pacificoastresraurant.com

There are five Stanford's in the Portland area but the Lloyd Center store is our favorite. They are all bright, super-clean and casual but definitely upscale dining establishments. The atmosphere is pleasant and the service is always superior—but we're including Stanford's because the food is so consistently good for either lunch or dinner. Stanford's offers a great selection of seafood, steaks, and chicken dishes and a good variety of vegetarian options. Stanford's grills are fired by oak, mesquite, and cherry woods giving off a tantalizing aroma. Their classic baby back ribs and open flame-broiled Pacific Northwest salmon are perennial favorites, and Stanford's Caesar Salad is one of the best around. The Stanford's restaurants also have great bars, with lots of polished wood, soft lighting, and friendly service. Stanford's are open from 11 A.M. until 11 P.M. Sunday through Thursday and they stay open until midnight on Fridays and Saturdays.

Super Burrito Express $
9019 N. Lombard St.
(503) 283–2181

This place has zero personality and even less atmosphere. Nevertheless, people flock here like bees to a hive. The attraction? Authentic, cheap, and fast Mexican food. Everything on the menu is under $4.50 and most of the items are under $3 and are quite good. Don't try to discuss the weather with the employees—they're too busy running a food assembly line to bother. But lest we complain, the El Super Burrito goes for just $3.25, is enormous, and is stuffed with shredded beef steak and other quality fillings. The best deal though, is probably the *carne asada*; a hot flour tortilla bulging with char-broiled steak, onions, chile, cilantro, refried beans, and Mexican avocado sauce. The dining area is terribly drab, so grab your goodies and take off to nearby Cathedral Park, which is just a few blocks south, and enjoy a Mexican feast under the city's most spectacular bridge. The Super Burrito Express is open seven days week from 8:30 A.M. until 11 P.M.

Sylvia's Italian Restaurant $$
5115 N.E. Sandy Blvd.
(503) 288–6828
www.sylvias.net

Do you like dinner theaters and Italian cuisine? If so, by all means go to Sylvia's, an award-winning authentic Italian restaurant. Sylvia's also offers Sylvia's Class Act Dinner Theater, showcasing local talent in well-known comedies, mysteries, dramas, and musicals Thursdays through Sundays. This place is also extremely popular with lovers of fine Italian food. You have a choice of soup and salad. The pasta and lasagna dishes are excellent and the veal parmigiana is highly praised. Some connoisseurs swear that Sylvia's Baked Lasagna and Minestrone are the best this side of old Italy. There's a full bar and an extensive wine selection as well as a children's menu. Sylvia's is open Mondays through Wednesday from 4 until 9 P.M., Thursday 4 to 10 P.M. Fridays and Satur-

days from 4 until 11 P.M., and Sundays from 3 until 9 P.M.

Tom's Pizza and Sports Pub $
2630 N. Lombard St.
(503) 283–4217
www.pdxguide.Toms.com

This blue-collar sports pub is open seven days a week serving up some serious sandwiches and burgers and a dozen superior pizzas. The sandwiches all have sports theme names. Our favorite is The Champ, an Italian submarine bulging with salami, pepperoni, Swiss and cheddar cheese, ham, and topped off with lettuce, tomatoes, and onion. The Philadelphia Flyer—with a half-pound of sirloin steak sliced paper thin, with onions, mushrooms, melted Swiss cheese, and special house seasonings—is a very close second. Tom's also takes great pride in its spicy pizzas served with generous amounts of topping and big, hearty burgers with unique garnishes. The Field Goal is an excellent choice for a slightly unusual pizza: The pepperoni, onions, and pepperoncini are topped with artichoke hearts, jalapeños, and tomatoes. The medium pizzas (14 inches) go for $11 to $13. Tom's offers a full espresso bar, thirty beers on tap (including many microbrews), and a limited wine selection.

Trio Restaurant & Bar $$-$$$
4627 N.E. Fremont St.
(503) 249–3247

This definitely out-of-the-mainstream, elegant, and intimate little restaurant will delight diners with creative yearnings. Trio offers adventurous fine dining and a great choice of wines. Appetizers range from chipotle honey baby back ribs and tomatillo chutney to eggplant with red bell pepper and goat cheese terrine. Get the idea? Seafood, pasta, and lamb are strong suites here, but the entrees change so frequently, you'll see plenty of surprises. Entrees are all under $20 and the appetizers are $6 to $8.

The wine list is quite extensive and the servers here are friendly and attentive.

Trio is open Tuesday through Saturday from 5:30 until 10 P.M.

Winterborne $$-$$$
3520 N.E. 42nd Ave.
(503) 249-8486

This very small but increasingly popular dinner restaurant features French- and Northwest-influenced cuisine in an intimate and friendly atmosphere. Although Winterborne is tiny and their menu offers not a morsel of beef, pork, or poultry, it is highly ambitious and offers some of the best seafood in town. Winterborne is truly a fish-lover's delight, as the seasonal menu showcases only the freshest of regional seafood. The Willapa Bay Oysters, which are sautéed to perfection and served with a horseradish, mayonnaise, and garlic sauce, are an excellent way to get started. Entrees change with the seasons, and all are served with delicious homemade soups and fresh baked bread. Following European fashion, the salads are served after the main course. The desserts—most notably the Lombard cake—are also delicious. Some local food critics can't find enough adjectives to praise this place, which is cozy and tastefully decorated. Winterborne is open Wednesdays through Saturdays from 5:30 until 9:30 P.M.

Vancouver

Chart House $$-$$$
101 E. Columbia Wy., Vancouver
(360) 693-9211

This popular chain restaurant serves lunch and dinner. The menu of hearty fare includes entrees such as Orange Basil Salmon, Coconut Crunch Shrimp, and herb-crusted chicken. For a savory side, try the Rock Salt Russet, a russet potato rolled in garlic butter and rock salt and cracked black pepper, served with butter, sour cream, and freshly cut chives. Now that's an impressive evolution of an old favorite. The Chart House also has a downtown Portland location; see our entry under Southwest Portland.

Dante's Ristorante $-$$
111 E. Main St., Vancouver
(360) 687-4373

This classic Italian restaurant offers affordable and sizeable dishes, including cannelonis, raviolis, and spaghetti. Try a glass of Chianti and a plate of your favorite pasta. Or you can build your own pizza from a big list of toppings, including sausage, pepperoni, and primavera.

Fa Fa Gourmet $$
11712 N.E. Fourth Plain Rd., Vancouver
(360) 260-1378

This authentic Chinese restaurant is a rare find for fans of this cuisine. Located in a suburb east of Vancouver, Fa Fa Gourmet offers five-spice duck, seaweed salad, bird's nest soup, and other crispy and tasty Szechuan and Hunan items.

Hidden House $$-$$$
100 W. 13th St., Vancouver
(360) 696-2847

This stately and beautifully refurbished Victorian home located in downtown Vancouver is graced with all the extras—gingerbread awnings, white trim, and stained-glass windows, while the inside, with old English china, lace curtains, and soft music, radiates warmth and hospitality. The dinners, which are served Tuesdays through Sundays, include vegetarian, seafood, and chicken dishes—and some wonderful treats such as the Escargots Chablienne—extra-large Burgundy snails baked under fresh mushroom caps with herbed curry-garlic butter and sour cream. Hidden House is currently expanding their lunch and dinner menus, so call for more information. Hours are 11 A.M. until 2 P.M. Tuesday through Friday for lunch, and for dinners Hidden House is open from 5 P.M. until 9 P.M. Tuesday through Saturday, and 5 until 8 P.M. on Sunday.

Sheldon's Cafe at the Grant House on Officer's Row $$
1101 Officers' Row, Vancouver
(360) 699–1213

Would you enjoy going back in time more than a century and being a dinner guest at a general's house? Built more than 150 years ago, Sheldon's Cafe is one of the oldest continuously used buildings in the Pacific Northwest and is brimming with atmosphere and lore. Diners may enjoy a wide selection of America's regional cuisine in a variety of settings: the classic dining room, the charming herb-garden patio, or under the covered veranda. Sheldon's regional menu pays tribute to the pioneers from other parts of the nation that settled in Fort Vancouver. From New England, for example, comes Seafood St. Jacques, a tasty platter of salmon, rock shrimp, and scallops baked in Mornay and mushroom cream sauce topped with Swiss cheese and served with rice and vegetables. The Northwest, South, and Midwest are also well represented by several standout entrees—but the hickory-smoked pork and chicken platter, complete with garlic mashed potatoes and salad and other fixings, was our favorite. Sheldon's is open for lunch, Tuesdays through Saturdays from 11 A.M. until 2 P.M., and for dinner between 5 and 8:30 P.M.

Outlying Areas

Amadeus at the Fernwood $$$
2122 S.E. Sparrow Rd., Milwaukie
(503) 659–1735

149 B Ave., Lake Oswego
(503) 636–7500

For elegance in dining and in atmosphere, Amadeus at the Fernwood is an excellent choice. Amadeus offers the finest continental cuisine in a romantic setting graced with period furniture, chandeliers, and flowers. Classic meals—such as the rack of Oregon spring lamb, steak au poivre Madagascar, and rockfish amandine—are skillfully prepared and complimented by an outstanding selection of Oregon and international wines. Amadeus at the Fernwood also offers outdoor dining on the scenic patio, live classic piano nightly, and a full bar. Call for dinner reservations, and don't forget about the exceptional Sunday brunches. Both locations are open seven days a week from 5 until 10 P.M. and on Sundays (for brunch) from 10 A.M. until 2 P.M.

Marine Polis Sushi Land $
4021 S.W. 117th Ave., Beaverton
(503) 520–0257

Ready for a party? Stop by this jam-packed Japanese diner disguised as a '50s Automat and hop on a stool to inspect the choices chugging by on a conveyor belt. Be prepared to wait for awhile, but if you're a social sort, you can join others cheerfully waiting to take their turn. Once you're in place, decide what you want, grab it, pop it in your mouth, and pay your bill later based on the color of the ring on your plates. It's quite a fascinating delivery system in this spirited sushi factory wedged into a strip mall in the suburban outback of Beaverton west of Portland. Sushi Land is open daily for breakfast, lunch, and dinner.

Newport Bay Restaurant $$
2757 S.E. Burnside Rd., Gresham
(503) 661–2722

(Tanasbourne Mall) 2865 N.W.
Town Center, Beaverton
(503) 645–2526

(Washington Square) 9699 S.W.
Washington Square Rd., Tigard
(503) 245–3474
www.newportbay.com

If you want very good seafood, excellent service, and an upbeat, casual environment, you can't go wrong at a Newport Bay. There are three Newport Bays in Portland's Outlying Areas—in Gresham, Beaverton, and Tigard. For more information on Newport Bay's great seafood choices, see the entry under Southwest Portland. Newport Bays are open seven days a week, from 11 A.M. until 10 P.M., except on Fridays and Saturdays when they close at 11 P.M. On Sundays they open at 9 A.M. for a special brunch.

Publisher's Cafe $-$$
2131 "B" St., Washougal, Washington
(360) 835–7637

Publisher's Cafe is one of those secret and delightful places you hear about only through word of mouth. It is a bit out of the way, but it's such a lovely drive on Washington Highway 14 to Washougal—and this charming cafe is so unique and appealing—that we had to include it. This isn't a place to bring the kiddies—but it is a wonderful spot for thinking adults. Publisher's Cafe truly offers nostalgic cuisine—and we don't mean pizzas and hamburgers—baking old-fashioned lemon-meringue pies every day. They also slow roast all the pork and beef for their dinners and sandwiches and make soups and gravies from scratch. Open seven days a week from 6:30 A.M., Publisher's Cafe isn't huge—it seats just forty-eight—so call if

possible to get reservations. You'll like the food, the service, and the old-fashioned hospitality. Call for closing times.

Saigon Kitchen $
14280 S.W. Allen Blvd., Beaverton
(503) 646–4611

There are three cheery and appealing Saigon Kitchens in the Portland Metro area, and all are popular. You can't go wrong at this Beaverton edition of the popular Vietnamese/Thai restaurant. The menu features a wide range of choices and everything is delicious and low priced. The service is pleasant and fast, but not rush-rush.

A particular standout is the Spicy Shrimp Rice Stick Noodle Soup, which includes shrimp, rice noodles, jalapeños, cilantro, and lime and comes in a bowl big enough to feed two people. All Saigon Kitchens are open every day of the week, from 11 A.M. until 10 P.M. (For other locations, see the entry under Southeast Portland.)

Swagat $$-$$$
2074 N.W. Lovejoy St.
(503) 227–4300

4325 S.W. 109th Ave., Beaverton
(503) 626–3000

"Swagat" is Hindi for "welcome," and that's how you feel when you stop by one of this authentic Indian restaurant's two locations. The food is a fulsome sampling of cuisine from both the north and southern regions of India, which are world renowned for their curries and tandooris. A favorite of many diners are the *dosas* (crepes made with lentil flours and stuffed with vegetable curry). Other tasty adventures are the lamb *biriyani* cooked with basmati rice and the Dal Curry (lentils cooked with spinach and tomatoes). Lunch and dinner are served daily.

Close-up

Chef Greg Higgins, Higgins Restaurant

It's 3:30 on a Thursday afternoon, and the small kitchen at Higgins Restaurant is fragrant, with a still puffing aromatically away, gleaning essences from herbs, and with pots of onions caramelizing. The kitchen is also noisy. The last of the lunch customers have straggled back to their offices, and the restaurant is gearing up for a busy evening. The phone rings. Bowls and knives clatter; handheld whisks whir sauces; food processors whine. The phone rings. Cooks rush about with large sheets of fingerling potatoes and roasted mushrooms. The pastry chef sets out samples from this week's dessert menu for the staff to try. The phone rings. Soon the din of preparation will settle into the background and the low hubbub of dinner conversation will saturate the room.

Higgins has been acclaimed as an outstanding restaurant since chef Greg Higgins and his partner Paul Mallory opened it in 1994. Greg Higgins had already made a national reputation for himself by serving as the head chef at the Heathman Restaurant down the street, so it wasn't difficult to persuade the customers to come through the door. Once they came in, they kept coming back, drawn by the exquisite food, the excellent wine and beer lists, and the knowledgeable, attentive service. They come to close business deals, get engaged, celebrate birthdays, but most of all, to eat and drink. And they come from all over: The distinguished international beer expert Michael Jackson wrote that Higgins is his favorite restaurant in the world.

Higgins looks like many other upscale restaurants, with its flowers, its engravings and prints decorating the walls, its tapestries and linens, its attractive, dark paneling. But the sophisticated appearance of the restaurant belies its true nature as a wellspring of food revolution, for Higgins is dedicated to serving locally produced seasonal food that is grown and harvested in sustainable ways. No beefsteak tomatoes in December here. Instead you'll find root vegetables and greens prepared so deliciously and inventively that you would think they were an exotic delicacy. That's because Greg Higgins intentionally turns the convention of American fine dining—that the best food must be from somewhere else, like France or Italy—on its head. Ironically, it was the chefs of France that taught him this lesson, that respecting the inherent properties of local food, its seasonal nature, and the soil that gave it life is the best way to create remarkable, timeless dishes. In the particular we find the universal.

So Greg Higgins has cultivated relationships with the particular farmers, gatherers, vintners, cheesemakers, and a battalion of other purveyors that inhabit the fertile Willamette Valley and its surroundings. On the backs of the menus, you'll find a manifesto on this topic, calling diners to respect and honor the small local farms that are good for the earth and the human communities that live by means of them. It calls on us to share with farmers the checks of season and ecological balance when we purchase food for our own kitchen.

Given his background, this vision is no surprise. During and after college, where he studied the fine arts, Higgins took up cooking as a way to pay the bills. Somewhere in the back of his mind were all the afternoons he had skipped school to forage in the wilds of upstate New York and then experiment with cooking what he had picked or dug that day. His family had little money; he had lots of brothers and sisters, and he had a single mother who was trying to educate herself and keep her family together. He was merely following an avocation, the way that the rest of us skip school to go to the beach. That doesn't mean we turn professional.

But Higgins did. Eventually, he traveled to France and studied with the great Alsatian chef Joseph Matter. In France he learned to discipline his art. Until then, he had preferred the romance of experiment, but the French taught him to respect his tools more. The painter learns discipline from the qualities of colors, the textures of the brushes and canvasses, the depth of the vision. The chef's discipline comes from the earth itself—the qualities of the soil, the textures of the food. "In France," says Higgins, "they have a long tradition of cooking that understands the essence of food, an understanding that has taken centuries to acquire." "In the contemporary U.S.," he continues, "our cooking has no depth. It is shallow."

While cooking is officially recognized as a fine art in France, here it is not. Americans have an estranged relationship with their food. This is hardly surprising—who could possibly trace the path of ingredients on the wrapper of a nutrition bar from the grocery store to the farm? Who could accurately explain to a child how a chicken transmogrifies into a nugget? The average American dinner has traveled 1,200 miles before it reaches the average American dinner table; en route, it must be processed, polished, and packaged; and before it's harvested, it must be grown with these packaging requirements in mind. Higgins worries about this disconnection between our lives and what sustains us, worries about what this lack of knowledge is doing to our air, land, and water, to our souls, to our communities.

He worries enough to spend as much time in outreach work as he does in the kitchen, educating growers about the possibilities of heirloom potatoes or apples and educating the palates of his customers. For him, outreach is both official and unofficial. Officially, he is on the board of the Chef's Collaborative, a national organization of chefs and other culinary professionals dedicated to teaching Americans about locally produced, seasonal food and sustainable practices with which to grow it. Officially he has written articles, appeared on television, been invited to numerous local festivals, and has otherwise spread his message. Moreover, the restaurant is consistently generous, donating food, time, and personnel to many local fundraising events.

Unofficially, too, Higgins is busy educating. You might say that it was a search for the best tools that led him to cultivate relationships with local purveyors, and it has not always been an easy sell because small farms are in a precarious enough position as it is. However, as the influence of the restaurant has spread, and as Greg's personal evangelizing has worked its magic, more area restaurants have begun to serve locally grown food and more purveyors have been willing to take a chance. And the more this happens, the more efficient the farmers become, too. In short, Higgins has been a catalyst for a whole subsector of the local economy.

You'd never know it from talking to him, however. He is remarkably unmodern in his lack of self-publicity. Though he has been lauded many times over, he doesn't like to talk about it. (For the record, he has been a finalist for the prestigious James Beard Award; called a "rising star," a "shining star," and a "luminary"; awarded a designation as a "Founder of the New Northwest"; it goes on like that.) While he has contributed to television shows, many magazines, and cookbooks, right now he is too busy to produce any of his own—no glossy coffee-table cookbooks for him. Instead, he writes policy papers on wild salmon.

And that brings us back to local food. If you ask him whether the Pacific Northwest or anywhere in the U.S. has a bona fide regional cuisine, Higgins will demur. "There's a lot of debate about that topic. It depends on your definition of regional cuisine, which generally has meant a commonly shared collection of recipes within geographic and climatic barriers using a number of specific ingredients." He expands on the topic: "Here, we have the commonly shared ingredients. What a number of us are doing," he adds, including other chefs in the area, "is to make use of the same ingredients. Yet you won't find any of us preparing them the same way, because we all bring different backgrounds and traditions with us into the kitchen."

Maybe, then, we are witnessing the birth of a new cuisine. The eminent food writer Jeffrey Steingarten once observed that the Pacific Northwest lacked a genuine regional food tradition; rather, it had ingredients in search of a cuisine. Thanks to Greg Higgins, those ingredients can lay aside their quest and get down to the business of evolving.

Chef Greg Higgins prepares an edible masterpiece of wild salmon. CREDIT: COURTESY OF HIGGINS RESTAURANT

Brewpubs, Cigar Bars, and Wine Bars

Throughout the ages, nothing has refreshed beer and ale lovers after a long day at the grindstone like a pint of their favorite beverage. Some anthropologists claim that beer, not bread, enticed Stone Age man to abandon his nomadic ways, to settle down, and plant grain to ensure a constant supply of fresh brew.

By 3,000 B.C. in Mesopotamia, suds-swilling Sumerians were becoming skilled brewmasters and had their own patron goddess of brewski, Ninkasi. It's a good bet that if Ninkasi were around today, she'd be living in Portland, a microbrew mecca. Within a few blocks, Ninkasi would discover an abundance of saloons and microbrew pubs serving up pints of ale for every taste imaginable. In fact, Portland has more microbreweries and pubs than any other city in the nation. Capitalizing on the abundance of the state's fourteen indigenous varieties of hops, Oregon-grown barley, and the sparkling fresh Cascade water, the city has all it needs to craft its own unique ales.

Also unique are the McMenamins (Mike and Brian), two brothers who cannot be ignored in any discussion of Portland microbrews. In the last fifteen years they've built up an empire of sixty pubs and other creative attractions, including Edgefield Manor (see Attractions), and the Crystal Ballroom (see Nightlife). We heartily endorse all of their casual and family-friendly neighborhood establishments, including their recent project, St. Johns Pub, and others you'll find as you browse the list of brewpubs below. Following our brewpubs, listed in geographical order, we also offer a sampling of some of Portland's cigar bars and wine bars.

Brewpubs

Southwest Portland

Full Sail Brewing
307 S.W. Montgomery St.
(503) 222–5343

Full Sail is a good name for a brewery located at the Riverplace Marina on the Willamette River just south of downtown Portland. A small operation that makes light, easy-to-sip ales and lagers, Full Sail is next door to McCormick and Schmick's Harborside Restaurant and Pilsner Room. Enjoy a notable seafood entree at this mothership of a national chain while sampling one of Full Sail's brews as you can gaze through a glass wall at brewers making a new batch. The Pilsner Room is also known for brewmaster's dinners held throughout the year at which chefs match each dish in a five-course meal with a particular beer made by a participating brewery. During the event the chefs and brewmasters talk about their creations.

Raccoon Lodge
7424 S.W. Beaverton-Hillsdale Hwy.
(503) 296–0110
www.raclodge.com

On the western outskirts of our tree-fringed metropolis you'll find the Raccoon Lodge, a large pub and brewery designed as a mountain lodge with high ceilings, ample dining space with wooden booths and Pendleton blanket cushions, wood trusses and wainscoting, and a monster stone fireplace surmounted by an elk's head and horns. Although this mammoth sip-and-nibble joint seems out of place in the 'burbs, it is packing them in with its smash hit: a variety of hand-cut French fries and dipping sauces. The choices of spuds are Yukon gold, shoestring, tater tots, sweet potatoes, or ale-batter steak fries, all of which arrive in a big bucket. The dipping sauces include country gravy, Creole tomato, red chili barbecue, raspberry habañero, tartar, white cheddar sauce, and buttermilk ranch. More substantial fare is also available: jerked pork loin, fish and chips, vegetable pot pie, and chicken turned on a rotisserie after a lemon, garlic, and ale marinade. As for the brew, the Black Snout Stout is superb and Ring Tale Pale and Bandit Amber are mildly pleasant. If you order vino you have a choice of ten reds or ten whites, mostly from Oregon and California with an Aussie Chardonnay or Cabernet tossed into the mix.

Rock Bottom Brewery & Restaurant
206 S.W. Morrison Ave.
(503) 796–2739
www.rockbottom.com

It seems like half of Portland's downtown workers cram into Rock Bottom at quitting time for a nosh and a brew named after a critter. Choices include Cryin' Coyote Western Ale, White Pelican American Pale Ale, Falcon Red Ale, Big Horn Nut Brown Ale, and Black Seal Stout. The brew kettles are in a long hall upstairs next to the pool room with its eight tables, while downstairs a full bar, wooden tables, and booths are all friendly zones in the tradition of a village pub. Grub favorites are the hickory burger, alder-smoked salmon fish and chips, buffalo fajitas, and Mrs. Chow's Sizzling Shrimp Salad. Fans of this hotspot can take home T-shirts, sweatshirts, hats, glassware, and other kinds of souvenirs. As the brewmaster says with a grin, "You haven't hit Portland until you've hit Rock Bottom."

Northwest Portland

Blue Moon
432 N.W. 21st Ave.
(503) 223–3184
www.mcmenamins.com

One of several McMenamin brothers' pubs, this ancient place is a short walk from the popular Cinema 21. After a fire in 2000, the place was remodeled and opened in March 2001. It's still a classic watering hole with the usual McMenamin amenities. There's friendly service here and a great menu. Try the burgers and fries.

Bridgeport Ales
1313 N.W. Marshall St.
(503) 241–7179
www.bridgeportale.com

The oldest of Portland's twenty-four microbreweries (by a whisker over those of the brothers McMenamin and the rest of the brew brigade), Bridgeport Breweries started rolling out barrels in 1984 with a production of merely 600 barrels of ale per year. Now this nationally recognized outfit produces 25,000 barrels annually in a one-hundred-year-old warehouse in the industrial portion of the booming Pearl District. This picturesque brick and ivy brewpub is reminiscent of the old German beer halls, especially the spacious upstairs, which is overflowing on the weekends. House standards, such as Coho Pacific and the Blue Heron, are available as well as cask-conditioned ales, which are naturally carbonated, unfiltered, and stored in kegs called firkins. Every Tuesday, brewers tap a firkin right on the bar for a fresh full-bodied taste direct from a gravity-fed spigot. Bridgeport offers a variety of British-style ales, including India Pale Ale, Extra Special Bitter, Black Strap Stout and Porter conditioned in a bottle, keg, or firkin cask. The flagship ale is Blue Heron Amber Ale brewed in honor of Portland's official city bird. Bridgeport also serves up a superior pizza, with dough made fresh daily from unfermented beer wort and topped with herbs and vegetables, feta cheese, or chorizo sausage.

McMenamins Tavern
1716 N.W. 23rd Ave.
(503) 227–0929
www.mcmenamins.com

This original tavern in the chain is the only one named after the "bros." It's a modest little spot a bit north of the cultural hubbub on 21st and 23rd Avenues. For a sense of history and a quiet brew, check it out. Try the Crystal Ale, an amber ale, or for a lighter taste, the Cascade Head Ale.

Mission Theater and Pub
1624 N.W. Glisan St.
(503) 223–4031
www.mcmenams.com

This McMenamin brothers' pub comes complete with a theater. Mixing microbrews and movies is a real kick, and the patrons are—for the most part—quiet and respectful during the shows, so don't be put off and afraid of a noisy free-for-all. Our movie experiences were very satisfying, so go for it! While you're there, try a Hammerhead, a perennial favorite here, or maybe the famous Terminator—a dark, stout, hearty brew that is McMenamins' all-time best-seller. Go for it! (For more on the Mission Theater see Nightlife.)

Portland Brewing Co. Taproom & Grill
2730 N.W. 31st Ave.
(503) 228–5269
www.portlandbrew.com

This huge brewery in the Guilds Lake Industrial District at the edge of Northwest Portland shows off its 140-barrel copper brewing vessels by making them a part of its brewpub's interior design. The kettles are from the Sixenbrau Brewery dating back to the sixteenth century in Bavaria. Added to this Teutonic touch are fancy steins and a menu of seafood, schnitzel, sausage, and other grilled meats cooked on an applewood rotisserie and grill. A covered patio is open for dining during the winter. As for the brew, other than a Bavarian-style Weizen, it is decidedly west of the continent. Dubbed new-American beer, the line includes Oregon Honey Beer, MacTarnahan's Scottish Style Amber Ale, Haystack Black Porter (named after an Oregon coastal mono-

Insiders' Tip

If you want to sample a variety pack of local microbrews, take the Portland Brew Bus, (888) BIG-BREW, on a three-to-four-hour guided tour of three or four local microbreweries. While on tour, you'll encounter fifteen to twenty brews, enjoy a light snack, and at the end of your arduous educational experience you'll be presented with a diploma. All of this costs $25.95 per person.

lith), and ZigZag Lager (a nod toward a resort town near Mount Hood in Oregon's northern Cascades).

The Ram's Head
2282 N.W. Hoyt St.
(503) 221–0098
www.mcmenamins.com

With its comfy couches, easy chairs, booths, and long bar, the Ram's Head has the feel of a private club for the rest of us. The grub at the McMenamin brothers' pub is particularly good, especially the French fries—cut and cooked on the spot. Located on the street level of a four-story apartment building at the corner of N.W. Hoyt Street and 23rd Avenue, this classy beer joint is dead center in the heart of the Northwest scene.

Ringler's
1332 W. Burnside St.
(503) 225-0543
www.mcmenamins.com

Yet another McMenamins' business, Ringler's brewpub is on the street level of a three-story operation including the Crystal Ballroom at the top and a brewery in the middle. A popular intermission zone for concerts and dance bands upstairs, Ringler's, with its madcap mosaics and Byzantine carvings, a long bar, booths, and tables, also offers free pool on Tuesdays and Sundays. If your thirst leans more toward the harder stuff than the brews trickling down from above, try McMenamins' Signature Margarita or the Crystal Ambush (Bushmill's Irish Whiskey, Amaretto, and coffee topped with whipped cream). Enjoy the pizza, prime rib sandwich, or linguine with artichoke hearts. Those with a Brit heart might want to try the bangers and mash.

Southeast Portland

The Bagdad Theater and Pub
3702 S.E. Hawthorne Blvd.
(503) 236–9234
www.mcmenamins.com

This is a Southeast Portland landmark and a great place to uncoil. You can watch a first-rate movie for a buck or sit out on the picnic tables and survey the scene on bustling Hawthorne Boulevard. One of the McMenamins' five movie-house brewpubs, the Bagdad underwent a comprehensive remodeling a few years ago and it has paid off handsomely. At first we were a bit leery about seeing a film in a pub where people are eating pizza and drinking Terminator Stout, but the audience noise wasn't a factor—seems like other people were there to get into the movie as well—and the lighting and sound quality were very good. The Bagdad carries the McMenamins' brews that you'd expect: the fruity Ruby Ale; Hammerhead, a malty, hoppy, English-style ale; the dark and stout Terminator; a light and refreshing Wheat Ale; and a rich, smooth, chocolatey Porter. Food choices include nearly a dozen pizza options and everything from hot Thai noodles to black bean burritos. Most of the small pizzas, sandwiches, and specialties cost around $6.

The Barley Mill
1629 S.E. Hawthorne Blvd.
(503) 231–1492
www.mcmenamins.com

This, the granddaddy of all the McMenamins' brewpubs, opened in 1983, but the Barley Mill's roots reach back to 1934 when it operated as The Scuttlebutt the year after the Prohibition was repealed. It's impossible to miss the cranky old barley mill stationed near the front door. Big picture windows shed light on this groovy place, which is funky with loads of Grateful Dead paraphernalia and posters. The pub plays their tunes during Grateful

Lucky Labrador Brewing Company is a big lodge of a brewpub with good grub and smooth brew made on the premises. CREDIT: DAVID JOHNSON

Dead Night every Wednesday night from 5 to 11 P.M. Seating in this place is excellent: You can choose between the large wooden picnic tables (inside and outside) or the cozy bar and smaller corner booths. The service is good—as at most McMenamins' brewpubs—and there is a nice selection of ales. We like the Nebraska Bitter, the Hammerhead, and the India Pale Ale. Ask the bartender about the daily special, and if you feel adventurous, try the Brewery Taster, a sampler of six different microbrews. The Barley Mill also offers a basic selection of Edgefield Wines, including Chardonnay, Pinot Gris, Riesling, and a few others. Wine by the glass is $4.50, by the bottle, $12 to $15. The Barley Mill offers plenty of good food, including hot and cold sandwiches and soups, salads, and pasta. We've consumed more than a few of their burgers and never been disappointed. The Com-

munications Breakdown Burger, with grilled onions, bell peppers, mushrooms, and cheddar cheese is our favorite.

Bridgeport Ale House
3632 S.E. Hawthorne Blvd.
(503) 233–6540

They're really not partial to Hawthorne establishments, although it may seem that way. Bridgeport Breweries is Oregon's oldest microbrewery and this, their newest venture, is one of our favorite spots for "rainy days and Mondays." The quality of beverages and food is consistently high and the neighborhood *Cheers* type of atmosphere is warm and earthy. This bright, airy pub offers two mellow cask-conditioned ales as well as six regular microbrews. Their most popular brew is the award-winning India Pale Ale. Our first choice, however, is Bridgeport's flagship brew, the incomparable Blue Heron

Amber Ale. The Hawthorne Street Ale House also does some very tasty seasonals, including the Summer Wheat Ale. Although there is no "happy hour" per se, on Mondays the India Pale Ale is served in twenty-ounce imperial pints for $2.50, as are all of the cask-conditioned ales on Wednesdays. Ale House serves lunch seven days a week and signature dishes include a wood-roasted oyster sandwich, a grilled eggplant sandwich, and the fire-grilled, seasoned ground-chuck Hawthorne Burger. The Ale-House Roast Beef Sandwich, served on grilled bread with sautéed onions, cheddar cheese, and homemade horseradish sauce is to die for. The sandwiches all go for about $5 and the wood-fired oven pizzas for $7.95 are another option. The hand-tossed, 10-inch pizza pies are baked to perfection and complemented with unusual toppings such as grilled zucchini, smoked chicken, and cilantro.

The Horse Brass Pub
4534 S.E. Belmont St.
(503) 232–2202
www.horsebrass.com

No visit to Portland is complete without a stop at the Horse Brass for a pint of bitters and a game of darts. This gem of a place is a pub in the finest and truest sense of the word, offering plenty of atmosphere and forty-six draughts of the finest microbrewed and imported beers, including Rogue YSB, the house beer for the Horse Brass Pub. Since 1976—more than decade before most Portlanders even heard of microbrews—the Horse Brass Pub has been a haven for crafted ales and authentic, home-style British fare. As the Horse Brass matchbox says, "It's a bit of England, where good companionship is the order of the day." Indeed, it is a noisy, gregarious place where folks have a smashing good time at the full bar or at one of the large round tables that brings friends and strangers together. The Bel-

mont Station (the Horse Brass outlet store next door) is also worth checking out. It is full of unique and fun gifts—all with an English motif. Besides beer, mugs, and T-shirts, you'll also find a bounty of British edibles—everything from chocolates to real English butter. If you can't find something, they'll do everything possible to order it for you.

Lucky Labrador Brewing Company
915 S.E. Hawthorne Blvd.
(503) 236–3555
www.luckylab.com

It's easy to miss the Lucky Labrador, which is located on the fringes of Southeast Portland's Industrial District. You don't want to do that because this is a big, sprawling, fun place with tasty, handcrafted microbrews. Gary Geist and Alex Stiles opened this popular and unpretentious brewpub on "hipper than thou" Hawthorne Boulevard four years ago. It is a refurbished warehouse and the atmosphere is open, spacious, and very casual. There is ample outside seating as well, with views of the surrounding industrial-area street scenes. We hope this place never changes, especially the large mural, a great takeoff on Andrew Wyeth's famous painting, *Christina's World*. There are no pool tables, no televisions, and no lotto machines. People go here in groups to have fun together, so there aren't the usual barflies hanging around smoking and nursing drinks. The brews are good, especially the robust Black Lab Stout, a slightly malty Konigs Kolsch, and the crispy Top Dog Extra Pale. Our favorite is Hawthorne's Best Bitter, which is an amber-hued, dry-hopped bitter, very characteristic of an English pint. The ales are served in twenty ounce pints and go for around $3, except for Mondays, when everything goes for $2. Plenty of cheap good food is available, including deli sandwiches, Bento, and a good selection of healthy vegetarian dishes.

Mickey Finn's Brew Pub
4336 S.E. Woodstock Blvd.
(503) 788-1587

Located in the original Portland Brewing brewpub that helped kick off the microbrew revolution in 1986, and a newer location in the percolating Woodstock neighborhood, Mickey Finn's is a favorite for those who delight in sampling a wide variety of lagers, ales, and weizens as well as hard liquor. Here in a dark-wooded climate amongst hanging Chinook salmon, fly-tying posters and other piscatory signage festooning walls and ceilings, pubsters can temporarily escape the Pacific Northwest drizzly outdoors. While sipping they can dip into "The Bait Box" for Brew City Onion Rings, Hot Shot Hot Wings, or Nestucca Bay Nuggets (Cod bits on a bed of lettuce, veggies, and tartar sauce). The pub also serves burgers, sandwiches, steak and chicken dinners, and the Angler's Platter consisting of a banger, bratwurst, cheese, fruit, Como bread (a chewy Italian peasant loaf), veggies, and garlic. (That ought to wake up the sleepiest angler.)

Philadelphia Steaks and Hoagies
6410 S.E. Milwaukie Ave.
(503) 239-8544
www.telepot.com/~tyhillws

You've got two reasons to visit "Philly's," Oregon's smallest brewery: great ales, and the most authentic Philadelphia cheese steak sandwiches this side of the Liberty Bell. The ten handcrafted ales on tap range from the crisp and light Betsy Ross Golden Ale, to the full-bodied Two-Street Stout. There's plenty of good food to choose from on the full menu, including beef and chicken cheese steaks and a bevy of huge hoagies. The secluded back deck is a splendid place to kick back on a sunny day.

North/Northeast Portland

Alameda Brewing Co.
4765 N.E. Fremont St.
(503) 460-9025

Look for the huge copper hop in front of the Alameda Brewpub—consider it a beacon for those seeking quality, handcrafted ales. Alameda's head brewmaster Craig Nicholls is preparing some of the finest microbrews in town, especially the Black Bear Double Stout, which aficionados are calling one of the best nitro-pours anywhere. (Nitrogen causes all those tiny little bubbles that make the "cascading effect" and gives ales that delicious creamy head.) Alameda offers nine unique regular micros along with two or three seasonals and their popular homemade root beer. With twenty-ounce pints going for $3.25, and even lower during happy hours, it's a great value. The food is excellent, affordable, and far more ambitious than standard pub grub. Entrees range from whiskey baby-back ribs to artichoke linguini to smoked chicken ravioli. Sandwiches and burgers are standouts too (our favorites are the super-fresh gardenburger and the smoked turkey breast sandwich), or you can nibble on some mouthwatering Porter smoked oysters. A children's menu is also available, as well as fresh baked pies and desserts. The atmosphere—galvanized metal, acid-stained floor, and the white maple/stainless-steel hop-yard theme—works splendidly as the brewery itself is located in the dining area. On every Saturday before Labor Day, the brewery presents the Big Guy Little Guy Brew Fest with live music and a celebration of breweries making less than a 1,000 barrels.

St. Johns Pub
8203 N. Ivanhoe St., St. Johns
(503) 283-8520
www.mcmenamins.com

This remarkably historic building with its distinctive dome was part of the 1905 Lewis and Clark Exposition held in Northwest Portland. After the festivities commemorating the centennial of that famous meander, the structure was barged across the Multnomah Channel of the Willamette River to St. Johns, a small 'burg now tied to the mainland by a lovely bridge with cathedral arches. After a long history as a church, fraternal lodge, and a watering hole called Duffy's, the McMenamin brothers bought the place and turned it into a roadhouse with lots of old-time signs and enough horns on the wall to hang half the hats in the West. It has the usual drinks and menu loaded with tasty sandwiches and burgers found in the historic theaters, schools, and hotels turned into emporiums of suds and grub by these omnipresent entrepreneurs. One of the most delightful beer gardens in town, it offers a charming and totally unique atmosphere, live music, and delicious microbrews (or wine). St. Johns is so different you have to go and experience it for yourself. With the long elegant wood bar, wood-burning stove, and a 7-foot tall bird of paradise standing sentinel, it is truly like stepping into a time machine. St. Johns, like most of the McMenamin brothers' brainstorms, is full of treasures, including stained-glass windows, a bizarre assortment of hanging lights, second-empire chairs, and an old-time piano that patrons sometimes play. There's extra seating upstairs, so come, have as much fun as you want, and it won't even put you in the poorhouse. Although the brew is imported from the brewery at the Kennedy School in N.E. Portland, this nostalgia-drenched quaffing parlor is well worth inclusion in our list of brewpubs. (See also our entry in Nightlife.)

Widmer Brothers Gasthaus
929 N. Russell St.
(503) 281–3333
www.widmer.com

The Gasthaus, in an old refurbished 1890s hotel adjacent to the Widmer's brewery, serves a complete menu, ranging from beer and appetizers to full dinners. There's plenty of exposed brick and wood lending character to this pub that seats around 120. The Gasthous serves twelve of Widmer's microbrews and our favorite is the sublime Hop Jack Pale Ale, which is almost a bitter. The sixteen-ounce ales go

Insiders' Tip

What's the best beer to go with a turkey sandwich? We know that this deeply meaningful question has occurred to you more than once. John Foyston, who trods the beer beat for *The Oregonian*, decided to toss this important question to a few knowledgeable brewmeisters. John Maler, brewmaster of Rogue Ales, stated unequivocally that Rogue Smoke was the perfect ale to wash down those slices of gobbler. We agree, but add that if you are without a turkey or any brand of sandwich, try the Rogues' Brutal Bitter Ale—a tasty treat all on its own.

for $3 except on Mondays, when all micros are discounted to $2.

Widmer Brothers Brewing Company is the top-selling craft brewer in the region, and produces seven original European- and Pacific Northwest-style beers. Their flagship ale is America's Original Hefeweizen, a cloudy-golden hued beer that's as easy to drink as it is to look at. Hefeweizen is bottled and kegged unfiltered and directly from the lagering tank, adding to its robust taste and unique appearance.

There are a few outside picnic tables and they fill up fast in the summertime. The food ranges from gourmet burgers, to German specialties, to grilled swordfish. This place is popular with everyone from the Wall Street set, to college students, to the shipyard workers on nearby Swan Island.

Vancouver

Bell Tower Brewery
707 S.E. 164th Ave., Vancouver
(360) 944–7800
www.thebelltower.com

Although the Bell Tower might be a bit off the beaten path, that's a strength, not a weakness to many of us. Brewmaster Eric Munger is creating eight very good ales at this wonderfully restored, turn-of-the-century Methodist Church that is loaded with character. Our favorites are the Wind River Extra Special Bitter and the Bell Ringer Rye, both distinguished takes on traditional English ales; during summer months, the crisp Hefeweizen and Marionberry ales are fine options. Besides the brews, there's a lot to enjoy here, including very good food, a delightful atmosphere, a beer garden, and an old-fashioned patio. The dining room, which seats 130, boasts plenty of wood and lots of historic photos of early Vancouver and Clark County's horse and buggy days—especially scenes from the Kaiser Shipyards and the old Star Brewery. A downstairs sports bar seats another one hundred folks and it is also laden with memorabilia. The menu is quite exten-

Insiders' Tip

Most stores display beer beneath fluorescent lights and can only stock the stuff that flies off the shelves. Not so at Belmont Station, a lively emporium of microbrews and imported beer located at 4520 S.E. Belmont, (503) 232-8538. Single bottles are displayed on shelves out front and the stuff actually for sale is kept in a darkened walk-in that has the somber, industrial demeanor of a bank vault. Stored this way, the beer lasts longer and tastes better. Belmont Station is open from noon to 10 P.M. Monday through Thursday and from noon to 11 P.M. on Friday through Saturday.

sive—an entire page is devoted to appetizers—and offers everything from steaks and pastas to oysters and blackened catfish. Come to the Bell Tower for breakfasts, as it opens at 6 A.M. seven days a week.

Hazel Dell Brewpub
8513 N.E. Hwy. 99, Vancouver
(360) 576–0996

Clark County's very first microbrew pub and restaurant, the Hazel Dell is worth a stop as it combines very good ales, carefully prepared food, and happy hour prices that will knock your socks off! From 3 to 6 P.M., pints of ten different varieties of delicious house-made brews go for the ridiculously low price of $1.75. As you imbibe, you can watch brewers preparing the next batch of ales in this cheerful "working microbrewery."

The pub fare isn't high cuisine, but the fish and chips are the best around. All food, beer, and wine are available to go.

Salmon Creek Brewery
108 W. Evergreen Blvd., Vancouver
(360) 993–1827

A delightful addition to downtown Vancouver, the Salmon Creek Brewery is a friendly, upscale establishment that features a handsome bar meticulously handcrafted from African hardwood and a ceiling of antiqued pressed tin. Accentuating the burnished atmosphere, the walls are decorated with old sepia photos recalling early Vancouver's heydays. Salmon Creek offers nine house brews, including Red Irish Ale, Golden Ale, Thunderbolt Porter, Nut Brown Ale, India Pale Ale, and the best-selling Scottish Ale. If it's your first visit, the friendly owner Ann Pratt will set up a sampler of all the house ales. Although Salmon Creek offers almost any kind of sandwich you can think of, including a hefty and exceptionally tasty Reuben, the menu is geared more towards fine dining than pub fare, with an emphasis on traditional steaks, seafood, chicken, and pasta dishes. Outdoor patio dining is a pleasant option during summer months with plenty of ivy, flowers, and plants gracing the patio, which is in the center of the horseshoe shaped tavern. There is a new dining room that seats forty-five.

Cigar Bars

Brazen Bean Cigar Bar
2075 N.W. Glisan St.
(503) 294–0636

This chic little restaurant in the Northwest District offers cigars in its cigar bar. If the weather is decent, you can puff outside on the porch or in the garden. While doing so, there is also a fine selection of cocktails, European food, and tempting desserts.

Greater Trumps
1520 S.E. 37th Ave.
(503) 235–4530
www.McMenamins.com

If you wish to sip a fine ale with your cigar, Greater Trumps is the right place to be. This intimate little room a half block down from the entryway to the Bagdad Theater on hustling Hawthorne has a large selection of Macanudos, Dunhills, and other fine cigars, as well as cigarettes. Yet another McMenamin brothers' affair, Greater Trumps offers a cruvinet of several vintage ports, including the house port, Fireside, made out at the Edgefield Winery. Or you can choose from a selection of wines and a small bill of fare, including smoked gouda with a slice of baguette and a bowl of nuts. There are a couple of McMenamin brews standing by.

Ringler's Annex
1223 S.W. Stark St.
(503) 525–0520
www.mcmenamins.com

Cigar connoisseurs can enjoy their smokes at Ringler's, 1332 W. Burnside, while shooting a game of pool or sipping a microbrew. The choice of a dozen cigars and cigarillos includes Rosa Cuba from Nicaragua, Partagas No. 1 from the Dominican Republic, and Macanudo Petit Corona from Jamaica. This tiny flat iron building also offers wine, beer, cocktails, sandwiches, and soup.

Wine Bars

Oregon Wines on Broadway
515 S.W. Broadway
(503) 228–4655

Located halfway between Nordstrom and the Benson Hotel, Oregon Wines on Broadway is a convenient stop for that relaxing glass after work in one of the Rose City's glass and steel palaces. This friendly nook boasts more Oregon wines available for tasting via its cruvinet than any other local wine bar, and offers samples of Adelsheim, Erath, Amity, and St. Innocent, a wine offered by the owner of Oregon Wines on Broadway since 1995. Prices are based on bottle cost. For example, wine under $20 costs $1 per taste and bottles over $20 cost $2. The congenial wine merchants explain how the system works: "Try it and buy it!"

Southpark Wine Bar
901 S.W. Salmon St.
(503) 326–1300
www.southpark.com or
www.citysearch.com

The wine bar annex to this stylish Mediterranean seafood grill is a textual delight for both eyes and palate. Caricatures reminiscent of Toulouse Lautrec adorn the wall, a tiled ceiling, sturdy decor, and metallic bar suggest a mélange of post-modern and medieval styles. Wine tasting can take various formats: There are bottles ranging from a $22 crisp French white to a $130 bottle of Bollinger champagne. Or try a two-ounce taste for $2.75 to $9 or a Wine Flight of various collections from $10 to $12. But there is no way you can lose by choosing the house Pinot Noir or Gris—both are delicious. All the while, you can nosh on a cheese plate with roasted grapes and candied walnuts or dive into the main menu. (We recommend the green-lipped mussels or the Ono crab cakes.)

Urban Wineworks
407 N.W. 16th Ave.
(503) 226–9797

After years of selling grapes to vintners, Reuel Fish got a great idea—Why not bring the winery in to town? The result is Urban Wineworks, where wine enthusiasts can savor their favorites next to oak barrels of aging wine. Located in the trendy Pearl District, Fish invites those coming to town for the "First Thursday Artwalk" (see The Arts) and workers commuting a few blocks to stop by for a glass.

Coffeehouses

Portland is well known for its spectacular beauty, unorthodox but congenial inhabitants, and damp weather, a perfect setting for a gourmet-coffee culture to explode, and it surely has. If you love fine coffees, welcome to Java heaven! On a chilly Oregon morning, it is almost impossible to think of anything more enticing than the tantalizing aroma of freshly brewed coffee or the hissing, whizzing, sputtering staccato sound of a little espresso machine hard at work.

Whether you are a discriminating coffee connoisseur or closet instant-coffee drinker beginning a new adventure, this chapter is created as a user's guide to start you on your quest for the perfect cup of coffee. Although we do talk about espressos, cappuccinos, and lattes, we also maintain an abiding respect for an honest, simple cup of good, fresh, coffee. In Portland and surrounding environs, most restaurants, delis, and coffeehouses still offer a house coffee of the day, and many places even offer a variety of different blends.

In the old days, it was coffee and a donut, or perhaps, a Danish. Today most coffee shops offer a tempting variety of scones, tarts, tortes, and perhaps bagels too, so we do talk about food a little bit as well.

All around Town

Boyd's Coffee Stores
1501 S.W. Taylor St.
(503) 241–6404

19730 N.E. Sandy Blvd.
(503) 666–4561, (800) 223–8211
www.boyds.com

Since 1900, Boyd's has maintained a reputation as purveyors of fine coffees. But their stores do a lot more than provide early morning customers with a jolt of their superior-grade blends. Boyd's stores offer an extensive selection of coffee/espresso drinks and carry many unique gift items for coffee lovers, including beans, coffeepots, grinders, fine china, and other quality items.

Coffee People
506 S.W. 6th Ave.
(503) 274–9332

737 S.W. Salmon St.
(503) 227–1794

533 N.W. 23rd Ave.
(503) 221–0235

100 N.W. 20th Place
(503) 223–4587

3500 S.E. Hawthorne Blvd.
(503) 235–1383

From a single cafe, Coffee People has expanded phenomenally, and now it nearly rivals Starbucks. After establishing a presence in such hip districts as Nob Hill and Southeast Portland's Hawthorne Boulevard, Coffee People has expanded into downtown and other parts of the city, plus the city of Beaverton.

Coffee People, which is famous for its "Good coffee and no back talk," slogan, hires super-friendly and knowledgeable people and gives its espresso drinks unusual names: The "Mindsweeper" is a latte supercharged with caffeine-packed Black Tiger espresso, the "Slamma-hamma" is a Mexican chocolate and Black Tiger blend, and our favorite—the "Double Depth Charge"—is a house coffee spiked with two shots of espresso. Coffee People also serves up great scones and cookies. For busy commuters who are drinking and driving legally, Coffee People's ten Motor Moka stations provide drive-through espresso and specialty coffee service. They are equally distributed through the metro area, so you are never far from one.

Java Man Coffee
1432 S.W. 6th Ave.
(503) 228–7578

9113 S.W. Barbur Blvd.
(503) 244–3202

220 N.W. 2nd Ave.
(503) 227–8851

4727 N.E. Fremont
(503) 287–5456

518 S.W. Taylor St.
(503) 279–0298

Another popular Portland coffee stop, Javas are exceedingly well maintained and staffed by courteous and hardworking folks. The espressos are superb and the lattes are very good. Most of the Java Man sites offer an extensive selection of tempting desserts and pastries.

Kobos Company
200 S.W. Market St.
(503) 221–0418

5331 S.W. Macadam
(503) 222–5226

2355 N.W. Vaughn St.
(503) 222–2181

1221 Lloyd Center
(503) 284–4831
www.kobos.com

Kobos specializes in specialty coffees, wonderful pastries, and a lot more. Teas, herbs and spices, chocolates and Torani syrups, and cooking utensils from around the world are temptingly displayed at their stores. The also sell gourmet kitchen utensils and supplies.

Starbucks Coffee Company

Based in Seattle, Washington, Starbucks first moved into Portland in 1989 when they opened up their first of many locations at Portland's Pioneer Square. Their popularity was enormous and the chain has now expanded to include forty-four separate stores in Portland. The Starbucks coffee shops, which have expanded across the United States and even into Japan, are known for their bright, cheery, shiny-clean atmospheres, and feature the

Insiders' Tip

For a people-watching feast, try to snag a sidewalk table at Starbucks, Coffee People, or Coffeetime along "Trendy-Third" Avenue on Saturday night. The crowds of stylish folk out for a stroll, on a shopping mission, or on their way to Restaurant Row are fun to gaze upon as they amble by.

company's own fine blend of coffee beans. They offer a classic espresso bar menu, an assortment of fine pastries and desserts, and also sell a wide selection of coffee paraphernalia, including grinders, mugs, flavoring syrups, espresso machines, and

coffeemakers. We're not going to list their operations because they operate more than seventy-five stores in the metro area outside of Portland, but we do give them a hearty endorsement.

Southwest Portland

Annie's Coffeehouse
1728 S.W. Broadway
(503) 497–1016

This funky little cave of a coffeehouse on the Portland State University campus is a classic hangout for students cramming for midterms or office workers in nearby administrative towers stopping for a quick refuel. Along with a mismatched cluster of chairs and tables, this cheerful, low-key place features a cartoon mural along the back wall.

Cup O' Cheer
808 S.W. 10th Ave.
(503) 243–1461

This aptly named watering hole is located conveniently across the street from the recently renovated central branch of the Multnomah County Library. After checking out that hot new piece of pulp fiction, stroll across 10th Avenue for a sip and a browse. Cup O' Cheer is also a handy coffee-break nook for harried journalists who work at Portland's alternative tabloid, *Willamette Week*, a few doors down the block. As well as a visually pleasing mini-gallery of rotating original art and photography, Cup O' Cheer offers a variety of coffees and an ample selection of pastries, including peach crisp and pineapple walnut scones. This coffeehouse also offers a full breakfast and ice cream in the summer.

Morning Star Espresso
510 S.W. 3rd Ave.
(503) 241–2401

This lively shoebox of a coffeehouse is on the ground floor of the historic old postal building in Old Town. Check out the crowded back area. The pierced-flesh and black-Levi's bunch will probably be sitting at touching tables or on the couch beneath an eye-popping exhibit of pop art and pseudo-tabloids. Legend has it that one of this crowd once shouted that he saw Elvis staring up at him from his coffee cup. As well as coffee with or without Mr. Presley, Morning Star serves gourmet sandwiches with monikers like "LeBob," "Yes M'Ham," and "Loony Tuna." A fun place to get revved for the day.

Park Avenue Café
1525 S.W. Park Ave.
(503) 225–9335

This coffeehouse and deli is a sleek little oasis in a stretch of aloof apartment buildings bordering the verdant blocks that pass as our town's version of Central Park. Not only does it attract students from nearby Portland State University, but on summer weekends it attracts the early birds at Portland Farmers' Market who are happy to get a Java-to-go before browsing for fresh fruits and vegetables.

Peet's
508 S.W. Broadway
(503) 973–5540

1441 N.E. Broadway
(503) 493–0192

With two locations on the same "Great White Way" stretching in different directions on both sides of the river, Peet's is easy to find. It's a California franchise in close competition with Starbucks. So if you give their downtown or Eastside outlet a try, you'll find a classy coffeehouse with lots of room to stretch out to enjoy your cup with an ample array of pastries.

Sweets Etc.
7824 S.W. Capitol Hwy.,
Multnomah Village
(503) 293–0088

Sweets is a bright, friendly spot that serves delicious Torrefazione Italian gourmet coffee, but they are more widely known for their terrific array of scrumptious confections, especially their many varieties of homemade fudge and chocolates. The enthusiastic servers crown their mochas with "criss-crossed" chocolate sweets and are known to tempt customers with chocolate-flavored Gummy Bears. Don't say we didn't warn you!

Northwest Portland

Aphrodite Espresso Bar
1037 N.W. 23rd Ave.
(503) 225–0746

Described by a local coffeehouse critic as Mediterranean minimalist, the Aphrodite Espresso Bar is an ultra cool scene with lean, curved sconces lining two walls like a troupe of sci-fi ballet dancers leaning on their bar. As well as coffee drinks, the menu lists Xanadu teas, fresh fruit smoothies, rice crispy bars, JaCiva's famous chocolate truffles, and ice cream scoops from the Great Northwest Ice Cream Company.

Anna Bannana's
1214 N.W. 21st Ave.
(503) 274–2559
www.citysearch.com

Billing itself as "a coffeehouse for the Northwest," Anna Bannana's is a classic old house converted into a comfy spot to rest and sip. Imagine a scene 180 degrees from the slick ambience of Starbucks. Toss in a ragtag collection of aging furniture, including a huge antique bellows for a coffee table, and books standing by for a browse ranging from a Dick Francis thriller to poems by Jim Morrison. One of the specialties here is a long list of special drinks, including chocolate with bananas and Hawaiian mocha sprinkled with macadamia nuts. For snacks you can choose from homemade scones, chocolate-chip cookies as big as Frisbees, and of course, banana bread. The management has one simple request: you have to spend $1 to hang out at Anna Bannana's. It's a tradition.

Anne Hughes Coffee Room
Powell's City of Books, 1005 W. Burnside St.
(503) 228–4651, ext. 234

This is a favorite place for coffee aficionados and book lovers to come together. The room is expansive and offers tables or little seats along the huge picture windows overlooking Burnside Street or 10th Avenue. It has a totally laid back atmosphere and a huge selection of current magazines as well as an in-house restaurant that serves great pastries and healthy soups and sandwiches. Try the house specialty, a Hell Cow, which is two shots of espresso with cold milk.

Coffeetime
710 N.W. 21st Ave.
(503) 497–1090

A mug's toss from Cinema 21, Portland's premiere artsy movie house, Coffeetime is a happening scene where Northwestern boulevardiers gather at sidewalk tables to kill time before the film starts or after the credits roll and it's time to critique the flick. Inside you'll find comfy booths and walls luxuriantly painted with scenes from Egyptian mythology. Beyond a counter where congenial baristas serve espresso, cappuccino, lattes, and a selection of pastries is another chamber even wilder than the main shop. This whimsically rococo parlor is decorated with leopard-skin chairs, a patchwork of patterned rugs, and more arcane artwork. Poets are encouraged to show up for open-mike readings on Sunday and Tuesday evenings.

Pearl Bakery
102 N.W. 9th Ave.
(503) 827–0910

Attached like a bright pendant to a gargantuan bakery in the Pearl District, the Pearl Bakery coffee shop is yet another indication that this once gray and grimy industrial zone is starting to sparkle. Set on a busy street corner, the shop has two full windows lined with counters, stools, and small tables and chairs. This open atmosphere is great for those overcast days when we need every errant sunbeam we can get. As well as the usual caffeinated suspects—coffee and espresso by Torrefazione Italia and tea by Republic of Tea—there are exotic sandwiches, desserts, and breakfast pastries. How about eggplant on Ciabatta or a fontina rosemary croissant? How can you walk away from a chocolate raspberry brownie or a rhubarb tart?

Torrefazione Italia
828 N.W. 23rd Ave.
(503) 228–1255

1140 Everett
(503) 224–9896
www.torrefazione.com

Torrefazione coffee can be sampled at a number of restaurants and coffeehouses around town, but it is here in the coffee company's two retail outlets that an elegant ambience is added to its robust brand of Java-like whipped cream on a cappuccino grande. An effective mix of ornately decorative cups, saucers, and plates and blond wooden chairs and tables sustains the notion of a classic Italian coffeehouse. An impressive lunch menu of a hearty selection of *Italia gastronomia* includes *panini, focaccia,* and pasta. One standout is the Cristoforo Columbo (tuna, artichoke hearts, sundried tomatoes, olives, red onions, and capers in a balsamic vinaigrette topped with baby spinach).

Insiders' Tip

A pleasant surprise for shoppers browsing through the imported food and furniture aisles at Cost Plus in the mini-mall at Burnside and 23rd Avenue: There's a coffee bar at the back of the store! During the dog days of summer, they offer iced coffees and teas—a real treat for those who have just about had it with their tour of Northwest boutiques, galleries, and shops.

Torrefazione Italia at its Northwest location in the stylish Pearl District. CREDIT: DAVID JOHNSON

Southeast Portland

Cafe Lena
2239 S.E. Hawthorne Blvd.
(503) 238–7087

This comforting little haven is located just outside the fringe of Hawthorne Boulevard's hottest retail section, and is an artist's haven. Besides great coffee drinks, Cafe Lena serves wonderful breakfasts all day long. Try Lena's French Toast with specially braided egg bread and genuine maple syrup. All of their pastries, breads, and desserts are fresh and homemade—treat yourself. And ask about the open-mike poetry readings and live music that is a regular feature of this neighborhood fixture.

Common Grounds
4321 S.E. Hawthorne Blvd.
(503) 236–4835

This coffeehouse, on the eastern side of the Hawthorne shopping district, is both a neighborhood draw and a destination point, one of the best places in the city to read and write with your latte. Graduate students, artists, and writers flock to the place. They stock a good selection of periodicals, from the *New York Review* to *Wired*, and the music is always good. Common Grounds also serves wonderful nosh to help fire up the neurons. Great cookies, pastries, and other desserts are made right there, and the *panini* will keep you going through writing that long chapter of your thesis.

Detour Café
3035 S.E. Division
(503) 234-7499

Owners of a new spot to get a decent cup of java told *The Oregonian* that "Portland just doesn't have a really developed coffeehouse culture." So they decided to do something about it. Not only do they offer good coffee, they have some tasty munchies to go with your brew. These include soups, salmon and herb cream cheese, and ricotta and tuna sandwiches. Lots of blocks from the nearest Starbucks, this cheerful hangout is indeed, a detour from the everyday.

Papaccino's
4411 S.E. Woodstock Blvd.
(503) 771-2825

This is a lively, neighborhood coffee shop with a decidedly Bohemian flavor. Besides excellent cappuccinos and lattes, the mocha, which is created from a secret recipe, is super-popular. Papaccino's gets a good share of "Reedies" from nearby Reed College and there is often a chess or backgammon game in progress.

The desserts and pastries are very good, particularly the Boysenberry Bavarian Cream Cake and the Peanut Butter Pie. Other beverages range from the coconut-flavored Thai iced coffee to fresh berry shakes. They sell imported coffee beans, teas, coffee grinders, mugs, T-shirts, and other good stuff here.

The Pied Cow Coffeehouse
3244 S.E. Belmont St.
(503) 230-4866

Belmont Street now boasts so many unique coffeehouses it is beginning to rival Hawthorne Boulevard and Northwest 23rd Avenue for the title of "Coffee Row." The Pied Cow is a wonderful, funky, old Victorian home that looks like a cheerfully haunted house. Inside it is decorated with brass chandeliers, and big comfortable sofas and pillows. It has a terrific porch too, and an outside dining area that is packed during the summer months. A favorite specialty is the Ice Mocha Float—rich vanilla ice cream, espresso, chocolate, and whipped cream. There is a good variety of coffee and tea drinks. The Yerba Mate, an Argentinean tea, and the Orange Cardamom Mint, are good choices. The Pied Cow offers very inventive and tasty soups, appetizers, and desserts and on some evenings, live music.

Rimsky Korsakoffee House
707 S.E. 12th Ave.
(503) 232-2640

One of the most unique stops in the city, Rimsky Korsakoffee House offers a wide

Insiders' Tip

If you are looking for a special treat slather some red-eye cream cheese on your choice of bagels at True Brew Cofeehouse, 3370 S.E. Milwaukie St., (503) 231-9992, in Old Friends Bookstore at the gateway to the working class-and-proud-of-it Brooklyn neighborhood. Made by owner John Asparro, this secret combination of over two dozen savory herbs and spices blended into cream cheese is not for sale unless it's on a bagel.

Coffee People, a local chain all over town, offers "Good Coffee/No Backtalk." CREDIT: DAVID JOHNSON

range of specialty coffees and live classical music. As you've no doubt concluded, this establishment is for aficionados of fine music and fine coffees and desserts. For a sinfully rich indulgence, feast on the Mocha Fudge Cake and the Rasputin's Vice—three scoops of coffee ice cream topped with raspberries. Another delight is the Tsar Sultan Suite—chocolate almond ice cream, almond syrup, and whipped cream.

North/Northeast Portland

Bravo Italia Café
4110 N.E. Fremont St.
(503) 282–2118

A delightful place for people who love to enjoy espresso all day long, Bravo Italia Café uses fine, organically grown European coffee beans for all their caffeine concoctions. Although they don't claim a house specialty, they cover all the basics and make them exceptionally well. Besides the espresso and cappuccino offerings, they serve great omelettes, light lunches, and wonderful desserts. For a change of pace, try a coffee-flavored dessert here. We like the simple and refreshing espresso a la mode.

Cadillac Café
914 N.E. Broadway
(503) 287–4750

We almost listed Cadillac Café under restaurants, but their coffees are so great and unique that we changed our minds. With plenty of plants, cheery windows, and its patented pink chairs and walls, the CC serves up some outstanding coffee drinks, particularly the "Oregonian," a cafe mocha with hazelnut topped with whipped cream and chocolate sprinkles. The "Irvington" is a cafe mocha with vanilla, whipped cream, and chocolate and vanilla sprinkles. Another big hit is the "Sullivan's Gulch" a cafe latte with blackberry, whipped cream, and vanilla sprinkles. The CC also serves great omelettes and French Custard Toast that is to die for.

Roslyn's Coffeehouse
1438 N.E. Alberta St.
(503) 288–8652

This classy, cheerful gift shop/cafe adds a much-appreciated touch of elegance to the Alberta neighborhood. With good food, excellent coffee, and pottery and other imported gifts, it provides a great atmosphere for conversation. Stroll about or sit and enjoy your cup of coffee on the patio and in the garden. There is also a light lunch of soup and sandwiches.

Hollywood Espresso Company
1805 N.E. 42nd Ave.
(503) 335–8131

It's all too easy to miss this fun spot, which is tucked away in the Hollywood District, but you don't want to do that. Hollywood Espresso Company makes exceptional specialty coffees and serves up fresh pastries, Italian sodas, and whole bean coffees. Hollywood names its coffee drinks after famous movies. The "Casablanca," a perennial favorite, is espresso, milk, Kahlua, hazelnut, and whipped cream. The "Dirty Harry" our choice, is espresso, milk, spicy chocolate, almond, and whipped cream. Ask about other great coffee drinks, including the "Moonstruck," the "Terminator," and the "Lethal Weapon."

Lew Jones, Portland's perennial folksinger/songwriter, can be heard at many of the clubs and cafes around town. CREDIT: DAVE JOHNSON

Nightlife

Unlike the Dixieland jazz of New Orleans, hard charging blues of Chicago, or upscale country of Nashville, the night side of the Rose City cheerfully refuses to settle into a particular pigeonhole. Instead, this town is known for a diversity of entertainment. It also has an unquenchable thirst for parties, including the Mt. Hood Festival of Jazz in nearby Gresham and the Waterfront Blues Festival in Tom McCall Waterfront Park. Those two fests are only the most notorious boogies in a calendar year that seems to have something popping every weekend. It's a long tradition that surged into national prominence in the late '80s and early '90s when Portland, along with its big sister, Seattle, became the proving grounds for bands like Nirvana that patented the Pacific Northwest grunge sound.

Today, Portland continues this lively heritage of providing a full menu of musical entertainment for all ages. Whatever your tastes, from cutting-edge fusion, funk, and electronica to laid-back blues or traditional folk, you'll find it here. So, adorned with plaid shirt or black turtleneck, tie-dyed tanktop, or Ann Taylor original, choose your watering hole for the evening.

Portland has hundreds of cozy taverns, most with pool tables, and one-seat video gambling parlors, ballrooms where you can swing to the Lindy Hop, and mega-blaster amphitheaters where you might take your chances in the mosh pit.

Like jazz? You could hang out at the venerable Jazz de Opus in the heart of Old town. You could disco at the Tiger Bar in the trendy Pearl District or listen to a Buddy Holly tune at the Bodacious Classics Restaurant and Pumphouse. Those who hanker for folksingers will find them under the antlerdome at St. Johns Pub.

Besides this eclectic menu of live music, DJs also provide a range of ambient music for Portland's many night spots, so you'll be surrounded by good sound nearly everywhere, once Portland's sun goes down.

But it's not just about music in Portland. There's also a thriving open-mike scene for poetry at Cafe Lena's and comedy at the Etcetera Tavern as well as at other clubs, bars, galleries, and coffeehouses. But if all you really want is a slice of pizza, a brew, and a cheap movie, then you still have lots of choices, including the Mission Theatre & Pub where, for a couple of bucks, you can see a flick, and for a few more you can have dinner and a drink. Or, if you time it right, you can sit on the hood of your car or on a handy boulder down by the river and watch fireworks for free. It seems that as well as staging one festival after another, Portlanders will set off a batch of sparkling starbursts for little or no reason at all.

While you're waiting for that next dazzling display, here is our list of dance clubs, nightclubs, pubs, and miscellaneous entertainment, all arranged by location.

Dance Clubs

Southwest Portland

Berbati's Pan
231 S.W. 3rd Ave.
(503) 248–4579
www.berbatipan.citysearch.com

A big L-shaped dance club connected to a Greek restaurant that serves ethnic food in the bar section, this venerable venue has three hard liquor bars and a stage that hosts a variety of action, from alternative rock concerts to jazz gigs to open-mike comedy to swing dance lessons to Songwriters in the Round. Berbati's Pan is also headquarters for the Portland Poetry Slam team, a nationally recognized contender for the Champion of the Known Universe, an annual national contest usually held in New York or Chicago. Cover charges range from $3 to $6, depending on whether you've come for a poetry slam, concert, or stand-up comedy.

Crystal Ballroom
1332 W. Burnside Ave.
(503) 225–0047
www.danceonair.com

The crown jewel in the McMenamin brothers' entertainment empire, the Crystal Ballroom is a renovated dance hall with a floating floor on ball bearings and rockers. Back when it opened in 1914 as the Cotillion Hall, Portlanders could be arrested for dancing the tango. Since then it's witnessed the likes of Rudolph Valentino, Ike and Tina Turner, Jimi Hendrix, Marvin Gaye, the Family Dog, and the Grateful Dead. The dance hall closed in 1968 and sat empty for thirty years until the McMenamins tackled a major rehabilitation. Now, Portlanders are once again enjoying this gracious space with its high-arched windows, curving balcony, rococo paintings, and, above all, that dance floor with a capacity for 1,500. Live bands play throughout the week and Sunday's bring ballroom dance lessons to the public. Ticket prices are $12 for most per-

formances. The dress code ranges from jeans and T-shirt for both genders to black cocktail dress or three-piece suit. There are a couple of bars serving microbrews and mixed drinks.

Polly Esther's
424 S.W. 4th Ave.
(503) 221–1970
www.pollyesthers.com

Labeled bachelorette headquarters, this new, hot dance club gets down with '70s disco and '80s retro and live music every Thursday. On Wednesdays, a male review for ladies only is presented with no cover from 8 to 10 P.M. Other hours are Wednesday 9 P.M. to 2 A.M. and Friday and Saturday 8 P.M. to 4 A.M.

Northwest Portland

Roseland Theatre and Grill
10 N.W. 6th Ave.
(503) 224–2038

Once a noisy, dingy dance hall called Starry Night that nabbed hard rockers blowing through the region, this site underwent a long-overdue renovation to be reincarnated as Roseland Theatre and Grill, a pleasant all-ages concert pavilion with a bar and roomy balcony upstairs for those over twenty-one. Now the bill of fare is an eclectic mix of national music and comedy acts, local groups' CD release parties, and DJ dance boogies. A bonus is the emergence of the Roseland Grill downstairs. This narrow slot of a bar has a festive wall covered with posters from the long history of the Roseland, and on Sunday evenings is the site of a Songwriters in the Round series.

Southeast Portland

Bodacious Classics Restaurant and Pumphouse
2433 S.E. Powell Blvd.
(503) 232–0852

For our money, this is one of the best values in town. Bodacious Classics isn't even close to upscale, but it has fun, high-energy 1950s rock 'n' roll music supplied by a lively but nonirritating DJ. BC's, as it is affectionately known, is the kind of place anybody, and we mean anybody, can go and have a ball. It offers a full-service bar with good prices and some terrific dinner specials. The menu isn't fancy or creative, but they make darned good steaks and chef salads. People here have a blast and the employees seem to be having as good a time as everyone else.

Grand Café & Andrea's Cha Cha Club
832 S.E. Grand Ave.
(503) 230–1166

This place, currently one of the hottest spots on the entire Eastside, throbs with activity on the weekends. This singles scene offers lots of action on the small, steamy dance floor. If you go here to groove, break out your ultra-chic clothes, and remember—people go here to work up a sweat to great world-beat sounds, not to stand around and stare. Drinks are steep—over $4 for microbrews, and there is a $4 cover charge for men. If you are a little rusty at "bustin' a move," shell out $8 for a cha-cha lesson, which will also get you a drink and free entry. There really is an Andrea, and she usually works the turntables herself on Fridays and Saturdays until closing.

The New Copper Penny
5932 S.E. 92nd Ave. and Foster Rd.
(503) 777–1415
www.newcopperpenny.com

This is a big, flashy place with a huge dance floor surrounded by video screens, a long bar, and sets of tables and chairs. The DJs spin popular dance music, including the standard top forties, until the wee hours of the morning. As you've guessed, this isn't a black tie establishment. The dress code for guys prohibits baseball hats, and for the ladies fashion jeans are fine, along with T-shirts or halter tops. Young and restless Portlanders in the outer Southeast area come here to meet people, and they do party-hearty at the "NCP."

North/Northeast Portland
The Refectory
1618 N.E. 122nd Ave.
(503) 255–8545

This isn't a rowdy college scene as some imagine, but a fun place for the mid-twenty to forty-something set to let their hair down. The Refectory is bursting at the seams with people out having a good time dancing and enjoying a few mixed drinks. The DJs play a lot of popular dance tunes along with some not too alternative music such as Matchbox 20 and Third Eye Blind. It's a casual but very

Insiders' Tip
Ready to flame out into the evening for a groovy sound to zing you into early morning? You can scan the ads in *Willamette Week* (in boxes and stacked in convenience stores on Wednesdays) and *The Portland Mercury*, a newer and wilder rag that hits the same bricks on Thursday. Both papers are jammed with ads from most of the musical venues featuring the funkiest and punkiest and the out-of-town wierdos blowing through Stumptown.

happening place with "high techno lighting" for the slightly older dance crowd.

Viscount Ballroom
722 E. Burnside
(503) 233-7855
www.viscountballroom.com

With the revival of swing dancing, the popularity of salsa, and the classic sizzle of Argentine tango, the Viscount Ballroom packs them in Monday through Tuesday and Friday through Sunday with a mix of DJs and live music. Located upstairs in an old Masonic Lodge nestled in the Industrial District near Eastside, Viscount charges $6 to $10 for early lessons and the all-night dancing.

Night Clubs

Southwest Portland

1201 Cafe & Lounge
1201 S.W. 12th Ave.
(503) 225-1201

This playful lounge and restaurant has a lot of options for a fun evening out. The Lounge opens at 8 P.M. Wednesday to Sunday. Music played by hip DJs starts nightly at 10 P.M. Wednesday dance to down tempo danceable electronics; Thursdays bring deep house music; Fridays are full of pure funk; Saturdays return to the old school, and Sundays are the best place to end your week!

Brasserie Montmarte
626 S.W. Park
(503) 224-5552
www.brasseriemontmarte.com

This stylish Pacific Northwest version of a Parisian bistro is a sophisticated, relaxed club where patrons pay no cover to listen to jazz seven nights a week. The newest change here is a second floor, added in Summer 2001. Breeze in and find a table beneath a ceiling whimsically collaged with playing cards and held aloft with faux columns as thick as a maitre d's midriff. While you're waiting for a martini or snack (try the French-fried artichoke hearts), capture the ambience with a crayon sketch of your own. For inspiration, the walls have an impressive collection of crayon art by the crème of Portland's art community. Come in an enjoy some cocktails in this very stylish place.

Candlelight Cafe & Bar
2032 S.W. 5th Ave.
(503) 222-3378

This reigning champion for the best blues in town adds to its popularity with no cover charge. A while back, this matchbox-sized juke joint on the eastern edge of PSU had loose jam sessions Sunday through Thursday. But that's tapered off as Portland's hottest blues artists are jamming a little tighter to the delight of a devoted crowd that packs the place. There is also a Cajun/Creole restaurant and audio performances on DSL for laptop hook-ups. So, enjoy a microbrew, mixed drink, or tasty snack while you listen to the blues, which kick off at 9:30 P.M. every night of the week.

The Riverside at The Four Points Sheraton
50 S.W. Morrison St.
(503) 221-0711
www.fourpointsportland.com

Down by the riverside, this swanky little bistro has a piano you can play. It also offers a full wine bar, local microbrews, and a menu that features fresh Northwest ingredients. For those who are jogging, biking, or strolling along the west bank of the Willamette through Tom McCall Waterfront Park or along the Greenway south of the park, The Riverside is a handy oasis with a touch of class.

A lively mural outside of the notorious bar, dance hall, and restaurant, the Lotus Cafe and Cardroom.

CREDIT: DAVID JOHNSON

Northwest Portland

Cobalt Lounge
32 N.W. 3rd Ave.
(503) 225–1003
www.cobaltlounge.com

The Cobalt Lounge presents the edgy outer envelope of local live music, performance art, go-go dancing, and comedy seven nights a week. This multi-genre scene mixes rockabilly, punk, indie rock, and serene soloists. You can watch a movie at the barside tube or slip into one of the blue-sparkle booths of the cafe. Enjoy exotic drinks with names like the Tiki Torch and Cobaltkazi Blue and scrumptious Tex-Northwest entrees. From 4 to 7 P.M. the Cobalt offers lots of happy hour munchies for $3.

Jazz de Opus
33 N.W. 2nd Ave.
(503) 222–6077

Entertaining jazz buffs since 1972, this venerable club in the heart of Old Town is Portland's most notable venue for live jazz. Every night of the week, seasoned musicians play at this intimate club, which has a cover charge of $5 on Friday and Saturday. Recently, an upstairs restaurant (Opus Too) has been added to the mix, with a broiler fueled by mesquite wood toasting a wide selection of seafood, steak, and lamb racks over the coals. In keeping with a tradition of employing masters at their craft, this quintessential Portland nightspot has hired a former chef to Her Majesty Queen Elizabeth II. The mixed drinks here are both tasty and affordable.

Jimmy Mak's
300 N.W. 10th Ave.
(503) 295–6542
www.jimmymaks.com

A Greek-American restaurant with an adjacent lounge, Jimmy Mak's, named after its savvy owner Jimmy Makarunas, was a hit from its first night out of the chute. Most of Portland's jazz, blues, and funk performers and more recently the hot new funk jazz bands have taken a turn on the small stage in this cozy, intimate club that was once known as The Long Goodbye. Now it's a hot joint where it's fun to sample the Souvlaki Kasa while leaning into the groove of a sax solo or guitar lick. Mixed drinks are served at Jimmy Mak's, which is open Monday through Saturday with live jazz every night. There's a $3 to $5 cover charge.

Ohm
31 N.W. 1st Ave.
(503) 223–9919

Once the locale of Key Largo, Portland's wildest boogy bar, this space has been transformed into a cutting edge electronic parlor. The new name for this avant-garde scene plays on two words: "ohm," the measure of electrical current, and the Sanskrit word "Om," a term that means "oneness," often chanted during meditation. Ohm also offers live theater, DJ spins, break dancing, hip-hop, and theme nights. All events are twenty-one or over; doors open at 8 P.M. Cover charges range from $4 to $7.

Satyricon
125 N.W. 6th Ave.
(503) 243–2380
www.clubsatyricon.com

Once a haven for neo-beat poets and a nerve center for punk rockers, Satyricon can claim the fame of first hosting bands like Soul Asylum and Nirvana, who then went on to Top-Ten notoriety.

Although the place still resembles a 3-D black-light poster from the 60's, it's a shade mellower than the days of Punk-a-

Rama. Now it's linked with a sleek eatery, Fellini, known for its Bangkok Ho, a heap of vegetables in peanut sauce. It also serves low-priced pitas, gyros, and burgers. Both places offer mixed drinks, beer, and wine.

Tiger Bar
317 N.W. Broadway
(503) 222–7297

With minimal signage and a mysteriously bland front door, Tiger Bar has the outside appearance of a private club. Inside it's an after-work, happening scene. For no cover charge you can join the artists, Bohemians, advertising execs, and other Pearl District habitués who come here to chat, sip an exotic cocktail like vodka-fueled "Liquid Love" or Damianas while nibbling tiger prawns, pad Thai noodles, and other Pan-Asian treats, all against the backdrop of a wall of electronic sound.

Southeast Portland

Meowmeow
527 S.E. Pine St.
(503) 230–2111
wwwthemeowmeow.com

Here's an answer to the classic teenage lament: "There is nothing to do." Well, at this feline rock parlor, all ages are welcome. Just leave alcohol, smokes, weapons, and drugs at the door. Covers for the shows runs from $5 to $6. Examples of bands that have played are Stereocrush, Slackjaw, Kind of Like Spitting, and All Girl Summer Fun Band.

Vancouver

Beaches Restaurant and Bar
1919 S.E. Columbia River Dr., Vancouver
(360) 699–1592
www.yagottahavefun.com

Beaches is a Vancouver hot spot with a great view of the Columbia. Here in this casual watering hole and eatery, Vancouverites relax at a lively bar or cafe side, sampling pastas, salads, hard-shelled clams, oven-fired pizza, and chicken wings flavored with Jack Daniels.

Pubs

Southwest Portland

The Cheerful Tortoise
1939 S.W. 6th Ave.
(503) 224–3377

Cleverly located on the edge of the PSU campus within easy reach of students who follow collegial and professional sports, this happy turtle with a couple of satellite dishes on its back, boasts twelve big screens filled with athletes darting, colliding, slam-dunking and base-running to victory. The Cheerful Tortoise's bar also has a full bar with twenty beers on tap.

Elephant and Castle
439 S.W. 2nd Ave.
(503) 222–5698
www.elephantcastle.citysearch.com

A stop on the London Tube, the Elephant and Castle is also one of Portland's most popular pubs. Englanders would feel right at home in this lively replica of one of their own. Don your tweeds and sensible shoes and stop by for a pint of Guiness, Boddington's Pub Ale, or a sip of Strongbow Cider. And if you have an inclination for a comestible, try the steak and mushroom pie or Icelandic cod and chips. You can also wait your turn to toss a dart.

Goose Hollow Inn
1927 S.W. Jefferson St.
(503) 228–7010

Tucked at the base of a draw leading into hills west of town, this pub got its start as Ann's Tavern in 1941. After a long run, Ann's morphed into the famous Goose Hollow Inn when former Portland Mayor Bud Clark took over in 1967 and imprinted this fun saloon with his jovial, savvy personality. There are photos and paintings of our quirky ex-mayor, historic shots of neighborhood trolleys, and cheerfully dingy memorabilia adorning the cluttered walls. Surrounding the inside bar is a deck with tables—a great spot to have a hearty lunch or dinner while discussing politics, sports, or the latest best-selling novel. Brews include a few reliable items such as Bridgeport IPA and Mirror Pond Pale Ale. The menu stretches from "The Best Reuben on the Planet," to crab cocktail to Goose Hollow Pizza.

Southeast Portland

Bar of the Gods
4801 S.E. Hawthorne Blvd.
(503) 232–2037

A unique selection of reasonably priced but heavenly-tasting microbrews, free pool, and an outdoor patio await you at Bar of the Gods. On some evenings they show films beneath hanging bunches of plastic grapes.

Biddy McGraw's Irish Pub
6000 N.E. Glisan St.
(503) 233–1178
www.biddys.com

This place is so authentic that it is cool without even trying to be. Don't bother to get dolled up going to this saloon—you won't impress anyone and you might draw stares or snickers. This is a working people's bar, and the people who come here, many Irish of course, are as real and unpretentious as the four Guinness taps and three ciders you can indulge in. Biddy's offers a lot more than stout ales and patrons oozing Celtic character. It serves up some of the best Irish food in the city, complimented with about twenty imports, microbrews, and hard liquor. Most evenings Biddy's offers live and authentic Irish music.

Mickey Finn's Brew
4336 S.E. Woodstock Blvd.
(503) 788–1587

This newer addition to the pub scene is winning over lots of fans and it's easy to see why. Mickey Finn's is a big, wholesome place that offers twenty-eight microbrews on tap, a very decent wine selection, and upscale pub grub such as gourmet burgers, specialty salads, hearty sandwiches, and homemade soups. It has a family atmosphere—although there are a few TVs, it isn't a hardcore sports bar. Mickey Finn's also has pool tables and dartboards.

Mt. Tabor Theater and Pub
4811 S.E. Hawthorne Blvd.
(503) 238–1646

A very unique and funky alternative pub, Mt. Tabor offers a selection of savory microbrews and alternative musicians hard rockin' in a 400-capacity music room. It also offers free pool and foosball seven days a week. This place isn't upscale but it is comfortable and uniquely charming.

Produce Row Cafe
204 S.E. Oak St.
(503) 232–8355

Although it's housed in a longtime Industrial District, make no mistake, this is no "hole in the wall." It's a fun, clean, and classy fixture among the microbrew set. Produce Row is easy to miss as it is hidden away in the bowels of Portland's Eastside. But it's worth the time to find it with its upgraded menu, excellent selection of beer and ales, genuine friendly service, and variety of live music offerings, rang-ing from jazz to bluegrass to folk. Produce Row recently underwent a total makeover with new carpet, chairs, and painted walls.

North/Northeast Portland

Etcetera Tavern
3276 N.E. Killingsworth St.
(503) 282–2411
www.etceteratavern.citysearch.com

This is a place where you really feel at home even if you don't know a soul in town. If the wise-cracking stand-up comics here don't tickle your funny bone, there are twenty-two beers on tap to help you smile. Etcetera also offers live music as well as tasty burgers, sandwiches, soups, and appetizers. There's also a big-screen TV for the sports junkies.

Laurelthirst Public House
2958 N.E. Glisan St.
(503) 232–1504

For the alternative folk music crowd, this is a premier nightspot, probably the trendiest place to go and be seen on the Eastside. Laurelthirst is far more than a "flavor of the week." They've built a great place with a talented and creative kitchen, a variety of microbrews, and a good wine selection. They also draw some of Portland's most sought-after musicians. If you've never heard the phrase "Eastside

Insiders' Tip

A little tight in the purse or wallet depart-ment? You can still dig some tunes on weekends at Beulahland, 118 N.E. 28th, a coffee and ale house with pints for a couple of bucks during happy hours (4 to 6 P.M.) and coffee for a buck. Not a bad expense for virtually free live music. You gotta be twenty-one or over after 9 P.M. but minors can still groove until then.

sound," that's okay. Come here and get a crash course. Laurelthirst also showcases some terrific and largely unknown talent during openmike nights. The pub itself has great atmosphere: Brick walls and plenty of rough-hewn wood lend it character, and the postage stamp-size stage is reminiscent of another era. Sadly, taverns aren't made like this anymore.

McGillacuddy's Grill and Pub
11133 N.E. Halsey St.
(503) 257–2337
www.mcgillacuddys.com

This here's a jolly good sports bar. McGillacuddy's serves up twelve on-tap microbrews, genuinely good burgers with fresh-cut French-fries, homemade soups, and garden-fresh salads. You will have to decide which ball game you are going to watch: Thanks to the wonders of satellite communication, McGillacuddy's ten TVs offer a wide variety of sporting events.

St. Johns Pub
8203 N. Ivanhoe St.
(503) 283–8520
www.mcmenamins.com

This renovated circa 1906 church offers a charmingly different atmosphere for a casual evening out with friends. The St. Johns Pub features one of the most delightful beer gardens in town, great live music, delicious microbrews, wines, and hard liquor to accompany your tasty sandwiches and burgers. This place is so unique you have to go and experience it for yourself. The long elegant wood bar and wood-burning stove make you feel like you're stepping into a time warp. The pub—one of the McMenamins brothers' brainstorms—is full of treasures, including a 7-foot-tall carving of a big bird of paradise, stained-glass windows, a bizarre assortment of hanging lights, second-empire chairs, and an old-time piano that patrons sometimes play. Go to this place and have as much fun as you want to, and it won't even put you in the poorhouse. For more information, see our chapter on Brewpubs.

Twilight Room
5242 N. Lombard St.
(503) 283–5091

This is a big, interactive place, with a horseshoe-shaped bar and plenty of booths, that serves up a half-dozen microbrews, hard liquor, very good sandwiches, great burgers, and fries. The Twilight has four full-size pool tables. People here don't sit staring at the tube like zombies—they're more inclined to strike up a conversation or shoot a game of 8-ball. If you want to blow off some steam on a Friday night, this neighborhood tavern is a good choice.

White Eagle
836 N. Russell St.
(503) 282–6810

Rocking, sweating, pulsating, the White Eagle—which is now one of the McMenamin brother's taverns—is indeed a raucous joint when the sun goes down. It doesn't look like much from the outside, but don't let that fool you. The old brick building is narrow and long, so when you go inside the place, it seems like you're in an elongated basement except for the high ceiling. The crowded feeling can be claustrophobic but that same closeness makes the enthusiasm more contagious when the bands turn up the heat. People go here to drink and dance to the blues and pile-driving rock of talented and hardworking musicians performing every night. Jeans and T-shirts are standard apparel. There is a new patio, new menu, and a renovated upstairs with eleven hotel rooms at the amazingly old-fashioned prices of $25, $35, and $45.

Vancouver
Dodge City Bar & Grill
7201 N.E. 18th St., Vancouver
(360) 253–6603

Dodge City is a pub where country rocks! Every night of the week you can learn to sashay and swing to Country and Western tunes spun by a DJ; dance lessons start at 8 P.M. There's a $3 cover on Friday and Saturday nights. If all this scuffling gets your appetite talking to you, Dodge City has buffalo burgers, tacos, and other hefty munchies. With tongue tucked deeply in its grizzled cheek, Dodge City also sponsors Jell-O wrestling, a mechanical bull, and a floor buffer rodeo.

McMenamins on the Columbia
1801 S.E. Columbia River Dr., Vancouver
(360) 699–1521
www.mcmenamin's.com

The first McMenamins' pub opened outside of Oregon, this tavern features a great view of the Columbia River, the usual Terminator and other brews by the bros, and a good menu of ales. Along with the regular McMenamins' menu of big burgers and monster fries, this spot offers a tasty salmon sandwich.

Insiders' Tip

If you or your high-energy kids want to start a rock and roll band, you or they can snag an easy booking at Meowmeow (see listings), a lively all ages nightclub. Aspiring bands can check out the booking action by visiting www.ethos-inc.com or call (503) 241-8824.

Miscellaneous

Southwest Portland

After Hours at the Portland Art Museum
1219 S.W. Park Ave.
(503) 226–2811

After Hours is presented every Wednesday evening from fall to spring in the museum's third-floor ballroom. For $6 you can see local and traveling musical talent. (Members pay $3.) Hors d'oeuvres and wine are available for an additional fee. While you're there, why not also take a tour of current exhibits?

Rialto Poolroom, Bar & Cafe
529 S.W. 4th Ave.
(503) 228–7605

Minnesota Fats would have felt at home in this downtown pool hall with its fifteen full-size Brunswick tables, full bar, sumptuous menu, and downstairs off-track betting. In fact, a photo of Jackie Gleason portraying the legendary stickman in *The Hustler,* is prominently displayed in the bar. Open every day of the year, the Rialto offers a rack of balls and

long stretch of green for $5 an hour before 5 P.M. and $7 per hour afterward. If hoisting a cue for a couple of rounds gets your appetite stirred, try their potato skins with sour cream, bacon, and scallions or their grilled halibut dinner. If you're a vegetarian still yearning for something on a bun, try the garden-burger, one of Portland's hometown products that is spreading to many of the nation's supermarkets.

Northwest Portland

Darcelle XV
208 N.W. 3rd Ave.
(503) 222–5338
www.citysearch.com

Darcelle XV, Portland's hilarious female impersonator and her/his Las Vegas–style cabaret revue strut their stuff Wednesday through Saturday. At midnight on Friday and Saturday, *Men of Paradise*, a Chippendale-style male strip show takes over. There's a $10 cover for all shows; cocktails are available.

Harvey's Comedy Club
436 N.W. 6th Ave.
(503) 241–0338
www.harveyscomedyclub.com

This is the longest-running comedy club in Portland. Locals sharpening their act, as well as well-known stand-up comics on national tours, crack up audiences that pay $8 to $10 to enjoy intelligent, witty banter rather than off-color cheap jokes. Harvey's is a nonsmoking club with no drink minimums and no purchase required other than tickets to the show.

Mission Theatre & Pub
1624 N.W. Glisan St.
(503) 223–4527
www.mcmenamin's.com

Looking for a sprawly, roomy place to watch a flick while downing a brew and slice of pizza? With its 300-seat capacity, the Mission Theatre & Pub is just the right spot for a relaxed evening. The movies cost $1 (except for the rare starred attraction), and once in a while, a musical performer or group will take to the stage for an evening concert. While you're waiting for the show to begin, check out the large windows and ornate balcony façade—hints that the place has a long history. This well-preserved brick building originated as a Swedish Evangelical Mission in 1912, then became a longshoreman hiring hall. Now it's yet another renovation project initiated by the McMenamins who have doubled as historical preservationists and brewmeisters. The Mission welcomes minors to Saturday and Sunday matinees with parents or guardian.

Southeast Portland

Aladdin Theater
3017 S.E. Milwaukie Ave.
(503) 233–1994
www.showman.com

This place lands all kinds of top-drawer acts from many different cultures in and outside of the U.S.A. Aladdin's focus is eclectic: They feature everything from grunge to polka music, to classical and neo-country. Once infamous for its record-breaking extended showing of *Deep Throat*, the Aladdin Theater is now famous for blurring the edges between musical genres and is the new darling of Portland's liberal-minded music scene. This place isn't just trendy, it's solid and innovative. Besides snagging some huge and widely respected talent, the Aladdin also books some terrific and often overlooked artists. Tickets are available at the box office out front from 1 to 6 P.M. and just before the show.

Grand Central Pool/Grand Central Bowling
808 S.E. Morrison St.
(503) 232–5166

Grand Central is an insomniac's delight. This place, just 3 blocks east of the Morrison Street Bridge, offers glow-in-the-dark, cosmic bowling, complete with black strobe lights, glowing bowling pins and balls, little machines spewing out fog, and a DJ playing top-forty dance music. Grand Central also features a full-service cocktail lounge, an around-the-clock restaurant and pizza, and eleven professional-style pool tables.

North/Northeast Portland

Sam's Hollywood Billiards
1845 N.E. 41st Ave.
(503) 282–8266

This is an excellent place to shoot pool. Sam's has thirteen gorgeous, 8-foot pool tables and quality pool cues to match. The bar offers a dozen microbrews, and the kitchen prepares a variety of reasonably priced sandwiches and fried foods. It's clean, basically nonsmoky, and very friendly. The pool tables rent for $8 an hour.

Window shopping in Sellwood is a visual feast. CREDIT: RACHEL DRESBECK

Shopping

No sales tax in Oregon. What else do you need to know?

All right, we'll tell you more. Portland is a great town for shopping. Here you will not only find the usual suspects—Gap, Pottery Barn, Banana Republic, and so on—but many interesting, chic, and homegrown shops. Portland's shopping is organized around its neighborhoods, and some of these neighborhoods have evolved into destination shopping districts; these composites of retail, business, and living spaces have blended in such a way to create local shops that reflect and sustain the neighborhoods they inhabit. And Portland also has other unusual shopping opportunities. Portland Saturday Market, which takes place every weekend under the Burnside Bridge, proffers some of the most engrossing shopping in town; it's a carnival of commerce from March through December. For more information, see the Festivals and Annual Events chapter or phone (503) 222-6072. Also see that chapter for information on the area's many fine farmers' markets.

Stores in Portland tend to open at 10 A.M., if not sooner. Closing hours vary—the smaller the store, the more likely it is to close by 6 P.M. The major downtown department stores stay open till 8 or 9 P.M. on some nights and close earlier on weekends. You'll find most of the larger stores and many of the small stores open six or seven days a week. Fred Meyer and the large grocery stores such as Safeway, Albertson's, Nature's, and Thriftway are usually open at 7 A.M.; some are open twenty-four hours a day, seven days a week. Mall hours are generally 10 A.M. to 9 P.M.

We begin with a look at the malls in the area, followed by an overview of the major shopping districts. Then we break the chapter into many categories, with shops listed alphabetically. (Since many shops have more than one location, we have deviated from organizing them by geography). Here you'll find sections on Antiques, Books and Periodicals, Clothing, Food, Home Repair and Decor, Shoes and ever so much more.

Malls

Southwest Portland

The Galleria
921 S.W. Morrison St.
(503) 228–2748

People scoffed at the late legendary entrepreneur Bill Naito when he created The Galleria, the first renovation of a historical building in downtown Portland—namely the circa 1910 Olds, Wortman, and King Department Store (the first department store west of the Mississippi). The Galleria proved that people would shop downtown if they were offered convenient parking and a variety of shops and restaurants. The Galleria has suffered a little from competition with the flashier and franchise-loaded Pioneer Place, but still offers an interesting range of shops and vendors, including the fashionable men's store Mario's, a large Made In Oregon store (another Bill Naito idea), and a Jantzen outlet packed with the company's trademark bathing suits and sporty, casual clothes for men and women. There are a few restaurants on-site. The Galleria is close to all the downtown hotels. There is an adjacent parking structure and a MAX stop.

Pioneer Place
S.W. Morrison, between 5th and 3rd
(503) 228–5800

Pioneer Place is the epicenter of shopping in downtown, with more than eighty different stores, including the only Saks Fifth Avenue in the Northwest, as well as a brand-new Tiffany & Co. A huge atrium fills the building with light on even the darkest day and is frequently decorated with amazing hanging creations and designs reflecting the seasons. While shoppers are protected from the rain, Pioneer Place reminds them that they are still in Oregon with a series of fountains and tiny waterfalls that evoke the landscape. In the atrium, a fountain surrounded by flowers and plants draws children and their parents, who are praying that the little ones won't tumble in as they wish on their pennies. In the food court, a whole series of waterways provides soothing white noise for diners engrossed in conversation. In the newest part of the mall, the rotunda, a large sculptural, floral fountain cascades water in controlled sheets; you're not supposed to touch it, but it is very difficult to obey this order. Escalators soar up the middle of the rotunda and the atrium all the way to the fourth floor (there are also elevators), providing fine vantage points for surveying the shopping landscape. A skybridge and an underground tunnel connect the rotunda and the atrium for those shoppers who wish to avoid the sidewalk route. And what can you find here? Only some of the most popular shops in the area, including J.Crew, Eddie Bauer, Victoria's Secret, April Cornell, various Gap stores, Banana Republic, Ann Taylor, Talbots, J. Jill, BCBG, and a Coach store. Once you've figured out what to wear, April Cornell and Ravenna Gardens will help you decorate; the Museum Store, Twist, and Gamekeeper will provide presents to lucky people; Present Perfect will supply the wrapping paper; the Paper Station will supply the thank-you cards; and Starbucks and Godiva Chocolate will supply the sustenance. Aveda and Origins also have small shops here, for a little shopping aromatherapy.

The food court, with a dozen or more vendors, fills the entire end of the lower level, and Todai, a popular Japanese restaurant perches atop the rotunda. Two Smart Park garages flank the mall, so parking is easy, except during the holiday season. But Pioneer Place is also a MAX stop, so getting there without a car is not only easy, but during the busy season, advised.

Southeast Portland

Clackamas Town Center
12000 S.E. 82nd Ave.
(503) 653–6913

This mall is a little out of the way but easy to get to since it's just off of Interstate 205 and Sunnyside Road. With Nordstrom, JC Penney, Meier & Frank, and Sears as anchors for its other smaller 180 shops, it's busy almost any time of year. Movie theaters and an ice-skating rink are a big draw. Across the road, the Clackamas Promenade supplies area residents with great bargains from Old Navy, Nordstrom Rack, and Target.

Mall 205
9900 S.E. Washington St.
(503) 255–5805

Mall 205 is off S.E. Stark Street and Interstate 205. There are some great values here, and you don't have to fight the crowds to find them. Among the seventy-five tenants are the larger anchors such as the Emporium; Tower vends books, music, and videos; smaller businesses including shoe stores, music shops, bookstores, and arts and crafts stores round out the offerings.

North/Northeast Portland

Jantzen Beach Shopping Center
I–5 at Exit 308, Hayden Island
(503) 247–1327

Long ago, Jantzen Beach was an amusement park, but since the national amusement seems to be shopping, it's fitting that this Columbia River-site is now a shopping mall. Good times and bad times have come and gone for this shopping center, but it now seems to have found its identity and settled into a newfound prosperity and retail success. While there is a mall with a Home Depot, Emporium, and a host of small specialty stores, this is a "big box" shopping center. Major draws include REI and Old Navy; you'll also find a Toys 'R' Us, Borders Books & Music, CompUSA, Circuit City, Kmart, a Copeland Sports superstore, and Pier 1 Imports, plus a good selection of local outlets of national restaurant chains scattered around the mall. The most exceptional feature of the mall is the beautifully restored C.W. Parker carousel in the atrium, a fragment of its history. The carousel operates from 10 A.M. to 10 P.M. daily; rides cost $1.

Lloyd Center
2201 Lloyd Center
(503) 282-2511

For many folks, shopping on the east side of the Willamette River begins at Lloyd Center, Oregon's largest and oldest mall, between N.E. Broadway and N.E. Multnomah Street and N.E. 9th and 16th Avenues, and the underpinning for the Broadway shopping district. Conveniently located a block north of a MAX station, Lloyd Center can also be reached by taking a colorful trolley to the mall from downtown at no charge. (You can also drive.)

A few years ago Lloyd Center underwent a multimillion-dollar facelift, and it paid off handsomely. With a spiffy new glass roof covering the entire structure, this place looks great inside and out. People from all walks of life visit its 200 shops spread out over three levels. Meier & Frank and Nordstrom are the two main anchor tenants. The mall is graced with plenty of good restaurants, movie theaters, and a large ice-skating rink; interesting carts along the promenade sell jewelry and other tchotchkes; and the usual folks are present—Gap, Victoria's Secret, The Limited. A Disney store is a big hit with the small fry, as is a Sesame Street store. It's always fun to have a bite to eat in a multiethnic food court on the second floor while watching skaters twirl and spin down below. Bring the kids here to escape the heat of summer or the cold of winter.

Vancouver
Westfield Shoppingtown—Vancouver
8700 N.E. Vancouver Mall Dr.
(on WA Hwy. 500, between I–205 and I–5)
(360) 892-6255

Also called simply "the Vancouver Mall," Westfield Shoppingtown—Vancouver features Meier & Frank, Nordstrom, and Mervyns, among others. Home Spun Crafters is a magnet for many folks; it offers an assortment of 200 mini-vendors selling a huge variety of one-of-a-kind gifts, goods, and food. Another 150 more traditional stores, kiosks, and small shops energize this two-level mall which has convenient access to Interstate 205 and Interstate 5. The only full-size shopping center in Clark County, the mall also hosts a lovely new branch of the Clark County Library.

Outlying Areas
Columbia Gorge Factory Stores
450 N.W. 257th Ave., Troutdale
(503) 669-8060

In most other major cities, the big factory outlet stores are hours away. This one is just twenty minutes from Portland proper, off Interstate 84. The outlet center boasts forty-two brand-name suppliers, including Haines, Adidas, Norm Thompson, Levi, Jockey, and Florsheim. You won't have any problem locating designer-label merchandise in women's and men's clothes, shoes, sportswear, and accessories. The discounts are sizable, ranging from 25 to 75 percent off regular department store prices. If you take the Marine Drive exit on the way back to the city, you'll enjoy a scenic view of the Columbia River, and if you time it right, perhaps even a spectacular sunset.

Washington Square and Square Too
OR Hwy. 217 at S.W. Greenburg Rd.,
Tigard
(503) 639–8860

This largest mall on Portland's suburban westside is anchored by JC Penney, Sears, Nordstrom, and Meier & Frank. Along with these four giants, you'll find about one hundred different specialty shops stretching out for what seems like miles. The second floor houses a food court and additional specialty shops. You'll find almost anything you could ask for here, including the ubiquitous Starbucks, a Nordstrom coffee counter, and several ATMs. OMSI operates a retail store here, and so does The Real Mother Goose (see Gifts and Crafts in this chapter). Oregon's own Kobos Company sells beautiful kitchen things, as well as coffee. Outside the mall proper there is another cluster of stores, including a 24-hour Kinkos, a Barnes & Noble, Drug Emporium, and the amazing Cost Plus.

Woodburn Factory Stores
1001 Arney Rd., Woodburn
(Exit 271, Interstate 5)
(888) 664–SHOP

Thirty miles or so south of town lies the area's newest collection of factory stores,

Insiders' Tip

Many downtown merchants will validate your SmartPark parking slips if you spend $25 or more at their shop. It never hurts to ask.

and since its opening, it has been constantly busy. Is it because of the spectacular savings on merchandise from beloved stores such as Gap, Eddie Bauer, Banana Republic, Brooks Brothers, and Ralph Lauren? Or is it that the designers planned this mall with actual humans in mind, providing them with grass, benches, and large eaves to keep off rain and sun? Either way, this mall is a great place to stock up on shoes by Rockport, Timberland, and Adidas; cookware by Le Creuset and china by Lenox; kidware by Gap, Carter's, and Oshkosh; and pianos from the Piano Liquidators.

Shopping Districts

The soul of Portland shopping can be found in its shopping districts. Because the city organizes itself around its neighborhoods, the shopping and business districts play a vital role in creating neighborhood identity and atmosphere. It is possible to find neighborhood shopping so compelling and comprehensive that you won't want to leave your own turf. But that would be a mistake, because the variety of shopping districts gives insight into the character of Portland.

Shopping districts are clustered throughout the city, and we feature some of them below. In addition to those featured, you may want to explore the shopping center at John's Landing and its neighborhood along S.W. Macadam Boulevard, south of downtown; the Hollywood District, (its epicenter is N.E. Sandy and 41st); Beaumont Village, along N.E. Fremont between 40th and 50th; and the small collection of shops at S.E. 26th and Clinton. These little aggregates serve primarily the nearby residents, but they are worth prospecting. We encourage you to stroll whatever neighborhood you're in—unless you do a little fieldwork on your own, who knows what fine harvests are in store?

Alberta Street, Sabin Neighborhood, and Northeast Martin Luther King Jr. Blvd. (Northeast Portland)

The north end of town along Martin Luther King Jr. Blvd. (locally known as "MLK") is the focus of a major city revitalization project that includes business development, transportation plans, and new housing. Community banks, city government, and neighborhood groups have converged to make this area one of the most vital places in the city. This gentrification is not without controversy, and not every citizen thinks that opening a new Starbucks counts as progress. However, the true source of this renaissance is homegrown business: local art galleries, coffee shops, retail stores, and other businesses. Northeast Alberta Street features much of the growth. There you'll find the marvelous **Tumbleweed**, 1804 N.E. Alberta, with clothes for women and children made right there on-site; **Rosyln's Coffeeshop**, 1438 N.E. Alberta, which also features the **Shades of Color Gallery**, is a local must-stop; **Delila's Attic** and **Salvage Works Furniture**, 1520 N.E. Alberta, for cool bookshelves reclaimed from scrapped lumber and linoleum, as well as secondhand finds; **RAJ**, 1600 N.E. Alberta, for hip infant, toddler, and children's clothing. **Plain Jane**, 2936 N.E. Alberta, is an art gallery that also sells supercool home decor items; in fact, the number of art galleries in this area is astounding. For more about them, see The Arts chapter. Or you can explore them for yourself at Last Thursday, an artwalk held on Alberta Street the last Thursday of each month from 6 to 9 P.M. This monthly festival is something of a counterpoint to First Thursday, which takes place in the Pearl District. Both events will give you a picture of the spirit of these neighborhoods.

Nearby, you'll find the shiny new **Nike Outlet Store**, 2650 N.E. MLK Jr. Boulevard, as well as an **Adidas retail store** at 5020 N.E. MLK Jr. Boulevard. At the **Standard Dairy**, 2808 N.E. MLK Jr. Boulevard, you'll find a number of interesting shops, including **Vessels & Co.**, for tableware, **World Village/Diana's Boutique and Home Accent Gallery** for clothing and home decor, and for beautiful ethnic clothing, **Sheba House of Elegance**. **The Best of All Worlds**, 424 N.E. Killingsworth, also carries exquisite clothing, gifts, and home accents. **Reflections Coffee & Bookstore**, 446 N.E. Killingsworth Street, specializes in African-American books, cards, and gifts; it is also a literary center with readings, exhibits, and discussion groups. And try some sweet potato pie from **Mother Dear's Tasty Pastries**, 438 N.E. Killingsworth.

Belmont (Southeast Portland)

Belmont is just to the north of the Hawthorne District, but this mixed-use neighborhood has seen so much interesting growth in the past few years that it deserves attention on its own. Neighborhood highlights include **Seaplane**, 3356 S.E. Belmont, for cool clothes; and **Hollyhocks Garden Essentials**, 2707 S.E. Belmont, for wonderful pots and plants. The **Pied Cow**, 3244 S.E. Belmont, with its attractive patio, is a favorite for coffee during the day and a glass of wine and dessert in the evening. **The Tao of Tea**, 3430 S.E. Belmont, is a truly inspiring tea shop, worth a trip on its own; the owners also run the tea house at the Chinese Garden (see Attractions). Up the street you'll find **Belmont Station**, 4520 S.E. Belmont, which carries British specialty foods, microbrews, imported beers, and many beer-related gifts.

Broadway District (Northeast Portland)

Northeast Broadway is a lively east-west stretch of shops, cafes, and offices; its new bike-and-foot-friendly design has helped to make it one of the most enjoyable shopping districts in the city. Some—by no means all—of the major shopping attractions include **French Quarter Linens**, 1444 N.E. Broadway, which also has a day spa attached; **Matisse**, 1411 N.E. Broadway, and **Vergotis**, 1433 N.E. Broadway, for beautiful women's clothes; **Halo**, 1425 Broadway, for shoes to go with them; and **Papillon**, 1320 N.E.

A young downtown shopper stops to visit a well-clad sculpture. CREDIT: RACHEL DRESBECK

Broadway for the lingerie to go under them. **Broadway Books,** 1714 N.E. Broadway, is an active, independent bookstore that carries a fine selection of history, local writers, and children's literature. **Dava Bead and Trade,** 1512 N.E. Broadway, will supply all your beads, findings, and other materials; **Ceramica,** at 15th and Broadway, will supply you with pottery for you to paint and then they'll fire it for you. **Kitchen Kaboodle,** at N.E. 16th and Broadway, has been purveying fine kitchenware and Northwest-casual furniture for more than twenty-five years; the new shop **Goodnight Room,** 1517 N.E. Broadway, will outfit your child's room. Two unusual shops are also worth mentioning: **Memories—Dolls of Distinction,** at 1405 N.E. Broadway, not only sells dolls but also repairs them, and **mary anne's wordshop,** 1139 N.E. Broadway, not only sells the cards and artwork of its owner, mary anne m.b.l. radmacher, but offers classes in journal writing, creative writing, collage-making, and other wordy pursuits. The anchor of all this glittery commerce is the **Lloyd Center,** Oregon's first indoor mall.

Downtown (Southwest Portland)

Department stores, fashionable boutiques, and a couple of pedestrian malls (Pioneer Place and The Galleria; see above) are the highlights of downtown shopping. **Nordstrom,** 701 S.W. Broadway, needs no introduction; this downtown branch flanks the west side of Pioneer Courthouse Square and furnishes area residents with stylish clothes, shoes, and accessories. The full-service department store **Meier & Frank,** 621 S.W. 5th, is now owned by the May Department Stores but has been in Portland since 1857. During the holidays, Portland children line up patiently to visit the exquisitely jolly Santa here, and to ride the Santaland monorail and look at the animated window displays. On the north end of downtown, across Burnside from Powell's, you will find cutting-edge bookstores, resale and vintage shops, and record stores. **Reading Frenzy,** 921 S.W. Oak, is especially striking—its collection of alternative periodicals is unparalleled. And on the other end of downtown, the **Oregon History Center,** 1200 S.W. Park, has an excellent museum store that provides artwork, books, jewelry, gifts, and other Oregon-related items. **Johnny Sole,** 815 S.W. Alder, purveys Kenneth Cole shoes, Doc Martens, and other stylish footwear for damp Oregon weather. More downtown enticements include a large, new **Williams-Sonoma** at 5th and Morrison; **Kathleen's of Dublin,** 860 S.W. Broadway, for beautiful Celtic clothing, jewelry, china, and gifts; **Finnegan's,** 922 S.W. Yamhill, for toys and gifts; **Jane's Vanity,** 521 S.W. Broadway, for alluring underthings; **St. John Boutique,** 814 S.W. Broadway, for upscale women's clothing; and **Mercantile,** 735 S.W. Park, for the same plus home decor items. Two other notable clothing shops are **Moda,** 615 S.W. Park, for chic urban wardrobes and shoes for women, and **Mario's,** at 811 and 921 S.W. Morrison, which equips male and female Portlanders with Prada, Armani, Helmut Lang, and other top designers. (Repeat after me: no sales tax in Oregon.)

Hawthorne District (Southeast Portland)

The Hawthorne District is Portland's left-coast hip shopping area, where granola meets granita. **Powell's** on Hawthorne, 3723 S.E. Hawthorne, and **Powell's Books for Cooks,** 3747 S.E. Hawthorne, the eastside siblings of the City of Books, are complemented by the women's bookstore **In Other Words,** 3734 S.E. Hawthorne, across the street. If you've brought the little ones along, a stop at the toy store **Kids at Heart,** 3445 S.E. Hawthorne, is a must; then drag them to **Presents of Mind,** 3633 S.E. Hawthorne, to pick up a bijou for yourself—it has a play area for children so you can concentrate on the jewelry, photo albums, cards, and other trinkets. Cool, fairly traded rugs, clothing, and other imports are available at **Ten Thousand Villages,** 3508 S.E. Hawthorne. Music lovers will find Hawthorne especially fruitful. **Crossroads Music,** 3130-B S.E. Hawthorne, is a music seller's co-op, and the selection of recordings and equipment here is astonishing. **The CD/Game Exchange,** 1725 S.E. 36th, is a smaller venue with a great selection of used CDs. **Jackpot Records,** 3736 S.E. Hawthorne, and **Reverb Records,** 3623 S.E. Hawthorne, specialize in rare, independent, and avant-garde music, and both carry new and used recordings. **Artichoke Music,** 3130 A S.E. Hawthorne, will help you make music instead of merely listening to it; they carry musical instruments, as does **Guitar Crazy** at 1736 S.E. Hawthorne. Need something to wear? Try **Fyberworks,** 4300 S.E. Hawthorne, for casual, stretchy women's clothing. **M. Sellin,** 3556 S.E. Hawthorne, car-

Insiders' Tip

Sometimes shopping is hard on a person. If you're suffering, make an appointment at Urbaca, (503) 241-5030, 120 N.W. 9th, for a massage, facial, pedicure, or haircut. You'll feel a lot better afterward, we promise.

ries stylish women's clothing in natural fabrics, as well as wonderful accessories. **Imelda's,** 1431 S.E. 37th Avenue, is a destination shoe store for fashionistas all over town; **Red Light,** 3590 S.E. Hawthorne, brings the same crowd for vintage clothes. **Blue Butterfly,** 3646 S.E. Hawthorne, will provide that Summer of Love look. And **Lena Medoyeff,** 3206 S.E. Hawthorne, is the home port for designer Lynn Solomon and her lovely dresses, skirts, and other clothes; she's the kind of person that make natives proud of their city. Hawthorne is the earthier alternative to the slick Northwest 23rd: you're more likely to get a whiff of patchouli than Chanel No. 5, although the **Perfume House,** 3328 S.E. Hawthorne, can supply either one.

Multnomah Village (Southwest Portland)

Multnomah really does feel like a village—it is a tight-knit community in addition to its identity as a retail, coffee shop, and hang-out mecca. Adding to the cohesive feel is the wonderful **Multnomah Arts Center,** 7688 Capitol Highway, which is a Portland Arts and Recreation facility that holds classes in everything from acrylic painting to Zen flower arranging, and **Annie Bloom's Books,** 7834 S.W. Capitol Highway, an outstanding bookstore that draws people from all over the city. Other Village highlights are antique-related: there are about a dozen antique, collectible, and resale shops in the Village. **Multnomah Antique Gallery** has two locations, 7764 and 7784 S.W. Capitol Highway; **Toby's Antiques & Collectibles,** 7871 S.W. Capitol Highway, is a good source for old toys.

Northwest 23rd District

This upscale, trendy neighborhood includes a number of shops on 21st, but is known to Portlanders simply as Northwest 23rd. Filled with lovely Victorian homes and countless trees, this neighborhood is one of the prettier balances of the domestic and commercial in Portland, and it's a great walking neighborhood—the pedestrian traffic here is at times so uppity that it stops the automotive traffic. The foot traffic has created a democracy of fashion: the pierced hipsters sipping martinis at the Gypsy coexist comfortably with the bourgeois denizens dining at Wildwood, and that's because there is something for everyone. Chain representatives include the **Gap,** 2302 W. Burnside, **Urban Outfitters,** 2320 N.W. Westover, **Restoration Hardware,** 315 N.W. 23rd, and the **Pottery Barn,** 310 N.W. 23rd. But the local hybrids are the real draw. For cool kitchen tools and accessories for the house, stop at **Kitchen Kaboodle,** N.W. 23rd and Flanders. For the culture hound, there is the staggeringly comprehensive **Music Millennium West,** N.W. 23rd and Johnson, and the enlightened **Twenty Third Avenue Books,** at 1015 N.W. 23rd. If you're feeling underdressed, stop at **Elizabeth Street,** 635 N.W. 23rd (for women) and **Irving's** 2322 N.W. Irving (for men). **Mimi & Lena,** 823 N.W. 23rd, carry beautiful dresses, many of them locally designed. **Urbino,** 521 and 628 N.W. 23rd, will help you make over your house with some of the most stylish furniture and housewares around; **Cargo,** 806 N.W 23rd, carries exotic and fashionable imports to wear and live with. **Coreen Salome + Apothecary 23,** 808 N.W. 23rd, is the best product shop in town, not only supplying fashionistas with cosmetics from Bliss and brushes from Shu Uemura, but carrying harder-to-find lines such as Chantecaille, Diptyque, and Supersmile. **Girlfriends,** 904 N.W. 23rd, is the Portland branch of the hip San Francisco store that sells clothing and gifts for girls and their big sisters. On the edges of the district, **Ellington Leather Goods,** which sells its sleek handbags worldwide, has an outlet store at 1533 N.W. 24th. And be sure to visit **Norm Thompson,** 1805 N.W. Thurman, which not only sells nice clothes and gifts, but was also awarded a "Founders of a New Northwest" designation for its commitment to using sustainable building materials at its headquarters.

Pearl District

Colonized by starving artists, then domesticated by hipsters, the Pearl District is now becoming the home of the haute bourgeoisie. Evidence of all three classes is readily apparent in the Soho of Portland. Not only are there dozens of art galleries (and a gallery walk the first Thursday night of each month) and an art school (the Pacific Northwest College of Art, 1241 N.W. Johnson), but the housewares, art supplies, furniture, clothing, hardware, and even light fixtures for sale in the area have a distinctly aesthetic quality to them. For clothing, try **Aubergine,** 1100 N.W. Glisan, for chic women's wear; **Baddoll,** 815 N.W. Glisan, for ultra-trendy shoes; **Odessa,** 718 N.W. 11th, for Diane von Furstenburg dresses and Earl Jeans; and **Hanna Andersson,** 327 N.W. 10th, for colorful, comfortable clothes for children and their moms. **Richard Calhoun Old Town Florist,** 403 N.W. 9th has elegant flowers. **F.U.P.,** 1200 N.W. Everett, will provide you with beautiful modern furniture; **Le Passe,** 120 N.W. 9th, with beautiful antiques; **Hunt and Gather,** 1302 N.W. Hoyt, with beautiful custom couches. Many gift and decorating shops pervade the area: standouts include but are by no means limited to **What the Wind Blew In,** 1314 N.W. Glisan, **Fifth Element,** 404 N.W. 10th, and **Blue Pear,** 1313 N.W. Glisan. **Circa A.D.,** 1204 N.W. Glisan, is known for its lovely European furniture and art objects, and **Bernadette Breu,** 1134 N.W. Everett, for vintage decorative arts. Need curtains? Try **The Whole Nine Yards,** 1033 N.W. Glisan, for beautiful decorating fabric. And be sure to visit the landmark **Winks Hardware,** 903 N.W. Davis, for the stuff you'll need to hang your curtains. **Dieci Soli,** 304 N.W. 11th, sells gorgeous Italian tableware; **Oblation Papers,** 516 N.W. 12th, sells handmade cards, invitations, and blank books. If all this walking around is making you hungry, stop at the excellent **Pearl Bakery,** 102 N.W. 9th, which supplies many restaurants in town, or **Piazza Italia,** 1129 N.W. Johnson, for a tiny bit of North Beach. **In Good Taste,** 231 N.W. 11th, can give you cooking supplies and lessons, if you'd rather go home to eat. Watch for a new Patagonia store and other retail shops in the Ecotrust Building, a century-old riverside warehouse undergoing "green" renovation. And keep an eye on the Brewery Blocks north of Burnside between 11th and 12th, for the next major development. The Pearl covers a large amount of territory, so wear good walking shoes when you shop here.

Sellwood District (Southeast Portland)

Sellwood, one of Portland's most distinctive and historic neighborhoods, is brimming with charming antique stores, particularly in the area along S.E. 13th Avenue, which is known as Antique Row. Because the shopping area is so condensed, you can park your car and then get around on foot. Laced in between the dozen blocks of antiques and collectibles stores you'll find numerous delightful espresso shops and cafes.

Many shopkeepers hang signs on their buildings explaining their original use and date of construction, but our sources say that Sellwood has been known as Portland's antique source since the middle of the last century. Since Sellwood was once a city in its own right (annexed in 1890), pride in the neighborhood runs deep. One could easily spend a day or two checking out the many stores, and if you do, keep an eye out for **Preservation Hall Antiques,** 7919 S.E. 13th Avenue, for antiques and textiles; **Douglas Grant,** 1226 S.E. Lexington, for handsome, handmade furniture; and the **Handwerk Shop,** 8317 S.E. 13th, for Stickley chairs and custom Craftsman furniture. **The Jealous Gardener,** 8301 S.E. 13th, supplies excellent garden tools in addition to ornaments and everlastings; **Nature in the City,** 8011 S.E. 13th, is a prime source for birdbaths, gifts, and garden ornaments; and check out **Two Blossoms,** 8233 S.E. 13th, for custom botanical arrangements. **Folk Art Friends,** 8624 S.E. 13th, is a treasure trove of folk art and country primitives. **American at Art,** 8203 S.E. 13th, sells reproduction Americana. **Rara Avis,** 8121 S.E. 13th, sells lovely European pieces; **Southern Accents,** 7718 S.E.

13th, sells handcrafted furniture and other decor items; **Royal Antiques,** 8035 S.E. 13th, specializes in jewelry and glassware. **Hollyhock Lane,** 8309 S.E. 13th, is a fine source for linens and gifts. And **Calamity Jane,** 7908 S.E. 13th, is one of the best women's clothing shops in the city. (And while you're on that end of town, stop by the **Columbia Sportswear Outlet,** 1323 S.E. Tacoma, for great buys on last season's jackets.) The **Antique Row Cafe,** 8235 S.E 13th, will refresh you with delicious soups and sandwiches before you head over to the Milwaukie Avenue section of Sellwood, which is actually called Westmoreland. There, you will find the three branches of **Stars,** a behemoth of antiques and collectibles. Stars alone will take you a day to browse. They may be found at 7027 S.E. Milwaukie, 7030 S.E. Milwaukie, and 6717 S.E. Milwaukie. For things that no one else has owned before, two good bets are **On the Avenue,** a splendid gift shop at 7007 S.E. Milwaukie, which doubles as a DIY pottery-glazing center, and **Haggis McBaggis,** 6802 S.E. Milwaukie, for truly wonderful children's shoes and accessories. Haggis McBaggis is so family friendly that they encourage local parents to stop by and use the attractive bathroom if their kids need a diaper change. (See more about Haggis McBaggis in the Kidstuff chapter.) If you're not at the diaper-changing stage yet, but would like to be, **Tres Fabu,** on the corner of Milwaukie and Bybee, has very fabulous wedding gowns and everything to go with them. (Except maybe a groom.) If, on the other hand, you require some boots made for walking, check out **John Newbury Boots,** 1665 S.E. Bybee, for handmade ones.

Antiques

Portland is the home of many, many antique stores. Here is a sample of them.

1874 House
8070 S.E. 13th Ave.
(503) 233–1874

This store, in Portland's historic Sellwood neighborhood, is jammed with a potpourri of old plumbing fixtures, stained glass, antique brass lighting fixtures, moldings, brass and copper hardware, and architectural items. Whether you need things for your doors, windows, or bathroom fixtures, this is the place to browse to your heart's content.

Classic Antiques
1805 Martin Luther King Jr. Blvd.
(503) 231–8689

Fine antiques from Europe and the United States, in addition to locally designed contemporary furniture, make this outpost a destination for citywide shoppers. Lighting and decor items are also good buys here.

Le Passe
120 N.W. 9th Ave.
(503) 916–1717

Their motto: "you can never be too old or too French"—too true, when it comes to furniture. A soothing, aromatic, light space, Le Passe specializes in eighteenth and nineteenth-century furniture and the stuff to put on it.

Preservation Hall
7919 S.E. 13th Ave.
(503) 238–9912

A newer contribution to Antique Row, Preservation Hall presents an eclectic mixture of antiques, accent pieces, and wonderful textiles and linens. The owners, a mother and daughter team, buy things according to the principle of whether they like them, a principle that has so far been a sound one. This attractive shop also carries luxurious European bath soaps and other necessities.

RD Steeves Imports
209 N. Yamhill St. on OR Hwy. 47 and
335 W. Monroe and OR Hwy. 47, Carlton
(503) 852–6519

RD Steeves carries an exceptionally high-quality inventory of furniture and antiques. See the complete listing in the Home Repair and Decor section.

The Sellwood Antique Mall
7875 S.E. 13th Ave.
(503) 232–3755

The Sellwood Antique Mall is perfect for either the serious or frivolous collector. It has more than one hundred different dealers, so the inventory changes constantly. The mall is one of the largest of its kind in the city, carrying a wide range of items from furniture to dishes to lighting fixtures. It also carries a good amount of nostalgia items from the 1950s.

Sorel Vintages
3713 S.E. Hawthorne Blvd.
(503) 232–8482

Many of the pieces at Sorel Vintages date from the early to mid-twentieth century. The genius of this shop is its inventive combinations of furniture and decor, so enticing that even if you never thought about putting 1950s modern furniture in your Craftsman before, you'll start thinking about it now. Sorel Vintages also carries interesting gifts. Real eye candy.

Stars
7027 S.E. Milwaukie
(503) 239–0346

Stars & Splendid
7030 S.E. Milwaukie
(503) 235–5990

More Stars
6717 S.E. Milwaukie
(503) 235–9142

Three hundred dealers and 27,500 square feet of antique and collectible furniture, linens, books, clothes, jewelry, dishes, and tchotchkes are here for the perusal of the antique hunter. Because there are so many different dealers, the Stars empire cannot be comprehensively characterized, but you're more likely to find a country primitive sideboard than a Federalist one, although you never know. The managers are very good about display—this is one of the most attractive antique malls around.

Bargains and Thrift Stores

Did we mention there is no sales tax in Oregon? For more savings, check out the stores below, as well as the two factory store malls listed in the Malls section above. Vintage clothing, used books and records, and secondhand furniture are listed in their respective categories rather than in this section

City Liquidators
823 S.E. 3rd Ave.
(503) 238–1367

Kids of all ages have a ball rooting through the odd stuff at this big store, which is packed to the rafters with bargains. Most of the stuff isn't super-high quality, but City Liquidators does a decent job of screening out the junk. Some of the hardware and tools are priced very low, as are carpets, planters, small pieces of furniture, and kitchen gadget-type items. The second floor is the furniture warehouse, and some of it is quite good. We've seen many low prices on couches, armchairs, dining room and bedroom sets, futons, and much more. From pots and pans to entertainment centers and bookcases, City Liquidators offers everything you need to cheaply furnish a home or apartment. They also have a good selection of office furniture, equipment, and supplies.

Columbia Sportswear Outlet Store
1323 S.E. Tacoma
(503) 238–0118

3 Monroe Pkwy.
(503) 636–6596

It is worth the drive to Sellwood or Lake Oswego to pick up that parka, rain hat, or down vest you've been eyeing at the downtown store for 30 to 50 percent off the price. This nationally distributed sportswear line is Oregon's own; they supply L.L. Bean and other companies in addition to distributing their own gear. Their handsome flagship retail store can be found at 911 S.W. Broadway, downtown.

Goodwill Store
1943 S.E. 6th Ave.
(503) 238–6165

No doubt, this is the Nordstrom of local thrift stores. It's big and sparkling clean, and has gotten national recognition for its inventive advertising and cheerful atmosphere. We've looked at plenty of resale shops and found a lot of them to be depressing, overpriced, and understocked. That isn't the case here. The selection of men's, women's, and children's clothes is extensive and reasonably priced. You won't waste time weeding out stained shirts and zipperless pants either.

The books section is remarkably free of culls and very well organized. The turnover in just one day is astounding, and the constant stream of new items can make you dizzy. Besides clothes and books, there are plenty of domestic items—dishes, fabrics, odds and ends, wall decorations—and a music section with a ton of LPs. This Goodwill store even has a little snack bar that offers sandwiches, burgers, and salads.

Hanna Andersson Outlet Store
7 Monroe Pkwy., Lake Oswego
(503) 697–1953

The long johns, dresses, tights, clogs, and sportswear you and your children have come to know and love are here offered at a reduced price. Hanna Andersson is known for its high-quality, Swedish-style soft clothing in wonderful colors and patterns. (See below, in Clothing, and the Kidstuff chapter for more information.)

Nordstrom Rack
401 S.W. Morrison St.
(503) 299–1815

(Location) Clackamas Promenade, 8930 S.E. Sunnyside Rd., Clackamas
(503) 654–5415

Almost every savvy Portlander knows about "the Rack." This is the closest Portland comes to Filene's Basement in Boston, and while you probably won't see anyone trying on clothes in the aisles, there is no lack of competitive shopping. This basement store is filled with clearance merchandise from Nordstrom stores plus some additional stuff. You'll find men's and women's clothing and shoes, plus a changing assortment of accessories, picture frames, and perfumes. Prices can be as much as 70 percent below the full retail price.

Norm Thompson Outlet Store
Oregon Mail Order Outlet Store
9 Monroe Pkwy., Lake Oswego
(503) 697–2931

Next to the Columbia Sportswear Outlet Store, these stores are worth the extra effort to find. The Mail Order Outlet Store is a Norm Thompson spin-off, with an eclectic mix of clothes, accessories, gadgets, household goods, cleaning solutions, cookware, outdoor clothes, and other things from Norm's lesser-known catalogs, Early Winters and Solutions. Call for detailed directions.

Pendleton Woolen Mill Outlet Store
2 17th St., Washougal, Washington
(360) 835–1118

This woolen mill, founded in 1909 and the leading producer of the Pendleton line of woolen clothing, is one of the most popular walking tours of the Portland-Vancouver area. The Washougal site offers the largest of the Pendleton Mill outlet stores and features great savings on new apparel, closeouts, and factory seconds. The tours, which are offered weekdays and Saturdays, afford an opportunity to see the looming of their extraordinary line of woolen blankets, which are collectibles and are still sold in trading huts in the southwestern corner of the United States.

Books and Periodicals

Portland is a city of readers. We have the largest bookstore in the nation, Powell's City of Books, which is made even larger by the fact that it has a number of branches. However, Powell's can sometimes overshadow the other fine independent bookstores in the area, including interesting book selections at places like the Oregon History Center, Portland State University, or the Portland Audubon Society of Portland. We also have the usual national chain bookstores here in town.

Annie Bloom's Books
7834 S.W. Capitol Hwy.
(503) 246–0053

Tucked into the retail center of the Multnomah neighborhood, this store attracts loyal readers from throughout the area who appreciate the selection, the suggestions, and assistance of the well-read staff, as well as the cozy armchairs. The store is also well known beyond Portland proper for its Children's Corner, with books and a play area, and for its collection of titles on Judaism and Judaic culture and art. Annie Bloom's is frequently mentioned as a contender for Portland's favorite bookstore.

B Dalton Bookseller
1021 Lloyd Center
(503) 288–6343

Mall 205, 9900 S.E. Washington St.
(503) 255–5650

This national purveyor of quality books isn't a mega-store but carries an excellent variety of general interest books, a very good cross-section of magazines, and is known for being service oriented. If they don't have a book, they'll find who does or they will special order it for you.

B Dalton also carries an excellent selection of tourism and business books and is famous for its section of discounted hardback best-sellers. As an added bonus, both of these bookstores are located in malls and are surrounded by good places to eat.

Broadway Books
1714 N.E. Broadway
(503) 284–1726

If bigger, sprawling chain bookstores are a bit daunting, try Broadway Books. One of a long stretch of shops and cafes along a bustling avenue that is defining itself as one of Portland's most exciting mercantile zones, this neat little bookstore fits like a glove. As well as a good selection of literary works, it sponsors poetry readings and author book-signing events.

Cameron's Books and Magazines
336 S.W. 3rd Ave.
(503) 228–2391

Before there was Powell's—before there was any other bookstore in Portland—there was Cameron's. Tucked into a downtown storefront, Cameron's windows are filled with well-cared-for copies of *Life, Time, Look, Saturday Evening Post, Colliers,* and other publications from the era of the general-interest magazine. They also have back issues of *Sports Illustrated* and *Playboy* as well as a massive collection of comic books. Cameron's claims to have 100,000 magazines, mass-market paperbacks, and comics in stock, and to be the home of the birthday magazine gift.

Great Northwest Bookstores
1234 S.W. Stark St.
(503) 223–8098

With 150,000 or so books in stock, this is Portland's largest, exclusively used bookstore. Some of the books here seem to have barely been opened, so "used" is somewhat of a misnomer. There is a good rare book collection, a large selection of Western Americana and maps, old photographs, and what is called in the trade "ephemera"—booklets, menus, letters, handbills, and leaflets. The store is just up the street from Jake's (see our Restaurants chapter), so you can take your newly purchased treasures and enjoy them over an Irish coffee or a glass of wine.

In Other Words
3734 S.E. Hawthorne Blvd.
(503) 232–6003

Once inside this cheerful, cozy outlet for women's books and resources, you'll find a bounty of magazines, videos, cards, gifts, and new and used books. Open seven days a week, the store also sponsors readings and workshops.

Laughing Horse Books
3652 S.E. Division
(503) 236–2893

This unabashedly progressive and vibrant bookstore advertises itself as a resource for social change. Inside are new and used books devoted to political issues, a bulletin board listing meetings and workshops held by local political action groups, and a gathering space where poets and authors read from their works and actors perform.

The Looking Glass Bookstore
318 S.W. Taylor St.
(503) 227–4760

In the more than thirty years that The Looking Glass Bookstore has been open, it's been the most successful of the downtown bookstores. It offers a well-chosen selection of new books, both paperback and hardcover, and if it doesn't have what you want in stock, the staff can find it and get it to you. The store has an intriguing selection of magazines and journals and an excellent selection of note cards, including those by Oregon and other Northwest artists. The poster selection,

displayed high on the walls, is also noteworthy. If you're visiting in the early spring, look for the annual wildflower mini-poster. The Looking Glass has been doing this promotion for years (you'll see past issues framed throughout the store), and these free oversize cards are nice enough to bring home as a souvenir.

Murder by the Book
3210 S.E. Hawthorne Blvd.
(503) 232–9995

As the name implies, this bookstore is devoted to mysteries—hard-boiled, tea-cozy, police procedural—name your poison and you'll find it here. There are $1 books on sale at the door, shelves of used books, and the newest releases in both hardbound and paperback. Patrons of this unique shop get a newsletter announcing new releases and readings by mystery authors.

Periodicals Paradise
3315 S.E. Hawthorne Blvd.
(503) 234–6003

This is a well-organized library/warehouse of vintage and new magazines. With a million issues in stock, it is said to be the largest collection on the West Coast. The prices on late-issue magazines are discounted about 75 percent from the regular retail price. We warn you, though—it's easy to lose track of time in this place, especially if you're a reader and love magazines.

Powell's City of Books
1005 W. Burnside St.
(503) 228–4651
www.powells.com

Powell's is getting pretty close to an empire. (And yes, there is a Powell: Michael Powell is the mind and the will behind Powell's growth, positioning, and well-known civic involvement.) With more than a million books in a store covering several levels in a building filling an entire city block, Powell's is the largest bookstore in the country. It even has its own (small) parking garage. Powell's has become an attraction in its own right and really does deserve a visit . . . or two . . . or three. This is a maze of a store, so pick up a map as you enter. Sections are color-coded, and there are plenty of signs to direct you. The staff is helpful, courteous, and knowledgeable in case you have to ask directions.

You'll find both used and new books and a separate rare book room. There are books in other languages besides English, and not surprisingly, a small selection of reading glasses. Powell's also has an excellent children's section as well as a selection of cards, blank journals, and other papery things. The Anne Hughes Coffee Room, with its coffee, tea, and snacks, would be a good place to look through potential purchases if one weren't always getting distracted by the interesting people wandering in and out of the room. The frequent literary readings are a big draw. Powell's is open every day of the year and is usually busy, if not downright crowded; there are other sites at the airport and in Beaverton, 8725 S.W. Cascade, in addition to the other branches listed below. If you're looking for science- and technology-related items, visit the nearby Powell's Technical Bookstore, 33 N.W. Park. Powell's Books for Cooks and Gardeners, 3747 S.E. Hawthorne Boulevard, is devoted to cooking and gardening books, and they have a comprehensive selection of these, as well as tools, toys, and crafted artifacts. It's a great spot to track down a birthday or holiday gift for those who like to cook or garden, or practically anybody else. Powell's Bookstore on Hawthorne, 3723 S.E. Hawthorne Boulevard, is a general-interest bookstore; it is smaller and perhaps, based on its scale, more user-friendly. This branch also sponsors weekly readings by writers, poets, and performance artists.

Powell's online service is incredibly well organized and useful. Don't tell them, but a lot of people look up the books that interest them before they get to the store. It helps make the experience less overwhelming.

Powell's Travel Store
S.W. 6th Ave. and S.W. Yamhill St.
(503) 228–1108

This tasty little bookstore on the southeast corner of Pioneer Square is laden with books, maps, packs, flashlights, and other travel paraphernalia. Whether you are planning an actual trip overseas, into the canyonlands, or up to the Arctic, or you are just suffering from wanderlust, stop by this handy info outlet. They also have a currency exchange.

Reading Frenzy
921 S.W. Oak
(503) 274–1449

Reading Frenzy, which specializes in publications by independent presses, sells things that you can't find anywhere else in Portland, and sometimes, anywhere else in the world. In addition to a fine selection of smart magazines, this shop carries locally and nationally published zines, literary quarterlies, and attractively published essays by people like Noam Chomksy. Reading Frenzy also serves as a meeting and distribution place for all kinds of alternative causes.

Title Wave
216 N.E. Knott
(503) 248–5021

The bookstore for discards from the Multnomah County Library, Title Wave is so good that we don't even really want to tell you about it. Prices start at about seventy-five cents for paperbacks and $1 for hardbound books; they go up from there—but not by much.

Tower Records Videos Books
Gateway Shopping Center,
102nd Ave. and N.E. Halsey St.
(503) 253–3116

Tower is perhaps better known for its music and videos, but you'll have to see the books and magazines to believe their wide selection. This store, Tower's only Oregon bookstore, operates as an independent in that they order all their own inventory largely based on customer feedback, so they have especially in-depth sections on science fiction, music, and popular culture. They also have a ton of books dealing with Portland and the Pacific Northwest. Tower, which is open 365 days of the year from 9 A.M. until midnight, also carries one of the top magazine selections in the entire state—with 3,000 different titles on the racks—and offers the largest selection of children's and young adult's books on the east side.

Twenty-third Avenue Books
1015 N.W. 23rd Ave.
(503) 224–5097

An excellent neighborhood shop for new books and periodicals like the *New York Review*, Twenty-third Avenue Books carries a general selection of books rather than specializing. However, it's a very good place to hear writers talk because the space is comfortable and intimate. It's much better to see Helen Schulman or David Sedaris here than on the stage at the Schnitz.

U.S. Government Bookstore
1305 S.W. Jefferson St.
(503) 221–6217

Don't laugh, this is a fascinating place. Not only does this store have books on an incredible range of topics, but there is also a great selection of posters, maps, and charts on everything from national parks to endangered wildlife to wildflowers. Right in the heart of Portland's Financial District, the store attracts lunchtime browsers as well as serious researchers, lawyers, government workers, writers, and the occasional conspiracy theorist. The history, foreign language, and travel sections (where else can you get a CIA country study to prepare for your next overseas trip?) are filled with unusual, valuable, and interesting works not found anywhere else.

Insiders' Tip

Why not check out the *Portland Tribune's* Jill Spitznass for intelligent and fresh fashion writing?

Waldenbooks
Clackamas Town Center,
12000 S.E. 82nd Ave.
(503) 659–3138
Lloyd Center, 9th Ave. and N.E. Halsey St.
(503) 284-9144

This eighty-year-old national chain is known for providing excellent customer service in its bookstores, as the staff is assigned to sections they specialize in. Walden's carries upwards of 100,000 titles and a ton of magazines and book-related gifts such as calendars and reading pillows. Inventory covers the gamut, but the store carries a lot of local interest books on subjects such as art, travel, music, history, and guidebooks. Waldenbooks, which is open seven days a week, also has a large selection of bargain books—a huge section of mostly hardbacks and gorgeous coffee-table books that are slashed up to 80 percent off.

Wallace Books
7241 S.E. Milwaukie Blvd.
(503) 235–7350

Just a couple blocks south of the Moreland business district with its cluster of great restaurants, antique malls, and small town shops, Wallace Books is an old house with bookshelves in every room. It's fun to browse upstairs and down to find the words you want to snuggle with later as the day winds down. The store has the newest releases as well as lots of new and used genre paperbacks.

Here's a list of other bookstores in Portland:

Barnes & Noble
1231 N.E. Broadway Ave.
(503) 335–0201

A Children's Place
4807 N.E. Fremont
(503) 284–8294

Borders Books & Music
708 S.W. 3rd Ave.
(503) 220–5911

New Renaissance
1338 N.W. 23rd Ave.
(503) 224–9995

Clothing

Calamity Jane
7908 S.E. 13th Ave.
(503) 235–3467

Since 1992, Calamity Jane has been supplying Portland women with clothes and accessories that are romantic and whimsical as well as simple and stylish. Their merchandise reflects the rustic-hip store showroom that occupies a funky, plank-floored, antique building in Sellwood. The shop supports local designers and carries a wide range of sizes so that all women can wear these artistic dresses, pants, skirts, and tops. Customers say that Calamity Jane makes it simple to look pulled together, not only because the clothes are great, but also because of the jewelry, shoes, and hats. The buyers have excellent taste and the service is outstanding, garnering an incredibly loyal clientele from all over the city.

Hanna Andersson
327 N.W. 10th Ave.
(503) 321–5275

Portland is headquarters for this nationally successful catalog shop featuring Swedish-style, high-quality clothing for kids and their moms. Designs are often, but not exclusively, made with cotton jersey. The underwear and pajamas are especially cozy and comfortable; and the clothes wear very well, through at least two children, and so are a good value. The store is clean, light, and wholesome. This civic-minded company passes along gen-

tly used Hannas to needy children—isn't that a good reason to shop here?

Langlitz Leathers
2443-A S.E. Division St.
(503) 235–0959

Over the past fifty years, Langlitz Leathers has forged a worldwide reputation for crafting the highest quality leather garments. Their shop is small—less than 3,000 square feet—and crowded. They have a total of fifteen people working in an old, crusty building with hundreds of garments hanging around. Far from snobby, they welcome visitors and will be happy to show you every aspect of how they create custom leathers. Langlitz only creates about six garments per day. Half are custom built, and the others are built to stock pattern sizes for walk-in customers. Because their prices are relatively low for custom work (between $500 and $1,000 per garment), their services are in constant demand. They have different products, but the Columbia was the first jacket Ross Langlitz designed in the mid-1940s and it remains the flagship of their jacket line, reflecting the traditional look of motorcycling in the middle of the century.

Mako
732 N.W. 23rd Ave.
(503) 274–9081

Here's a chance for kids of all ages to enliven their wardrobes. Mako carries hand-knit cotton sweaters and also sells leggings, T-shirts, and fancy socks, none of which would ever make it to JC Penney's.

Mario's
Men's Store: 921 S.W. Morrison St.
(503) 227–3477

Women's Store: 811 S.W. Morrison St.
(503) 241–8111

Mario's is the best source in town for urbane designer clothing, shoes, and accessories. Some readers may be familiar with the clean, spare luxury of the Mario's in Seattle, but this one is the original; it was one of the first residents of The Galleria and therefore may be regarded as a chief contributor to the beautification of downtown—and its residents. In 1999, the women's store underwent a stunning renovation; something similar is planned for the men's store in the near future.

Matisse
1411 N.E. Broadway
(503) 287–5414

While Matisse does carry chic everyday clothes, many women shop here for the evening clothes, which are flowing things made out of gorgeous fabrics in flattering styles. Savvy Portlanders choose this shop for their Academy or National Book Awards dresses, and when they do, they can be confident that not only will their clothes be beautiful and stylish, but they won't look like everybody else either. Matisse also sells lovely shoes and jewelry, and they always have a little basket of markdowns right outside the door.

Moda
615 S.W. Park
(503) 227–6522

Tucked away on a downtown side street, Moda's merchandise belies its location because there's nothing obscure about the clothes here, which include sophisticated urban daywear and more. Actually, the shoes are a big draw for this store— they carry beautiful Italian shoes from lines such as Donald Pliner. It's conve-niently sited across the street from the new Westin, so if any of you are staying there, don't miss this shop.

M. Sellin
3556 S.E. Hawthorne Blvd.
(503) 239–4605

M. Sellin's strong suit is stylish women's clothing in natural fibers (mostly—a little Lycra is a good thing). This Hawthorne Boulevard boutique also carries a sampling of fashionable shoes, luscious accessories, and products by Bliss. Easy dressing is the principal look—cotton skirts, linen pants, handknit sweaters, and pretty summer dresses are typical of this shop, but you can also find nicely draping jackets and other, more structured pieces. M. Sellin thoughtfully provides a basket of toys to occupy the little ones while you decide whether mauve is really your color.

Norm Thompson Outfitters
1805 N.W. Thurman St.
(503) 221–0764

Norm Thompson is probably best known outside of Portland for its catalogs. Some believe that the store is the real Norm Thompson, and the catalog is just a poor shadow of reality. The company is trying to change the demographics of its customers, particularly mail-order customers, to reach a younger audience. Even if the catalog may not be your thing, the store, which filled with classic wool, leather, silk, cashmere, and cotton clothing for men and women, is worth a visit. There are shirts, sweaters, vests, blouses, skirts, scarves, gloves, ties, pants, slacks and trousers, and bathrobes. You'll find a large offering of specialty food items, including imported and domestic cookies, pastas, and chocolates. Norm Thompson also carries a nice range of pricey gadgets and adult toys, including a sleek Porsche-designed, leather-covered portable radio for about $150. There's also a Norm Thompson Outlet Store in Lake Oswego (see listing in the Bargains and Thrift Stores section of this chapter).

Odessa
718 N.W. 11th Ave.
(503) 223-1998

Odessa, in the Pearl District, sells fashionable clothes with a downtown feel; they have a good eye for singular pieces with distinctive lines. Most lines are from New York, London, and Los Angeles, and they include Katayone, Adeli, and Jane Mayle. Odessa has beautiful evening clothes but also carries beguiling everyday clothes for the fashionista, such as Petite Bateau T-shirts and Earl Jeans. You'll find some shoes and handbags, as well.

Papillon
1320 N.E. Broadway
(503) 284-1023

The truly chic have underthings as nice as their outerwear. This tiny shop on Broadway furnishes women with the choicest lingerie from Lejaby, Chantelle, Frou Frou, and Cotton Club. Papillon is also a good place to obtain Wolford tights.

Portland Pendleton Shop
900 S.W. Taylor St.
(503) 242-0037

On the east side of the Standard Insurance Building, this store offers the most complete collection of Pendleton clothing for men and women in all of Oregon. Despite fashion's follies and foibles, Pendleton has always offered classic styles for men and women and excellent value. They've updated their clothing lines with a more contemporary look while retaining their well-known fabrics and colors. In addition to clothing, the store carries an excellent selection of blankets and pillows with dramatic designs and colors based on Western and Native American art and symbols.

Red Light
3590 S.E. Hawthorne Blvd.
(503) 963-8888

Some of the best vintage clothing in Portland is found in this large, trendy shop, in addition to resale modern clothes from BCBG, Betsy Johnson, Urban Outfitters, and Bébé. The vintage selection is comprehensive and reasonably priced, with everything from slips to coats. Men and women alike will find wonderful old leather jackets, evening wear, sweaters, and, well, everything you could imagine.

Savvy Plus
3204 S.E. Hawthorne Blvd.
(503) 231-7116

Definitely a one-of-a kind shop, Savvy Plus specializes in high-quality women's clothes size twelve and up. Most of the apparel is created using natural fibers and made in the good old U.S.A. They also carry some unusual jewelry that is handcrafted by local artisans who thrive in the busting Hawthorne area. Ask if they have a sale rack; they mark down selected items almost every month.

Florists, Nurseries, and Greenhouses

The Jealous Gardener
8301 S.E. 13th Ave.
(503) 231-4500

If you're looking for something to inspire envy in your gardening neighbors, this shop is for you. Owner Chris Bolesky says that it's the motivating kind of jealousy that draws gardeners to her pretty shop in Sellwood, which sells choice garden tools and garden accessories. Even if you're not a gardener, however, you are sure to find something botanical to spruce up the house; the shop carries an extensive array of garden-related gifts, which are sure to inspire you to get out and start digging.

Plant Peddler
3022 E. Burnside St.
(503) 233-0384

This popular plant store isn't huge, but they might sell as many ferns as anybody in town. That's why they can price a vigorously healthy fern or spider plant in a 6-inch pot at a mere $6.99. They also have a wide variety of potted flowers in stock, all for much more reasonable prices than you'll find in a regular florist's shop. These are really nice folks who seem to love people as much as they do plants, and they also carry the largest inventory of rare and unusual cactus plants in Portland. Prices are so low here you won't always find a sale going on. But if you're in a nurturing mood and see a droopy plant, ask if they'll knock a buck off. They try to keep inventory moving and like to find a home for every plant.

Portland Nursery
5050 S.E. Stark St.
(503) 231–5050

9000 S.E. Division
(503) 788–9000

This is one of the highest quality nurseries in the area, with a fine, well-organized selection of trees, shrubs, plants, bulbs, seeds, and supplies in two Portland locations. On a sunny Saturday morning in April, you are sure to run into half the people you know, all doing what you are doing. The staff really knows their stuff, so if you don't have a green thumb, ask questions; they have information counters set up for this.

Richard Calhoun Old Town Florist
403 N.W. 9th Ave.
(503) 223–1646

Before anybody was in the Pearl District, Richard Calhoun was—this urban pioneer was one of the first to appreciate the possibilities of the district. The shop is now owned by Wendi Day, who upholds the firm's outstanding reputation for high-design, Asian-inspired floral arrangements. Richard Calhoun supplies the flowers for many of the major spaces and events in the city, but they will also do flowers for your own house or event, so don't be shy about asking. The shop carries some handsome garden accessories and fountains in addition to its made-to-order arrangements.

Two Blossoms
8235 S.E. 13th Ave.
(503) 236–6111

Working with a blend of fresh and dried botanical elements, Two Blossoms designs and crafts beautiful arrangements for the office, house, and event (weddings, in particular). This tiny shop in Sellwood also carries wreaths, jewelry, skin-care lines, and other gifts, but their major contribution to Portland is their exquisite custom work.

Food

Along with the usual chain supermarkets such as **Albertsons**, **Safeway**, **Thriftway**, and **Fred Meyers**, Portland is also home to a variety of Korean, Vietnamese, Japanese, Lebanese, Mexican, Russian, and German stores and delis. **Nature's Northwest Grocery** specializes in organic and natural foods; they are now part of the Wild Oats chain and have stores scattered throughout the city. **Trader Joe's**, the California-based chain, has four stores here: look for them in Portland at 4715 S. E. 39th Avenue and in the Hollywood District at 4218 N.E. Sandy Boulevard; and in Beaverton, 11753 S. W. Beaverton Hillsdale Highway, as well as Lake Oswego, 15391 S. W. Bangy Road, next to the Ethan Allen Furniture Gallery.

The Hawthorne District offers everything to feed the body and the mind. CREDIT: RACHEL DRESBECK

The Bee Co.
800 N. Killingsworth St.
(503) 283–3171

This place always carries some good values, and sometimes offers some great deals on everything from breakfast cereal to California wines to navy beans. The Bee offers substantial discounts (often 20 to 40 percent) off a wide range of items including canned goods, salsas and sauces, cereals and snacks, soaps and household products, and all kinds of beverages and juices. When you go to The Bee, you take potluck. We've seen some very good wines selling there for low, low prices. They also sell milk, yogurt, and cheese products, and a variety of hot dogs and sandwich meats such as sliced ham and turkey breast. They always carry a large selection of coffee, tea, jellies, mustards, condiments, pickles, olives, and spices. The Bee is no giant, but it's a very worthwhile adventure—and you'll never get stung by high prices.

Bob's Red Mill
5209 S.E. International Wy., Milwaukie
(503) 654–3215

If you are into 100 percent stone-ground flours, Bob's Red Mill is an absolute must-stop. When their painstakingly restored, turn-of-the-century grist mill burned in an arson fire, Bob Moore and his wife and business partner Charlee built up an amazing national business from the once relatively small retail operation. But although Bob's Red Mill is now a giant, it still does things the old fashioned way. The huge, 120-year-old millstones they salvaged from the fire still operate twenty-four hours a day, grinding out every grain under the sun—into flours, cereals, meals, farinas, and cracks. Bob's Red Mill is also a certified organic processor and carries a vast amount of organic whole grain products. Their goods—which are free of chemicals, additives, and preservatives—are also kosher certified by the Rabbinical Council of America. Ask for a tour of the plant, which is on a gorgeous, landscaped setting complete with a duck pond, and stop at the attractive and well-organized on-site retail store for everything from rice, beans, nuts, seeds, milk powders, pastas, dried fruits, sweeteners, and other related products, in either bulk or small packages. Bob Moore still works at his plant most days—he's easy to spot because he looks just like the picture on his products—and he'll gladly take the time to answer your questions or show you around.

Insiders' Tip

Surrounded by fertile plains and valleys, Portland has access to a rich source of small, local farms that will deliver organic produce each week to a location near your house. These subscription farms are good for the community too. For more information, check out the USDA's Web site that lists farms in Oregon: www.nal.usda.gov/afsic/csa/states/ORfarm.htm.

In Good Taste
231 N.W. 11th Ave.
(503) 248–2015

Gayle Jolley, who for years taught cooking classes at Sheridan (see below), opened this industrial-chic cooking arena in the Pearl District in 1999. Not only will you find the best, professional-quality cookware here, but you will also find specialty foods and a great wine selection. A bridal registry is available. But people really come here for the cooking classes taught by excellent local chefs. In Good Taste also offers full-service catering and a lunchtime bistro to refresh those hungry Pearl District shoppers.

New Seasons
1214 S.E. Tacoma
(503) 230–4949

7300 S.W. Beaverton-Hillsdale Hwy.
(503) 292–6838

After the formerly locally owned Nature's was sold and resold to big corporations, the original owners apparently missed having stores that were integral parts of neighborhood communities and driven by local interests. Thus, they founded New Seasons, which is designed to help bring back the local to seasonal and organic food. New Seasons is a full-service grocery store that features natural and organic foods, with exceptional produce and takeout in addition to traditional groceries, wine, and health and beauty aids. Moreover, the service is remarkably friendly and knowledgeable. Plans are well underway to add more stores.

Pastaworks
3735 S.E. Hawthorne Blvd.
(503) 232–1010

735 N.W. 21st
(503) 221–3002

Pastaworks makes fabulous fresh pasta and sauces right on-site, from light-as-air fettuccine to superbly flavorful ravioli. But Pastaworks is not only for pasta—it also sells everything you need to go with it, from the best produce to the most exquisite cheeses to the choicest organic meat. You'll find many local and imported specialty items are here, including truffled olive oils from Italy and melt-in-your-mouth ginger cookies from Sweden. Wines are also a strong suit of the store; the Hawthorne branch offers tastings, as well as a fine selection of stemware, cookware, and cooking classes. In addition, there are a few tables outside where you can sit with coffee and rolls while you watch people buy flowers from the Hawthorne Flower Girl, who plies her floral trade right outside.

Sheridan Fruit Co.
408 S.E. 3rd Ave.
(503) 236–2114

Sheridan Fruit Co. is another Portland institution, offering many unusual herbs, exotic plants, and vegetables. It's a big, fun, bustling place to visit, and many people come to the Sheridan market from all around the Portland-Vancouver area. Sheridan's is known for its produce, but also carries an excellent selection of pasta, wine, meat, and cheese. Sheridan's also has a vast bulk section—and they make good espresso, too.

Gifts and Crafts

African Rhythm Traders
825 N.E. Broadway
(503) 288–6950

This is a unique, fascinating store in the bustling Broadway District that offers many food, art, and craft items imported directly from Africa. Here's a sample of the goods: batik tie-dye fabrics, Holland and Java prints, Mud cloth, Sad George fabric, and a variety of stunningly elegant handmade jewelry.

Daisy Kingdom
134 N.W. 8th Ave.
(503) 222–9033

There is no place on earth like Daisy Kingdom, a fabric store that specializes in the special. Daisy Kingdom is beloved by quilters, home decorators, brides, and parents-to-be for their vast selection of beautiful and unusual fabrics and everything to go with them. An entire section is devoted to calico alone. In addition, they carry some ready-to-wear clothes, as well as accessories, decor items, and gifts. Children think that nothing on earth is as boring as looking at fabric, so Daisy Kingdom thoughtfully provides a playroom where you can deposit them.

Kathleen's of Dublin
860 S.W. Broadway
(503) 224–4869

This is a wonderful shop with a staff that is helpful and knowledgeable about their wares, which include Irish woolen sweaters and vests, linen shirts, and statues of St. Patrick. The shop is usually filled with the haunting sounds of Celtic music, ranging from the mournful wail of the pipes to IRA drinking songs and New Age melodies based on centuries-old music.

mary anne's wordshop
1139 N.E. Broadway
(503) 284–4212

The Portland outpost of writer and calligraphy artist mary anne m.b.l. radmacher, this shop not only offers mary anne's cards, journals, posters, and specialty papers, but also offers a whole course catalog of special classes. The courses include everything from photo journaling to collage making to creative writing; they are very reasonably priced and taught by Ms. radmacher herself and other fine local artists. This is a splendid place to explore the convergence of artistic media.

Memories—Dolls of Distinction
1405 N.E. Broadway
(503) 284–9198

This shop is unlike any other in Oregon, for not only does it sell antique, custom-made, reproduction, and collectible dolls, but it also serves as a doll hospital. Look here for Ginny and Madame Alexander dolls, antique dolls with porcelain heads, and contemporary dolls made by artists. The shop also conducts classes in doll making and supplies the greenware and other things you'll need to make them. Suzanne Wilson, the owner, can perform appraisals too.

Menagerie Works
2515 S.E. 22nd Ave.
(503) 231–8647

Want to buy a unique, gallery-quality gift without dropping a bundle? Stop in at Menagerie Works, which is a workshop rather than a retail business. Doug Cooper blends the ancient craft of sand casting with modern volume-based die-casting technology. Menagerie Works, a tiny business that Cooper jump-started in his basement in 1990, creates metal sculpture gifts for the home, lawn, and garden. In the early days, when castings came back from the foundry, Cooper hand-filed the burred edges down himself until they were smooth, and during the Rose Festival, he sold his goods out of a Made in Oregon tent. Today, Menagerie Works's plant hangers, shelf brackets, mailbox supports, and door knockers are featured in catalogs such as Norm Thompson, Country Store, Earthmade, L.L. Bean, and Plow and Hearth. Cooper is an incredible stickler about quality, so anything scratched or nicked is sold as a "second" and marked down. The designs of his first four products, castings of a duck, fish, rabbit, and horse, are still among our favorites, but we give our top vote to his elegant bronze heron door knockers.

The Real Mother Goose
901 S.W. Yamhill St.
(503) 223–9510

Visit this store! The Real Mother Goose is an eclectic cross of art gallery, potter's guild, and jewelry store—actually, that's a very limited description. Venture inside and you'll find fine-crafted silver and gold jewelry, glass and pottery lamps, vases, dishes, and art objects as well as a small selection of handmade clothing. The furniture gallery in the downtown store features sophisticated, one-of-a-kind pieces done in fine and rare woods. The quality of design and construction are superb. If you would like something to carry home, look over the display of wooden boxes. You can imagine what this place is like during the holiday shopping season. There are three stores in all—one at the airport, where the selection is a little more limited, one in the Washington Square Shopping Center, and this original store in downtown.

Uncommon Treasures
3526 S.E. Hawthorne Blvd.
(503) 234–4813

This shop is hard to categorize, so we won't. We'll just say it is brimming with jewelry, gifts, and art from the past and present. These one-of-a-kind gifts items are created by everyone from nearby neighborhood artisans to sculptors in the far regions of Siberia, and many items are priced in the $20 to $40 range. It's fun just to walk around, poke into the shop's nooks and crannies, and find treasures ranging from regional totems to mythological hand-carved dragons to an array of whimsical mechanical wooden toys. You will also find a diverse collection of jewelry encompassing Celtic, Native America, artisan, amber, and vintage pieces. Peter Diehl, the shop's owner, is usually on the premises, and he's knowledgeable and fun to visit with. Ask him about the hand-crafted Celtic torques, the matched pair of peacock champagne flutes, or the hand-carved nesuke and he'll give you an earful.

Yarn Garden
1413 S.E. Hawthorne Blvd.
(503) 239–7950

We should all honor our work by using the best materials available, and if knitting is your work, Yarn Garden is the place for the best tools. Luscious yarns in every weight, color, and texture, needles, patterns—all your knitting needs are served here. The staff is so knowledgeable and helpful for beginners and experienced knitters alike that you'll find half the afternoon has passed before you know it. They are open on Wednesday evenings until 8 P.M.; that's when they hold knitting circles at which you can solicit and receive advice, trade ideas, or meet other knitters. Yarn Garden also has a good selection of books.

American at Heart
8203 S.E. 13th Ave.
(503) 235–5115

Though it is in Antique Row, American at Heart actually sells top-quality reproductions of eighteenth-century and Shaker-style American furniture. They offer an attractive signature pencil-post bed made here in Oregon, as well as beautiful Shaker boxes, some of which are as large as coffee tables. Room after room of lamps, rugs, decor items, and gifts will also draw your hand to your wallet. So will the Walnettos by the register.

Cargo
806 N.W. 23rd Ave.
(503) 241–3532

Those pictures in *Elle Decor* of lofts decorated with tansu chests and Indian saris have always looked appealing, but where do you get the saris and tansu chests to decorate with? In Portland, you get them at Cargo, which is a kind of upscale Cost Plus with many beautiful imports, mainly from India and Asia. High-quality silk pillows, baskets, wooden tea chests, bamboo blinds, and so on are all here, as well as sake sets and chopsticks. Cargo is also an excellent place for gifts.

Chrisman Picture Frames
8002 S.E. 13th Ave.
(503) 235–3287

2912 S.E. Burnside St.
(503) 231–7462

The staff at these Chrisman stores is extremely friendly and helpful for the do-it-yourselfers. They will cut the frame, mat, and glass, as well as advise you in the best way to frame your artwork. They offer a good selection of ready-made frames, as well as the inexpensive "uniframes" that clip the poster or art onto glass without a frame. They also have frequent sales, reducing the price of custom framing by 15 to 20 percent.

Dieci Soli
304 N.W. 11th Ave.
(503) 222–4221

If you can't afford to rent a villa in Tuscany for the month of April, you can always shop here for colorful Italian dishes, table linens, and bedding and just pretend you're there. Here you'll find majolica ceramics, Renaissance Deruta designs, and modern Italian decor. While they specialize in Italian designs, they are also starting to carry more things from Provence. One of our friends told her husband that anything from this store at any time for any occasion would be fine with her, so you may be glad to know that they have a bridal registry too, with which to train husbands and others.

French Quarter Linens
1444 N.E. Broadway
(503) 282–8200

536 N.W. 14th Ave.
(503) 223–3879

You spend one third of your life in bed—shouldn't you be comfortable while you're there? French Quarter Linens thinks so, and to that end, they sell the accoutrements to make it happen. Sumptuous European linens are the specialty here, woven with heirloom quality out of the finest linen and cotton threads, in classic patterns. They supply the best hypoallergenic down pillows, duvets, and featherbeds that money can buy. They also offer wine tastings, which may seem incongruous at first, but makes sense when you think about it; in addition, the knowledgeable staff will help you learn to care for all these exquisite things in case you spill red wine on them. French Quarter is inspired not just by Europe but by New Orleans, and many of their bedroom looks evoke that colorful city. Their Broadway location has a day spa.

Full Upright Position (F. U. P.)
1200 N.W. Everett
(503) 228–6190

Usefully located in the land of lofts, Full Upright Position specializes in modern furniture from Eileen Gray, Eames, Neo, and all the great modern classic designers, as well as adding to the pantheon themselves. Here you'll find pieces like the Marshmallow Sofa by the American designer George Nelson, as well as groovy Aalto chairs. Notable also is F.U.P.'s own signature sofa, which is so well designed that it can adapt itself to any interior—really.

The Handwerk Shop
8317 S.E. 13th Ave.
(503) 236–7870

A lovely shop with exceptionally competent and informed staff, The Handwerk Shop is one of the best sources for Mission furniture to go with your Craftsman. Owners Brent and Linda Willis specialize in American Arts and Crafts furniture, particularly in the style of Gustav Stickley. While they sell the original lines, they are true to the movement by making much of the furniture themselves by hand: this is primarily a custom operation. They also sell the fabrics, pottery, and lamps to go with their designs.

Hippo Hardware and Trading Company
1040 E. Burnside St.
(503) 231–1444

Hippo Hardware, a well-known Portland fixture for many years, carries a wonderfully eclectic assortment of plumbing fixtures, doors, lighting fixtures, and salvaged items for older homes. This place is far more entertaining than the average nuts-and-bolts hardware store and is jam-packed with functional curios and odd stuff that can be very useful if you know what to do with it (if you're like us and have no idea what it's supposed to do, just ask and someone will be glad to help you). It takes a long time to search through all the offerings, so plan accordingly. They will also custom build lighting fixtures. Don't forget to bring your old broken antique fixtures in here for a swap. It is a trading company, after all.

Home and Castle
11960 S.W. Pacific Hwy., Tigard
(503) 620–4534

19027 S.E. Stark, Gresham
(503) 669–1944

These two stores are open 10 A.M. to 6 P.M. Monday through Saturday to offer folks a wide variety of ways to enliven their home. They sell spas, whirlpools, above and in-ground pools, and swim-spas—a special pool with a flow of water allowing you to swim in place, thus vigorously exercising at home. Also as a service, they offer complete water testing from samples brought to the store.

Once out of the pool you might want to relax in one of their chairs, chaise lounges, or another piece of patio furniture on display. Or if you're chilly you might want to warm up in front of a wood, pellet, gas, or oil stove. And if you've worked up an appetite, fire up the barbecue from a large selection of high-end outdoor grills.

Katayama Framing and Gallery
2219 N.W. Raleigh St.
(503) 224–3334

Old-world craftsmanship and gold laying techniques dating back to the thirteenth century are all in a day's work at Katayama Framing, which has forged a reputation as one of the highest quality custom-frame designers on the entire West Coast. With more than 250 years of combined picture-framing experience, the Katayama team of thirteen employees includes a gold and silver gilder, a Japanese and European carving expert, a colorist and frame restorer, and tapestry specialists. With their combined skills and experience, the shop can create replicas of any historical or period frame. Last year the owners moved their business across N.W. Raleigh Street into its new building, doubling their space to 10,000 square feet. Fixtures on the local art scene for more than a decade, Katayama's frequently hosts art fundraisers and other civic charities, and unlike other galleries, they showcase nearly all the artists from all the galleries in the region. (See also our entry in The Arts.)

Kitchen Kaboodle
S.W. 6th Ave. and Alder St.
(503) 464–9545

N.E. 16th and Broadway
(503) 288–1500

Clackamas Town Center
(503) 652–2567

S.W. Hall Blvd. and Scholls Ferry Rd.
(503) 643–5491

N.W. 23rd Ave. and Flanders
(503) 241–4040

Their motto is "We make your house a home," and they've been doing just that since 1975. Kitchen Kaboodle sells functional, unique house accoutrements, providing not only every possible gadget you might use someday, but the storage unit to put it in. This Portland institution has stores all over town; and whether you need an electric egg cooker, a potato ricer, an enameled French casserole, or a maple sideboard, you can find it here. The staff is very knowledgeable and friendly—make use of them. That's what they're paid for.

RD Steeves Imports
209 N. Yamhill St. on OR Hwy. 47 and
335 W. Monroe and OR Hwy. 47, Carlton
(503) 852–6519

This place is a bit out of the way, but we're including it for two reasons: They carry an exceptionally high-quality inventory of furniture and antiques and are such a draw that they supply more than one hundred antique dealers in five western states. Located in Northwest Yamhill County in the quaint town of Carlton, RD

Steeves offers two large warehouses full of imported (mostly from Europe) treasures, including English armoires, sideboards, bedroom suites, bureaus, china cabinets, stained-glass windows, and all sorts of unusual surprises such as hand crank sewing machines, chimney pots, and paddles—that are not for a canoe! RD Steeves, which is open Tuesdays through Sundays, receives huge 40-foot containers of goods direct from overseas every few weeks—and when they do, it's a race to their front door because they wholesale to the general public and sell below wholesale to dealers.

To reach Carlton, take Oregon Highway 47 south of Forest Grove or north from McMinnville. You can also take Oregon Highway 240 from Oregon Highway 99 West in Newberg. Time permitting, your trip may include a visit to one or more of the several outstanding wineries in the area and a stop for a picnic at one of the two beautiful parks in Colton. The Upper Park is in the heart of downtown next to a public swimming pool and has been refurbished with new playground equipment for the kids. The other option, Wennerberg Park, lies alongside the North Yamhill River and is the seasonal home to migrating geese and deer.

The Rebuilding Center
3625 N. Mississippi
(503) 331–1877

2015 N.W. 23rd Ave.
(503) 221–3193

A nonprofit salvage outlet, the Rebuilding Center sells reclaimed, well, everything—hardware, windows, doors, plumbing fixtures, moldings, lumber. This is the retail outlet of a firm that disassembles houses and other buildings; what is not immediately reused in other projects is sold here. For the recycling-conscious do-it-yourselfer, this place is heaven.

Rejuvenation
1100 S. E. Grand Ave.
(503) 238–1900

Another Portland landmark, Rejuvenation is well known nationally for its period lighting fixtures, but also carries new and salvaged plumbing, doors, windows, moldings, and lumber. They also carry handsome furniture and garden ornaments. This is a terrific resource center for home improvements; Rejuvenation has built a thriving business around helping people restore classic, turn-of-the-century houses. A knowledgeable staff provides useful information and referral lists of competent home rehabilitation specialists. There's a tiny nook for children to play in while their parents browse; the Daily Cafe, inside the store, is a good place for eating lunch while you figure out what to do with the salvaged staircase that you've just bought. Rejuvenation also sells their seconds, which can be a fine source for well-priced lighting fixtures and other things.

Sweetwater Farm
1317 N.W. Hoyt
(503) 227–4947

Richard Friedman sells furnishings that put the fun back in functional. This shop deals in colorful, funky furniture—everything from armoires to entertainment centers—and singular treasures made by artisans from all over the country. David Marsh and Shoestring Creations are two featured artists, but there are many more. In addition to the furniture, you'll find a striking array of jewelry, lighting, pillows, toys, and other surprises. Sweetwater Farm might be just the place to find the necessary touch of whimsy to go with the Eileen Gray daybed (see F.U.P) in your modern rowhouse.

Versatile Sash & Woodworking
1100 S.E. Grand Ave.
(503) 238–6403

These folks have developed a high level of expertise by specializing in wooden windows and doors for historic homes and businesses. Besides having parts and supplies, they are equipped with extensive knowledge. If they can't help you, you're in trouble.

The Whole 9 Yards
1033 N.W. Glisan St.
(503) 223–2880

Specializing in interior fabrics and trim, The Whole 9 Yards has developed a national reputation for its gorgeous fabrics, inventive combinations, and original style. Their chenilles, jacquards, and

Insiders' Tip

The Central Eastside Industrial District is not just for container trucks full of vegetables and office supplies. There you will also find a range of the finest sources for house remodeling. In addition to Rejuvenation (see above), lucky hunters will find discounted upholstery fabrics at Bits and Pieces, 715 S.E. Grand, exquisite tile at Ann Sacks Tile & Stone, 1210 S.E. Grand, and classic marble at Oregon Tile and Marble, 1845 S.E. 3rd.

velvets are renowned, but they carry everything from duponi to cotton. They'll help you put together your drapes and upholstery, as well as providing you with general expertise, curtain rods and trim, and their own line of freshly designed, competitively priced furniture. The shop also offers two brilliant services: classes in fashioning slipcovers, curtains, and pillows, and a big, comfortable playroom for restless children.

Music

2nd Avenue Records
400 S.W. 2nd Ave.
(503) 222-3783

A voluminous outlet for all musical genres, 2nd Avenue has the biggest selection of hip-hop in town. You can also track down obscure performers on independent labels.

Artichoke Music
3130 S.E. Hawthorne Blvd.
(503) 232-8845

Don't settle for banging a gong; stop by this friendly music shop and strum an Autoharp or thump an Irish bodhran with a double drumstick. Everyone in Southeast Portland knows about Artichoke Music's live folk performances and high-quality musical instruments. You name it, they've got it, including guitars, banjos, mandolins, dulcimers, harps, accordions, and a fascinating assortment of unusual folk instruments. They also buy and sell all kinds of musical instruments and are extremely knowledgeable about the local music scene. Artichoke hosts an open-mike session every Thursday evening that features a blend of folk music, storytelling, song writing, and poetry; there is no cover charge.

Django Records
1111 S.W. Stark St.
(503) 227-4381

Named after a legendary jazz guitarist, this shop has tons of vinyl from oldies to the latest rock, jazz, blues, soul, and R&B pressed into a disk. Many of these records go for $2 or less.

Music Millennium/Classical Millennium
3158 E. Burnside St.
(503) 231-8926

801 N.W. 23rd Ave.
(503) 248-0163

Music Millennium offers the widest selection of classical CDs in the entire city. They also have a ton of New Age, blues, rock, reggae, and whatever else gets your toes to tapping. Music Millennium, which has been around for nearly thirty years, usually offers several good-size bins of discounted tapes and CDs.

No LPs are to be found in this place, but they always play great and unusual music that you might not ordinarily be exposed to, and they know about all the upcoming concerts. If you can't find the release here, it hasn't been released. One of the notable features of this remarkable shop is an ongoing series of in-store performances by national acts with new albums.

Here are some other great Portland record stores:

CD/Game Exchange
2735 N.E. Broadway
(503) 287–0382

1725 S.E. 36th Ave.
(503) 233–1708

2605 S.E. 122nd Ave.
(503) 761–0312

Everyday Music
1313 W. Burnside St.
(503) 274–0961

1931 N.E. Sandy Blvd.
(503) 239–7610

Locals Only
916 W. Burnside St.
(503) 227–5000

537 S.E. Ash
(503) 232–4870

Ozone
1036 W. Burnside St.
(503) 227–1975

Reverb
3623 S.E. Hawthorne Blvd.
(503) 736–9110

Outdoor Gear and Apparel

See the Recreation chapter for more stores that sell gear.

Captain's Nautical Supply, Inc.
138 N.W. 10th Ave.
(503) 227–1648

Portland and Vancouver are more aware of the Columbia and Willamette Rivers than they are of the Pacific, despite the historical and contemporary economic importance of maritime affairs. Though everyone is welcome, this is no touristy shop but a store for merchant sailors, fishing boat crews, and serious recreational sailors. It carries real gear, equipment, and hardware that will stand up to the wear and tear of an oceangoing craft. For those not immediately heading across the Columbia Bar, there is a good selection of local and regional charts, books about sailing and the sea, instruments for navigation, and brass items for boats and homes.

Citybikes Workers Cooperative
1914 S.E. Ankeny St.
(503) 239–0553

This is a very good place to purchase a high-quality reconditioned bike at well below the original selling price. Citybikes doesn't carry any cheapos, just name brands and many European models. They also have some older classic bikes that have been beautifully reconditioned. Last time we stopped by, they had forty-some bikes for sale, all different kinds and styles, and another huge batch being serviced in the work area. These people take a huge amount of pride in their work, and it shows.

Columbia Sportswear
911 S.W. Broadway
(503) 226–6800

You may have noticed Oregonians' affinity for Gore-Tex jackets and parkas, substantial shoes and boots, and all manner of Polartec garments. We're also easy marks for expensive racks that can carry canoes, kayaks, and bikes atop our cars and trucks. Here's where we get all these goodies. This is the flagship store for Columbia Sportswear—two floors of high quality, well-designed, functional clothes, shoes, and assorted accessories. The prices, despite some good sales, are full retail.

G.I. Joe's
3485 S.W. Cedar Hills
(503) 644–9936

3900 S.E. 82nd Ave.
(503) 777–4526

15600 S.E. McLoughlin Blvd.
(503) 653–5616

1140 N. Hayden Meadows Dr.
(503) 283–0318

17799 S.W. Boones Ferry Rd., Tualatin
(503) 635–1064

Long ago, this store began life selling industrial and military surplus. Now, these are huge stores filled with everything from sunglasses, rifles, tons of fishing and hunting gear and clothing, a huge automotive section, and an even larger selection of athletic clothes and shoes. You can also get hunting licenses, fishing licenses, duck stamps, reservations for state campgrounds, and tickets to a rock concert here.

Photography

Advance Camera Repair and Sales, Inc.
8124 S.W. Beaverton-Hillsdale Hwy.
(503) 292–6996

Not only does this shop offer a staff of knowledgeable experts who can unjam that roll of film or tell you that you need a new battery, but it also has several display cases full of used camera equipment at excellent prices. Advance Camera guarantees its work and its merchandise.

Camera World
500 S.W. 5th Ave.
(503) 205–5900

A supermarket-size store largely devoted to still photography (the exception being video recorders), Camera World's selection of cameras includes Canon, Nikon, Leica, Pentax, Yashica, Polaroid, Minolta, Ricoh, Bronica, Mamiya, Konica, Hasselblad, and Contax. Both bodies and lenses are sold here. It also has an extensive range of black-and-white and color film for professional and amateur photographers, developing chemicals and tools, paper, and enlargers. The staff is knowledgeable and polite, but the place can get busy during lunch hours on weekdays. The shop has frequent sales; at times you may see customers lined up waiting for the store to open. There is also a good selection of books on photography.

Hollywood Camera Store
4039 N.E. Sandy Blvd.
(503) 284–2060

This store should be a registered treasure for camera lovers. Hollywood specializes in repairing and selling quality used cameras and offers excellent value for your dollar. Can't find the Canon AE-1 or Pentax K-1000 you've been yearning for? Stop by Hollywood's. They sell fine, brand-name cameras—no junk—and put warranties on many of their items.

Photo Kinon
7505 N.E. Glisan St.
(503) 256–4934

Although Photo Kinon is small and easy to miss, it carries very good equipment, including camera bodies, lenses, flash units, and accessories such as lens caps, tripods, bags, and straps. John, the owner, is extremely knowledgeable and helpful. If you buy something from him, he'll back it up. He's also good at fixing things, and if it is something he can't figure out, he'll send it in to a factory-authorized repair specialist. If you are trying to find a special piece of equipment—a fish-eye lens for example—John will try to get one for you and call you up and tell you when he has it in stock.

Shoes

Be sure to look in the Shopping districts section for more great shoe stores.

Al's Shoes
5811 S.E. 82nd Ave.
(503) 771–2130

It seems as though this family-owned business, nearly a Portland icon, has been around for more than fifty years. You can bet your booties that the people here know quality shoes. Al's carries almost every kind of shoe or boot you can imagine. There's no cheap stuff—all name brands—but a good amount of their stock is discounted between 10 to 15 percent off the regular retail price. We've never seen a better selection of all sizes of men's shoes for work, show, or play; the selection is supposed to be the biggest on the entire West Coast. If you poke around, you might find a great bargain. There is always an on-sale shoe rack, and there are sometimes huge discounts on misfits, odd sizes and/or closeouts. If you love shoes (and don't we all?), you can have a blast just looking.

Baddoll Shoes
815 N.W. Glisan St.
(503) 525–2202

Connecticut Winkler sells the most cutting-edge shoes in Portland in her little shop on Glisan in the Pearl District. And that's all you need to know.

Danner Factory Outlet Store
12722 N.E. Airport Wy.
(503) 251–1111

Boots, boots, boots. This is another great spot to treat your feet to the best leather around. This Danner Factory Outlet offers high quality factory firsts for between $175 and $250 and seconds between $100 and $150. Seconds just means there is a slight defect someplace, which may be as minor as a goofed-up stitch. In some cases we couldn't even find the boo-boo, but a tag is attached to the footwear to let you know where it is. This is the place to visit if you need comfortable

and long lasting hiking boots, work boots, or hunting boots. Sorry, dudes and wranglers, there are no cowboy boots.

Hollywood Shoe Repair Shop
4041 N.E. Sandy Blvd.
(503) 284–5863

Investment bankers with shiny Florsheims, ditch diggers with muddy boots, ballet dancers, waitresses, and every spectrum of society's rainbow visit Sang Hui Lee's shop, where he holds court six days a week. Lee's excellent service and high-quality craftsmanship draw customers from as far away as Pendleton, Coos Bay, and Astoria; they all rave about his consistency and attention to detail. Lee opened this little shop fifteen years ago and now repairs upwards of thirty shoes a day.

Imelda's
1431 S.E. 37th.
(503) 233–7476

Alluring shoes at reasonable prices: that's why stylish Portlanders seek out Imelda's, which is just north of Hawthorne. Franco Sarto, Diba, and Secs are some of the lines that Imelda's carries; but also look for special handmade shoes from New York, groovy handbags, and really pretty jewelry. Imelda's started out as a women's shoe store, but a couple of years ago doubled its space and added men's lines too. Everybody buys shoes here.

Nike Factory Outlet
2650 N.E. Martin Luther King Jr. Blvd.
(503) 281–5901

If athletic footwear is your bag, this is a place to check out. Basketball shoes, jogging shoes, cross trainers, walking shoes—plus, this place has shoes for activities we didn't even know existed. This fun and affordable Nike Outlet sells last season's merchandise and a variety of closeout items.

Close-up

Local Design

Portland has a history of supplying the nation with stylish, well-made clothing, and you've probably heard of Hanna Andersson, Jantzen, Columbia Sportswear, and Nike. But Portland's increasing urbanity is reflected the growing number of successful local designers who have set up shop in the past few years, designers that are also receiving national attention. The following shops carry locally made and designed clothing by Portland's rising design stars.

Ellington Leather Goods
1533 N.W. 24th Ave.
(503) 223–7457
Ellington makes Italian-inspired handbags, wallets, luggage, and other leather items, as well as a sophisticated line of microfiber bags. Their backpack purses are modern classics. Ellington also has good webstore; find it at www.ellingtonleather.com

Fyberworks
4300 S.E. Hawthorne Blvd.
(503) 232–7659
Street clothes and workout wear are the specialty here, most of which are sewn right in the shop. We go here for the great leggings, shirts, and shift dress, but we have also been attracted to the jackets lately. Fyberworks makes really great baby leggings in bright prints in addition to clothes for women. The shop also supports other local designers and will carry their stuff.

Lena Medoyeff
3206 S.E. Hawthorne Blvd.
(503) 230–7259
Well-cut clothes in stunning fabrics: this is the hallmark of Lynn Solmonson, the designer behind the name Lena Medoyeff. These dresses, skirts, pants, and jackets for day or evening are truly alluring, and they'll make you so as well. You'll see a lot of embroidery; in fact, some of the Lena Medoyeff designs carry hand-embroidered flowers by Alicia Paulson, the local artist responsible for Posie custom embroidery. (Posie's Web site is www.posiedesigns.com; they'll take orders from all over the nation.) Depending, of course, on the season, you may also see duponi, velvet, or lightweight wool, but

whatever you see, it will be a simple design that allows the beauty of the fabric to stand out. These clothes are rather dressy, but for Portland, a Lena Medoyeff skirt with a T-shirt and flip-flops fits in just right.

Seaplane
3356 S.E. Belmont
(503) 234–2409
Seaplane carries clothes that are a modern hybrid of Bond girl, Grace Jones, and Debbie Harry. Designers and proprietors Holly Stadler and Kathryn Towers feature beautifully sculpted dresses, sweaters, and skirts. They also carry luscious, sexy dresses by another Portland designer, Kwai Toa. Her line is called G-Spot.

Tumbleweed
1804 N.E. Alberta
(503) 335–3100
www.kara-line.com
Tumbleweed is the home base of designer Kara Larson and her Kara-Line brand of clothing. These urban cowgirl clothes are available throughout the city and the country. Her simple skirts and dresses are charming without being the least bit fussy; they are made of pretty prints in cottons and rayons. We also love the fact that you can talk to the woman who made them. They purvey an entire "rustic romantic" look, but the pieces blend well with things you already own and can really individualize a wardrobe. Dresses for little girls, vintage cowboy boots, pantaloons, sweaters, and other fabric delights (including a fun basket of remnants) round out the selection. They're on a personal mission to revive the dress—the store's motto is "Wear more

dresses!" and after fifteen minutes inside you can't help but think—all right, then! I will!

Vergotis
1433 N.E. Broadway
(503) 284–4065
Kelli Vergotis designs and sells her sophisticated wardrobe here (it's fun to walk in and see the pattern book on the little table that serves as a counter). These simply cut, lovely suits, trousers, and dresses are perfect for work and beyond. Vergotis also sells Policy jeans, clothes by Theory, White and Warren sweaters, and other fill-in pieces. She carries local jewelry and handbags too, as well as some lingerie.

Also visit **Calamity Jane**, 7908 S.E. 13th, and **Mimi & Lena**, 823 N. W. 23rd, which carry many of the above lines, as well as other natives.

Local designer Kara Larson supplies dresses for urban cowgirls. CREDIT: VINCE RADOSTITZ

Niketown
930 S.W. 6th Ave.
(503) 221–6453

If shopping were a secular religion, Portland's Niketown, the progenitor of all other Niketowns in the entire world, would be the Vatican. This store is a shrine to consumerism and marketing—living, concrete proof that form and image are more vital than reality. Niketown is made of equal parts of museum, gallery, temple, and store. Yes, you can buy shoes and other things here, but the real purpose of a visit is to honor the "swoosh" with generous offerings of currency and plastic. From the young, hip Nike-clad greeters to the spotlighted and enshrined sneakers, this is a cultural icon.

Smoke Shops

Cascade Cigar & Wine
518 S.W. 6th Ave.
(503) 790–9045

This recent addition to the shopping scene capitalizes on the renewed interest in cigars. It stocks a good selection of magazines too. Those so inclined will find cigarette and cigar lighters, cases and tools, and a range of imported cigarettes and pipe tobaccos. The store also offers those relics of days gone by—wooden and paper cigar boxes. They also have a small selection of T-shirts with cigar band and logo artwork.

Rich's Cigar Store
820 S.W. Alder St.
(503) 228–1700

706 N.W. 23rd Ave.
(503) 227–6907

Before *The New York Times* went national with regionally printed editions, Rich's was just about the only place in Portland where you could get *The Times*. It came by train (according to some accounts) from New York City and arrived in Portland on the following Wednesday. Rich's was also the place where you bought good cigars before they were trendy, as well as French, English, and other imported or hard-to-find cigarettes. For more than a century, Rich's has set the standard in Portland for the range of U.S. and imported magazines and journals it stocks and for the number of American and foreign newspapers it carries. They also have a good selection of books and maps, and you can find most of Portland's free papers piled on a shelf. If you want to find out what's happening in your hometown while you're in Portland, Rich's downtown store is the place to go. The Rich's outpost on N.W. 23rd Avenue, is somewhat smaller, with a reduced range of offerings.

Vancouver

The Den
1002 Main St.
(360) 694–5958

Open every day of the week, The Den, in the heart of historic downtown Vancouver, is a combination of old-fashioned newsstand/smoke shop and wine store. Besides carrying an extensive collection of newspapers and magazines, The Den offers one of the largest selections of premium cigars and cigarettes in the area and also carries an excellent assortment of fine wines, both imported and domestic. If that isn't enough, they also carry a wide range of greeting cards for all occasions.

Close-up

In Vino Veritas

Oregon is wine country and is justly famous for its Pinots. Some passionate souls devoted to the blood of the Oregon soil have set up shop, making local wines available and bringing good international wines to the attention of Portland citizens. Each of the shops below likes to focus on boutique or hard-to-find wines; the ambience of each, their tasting events, and their prodigious variety of stock make them all worth visiting (perhaps not all on the same day). Many hold classes and other events, as well. The people who own the shops are as varied and fascinating as the wine that they sell, so ask them about their passions.

750 ml
232 N.W. 12th
(503) 224–1432
Rena Vatch started this unorthodox wine shop, where wines are arranged by quality ("luscious," "sassy") instead of origin, and where customers can taste featured wines before they buy them, to make wine-buying less intimidating. Most wines are priced around $15.

Great Wine Buys
1515 N.E. Broadway
(503) 287–2897

Liner & Elsen
202 N.W. 21st
(503) 241–WINE

Mt. Tabor Fine Wines
4316 S.E. Hawthorne Blvd.
(503) 235–4444
This shop was named as one of the best wine shops in America two years running (1999 and 2000) by *Food & Wine Magazine*.

Portland Wine Merchants
S.E. 35th and Hawthorne Blvd.
(503) 234–4399

Urban Wineworks
407 N.W. 16th Ave.
(503) 226–9797
Urban Wineworks sells wine that other people make; they also are a winery themselves and purvey their own label. Stepping into their warehouse, you suddenly feel like you're in Napa.

Vino
1226 S.E. Lexington
(503) 235–8545, (888) 922–8545
Vino is a charming spot that features value-priced wines that would be difficult to find without the hard work of the owner, Bruce Bauer.

The Oregon History Center with murals of pioneers (left) and Lewis and Clark. CREDIT: DAVID JOHNSON

Attractions

To paraphrase an old Broadway song, there is something for everyone in Portland today.

Visitors come from all over to see what makes the Portland area different from other parts of the country and world. This chapter emphasizes the local and regional attractions—natural, historical, and contemporary—that define and characterize our area.

Downtown Portland, which is encompassed in our Southwest Portland section, is agreeable for walking, and even if the weather is not entirely cooperative, the distances are relatively short. Fareless Square, a downtown zone along the bus mall (in which bus fare is free), invites visitors to join local residents on Tri-Met's buses and light rail cars to get around downtown more easily. In good weather, visitors can take advantage of the many downtown parks and fountains with their benches and sitting areas to take a break and watch the Northwest world go by.

Visitors to Vancouver and Clark County, Washington, will be more dependent on cars to get around, though downtown Vancouver does lend itself to a walking tour.

The entire Portland Metro area is a work in progress. Expect to encounter new construction on downtown buildings and work on various streets and bridges throughout the region. During the spring and summer, expect the occasional parade, especially during the Rose Festival and on the Fourth of July, as well as street festivals, bike races, weekend runs, and even the occasional protest outside some government building. For more information about special happenings, see our Festivals and Annual Events chapter, and for other attractions, like galleries and museums, see The Arts chapter. Additionally, if you're traveling with kids, you may want to check out the children's museums and amusement parks in the Kidstuff chapter.

We have made every effort to report the most current and accurate hours and addresses. However, given the rate of change in the area, visitors are advised to call their destination beforehand to make sure the information is accurate.

Southwest Portland

Berry Botanic Garden
11505 S.W. Summerville Ave.
(503) 636–4112
www.berrybot.org

Rae Selling Berry was by all accounts a legendary plantswoman, and her legacy lives on at the Berry Botanic Garden, the site of her estate. This garden shouldn't be missed, especially during the spring and summer. The six and one-half acre estate features a collection of endangered plant species, the largest public rock garden on the West Coast, and major collections of lilies, native Northwest plants, and rhododendrons in settings that vary from a damp woodland to streamside plantings. The Berry Botanic Garden was the first seed bank in the nation to dedicate itself to the preservation of the flora of an entire region (the Pacific Northwest), and part of its mission is to sustain the botanical heritage of the area through an extensive research program. Classes and events are offered regularly. The garden is open by appointment every day from dawn until dusk with free admission during July and August. Admission for the rest of the year is $5 per person. Because the garden is in a residential area, you'll need to call to make an appointment, but it's not difficult to get one. Also call for directions to the garden. A recorded message will give them to you—be sure to have your pencil ready because they're delivered rapidly. Alternatively, you can look up directions on the useful website, which also has information about current classes and events.

Hoyt Arboretum
4000 S.W. Fairview Blvd.
(503) 823–3654,
(503) 228–8733 (visitor center)

Hoyt Arboretum, which is part of Washington Park, not only provides more than 900 species of trees and shrubs to observe, but it also provides 183 acres and 10 miles of trails with striking views of the city, Mount Hood and Mount St. Helens, the Coast Range, and the rolling hills to the west, north, and east. Oaks, maples, cherry trees, Douglas fir, redwoods, blue spruce, Himalayan spruce, and bristlecone pine are but a few of the species that keep the arboretum fragrant in the spring, fresh and cool in the summer, and flushed with color during the fall. For those of us who weren't paying attention during Outdoor School, most species are labeled, and for those who want to learn more, tours are offered during the weekends from April through August. The trails do twist up and down the hills, so comfortable and sturdy footwear is suggested. A ¾-mile section of the Bristlecone Trail is paved for wheelchair access and offers a good introduction to Washington Park. The grounds are open from 6 A.M. to 10 P.M. The visitor center is open from 9 A.M. to 4 P.M. daily, except for Thanksgiving, Christmas, and New Year's Day.

International Rose Test Garden
400 S.W. Kingston in Washington Park
(503) 823–3636

For some residents and visitors, this park is what Portland is about. High above the city, offering a priceless, rose-framed view of the skyline, the Willamette River and its bridges, the snowcapped peaks of the Cascade Mountains (Mount Hood, Mount St. Helens, Mount Adams, and even Mount Rainier, on some days), the

Rose Test Garden is an almost obligatory stop for visitors. This place is totally dedicated to the proposition that one should stop and smell the roses (or any other flowers that happen to be on hand), and underscores this principle by offering many summer concerts, plays, and other outdoor events in addition to its lovely views. This site has been a public rose garden since 1917—it's the oldest public rose test garden in the nation. The five-acre gardens offer visitors the sight and scent of 8,000 plants representing some 500 varieties of roses, from those producing fragile miniatures to some with blossoms nearly 8 inches broad. The roses begin to bloom in May and usually reach their peak sometime in June, depending on the weather. But there will be flowers on the bushes until October, long after all but the most faithful rose fancier has gone home. Visitors are free to wander through the gardens, admiring the flowers, inhaling the sweet fragrance, and capturing the colors on film.

The rule here is simple: look closely, breath in deeply the rose's aroma, admire, paint, photograph, and even envy the garden's bounty, but don't be tempted to pick a single stem, no matter how overcome by the passion for possession. There are no admission fees or formal operating hours, but there is a $500 fine for picking a flower.

See the Portland's Parks chapter for information on other public rose gardens in Portland.

Ira Keller Memorial Fountain
S.W. 3rd Ave. and S.W. Clay St.

Named after Ira C. Keller, a self-made millionaire with a well-developed social conscience and fine-tuned sense of the city, this water sculpture with misty falls and rectilinear pools is across from the Keller Auditorium in downtown Portland. In spring and summer, downtown workers eat lunch, nap, talk with friends, read, and sun themselves to the soothing sounds of water cascading down the structure's various levels. Children, unintimidated by adult mores and the structure's aesthetics, splash in the cooling waters and delight in the fountain's different waterfalls, pools, concrete and metal islands and terraces, and the design's overall human scale.

Ada Louise Huxtable, *The New York Times's* respected architecture critic, described the fountain as "perhaps the greatest open space since the Renaissance"—no faint praise for a work of public art, especially in a city with many public spaces.

Japanese Gardens
611 S.W. Kingston Ave.
(503) 223–1321, (503) 223–9233 (for tours)

A Japanese ambassador to the United States once commented that this site in Washington Park is the most beautiful and authentic Japanese garden outside of Japan. Established in 1963, the Japanese Garden was designed by Professor Takuma Tono, a distinguished landscape and garden designer, and his achievement is remarkable, compressing five different garden spaces—the Flat Garden, the Strolling Pond Garden, a Tea Garden with a *chashitsu* (a ceremonial tea house), the Natural Garden, and the Zen-inspired Sand and Stone Garden—into a little more than five acres. The trees and plants, water, and rocks here change with the season, offering visitors different perspectives of color, texture, shape, shadow, and sound throughout the year. In spring, azaleas and flowering cherry trees illuminate the garden. During the summer, flowering shrubs and annuals create dramatic spots of color contrasting with differing tones and shades of green. The garden's varieties of graceful irises provide accents of purple to the garden's green.

In fall, the garden is aflame with color as the delicate leaves of the Japanese maples turn and brilliantly burst into heated reds and oranges, yellows, and golds. Though the winter months are less flamboyant, these gardens can be restorative to your soul even during the long

weeks of gray, damp days. At least once a year, a covering of snow creates an ethereal but short-lived monochromatic landscape that equals in its own right the beauty of the other seasons.

Managed by the nonprofit Japanese Garden Society of Oregon, the gardens are open daily, except on Thanksgiving, Christmas Day, and New Year's Day. Hours vary according to the season, but visitors can be assured of admission between 10 A.M. and 4 P.M. Guided tours are available, as well as special annual events, including a moon viewing in September, a bonsai exhibition in October, and an excellent art and gift exhibit and sale in December. A fine gift shop lists a wide range of books on Japanese art, culture, and gardens among its offerings. Admission to the Japanese Gardens is $6 for adults and $3.50 for children age six to seventeen, as well as college students with proper identification. Guests sixty-two and older are also admitted for $4; and there is no charge for children younger than six. The Japanese Garden, save for a few areas, is wheelchair accessible.

Multnomah County Library, Central Branch
801 S.W. 10th Ave.
(503) 988–5123
www.multnomah.lib.or.us

Each day of the week, thousands of citizens stream through the handsome doors of the Central Branch of the Multnomah County Library. While the library's holdings are extensive, it isn't a mere warehouse for books: it's a major component in the cultural life of the city. The Central Branch is an exemplary balance of intimate and public space, of cool marble and warm wood, of airy reading rooms and snug alcoves, of formal exhibits and cafe conversation. Its popularity attests to the success of this balance.

The library has dozens of programs, workshops, groups, and events that draw in visitors from all over the area. These range from lectures and roundtable discussions with regional writers to Saturday

The Central Branch of the Multnomah County Library is housed in an attractive building.

afternoon concerts to brownbag forums on stress relief to printmaking workshops. The Central Branch is, in fact, dedicated to the principle of lifelong learning, and therefore offers classes, tutoring, and other resources for every age group, from senior-focused lectures and computer workshops to story times, art projects, and other child-focused events to delight small patrons. Its flourishing programs prompted Portland writer Sallie Tisdale to wonder whether the Central Branch wasn't getting too noisy. Fortunately, the Sterling Room for Writers, available by application only, can provide writers with some peace and quiet.

Some, but only some, of the highlights include the Beverly Cleary Children's Library (see our Kidstuff chapter), with both cozy reading nooks and high-tech media capabilities. This enchanting room recruits thousands of small new book lovers each year, sustaining their devotion as they get older with good research facilities for school reports and with splendid books, videos, and CDs to entertain them. The Henry Failing Art and Music Library contains one of the most significant sheet music collections in the nation, along with robust collections in the history of painting, photography, and handicrafts. The Grants Information Center provides the necessary data for those who would like the financial support to study the collections more thoroughly (or to finance any other worthy project). The John Wilson Room houses rare books and artifacts, such as the Nuremburg Chronicle (dating from 1493); and the Meyer Memorial Trust libraries for science and business and for government documents are among the most-used collections in the library.

The library is open every day; Monday through Thursday from 9 A.M. to 9 P.M.; Friday and Saturday from 9 A.M. to 6 P.M.; and Sunday from 1 to 5 P.M. Free tours are available on Saturdays at 11:30 A.M. and at 3:30 P.M. Portland citizens don't like to be far from coffee, so Starbucks operates a small store, and the coffee scenting the air on the main floor adds a piquant Portland touch.

Oregon History Center
1200 S.W. Park Ave.
(503) 222–1741;
(503) 306–5198 (information line)
www.ohs.org

The Oregon History Center, operated by the Oregon Historical Society, is a fine place to begin a visit to Portland; it covers the history of Oregon from the earliest Indian civilizations through the saga of the Oregon Trail right up to the issues surrounding Portland's light rail. Before you even enter the building, the two eight-story-high trompe l'oeil murals by Richard Haas present dramatic views and symbols of Oregon's past. The West Mural, at S.W. Park Avenue and Madison Street, captures in larger-than-life scale the key members of the Lewis and Clark Expedition, including their dog, Seaman; Sacagawea; her child Baptiste; and Clark's slave, York. The other mural, visible from Broadway and Jefferson Streets, symbolically depicts early Oregon characters, among them Native Americans, trappers, and settlers.

The Oregon History Center is neither dusty nor staid. Part museum, part research facility, it's a leading and influential force in the city and state, sponsoring seminars, workshops, festivals, and celebrations, in addition to its extensive library and its own publications. The center holds an astonishing collection of historical photos (an estimated three million), documents, and artifacts. Although its choice of displays is limited by space, the exhibits and collections could nonetheless occupy a week of rainy afternoons.

The Portland Exhibit traces the city's history with interactive computer programs and displays of maps, photos, and paintings; other galleries feature fascinating exhibits of textiles and Native American artifacts. Engrossing presentations of the ephemera of daily life, from clay marbles, to shaman's knives, to menus from historic hotels, will spark anyone's historical imagination.

The Museum Store offers a well-chosen selection of books on Oregon and Northwest history, attractions, and personalities, many of which are written by Oregonians and other regional authors, and some of which are published by the OHS's respected press. The shop also has maps, trinkets, and jewelry, as well as an excellent selection of postcards, note cards, and prints, many produced by local artists and photographers. The Oregon History Center is open Tuesday through Saturday from 10 A.M. to 5 P.M. On Sundays, the museum is open from noon to 5 P.M. The library is open Wednesday through Saturday from 11:30 A.M. to 5 P.M. Both the library and the History Center are open until 8 P.M. on Thursday. Admission is $6 for adults, $3 for students with ID, and $1.50 for children ages six to twelve; seniors are admitted at no charge on Thursdays, and there is no cost for children younger than five. Multnomah County Library cardholders receive free admission to the library if they present their cards.

Oregon Maritime Center and Museum
113 S.W. Naito Pkwy.
(503) 224–7724

Looking like an ordinary storefront at the east end of Skidmore Square, this small museum is a treasure chest filled with artifacts, models, historic paintings, and a collection of navigational instruments recounting Oregon's seagoing history. One room details the regional shipbuilding industry during World War II. Housed in the Smith Block, a restored brick building dating from 1872, the museum includes a small gift shop with a selection of nautical items and books. Admission to the museum ($4 for adults, $3 for seniors, $2 for youth ages eight to seventeen) includes a tour of the steampowered stern-wheeler tug *Portland*, moored on the Willamette River across S.W. Naito Parkway from the museum. The museum's hours vary by season. During the summer (Memorial Day to Labor Day), the museum is open from 11 A.M. to 4 P.M., Wednesday through Sunday. During other months, the museum's hours are 11 A.M. to 4 P.M., Friday, Saturday, and Sunday.

The Oregon Zoo
4001 S.W. Canyon Rd.
(503) 226–1561
www.oregonzoo.org

The Oregon Zoo is the newest name for a zoo originally established in 1887 with the gift to the city of an animal collection from a wealthy and idiosyncratic Portland pharmacist, Richard Knight. The Oregon Zoo has evolved from a hodgepodge of animals kept at the back of a pharmacy into a world-class research facility, offering a constantly changing mix of exhibits and other amusements. It's an internationally recognized and respected center for breeding Asian elephants, and it features an imaginative re-creation of the African rainforest. It's undergone a signif-

icant overhaul and renewal in the past few years, including a major new contribution to educating visitors about the animals of the Pacific Northwest, with striking facilities for sea otters and other marine life. All these combine to provide visitors with more information about and a context for the animals they see.

More importantly, The Oregon Zoo has made, and continues to make, a serious effort to improve the areas where the animals are kept. The cold concrete and steel bars associated with zoos in the past are being phased out of The Oregon Zoo's exhibits. As if in response to a homier atmosphere, the zoo's animal population is remarkably fertile, and the nursery is one of the most popular exhibits with adults, children, and the Portland media.

This well-liked attraction, second only to Multnomah Falls in the number of visitors it receives each year, offers a variety of other diversions that do not focus on animals. The Zoo Railway is a narrowgauge railroad running two trains, including a replica of the 1960s streamlined but unsuccessful Aerostar, along a route through part of the zoo, into Washington Park and the Rose Gardens. The zoo railroad has the only surviving railway post office in the country and you can amuse your friends back home by sending them mail with its unusual postmark. During Halloween and the Christmas season, The Oregon Zoo hosts many special events in which the train plays a role, such as a festival of lights, which is best seen from the train (see Festivals and Annual Events).

As you might predict, the zoo has a terrific gift shop and several restaurants and refreshment stands, including the AfriCafe, a restaurant that suggests huts found in a traditional African village.

During the summer, the zoo hosts a series of concerts on a stage surrounded by terraced lawns. Many of these concerts are free with zoo admission; others cost more. The mild evenings, popular artists, and availability of catered food, regional wines and beer, and coffee combine to make these concerts into events that express the very essence of Portland. Many people bring a picnic (you can bring anything edible except alcohol into the zoo) and sprawl on blankets in the late afternoon sunshine before the music begins. Spontaneous outbursts of dancing will occur in front of the stage. It's a fine thing to see people of all ages and ways of life come together at these events; everyone loves to sit on the big lawns listening to great music under the lovely skies at twilight with friends and families.

The Oregon Zoo is open every day except Christmas Day. Gates are open from 9 A.M. until 6 P.M., except from October 1 to March 31, when they are open from 9 A.M. until 4 P.M. The zoo stays open for an hour after the gates close, unless you're attending a special event or concert, when you can stay longer. Admission to the zoo is $6.50 for adults, $4 for children ages three to eleven, and $5 for older adults. Admission is free after 1 P.M. on the second Tuesday of each month. The Zoo Railway has a separate charge of $2.75 for adults and $2 for kids and seniors sixty-four and older. By car, the zoo is best reached by a well-marked exit from westbound U.S. Highway 26 as it leaves downtown Portland. There is a light rail station at the zoo, and ART the Cultural Bus also stops at the zoo. On summer weekends and during many concerts, parking can be particularly scarce, so light rail may be the least frustrating way to get here. (See our Portland's Parks chapter for more information on the zoo.)

Pioneer Courthouse Square
Between Broadway and S.W. 6th Aves. at S.W. Yamhill and S.W. Morrison Sts.

Pioneer Courthouse Square has been many things during its long life. The site was home to the city's first public schoolhouse; then home to the Portland Hotel, a massive and impressive building that was torn down, to much local dismay, to make way for a parking lot. Now, however, this wonderful piece of real estate is known as "Portland's living room" for its warm blend of red brick, park benches, flowers, sculpture, coffee, and books. Look at the bricks in the square's open spaces, and you'll see the inscribed names of more than 64,000 Portland residents, companies, and Oregonians who paid $25 each to buy the bricks: the citizens of Portland rallied to install this project against some local ill will. (You can still buy a brick, but in these inflationary times, the price has gone up to $100.)

By the early 1970s, downtown Portland was choking on its own traffic and a decline in air quality, and stores and other businesses were fleeing to the suburbs where parking was easier and the surroundings less threatening, if more bland. Instead of prolonged municipal handwringing and gnashing of teeth, Portland ripped up a freeway, tore up almost the entire downtown and invited pedestrians back into the city's core with a transit mall and free bus rides, wider sidewalks, parking restrictions, trees, flower-filled planters, public art, and a squad of uniformed workers paid to keep the streets and sidewalks clean, give directions to visitors, and prevent crime by simply being visible and pleasant. The result has been one of the most accoladed urban renaissance projects in the nation and Pioneer Courthouse Square is its epicenter. Food vendors, a flower stand, a Starbucks, and public restrooms add to the charm, and the city's light rail system runs on two sides of the square, making it accessible to everyone. The Portland Oregon Visitor Association and Tri-Met both have major offices here, along with maintaining rooms for meetings and other occurrences, and a new facility, Ticket Central, allows people to buy tickets for events around town. Powell's has a branch here devoted to travel books, Nordstrom is just across the street, and the Pioneer Courthouse Post Office, in a classic stone building across the street, still sells stamps.

One thing about the decor of Portland's living room: it can surprise you. The square attracts diverse crowds that tolerate and even amuse each other and who, with very rare exception, get along quite well, illustrating the city's acceptance of individuality. Expect to see street musicians, jugglers, pierced and tattooed teenagers, and street people with their studded leather jackets, army surplus camouflage, and assortments of pet dogs, snakes, kittens, and birds. This is the rich urban tableau presented as street theater at its best. The Weather Machine, a piece of whimsical but functional sculpture, informs passersby of the weather: a blue heron means mist and drizzle, a golden sun goddess predicts clear skies, and a copper dragon warns of approaching storms, heavy rain, and winds.

Pioneer Square hosts an unending series of special events (see Festivals and Annual Events), including contests, cultural festivals, a giant civic Christmas tree, a yuletide tuba concert, a mini-Oregon State Fair, officially sanctioned skateboarding competitions, and anything else residents can get approved.

Pioneer Courthouse
555 S.W. Yamhill St.
(503) 326–5830

Pioneer Courthouse was Portland's first restoration project back in the 1970s. Built in the late 1860s, the Italianate building survived ill-considered plans that would have had it demolished for a mundane office building in the 1930s, for a parking lot in the 1940s, and for a new federal office building in the 1960s. Most of the city's residents don't know it, but you can climb to the cupola of Pioneer Courthouse for a rarely seen view of the city. This is a free trip back to 1877. Hanging between the cupola's eight windows are a series of restored photos of the city in that year by a local photographer, A.H. Wulzen. Many of the photos were taken from the cupola and offer the viewer a most unusual "before and after" scene. To reach the cupola, enter the courthouse (not the Post Office on S.W. 6th Ave.) from S.W. Yamhill Street. There is a stairway to the cupola, though you may have to pass through a metal detector, the times being what they are.

Pittock Mansion
3229 S.W. Pittock Dr.
(503) 823–3624

Henry Pittock, founder of *The Oregonian*, the city's daily newspaper and the largest paper in the state, built himself a château 1,000 feet above the city. The mansion stayed in the family for fifty years, until 1964, when it was sold to the City of Portland. This twenty-two-room, 16,000-square-foot, antique- and art-filled house is now open to a public interested in how the other half lived in less egalitarian times. Guided tours of the house are offered each afternoon, and visitors can wander through the gardens of roses, azaleas, and rhododendrons. In spring, flowering cherry trees add their color to the grounds. The view is spectacular. The adjoining Pittock Acres offer hiking and walking trails and are part of the Audubon Society's Wildlife Preserve.

The mansion's gatehouse, which once was the gardener's cottage, is now the Gate Lodge Restaurant. Lunch and afternoon tea are available every day except Sunday. The Pittock Mansion is open for public viewing seven days a week from noon to 4 P.M. The mansion is closed on major holidays, for a few days in late November when holiday decorations are being put up, and during the first three weeks of January for annual maintenance. Admission for adults is $5. Adults sixty-five and older are admitted for $4.50, and children and students (ages six through eighteen) pay $2.50. The Pittock Mansion is often rented by businesses, private groups, and families for dinners, receptions, meetings, and weddings, but these events are limited to evening hours.

Police Historical Museum Justice Center
1111 S.W. 2nd Ave.
(503) 823–0019

You may not want to know the motives of some of the other people visiting here with you, but don't miss this small museum, which highlights the fascinating history of crime and punishment.

The museum displays a retired police motorcycle, a working traffic signal, a collection of badges, uniforms, weapons, handcuffs, and other tools of the trade representing both sides of the cops-and-robbers paradigm. There is also a great collection of historical photos. Current and retired Portland police officers make up the volunteer staff, so mind your manners. Entry to the museum is free, though donations are welcome. The museum is open Monday through Thursday from 10 A.M. to 3 P.M. There's also a gift shop.

Portland Art Museum
1219 S.W. Park Ave.
(503) 226–2811

The Portland Art Museum, the oldest museum in the Pacific Northwest, has become an attraction with new dimensions, an attraction that extends beyond the striking allure of the Pietro Belluschi-designed building and the art within it. Under the direction of John Buchanan, the museum has gained much attention for its major exhibitions and even more major fundraising capabilities. The results have been impressive: after an extensive expansion, the museum now has the space for new galleries, educational facilities, a multimedia room, an appealing public sculpture garden, and a cafe. This new wealth of space has allowed the museum to better feature its important collections in Northwest and Native American art and in European painting, as well as creating space for recent acquisitions. (In 2000, the museum procured the collection of the distinguished New York art critic, Clement Greenberg.) But the museum has also become a lively force in the cultural life of the city, enlisting young patrons in its philanthropic drives, arranging family programs, sponsoring lectures and evening events, and generally making a big splash. Hours are Tuesday through Saturday, 10 A.M. to 5 P.M.; Sundays from noon to 5 P.M. Tickets are $7.50 for adults, $6 for seniors and students, and $4 for youth ages five to eighteen. For more information, see our Arts chapter.

Portland Building
1120 S.W. 5th Ave.
(503) 823–4000

Built in 1982, this wonderful, controversial, fifteen-story building still evokes potent reactions from local, regional, and national architects, designers, and critics, local politicians making some point about public spending and public art, and almost everyone who views it. Designed by Michael Graves in his distinctive postmodern style, the colorful Portland Building houses an administrative wing of Portland city government, next door to Portland City Hall, so between 8 A.M. and 5 P.M. you can walk around the lobby and other public areas where local artists' works are on display. Just beyond the main ground-floor lobby, you'll find a supply of many of the free weekly, monthly, and occasional newspapers produced in Portland. On the second floor there is a display detailing the building's design and construction as well as information about the equally controversial but now-beloved statue of *Portlandia*, looming over the street from a three-story ledge.

Portlandia was installed in 1985 after being barged up the Willamette River and trucked through downtown. This large, hammered-copper statue, which is second in size only to the more traditional Statue of Liberty, represents a modern mythological incarnation or descendant of Lady Commerce, the classic female figure on the City of Portland's official seal. With strong, 9-foot-long thighs and a plunging bronze decolletage, *Portlandia* has been called heroic, revealing, X-rated, and even "statuesque." While some still dissatisfied citizens want her relocated to a more (or less) visible location, the statue was designed for this location. She will remain where she is.

Portland City Hall
1221 S.W. 4th Ave.
(503) 823–4000

Portland City Hall, built in 1895, underwent extensive renovation during the late 1990s. This ambitious project not only restored this Italianate building's original floor plan and reestablished its original look and feel, but also preserved one of the most historically important buildings in the city. While the building retains much of its traditional appearance on the outside, its infrastructure is modern and energy-efficient. The building has also been made more accessible to the public, and a number of very Portland touches have been added, including a coffee bar, a secured bicycle parking shelter, and a rose garden that replaced a small, inefficient parking lot. The renovation has also restored natural light, air, and color to the interior of the building by uncovering the original skylights, by refurbishing the beautiful woodwork and floor tiles, and by ripping out walls that had enclosed the stairwells, exposing the decorative copper plating that had once adorned them.

The new City Hall displays a number of artworks commissioned for the building, adding to the city's growing inventory of public art. On the northwest side of the first floor, you will find the "Evolution of a City," a television screen display of photos taken over the past one hundred years of all parts of the city. Created and produced by two local artists, the installation presents a series of high-resolution digital images of the archival photographs. In addition to the photographs, works from the City's special collection, the "Visual Chronicle of Portland," are displayed in the lobby on the first floor. This collection of works on paper was established in 1985 and is continually updated; each work renders the artist's view of the distinctive characteristics of Portland. As you wander through the building, you will find other works of art, permanently or temporarily displayed. The friendly folks at the Information Desk can help you find out about them. City Hall is open from 6 A.M. to 7 P.M. Monday through Friday.

Portland Vintage Trolley
Lloyd Center/Downtown Transit Mall
(503) 22–TOOTS

Portland's Vintage Trolley uses four oak-paneled replicas of the city's now discarded Council Crest Streetcars. You can catch the trolley on any MAX stop from The Galleria to Lloyd Center. The trolley's schedule of operations varies with the season, but in general, trolleys run on

Insiders' Tip

The outside of the Portland Art Museum is as aesthetically interesting as its inside. That's because it was designed by Portland's Pietro Belluschi, the renowned architect of many buildings in the International style, including the Julliard School and the Met Life Building in New York City.

weekends year-round and more frequently during the summer. The ride is free for children younger than six. A $1 donation is requested of other riders. (See our Getting Here, Getting Around chapter for more information.)

Tom McCall Waterfront Park
Bordering Naito Pkwy. and the Willamette River from Broadway Bridge south to River Place

If Pioneer Courthouse Square is Portland's living room, then the Tom McCall Waterfront Park is the city's front yard. The park starts at the Broadway Bridge, stretches for about 2 miles and then converts into a portion of the Greenway, a path continuing south to Willamette Park, a total distance of 3.25 miles. Once upon a time there was an ugly freeway in Portland that cut off the downtown from the Willamette River. Led by Governor Tom McCall, planners came up with the Downtown Plan of 1972, which included the removal of the freeway and the creation of open space that would again reunite the city and river. This space would eventually be named Tom McCall Waterfront Park for the Oregon governor who was instrumental in restoring the space to the public. Portlanders have adopted the park with such fervor that it is in danger of being loved to death by an unending series of events, including the Rose Festival Fun Center, the Bite, Brewers' Festival, Cinco de Mayo, Blues Festival, Tulip Festival, Fourth of July fireworks, and the Race for the Cure (see our Portland's Parks chapter for more on this park and our Festivals and Annual Events chapter for more on these special outings). The city recently limited the number of permits for events while it installed hardier sod, improved drainage, and made other changes to help the park bear the wear and tear of all these festivities.

Center stage for Waterfront Park is the Salmon Street Springs Fountain at the foot of S.W. Salmon Street. In hot weather, this fountain, with its spurting jets of water, attracts crowds of adults and children who unabashedly play and splash in the streams of water and the shallow pool. The dock for the *Portland Spirit*, an excursion boat offering cruises on the Willamette, is also nearby.

The Waterfront Story Garden, a lighthearted cobblestone and granite monument to storytellers, is one of a small number of memorials. Another is the Japanese American Historical Plaza, sometimes referred to as the Garden of Stones. This solemn memorial is best walked from south to north. Along the memorial's formal plaza are stones, some broken, some cut, some shattered, to represent the disrupted lives of 110,000 Japanese Americans interned in camps throughout the western United States during World War II. The stones are carved with inscriptions in English (quotations from Oregonians of Japanese ancestry who were interned), and in Japanese (often written in Japan's unique poetry, haiku). Farther north, near the Steel Bridge, is the Friendship Circle. This sculpture emits the sounds of a Japanese flute and drum and honors the Sister City relationship between Portland and Sapporo, Japan.

Across from the Oregon Maritime Museum is the stern-wheeler *Portland* and the Battleship USS *Oregon Monument*. Oregon, known as "McKinley's Bulldog" because of its role in the Spanish-American War, was a turn-of-the century battleship launched in 1893. Having played its part in three wars, the ship was cut up for scrap following World War II. Between the two world wars, the *Oregon* was tied up along the sea wall at the foot of S.W. Jefferson Street as memorial and museum, but in 1942, as a patriotic gesture, the ship was returned to the U.S. Navy. One of the ship's masts was removed before she was reclaimed by the navy, and it is that battleship gray mast from which the American and Oregon flags fly along the river.

The final monument along Waterfront Park is, unfortunately, little noted. In a tribute to the staff of the Canadian Embassy in Tehran, Iran, who helped a number of American diplomats and their families escape during the yearlong Iran Hostage Crisis, a small group of Portlanders commissioned a plaque honoring their bravery. The monument is often overlooked and at times is not well maintained, but it is a heartfelt tribute to the quiet bravery of the Canadian diplomatic corps and the Canadian nation.

24-Hour Church of Elvis
720 S.W. Ankeny St.
(503) 226–3671
www.churchofelvis.com

This wacky Portland landmark may be the world's only coin-operated church/ art gallery. You can play it safe and merely visit the displays of kitsch, but you may find yourself entering the bonds of matrimony: you can have a legal wedding for $25, with lovely extras such as refrigerator magnets thrown in for a few dollars more. For $5 you can have a cheap, though not legal, wedding. This may be the wiser choice for those of you who are prone to be moved by the Mystery of the Spinning Elvi (plural for "more than one Elvis"), which will prophesy for you if you drop a quarter into the box.

Vietnam Veterans' Memorial
World Forestry Center,
4033 S.W. Canyon Rd.

Oregon's tribute to the sacrifices of a generation sits on eleven acres of land in the southwest corner of Hoyt Arboretum, above the large wooden structure of the World Forestry Center. The Vietnam Veterans' Memorial honors the 57,000 Oregonians who served in Southeast Asia, listing by name and date of death the state's nearly 800 known dead and still missing. The memorial puts those deaths in a historical context by including references to state, national, and international events occurring at the same time. The site is reverent, graceful, and solemn, and often the only sounds are those of quiet footsteps, the wind, and the hum of distant traffic. As at the national memorial in Washington, D.C., visitors often find personal remembrances—military insignia, campaign ribbons and medals, faded pictures, flowers, toys, candles, photos of sons and daughters, grandsons and granddaughters—left near a name. Each Memorial Day, an honor guard of ROTC cadets from the University of Portland stands a silent twenty-four-hour guard at the memorial. The ceremony and vigil ends with all the names of the dead being read aloud, to show they are not forgotten, and with the haunting sounds of taps echoing through the trees and hills. The monument is open for viewing during daylight hours.

Washington Park
S.W. Park Place at S.W. Vista Ave.
(503) 823–7529

Overlooking downtown Portland, the Willamette River and the entire east side of the city, Washington Park is set on 546 acres on the city's West Hills and includes many of the city's most important attractions. The park has existed since 1871 when the land was purchased by the city. The simplest way to the park is a clearly marked exit from westbound U.S. Highway 26 as it leaves downtown Portland and climbs over the West Hills toward Beaverton (follow the exit signs that say "Oregon Zoo" and "World Forestry Center"). This highway is easily accessible (and well marked) from I-5 via I-405. Visitors coming from Portland's Eastside can use either the Fremont Bridge or the Marquam Bridge. If you're downtown already, the two easiest ways to enter Washington Park are from S.W. Vista Avenue above Civic Stadium, and close to the intersection of Burnside Street and N.W. 23rd Avenue, at the Uptown Shopping Center. This entrance is the most convenient from Northwest Portland.

A light rail station at the zoo is handy for visitors going to attractions in

The Portland Art Museum showcases Northwest, Native American, and European art.
CREDIT: COURTESY OF THE PORTLAND ART MUSEUM

Washington Park, including the Oregon Zoo, World Forestry Center, Japanese Garden, and the Rose Gardens (all included in this chapter), and the Children's Museum (see our Kidstuff chapter). All of these attractions are within walking distance, if you're a sturdy walker. The Zoo, Forestry Center, and the Children's Museum are right off the MAX stop. The Japanese and Rose Gardens require a longer walk, as they are about a mile away along the roads or trails of Washington Park. Bus Line #63, which goes to and through the park, can take you from the MAX station to the parts of the park that may be too far to walk. You can also take the Zoo train, which has a station at the Rose Gardens. Another vehicle to take to get to Washington Park is ART, the Cultural Bus. ART, a propane-powered bus painted by Henk Pander, one of Portland's best-known artists, runs on Line #63.

This is one of Portland's most popular parks. On summer weekends, especially during Rose Festival, and during any special event or concert in the park, traffic can be vicious and parking all but impossible. Seriously consider light rail, bus, or even a taxi as an alternative to driving. This option may save your nerves and let you leave with a memory of a nice outing, not the frustration of a traffic jam.

World Forestry Center Museum
4033 S.W. Canyon Rd.
(503) 228–1367
www.worldforest.org

Before Oregon's Silicon Forest, there were real forests where giant trees were felled by handsaws and axes, hauled or floated to mills, and then cut and finished to build the nation's houses and factories. Built by a consortium of timber and related industries, the World Forestry Center Museum offers information and exhibits emphasizing the Pacific Northwest's forests as well as an exhibit from the Smithsonian Institution about the tropical rain forests. There are exhibits of petrified wood and a sculpture of a tiger carved from a 1,000-year-old tree for the 1988 Olympics. An intriguing 70-foot talking Douglas fir tree is designed to interest children as it explains to them how it grows.

The Forestry Center also hosts a range of special activities, including an annual show featuring Oregon woodworkers and carvers and an exhibit of wooden toys. A gallery features rotating exhibits of photography and other art. The Forest Store, the center's gift shop, offers wooden gifts and other items in keeping with the forest theme.

The World Forestry Center Museum is open daily from 9 A.M. to 5 P.M. Admission is $4.50 for adults and $3.50 for adults older than sixty-five and children older than five.

Northwest Portland

American Advertising Museum
211 N.W. 5th Ave.
(503) 226–0000

Claiming to be the first museum of its type in the world (what else would you expect from an advertising museum?), this small museum displays an eclectic collection of advertising artifacts, audio and videotapes, and print ads. Items in the collection range from a gas station sign with a red neon winged-horse (Mobil) to one of the original California Raisins claymation figures created by Portland's Will Vinton to featured campaigns from Weiden + Kennedy, Portland's major contribution to the advertising world. Some exhibits have particular themes, such as how women were and are portrayed in ads, but the displays rarely probe beneath the surface of the ads, following in the tradition of the advertisements we encounter every day.

Oregon Jewish Museum
2701 N.W. Vaughn St., Ste. 715
(503) 226–3600

After an initial home in the Oregon History Center, the Oregon Jewish Museum is now at Montgomery Park, once the huge warehouse for Montgomery Ward but now remodeled for office space. The museum, which is the only institution in the Pacific Northwest devoted to Jewish history and culture, features an archival library with papers and oral histories about the history of Jews in Oregon, permanent exhibits, and changing exhibits of Jewish history both in Oregon and throughout the world. Call for hours, which vary, and to make an appointment to visit the museum.

Portland Audubon Society Sanctuary
5151 N.W. Cornell Rd.
(503) 292-6855

The Portland Audubon Society, a nonprofit group with a long and established concern about the Oregon's ecology and wildlife, has worked closely with government agencies to further protect Oregon's natural beauty. A leading example is the Audubon Sanctuary, a 160-acre tract surrounded by Forest Park, a 5,000-acre municipal park, and linked to that park's Wildwood and Macleary Trails. Most visitors arrive by car not only to walk the trails and spot birds, but also to visit the Wildlife Care Center. Here injured owls, hawks, herons, cranes, and other birds and waterfowl are cared for until they can be returned to the wild.

Audubon House includes one of the best selections of books on natural history and wildlife. There is also an interpretive center, a nature store, and a viewing window overlooking the feeding platforms for resident songbirds. Hours for the sanctuary and gift shop are 10 A.M. to 6 P.M. Monday through Saturday and 10 A.M. to 5 P.M. on Sunday. There is no admission charge to visit the sanctuary.

Portland's beautiful Chinese Garden mingles nature with clever nurturing. CREDIT: ROGER LEUDTKE

Portland Classical Chinese Garden
N.W. 3rd and Everett
(503) 228–8131
www.chinesegarden.org

In September 2000, the ribbon was cut on Portland's newest attraction, the exquisite Portland Classical Chinese Garden, more formally known as the "Garden of Awakening Orchids." This double-walled oasis, which was built in a traditional Chinese style with extensive help from Portland's Chinese sister city Suzhou, inhabits a city block at the north end of Chinatown and serves as a retreat from the chaos of urban life. But it's more than a retreat. The garden integrates the elements of water, stone, light, shadow, color, texture, and fragrance to form an enclosed small world that mysteriously feels as though it unfurls the entire universe within its walls.

Mysteries are at the soul of this place, but its physical existence is due to attentive design and careful building. Clever planning makes good use of views and space; you would never know from the outside that the garden holds a lake of 8,000 square feet, and from the inside, it's hard to remember that the sidewalk is 12 feet away. You enter through a series of courtyards designed to help you make the transition from the outer world of hurry and work, and wander along paths, over bridges, beside water, and through rooms with enticing names like "Celestial House of Permeating Fragrance" or "Reflections in Clear Ripples." Similarly, pavilions are named after the meditations they are meant to inspire—"Flowers Bathing in Spring Rain," or "Painted Boat in Misty Rain." The Tower of Cosmic Reflections is a tea house run by Portland's Tao of Tea (see the Shopping chapter).

Within each discrete space is a carefully arranged display of stones, trees, shrubs, flowers, or other components.

Classical Chinese gardens, unlike the gardens of the emperor, were built by gentlemen scholars for their own use, so their scale is small, focusing on the well-wrought detail. No pebble is insignificant. Latticed windows give sunshine a template to decorate the elaborate mosaic floors. Banana plants live underneath the rain gutters to allow a beautiful sound to permeate the garden when it rains and the water splashes onto them. Rocks left in Suzhou streams sixty years ago by grandparents to be naturally sculpted by the water have been harvested by grandchildren and placed with delicate care. All five senses are honored in the feel of the stones, the fragrant blossoms, the sound of water, the taste of tea in the tea house, and the sight of, well, everything.

The deliberate recreation of nature's spontaneous workings: the Chinese garden is meant to inspire you to think about this paradox and others like it. For the scholars who possessed them—scholars who today would be bureaucrats or businessmen—gardens were places of freedom from the pressure and constraints of official life, where their owners could meditate upon the paradoxes of the freedom found in duty or the nature found in culture. One reason the Chinese Garden is powerful is that such paradoxes are not foreign to us moderns. We buy cars and houses in order to be free but then must slave away to pay for the houses and cars.

It is easy to enjoy the garden on your own, but if you want to learn more about its history, traditions, and symbolism, we strongly recommend taking one of the tours offered throughout the day. The garden is open daily, from 10 A.M. to 5 P.M., November through March, and from 9 A.M. to 6 P.M., April through September. Tickets are $6 for adults, $5 for everyone else over the age of five.

Union Station
800 N.W. 6th Ave.
(503) 273–4866

The neon GO BY TRAIN sign on the tower of Portland's Union Station harkens back to an earlier era of travel, but this large brick building still plays a key role in the city's transportation network. Amtrak trains on long-distance journeys stop at Union Station, heading for Seattle, Chicago, San Francisco, and Los Angeles, and there are daily, super-modern trains to Seattle that contrast with the old-fashioned setting of the station itself. A visit to Union Station is an exercise in nostalgia, with its massive, dark ticket counter, its echoing marble floors and walls, and its majestically high ceilings. There is a small snack shop in the station offering microwave meals, soft drinks, sandwiches, postcards, trinket souvenirs, and T-shirts; outside the snack shop are quaint paintings of railway scenes. Next to the waiting area is Wilfs, a long-established restaurant and lounge. With its Victorian red-flocked walls, terrific piano bar, honest bartender, and good food, it has drawn an eclectic crowd for lunch, dinner, and evening drinks for most of this century. On a damp rainy Portland night, an Irish Coffee at Wilfs, savored while listening to the pianist, is good for the soul.

The face of Union Station is a graceful curve, and the tower clock still accurately tells time. The station has a new lease on its downsized life as part of a multimodal transportation center (in urban planner-speak). The intercity bus terminals are nearby, and Tri-Met has extended the city's transit mall to the station.

The station's large rail yards are gone, much to the horror of those who hoped for a larger rail renaissance, and are being replaced by town houses, condos, and retail and commercial space. Adjacent to Portland's trendy Pearl District, the in-progress River District will reshape the entire area into a new neighborhood. A long-buried urban stream will be restored as part of the project, creating a natural oasis in the area. To make all this possible, the city, the Portland Development Commission, and other government agencies agreed to pour a great deal of public money into the project.

Crystal Springs Rhododendron Garden
S.E. 28th Ave.
(1 block north of Woodstock Blvd.)
(503) 823-3640

Long periods of gray days create a great sense of appreciation of color in many Oregonians. You can see this in the well-tended public and private gardens that celebrate the coming of spring and summer with tulips, lilacs, daffodils, azaleas, magnolias, roses, and rhododendrons. Beginning in April, Oregonians flock to the seven-acre Crystal Springs Rhododendron Gardens to rejoice and revel in the brilliant colors of the garden's 2,500 rhododendrons, azaleas, and other plants. While spring is prime time here, the gardens are a delight at any time of the year. In the fall, the Japanese maples and sourwood trees burst into flame, a final defiant gesture against the coming dark monotones of winter. A spring-fed lake attracts a permanent colony of ducks and other waterfowl, not to mention the area's population of birders. Even when the seasons' colors have peaked, the garden attracts visitors looking for solitude and a temporary respite from urban life.

From the first of March through Labor Day, there is a $3 admission charge, but children under twelve are always admitted free, and Tuesdays and Wednesdays the fees are waived. The park is open from dawn to dusk. (For further information, see our Portland's Parks chapter.)

Kidd Toy Museum
1301 S.E. Grand Ave.
(503) 233-7807

The bumper sticker proclaiming "whoever dies with the most toys wins" may have been inspired by Kidd Toy Museum. This world-class collection of toys, particularly toy cars and other transportation vehicles, originated as one person's hobby gone wild over twenty-five years. The collection also includes toy trains and planes, railroad items, police badges, and a range of mechanical banks. To preserve the collection (and avoid paying inheritance taxes), the owner created a museum that is open to the public free of charge.

Insiders' Tip

Rather than simply drive to Oaks Amusement Park make it the destination of two lovely nature walks. First, you can start at the trailhead of the Oaks Bottom Trail on Milwaukie Boulevard just south of the intersection of Holgate and Mcloughlin. Here you can meander down into a large swale running along the Willamette River that leads to the amusement park. The other approach takes off from Oaks Park just north of the Sellwood Bridge. Head down to the Willamette and follow a broad trail to the amusement park.

The Kidd Toy Museum is closed on Sundays and open Mondays through Fridays from 8:30 A.M. until 5 P.M. and from 8:30 A.M. until 1 P.M. on Saturdays. (See our entry in Kidstuff.)

Leach Botanical Garden
6704 S.E 122nd Ave.
(503) 761–9503

Come see this delightful and unique garden that is free to the public. Beginning in the 1930s, Lila and John Leach, two amateur botanists, started their five-acre garden along Southeast Portland's Johnson Creek. Credited with discovering eleven new species of Northwest plants, the Leaches eventually grew their garden to include some fourteen acres. More than 1,500 species of native ferns, wildflowers, shrubs, and irises contentedly grow in the garden. Rock gardens, bog gardens, and an experimental recycling and composting center have recently been added. The garden is open Sundays from 1 P.M. until 4 P.M. and Tuesdays through Saturdays from 9 A.M. until 4 P.M. (Also see our entry in Portland's Parks.)

Oaks Amusement Park
S.E. Spokane St. at the east end of the Sellwood Bridge, on the Willamette River
(503) 236–5722
www.oakspark.com

Offering lots of good, clean, old-fashioned fun, Oaks Park is a throwback to the days when municipal or private streetcar companies built residential developments and amusement parks to stimulate riders. Originally opened in 1905, Oaks Park has survived the demise of the streetcars, the introduction of television and video games and several floods to amuse and entertain yet another generation of Portlanders. This isn't Disneyland and it isn't high-tech. However, there are enough stomach-churning, neck-snapping rides for the bigger kids as well as many milder rides for the smaller, younger, or more timid thrill seekers. For an afternoon or evening of excitement and laughter, you can't go wrong.

Besides the games of skill and chance, Oaks Park offers a sedately scary tunnel of love, a giant slide, and a small merry-go-round. New rides are in the works as well as remodeling some of the creaky buildings. Picnic tables and fireplaces are available for family use, and there are no rules prohibiting bringing in your own food. The usual amusement park menu of cotton candy and deep-fried "food-on-a-stick" refreshments are also offered. The park's roller-skating rink clearly harkens back to a different era of entertainment, but it is still very popular. It is one of the oldest continually operating roller rinks in the country and the only one with a live Wurlitzer organ. If you don't travel with your own roller skates, rentals are available. The park is open throughout the year, but its high season is clearly during the summer. It is also sponsors Fourth-of-July fireworks, weather permitting. For more information, please refer to our Kidstuff chapter.

Oregon Museum of Science and Industry (OMSI)
1945 S.E. Water Ave.
(503) 797–4000
www.omsi.edu

One of the most popular attractions in Oregon and one of the five largest science museums in the nation, the Oregon Museum of Science and Industry is really a series of very different exhibits and elements. OMSI is a hands-on museum where visitors, especially children, are encouraged to touch things, to try experiments, and to question why things happen. While not specifically a children's museum, this is a learning center disguised as a museum.

Adults and children alike will enjoy the presentations in the large-screen OMNIMAX theater and the variety of programs in the Murdock Sky Theater, a domed theater for programs on astronomy. The core of the museum is a series of specialized exhibit halls, each with a different emphasis and exhibits. The Earth Science Hall shakes things up with its

The USS Blueback, *the last diesel-powered submarine built, is now decommissioned. It is docked at OMSI and is open for tours.* CREDIT: DAVID JOHNSON

realistic Earthquake Room. Recently, OMSI offered an exhibit that captured the kids' attention. *Grossology: The Impolite Science of the Human Body* explains tummy acid, burps, and why you shouldn't eat boogers. Other exhibits present information about natural phenomena and allow visitors to discover the complex interrelationships of the earth's seemingly unrelated elements. The Life Science Hall focuses on human growth in the fullest sense of the term and includes a house and an office illustrating designs for accessible living and assisting technology. At the Information Science Hall visitors can beam a personal message into the vastness of space and receive information on the knowledge and skills that created technology as we know it and constantly expands it.

While there is a separate admission charge for USS *Blueback*, the U.S. Navy's last diesel powered submarine, visitors should not miss a tour of this vessel. The *Blueback* tour lasts forty minutes, and visitors should carefully read the "Tips for USS *Blueback* Visitors" brochure before buying a ticket. This is a real submarine, with confined spaces, no windows, and no onboard restrooms; access is by ladders instead of stairs. Children must be at least four years old and 36 inches tall to tour the submarine.

OMSI also brings a series of special exhibits to Portland, many of which appeal to children and adults. Giants of the Gobi capitalized on the interest in dinosaurs, and Missing Links Alive used exhibits of rare fossils, multimedia presentations, and lifelike animatronics to travel several million years back in time to see how our long-forgotten ancestors lived.

Now located in a dramatically domed new building on the east bank of the Willamette River, OMSI is closed on

Mondays except when a public school holiday falls on a Monday. It is open Tuesday through Sunday 9:30 A.M. until 5:30 P.M., except for Sundays when it is open from 9:30 A.M. until 7 P.M. Summer hours are Monday through Sunday 9:30 A.M. to 7 P.M. During the year, OMSI offers a variety of camps, classes, field trips, and special programs for students, adults, and families. The facility has an ATM, a cafe, and vending machines. Not surprisingly, there is a large, well-stocked gift shop with a wide range of science-oriented objects, toys, T-shirts, games, and books. There is also an OMSI Science Store in the Washington Square Shopping Center in Beaverton, Oregon. Parking is free, and admission to OMSI is $7 for adults and $5 for youth and seniors.

North/Northeast Portland

The Grotto
N.E. 85th Ave. and Sandy Blvd.
(503) 254–7371
www.thegrotto.org

This long-established, sixty-two-acre Catholic sanctuary is an oasis in Portland's urban cityscape. The Grotto is both a religious shrine and a garden. Staffed by the Servites, or the Order of the Servants of Mary, the grounds include lush groves of towering fir trees, ferns, rhododendrons, and other native plants. Our Lady's Grotto, a rock cave carved into the base of a 110-foot high granite cliff sheltering a marble replica of Michelangelo's *The Pieta*, is the central attraction. The Grotto's upper level contains well-tended gardens, streams, and ponds while offering incredible views of the Columbia River Gorge, Mount St. Helens, and the Cascades. The Meditation Chapel features a floor-to-ceiling glass wall with a panoramic view of the Columbia River, and on a clear day, Mount St. Helens and Mount Adams. A Servite Monastery, a Peace Garden, and an interesting collection of wood sculpture are also within The Grotto's boundaries. Parking is free, but there is a $2 fee for the ten-story elevator ride to the upper level. During Christmas, The Grotto takes on a seasonal air, and crowds come to see the story of the nativity told with light sculpted figures. The Grotto is open seven days a week from 9 A.M. until 8 P.M., and in the winter, from 9 A.M. until 5:30 P.M.

The Oregon Garden
879 W. Main St., Silverton
www.oregongarden.org

Opened in April 2000, this 240 acres of impressive horticulture is a flowery blossom on the West Coast designed to show off Oregon's nursery industry. The Oregon Garden contains a water garden with waterfalls and ponds, a Weird Plant Garden, and a Children's Garden with animal topiaries. If you go from Portland, take Interstate 5 south to the Woodburn exit, go east on Oregon Highway 21 approximately 11 miles to Oregon Highway 213, go south, (right) about 15 miles to Silverton. Large signs will guide you through Silverton to the gardens. Hours are 9 A.M. to 3 P.M. daily. Entrance fees are $6 for adults, $5 for seniors (sixty and older) and students (ages fourteen through seventeen), $3 for children ages eight through fourteen, and children seven and younger are admitted free.

SamTrack (Near Oregon Museum of Science and Industry)
1945 S.E. Water Ave.
(503) 653–5452

The delightful SAMTRAK train offers a leisurely paced ride on rails along the east bank of the Willamette River, through some industrial and residential sections of the city, on to the amusement center at Oaks Park, through the Oaks Bottom Wildlife Preserve, and then to the Sellwood Bridge. While you can board the train at any of the stations, it is most convenient to start at the OMSI in Southeast Portland. This is an open-air ride, and the train runs from May through October, when there is the highest probability, but no guarantee, of good weather. This is Portland, so dress appropriately, or at least defensively. That means rain coats, hats, and umbrellas. For more specific information, please see our Kidstuff chapter.

Vancouver, Washington

Europeans settled in Vancouver in the early 1800s as a Hudson's Bay Company trading post. Now Vancouver is the fourth largest city in Washington, with a population of more than 200,000. Vancouver's diverse attractions range from the restoration of original Fort Vancouver and Officer's Row to the Ridgefield Wildlife Refuge. While Vancouver shares the Columbia River with Portland, the city has developed its own identity and should not be viewed as a lesser Portland or even as a Portland suburb, but as a historic and vibrant city in its own right. The area code for all attractions in Vancouver and Southwest Washington is 360, so it's always a long-distance call from Portland.

The Academy
400 E. Evergreen Blvd.
(360) 694–3271

American and Northwest history is filled with the pioneering efforts of religious orders to help settle and develop new territories. Mother Joseph, a Catholic nun from the Midwest, arrived in Washington in the early 1870s and eventually founded and built a number of charitable institutions. The Academy was built out of local brick. It housed the first school, hospital, orphanage, and convent in Clark County. While the Sisters of Providence no longer own the building, the structure, now restored, remains as a local landmark with its distinctive architecture and highly visible and central location. The building is still active, housing private offices and a cozy bistro.

Clark County Historical Museum
1511 Main St.
(360) 695–4681
www.fvhscc.org

A good starting place for a visit to Vancouver, the museum displays a range of historic artifacts relating to the founding and growth of the area. Additional displays and exhibits document the original Native American residents of the region. There is also an exhibit detailing how the expansion of the railroads across the country and along the Pacific Coast changed the area's economy, population, and contact with the rest of the nation.

The museum is open all year (except on major holidays) Tuesday through Saturday from 12:30 P.M. until 4:30 P.M. Although the museum is free, donations are accepted. The museum is not wheelchair accessible.

Columbia Arts Center
400 W. Evergreen Blvd.
(360) 693–0350

Located in a former Presbyterian Church originally built in 1911, this community center for the performing and visual arts reflects local interest and support of the arts and offers a year-round schedule of live theater as well as musical and dance performances. The center's gallery, with its rotating exhibits of work by local and regional artists, is open to the public without charge Monday through Friday from 8 A.M. to 6 P.M., but is closed on Saturdays. Space can be rented on weekends.

Columbia River Waterfront Trail

This flat, one-way trail runs 4 miles from the Captain Vancouver Memorial at the foot of Columbia Way, passes through Marine Park near the Henry J. Kaiser Memorial and Renaissance Promenade, and ends at Tidewater Cove. It also passes a larger-than-life bronze statue honoring Ilchee, the daughter of a nineteenth-century chief of the Chinook tribe, and a

Marine Park Interpretive Center before ending at Tidewater Cove. Even on a warm day, there can be a brisk wind along the river, so a light jacket, a hat, and sunglasses might make the walk more enjoyable.

Henry J. Kaiser Shipyard Memorial
In Marine Park on Boat Launch Rd. at the end of Marine Dr.
(360) 696–8171

During World War II, the Henry J. Kaiser Shipyards in Vancouver and Portland turned out 140 Liberty ships, T-2 Tankers, and escort carriers ("baby flat-tops") for the war effort. The city of Vanport north of Portland was built to house the 38,000 workers who migrated to the region from throughout the country to build the ships. The workforce included a large number of African Americans who were recruited in the South and brought to Oregon and Washington by the trainload. The descendants of these workers who stayed after the war formed the core of the area's African-American population, which added to the region's cultural diversity.

The shipyards closed shortly after the end of the war and Vanport was destroyed in a postwar flood. Now, only faint traces of the shipyard's wooden ways remain along the river. The three-story Henry J. Kaiser Shipyard Memorial and Interpretive Center recognizes and honors the contributions of these workers not only to the Allied victory in World War II, but also for their continuing contributions to the region's culture and economy. (For more on Vanport and shipbuilding during the war years, see our History chapter.)

Esther Short Park
6th St. and Columbia Dr.
(360) 696–8171

This five-acre site is the state's oldest public square and includes the Victorian Rose Gardens and the 1867 Slocum House, an Italianate structure that is one of the few remaining buildings from Vancouver's earliest residential neighborhoods. Moved from its original site during an urban renewal project, the Slocum House now serves as a theater. With downtown Vancouver experiencing a period of renaissance and revitalization, this park, with its gardens and Victorian-era benches, fountains, and lights, serves as an anchor to the city's past.

Fort Vancouver National Historic Site
1501 E. Evergreen Blvd.
(800) 832–3599, ext. 17
www.nps.gov/fova

Fort Vancouver was originally built by the British not only as a fur-trading center,

Insiders' Tip

A worthy day trip on a sunny day would be a jaunt to the Oregon Garden with a small detour en route to the hamlet of Aurora. Here at the junction of ORE 219 and Highway 99 E, this richly historic town offers a terrific museum with artifacts from the days when Aurora was a religious commune dominated by a brusk tyrant, and a number of bustling antique stores for a pleasant afternoon of browsing and then on to the garden for more to appreciate down the valley.

but also as an attempt to solidify Britain's claim to the entire Northwest Territory. One of thirty-four such forts the Hudson's Bay Company built, Fort Vancouver became an American outpost in 1846 when a treaty between the United States and Britain established the 49th parallel as Canada's southern border. Now restored and administered by the National Park Service, Fort Vancouver offers a look back at frontier life through a range of restored buildings, exhibits and displays, and recreations.

Adjacent to Fort Vancouver National Historic Site sits Vancouver Barracks, the first military post in the Oregon Territory. From this base, Americans explored Alaska, fought the Indian Wars, provided security to settlers, and developed an early network of roads, dams, and locks. From May 1849 to the present, Vancouver Barracks has been an active military post. To the north of the Fort Vancouver National Historic Site and just across a vast park-like green is Officers' Row, an immaculately restored and rare collection of twenty-one Victorian-era homes built between 1850 and 1906 by the federal government. The houses were the residences for the military officers and other government officials and their families assigned to Fort Vancouver, Vancouver Barracks, and the army's Department of the Columbia. Homes such as these were once common on American military bases, but this is the only entire Officers Row preserved in the nation. Among the army officers who lived on Officers Row were Generals Phillip Sheridan, Benjamin Bonneville, and Omar Bradley. Guests at Officers' Row included three U.S. presidents: Ulysses S. Grant, Rutherford B. Hayes, and Franklin Delano Roosevelt. This site is open from 9 A.M. to 4 P.M. daily during winter and 9 A.M. to 5 P.M. during summer.

The George C. Marshall House
1301 Officers Row
(360) 693–3103
www.ci.vancouver.wa.us
This Officers Row house, now called The George C. Marshall House, was the home for the commanding officer of Vancouver Barracks. Originally built in 1886 and now completely restored and furnished with antiques from the 1880s, the house is home to the local office of Washington's governor. General Marshall, who was awarded the Nobel Peace Prize in 1953, served as Vancouver Barracks' commanding officer from 1936 to 1938 and lived in the house during that period. In 1937 Marshall opened his home to the three Russian fliers who landed at Pearson Airfield after their transpolar flight. The building was later renamed to honor his service to the nation as the U.S. Army's Chief of Staff during World War II and later as Secretary of Defense and Secretary of State. The George C. Marshall House is open seven days of the week from 9 A.M. to 5 P.M.

The Grant House
1101 Officers Row
(360) 694–5252
The Grant House is the oldest building on Officers Row and was named after Ulysses S. Grant, who served as the base quartermaster in the 1850s and returned to visit the base in 1879 after winning fame in the Civil War and serving as U.S. president.

The Grant House, which is open Monday through Saturday from 11 A.M. to 5 P.M. and Sunday 10 A.M. to 2 P.M., now sees action as the Grant House Folk Art Center. In addition to exhibits of American and Northwestern folk art, there is a gift gallery featuring work of regional artists, and Sheldon's Cafe (see our entry in the Restaurants chapter). There is no admission fee to the Grant House, but donations are accepted.

Hidden House
110 W. 13th St.
(360) 696–2847
This elegant, restored Victorian mansion was built by Lowell M. Hidden and his son Foster. A classic Victorian entrepreneur, Hidden made his fortune with a

brick factory, hotel development, railroad construction, and banking. The family brick factory is still in operation, but these beautiful homes are no longer in the family. Visitors are invited to tour the home with no admission fee before or after lunch at the Hidden House Restaurant from 11 A.M. to 2 P.M. from Tuesday to Friday and dinner Tuesday through Sunday from 5 to 9 P.M.

**M.J. Pearson Air Museum at
Pearson Air Field
1105 E. 5th St.
(360) 694–7026
www.pearsonairmuseum.org**

Interested in aviation? If so, this place is a must stop. At the east end of the Ft. Vancouver National Historic Site, this newly expanded aviation museum captures the achievements and excitement of the Golden Age of Aviation in the 1920s and '30s. As part of Vancouver Barracks, Pearson Airfield was established in 1905 as a dirigible base. The early, unwieldy lighter-than-air ships displaced the officers' polo ponies, as the airfield is built on a former polo field.

Having welcomed its first airplane in 1911, Pearson Airfield is the oldest operating airport in the nation. The museum's recently expanded facilities include an airplane hanger dating from the 1920s as well as a new theater, computerized flight simulators, and a working aircraft restoration center. While there are some contemporary aircraft on display, the heart of the museum's aircraft collection and related exhibits reflect earlier eras, concentrating on civilian aviation developments during the two decades before World War II.

Pearson Airfield played an important role in the development of airmail service as a center of early commercial aviation and as an early Army aviation base. Tex Rankin and Charles Lindbergh flew from this field, and in 1937 the Russian aircraft making the first nonstop transpolar flight landed here. The Soviet Transpolar Monument, displayed outside the museum, commemorates the accomplishments of the three Soviet aviators who made that historic flight. After unexpectedly landing at Vancouver (they were trying to reach California), the aircrew was greeted by General George C. Marshall, then the officer commanding Vancouver Barracks.

The museum also has a well-stocked gift shop and hosts a variety of lectures and presentations on aviation history and several aviation-themed special events throughout the year, including flights of vintage aircraft. If you want to break for a sack lunch, there are a few picnic tables in a very nice open green space directly across from the museum. Admission is $5 for adults, $4 for seniors, $3 for students ages thirteen through eighteen and $2 for children ages six through twelve. On Father's Day, all dads are admitted free and get a chance to win a ride in an antique aircraft. The museum is open Tuesdays through Sundays from 10 A.M. until 5 P.M.

**Ridgefield National Wildlife Refuge
N.W. 269th St. (WA Hwy. 501) at 1–5, exit 14
(360) 887–4106
www.r1.fws.gov/ridgefield**

Between Vancouver and Woodland, Washington, this 5,100-acre refuge features pasture, woodlands, and marshland. Much of the wildlife that sustained the area's Native American population (decimated by epidemics in the 1930s) and the later European settlers, is still found here. The refuge's population includes deer, coyotes, nutria, foxes, rabbits, beavers, and otters. The population swells as 200,000 or more migratory birds and waterfowl travel the Pacific Flyway (depending on the season) and either stop and rest in the preserved wetlands or decide to spend the winter there. The refuge's permanent waterfowl and avian population includes herons, cranes, swans, geese, and eagles. There is a well-marked 1.9-mile loop trail that is an easy, if sometimes muddy, walk, even for children. This is a day-use only area. Though hiking and fishing are allowed, fires and off-road vehicles are not permitted. Binoculars, spotting scopes, and cameras with tripods and long lenses may make viewing and wildlife photography easier. Boots or old, comfortable shoes, jackets, hats, sunglasses, and sunscreen as necessary, may make the visit more enjoyable. A footbridge over a set of busy railroad tracks is an added attraction, allowing an unusual perspective on the Amtrak trains and the hardworking freight trains running up and down the Pacific Coast. The Ridgefield Refuge Office, 301 N. 3rd Street, is open weekdays from 7:30 A.M. to 4 P.M. and it has dozens of informative brochures and a useful map/user's guide to the refuge. Open from dawn to dusk all year long, the refuge is free to all ages.

Outlying Areas

Bonneville Dam
Off I–84 (Exit 40)
(541) 374–8820
www.bpa.gov

A half-hour of scenic driving through the Columbia River Gorge will take you to the Bonneville Dam, which has an attractive visitor center brimming with interactive exhibits, short films, and displays that illustrate the history and culture of local and regional Native American tribes. You can watch steelhead and Chinook salmon climbing the fish ladders, and boats passing through the locks. There isn't a restaurant nearby, so pack a few brown bags and enjoy a leisurely sack lunch on one of the numerous indoor and outdoor picnic tables. On the return trip, stop and stretch your legs on one of the many trails at Multnomah Falls (see Daytrips), one of the area's premier attractions any time of year.

End of the Oregon Trail Interpretive Center
1726 Washington St., Oregon City
(503) 657–9336
www.endoftheoregontrail.org

The End of the Oregon Trail Interpretive Center is in Oregon City, and officially designated as the true end of the Oregon Trail. On Abernathy Green, just off I–205, the center has created a new local landmark with its three stylized 50-foot-tall covered wagon-shaped buildings. While everyone in Oregon talked about the sesquicentennial (150th anniversary) of the Oregon Trail, and there were all sorts of events, both silly and serious, during the yearlong celebration in 1993, these people went out and did something. Admittedly this is a made-to-order historical attraction. But it is in the correct location, and the organizers have done a good job of telling not only the settlers' stories but the effect this large migration— 300,000 people over the course of thirty years—had on the indigenous peoples and the land. Just as importantly, the center's organizers had the courage and determination to make something new, a trait they share with the people they honor.

The first years of the center were difficult: The year after the center opened, the site was flooded in one of the worst winters in recent Oregon history. The next year, high winds ripped apart the canvas coverings on the huge wagons. Undaunted, organizers recovered. Costumed trail guides lead visitors through a tour of the center that includes a multimedia dramatization of three representative journeys across 2,000 miles of frontier. The tour also uses live presentations, demonstrations, and well-researched and well-prepared exhibits of artifacts and heirlooms to retell the pioneers' epic stories.

The shows are scheduled for specific times, so this is not a self-guided museum. Visitors spend an average of ninety minutes at the center. Advance tickets can be purchased at all TicketMaster outlets, (503-224-4400). On summer (May through September) weekdays and Saturdays, there are eight scheduled

The Center for Northwest Art at the Portland Art Museum has natural light and expansive spaces. It is a beautiful new space for displaying the work of regional artists. CREDIT: COURTESY OF THE PORTLAND ART MUSEUM

presentations. On summer Sundays, when the center opens at 10 A.M. instead of 9 A.M., there are seven. The winter schedule (September through May) allows five daily presentations. During the summer, the center hosts a locally written presentation called the Oregon Trail Pageant, which mixes music (some of which is performed on authentic and reproduction instruments of the era), dance, and drama to tell the story of the Oregon Trail. Not unexpectedly, there is a gift shop, the George Abernethy & Co. Merchandise museum store, featuring the usual variety of souvenirs, called heritage items, and Northwest handicrafts. Hours are Monday through Saturday 9 A.M. to 5 P.M. and Sunday 10 A.M. to 5 P.M. Admission is $5.50 for adults and $3 for children between the ages of five and twelve. Seniors may enter for $4.50.

Hulda Klager Lilac Gardens
115 Pekin Rd., Woodland, Washington
(360) 225–8996

Well worth the twenty-five-minute drive, the Hulda Klager Lilac Gardens are easy to find. Just take I–5 north of Vancouver, look for exit 21, and follow the signs. It's a lovely garden, especially during the annual Spring Lilac Week when dozens of varieties of lilacs are in full bloom. Depending on the weather, Lilac Week is held during the last week in April or the first week in May. The lilacs truly flourish and flower on these well-kept and fertile grounds. The Mager House is listed on the National Register of Historic Places and features a large collection of antique dolls and period furniture and artifacts. There is also a small gift shop. The Lilac Gardens are open year-round, but are most popular, and most crowded, when the blossoms are in flower in late spring or early summer. Gardeners from throughout Washington and Oregon come to buy cuttings and seedlings to plant in their own gardens. The Mager House is open for tours during Lilac Week and by appointment at other times. There twelve years of age and over.

Oregon Military Museum Camp Withycombe
Hwy. 212, Clackamas
(503) 557-5359
www.swiftview.com\^ormilmuseum|join.html

The Oregon Military Museum is housed in a Quonset Hut on an Oregon Army National Guard facility. To get here, take Interstate 205 to Oregon Highway 212, which heads toward Estacada. After ⅛ mile, turn left on S.E. 102nd and follow to the maingate entrance of the camp. Its displays and exhibits emphasize the history and accomplishments of the Oregon Army, Oregon Air National Guard, and Oregon veterans. With limited space and resources, the museum's collection includes uniforms, artifacts, models, paintings, a small but impressive library and archives, and, perhaps most importantly, a knowledgeable and helpful staff. The museum also has a significant collection of restored and functional wheeled and tracked military vehicles and artillery pieces. When visiting, ask to see what was called on national television the "Oh, My God Room." This is actually a very large vault containing the museum's significant collection of handheld weapons. Admission is free though donations are welcomed. The Oregon Military Museum is open on Fridays and Saturdays from 9 A.M. to 5 P.M. or by appointment. The staff is very cooperative in arranging private tours.

Vista House at Crown Point
Columbia River Historic Hwy.

Officially Crown Point State Park, Vista House was conceived as a monument to the completion of the Columbia River Highway from Portland to Hood River in 1916 (see our Daytrips chapter's section on the Mount Hood/Columbia Gorge Loop). Two years later, the slightly Art Nouveau building was completed. The view from Vista House, which is 733 feet above the Columbia River, is one of the state's most popular, dramatic, and beautiful sights. It can be reached by taking the Historic Columbia River Highway (Oregon Highway 30) off of U.S. Interstate 84 at Corbett (exit 22), 15 miles east of Portland. Designated a Natural Landmark of national significance, Vista House is also listed on the National Register of Historic Places. Visitors will not only be impressed by the sweeping views of the Columbia River, the Cascades, and the Columbia Gorge, but also by the endurance—and perhaps masochism—of the cyclists who pedal their way up the winding hills to Vista House. Sunsets and sunrises are spectacular. If you plan on photographing the evening or morning colors, bring a tripod because the winds can cause a handheld camera to vibrate. There is a small gift shop and snack bar inside the building, but the real attraction is the view. Standing on the edge of the viewing area, often facing into the east wind, the sheer magnitude of the meeting of the mountains and river is dramatic. Although Vista House will be closed through 2001 for restoration, Crown Point will still be open with a modular office. Office Hours are 8:30 A.M. to 6 P.M. April 15 to October 15.

Willamette Shore Trolley
HarborPlace Station (south of the RiverPlace Hotel in Portland and State St. Terminal or 311 State St., Lake Oswego
(503) 222-2226
www.trainweb.org-orehs-wst.htm

This is hardly either rapid transit or mass transit, but a ride on the Willamette Shore Trolley between Portland and Lake Oswego or the reverse offers a different perspective on the river and several Portland neighborhoods. The trolley runs on a once-abandoned track between Macadam Avenue and the river, and provides riders with close-up views of close-in east bank neighborhoods, river traffic, residential and commercial development at Johns' Landing in Southwest Portland, and some nice riverfront homes in Lake Oswego.

A host of unresolved and perhaps unresolvable issues may keep this route from being developed as anything more than an enjoyable ride. You may notice that the trolley pulls or pushes a small vehicle, called a donkey, which generates power for the electric motor: There are no wires along the route, so the trolley has to create its own power. The Lake Oswego station is in downtown Lake Oswego, a section with several galleries, small shops, restaurants, taverns, and coffee shops within walking distance. The actual streetcar used for the trip may vary: In the past, the trip has used an Australian streetcar; a double-decker Blackpool tram from the United Kingdom is now on the tracks. During December, the trolley makes some evening runs for riders to view the Parade of Boats, Portland's annual display of decorated and illuminated boats. Round-trip fare for adults is $8; $4 for children under twelve, and $7 for seniors. One-way trips are $7 for sen-

Insiders' Tip

Portland's Chinatown was home one-hundred years ago to the second-largest Chinese community in the nation. Now it's known for its shops, grocery stores, and restaurants, and especially for its magnificent gate at N.W. 4th and Burnside.

iors and adults and $2 for kids. There are special fares for families. Trips run during spring Saturday and Sunday noon to 2:30 P.M. from Lake Oswego and 1 to 3:30 P.M. from Portland.

Close-up

Souvenirs

We all need, along with world peace, an honest car mechanic, a broker who can predict the future, and another souvenir T-shirt, sweatshirt, or logo baseball cap. Fortunately, you will not lack the opportunity to purchase these necessities during your visit to Portland.

If you need something concrete to remind yourself of your trip, the following shops may help you. The information may be also of value if you made promises to friends, co-workers, distant relatives, or significant others to remember them with something material from your visit here.

To begin with the traditional fare, almost every Fred Meyer store has a small section of Oregon souvenirs. These are classic souvenirs in the fullest sense of the word, including shot glasses with maps of Oregon, miniature spoons decorated with a salmon or log truck, decals for your car's back window, postcards and souvenir photo books, and key chains with miniature Oregon license plates featuring various first names.

The downtown Visitors' Information Center (in Pioneer Courthouse Square), run by the Portland Oregon Visitors Association (POVA), is an excellent source of good advice, easily understood directions, insiders' tips from knowledgeable staff and volunteers, local publications, and a gazillion brochures. Oh, yes, they also sell a nice range of souvenirs. These include T-shirts, sweatshirts, posters, books, and assorted other logoed trinkets.

Among the accomplishments of Portland's late pioneer redeveloper Bill Naito is **Made In Oregon**, a chain store that carries homegrown products. The flagship store is in The Galleria at 921 S.W. Morrison, (503) 241–3630; other stores are located at the airport, in Washington Square, and in Depoe Bay on the Oregon coast. The stores are filled with Oregon wines and beers, Pendleton products, locally produced foods such as cheeses, assorted smoked meats, smoked salmon, hazelnuts, jams and jellies, and other items made or grown in Oregon. If nothing else, you owe yourself a visit just to see what is here.

Then there's always the university souvenir. Oregon's official state mammal is the American Beaver (aren't you glad you know that now?). The furry and toothy little animal is also the mascot for Oregon State University (OSU) in Corvallis, one of the state's two major universities. OSU's arch-rival is the University of Oregon (U of O or simply "Oregon") in Eugene. Oregon adopted a duck as a mascot. Both schools have lots of alumni and outposts in Portland. Both universities have centers in Portland that offer classes and programs, as well as critical sportswear items such as sweatshirts, beanies with propellers, and boxer shorts with college pennants, as well as more sophisticated pullovers and jackets. (Please note that we're not talking about chic understatement here. Oregon's colors are green and yellow; OSU's are black and orange.) Pick your colors at **OSU II**, 240 Yamhill Street, (503) 725–5765, or around the corner at the **U of O Center**, 772 S.W. Second Avenue, (503) 725–3057.

For something a little different, the gift shop or store at the **Oregon History Center**, 1200 S.W. Park, (503) 306–5230, may be the most underrated source of useful, intelligent, and attractive "souvenirs." There is an excellent selection of books on Portland, Oregon, and the Northwest. These range from serious political, social, and natural histories to coffee table photo essay books, many (if not most) produced by local authors and photographers. The shop stocks a wide selection of note cards, art cards, and postcards created by local graphic artists, designers, and photographers.

The center's store also offers a small selection of Northwest crafts (pottery, silver jewelry, and scarves) and toys, including model covered wagons. They have a well-chosen selection of

T-shirts, sweatshirts, coffee cups, and well-made denim shirts decorated with copies of petroglyphs and other designs inspired by regional Native Americans. The store also carries a range of Pendleton woolen products, including blankets and pillows, featuring both the company's classic designs and patterns and more contemporary interpretations of Western and Native American art and designs. These are not inexpensive, but they wear well and have excellent value, and the designs and colors are original, sophisticated, and dramatic.

At the Oregon History Center store and at other gift and specialty shops around Portland, look for historical photos from the Oregon Historical Society's massive photo archives. Recording both the dramatic and mundane from the turn of the century through the mid-1950s, the matted, 8"x10" black-and-white prints sell for less than $20.

Over in Vancouver, checkout the museum shop at **Pearson Air Museum**, 1115 E. 5th Street, Vancouver, (360) 694–7026, for gifts (T-shirts, die-cast toys, plastic and paper models, books and magazines, military insignia, and aviation "art") with a historic aeronautic bent.

The region's extensive network of brewpubs is a good source of original, inexpensive, and always practical gifts. These include pint glasses with the pub's logo, bar towels, and, of course, baseball caps, jackets, T-shirts, and sweatshirts proclaiming one's choice of brews. You can also usually leave with a small supply of the pub's coasters without too much trouble.

The Central Branch of the **Multnomah County Library**, 801 S.W. 10th Avenue, (503) 988–5911, has a small gift shop in the main foyer. Proceeds from sales help support the library. They don't have books, surprisingly, but most of the items—cards, coffee mugs, jewelry—have literary or book themes. One original item is a silk necktie ($30) with detailed images of bridges like those spanning Portland's Willamette River.

The **Oregon Maritime Museum**, 113 S.W. Naito Parkway, (503) 224–7724, has a small gift shop offering a selection of model boats handmade by a local artisan. Model ship builders and battleship history fans may consider a detailed plastic model of the USS *Oregon*, produced by Glencoe. These can be had for less than $20 and are available at better Portland hobby shops, including **Bridgetown Hobbies**, 3350 N.E. Sandy Boulevard, (503) 234–1881.

The Real Mother Goose, at 901 S.W. Yamhill, (503) 223–9510, is a locally owned one-of-a-kind store that is a cross between a fine art gallery, a sophisticated craft shop, and a jewelry store. The selection of pottery, handcrafted wood products and furniture, art glass, fabric art and handmade clothing, and art is superb. Prices are fair given the quality of the items. The staff is knowledgeable, intelligent, and courteous. If you want your purchase shipped home or sent as a gift, they can make the necessary arrangements and you can be assured that the item(s) will arrive in good condition.

The gift shops at the **Oregon Museum of Science and Industry**, 1945 S.E. Water Avenue, (503) 797–4626; the **Oregon Zoo**, Washington Park, (503) 525–4220; and the **Nature Store** at the **Portland Audubon Society**, 5151 N.W. Cornell Road, (503) 292–9453, all offer meaningful souvenir opportunities.

The city is also filled with locally owned small art and craft galleries that offer items that are ideal as mementos of your stay in Portland. The **Contemporary Crafts Gallery**, 3934 S.W. Corbett, (503) 223–2654, offers pottery, glass, furniture, jewelry, weavings, enamelware, and paper art made by local and regional artists and craftworkers. **Quintana Galleries**, 501 S.W. Broadway, (503) 223–1729, specializes in contemporary Northwest Native American art. They also offer folk art and antique art and artifacts from other Native American tribes and cultures and from Mexico and Central and South America. The **Hoffman Gallery**, 8245 S.W. Barnes Road (503) 297–5544, is on the wooded campus of the Oregon College of Art and Craft. The college, founded in 1906, is a nationally respected art and craft education center. The Hoffman Gallery, as well as the campus itself, a small cafe, and an excellent gift shop filled with art, glass, ceramics, weavings, and jewelry, make this often-overlooked attraction the source of some unusual souvenirs.

Succumbing to the economics of running a bookstore, Powell's City of Books has a selection of appropriately decorated T-shirts and sweatshirts and a few posters and coffee mugs.

Finally, for the really off-beat, **Tri-Met**, the regional transit agency, has a small "company store" in its headquarters in Southeast Portland at 4012 S.E. 17th Avenue, (503) 962–2400. The store features a variety of clothing and other items adorned with images of buses, light rail vehicles, and the agency's logo. Likewise, the **Portland Police Museum** on the 16th floor of the Justice Center, 1111 S.W. 2nd Avenue, (503) 823–0019, is the only place in town to buy a Portland Police Bureau sweatshirt, baseball hat, and other rare and desirable items. The museum is open Monday through Thursday from 10 A.M. to 3 P.M.

A neon insignia at the Portland Police Museum. CREDIT: DAVID JOHNSON

A spooky tree will bewitch visitors to the Enchanted Forest. CREDIT: MARY ALLISON

Kidstuff

"If a place has a reputation as being great for children," one of our friends once observed, "it's probably no good for adults." Fortunately, he wasn't referring to his native city. Portland is a great place for children and the adults who live with them. Many of the area's major attractions—Washington Park, the Chinese Garden, the Oregon History Center—appeal to persons both small and large, and many of the attractions designed just for children hold a kind of giddy appeal for their guardians. Here, then, are some of our favorite places to go with children in the Portland Metro area and a little beyond.

Attractions

Portland

Alpenrose Dairy
6149 S.W. Shattuck Rd.
(503) 244–1133

This working dairy holds surprises for any visitors who stop by for a simple glass of milk. As well as a menagerie of cows, sheep, horses, and goats, Alpenrose features a Western village, a museum of old cars and tractors and other farm implements, and a collection of antique toys. Seasonal events entertain the children during Christmas, Easter, and other times throughout the year. An old-fashioned velodrome with steep banks for bike races, several Little League fields, and an opera house make this an interesting and unusual place. Call for times, rates, and events; many exhibits and events are free.

Grant Park
N.E. 33rd Ave. and U.S. Grant Place

If your children are fans of Ramona Quimby, the young heroine of Beverly Cleary's whimsical books set in Northeast Portland, you ought to visit Grant Park. Its Children's Sculpture Garden features bronze statues of Ramona, Henry Huggins, and the matchless Ribsy. The fountains under Ramona's and Ribsy's feet are perfect for kids to splash in during warm weather, and around the concrete fountain, you'll find granite plaques engraved with all the titles of the Cleary books that take place in Portland. The sculpture garden is just south of the playground in Grant Park on N.E. 33rd Avenue between Knott Street and Broadway, adjacent to Grant High School where Cleary attended school in the 1930s. Four blocks away, you'll find Klikitat Street. Grant Park also has plenty of amusement outside the Cleary connection, with sports fields, playground equipment, tennis courts, lovely tall trees, and a pool.

Oaks Amusement Park
S. E. Spokane St. at the east end of Sellwood Bridge
(503) 236–5722
www.oakspark.com

There's plenty of action at this charming, old-fashioned amusement park dating back to the Lewis and Clark Exposition in 1905. Easy to find, on the east end of the Sellwood Bridge, the park offers twenty-eight rides. Highlights include a Ferris wheel, Noah's Ark carousel, a roller-skating rink, 360-degree looping roller coaster, and bumper boats for tots. Bring a sack lunch and enjoy lunch on the banks of the Willamette River. Don't forget to bring your camera—this is a totally unique place and you'll want to savor the memories. The park closes during the winter, but the roller rink stays open all year-round. Their Web site has good directions and information about hours and prices; you can also call, of course. (See our Attractions chapter for more information.)

SamTrack
Boarding stations at S.E. 11th Ave. and Linn St., Oaks Park, and Oregon Museum of Science and Industry
(503) 653–2380

Kids love to ride on trains, especially this flashy mini-locomotive, a fire engine-red diesel engine pulling two open-air cars through scenic Oaks Bottom Wildlife Refuge en route to either Oaks Amusement Park or the Oregon Museum of Science and Industry. The 6-mile trip lasts about an hour and affords nice views of the Willamette River. Tickets are $6 for adults, with discounts for senior citizens and kids younger than ten years of age. On Father's Day, all dads accompanied by a daughter or son get to ride for free. (See our chapter on Attractions for more information on SamTrack.)

Outlying Areas
Bonneville Dam
Off I–84 (Exit 40)
(541) 374–8820

Kids and their parents will love the beautiful half-hour drive from Portland through the Columbia River Gorge to the Bonneville Dam. The dam's attractive and informative visitor center is brimming with interactive exhibits, short films, and displays that illustrate the history and culture of local and regional Native American tribes. Watching the big boats pass through the locks is truly compelling, as are the dam's huge generators inside the powerhouse. Little ones are entranced by the sight of steelhead and Chinook Salmon stubbornly climbing the fish ladders, though sometimes older siblings grumble about dam breaching and salmon policy. There isn't a restaurant nearby, so pack a few brown bags and enjoy a leisurely sack lunch on one of the numerous indoor and outdoor picnic tables. On the return trip, take a hike along one of the many trails at or near

Multnomah Falls, one of the area's premier attractions any time of year.

Duyck's Peachy-Pig Farm
34840 S.W. Johnson School Rd., Cornelius
(503) 357–3570

The Portland Metro area is surrounded by some of the most fertile farmland in the nation, and farms like this one still dot the landscape just outside the city, though they are rapidly becoming endangered by Home Depots and tract houses. This traditional farmstead, a thirty-minute drive west of town on U.S. Highway 26, is worth the short trek so that the youngsters can see what a working farm is all about. Here they can watch the horses, cows, goats, and pigs living their lives far beyond petting zoos. Not only can they climb onto the seat of a tractor or other piece of farm equipment, but they can also be junior farmers picking strawberries and blackberries in season.

Enchanted Forest
8462 S.E Enchanted Wy., Turner
(503) 363–3060, (503) 371–4242
www.enchantedforest.com

We were grateful to have our own children so that we could have an excuse to visit the Enchanted Forest, 7 miles south of Salem and a little bit less than an hour's drive south from Portland. This amusement park features imaginative rides, displays, and activities for children of all ages (though some rides have height requirements). One of the nicest things about this place is the balance between thrilling rides and gentler activities. A half-timbered English Village and a replicated Old West town are fun to poke around, while a roller coaster designed to feel like a bob-sled and a scary haunted house provide more adrenaline-inducing entertainment. The Big Timber Log Ride is a fun, splashy way to cool off on a hot summer day. In addition, you'll find bumper boats, a Ferris wheel, fountains, storybook characters, and many other appealing things. Prices are reasonable: $6.95 for adults, $6.50 for seniors, and $6.25 for children

The roller coaster at Oaks Amusement Park is a family favorite. CREDIT: MARY ALLISON

ages three through twelve. (Children two and younger are admitted at no charge.) Take I–5 exit 248 (Sunnyside-Turner) to get here.

Fir Point Farms
14601 Arndt Rd., Aurora
(503) 678–2455

Pack up a picnic lunch and take the kids to see farmer Ed and one of the most beautiful farms in Oregon. A twenty-five-minute drive from downtown Portland, Fir Point Farms offers flowers, fresh produce, tours (by reservation), a deli, gift shop, and Tillamook ice cream. In the fall, Fir Point Farms is the host to swarms of pumpkin-picking schoolchildren, and every weekend in October feels like a farm exhibit in Central Park instead of Oregon, but between the homemade doughnuts and the hayrides, it's not easy to resist, even with the crowds. Other allurements include a spooky hay maze, pony rides,

and the chickens, turkeys, cows, horses, and goats. You can feed most of the animals, and the owners have capitalized on the attraction of this activity for city folks by charging twenty-five cents for a handful of chow. The greedy goats are the most fun to watch as they storm unwary visitors. In addition to their large, wooded pen, the goats have a tree house for their amusement and scamper along platforms 12 feet in the air, peering down at gawking parents and children. You can send food up to the goats by means of buckets on pulleys. That alone is worth the trip.

Flower Farmer and Canby Ferry
2512 N. Holly Rd., Canby
(503) 266–3581
www.flowerfarmer.com

Hordes of kids visit the Flower Farmer, 17 miles south of Portland, to see Sparky and Fred. Sparky is a pint-size, thirty-horsepower diesel engine that pulls the

Phoenix and Holly Railroad's 15-inch narrow gauge train through flowerbeds on a winding 1/2-mile circuit of tracks leading to a petting zoo and a pumpkin patch. The bright red caboose is named Fred. The train stops on the way to feed the horses and mules. The Flower Farmer is a blast for kids, especially around Halloween and Christmas. There's a hay pyramid that kids love and parents hate. There's also a gift shop with a staggering selection of dried flowers, as well as fresh flowers and produce when in season. (They'll also build you a train, given enough notice.) On the way home, if you follow Holly Road north to the end, it will take you to the charming Canby Ferry, in operation since 1914 and one of the few remaining river ferries on the Willamette. For $1.25, the friendly ferry operator will take your car full of people across the river on a platform ferry that holds about six vehicles. After you cross, you can take Mountain Road north; it will turn into Stafford Road and take you to I-205. The number for ferry information is (503) 655-8521.

Pacific Northwest Live Steamers
31083 S. Shady Dell Dr., Molalla
(503) 829-6866
Something about the Molalla area inspires train building. With up to eight operating ⅛-scale model trains running the rails, Pacific Northwest Live Steamers is Choo-Choo heaven. Approximately 25 miles from Portland on Oregon Highway

213, this beautiful, four-acre private park is open from May to October on Sundays and holidays. Admission is free, but donations are welcome. In the summer months, bring a jug of lemonade, a blanket, and a sack lunch and plop underneath one of the many gorgeous shade trees.

Summer Action Park
Mount Hood Ski Bowl on U.S. Hwy. 26
(503) 222-2695
Think the only action on the slopes is in the winter? Think again. The clever people at Mount Hood Ski Bowl maintain the Summer Action Park, which offers more than twenty-five attractions, including the Northwest's only Alpine slide, as well as Indy Karts, bungee jumping, adventure river rides, kiddy jeeps, batting cages, and horse and pony rides. Visit on the way to or from Ski Bowl at Camp Creek, Tollgate Campground, or one of the many gorgeous campsites in lush Mount Hood National Forest just off of U.S. Highway 26. Prepare a picnic basket or stop at the Dairy Queen in the nearby village of Rhododendron. Mount Hood is an hour's drive east of Portland on Oregon Highway 26. (For more information see our Daytrips and Recreation chapters.) Individual featured activities will set you back $1 to $5; all-day passes, which include unlimited rides down the 1/2-mile Alpine slide, are about $25.

Museums

Children's Museum
Washington Park, across from the Oregon Zoo
(503) 823-2227
www.pdxchildrensmuseum.org
The Children's Museum, a favorite of Portland children since 1949, reopened in June 2001 in a site that formerly housed OMSI, with three times the previous size for its innovative, hands-on play struc-

tures and materials that include digital storytelling, water play, and scope for the imagination. One feature of the new museum is a climbing structure that is also a musical instrument. The museum still offers amusements just for babies and spaces for birthday parties, as well as for field trips and group tours; a large public plaza is also open. The museum is open Tuesday through Sunday, from 9 A.M. to 5 P.M.; admission is $4. Check the website for updates.

Jeff Morris Fire Museum
55 S.W. Ash
(503) 823–3083, by appointment only

Located in a glass-enclosed room at the north end of the Portland Fire Station at 55 S.W. Ash, a collection of antique fire equipment helps kids learn about the history of fire fighting. Here, modern trucks and trailers sit close to their predecessors, an 1863 hand-pumper, an 1870 hand-drawn ladder truck, and an 1870 steam-pumper engine. One of the attractions that engages the avid attention of young and old is a 4,000-pound fire bell. Imagine the sound of that big ringer alerting firefighters to hop into their boots and slide down the pole.

Oregon Museum of Science and Industry
1945 S.E. Water Ave.
(503) 797–4000

The futuristic center known as OMSI (pronounced Ahm-zee) is nestled on the banks of the Willamette River and is home to the state's biggest science exhibits and laser light shows. OMSI is a preferred destination for wiggly preschoolers on rainy afternoons, as well as for older children on field trips. OMSI has the gift of making science and technology interesting without reducing it to mindless entertainment, and children really love this place. They also love boarding the USS *Blueback*,

a genuine diesel-powered submarine now permanently moored on the banks of the Willamette, and the larger-than-life OMN-IMAX theater with its million-dollar projector and five-story screen. Admission is $5 for kids four to thirteen years of age and $7 for adults. Expect to pay a separate fee for OMNIMAX, laser, and other shows. If you think you'll go a lot, you should buy a membership. (For more details, see the Attractions chapter.)

The State of Oregon Sports Hall of Fame
321 S.W. Salmon
(503) 227–7466

This museum, located in downtown Portland, is dedicated to athletes who have added to Oregon's sports history and the inspirational lessons we can learn from them. Exhibits include a life-size statue of Trailblazer star Bill Walton wearing his 1977 NBA Championship jersey, a swimsuit worn at the 1948 Olympics, a football from the 1917 Rose Bowl, an Oregon sports timeline, and football star Terry Baker's Heisman Trophy. There are also lots of videos, uniforms, and plaques. Hands-on exhibits let visitors ride a rodeo saddle, try on a catcher's mitt and feel the impact of a fastball, or try racing against a wheelchair track star. The Hall of Fame is open Monday through Saturday 10 A.M. to 6 P.M., and Sunday noon to 5 P.M. Admission is $4 for adults, $3 for students and seniors, and $10 for the whole family. If you take your kid's school class, everyone gets in for free.

Restaurants

Portland

The Carnival
2805 S.W. Sam Jackson Rd.
(503) 227–4244

This big rambling place on the way up Pill Hill looks like a carnival, with red and white striped awnings and walls. Outside

there's a fish pond that's a hit with kids. Inside, they can see an antique carousel horse and circus posters, while enjoying hot dogs, burgers, shakes, and fries. Lots of other menu items will appeal to youthful palates. It's a common stop for medical professionals and salesman, so the mix of conversation can be intriguing. The Carnival is open 11 A.M. to 8 P.M., Monday through Saturday.

The Ivy House Restaurant
1605 S.E. Bybee St.
(503) 231–9528

It's Mother's Day and kids' day too, all year long at the Ivy House. The Ivy House has reinvented family dining based on the premise that just because a three-year-old will eat nothing but grilled cheese sandwiches doesn't mean that mom and dad have to be deprived of real food. The food for the children is simple and inexpensive, and the food for adults is carefully prepared, delicious fine dining, with items such as rib eye steaks, hazelnut-crusted salmon, and specialty salads enlivening the menu. Meals in this refurbished 1911 house are served on two floors. While you're waiting for your meal, the kids can enjoy the playroom upstairs, which comes with train sets, dollhouses, and lots of books and games. On warm, sunny days, you can sit on the outside porch or covered patio. On cold, wintry days, try for a table inside by the fireplace. The Ivy House is open seven days a week for lunch and dinner.

Old Wives' Tales
1300 E. Burnside
(503) 238–0470

This restaurant is popular with kids and has built up loyalty with their parents too, for providing a large, well-stocked playroom in addition to the good children's menu and savory sandwiches, soups, and other light fare. Sit in a booth by the window and watch the street theater of Burnside. Old Wives' Tales also serves beer and wine and is open for breakfast, lunch, and dinner, seven days a week. (See the Restaurants chapter for more information.)

Original Portland Ice Cream Parlour
613 N.E. Weidler St.
(503) 281–1271

This jaunty place used to be a Farrell's, and it still retains some of the ambience of the St. Louis World's Fair. But what it mostly retains are the luscious sundaes, banana splits, and every other form of deliciously irresponsible ice cream dessert. The desserts come in every size and flavor, and if they're not enough, a carnival of bright candy lurks right by the cash register. Birthday children get a drum roll and a happy birthday—it's not quite the chaos of yesteryear (thank

Insiders' Tip

The Portland Saturday Market, which also runs on Sunday, is a characteristic Portland experience that children love. In addition to the vendors of tie-dye, candles, jewelry, pottery, and stained glass, you'll find lively entertainment of every variety (especially music). The food is delicious, and the eye candy is even better. Saturday Market takes place underneath the Burnside Bridge between S.W. First Avenue and S.W. Ankeny Street from the first weekend in March to Christmas Eve. Saturdays, the market opens at 10 A.M. and closes at 5 PM; Sunday hours are 11 A.M. to 4:30 P.M. For more information, call (503) 222-6072.

heaven), but instead the right proportion of deference and attention. It is possible to eat lunch or dinner here, but we take the kids after they've already eaten so they won't get distracted by dessert.

Outlying Areas

Lacey's Bomber Restaurant & Catering
13515 S.E. McLoughlin Blvd., Milwaukie
(503) 659–9306

For many years "the Bomber," a restored B–17 Air Fortress, has been the biggest tourist attraction in Clackamas County, and it continues to draw good crowds year-round. Kids love eating a meal in a huge airplane, and they also appreciate the complimentary ice-cream cones and the excellent children's menu. This place is a gold mine for aviation and history buffs and is full of nostalgic old pictures, knickknacks, and military paraphernalia. The Bomber, just a few miles south of Portland's city limits, opens at 6 A.M. and serves breakfast, lunch, and dinner seven days a week.

Sports and Games

Portland

Portland is a city full of outdoor enthusiasts, and they seem pretty much born that way with their inclinations abetted by facilities all over the city. Portland Parks and Recreation offers the greatest variety of sports and other athletic activities in the city, including dancing, swimming, even snowshoeing. They run class sessions continually and also sponsor team sports like soccer and basketball. Call them at (503) 823–PLAY. You can also find out about organized team sports by contacting your child's school.

In general, Portland's parks, sports programs, and trails are filled with children. The city has many parks with playground equipment, and thanks to a recent bond measure, much of that equipment has undergone a renaissance in the past few years. Exceptional playgrounds include Washington Park, where the considerable bright red, blue, and yellow equipment looks like a four-year-old's idea of a castle; Laurelhurst Park has a series of bridges that are good for playing tag; Gabriel Park, has bright green grassy hills that look like they're straight out of *Teletubbies*; Sellwood Park is full of wonderful tall fir trees; and Mt. Tabor Park has views of Mount St. Helens in addition to its climbing structure and swings. Many school grounds are adjacent to parks and have good equipment, as well. Places that inspire bursts of running in children include Waterfront Park, Pioneer Courthouse Square, the plaza in front of OMSI, and the big lawn at the Oregon Zoo. The Hoyt Arboretum draws families who love to hike, and Powell Butte, just east of town, offers a network of easy trails so that children can explore the vestiges of the old farm. Powell Butte provides a glimpse of what things might have looked like in a different era, in spite of the new houses that flank it. More information about the parks in the area may be found in the Portland's Parks chapter of this book.

The Children's Gym
1825 N.E. 43rd Ave.
(503) 249–5867

Looking for fitness and fun activities for kids who are glued to the boob tube? Look no further. The Children's Gym is a preschool gymnastics and motor development program designed to build confidence in children ages eighteen months to twelve years. The kids have a lot of fun in the process, working out on the rings and bars, tumbling, dancing, and jumping on the trampolines. Birthday parties are held on-site, and gymnastic camps are offered during the summer.

Electric Castles Wunderland
3451 S.E. Belmont St.
(503) 238–1617

11481 S.E. 82nd Ave.
(503) 653–0880

10306 N.E. Halsey St.
(503) 255–7333

2043 N.E. Burnside St., Gresham
(503) 667–3394

11955 N. Center Ave.
(503) 285–6044

8080 E. Mill Plain Blvd., Vancouver
(360) 699–6131
www.wunderlandgames.com

Five cent video games? Yup, it's the truth at Wunderland. Admission for children is $4, and the games are free, or cost a nickel (at some locations). Wunderland carries all the hottest video and pinball games, including test games. New games arrive all the time. If you're a pinball wizard, some of the payoffs from video and pinball games can be redeemed for prizes. The place is also tailor-made for kids' parties and birthday fun.

The Ice Chalet
953 Lloyd Center
(503) 288–6073

Clackamas Town Center
12000 S.E. 82nd Ave.
(503) 786–6000

Young kids, teens—even mom and dad—can have a blast at The Ice Chalet, cutting up on and off the ice. Besides offering ice-skating and hockey lessons, this is a favorite place for birthday parties and all sorts of festive occasions. Tired of baseball and basketball? Try Broomball for a change of pace! The Ice Chalet also offers a summer camp for youngsters who are serious about wanting to learn to skate. Admission is $5.25 for kids under eighteen years of age, and $6.25 for all others. Sometimes you can find two-for-one discount coupons in *The Oregonian*. Ice skates rent for $2.50.

Metro Family YMCA Center
2831 S.W. Barbur Blvd.
(503) 294–3366

The indoor playground at the Metro YMCA Center has hoops, tunnels, slides, and a huge ball pit. Kids ages two to ten and their parents can play together for free for one hour, or kids can be left on their own. Fees to leave children are $3.75 per child per first hour if you are member or guest of a member. For each additional hour, add $2.25 per child. Everyone must wear socks! Another site at the Metro Y is the Fun Club upstairs in the exercise room. Admission for children (ages five to thirteen) of Y members is $5. Here, staffers guide youngsters through a variety of activities, including basketball, racquetball, volleyball, and floor hockey.

Vancouver and Outlying Areas

Family Fun Center and Bullwinkle's Restaurant
29111 S.W. Town Center Loop W., Wilsonville
(503) 685–5000

If the dog days of summer are becoming a drag for the kids, take them to the Family Fun Center. Bound to distract the kids from boredom, the place offers a double-story game arcade, batting cages, go-carts, and bumper boats. Miniature golf helps them work on their hand-eye coordination, while a flight simulator provides some high-tech fun. Laser tag is featured as well. The restaurant, Bullwinkle's, specializes in kid-friendly cuisine like pizza and burgers.

Mountain View Ice Arena
14313 S.E. Mill Plain Blvd., Vancouver
(360) 896–8700

Whether it's hockey, lessons, or just a good tour around the rink you're after, the Mountain View Ice Arena will help you. Public skating times are Mondays through Fridays, 9 A.M. to midnight and 2 to 5:15 P.M. You can also skate Sunday, Tuesday, and Thursday evenings from

7 to 9 P.M. Skates rent for $2.25; admission is $3 for the five-and-under crowd, $6 for everyone else.

Ultrazone
Holly Farm Center
16074 S.E. McLoughlin Blvd., Milwaukie
(503) 652–1122

The kids will have plenty of fun here, playing high-tech interactive, laser-tag games.

The futuristic atmosphere, with mazes, strobe lights, and special sound effects, adds to the enjoyment. Ultrazone is recommended for kids older than five. Adults like to play too, and corporations will sometimes sponsor team-building events here, so don't be surprised if you spy Joe from Accounting. Tickets cost around $6.

Shopping for Toys, Books, and More

Portland

Annie Bloom's Books
7834 S.W. Capitol Hwy., Multnomah Village
(503) 246–0053

This kid-friendly outfit has songfests, craft demonstrations, and storytimes, including those that are in sign language.

Barnes & Noble Bookstore
18300 N.W. Evergreen Pkwy., Beaverton
(503) 645–3046

This Barnes & Noble Bookstore not only offers books, but has storytimes for preschoolers on Thursdays at 10 A.M.; children ages five to eight are read to on Saturdays at 11 A.M.

Borders Books
708 S.W. 3rd Ave.
(503) 221–5911

2605 S.W. Cedar Hills Blvd., Beaverton
(503) 644–6164

16920 S.W. 72nd Ave., Tigard
(503) 968–7576

Borders not only has books for children but also offers them storytimes. The downtown stores holds its storytimes at 2 P.M. on Saturdays; the Beaverton store schedules its storytimes on Tuesdays at 10 A.M. and Saturdays at 11 A.M.; and the Tigard store offers stories for kids on Fridays and Saturdays at 10 A.M.

Bridges
402 N. State St.
(503) 699–1322
www.bridgestoys.com

This shop, which parents regularly mention as one of the best in the area, is full of a great variety of dolls, stuffed animals, books, and other imaginative and fun toys. Featured lines include Playmobil, Brio, Lego, Madame Alexander, and Corolle. Their worthy motto: "Connecting play with learning."

Children's Place
4807 N.E. Fremont
(503) 284–8294

Children's Place has books galore—more than 30,000 titles geared for younger readers—and a large music selection for kids, but that's just for starters. You can also buy a wide variety of educational toys and puzzles here, as well as games to stimulate those fertile imaginations, a good stock of art supplies, and musical instruments. Children's Place hosts book fairs as well as Saturday-morning readings by authors of popular children's books.

Child's Play
907 N.W. 23rd Ave.
(503) 224–5586

A fine neighborhood shop in the Northwest Portland District, Child's Play features well-made, inventive toys. You'll

Children will have fun learning about the animals at the Oregon Zoo. CREDIT: YU-WEN LIN

find a decent selection of seasonal toys and dress-up clothes, as well as lines like Playmobil, Lego, and Brio. The wide array of Breyer horses and accoutrements draws many children. The store also carries books. Some useful additional information: the shop has a parking lot (a rarity in the area) and is conveniently located next to a place that carries wrapping paper and party supplies.

Finnegan's
922 Yamhill
(503) 221–0306

At Finnegan's you'll find whole cities of dolls, lots of building blocks, sidewalk chalk, ant farms, flower presses, boomerangs, dump trucks—in short, every kind of toy a child could imagine. Though it is large, it never has that frantic feeling that so many of the big chain toy stores cultivate; even during the holidays

when it's really busy, Finnegan's manages to exude serenity. It could be the well-organized and competent staff, or perhaps its high quality toys. They carry a vast selection of Brio, Plan, and Playmobil toys, lovely Ravensburger puzzles, great craft kits, plush toys, books, and more. And you'll find a lot of cool toys for party bags—bubbles, tops, creatures, chalk. The Hello Kitty Photo Sticker Machine, which will turn your image into stickers, is worth a stop even if you don't have any kids.

Generations
4029 S.E. Hawthorne Blvd.
(503) 233–8130

Beautiful natural-fiber clothing for children and their mothers (their pregnant and nursing mothers, that is), as well as a fine selection of baby accessories and some toys, draw people from all over town to this cozy shop on Hawthorne. The clothing and accessories for pregnant and nursing women are excellent, and the children's clothing is adorable. You will also find some consumer-tested clothing and shoes for resale.

Haggis McBaggis
6802 S.E. Milwaukie Ave.
503-234–0849

Finally, a store that understands the parental shopper: we are buying things for our children that secretly we want to wear ourselves. So the fancy shoes, wonderful tights, jewels, and very imaginative accessories that also come in adult sizes are a few reasons to shop in this colorful, attractive store. Another reason is the beautiful, clean, and spacious bathroom that stocks disposable diapers for emergencies. And still another are the kids toys. Yet one more is the big cookie jar. Did we mention the adult sizes?

Hanna Andersson
327 N.W. 10th Ave.
(503) 321–5275

Beautiful, well-made cotton clothes that look good and feel good are the specialty of this amazing Portland store, and it has acquired an international following through its catalogue sales since its founding here in 1983. These clothes last a long time—even the tights. The clothes are meant to last for more than one child, so the company has a program to pass on gently used Hannas to needy children. Hanna Andersson is open Monday through Friday, 10 A.M. to 6 P.M. and on Saturday, from 10 A.M. to 5 P.M. See the Shopping chapter for more details.

Kids at Heart
3435 S.E. Hawthorne Blvd.
(503) 231–2954

Kids at Heart is a sweet neighborhood store in the Hawthorne shopping district; it keeps area residents supplied with birthday presents, art supplies, Playmobil sets, and Brio trains, but it's worth a trip for nonresidents too. Kids at Heart has a fine collection of dress-up clothes, games, and

science-oriented toys—kits turning children into spies and explorers have been recent hits at parties. You won't find Barbie, but you will find Madeline dolls and Groovy Girls, in addition to a whole wall of trains and building toys. They also carry many clever and ingenious baby toys.

Niketown
930 S.W. 6th Ave.
(503) 221–6453

When kids are visiting Portland from as far away as Japan or Argentina, often the first place they want to check out is Niketown, a high-tech, ultra-modern retail outlet for shoes, shirts, caps, and other sports apparel with that famous swoosh logo. The corner store is easy to spot with a life-size metallic silhouette of His Airness, Michael Jordan on the south wall. Inside are plaques celebrating other noted athletes, interactive displays, multimedia delights, and video theatrics. (See the Shopping chapter for more information on Niketown.)

Powell's City of Books
1005 W. Burnside
(503) 228–4651

While Powell's City of Books is fully covered in our Shopping chapter, it is worth noting that the children's resources at Powell's are phenomenal. Not only do they carry current favorites, but they have vast holdings of used books, classics, collector's items, and, most important, a knowledgeable staff to help you find the perfect book for your child. Furthermore, they carry excellent educational materials; whether you are a homeschooling parent, or a teacher, or simply an interested adult, you will be astonished at the wealth here. Visiting the store is a fine way to spend a day—while Powell's wants parents to watch their little ones and to refrain them from terrorizing the place, they also want to cultivate future readers, so exploring the wares is encouraged. The Hawthorne branch also has a good, though smaller, children's section.

Water Babies
3272 S.E. Hawthorne Blvd.
(503) 232–6039

Water Babies carries wonderful children's clothing and accessories, both the kind of dresses, coats, jackets, and trousers that grandparents like to buy for little ones and the kind they like to choose for themselves. You'll find delightful polar fleece hats and coats, beautiful summer sandals, and the perfect back-to-school outfit here. While Water Babies features clothes for younger children, you can also find some good buys for children size ten and a little bigger. The shop is also excellent for gifts.

Zipadees
4225 N.E. Fremont
(503) 493–3390

Super funky, colorful, and original children's clothing and accessories attract shoppers from all over the city to this shop in the Beaumont District. The sizes run from newborn to preteen, for both boys and girls. Some of the lines are locally made and designed, and it's refreshing to shop at a children's store that is as cool as this one—it is definitely worth a visit.

Vancouver

Once Upon a Child
11505 N.E. 4th Plain Rd., Vancouver
(360) 253–7742

This place is worth checking out because of its wide variety of inventory and exceptional values. Once Upon a Child carries everything from games, books, and toys, to lamps, car seats, school clothes, and strollers. They buy, sell, and trade "gently used" children's items and seem to have a fast turnaround. This isn't a typical secondhand store. You won't have to sort through any broken junk; everything is shiny and clean. If your kids have outgrown their shoes and clothes, bring them in for cash on the spot or a trade-in.

Summer Activities

What should we do this summer? Portland has so many parks and playgrounds and is so close to both the mountains and the ocean that this question should have lots of answers. Our chapters on Recreation and on Portland's Parks give comprehensive and plentiful accounts of the Parks and Rec activities and programs.

There are also lots of summer camps in the area, with focuses in equestrian pursuits, sports (golf, baseball, soccer, basketball, and roller hockey), arts, theater, science, African arts, music, and even computers—all in addition, of course, to plain old sleep-away camps with singing around the campfire. (Nostalgic parents don't have to be left out, either: Camp Westwind, on the Oregon coast, organizes a few sessions each summer for parents and children.) OMSI and the Oregon Zoo both offer popular summer camps. The free monthly papers *Portland Parent* and *Portland Family* provide comprehensive lists of camps each year. You can pick them up at any local library, most schools, and many children's stores. *The Oregonian* also publishes a special section every spring that lists camps in the Portland area. In addition, you can attend the annual Summer Camp and Vacation Show, held at the Convention Center each spring. More than eighty organizations sponsor booths and tables for families to peruse. The tickets for this extravaganza are very inexpensive ($1 for children, $2 for adults), and some of the proceeds benefit local organizations that help low-income children attend summer camps or other worthy causes. For more information, call (503) 230-0272. Insurance giant MetLife has a useful, free brochure, "Choosing a Summer Camp," that can help you make an informed choice. Call them at (800) 638-5433. Financial aid for camps is often available; your camp can provide information.

Other Park Programs

Children's Programs
Metro Regional Parks and Greenspaces
(503) 797–1850

Metro Regional Parks and Greenspaces Department runs many engaging activities and programs at their various sites throughout the Metro area. Especially for Kids, an eight-week outdoor series, takes place at popular Blue Lake Park, (8 miles east of downtown Portland off of Marine Drive in Gresham). Four- to ten-year-olds enjoy the fun programs, which focus on interactive entertainment emphasizing the performing arts, cultural awareness, and nature themes. The outdoor performances, which are free with park admission, are held on Wednesdays, rain or sunshine, from June through the middle of August at Blue Lake Regional Park off of Marine Drive. Call for more information about the summer schedule of performances, which include everything from comedy and jugglers to live rain forest animals and folk music. Blue Lake is also the site of summer day camps, as well as interesting crafts instruction in things such as pioneer candle-making and animal-track casting.

Oxbow Adventures, held at Oxbow Park, is perfect for curious kids—and parents—who would like to learn about plant identification, bird and animal habits and habitat, and other useful stuff. Wetland Explorers teaches children about wetland habitat and the birds, bugs, turtles, and other creatures that live in them; these workshops are held at different wetland areas in the region. Dress comfortably and bring a sack lunch and your own soft drink. Call the phone number above or visit Metro on the Web at www.metro-region.org/parks/greenscene/greenkids.html for further information on kids' activities in the Metro's parks, and see the Portland's Parks chapter for more general information on these parks.

Nature Crafts for Kids
Blue Lake Regional Park
(503) 797–1850

Another great program offered at Blue Lake Park, this fun series is geared at chil-

Insiders' Tip

What should you do when it rains? Oregonians learn early on to amuse themselves in spite of the weather, but a list of activities can come in handy when the small fry are soggy with boredom. In addition to the staples—OMSI, the Children's Museum, and any branch of the library—try taking them ice-skating or to a paint-your-own pottery shop. The airport, especially the play area, is fun to visit, and you'd be surprised at how calm you feel there when you're not rushing to get a plane. Or try downtown: Niketown, Powell's, and the food court at Pioneer Place offer many diversions. The food court has an enticing series of fountains for making wishes. You can also just bundle them up and go for a splashy walk.

dren ages seven through twelve, and runs from July to early September. It covers a wide range of wholesome and educational activities such as making pioneer candles from scratch, carving animal figures from stone, and sand painting. All children must be accompanied by an adult. Craft activities are $2 per child for materials, payable the day of the event. The park entrance fee is $3 per car or $6 per bus.

Arts Programs

Art House
3223 N.E. Broadway
(503) 287-8138

All kids are artists—some more than others—and this place strives to bring out the dormant genius in youngsters. Art House offers cool arts and crafts workrooms, as well as scrap-booking and rubber-stamping activities, all supervised by adults. They also offer a wide variety of art classes for kids as well as adults and host art parties. In the summer months this is a great environment for kids to practice fun, yet cerebral pursuits in a nurturing and supportive environment.

Children's Library at Central Multnomah County Library
801 S.W. 10th Ave.
(503) 248-5235

Once you enter the recently renovated Central Library, take a right turn and enter the Children's Library. As you enter this brightly illuminated treasure trove of books, videos, and artwork for kids, a bronze tree catches your eye. This arboreal fantasy has a hollow trunk for play and storytelling inside. The library has one activity that should keep kids busy during the summer: the summer reading program, which is theme-based and offers prizes. It also offers storytimes. While you're there, pick up a copy of InfoLines, the library's newsletter, which gives information about other library programs and events.

Metro Arts Kids Camp at Portland Center for Performing Arts
S.W. Broadway and Main
(503) 245-4885

This terrific program gets kids up on the big stage at the Performing Arts Center downtown. Professional educators, visual artists, and performers from the Oregon Symphony, Oregon Ballet Theatre, and various theater companies help students create their own works of art, sing, play instruments, paint, dance, and act in live performances. To get a brochure, call the above number.

Pottery Paint Box
3551 S.E. Division
(503) 736-9990

While it's not exactly an arts program, so many children enjoy spending rainy afternoons here that it's worth a mention. Lots of pottery painting places operate in the area, but we have come to like this one enormously for its mellow atmosphere, reasonable prices, wonderful party room, and friendly and thoughtful owner. Another reason to like this place: the basket of activities for little sisters and brothers too young to paint. The Pottery Paint Box offers parties and gift certificates, too.

Swimming Holes and Water Parks

Portland

The City of Portland Parks and Recreation Department
(503) 823-7529

The City of Portland offers a host of fun, healthy, year-round activities. In the summer, the aquatics programs are exceptionally popular; the swimming lessons are a cherished summertime ritual. The department offers swimming lessons for kids, toddlers on up (adults too!). Young swimmers can get advanced lifeguard certification, take diving lessons, or just come to splash at open swim time. Classes are offered at every pool listed below. Drop-in swim fees are $2.50 for adults and $1.50 for children three to twelve, except at the Southwest Community Center and at Mt. Scott, where they are a wee bit more. Most of the swimming pools are open from early in the morning until late at night and many offer amusing activities such as dive-in movies and water basketball. The pools at the Southwest Community Center and at Mt. Scott have been beautifully refurbished with water toys, water slides, current channels, and other enticements. Call the park nearest you for specific information and rates. (See the Portland's Parks chapter for more information.)

Indoor Facilities

Buckman Swimming Pool
320 S.E. 16th Ave.
(503) 823-3668

Columbia Swimming Pool
7701 N. Chautauqua Blvd.
(503) 823-3669

Dishman Pool
77 N.E. Knott St.
(503) 823-3673

MLC Pool
2033 N.W. Glisan St.
(503) 823-3671

Mt. Scott Swimming Pool
5530 S.E. 72nd Ave.
(503) 823-3813

Southwest Community Center
6820 S.W. 45th Ave.
(503) 823-2840

Outdoor Facilities

Creston Swimming Pool
4454 S.E. Powell Blvd.
(503) 823-3672

Grant Swimming Pool
2300 N.E. 33rd Ave.
(503) 823-3674

Montavilla Swimming Pool
8219 N.E. Glisan St.
(503) 823-3675

Peninsula Swimming Pool
700 N. Portland Blvd.
(503) 823-3679

Pier Swimming Pool
9341 N. St. Johns St.
(503) 823-3678

Sellwood Swimming Pool
7951 S.E. 7th Ave.
(503) 823-3680

Outlying Areas

North Clackamas Aquatic Center
7300 S.E. Harmony Rd., Milwaukie
(503) 794-8080

This Disneyland-ish "water world" is a wonderfully wet place for the kids to cool off during the long hot days of July and August. With wave pools, wading pools, diving pools, three water slides, and a whirlpool, you can bet the little ones will return home waterlogged. Kids nine through seventeen are admitted for $6.99; youths three to eight years pay $4.99; adults pay $9.99.

Giggles the Clown
(503) 655–7997, (503) 655–1571

Many fine clowns live in Portland, but Giggles is the only one that didn't make our children cry in terror. She does magic tricks, balloon animals, and fun games. Her face painting is extraordinary. But it's her calm demeanor that really wins us over.

Mad Science Birthday Parties
(503) 230–8040

With "hands-on" vortex generators, light shows, cool chemical reactions, and slippery slime, Mad Science transforms ho-hum birthday parties into fun-filled, memorable events. They specialize in entertaining youngsters from ages five through twelve with their hour-long, action-packed science presentations that include rocket launches, sound effects, and even cotton candy.

Besides parties, Mad Science offers a variety of after-school courses, workshops, and camp programs.

Run for the Arts
(503) 225–5900

Every year, Portland children do their part to raise moral and financial support for

Insiders' Tip

Children have many opportunities to both participate in and watch the performing arts in Portland. In addition to the annual Nutcracker performances by the Oregon Ballet Theater and the summer concerts at the Oregon Zoo, you'll find a variety of child-centered theater programs. The puppet theater, Tears of Joy Theater (503) 284-0557 and the Oregon Children's Theatre Company (503) 228-9571 perform seasonally for children and adults; the Ladybug Theater (503) 232-2346, has ongoing performances for small and big children. And the respected Northwest Children's Theater and School, (503) 222-4480, produces frequent and imaginative shows with children in starring roles. Portland Center for the Performing Arts Kids' Events, (503) 796-9293 (events line) or www.pcpa.com, runs a number of child-friendly theater, dance, and music performances each month throughout its season. Shows vary, of course, but an annual essential is the excellent production of *A Christmas Carol*. To train younger children in how to behave at a live performance, take them to the free brown bag previews at noon in various locations.

A visit to the pumpkin patch is an annual ritual for Portland children. CREDIT: DEBRA LEAVITT

the arts in their schools by running laps for bucks. The run, which is sponsored by Young Audiences, a nonprofit arts group, is organized around pledges made and then fulfilled when these youthful track stars chug around their playgrounds or nearby parks throughout the months of October or April. Each school schedules its own run during one or both of these months. Among the projects funded by the Run for the Arts are presentations by a touring African-American ballet troupe, a quilt-making workshop, and mosaic sculptures decorating the front steps of one of the schools. More than one hundred schools from Vancouver to Beaverton participate in this annual run.

Sand in the City Beach Party
Pioneer Courthouse Square
(503) 246–5818

Held in early July, this benefit for the Kids on the Block Awareness Program transforms Portland's festive downtown patio into an ocean beach when more than 250 tons of sand are shaped, slapped, and molded into sandcastles, dragons, and other wild critters by teams of local businesspeople. In addition to this jovial competition, master sand sculptors give demonstrations and children can create their own works of art in a kids' sandbox. Food and craft booths are plentiful, too, as well as live music, clowns, and puppet shows. For further information on Sand in the City, see our Festivals and Annual Events chapter.

The Multnomah County Fair gives city kids the chance to bond with furry friends. CREDIT: MARY ALLISON

Festivals and Annual Events

There is no shortage of local events or annual festivals in Portland, Vancouver, and the surrounding areas. Almost everything, from the sacred to the mundane, seems to have its own festival or event. In this chapter we cover everything from the annual release of new Oregon Pinot Noir vintages, a road race from Mount Hood to the Pacific Ocean, a weekend devoted to saving (and eating) salmon, an annual Native American Powwow, and a yearly rejoicing at the hops harvest. We also include the myriad festivals, celebrations, and annual events in Portland and the metro area, the more rural surrounding Oregon counties, and in Vancouver and Clark County, Washington.

In a culture of mass marketing, mass media, and mass consumption, these celebrations help define and distinguish a particular area, preserving an awareness of local identity and history. Most importantly, they preserve a sense of place.

Annual events in and around Portland include an African arts festival, Thanksgiving, and Memorial Day weekend wine tours and tastings, fly-ins of antique and classic airplanes, a creative conference, a potters' show and jazz, and blues and chamber music festivals.

The following calendar includes some of the major, or most popular, running and bicycle events around, due in part because Nike and Adidas are headquartered here. Regardless of any connection with corporate athleticism, folks of all ages bike, run, walk, hike, canoe, kayak, climb (mountains and rocks), row, fish, hunt, hang-glide, soar, skate, swim, ski, sail, snowboard, snowshoe, parachute, windsurf, and parasail in many events around town that highlight these activities.

The Portland Marathon is ranked as one of the best-organized marathons in North America. The Hood to Coast Relay sees teams of lemming-like runners starting at a 7,000-foot level on Mount Hood and covering more than 100 miles before the race ends (often in sheer exhaustion) on the beach at Seaside.

Other popular endurance events include June's 186-plus-mile Seattle to Portland Bicycle Ride (STP) and September's Cycle Oregon Bike Tour. The latter, created in 1988 by the Oregon Department of Tourism, is a muscle-draining, seat-numbing, weeklong bike ride over a challenging (read mountainous) route that changes from year to year. Spaces in both events fill-up almost immediately. Each year, for example, 2,000 riders start (but do not necessarily finish) Cycle Oregon. During these events, well-organized hordes of essentially happy Lycra-skinned bikers pay to spend days riding on hard, narrow seats atop skinny wheels for hours at a time. Like a colorful migrating tribe, band, or herd, they take over back roads and country byways. Camping out in small towns and consuming immense quantities of all sorts of foods, but especially cookies, bananas, and water, they stimulate the state's economy by exchanging their hard-earned dollars for food prepared by local residents, bathroom privileges, and visits to local hospital emergency rooms.

Most of the events we've listed here take place in Portland and Vancouver. There are a small number of events, the Salem Art Fair, the Vintage Festival, the Lilac Festival, the Gorge Games, and the Oregon Country Fair, that are out of the immediate area, but included because of their quality and uniqueness.

As the largest city and metro area in the state, Portland attracts an increasing number of regional, national, and even international trade shows, conventions, and meetings. The city also hosts the touring boat, car, fishing, dog, cat, antiques, manufactured home, hunting, gardening, gun, knife and camping, and gift shows. These include shows making a national circuit and those originating locally.

In the summer, Portland's Tom McCall Waterfront Park hosts the Oregon Brewers Festival, the Rose Festival Fun Center, and the Waterfront Blues Festival. The area also has a chance to showcase its increasing number of Farmers Markets during the summer. Shoppers and browsers find specialty and organic food products, flowers, and nursery stock, not to mention the area's agricultural bounty (see the Close-up on the Portland Farmers' Market in this chapter). Portland's Old Town hosts the Saturday Market, an open-air craft and food event held each weekend from March until Christmas. Downtown's Pioneer Square is another popular site for performances of all sorts and smaller ethnic, art, food, and other festivals.

The Mt. Hood Jazz Festival, held in early August at Mt. Hood Community College in Gresham, just east of Portland, attracts noted musicians such as Bruce Hornsby, David Sanborn, and Mose Allison, and an audience from throughout the western United States and Canada.

In Vancouver, the Fourth of July is celebrated all day at Ft. Vancouver, Officers Row, and the Pearson Air Museum. The day ends with the largest fireworks display west of the Mississippi. And some years, the July weather even cooperates.

So this chapter is a taste of what is here that makes this area different and special. Local newspapers are the best source of what is going on when you are visiting. *The Oregonian's* Friday A&E section and "Homes & Gardens of the Northwest" insert all carry detailed listings and calendars of a wide assortment of events in the entire region. The area's weekly and monthly newspapers and special interest publications, including *The Asian Reporter, Just Out, Oregon Wine, Portland Palette, The Scanner, The Freshwater News, Willamette Week,* and *The Columbian* (Vancouver, Washington) also carry detailed calendars of local special-interest events. These usually include detailed information on numerous events, including time, place, parking, and admission fees (if any). There is usually a telephone number for more information. A quick call can also provide the best directions if you are unfamiliar with the area. If no contact number is listed, a call to the Portland Oregon Visitors Association (POVA), at (503) 222–2223, can most likely get you the information you need.

Three of our local radio stations are also good sources for information about events and performances. KPBS-FM, a 24-hour classical music station updates listeners about music, choral, and arts events. KBOO is a community radio station run by a highly politicized board determined to give management by chaos theory and anarchy a try. Portland is also home to KMHD-FM, the region's only all-jazz radio station, and a good source of information about who is playing what, where, and when.

Keep in mind that events at the recently remodeled Expo Center, the Convention Center, and the Rose Garden will have a separate parking fee. Amounts will vary, so you may want to call ahead to prevent unpleasant surprises. Most major venues are served by either Tri-Met's buses or the light rail system. Some special events, like the Rose Festival Air Show and the Lake Oswego Festival of the Arts, understand the advantage of mass transit and the problems associated with parking and have special, often free, shuttle buses.

Finally, this is Oregon. Outside events are rarely canceled because of weather. Weather may cause changes in schedules and performances, but in general, the show goes on. Dress accordingly.

January

All Breed Dog Show
Expo Center, 2060 N. Marine Dr.
(503) 248–5144

Obedience, agility, grooming, intelligence—no, this is not a singles bar. Portlanders love their dogs and this event allows owners from throughout Oregon and southwest Washington to show off their pets (or vice versa). Breeders bring their offspring and vendors peddle everything dogs, or their masters, might need. And, yes, master and faithful companion do tend to look alike. Step carefully, but this is a fascinating place to people and dog watch. Sit, Spot, sit.

Reel Music
Northwest Film Center, 1219 S.W. Park
(503) 221–1156

The annual celebration of music on film is one of two popular winter events sponsored by the Northwest Film Center. It's held at Guild Theatre, S.W. 9th Avenue and Taylor Street (503–221–1156), and other art film houses in Portland. The event features film showings, concerts, and speakers. Admission fees vary, so call ahead.

Rose Quarter Pro-Rodeo Classic
The Rose Garden, 1 Center Court
(503) 235–8771
www.rosequarter.com

Real cowpersons shine up their boots, dust off their jeans, and check their medical insurance for three days of riding, roping, and bucking that brings the West to the big city. Admission fees change from year to year, but usually include reduced rates for children. Head 'em up, move 'em out, keep them doggies rollin'.

February

Doll & Teddy Bear Show
Expo Center, 2060 N. Marine Dr.
(503) 284–4062

Long before the creation of Barbie and Beanie Babies, there were dolls and teddy bears. And, most likely, long after Barbie gets her (or Ken's) last social security check and Beanie Babies are the answer to a trick question in some future version of Trivial Pursuit, there will be dolls and teddy bears. This show is for both children and adults. General admission is $5; those over sixty-five are charged $4, and children twelve and under and those with disabilities get in for $2. There is also an additional parking fee.

Greater Portland International Auto Show
Oregon Convention Center,
777 N.E. Martin Luther King Jr. Blvd.
(503) 235–7575

New cars, old cars, minivans with more cup holders than wheels and spark plugs, tricked-up pickup trucks, and concept cars that will never dirty their tires on a real city street are all polished up and sparkle and gleam for this annual paean to our love affair with the automobile.

Oregon Cat Fanciers' Show
Portland Expo Center
(503) 248–4338

Lots of pussyfooting around here as hundreds of cats from thirty-five or more breeds, preen, purr, pose, and get really catty for those judges. There are also information booths about cats, breeding, showing, and animal welfare. Vendors' booths are stocked with necessities and luxuries for Fluffy and Socks. Almost everything one can imagine is available decorated or adorned in a feline theme or motif. Admission to this event is modest. Cat fans can avoid paying for parking by riding MAX.

Pacific Northwest Sportsmen's Show
Portland Expo Center, 2060 N. Marine Dr.
(503) 246–8291, (503) 285–7756

The region's oldest and largest show of its type, this adult toy show is for those who fish, camp, hunt, and hike. There are hundreds of new products and services along with free seminars, exhibitions, and hands-on demonstrations. Be prepared to pay admission and a parking fee unless you take public transit. Admission in 2001 was $7 for adults and $4 for kids six through sixteen.

Portland International Film Festival
At various locations
(503) 221–1156

Whether you're the type who goes to movies or critically views a cinema, you can sit in the dark for hours and hours looking at professional, experimental, traditional, and avant-garde film during this well-attended event sponsored by the Northwest Film Center. Admission fees vary, but in general, the more movies you attend, the lower the cost per viewing, if you buy a pass or block of tickets. Movies (as many as eighty) are shown in local theaters over a three-week period. The opening and closing nights feature the Portland premiers of new major movies. Tickets run $7.50, which is average for a movie shown after discounted afternoon and early evening shows (which average $4).

RAW, the Reed Arts Weekend
Reed College, 3203 S.E. Woodstock
(503) 777–7708

Reed is the local college Oregonians love to make fun of—"those hippie/perverted/pointy-headed intellectual Reedies." While the school's nuclear reactor—the only one in the state—is not open for visits, this four-day orgy of dance, poetry and prose readings, exhibits, and musical performances is intellectually stimulating and challenging. This event helps in a small way to dispel the myth that Portland is bland and boring. Besides, the college's southeast Portland campus is beautiful, with a small but excellent art gallery, a superb performing arts center, and a great bookstore. If you're impressed with what you see and hear, and have a college-bound son or daughter, have someone qualified in CPR nearby before you check out the tuition cost. (For additional information about Reed, see the chapter on Education.)

Insiders' Tip

Local newspapers, hotel concierges, and online services are excellent and reliable sources of information about special events and celebrations, but don't overlook the Portland Oregon Visitors Association (POVA), a fine resource. Their services are free and the Downtown Visitors Information Center (in their brand-new offices at Pioneer Courthouse Square) is staffed by helpful, friendly, and well-informed people. Call (503) 222-2223 or (800) 345-3214.

March

Antique & Collectible Shows
Portland Expo Center, 2060 N. Marine Dr.
(503) 282–0877, (503) 285–7756

"I used to have one of those" or "my parents had one just like that" are among the frequently heard laments at this popular show that encourages some people not to throw anything away. Admission is $5, but there is an additional parking fee that nearly doubles the cost of this show that has 1,350 booths filling the Expo Center with intriguing items from the past.

Northwest Quilters Show
Portland State University,
724 S.W. Harrison
(503) 222–1991

This growing annual event is one of a very small number of local shows devoted to quilting. This modest event draws experts, novices, and admirers from throughout the region. It is free and open to the public.

Portland Saturday Market
Under the Burnside Bridge on S.W. lst Ave.
(503) 222–6072

This is big city Portland's version of an event created down the valley in that cen-

ter of rebellion, liberalism, and the counter-culture, Eugene, home of the University of Oregon. Now approaching adulthood, having run for more than twenty-five years, Saturday Market (it is open on Sunday too) is another "must see" for visitors. You can enjoy street theater (some intentional, some not), a range of food booths, and buy everything from candles, macramé, pottery, stained glass, clothing, hemp products, local produce and handmade housewares, furniture and toys, and tools and trinkets. Not as counter-cultural as they once were, vendors may dress like Deadheads but in reality are small business owners, and there is a fair amount of gray hair and middle-aged spread under the embroidered denim and sandals. Everything is made by hand. The market runs until Christmas. During the holiday-shopping madness, it is as packed as any department store or mall.

St. Patrick's Day
Various Locations

Yes, they do green beer here, too. For some inexplicable reason, Portland has turned

---

Insiders' Tip

You can get ready for St. Patrick's Day at Kathleen's of Dublin, 860 S.W. Broadway, (503) 224-4869, one of the best shops for Irish (and Scottish) merchandise, including clothing, tapes and CDs, Celtic-inspired jewelry, and tea cups and tea pots. The Irish Corner & More in the Water Tower at 5331 S.W. Macadam Avenue, (503) 222-7080; and the Celtic Corner, 4142 N.E. Sandy Boulevard, (503) 287-3000, are two other good sources of St. Patrick's Day supplies. If you should be at a loss on how to properly celebrate this occasion, call the Irish Cultural Society, (503) 286-4812.

St. Patrick's Day into a multiday party. Kells Irish Restaurant and Pub hosts a street fair, live Irish and Celtic music, and demonstrations of Irish crafts. They also serve beer (Harp and Guinness flows freely) and you can ward off the damp chill with an Irish coffee or some Irish whiskey. Look for the menu to improve, as Kells just snared one of the city's best chefs. Other shops, restaurants, pubs, and bars flaunt their Irish heritage or make it up for a day as they join in the celebration.

Shamrock Run
Tom McCall Waterfront Park
(503) 226–5080

One of Portland's most popular running events, the Shamrock Run is a fund-raiser for Doernbecher Children's Hospital Foundation, one of the state's most popular and successful charities. The event includes a Leprechaun Lap, a 1-kilometer run, walk, or jog; the Shamrock Stride, a 4-mile walk; and an 8-kilometer race. The entry fee varies with the runner's age and

selected event but includes a souvenir T-shirt. There are usually a variety of freebies for runners, walkers, and their supporters, including food items and beverages.

Winter Games of Oregon
Mount Hood Meadows, Timberline,
SkiBowl, Mount Hood National Forest
(503) 520–1319

Skiing is not only possible but also can be very good into the late spring and through the summer at the Timberline Ski Area on Mount Hood. The Winter Games of Oregon include Nordic and Alpine Skiing events at three Mount Hood ski areas. If you go to participate or just watch, do not forget to get the required SnoPark pass for parking at Ticketmaster (503) 224–4400 and G.I. Joe (503) 790–2787. From October to April the pass costs $2.50 per day or $10 for the season. This fee goes toward the cost of plowing the parking lots. (For more information on Mount Hood Meadows see the Skiing section in Recreation.)

April

Children's Tree Trail
World Forestry Center, Washington Park,
4033 S.W. Canyon Rd.
(503) 228–1367

This is a most appropriate (and perhaps somewhat ironic) setting for an Arbor Day celebration. At the entrance to Washington Park, the timber-industry funded World Forestry Center hosts a range of free activities, including a guided walk through the Hoyt Arboretum, a picnic with Smokey the Bear, and a variety of hands-on activities. Best of all, admission to the Forestry Center and its exhibits, galleries, and gift shop, is free.

The 5th Annual Highland Eurofest
Highland Pub & Brewery
4225 S.E. 182nd, Gresham, Oregon
(503) 665–3015

An invitational gathering of McMe-

namins' brewers, this event focuses on the beer styles of Europe and features interpretations of traditional Belgian, German, Czech, and British beers.

Lilac Festival
Hulda Klager Lilac Gardens, Woodland,
Washington
(360) 225–8996

If your visit coincides with the Spring blossoming of lilacs, the thirty-minute trip north from Portland to Woodland is worth it. Set on five and one-half acres near the Columbia River, the Hulda Klager Lilac Gardens holds the promise of spring when the fragrant bushes burst into color. This is a popular event for color-starved Pacific Northwesterners who spend hours wandering the grounds admiring the hues and smelling the fragrance of both rare and more common varieties of the plant. Bouquets and cuttings are also available for purchase. There is a small gift shop in the farmhouse and refreshments are available. Admission is $2 to $3.

Portland Juggling Festival
Reed College, 3203 S.E. Woodstock
(503) 282–1429

Keep your eye on the ball here. This may be the largest regional juggling festival in the nation. There are performances by skilled professionals and gifted amateurs and more than two dozen workshops about, well, juggling and related matters, whatever those are. There are no mimes in sight and spectators are welcome.

Rhododendron Show
Jenkins Estate, 8005 S.W. Grabhorn Rd., Aloha
(503) 642–3855

Slightly off the usual visitor's path in the suburban hills, the Jenkins Estate alone is worth a visit, but during early spring, the estate's two and one-half-acre rhododendron garden is ablaze with blossoms. The gardens are also filled with daffodils, Japanese and other plum and cherry trees, camellias, and azaleas. Best of all, next to the sheer beauty of the blossoms, the event is free and visitors can stroll the well-kept grounds and visit the big house from Portland's past.

RiverPlace Tulip Festival
Riverplace Esplanade, 1510 S.W. Harbor Wy.
(503) 228–5108

Another celebration of spring and Easter, this free riverside festival fills the city with color and other signs of hope that the winter is almost over. The tulips are for sale and there is an Easter Egg Hunt for kids, and other child-oriented entertainment and activities.

Trillium Festival
Tryon Creek State Park
11321 S.W. Terwilliger Blvd., Lake Oswego
(503) 636–4398

The Trillium Festival celebrates a native Oregon plant at this quiet 635-acre park, tucked away between Lewis & Clark College and Lake Oswego, less than ten min-

Insiders' Tip

The Hood River Valley, east of Portland, is prime orchard country, and during late March and all through April, it is blanketed in pink and white blossoms. A drive to see the peach, apple, pear, and cherry blossoms makes a perfect half-day trip, and whether you take the long route over Mount Hood on U.S. Highway 26 or the shorter way (east along the Columbia Gorge via I-84), your drive will be spectacular. Call the Hood River Chamber of Commerce and they'll send you a blossom-time brochure: (800) 366-3530.

utes from the busy concrete ribbon of Interstate 5. The free event features a variety of nature-related and craft activities for children at the visitor/learning center. Visitors can purchase plants, trees, and shrubs to help support the park's educational programs and maintenance. There are easy walks along the park's rolling trails and streams and food and music for the body and soul.

Woodburn Tulip Festival
Woodburn
(800) 711–2006
www.woodenshoe.com

Emerging from the gray Oregon winter, hundreds of thousands of tulip bulbs burst into color each spring at several nurseries in this small town just south of Portland. Oregonians flock to the varied colored fields, rejoicing at this welcome sign that they survived another winter. Entry is free and visitors can purchase cut flowers, order bulbs, snack on local foods, and be tempted by the nurseries' bounty and gift shops. The actual dates vary slightly in response to the severity of the winter, but this event, like spring, is worth the wait.

May

Alberta Street Fair
Between 18th Ave. and 30th Ave. along Alberta St.

This blossoming mercantile strip in Northeast Portland celebrates its recovery from urban blight with a multicultural neighborhood celebration featuring artwork, music, food, children's activities, and a free trolley. If you miss this event you can enjoy the art galleries, restaurants, and boutiques that are popping up along this busy street by attending Last Thursday Walks every month. (See The Arts chapter for more information on Last Thursday Walks.)

Ceramic Showcase
Oregon Convention Center,
777 N.E. Martin Luther King Jr. Blvd.
(503) 238–0973
www.ceramicshowcase.com

If you want to know what Oregonians do when it can rain from October to May, visit this annual event sponsored by the Oregon Potters Association. The show fills several huge rooms with pottery and ceramics by dozens of potters from throughout Oregon and Washington. Admission is free. If you buy something, these people know how to pack it so it gets to your home unbroken.

Cinco de Mayo
Tom McCall Waterfront Park, between the banks of the Willamette River and Bill Naito Pkwy.
(503) 823–4572

Portland is a Sister City to several cities throughout the world, including Guadalajara. This is a large event celebrating the country's holiday and featuring Mexican and Latino food, crafts, art, music, and dancing. Entry is free or very modest, but you will have to buy your refreshments.

Doggie Dash
Tom McCall Waterfront Park, between the banks of the Willamette River and Bill Naito Pkwy.
(503) 222–5103

This is a very enjoyable and light-hearted take on your basic road race. Sponsored by a local radio station, the Doggie Dash is a 2 mile run/walk/trot for canines and their owners. A modest entry fee includes a T-shirt (for the runner) and doggie treats (for the dogs). Costumed runners, both canine and human, are not uncommon. For more on this race see Spectator Sports. Prices for the doggie costumes are $10 and $20 depending on size. (For more information, look for the entry under Multnomah Greyhound Park in Spectator Sports.)

Festival of Flowers
Pioneer Square, between 6th Ave. and Broadway, Morrison St. and Yamhill St.
(503) 223–1613

This event mixes a fair amount of flat, open space and the talent and imagination of an artist, hundreds of volunteers, and 25,000 or so potted annuals. The volunteers turn the flowers into a work of art (one year a huge quilt, another year a scaled-down rendition of the city's Japanese Gardens. You get the idea. After a few days, when thousands of onlookers have admired the piece, the flowers are sold to the public at wholesale prices.

5th Annual Olympic Club Brew Festival in May
Olympic Club, 112 North Tower Ave., Centralia, Washington
(360) 736–5164

The historic saloon hosts a cozy festival where you can saddle up to the bar and sample ales brewed from McMenamins' Washington breweries as well as guest beers from regional neighbors.

Yamhill County Wine Country
Memorial Weekend
Yamhill County Wineries Association
(503) 646–2985

This is an increasingly popular self-guided tour of some twenty-five Yamhill vineyards and wineries, including some not open at any other time of the year. The event features wine and food matches from some of the region's best chefs and vintners. Maps, lists of participating vineyards and wineries, and other details (telephone numbers, open hours, etc.) are available from calling the number above. For a feel for the region, see the section in Daytrips on touring the Wine Country.

June

Africa Fete
Oaks Park, at the eastern foot of the Sellwood Bridge
(503) 224–4400

When the music starts at one of Portland's newest festivals, visitors easily overcome the incongruity of the location, a small town amusement park, in which the performers set up an African village. With heavy-weight national sponsors, American Express and The Kennedy Center, this event turns cultural diversity into cultural awareness using the energy of music and dance and the lure of food booths.

Chamber Music Northwest
Reed College, 3203 S. E. Woodstock
Catlin Gabel School, 8825 S.W. Barnes Rd.
(503) 223–3202, (503) 294–6400
www.cmnw.com

Brilliant, challenging, soothing, and inspiring are all words to describe this series of twenty-five performances and concerts held on two beautiful, but frequently overlooked campuses. Pre-concert picnics feature gourmet foods, wines, coffees, and desserts. The admission fee is reasonable, series tickets are available, and the events show that music and talent are alive and well in the Northwest.

Father's Day Brewfest and Golf Tourney at Edgefield
2126 S.W. Halsey, Troutdale, 97060
(503) 669–8610

McMenamins' brewers offer favorites along with new brew recipes while two-person-scramble golf tournaments begin at 10 A.M. and 2 P.M. on the Pub Course. Prizes are awarded after the tournament. Brewfest admission is $5, tournament admission is $50 per pair, which includes brewfest admission, and beer tasters cost of $1 each. Call (503) 669–8610 to reserve your spot in the tournament.

Good in the Hood
Holy Redeemer School,
127 N. Portland Blvd.
(503) 283–5175

A three-day neighborhood event attracting people from throughout the city to this North Portland neighborhood, Good in the Hood celebrates Portland's commitment to multiculturalism, with an emphasis on music and food, including some outrageous barbecued chicken. The music ranges from funk and salsa to African pop while the dance numbers cover everything from tap to hula to Irish jigs. This is a view of a different Portland, but one that is as vital and real, maybe even more than anything downtown.

Mid-Summer's Eve Festival
Sellwood Moreland Business Association,
P.O. Box 82456, Portland, OR 97282

A celebration of arts, antiques, food, and music kicks off in late June in and around the big parking lot in downtown Moreland. This modest event started in 1998 as a project of the Sellwood Moreland Business Association. It features a street dance with nine bands, a collection of crafts booths, and lots of food kiosks like Tennessee Red's BBQ and Kathmandu Café. It is also close to a number of antique stores with doors wide open.

Lake Oswego Festival of the Arts
George Rogers Park, Lake Oswego,
Hwy. 43 and McVey Ave.
(503) 636–9673

A small, free, family-oriented event in this upscale suburb, the festival includes art and craft booths, a juried art competition, food booths, and activities for children and families. Somewhat low-key, it is a good example of a community event that retains its human scale while drawing a good crowd and some excellent artists.

Native American Powwow
Delta Park, N. Denver and
Martin Luther King Jr. Blvd.
(503) 630–5195

The largest regularly scheduled gathering of Native Americans in Portland, this festival includes members of various tribes who share their dances, ceremonies, crafts, music, and indigenous foods with guests. The event turns this urban park into a large encampment that attracts residents and visitors from throughout the region.

Portland Celtic Festival
Oaks Park at the eastern foot of the
Sellwood Bridge
(503) 231–8926

Created and sponsored by Music Millennium, one of the best record (and tape and CD and DAT, etc.) stores in the Pacific Northwest, this event proves that the region's interest in Irish music extends beyond St. Patrick's Day. Tickets are essentially within reason ($15 to $25, but watch that service charge). The festival features a full range of Celtic music and performers, from punk-Celt to more traditional genres. The lilt of the Celtic language and performances can be everything from stirring to haunting.

The Rose Festival provides an array of amusements for all ages. CREDIT: RACHEL DRESBECK

Portland Rose Festival
Portland Rose Festival Association
Various venues citywide
(503) 275–9750,
(800) 745–0888 (ticketed events)

There are more than one hundred different official Rose Festival events, including three parades, dragon boat races, a carnival-like fun center on the waterfront, several art exhibits, tours of ships from the U.S. and Canadian navies and Coast Guard, an airshow, a ski race, a hot-air balloon race, the CART (Championship Auto Racing Teams) Races, and a world-class rose show. The 2000 Rose Festival will take place June 1 to June 25.

Pride Northwest
Location/date varies, Portland
(503) 295–9788

Pride Northwest is Portland's annual Gay, Lesbian, Bi, Trans celebration that includes a rally with speeches, music, and parades (the official Pride Parade occurs the night before by the Lesbian Avengers' Dyke March). There is also a festival of food, crafts, and booths by Gay/Lesbian-friendly organizations and services.

A Taste of Beaverton
Griffith Park on Griffith Dr. in downtown
Beaverton
(503) 644–0123

We do like to eat here, as should be obvious from the number of festivals and other events focused on food and eating. Actually, this free event offers a three-day feast for all the senses, with some very good music and a range of crafts, arts, displays, and activities by local organizations and businesses. The event also calls attention to the diverse cultures that have found a home in this suburb. There is a hotline, (503) 778–5811, for a calendar of events during the "Taste."

A Northwest Fourth of July

As in other parts of the country, the Fourth of July celebrates not only the national birthday, but the full-fledged arrival of summer. Local celebrations of this national holiday reflect a sense of national and local identity, and picnics, barbecues, local concerts, parades, and fireworks are as a traditional as, well, as the Fourth of July.

Local weather lore indicates that summer in Oregon begins on July 5. Moist, low clouds can sometimes affect fireworks displays and chilly temperatures can keep residents bundled up. On one such holiday several years ago, *The Oregonian* didn't want to disappoint its readers, so they ran a front-page color photo from a previous year when the weather was better. Local residents who had attended the fireworks display and didn't recognize the photo inundated the paper with questions and complaints until and the editors finally confessed to their use of a "historical photo." (Can't put one over on us!)

There are dozen of neighborhood celebrations and festivals, as well as several large displays of fireworks along the Willamette and Columbia Rivers. Oaks Park and Waterfront Park along the Willamette have the two most central displays, and if you position yourself just right along the river, you can see both of them at once. Other venues, such as the Portland International Speedway and Civic Stadium (now PGE Park) have also displayed fireworks in the past. Vancouver (see below) also has a wonderous pyrotechnic display. All over town, you'll find live outdoor music (especially at the Waterfront Blues Festival, below), barbecues, picnics, block parties, and festivity. Two special regional traditions are listed below, one at Ft. Vancouver and one in the little town of St. Paul, south of Portland.

Ft. Vancouver (Washington) Fourth of July
612 E. Reserve, Vancouver
(800) 832-3599

The Ft. Vancouver celebration is a day-long free event offering tours of the M.J. Pearson Air Museum, Officers Row, and the recreated outpost of Ft. Vancouver. The air museum offers rides in classic biplanes as well as a range of aviation-based activities for children. The museum charges a very modest admission fee.

The Fort Vancouver Brigade Encampment is a reenactment of the annual return of fur trappers to one of the Northwest's oldest European settlements, complete with participants in full period costume and equipped with all of a trapper's equipment. The all-day festival offers free picnic space as well as food booths and free entertainment. Around dark, close to 9 P.M., barges on the Columbia start launching almost an hour's worth of fireworks. After the fireworks, visitors, now tired, sunburned, and potentially cranky, spend an hour fighting some of the heaviest traffic of the year. (For more about the M.J. Pearson Air Museum, see our Attractions chapter.)

The St. Paul Rodeo
St. Paul, Oregon
(503) 633-2011, (800) 237-5920

St. Paul, a small rural Willamette Valley town south of Portland off of Interstate 5, holds a rodeo that's one of the best in the country, with riders competing for prizes in several categories. Even the big city folks get out their jeans, Western shirts, and cowboy boots and join the fun. There are food and beverage booths, a carnival with rides and games of chance and skill, Western dancing for grown-ups, lots of music, a traditional small-town Fourth of July Parade, and, of course, fireworks. This is a real slice of Americana. If you are in town and without other plans over the 4th, this is worth the short ride. To see the rodeo, you'll need a ticket; these run from about $10 to $15, depending on the luxuriousness of the seat. And it's best to order them ahead. Parking is free.

Carifest
South Park Blocks, Portland State
University campus
(503) 725-3000

Portland State University (PSU) is the city's largest urban university and the school has been working hard to define its role in Portland, seeking to end any of the traditional "town and gown" issues. Carifest is a free, daylong celebration of Caribbean arts and cultures. Overseas students, cultural and musical organizations, dancers, artists, and food vendors gather, perform, and exhibit on the South Park Blocks near campus. This free event spices up the Portland summer and adds a dash of color to the city.

Concerts in the Parks
Citywide
(503) 823-PLAY

Summer in the city: early evening light softens but still gleams off the river; the current laps gently at the river's banks, a counter-point to the fading, distant hum of traffic; and music soothes and stimulates the quiet crowd that has gathered at Waterfront Park to hear the Oregon Symphony. Or perhaps the crowd is on its feet and dancing the rhumba at Mt. Tabor. Whatever the music and wherever the park, these free concerts are held during the month of July (and often into August) throughout the city. You'll find a free concert of one kind or another just about every night of the week. Information about these concerts is available at all Portland Parks and Recreation facilities, as well as libraries throughout the city. You can also find concert schedules and locations at the Portland Parks Web site: www.PortlandParks.org. When Portland's summer is good, it is very good.

Concours D'Elegance
Pacific University, 2043 College Wy.,
Forest Grove
(503) 357-2300
info@forestgroveconcours.org

More than a quarter of a century old, this Concours D'Elegance is the largest event of its type in the Pacific Northwest. Organized by the Forest Grove Rotary Club, the event is held on the pastoral campus of Pacific University, and features more than 350 classic, vintage, and antique touring and sports cars from virtually every era of automotive history. This is a one-day event, usually held on a Sunday

Insiders' Tip

Do you want to enjoy the fireworks but avoid the crowds? Early in the evening, pack an evening snack (sorry, no alcohol in the parks) and maybe a sweater, then head up to Washington Park. Find a place to park before the crowds arrive. Smell the roses. Find a spot overlooking the city and then wait until dark. The fireworks from the Blues Festival will be closest, and most dramatic against the city's skyline, but you will also be able to see the fireworks from Vancouver, Oaks Park, and the Portland Speedway.

in mid-July. Admission for adults is $12, and for children six through twelve, $6. (Some discounts are available if you buy your tickets ahead of time.) In addition to the display of cars as art and investments, there is a range of musical entertainment and assorted refreshments. If you go, plan on spending a full day in Forest Grove. This is a neat little town where, in typical Oregon fashion, loggers and mill workers share neighborhoods with college students and professors and those who commute to downtown Portland. There are a growing number of small retail establishments, antique stores, restaurants, and coffee shops. Don't miss the gallery operated by the Valley Art Association.

da Vinci Days
Oregon State University, Corvallis
760 S.W. Madison, Ste. 200, Corvallis 97333
(541) 757–6363
www.davinci-days.org

If you can go to this event—based on the idea that Leonardo da Vinci's genius was to integrate art and science—you ought to go. You won't regret it. It's a three-day celebration that includes everything from a regional art show to performances of original dance. (Dancers were suspended from trees in a piece presented one year.) There are skateboard and teen band competitions, a film and video festival, jazz performances, a childrens' parade, Ultimate Frisbee, and street theater. A range of demonstrations and hands-on activities related to the yearly theme are also scheduled. This is a terrific event for both adults and children.

Frog Day
Downtown Silverton, Oregon on OR Hwy.
213, south of Oregon City
(503) 873–5440

While this is not Mark Twain's Calaveras County, Silverton's Frog Day is a low-key event about fun, summertime, and other traditional elements of small town life and character. The free event, which draws a couple of thousand visitors each year, includes an amphibian petting zoo,

displays of frog collectibles and clothing, as well as a frog-coloring contest. A frog-judging contest is also held, with prizes and some degree of honor for the Best of Show. Contestants and visitors are also educated and urged not to take frogs from their environment for the contest.

This small, semi-rural town (about 7,000 residents) is one of those relatively undiscovered Oregon gems. Set in the rich agricultural land of the northern Willamette Valley, Silverton has defined itself with a delightful downtown filled with local shops and an increasing number of good restaurants and galleries. The local culture reflects the Anglo, Hispanic, and Russian origins of its population and the importance of agriculture in a digitized, silicon age. Too many people pass through Silverton on their way to Silver Falls State Park (see Daytrips). They are not only missing the frog thing but a Spring Iris Festival at Cooley's Gardens, (503) 873–5463, and Schreiner's Iris Gardens, (503) 393–3233, and a popular Volkswalk.

The Gorge Games
Hood River
(541) 386–7774
www.gorgegames.com

Subaru sponsors this weeklong sports competition (kayaking, mountain biking, and windsurfing) that draws more than 30,000 each year. Professionals, skilled recreational amateurs, and total novices are all welcome here, with separate events for different levels of skill. This event includes a sports expo, eleven how-to clinics, outdoor concerts, twenty sports competitions, lots of activities, and a generous offering of local foods and brews, and it's a great opportunity to try some of those scary-looking extreme sports you've been watching on ESPN. Hood River is about an hour's drive east of Portland up the Columbia Gorge. If you plan to play, remember that the Columbia and other local rivers are very cold, even in the summer. Admission fees vary, but a lot of stuff is free, such as the Street Dance on

Sunday. When your knees and arms need a rest, take a break and visit the Columbia Art Gallery at 207 Second Street, Hood River, (541) 386-4512. It's an excellent local gallery showcasing the impressive talents of local artists.

Hood to Coast Relay
Government Camp
(503) 292-4626

For more than twenty years, teams have gathered at Government Camp, on Mount Hood, to run a 195-mile relay race all the way to Seaside at the Oregon coast. Twelve people are on each team. The race, which is billed as the largest relay race in the world, attracts more than 12,000 people—runners, walkers, spectators—from all over. Walking events are offered in addition to running events, and some of the racewalkers are impossibly fast. This race is very exhilirating, and therefore popular; many teams are made up of people who wouldn't ordinarily find themselves in any kind of race whatsoever. Because of its popularity, the organizers have a strict registration policy, and expect you to register well in advance. But even if you're not racing, the event is fun to follow, whether you're watching the runners speed through Portland or joining them in celebration at Seaside.

International Pinot Noir Celebration
Linfield College, 900 S.E. Baker, McMinnville
(503) 472-8964, (800) 775-4762

This is Oregon's most prestigious wine event. The celebration draws oenophiles and wine experts from throughout the country to this small college for three days of tastings, talks and tours, eating, and entertainment. Half of the sixty pinots are from right here in Oregon and the other half arrive from the world over. Advance reservations are mandatory—fewer than 400 tickets are sold for this event, and tickets sell out within hours, despite the very steep prices. If this is for you, you may want to consider calling a year in advance.

Molalla Buckeroo
The Buckeroo Grounds, Molalla
(503) 829-8388

Since 1913, professional riders, ropers, and other persons skilled in the arts of the Western ranch have been coming to the Molalla Buckeroo (that's Oregon-speak for rodeo). Admission prices vary from about $5 to $12, depending on how old you are and where you sit. This event includes dances, barbecues, trail rides, parades, and, of course, three days of professional rodeo.

Mt. Angel Abbey Bach Festival
Mt. Angel Abbey, Angel
(503) 845-3321

While the state's largest celebration of Bach is held in Eugene, this event is an opportunity to hear some of the master's music superbly performed in an unusual setting. Each night of the festival opens with a vespers service and then a recital, after which the entire audience gathers outside in groups of four for picnic suppers before heading in for the evening's featured performance. Held on the final Wednesday, Thursday, and Friday in July, the festival's 500 nightly seats are sold out months in advance. If you want to attend, call well ahead and get your name on the waiting lists.

Mt. Angel is best known for its annual Oktoberfest (see the October section), an event that has been called the state's largest party. On the other hand, the town is worth visiting at other times of the year, even if you don't have tickets to the Bach Festival. The drive down, especially on the back roads, takes you through some of the richest farmland in the world. The century-old Benedictine abbey and seminary sit on a 300-foot-high hill overlooking the town of Mt. Angel and the area's fertile valley. The abbey has a small, eclectic museum and gift shop and tours are available by prior arrangement.

In downtown Mt. Angel, St. Mary's Church, 575 E. College Street, (503) 845-2296, is an inspiring and historic example of Neogothic architecture. Originally built in 1912 to serve the religious needs of the German Catholics who settled in the area, the church was severely damaged in 1993's Spring Break Earthquake. The restoration was expensive and painstaking, but the results are incredible. The Mt. Angel Brewing Company, 210 Monroe Street, Mt. Angel, (503) 845-9624, a locally owned brewpub and restaurant, also makes a nice stop.

Mt. Hood Oregon Trail Quilt Show and Old-Time Fiddler's Jamboree
Brightwood, Oregon
(503) 622-4798

This two-day free event is held in a small town at the base of Mount Hood, 45 miles from Portland. The festival includes a display of antique quilts dating back 150 years to the era of the Oregon Trail. Contemporary quilts, other quilted items, quilting supplies, and demonstrations as well as traditional folk music and local history exhibits sew up this event. All of the quilts are for display only.

Oregon Brewers Festival
Tom McCall Waterfront Park,
between the Bill Naito Parkway and the Willamette River
(503) 241-7179, (503) 281-2437

Oregon has a reputation for making fine brews, and so it's not surprising that this popular festival draws 80,000 to 90,000 people, who come to Portland's waterfront to taste our region's excellent local beers and ales, as well as those from elsewhere. The festival invited seventy-two brewers from across the continent to show off their crafts, and about a third of these brewers are from right here in town. You can expect to find more than a dozen styles of beer and ale ranging from stouts to wheat beers and porters (but only one product from each brewery is allowed). And for those who don't indulge, craft-brewed root beer and cream soda, lemonade, cider, and coffees are also available. A selection of locally prepared specialty foods, most of which may be eaten with-

out utensils, is also available. Local musicians, including some of the area's best performers, offer entertainment. Moderation as well as the use of mass transit, taxis, and designated drivers are all seriously encouraged. While clearly not a family event for those with underage offspring—though children are allowed—the festival encourages enjoyment, beer tasting, and a little bit of education about the brewer's art and product. There is zero tolerance for any type of boisterous, unruly, or other anti-social behavior. All local laws are well enforced by Portland's blue-clad finest and the event is monitored by the sponsoring association and the Oregon Liquor Control Commission. Admission is free, but visitors must purchase a $3 mug for tasting and purchase tokens in advance in order to fill it (Tokens and mugs are sold at the same site). Tokens are $1 each; a full glass of beer is $3, while a 1-oz. taste is $1. All of this must be paid for with cash; an ATM is available on-site. No credit cards are accepted.

Oregon Country Fair
Veneta, Oregon
(541) 343-4298
www.oregoncountryfair.org

The Oregon Country Fair is a wondrous alloy of beautiful handicrafts, displays of alternative energy sources, acoustic music, funky vaudeville acts, excellent food, arts displays, and much more. If you have the time (Veneta, near Eugene, is a good two-hour drive from Portland), check this one out. It's a cultural experience unique to Oregon. Be sure to call the above number for directions and order advance tickets through FASTIXX, (800) 992-8499—none will be sold at the site. Friday, the fair's first day, offers the complete experience with fewer visitors. Don't bring your dog, alcohol, glass containers, or video cameras. Meet jesters and jugglers, musicians, mimes and magicians, crafters and cooks. Some childcare is available on-site. This event is extremely popular, so parking and traffic may give you a lot of headaches. You might instead take one of the buses that Lane County Transit thoughtfully sends out to the fair site. If you do park at the fair, be sure to respect the residents who live near the grounds.

Portland International Performance Festival
Location and sites vary
(503) 72–LEARN.

And now for something completely different. . . . This is not about jazz, the blues, Shakespeare, rock, dance, crafts, food, or chamber music. This is, in the end, about the human condition and about art and about performing and performance. Each year's festival varies: There is no paradigm for this event other than sheer creativity. The most recent festival, with performances at Lewis & Clark College, Portland State University, and in private homes, included musicians, poets, actors, storytellers, dancers, and puppeteers. Admission varies, but is in the $8 to $16 per performance range. This is a Portland few people, including most of the city's residents, know about, and it is a good opportunity to get close to the creative consortium that is alive and well in our town.

Portland Scottish Highland Games
Mt. Hood Community College
26000 S.E. Stark, Gresham
(503) 293–8501

Bring your bagpipes and wear your kilts and clan tartans if you want to fit in at this celebration of all things Scottish. There are bagpipe bands and soloists, Highland dancers, fiddlers, and those unusual and muscle-straining Scottish athletic competitions. Visitors can enjoy ethnic Scottish foods and beverages and browse a range of imported clothes, jewelry, and other items. Admission is in the $10 per person range. Gresham is at the east end of the light rail system, but the college is a couple of miles from the station, so a car may be the best means of getting there.

Salem Art Fair & Festival
Bush's Pasture Park, Salem
(503) 581–2228

This event is one of the best on the entire West Coast, and well worth the short drive down Interstate 5 to Salem from Portland or Vancouver. Approximately 200 artists and craftspeople from throughout the entire West display (and gladly sell) their works. Children and adults will enjoy the range of entertainment, concerts, demonstrations, and puppet shows. The event is also an opportunity to walk through and admire a superb rose garden, a Victorian home, and an excellent community gallery. Admission, parking, and a shuttle service are free.

Sand in the City
Pioneer Square between 6th Ave. and
Broadway, Morrison and Yamhill
(503) 246–5818

Now you can get even with your parents for all the times they told you "don't bring the whole beach home with you." It's not the whole beach (Oregon has some 300 miles of coastline) but it's enough—270 tons—to allow eighteen teams of architects and others to design and build sand castles and other structures in the center of downtown. Amused and intrigued onlookers are allowed to provide unsolicited advice during this three-day fundraising event for Kids on the Block, an organization that reaches out to disadvantaged youth. The event also includes puppet shows, music, and a children's sandbox.

State Games of Oregon
Venues vary
(503) 520–1319

The State Games involve more than three dozen "grassroots" sports ranging from armwrestling and badminton to footbag (hackey-sack) and roller hockey, indoor soccer, and water polo, most with at least two or three categories of competition. More than 16,000 people from throughout Oregon and neighboring states will participate at sites throughout the metro area. The State Games of Oregon are a statewide, multisport, Olympic-style competition (individual and team sports) created by the Oregon Amateur Sports Foundation and supported by proceeds from the Oregon Lottery. With some exceptions, only Oregon residents can compete. Admission for spectators is free. Registration fees vary; call for information.

Street of Dreams
Location and specific times vary, Portland
(503) 684–1880

To showcase their talents each year, between seven and ten local builders create a custom-designed, decorated, and landscaped house in a selected enclave. These are clearly not starter, or even average, homes: prices begin at about $400,000 and up, and up, and up. Extravagance is the word here. But for a modest admission fee ($10 per person for adults), it is a pleasant way to spend an afternoon seeing how and where the affluent plan to live. The event, a fund-raiser for local nonprofit organizations, opens with a black-tie tour. Hors d' oeuvres and liquid refreshments are included. See our Neighborhoods chapter for additional information.

Waterfront Blues Festival
Tom McCall Waterfront Park, between the banks of the Willamette River and Bill Naito Pkwy.
(503) 973–FEST

There may be some irony about a four-day blues festival held over the Fourth of July weekend in one of the most livable cities in the nation. The blues are perhaps *the* American musical genre, rooted in hard times and forged with heartache.

If you've been down so long that it looks like up to you, then you may not notice that the festival is held on the green sloping banks of a river with a snowcapped mountain bathed in evening light as a backdrop. Nor would you notice the free fireworks that end the Fourth of July concert or the fact that the festival brings some of the nation's, and the Northwest's, finest blues artists to the city. One of Portland's premier events, the Waterfront Blues Festival has been packing them in by land and sea (boaters anchor off the seawall to listen to the music sans admission charge) for fifteen years or more. If you don't mind not seeing the performers, spread a blanket on the grass beyond the festival area, close your eyes, and listen with all your heart. Admission is by donation—the common suggestion is $3 and a couple cans of food for the Oregon Food Bank.

August

The Bite—A Taste of Portland
Tom McCall Waterfront Park, between the Bill Naito Pkwy. and the Willamette River
(503) 698–3400

Portlanders do love their summer festivals: it must have something to do with being able to get outdoors without an umbrella, layers of Gore-Tex and Polartec fleece, waterproof Danner boots, and a rain hat. The Bite is another local celebration of food, eating, and conspicuous food consumption, and it draws people from all over to eat their way from one end of Waterfront Park to the other. (One year, the ingenius maker of a new antacid had people giving out free samples.) The idea is that if you run, jog, hike, or bike enough, you can work off those calories and keep the arteries open and the waist size within reason. The admission charge of $3 supports the Oregon Special Olympics. Music and dancing are also featured.

Evergreen Antique and Classic Fly-In
Evergreen Airport,
13800 E. Mill Plain Blvd., Vancouver
(360) 892–5028

This event is on the endangered species list as commercial development encroaches on the airport's historic grass runways. The fly-in (and camp-in for pilots and visitors) draws as many as 300 aircraft and is the closest thing to the Barnstorming Era of the 1920s and 1930s on the current airshow circuit. The grass runway limits the type of airplanes that can land and take off, but there are dozens of aircraft from restored fabric and wire biplanes of the late 1920s to World War II-era trainers. A local pilot is known to fly in his immaculately restored Battle of Britain-era Hawker Hurricane. The event is free and there are few barriers so you can kick a few tires, talk to the pilots, and watch a flour-bombing competition. When the event is over, don't rush off; stay to watch the aircraft as they fly-out for home. Tickets for the Fly-In, which has been going strong for more than forty years, are $5 for adults, $4 for seniors, and $3 for kids six to twelve.

Homowo Festival of African Arts
Location varies
(503) 288–3025

Portland wants to honor cultural and ethnic diversity and this family-oriented festival does so by featuring the art, music, dance, food, and crafts of several African nations and cultures. The free event also features traditional African storytelling. Homowo has been held in Cathedral Park, with the soaring spires of the St. Johns Bridge and the Willamette as a backdrop and in Washington Park with the city's steel and glass skyline, the Willamette River and Mount Hood as a cultural counterpoint.

Mt. Hood Festival of Jazz
Mt. Hood Community College,
26000 S.E. Stark, Gresham, Oregon
(503) 219–9833

This is a big one. While tickets are expensive, starting in the $20 per person range for general admission and going up to $50 per person, the open-air Mt. Hood Festival of Jazz celebrates music and the Oregon summer by attracting some of the biggest and most respected names in jazz. Ray Charles, Chick Correa, and Al Jarreau have been headliners, but the depth of talent and skill of the other twenty or so performers, soloists, singers, and groups from a trio on up in size, is equally as impressive. The largest jazz festival in the state, this is a popular event inspiring both patrons and performers to return year after year. The festival recognizes that having fun is as important as the music and manages to balance those concerns very well. Parking is $3, but a shuttle from MAX to the college is an attractive alternative.

Festa Italiana
Pioneer Square, between 6th Ave.
and Broadway, Morrison and Yamhill
(503) 771–0310
www.festa-italiana.org

Still another free festival in Pioneer Square (which has been called Portland's Living Room), this event is full of strolling musicians, art displays, and the culinary arts of a dozen or so Italian restaurants offering pizza, pastas, garlic bread, Italian ices, and coffees. All of this and a wine garden draw an afternoon and early-evening crowd from the suburbs and downtown offices. The festival spills beyond the bricks of Pioneer Square, however. The purpose is to celebrate all things Italian, and to this end, a mass is celebrated at St. Michael the Archangel, a local Catholic Church with an enthusiastic Italian-American population (the mass is followed by a bocce ball tournament at the Ponzi Vineyards, west of town).

The Homowo Festival of African Arts features music, dancing, and storytelling. CREDIT: MARY ALLISON

Fiesta Mexicana
Legion Park, Woodburn
(503) 982–2563

Just down the freeway (south on Inter-state 5) from Portland, Woodburn is a growing city in its own right, not a true suburb. A growing Hispanic population in the Willamette Valley adds diversity, color, and a continuing cultural influence to Oregon. Less commercial and flashy than Portland's Cinco de Mayo celebra-tion, this event reflects the real lives, food, art, music, and traditions of Hispanic Americans. Admission is free and the event is well worth the short drive.

Fred Meyer Challenge
The Reserve Vineyard and Golf Course,
4805 S.W. 229th Ave., Aloha
(503) 526–9331

Locally known as "Peter's Party," the Fred Meyer Challenge, organized by golf pro Peter Jacobson and his event company PJP

Productions, is a popular golf tourna-ment featuring foursomes of golf profes-sionals, celebrities, and skilled amateurs. In Portland this event usually makes the society page, the sports page, and the business page. Ticket prices are $40 per day or a season ticket for $100; this gets you into all three days of the event. (See Spectator Sports for more information.)

India Festival
Pioneer Square between 6th Ave.
and Broadway, Morrison and Yamhill
(503) 223–1613

The India Festival draws Oregonians whose families originated on the Indian subcontinent, as well as everyone in town who loves Indian food, spices, art, jewelry, arts and crafts, music, and dance. It's a sensory carnival, with colors, music, and aromas blending intriguingly. There's no admission charge for this Pioneer Square event.

**Mt. Hood Huckleberry Festival &
Barlow Trail Days
Welches
(503) 622–4798**

Events like these are important for the area's suburban and urban populations because they help maintain awareness of the state's agricultural heritage and bounty. While Oregon is currently known for high-tech products, expensive athletic shoes, and tourism, agriculture remains one of the three largest industries. This free event emphasizes the region's history, for it takes place on part of the Oregon Trail, and the state's natural wealth—in this case, berries. You can buy jams, pies, sauces, tarts, and syrups, enjoy a salmon bake, and take three tours of the historic Barlow Trail, which led pioneers around Mount Hood and down into the Willamette Valley.

**OBT Exposed
South Park Blocks, between Salmon
and Main Sts.
(503) 227–0977**

Much more than just very limber and graceful men and women in black tights, this open-air studio with no admission charge, brings viewers "backstage" to see how much work, practice, and skill is involved in the dance world of Oregon Ballet Theater. A fascinating marketing and awareness-building effort, this event features ballet members who spend two weeks practicing in tents as part of their preparation for the new season. Much more than a publicity ploy, it's a traffic-stopping effort to bring art into the light.

**ObonFest
Oregon Buddhist Temple, 3720 S.E. 34th Ave.
(503) 254–9536**

Out in a residential neighborhood, this is a Japanese-American Buddhist Festival of the Ancestors, which offers another perspective on multicultural life in Portland. The free festival is also an opportunity to learn about the long and not terribly comfortable history of Oregon's Japanese-American community. More cultural than strictly religious, the fest includes Japanese and other Asian foods, crafts, music, and dancing.

**Tualatin Crawfish Festival
Tualatin Commons and Community Park,
8535 S.W. Tualatin Rd., Tualatin
(503) 692–0780**

As this once-rural suburb grows into a city, it continues to celebrate a tradition that is more than a half-century old. The event is split between the Commons in downtown Tualatin and the Community Park just a short stroll away. It features music, craft, and food booths, a street dance, and plenty of crawfish in gumbo, a la carte, and various other delivery systems. There is also a crawfish-eating contest.

Insiders' Tip

With their farm animals, 4-H kids, crafts exhibits, carnival rides, and country music, county fairs provide some of the best summer entertainment around. In July, look for the Multnomah County Fair (right here in Portland), (503) 248-5144, the Hood River County Fair, (541) 354-2865, and the Washington County Fair and Rodeo, (503) 648-1416; in August, try the Yamhill County Fair, (503) 472-9371, the Clackamas County Fair (503) 266-1136, and the Clark County Fair, across the river, at (360) 397-6180.

September

Art in the Pearl
Northwest Park blocks (between W. Burnside and N.W. Glisan at N.W. 8th Ave.)
(503) 722–9017
www.artinthepearl.com

More than one hundred artists gather here each Labor Day weekend for a lively three days of culture and commerce. In addition to artists selling their wares, musicians and theatre groups perform on a central stage. And you can try out artistic pursuits for yourself in the Education Pavilion, which has activities for children and their grown-up friends. And, naturally, you'll find the usual festival food booths.

Celebration of Cultures
Downtown Gresham
(503) 618–3000

Once a quiet, distant city of farms and fields, Gresham has changed in the last twenty-five years, welcoming light rail and building new neighborhoods and restoring the downtown. For a long time, people felt, to paraphrase Gertrude Stein, that "there was no there, there." That's not true anymore. This free event is sponsored by the Gresham Sister City Association to honor the city's own increasingly diverse population and identity as well as its three overseas sister cities: Ebetsu, Japan, Sok-Cho, Korea, and Owerri, Nigeria. The event includes foods from different countries and cultures and ethnic entertainment.

Dada Ball
Locations vary
(503) 242–1419
www.pica.org/htdocs

A fund-raiser for the Portland Institute of Contemporary Art, the Dada Ball brings out the latent druid in attendees, who tend to dress both sparingly and inventively for this wild evening. It's Portland's version of Carnivale and it's a favorite of the Beautiful People. Tickets are about $35 at the door, and slightly discounted if purchased in advance. A catered patrons' dinner and auction is held before the dance; these tickets run close to $200.

North by Northwest (NXNW)
Old Town and other locations
(512) 467–7979
www.nxnw.com

Three hundred bands and a whole lot of other musicians, producers, composers, writers, and recording industry types fill the city's clubs for this four-day musical conference and festival. It showcases new music and artists performing everything from jazz to hip-hop to grunge to that indefinable "alternative rock," with a special, though not exclusive, emphasis on homegrown music.

Oregon State Fair
Oregon State Fairgrounds, Salem
(503) 947–FAIR
www.fair.state.or.us

The Oregon State Fair is an updated American tradition, held the last week before Labor Day (which means it sometimes falls in the month of August.) The fair still has strong roots, and support, in the state's rural areas and agricultural and ranching communities and industries, but in a larger sense, the fair celebrates and honors Oregon's past, acknowledges the present, and recognizes the future. The fair offers 4-H and Future Farmers of America displays, animals, and products along with a carnival, horse racing, and booth after booth of food and other products. The fair draws visitors from throughout the state and region. Tickets at the gate are $6 for adults, $4 for seniors, and $3 for children ages six to twelve. Parking is $4.

Portland Creative Conference
Portland Center for the Performing Arts,
S.W. Broadway and Main St.
P.O. Box 6943, Portland, Oregon 97228
(503) 234–1641, (800) 597–0099
www.creativeconference.org

Advertising types, movie folks from Hollywood, New York, and Utah, actors, agents, producers, writers, composers, entertainment enthusiasts, and hangers-on come to Portland for this three-day event in which creativity is explained to those who lack it. A major schmooze-fest, the conference is replete with ultra-hip souls who watch movies and videos and listen to speakers discuss art and mammon. The admission fee for this conference is very expensive—upwards of $600. You are advised to get on the mailing list by writing to the post office box listed above to receive the program before getting your heart set on finding someone to read your screenplay.

Swan Island Dahlia Conference Show
Clackamas County Fairgrounds, Canby
(503) 226–7711

Nursery stock—everything from grass seed to irises, tulips, and ornamental bushes—is a huge industry in northwest Oregon. Large fields of Dahlias and other flowers flourish in the fertile soil around Portland, and this free event offers information for both professionals and enthusiasts. The fairgrounds are 30 miles south of Portland on U.S. Highway 99 East.

Vintage Fair
Sportsman Airpark, Newberg
(503) 538–2014

There are lots of harvest festivals to mark the turn of the season in Oregon, but this is one of the best. Not only is admission very modest ($5 or so), but the event retains its human scale. And it really is in the country. Newberg was basically an agricultural community for a long time, with strong Quaker roots, and has escaped most of the unplanned growth that turns nice little towns into ugly suburbs. The Vintage Fair showcases vintage airplanes, cars, motorcycles, bicycles, and tractors, and some owners dress in period costumes to accompany their vehicles. There are craft booths and demonstrations. And, of course, there is food and drink, including locally brewed beers and local wines.

October

Greek Festival
Holy Trinity Greek Orthodox Church,
3131 N.E. Glisan St.
(503) 234–0468

This is a very popular free event drawing visitors from throughout northwest Oregon and southwest Washington who come to enjoy . Greek music and dancing, arts and crafts displays, and, of course, lots of food.

Halloween Pumpkin Fest
Fir Point Farms, 14601 Arndt Rd., Aurora
(503) 678–2455

This is another "see the real Oregon" must-see. Fir Point Farms is a real, working farm producing flowers and nursery stock, pumpkins, hay, and a variety of fruits and vegetables. It is also a roadside fruit and vegetable stand where you can buy locally grown produce and flowers. They have an excellent selection of locally made baked goods (like strawberry-rhubarb pie), dried fruits, mustards, jams and jellies, and fruit butters. There is a small "country store" full of all sorts of country merchandise. A couple of times a year, the owners attract good crowds of city dwellers, visitors, and locals for a series of holiday events.

At Halloween there is a maze made of hay, as well as a "haunted trail." The grounds are filled with carved and decorated pumpkins and there are pony and cart rides, face painting, and entertainment for children.

Rabbits, chickens, and turkeys are on hand for petting and watching, and the farm's goats climb a series of ramps and tree branches to get an aerial perch on the activities. For a quarter you can buy a handful of goat food and winch it up to a platform where the goats are waiting for their reward.

No admission is charged, though there are small fees for rides, and while picnics are welcome, refreshments are available for modest prices. This is great fun not only for children but for adults too. The farm is a few minutes off Interstate 5 at the Aurora/Canby exit and there are lots of signs pointing you in the right direction. (See Kidstuff for more on Fir Point Farms and other pumpkin patches.)

Howl-a-Ween
The Oregon Zoo, 4001 S.W. Canyon Rd.
in Washington Park
(503) 226-1561

Kids are invited to the zoo to go on a scavenger hunt and trick-or-treat combination event (see Attractions) This event happens on October 30 and 31. (For more on the zoo, see Attractions.)

Oktoberfest Celebrations

Is this just another excuse to put on costumes we wouldn't be caught dead in any other time of the year, drink beer, eat sausage, and dance around? Perhaps, but does it really matter? Years ago, Oktoberfest meant going to the little faux-Bavarian village of Mt. Angel south of Portland. But now other communities, restaurants, brewpubs, including the Portland Brewing Co. and Widmer Brothers Gasthaus (see chapter on Brewpubs), and social and cultural groups have gotten in on the cultural act. The result is that there is a lot more to do, to eat, and to drink.

Horst Mager's Rheinlander Oktoberfest
Oaks Park at the east end of the
Sellwood Bridge
(503) 233-5777

Horst Mager's restaurants, Der Rheinlander and Gustav's Bier Stube, 5035 S.E. Sandy Boulevard, (503) 288-5503, and Gustav's Bier Stube-Sunnyside, 12605 S.E. 97th Avenue, Clackamas, (503) 653-1391, are traditional Portland favorites that have been providing Portland residents with a taste of German food and culture for years. Horst has taken his talents and taste on the road with an outdoor Oktoberfest at Oaks Park on the banks of the Willamette River. Visitors will find traditional German foods and music as well as ample supplies of German and local beers and wines.

Mt. Angel Oktoberfest
Throughout downtown Mt. Angel, Oregon
(503) 845-6882

Despite a long history of German settlers, Mt. Angel didn't make Oktoberfest a commercial activity until 1965. Now the free event lasts four days, beginning with the traditional Webentanz, or May Pole dance. There are four stages with nearly continuous live music, demonstrations of traditional Bavarian folk dancing, and street dances on Friday and Saturday nights. Visitors will also find food booths (German and other) and craft booths. In addition to the traditional Biergarten and Wiengarten, there is now a Microgarten with locally brewed beers. For younger visitors, there is a Kindergarten with rides and other entertainment geared for youngsters.

Portland Marathon
(503) 226-1111

While the 26.2-mile run is the logical centerpiece of this event, this well-organized open marathon, now in its fourth decade, includes a 26.2-mile walk, a 5-mile run, a 10-kilometer (6.2 miles) run, a 10-kilometer

Mayor's Walk, a non-competitive 2-mile kids' run, and a 2-mile Special Olympics run. For those who haven't entered the marathon—a 24-hour ultra-track run—there is also a sports medicine and fitness fair. The Portland Marathon is sponsored by Nike, Gatorade, Crown Pacific, and the Portland Hilton. For more information, see the Recreation chapter.

Salmon Festival
Oxbow Regional Park, Sandy
(503) 797–1850

A regional icon, the native and wild salmon is clearly an endangered species. This festival is a chance to see the Chinook swim upstream to spawn, to learn about their habitat, and to understand that we all are involved in their ultimate fate. Among other activities are a salmon bake (it's still okay to eat them) and displays by various organizations committed to the environment and the restoration and health of the salmon habitat. Recent admission prices were $6 per car. To get to the park, drive 6 miles east of Gresham on Division Street.

Sauerkraut Festival
Scappoose
(503) 543–6895

About thirty minutes outside of Portland along the Columbia River, Scappoose is home to those crispy Steinfeld's Pickles and an annual outdoor Sauerkraut Festival held in early October (a time of year with some of the region's best weather). There are also craft booths and entertainment, a Volkswalk, and, of course, food booths with lots of sauerkraut. Admission is free.

November

Christmas at the Pittock Mansion
3229 N.W. Pittock Dr.
(503) 823–3624

Perched 1,000 feet above Portland's downtown, the Pittock Mansion (see the Attractions chapter) is the grandest of all Portland's mansions. As such, it is appropriately decorated and lighted for Christmas. During the festivity, a small restaurant and tea shop is open. The usual admission fee applies ($5 for adults, $4.50 for older adults, and $2.50 for children), but there are often performances of choral and other musical works requiring additional admission during this time of year, so call ahead in order to know what to expect.

Meier & Frank Holiday Parade
Downtown Portland
(503) 241–5329

Holiday shopping takes a short break as this Portland tradition fills the streets with floats, balloon figures, bands, midget autos, and other moving amusements to jump-start the season. The parade is held, rain or shine, the day after Thanksgiving. Shopping commences immediately after the parade.

Pioneer Courthouse Square
Holiday Happenings
Pioneer Square between 6th Ave. and
Broadway, Morrison and Yamhill
(503) 223–1613

The one Portland tradition visitors must hear (and see) to believe is the annual Tuba Concert. With one hundred or more tuba players ranging from symphony members to enthusiastic novices risking badly chilled lips and fingers, the downtown echoes (and echoes) with unique renditions of favorite holiday songs and carols. At times, you can almost hear the carolers making a good-faith effort to match to the tuba sounds. Don't miss it.

The city's Christmas tree is displayed here too, delivered from a local tree farm by a log truck, an event guaranteed to tie-up traffic, but only the real Scrooges get upset. The city's official menorah is lit nearby when Hanukah begins.

Pioneer Harvest Feast
Welches, Oregon
(503) 622-4798

Long before Oregon was known for high-tech electronics and other products—high-tech running shoes, high-tech clothes, and even high-tech food—there was the richness borne of the land that brought people to the state. So, as in New England and in other farming areas, a harvest festival makes sense. While the roses, berries, and peaches are gone, fall means apples and filberts, pears, and pumpkins. This celebration, at the base of Mount Hood, combines history, agriculture, and local lore.

Portland Lo/Op
Oregon Rowing Unlimited
(503) 233-9426

Since a river runs through it, Portland has become a regional rowing center, and the Portland Lo/Op (pronounced "loop"), held the first Saturday in November, is a 4.5-mile race on the Willamette. Some of the best collegiate crews (men and women) from Stanford, University of Washington, UC-Berkeley, Harvard, Cornell, as well as the University of Oregon and Oregon State University and Portland's own Lewis & Clark College, compete on the chilly waters.

Winter Wunderland: A Celebration of Lights
Portland International Raceway West
Delta Park and N. Victory Dr.
(503) 232-3000

Given the region's hydroelectric riches, electricity is usually—though not always—plentiful, so in the darkest months of the year, it is okay to turn on the lights. This is a drive-through attraction: thousands of colored lights are strung on frames and other structures to create illuminated representations of Christmas and other seasonal creatures and symbols. Admission is generally less than $10 per car, but goes up if you have a lot of people in a large vehicle.

Wooden Toy Show
World Forestry Center,
4033 S.W. Canyon Rd. in Washington Park
(503) 228-1367

A three-day show, this Portland tradition brings talented toy makers from throughout the Northwest to display, demonstrate, and sell their wares. If you think craftsmanship, talent, skill, and originality are lost, your faith will be restored by attending this event. There is an admission fee of $4.50 for adults and $3.50 for seniors and children six to eighteen. By taking light rail to the Washington Park station, patrons can avoid automobile anarchy.

Yamhill County Wine Country Thanksgiving
(503) 646-2985

This popular tour is held the fourth weekend in November, following Thanksgiving Day. Sponsored by the Yamhill County Wineries Association, the event highlights more than two dozen wineries and vineyards with new vintages, winery tours, sale prices, and lots of food, crafts, and music.

Close-up

Portland's Farmers' Market

From the 1850s to 1941, Portland had a thriving public market. As late as the 1930s, the Yamhill Public Market, in what is now Old Town Portland, was a 5-block spread of booths, stalls, tables, and baskets all loaded with fresh produce, meat, and poultry brought into town daily by farmers and ranchers. The city rented these curbside stalls for sixteen cents a day.

In those days you could heap a pickup bed with tomatoes, potatoes, carrots, onions, apples, and plums for a buck or two. Now, six decades later, the tradition continues with the Portland Farmers' Market held in the Park Blocks on May through October weekends at S.W. Broadway and Montgomery Street near Portland State University, and June through September on Wednesdays at S.W. Park and Salmon.

Founded in 1992, the market has more than fifty vendors selling farm-fresh produce, cut flowers and bedding plants, vegetable and herb starts, smoked seafood, and artisan breads and cheeses. Much, but not all, of the produce is organically grown.

It's a good idea to visit the market as soon as you can get there in the morning to get the best choices of produce and products. It's also a treat to savor sights, sounds, and smells stirring ancient memories of open air markets that have been the heartbeat of villages for thousands of years and can still be found around the globe by travelers searching for the real feel of a land and its people.

Here in Portland that feel includes the image of mounds of green lettuce heads or a huge tub full of sugar-fried popcorn, the sounds of a fiddle player bowing a jump tune next to a farmer from the Coast Range town of Alsea bagging up a half-pound of goat cheese, and the crisp scent of smoked tuna and salmon, making it hard to pick which fish to munch. You'll find cinnamon twists, croissants, and pastry here, as well as shitake mushrooms, and organically grown tomatoes. Gardeners can take home honeysuckle starts, and dahlia tubers, and other plants.

As well as the wealth of good food at great prices, the market offers a series of events throughout its season. Garden Talks take place each Saturday, May through June at 10 A.M. with Northwest gardening celebrities dispensing advice. Chef-in-the-Market cooking demonstrations let you watch some of the best chefs in Portland cooking with farmers' market produce on Saturdays at 10 A.M., June through October.

Monthly celebrations are an important feature of the market because they underscore the seasonal nature of food. During the July Berry Festival, 1,000 free berry shortcakes are given away by Oregon's Dairy Princesses. In late July, The Pickle Frenzy features samples and demonstrations starring those juiced-up cukes. A wildly popular Summer Loaf Bread festival held in August brings more than twenty area bakeries to the market, along with a wood-burning demonstration oven, featured bread-baking speakers, and amateur and professional baking contests. In September, at the Tomato Turn-On, more than fifty peak-season tomato varieties are cut into nibble-sized pieces and placed on paper plates with name tags along a row of tables. It's your tough assignment to taste them and write down your comments. Lastly, a Harvest Festival, held in late October, wraps up the season with a pumpkin pie contest, jack-o'-lantern carving, and other fall traditions.

The Portland Farmers' Market—and all the farmers' markets in the area—give Portland citizens the chance to connect with the important people who sustain us, a chance that we don't have very often. It may be the Age of Information, but we still have to eat food that someone grows. And what better way to appreciate your food than to meet the person who grew it? So although farmers and other marketeers pay $30 for a booth space and a percentage of their sales, rather than the sixteen cents of yesteryear, they aren't complaining about inflation. They smile on their side of the counter as they weigh bags full of green and yellow vegetables, red and purple fruit, and hand them over to even bigger smiles.

Portland Farmers' Market
Portland State University
1800 S.W Broadway at Montgomery
(503) 241–0032
May through October, Saturdays, 8 A.M. to 1 P.M.

A second location is open for a shorter season:
S.W. Salmon and Park
(503) 241–0032
June through September, Wednesdays, 10 A.M. to 2 P.M.

Regional Farmers' Markets

The Portland Farmers' market is only one of many in the region. Here's a list of others in Portland and in Outlying Areas. The Oregon Department of Agriculture will also send you a pamphlet with all of the Farmers' Markets in Oregon. Contact them at (503) 872-6600 or by email at agmarket@oda.state.or.us.

Portland

Cedar Mill Farmers' Market
Milltowner Shopping Center,
12505 Northwest Cornell Rd.
(503) 643–9962
June through September, Saturdays, 8:30 A.M. to 1:30 P.M.

Hollywood Farmers' Market
N.E. Hancock, between 44th & 45th Sts.
(503) 233–3313
May through October, Saturdays, 8 A.M. to 1 P.M.

Lents Community Market
S.E. 92nd & Foster Rd.
(503) 227–5368
May through October, Saturdays, 9 A.M. to 2 P.M.

Peninsula People's Farmers' Market
N. Lodge and Lombard
(503) 978–0540
May through October, Sundays, 1 P.M. to 4 P.M.

People's All Organic Farmers' Market
3029 S.E. 21st Ave.
(503) 232–9051
April through November, Wednesdays, 2 P.M. to 7 P.M.

Outlying Areas

Beaverton Farmers' Market
Hall Blvd., between 3rd and 5th Aves.
(503) 643–5345
May through October, Saturdays, 8 A.M. to 1:30 P.M.

In July, a second day is added: Wednesday, 3 to 7 P.M.

Forest Grove Farmers' Market
Corner of 19th Ave. and Ash
(503) 357–7111
May through October, Saturdays, 8 A.M. to 1 P.M.

Farmers' Market at Wilco Farm Stores
2741 N. 99 W., McMinnville
(503) 472–6154
August through September, Saturdays, 8 to 11 A.M.

Gresham Farmers' Market
Roberts Avenue between 2nd and 5th
(503) 695–2698
May through October, Saturdays, 8:30 A.M. to 2 P.M.

Hillsboro Farmers' Market
There are two Hillsboro Farmers' Markets:
2nd and East Main on Courthouse Square
(503) 844–6685
May through October, Saturdays, 8 A.M. to 1 P.M.

1st and 3rd on Main St.
(503) 844–6685
June through August, Tuesdays, 5:30 to 8:30 P.M.

Milwaukie Farmers' Market
Main St., between Harrison and Jefferson
(503) 353–9123
May through October, Sundays, 10 A.M. to 2:30 P.M.

Molalla Saturday Market
City Park
(503) 266–6599
May through October, Saturday, 9 A.M. to 2 P.M.

Sandy Farmers' Market
Highway 26 and Route 211, Estacada
(503) 630–4058
May through September, Sundays, 10 A.M. to 3 P.M.

Tigard Farmers' Market
Parking lot at Hall Blvd. and Oleson Rd.
(503) 244–2479
May through October, Saturdays, 8 A.M. to 1 P.M.

Vancouver Farmers' Market
Downtown Vancouver, next to Esther Short Park
(360) 737–8298
April through October, Saturdays, 9 A.M. to 3 P.M.

December

Festival of the Trees
Oregon Convention Center,
777 N.E. Martin Luther King, Jr. Blvd.
(503) 215–6070

To benefit the Providence Medical Foundation, local designers and celebrities decorate sixty-five 8-foot trees. The trees are auctioned off during opening night, with bids beginning at $500. There are also gingerbread and other displays, holiday entertainment, and demonstrations of arts and crafts. Admission is $5 for adults, and $4 for seniors; children twelve and younger are admitted free.

Holiday Lights Displays
Various Locations throughout the city, including:

Festival of Lights at the Grotto,
Sandy Blvd. and N.E. 85th Ave.
(503) 254–7371

ZooLights Festival at the Oregon Zoo
4001 N.W. Canyon Rd. in Washington Park
(503) 226–1561

The darkness of winter nights is charmingly dispelled by these glimmering displays of holiday lights in various neighborhoods and at the Grotto and the Zoo. Admission is charged at both the Oregon Zoo and the Grotto. The Grotto hosts the largest choral festival in the Pacific Northwest with singers from 130 or more school, church, and civic choral groups performing in a 600-seat chapel. The chapel's acoustics are cathedral quality, enhancing the practiced voices of the choirs. The nativity story is told in lighted dioramas and there is a petting zoo for children. Suitable refreshments—hot chocolate, cider, and the like—are available here.

The Oregon Zoo hosts a monthlong display with thousands of lights on trees and buildings and holiday lights arranged into animal silhouettes that raise and lower their heads or perform other animated gestures. The zoo stays open late,

and evenings feature local choirs performing holiday music and adult-size elves bearing treats. The additional charge to ride the Zoo Train is worth it to see the displays from a different perspective. Zoo Lights can get very crowded, so be prepared for a wait for the Zoo Train and dress warmly!

Various neighborhoods compete with each other for the most lavish displays, though the traditional winner is Peacock Lane. A must-visit street for many years, residents on Peacock Lane have now enlisted computers and fiber optics to enhance their displays. The lights and displays draw visitors like moths to electric flames. Some visitors prefer to drive down the 2 blocks or so, but the traffic backs up fast. Others park nearby, bundle up, and walk up and down the street to admire the displays. Hot chocolate is sold from a little booth to warm those who choose to see the lights on foot.

Parade of Christmas Ships
Willamette and Columbia Rivers
(503) 222–2223
www.christmasships.org

Local boat owners decorate their crafts, then form a floating convoy and sail up and down the Columbia and Willamette Rivers each night for several weeks in December. Owners have an informal competition among themselves for the most colorful display and some boats broadcast Christmas carols. If the weather is bad, find a riverside restaurant or bar, order an Irish Coffee or a local stout, and enjoy the floating spectacle snug and warm. If the weather is tolerable, try standing on the Sellwood Bridge over the Willamette south of Portland as the twinkling fleet sails under the bridge upstream and back. Park in East Sellwood and then stroll out onto the bridge. Dress for chilly winds.

The Nutcracker
Oregon Ballet Theater, Keller Auditorium
S.W. 3rd Ave. and Clay
(503) 227-6867

Oregon Ballet Theater director James Canfield's lovely rendition of the holiday classic sells out every year—though tickets are usually available because they give many performances—and has been a tradition among some Portland families for generations. Prices range from $5.50 to $89, depending on seating. Reservations are mandatory.

A Christmas Carol
Portland Center Stage,
1111 S.W. Broadway
(503) 274-6588

The Portland Center Stage has adapted this classic Dickens story for the stage in a notable production for a number of years, and now Artistic Director Chris Coleman has imparted his own stamp. Tickets sell out quickly, so reserve yours well ahead.

Lucky ducks play at the Multnomah County Fair. CREDIT: MARY ALLISON

Oregon Children's Theatre's production of Tom Sawyer. CREDIT: OWEN CAREY

The Arts

One easily apparent reason Portland has a reputation as a city with an enticing quality of life is the bounty of art everywhere you look and listen.

Once a brawling timber town with dangerous docks and Shanghai saloons, Stumptown has mellowed into Rose City, a cosmopolitan center with public art on just about every block. Fountains bubble up and stream down granite slopes, clever murals are broadly stroked across the walls of office buildings, life-size bronze beavers, ducks, and other critters cavort along sidewalks, and sculpted personalities like the business exec with umbrella at Pioneer Square and the bronze damsel at Washington and 5th Street that prompted our ex-mayor to "expose himself to art" in a famous poster, remind Portlanders that there is more to life than making a living. For those who commute to and from their jobs on the Westside MAX, a light rail trolley stretching to Hillsboro, there's a striking linear exhibit of public art on view along the route at every station.

And when folks find time in the hubbub of this new millennium to enrich their lives with an encounter with indoor arts, there is a remarkable abundance of fine music, theater, dance, and film to be found in a culturally booming town that seems to attract artists, actors, writers, dancers, filmmakers, cinematographers, and animators. Thanks to this influx of talent, you don't have to zoom to big sister Seattle or the Big Apple to enjoy top-notch performances in one of four venues under the heading of the Portland Center for the Performing Arts. Also, if you're willing to take a chance with the local version of Off-Broadway, you can stop by one of those warehouses painted black inside and thus turned into mini-theaters. Chances are you won't be disappointed regardless of whether you go black tie or turtleneck.

Speaking of the beat look, Portland is well-known for its hot Poetry Slam Team that's competed regionally and nationally. There are also plenty of verbally deft poets who have chosen a more traditional style to try out their poesy on audiences in coffeehouses, pubs, bookstores, and libraries. Even if you stay home at night, happily cozy with a book or a vid on the tube, you just might glance up while getting there, riding one of the Tri-Met buses, and see a poem picked for the "Poetry in Motion" project, which was first started in New York City.

If it's visual art you crave, there are over seventy art galleries on both sides of the river. Taking a tip from the Seattle art community's First Thursday Artwalk, Westside Portland's gallery owners have had great success staging open houses with nibbles and live music as well as new artwork during their First Thursday. To round out this monthly smorgasbord, gallery and shop owners along Alberta Street in Northeast Portland have added Last Thursday as yet another chance to see exciting new artwork.

To find the where, what, who, and perhaps why of most of the above, here's a selection of the most intriguing, vital, happening arts outfits in the Portland area. The listing includes performance and cultural centers, arts organizations, dance assemblies, literary venues and groups, a profile of the Portland Art Museum, musical ensembles, arts schools, theatrical troupes, and visual arts opportunities.

Cultural Centers and Arts Organizations

The Portland Center for the Performing Arts
1111 S.W. Broadway
(503) 248–4335, (503) 796–9293 (events)

Looming as the centerpiece of the city's cultural district, The Portland Center for the Performing Arts hosts over 900 events, entertaining more than one million ticketholders.

The center is comprised of three main buildings:

The Keller Auditorium on S.W. 3rd Avenue between Market and Clay Streets (503) 248–4335, is a big box of a place with a capacity of 3,000 seats. It's where audiences watch Broadway musicals and operas and enjoy concerts by out-of-town performers. Built in 1917, it was renovated in 1968. The on-site box office is open on show days only, but tickets can be purchased at other times at the Portland Center for the Performing Arts ticket office located in the lobby of the New Theatre Building. Hours are Monday to Saturday, 10 A.M. to 6 P.M.

The Arlene Schnitzer Concert Hall, S.W. Broadway at Main Street (503) 248–4335, is the grande dame of the performance halls (see Close-up profile of "The Schnitz"). A building with a grand past, it's currently the home of the Oregon Symphony, and host to several traveling theater productions, lectures, and other entertainment.

The New Theatre Building, just south of The Schnitz, features an award-winning lobby/reception area with a stunning rotunda topped by a glittering, reflective dome. The lobby leads to two theaters: the Dolores Winningstad Theatre, an Elizabethan or "black-box" theater with 292 seats; and the Newmark Theatre/Brunish Hall, a 916-seat room designed to emulate the Edwardian-style theaters of Europe. Free tours of these performance spaces are offered Wednesdays at 11 A.M., Saturdays every half-hour from 11 A.M. to 1 P.M., and on the first Thursday of every month at 6 P.M. Tours leave from the lobby of the New Theatre Building at S.W. Broadway and Main Street.

Community Music Center
3350 S.E. Francis
(503) 823–3177
www.portlandparks.org

A long, tranquil block south of Powell Boulevard at S.E. 33rd Place and Francis Street in the historic Francis Street Fire Station, is the newly renovated Community Music Center. This charmingly eccentric old building built in 1912 served the neighborhood until it was abandoned mid-century. Now instead of a fire station with a four-story brick tower to dry draped fire hoses, it's a training center for hundreds of music students in the Portland area who present their recitals at the center. Most of those school-age musicians who train at the center are learning to play stringed instruments, including violin, viola, cello, and bass. Many students go on to play with the Metropolitan Youth Symphony and Portland Youth Philharmonic. The center, a member of the National Guild of Community Schools of the Arts, is also a recipient of Chamber Music Program grants from the Amateur Chamber Music Players Foundation.

Interstate Firehouse Cultural Center
5340 N. Interstate Ave.
(503) 823–4322

This fire station that was renovated into a community-based theater/art gallery is a cultural vortex with an emphasis on multicultural art, music, drama, and social issues. Recent exhibits have included paintings and poems by a survivor of the Japanese-American internment camps and artwork celebrating Gullah Islanders living offshore of the Carolinas. Then, downstairs in the theater, patrons can watch comedies or tragedies such as *Tell Me, Janie Bigo* and *Lady Buddha*, both by award-winning playwright Dmae Roberts. Facility hours are Monday to Saturday 10 A.M. to 5 P.M. and gallery hours are noon to 5 P.M.

Multnomah Arts Center
7688 S.W. Capitol Hwy.
(503) 823-2787
www.portlandparks.org

Nicknamed "MAC," this former middle school on the northern edge of Multnomah Village, is now a learning center for artists, musicians, and craftspeople from all over the Portland Metro region. Surely a crown jewel of Parks and Recreation, MAC offers a full menu of tai chi, yoga, and art classes for everyone, from toddlers dabbling with mom and dad to preteens learning cartooning, to serious graphic artists using the right side of their brains. There are burgeoning theater, music, and dance departments as well as classroom and hall rentals. It is also home to the Basketry Guild and Portland Handweavers Guild. All of this is reasonably affordable, with fees ranging from $20 to $170. A catalog, available at the center or through Portland Parks and Recreation, describes this bounty of opportunities along with a credo that says MAC "empowers the people in Portland to live life artfully."

Oregon Potters Association
(503) 222-0533
www.oregonpotterrs.org

The nonprofit Oregon Potters Association presents a large exhibit of works by more than 400 Oregon and southwest Washington clay artists every spring at the Oregon Convention Center, 777 N.E. Martin Luther King Jr. Boulevard. Admission is free to the exhibit, which features clay art including dinner and functional ware, jewelry, sculpture, outdoor garden sculpture, tile work, fountains, and vessels. Throughout each day, artists will demonstrate their individual techniques. Attendees can learn how to make a vessel with a potter's wheel, or be entertained with a bit of pioneer history while watching artists throw pots on an old wagon wheel.

Portland Institute for Contemporary Art
219 N.W. 12th Ave.
(503) 242-1419
www.pica.org

Affectionately dubbed PICA, as in the printer's measurement of six picas per inch, this seriously and often not so seriously hip outfit has been up and running since 1994. Dedicated to bringing innovative and relevant contemporary art, music, and theater to Stumptown, U.S.A., PICA is best known for its annual Dada Ball at which even the most staid bureaucrats have been known to astonish the crowd with their outrageous costumes. Other memorable events presented by PICA were Monsters of Grace, a new multimedia opera by Robert Wilson and Philip Glass, a talk by raconteur Spalding Gray, and a chocolate bonbon in the shape of performance artist Karen Finley. The notable thrust of PICA is that it sponsors the avant-garde all over town, thus spreading the word that the theater of the absurd is alive and willful. There is a permanent gallery and a resource room. Hours are Wednesday to Sunday noon to 6 P.M.

Dance

Oregon Ballet Theatre
818 S.E. 6th Ave.
(503) 222–5538
www.obt.org

Leaping, pirouetting, and gliding since 1989, the Oregon Ballet Theatre not only presents classics such as *Giselle* and *The Nutcracker*, but stretches its collective creativity with showcase work including Bebe Miller's *A Certain Depth of Heart* and Love and Trey McIntire's athletically urban mood piece, *Speak*. Also memorable was recently produced *Signatures*, a ballet by OBT director James Canfield that explores the life of fashion designer Coco Chanel. The OBT also features signature Canfield works including *Jungle*, *Drifted in a Deeper Land*, and *Go Ask Alice*. Although most of the performances are at the Keller Auditorium and the Newmark Theatre (see the Portland Center for the Performing Arts for more information), Oregon Ballet Theatre also takes to smaller stages such as Lincoln Hall at Portland State University as well as touring engagements throughout the United States.

Northwest Afrikan American Ballet
P.O. Box 11143
(503) 287–8852
www.nwaab.org

A high-energy ensemble founded in 1982, Northwest Afrikan American Ballet blends dance movements from Senegal, Guinea, and the Mali regions of West Africa to create memorable performances. With its vibrant dance, authentic, elaborate costumes and sets, this group invokes the feel of a tribal village celebrating its folklore. Along with its signature piece, South African Boot Dance, Northwest Afrikan American Ballet has performed *Rites of Passage*, a popular African ballet exploring the passage of young boys into manhood, and *The Heritage Concert*, a look at Black history. This dance troupe has done residencies from Alaska to California and has toured Scotland and South Africa. In Portland the group performs for many outreach programs and also performs annually in *The Heritage Concert* in mid-February at the Arlene Schnitzer Concert Hall, 1111 S.W. Broadway, (503) 796–9293. Tickets are $24 and $20 purchased through FASTIXX, (503) 224–8499.

White Bird Dance
5620 S.W. Edgemont Place
(503) 245–1600
www.whitebird.org

White Bird Dance brings exciting dance performances to Portland with most shows staged at the Arlene Schnitzer Concert Hall, but a few performances require more intimate venues. Recently, White Bird Dance sponsored the Paul Taylor Dance Company led by a legend who *Newsweek* called "The world's greatest choreographer"; Ballet Hispanico, the nation's leading Hispanic-American dance company; and the Diavolo Dance Company, a group that leaps, spins, and flies through the air. White Bird is collaborating with Portland State University in a new dance series.

Cinema 21
616 N.W. 21st Ave.
(503) 223–4515
www.cinema21.com

Cinema 21 is easily the front-runner in the small contingent of art and foreign film houses in town. With its single screen, loose-sprung seats, less than impeccable sound, and vaguely shabby lobby, this comfy parlor is an aging neighborhood movie house redefining itself as the place to catch a cult favorite, the big hit at Cannes, a black-and-white B-flick, or a martial arts marathon just in from Taiwan. Their quarterly program calendars on a newsprint poster look great on the fridge. Tickets are $6 with a packet of five for $20.

Cinemagic
2021 S.E. Hawthorne Blvd.
(503) 231–7919

This little blue box is a classic with a juke-box in the lobby and a steady parade of oldie-goldie flicks intermixed with artsy contemporary films. It is a tradition here to keep the same movie up on the marquee for what seems like months. If you want to catch a second run or a foreign hit, yet have a hectic life, Cinemagic is a good place to aim towards. Tickets are $4 before 6 P.M. and $6 adults and $4 for children and seniors after 6 P.M.

Clinton St. Theatre
2522 S.E. Clinton St.
(503) 238–8899

Once exclusively a film theater, this multipurpose rumpus room for the pierced-flesh folks and other rads offers poetry slams, performance art pieces, and movies of various genres, including science fiction, foreign, artsy, and high velocity irreverence. New owner Dennis Nyeback brings the vast archive of his eccentric and wacky films of the '20s, '30s, and '40s to Clinton Street. Tickets for most shows are $5.

Hollywood Theater
4122 N.E. Sandy Blvd.
(503) 281–4215
www.hollywoodtheatre.org

Open since 1926, this opulently rococo castle in the grand tradition of movie parlors designed as exotic mansions back in the '20s and '30s, has been recently renovated by the concerted efforts of a neighborhood that didn't want to see it tumble. After all, it lent its name to the Hollywood District, a stretch of lively if mainstream restaurants, bars, bowling alleys, and shops along Sandy Boulevard from 40th to 45th Avenue. After funds were raised to return the Hollywood Theater to its earlier glamour, the film house now shows foreign, art, and second-run movies for $2 to $3.

Laurelhurst Theater and Pub
2735 E. Burnside
(503) 232–5511
www.laurelhursttheater.com

This newly-renovated classic neighborhood movie house offers pizza, wine, and microbrew beer with second-run films at

Insiders' Tip

To check out new flicks just hitting local theaters, call (503) 777-FILM, or go to moviefone.com for all the details on where and when it's playing, what it's about, and who's starring in this movie. Or to access more national movie news try fandango.com.

$2 per show. Check it out for its neon swirl out front and along the ceiling. Once a shabby boarded-up wreck, The Laurelhurst is now a hot spot that's jump-starting the vitality of the surrounding outer Burnside District.

Northwest Film Center
1219 S.W. Park Ave.
(503) 221–1156
www.nwfilm.org

An adjunct of the Portland Art Museum, the Northwest Film Center is an educational facility with a broad curriculum of filmmaking, screenwriting, and similar classes that can lead to a certificate of film study. The film center also houses a media arts resource center, and happily for the rest of us, it is also a terrific conduit of current and classic art and foreign films. Costs for classes varies depending on length and topic. Call the center for more information on tuition. Every year, the center sponsors an international film festival that brings dozens of award-winning movies from all over the globe, the Northwest Film and Video Festival featuring work by regional filmmakers, animators, and cinematographers, and Young People's Film and Video Festival. Following the major renovation at the Portland Art Museum, films are screened at the museum's Whitsell Auditorium, S.W. Park and Madison, the Guild Theatre, S.W. 9th Avenue, and local Regal Cinemas. Tickets are $6.50.

Literary Arts

Berbati's Pan
10 S.W. 3rd Ave.
(503) 248–4579

A brightly blinking light on the international Poetry Slammer's map, Berbati's Pan, a restaurant, nightclub, and reader's theater, hosts almost monthly slams in which poets recite and regale while audiences hoot their critiques. This cheerfully competitive entertainment is a noisy alternative to the often staid and painfully formal academic events that have given poetry readings a grim name. Successful competitors are often asked to join the Portland team that competes on the regional and national level. (See our Nightlife chapter.)

Cafe Lena
2239 S.E. Hawthorne Blvd.
(503) 238–7087

Since 1991, this little bistro with its walls and tables slathered with pix of famous writers, has been poetry central for Southeast Portland literati. Every Tuesday evening at 9:30 P.M. an open mike jams the joint with the good, bad, and verbally ugly while other nights are picked for music, performance art, and other cultural surprises, including the written word lifted off the page and into the raucous air. Stop by with your poems if you're ready to be patient and able to withstand the critical feedback from a group that is both tough and loyal to the art form. (For more on Cafe Lena, see Coffeehouses.)

"I Love Monday!" Readings at Borders
708 S.W. 3rd Ave.
(503) 220–5911

Each Monday in the cozy tea nook of this bookstore, rambunctious poet and MC Dan Raphael hosts readings by visiting writers and locals signed up for open mike night. He also uses one of the Mondays to present a forum on various literary subjects. The get-togethers are free and usually start at 7 P.M.

In Other Words
3734 S.E. Hawthorne Blvd.
(503) 232–6003
www.inotherwords.org

"The Last Word" reading series is held at In Other Words bookstore, a bookstore focused on women's literature. Women of all ages are invited to bring poetry, short fiction, journal musings, personal essays, and other written and spoken words to read for up to five minutes.

The free event takes place on the last Friday of every month at 9 P.M. For more information on the readings contact Daly at the above number.

KBOO 90.7 FM in Portland;
92.7 FM along the Columbia Gorge
20 S.E. 8th Ave.
(503) 231–8032
www.kboo.org

Portland's alternative audiovortex, KBOO, offers a couple of literary radio shows worth a listen for scribblers and fans of scribbling. *The Talking Earth*, celebrating the art of the spoken word, airs on Mondays from 10 to 11 P.M. Seasoned Portland poets Walt Curtis and Barbara LaMorticella take turns hosting this program, which presents visiting writers reading their work and talking about writing. A popular portion of the show is a chance to phone in your favorite poem and read it over the air. KBOO's other literary program, *Between the Covers*, can be heard on Tuesdays at 9 A.M. during a *Morning Radiozine* that runs Monday through Friday after the morning news. This show features interviews with nationally recognized authors.

Literary Arts, Inc.
219 N.W 12th Ave. #201
(503) 227–2583
www.literary-arts.org

This busy bunch sponsors the Portland Arts and Lectures, Oregon Literary Fellowships, including the Friends of Lake Oswego Library/William Stafford Fellowship from Literary Arts, Writers in the Schools, and the Poetry in Motion project. Sponsored by Tri-Met, Literary Arts, Inc., the Portland chapter of the American Institute of Graphic Arts, OBIE Media and the Poetry Society of America, twenty poems were chosen to be displayed on 350 MAX trains and buses on view for thousands of daily riders. Among the local poets chosen were Vern Rutsala, Barbara La Morticella, and Peter Sears. Poems picked from the Poetry in Motion Anthology also included those by William Butler Yeats, Nikki Giovanni, and Shel Silverstein. Portland was the first city on the West Coast to launch a Poetry in Motion program. The first was inaugurated in New York City in 1992. Since then it has expanded to Chicago, Boston, and plans are in the works to have bus poems in Los Angeles, Atlanta, Dallas, and Washington, D.C. In all, Poetry in Motion poems are seen daily by over seven million people riding subways, buses, and trains across the country. A special feature has been added to the Portland project this year. Called "Kidspeak," it will add three poems and art from students at Westview High School and another three from students at Sellwood Middle School. Literary Arts also sponsors the Oregon Book Awards at which every year, writers and their friends gather to watch as book awards are presented for poetry, fiction, literary nonfiction, drama, and work aimed at young readers.

Mountain Writers Center
3624 S.E. Milwaukie Ave.
(503) 236–4854
www.pdxmws.org

It wasn't much to look at when Director Sandra Williams and her colleagues at the Mountain Writers Center first toured the modest, run-down Victorian house in the Brooklyn neighborhood that is now the physical site of one of the largest literary networks in the United States. But after three years of putty, paint, and spackle, the facility has emerged as a resource library, performance venue, residency for visiting writers, and a meeting spot for poets, novelists, essayists, and other ink-stained or keyboard/weary wretches who often work in lonely isolation.

The center has a lot to offer its members (dues start at $45 per year) and the welcome public. In the front room a large table circled with chairs is the focus of feedback and critique sessions called "workshops." The center runs a quarterly workshop series eight to ten weeks long for $200 as well as weekend and one-day workshops. Write to or call the center and they will send you a calendar of events and workshops or visit their website. The room also serves as a reading space for performers, including Portland poet Dan Raphael joined by bassist Glen Moore and award-winning poet Sandra McPherson. Upstairs, a library invites the visitor to cocoon with a collection of poetry, short stories, fiction, and criticism donated by members and supporters. At the heart of this impressive archive is a television, VCR, and a collection of author videos, including some featuring Gary Snyder, Carolyn Forché, Octavio Paz, Sharon Olds, and Barry Lopez. Williams explains that the center has four areas of operation: block booking of writers, high school programs, internships for college students, and writing services, resources, and events. For a current schedule of events, try the center's Web site.

PoetSpeak
Koinonia House, 633 S.W. Montgomery St.
(503) 925–9833

Held on Sunday afternoons in the Great Hall of Portland State University's Koinonia House throughout the year, this reading series features Northwest poets often reading from their latest publications. A $5 general admission is charged to cover administrative costs as well as provide a stipend for the visiting authors. Local poets are encouraged to call to arrange a slot on the performance schedule.

Powell's Bookstores
1005 W. Burnside St.
(503) 228–4651

3747 S.E. Hawthorne Blvd.
(503) 238–1668

8725 S.W. Cascade Ave.
(503) 643–3131
www.powells.com

The preeminent venues for literary readings in the Portland area are arguably the three Powell's bookstores: the Mothership on Burnside, the Eastside store in the heart of the Hip Strip, and the newest store in Beaverton. All three have author's readings in the evenings throughout the week. Expect everything from writers who are on the top-ten list to those who are just starting their careers or causing a hubbub with offbeat books. Schedules are available at all stores and advertised in local newspapers and magazines. Often, while the novelist, poet, or journalist is signing books after the reading you can have a chat with these intriguing scribes.

(Lots of other bookstores sponsor literary readings, too. The A&E Section of Friday's *Oregonian* has a good listing of lyrical utterances to be heard at Looking Glass Books, Annie Bloom's, Borders, Wallace Books, Laughing Horse Books, Broadway Books, 23rd Ave. Books, Barnes & Noble, and usually a killer show, Murder By The Book.)

Music

The Academy
400 E. Evergreen Blvd., Vancouver
(360) 694–3271

American and Northwest history is filled with the pioneering efforts of religious orders to help settle and develop new territories. Mother Joseph, a Catholic nun from the Midwest, arrived in Washington in the early 1870s and eventually founded and built a number of charitable institutions. The Academy was built out of local brick. It housed the first school, hospital, orphanage, and convent in Clark County. While the Sisters of Providence no longer own the building, the structure, now restored, remains as a local landmark with its distinctive architecture and highly visible and central location. The building is still active, housing private offices and a bistro.

Oregon Repertory Singers
St. Philip Neri Catholic Church,
S.E. 18th Ave. and Division St. and
St. Mary's Cathedral, N.W. 18th and Davis
(503) 230–0652
www.oregonrepsingers.org

Entertaining its audiences for two decades in the sumptuous chambers of St. Philip Neri Catholic Church, the fifty-voice Oregon Repertory Singers present neglected classics as well as contemporary pieces. Directed by versatile conductor Gilbert Seeley, the group often joins the Portland Baroque Orchestra to reinterpret work by Handel, Mozart, and Bach. They also have four youth choirs with 140 children.

Oregon Symphony
923 S.W. Washington St.
(503) 228–1353
www.orsymphony.org

Perhaps the most telling aspect of Oregon Symphony is its exuberant refusal to fit the stereotype of a bunch of stuffed shirts playing dull music for other stuffed shirts. Rather, this ensemble of world-class performers and a lustrous list of conductors and musicians stopping by, combine to offer a remarkable package of series for all ears. The "Bravo" series is the mainstay of this menu during which the symphony presents work by Beethoven, Brahms, Mozart, and Tchaikovsky. At the other end of things, "nerve endings" is a delightful series with titles such as "Do the Tango and Get Arrested," and "Did You Hear the One About," or "Can Classical Music be Funny?" Recently, the series combined classical pieces with short films by local filmmakers. The "Applause" series brings guests to the stage, including Peter Serkin on piano and Stanislaw Skrowaczewksi as conductor. On "Symphony Sundays" afternoons are filled with low-priced performances led by the symphony's three conductors, James DePriest, Murray Sidlin, and Norman Leyden. Lastly, the Oregon Symphony

sponsors special events including appearances by Bill Cosby, Itzhak Perlman, Ravi Shankar, and Nadja Salerno-Sonnenburg.

Portland Baroque Orchestra
909 S.W. 11th Ave.
(503) 222–6000
www.pbo.org

It would be worth attending a concert by the Portland Baroque Orchestra to listen to the orchestra play music written between 1600 and the mid-nineteenth century on early instruments. To enhance this time travel, visiting soloists on violin, cello, and harpsichord join the orchestra to render historical versions of Handel, Haydn, and Mozart.

Portland Youth Philharmonic
1119 S.W. Park
(503) 223–5939
www.portlandyouthphil.org

Portland Youth Philharmonic has a long and lustrous history as the country's first youth orchestra. In 1912, Oregon's first children's orchestra was christened as the Sagebrush Symphony. This group turned into the Portland Junior Symphony in 1924 and then in 1930 it settled into its current title. In the past seventy-five years, this assembly of young musicians has performed at the Arlene Schnitzer Concert Hall, recorded six CDs, performed in Washington, D.C., and New York City, and toured overseas including three weeks in Australia to the delight of music lovers worldwide. Most recently, the orchestra represented the U.S. at the Banff International Festival of Youth Orchestras in Canada. Examples of the sort of music this talented group presents are Tchaikovsky's "Violin Concerto," Schubert's "Unfinished Symphony," and Gershwin's "Rhapsody in Blue."

Third Friday Coffeehouse
4312 S.E. Stark St.
Sponsored by the Portland Folklore Society
(503) 282–1327

Every third Friday from September through May, the two-story Multnomah

Friends Meeting House rearranges itself into a coffeehouse with a growing reputation as a nationally recognized venue for folksinger/songwriters, banjo and guitar strummers, and other acoustic musicians. Sponsored by the Portland Folklore Society (PFS), this low-key performance space sans noisy espresso machine and smoky haze, seats 120 fans of contemporary and traditional folk, bluegrass, old-time, and the blues. On any given third Friday, melodious melées of guitar, mandolins, fiddles, basses, banjos, accordions, and singers often lead audiences to join in sing-alongs. A roster of those who've performed include acoustic musician Doug Smith, bluegrass group Misty River, popular country band No Strings Attached, a didgeridoo player Michael Sterling, and American Indian storyteller Ed Edmo. During the intermission between the second and third sets, folks head downstairs for coffee, tea, juice, and sweet treats sold by the young members group of the Multnomah Friends.

Schools

Oregon College of Art & Craft
8245 S.W. Barnes Rd.
(503) 297–5544
www.ocac.edu

Located on a nine-acre wooded knoll, the Oregon College of Art & Craft was founded in 1907 as part of the Art & Craft Movement that emerged as a response to the Industrial Revolution. The emphasis of this movement was on beautifully crafted, handmade objects rather than those created via the assembly line. Almost a century later, OCAC continues this tradition with classes in painting, drawing, printmaking, book arts, ceramics, photography, and woodworking. The school also offers "Art Adventures," a kids' summer camp with classes in metalsmithing, watercolor, photography, printmaking, and other opportunities to create art and craft.

Pacific Northwest College of Art
1241 N.W. Johnson St.
(503) 226–4391
www.pnca.edu

Pacific Northwest College Of Art has been providing visual arts education for over ninety years by offering a bachelor of fine arts degree, as well as continuing education and community outreach programs. Founded in 1909 as the School of the Portland Art Association, the school was part of the Portland Art Museum complex on Southwest Park in a five-floor facility designed by Pietro Belluschi, retired Dean of the School of Architecture at M.I.T. who was a student at the Museum Art School. In 1981, the school changed its name to the Pacific Northwest College; in 1994, the college became institutionally separate from the museum and in 1998, the college moved to its new location, a former warehouse at 1241 N.W. Johnson. An intriguing feature of this new space is the Swigert Common, a 26-foot-high space where student, regional, and national artistic talent will be exhibited.

The School of Oregon Ballet Theatre
1120 S.W. 10th Ave.
(503) 227–0977

This ballet school provides dance instruction to nearly 300 children and adults each year. Students perform with the professional company in selected performances and in the school's annual performance each spring. One of the highlights of this school is its Summer Dance Program with a curriculum that includes studying with guest instructors in classical ballet technique, pointe work, Spanish classical, flamenco, modern dance, and Russian character dance. Students also get a chance to attend other summer dance programs throughout the nation through scholarships awarded in the spring.

Theater

Artists Repertory Theatre
1516 S.W. Alder St.
(503) 241–9807 (info.),
(503) 241–127 (box office)
www.artistsrep.org

A charming little black-box theater is home to this tight little company of some of the city's best actors known for taut performances of new plays. A good example is Margaret Edson's Pulitzer Prize-winning play, *Wit*. Out on the edge, ART will find its way under your skin, all the while entertaining you with the brightest theater emerging in America. Tickets are $26 on Fridays and Saturdays and $22 on Sundays, Wednesdays, and Thursdays.

Do Jump!
1515 S.E. 37th Ave.
(503) 231–1232
www. Dojump.org

After establishing itself as a one-of-a-kind physical theater troupe known for aerial acrobatics and live music incorporated into their original pieces, Do Jump! has stretched beyond its home base in the Echo Theatre just off Hawthorne Boulevard to the Newmark Theatre downtown where their new work, including the heart-stopping *Threads*, has been turning heads and dropping jaws. *The Oregonian* summed up Do Jump! as an ensemble with "limitless theatrical intelligence apparently immune to gravity, to centrifugal force, to human limitations."

Imago Theatre
17 S.E. 8th Ave.
(503) 231–9581
www.imagotheatre.com

Two decades ago, actors Carol Triffle and Jerry Mouwad co-founded Theatre Mask Ensemble, an experimental performance group that has since changed its name to Imago and perfected its signature piece, *Frogz*, a hilarious physical romp starring all of the above. Easily Portland's most avant-garde theater ensemble, Imago tackles edgy drama that slices across theatrical history from Japanese Noh to Sartre's *No Exit* to contemporary playwright Richard Foreman's current *Confusions of the Soul*. When the Imago gang is not touring the globe, Portlanders line up to see their newest, strangely-captivating drama. A recent example is *Oh Lost Weekend*, written, directed by, and starring Triffle as a woman who thinks she is Queen Victoria who ends up in a 300-gallon tank of water. But Imago is not just about bold, innovative acting, the sets are also always a surprising treat. For its version of *No Exit*, Mouwad envisioned hell as a raised platform with minimal furniture that tilted right when an actor walked to the right. By the end of the play, audience members were reaching for their Dramamine. Tickets for most performances are $16 for adults and $14 for students and seniors.

Ladybug Theater
8210 S.E. 13th.
(503) 232–2346
www.ladybugtheater.com

Ladybug Theater offers kids three years and older classics such as *The Three Pigs*, and other fables, legends, tales, and stories from children's literature. Shows are usually held on the weekend, cost $5 per person, and can be attended with reservations by calling the number above.

Miracle Theatre Group
425 S.E. 6th Ave.
(503) 236–7253
www.milagro.org

Comprised of Miracle Mainstage, Teatro Milagro, and Milagro Bailadores, this Portland-based operation is the largest Hispanic arts and cultural organization in the Pacific Northwest. Since it started in 1985, Miracle Theatre has offered Hispanic theater, arts, and cultural experiences throughout the region, particularly to low- and moderate-income Spanish-

Imago Theatre's Oh Lost Weekend *by Carol Triffle.*   CREDIT: JERRY MOUAWAD

speaking audiences and those in rural settings who often don't get to see quality drama. Mainstage presents four English-language plays by Hispanic playwrights and two festivals each season on the Portland stage. Recent hits include *Deporting the Divas*, an outrageous comedy in which an INS agent confronts his sexual identity crisis, and *Burning Patience*, a play about the poetry of Chilean poet Pablo Neruda and a young postman, which inspired the hit film *Il Postino*. Teatro Milagro is the group's touring theatrical company that journeys to rural communities in Oregon, Idaho, Montana, Washington, and Wyoming where it invites local amateur actors and youth-at-risk to join the troupers onstage. Milagro Bailadores, a touring dance company, travels to schools throughout the western United States where it entertains as well as informs audiences about Latin American dance and music.

Oregon Children's Theatre
600 S.W. 10th Ave., Ste. 543
(503) 228–9571
www.octc.org

This professional theater company takes props, makeup, and sets to Portland-area schools to ignite the magic of drama in classroom workshops and assemblies. And then, at Keller Auditorium, this marvelous outfit turns it around by bringing local kids onstage to help present plays and musicals. One good example was the staging of *James and the Giant Peach*, a popular daytime show enjoyed by thousands of kids who took the bus to the auditorium to enjoy their pals trodding the boards.

Pans Plays
Berbati's Pan, 10 S.W. 3rd Ave.
(503) 248–4579

Just one of many tunes played by the mythological piper Pan at this nightclub, restaurant, poetry slammer's headquarters, and reader's theater, this event, staged every second Sunday of the month, is free to members of the public who are happy to take their chances. Budding playwrights and screenwriters read from their works in progress or completed plays and films scripts. One example is *The Love Brothers*, a lighthearted comedy about renegade puppeteers staging a bonsai audition in Hollywood.

Paula Productions
2820 N.E. Sandy Blvd.
(503) 238–9692

Paula Production has moved to a new venue—Jack Oakes Theater, named after Artistic Director Guy Peter Oake's father. Even more intimate than the company's inner-Eastside warehouse morphed into grungy performance space, this new and even more intimate theater has only fifty seats. To commission the Jack Oakes Theater, the troupe presented a pair of Pinter one-act plays, *The Room* and *The Dumb Waiter*. Theater buffs who have been attending the avant-garde, experimental, and classically-edgy dramas dished up by Paula and her gang can expect more of the same in this new location. Tickets for performances are usually $10.

Portland Center Stage
1111 S.W. Broadway
(503) 274–6588
www.pcs.org

Portland Center Stage, our city's only fully professional resident theater company, presents its dramas and comedies in the Newmark Theatre. Recent productions have gone from the timeless agonies of *Hamlet* to the American classic *Bus Stop* to Tom Stoppard's witty and timely *Rosencrantz and Guildenstern Are Dead*. The Shakespearean flavor of this company reflects its history as a former component of the Oregon Shakespeare Festival in Ashland near the California border. Center Stage also offers The Forum Series, with in-depth discussions of plays presented as Sunday matinees; The Talkback

Series, when the cast returns to the stage to discuss their efforts; and The G.A.L.A. Series, providing an opportunity for the gay/lesbian community to join the cast for post-show gatherings at various venues. Tickets range from $12 to $39 depending on seating and day of the week.

Portland Opera
1515 S.W. Morrison St.
(503) 241–1401
www.portlandopera.org

Since the early '60s, the Portland Opera has been presenting operas that have earned the group a ranking in the top fifteen opera companies in the U.S. It was also the second company in the United States to use supertitles (English translation projected above the stage). This will come as good news to those who find it difficult to follow the plot through aria after aria. As well as presenting classic operas such as *Aida*, *Carmina Burana*, and *The Mikado*, Portland Opera became the first opera company in the world to sponsor a subscription series to national touring Broadway musicals. This "Best of Broadway Series" has brought *The Sound of Music*, *Sunset Boulevard*, *Les Miserables*, *The Wizard of Oz*, and many more crowd-pleasers to the Keller Auditorium. All operas are also held at Keller Auditorium with tickets ranging from $25 to $125 depending on seating and day of the week.

Sowelu
4319 S.E. Hawthorne Blvd.
(503) 230–2090

Dubbed Sowelu (So-way-loo) after a lightning-bolt druidic rune meaning "life process," this fresh resident, award-winning company is comprised of thespians who have collaborated on plays and projects over the past five years. Artistic director Barry Hunt explains that Sowelu is rooted in how its members do what they do. "It's a workshop atmosphere," he says. "While we are in our workshops, we develop new ways of working together. It's less result-oriented and more for the sake of the exercise." Their first plays were *Savage in Limbo*, an Italian-American barflies-seeking-the-meaning-of-life drama by New York playwright John Patrick Shanley who scripted the film *Moonstruck*; and *The Further Adventures of Anse and Bhule in No-mans Land*, a post-apocalyptic buddy tale of life, death, and transfiguration by local playwright Tania Myren which won a local "Drammie." The venue is located behind Common Grounds Coffeehouse.

Stark Raving Theatre
2258 N.W. Raleigh St.
(503) 231–4872

This popular theatre will be relocating to a new one hundred-seat theatre they will share with CoHo Productions in the Pearl District. A significant aspect of Stark Raving is its focus on new plays dealing with social issues such as sexual harassment, self-esteem, and youth-at-risk. A project of Stark Raving is the New Rave Festival when six playwrights get invaluable feedback from audiences responding to works-in-progress.

Tears of Joy Theatre
P.O. Box 1029 Vancouver,
WA 98666
(360) 695–3050, (503) 248–0557
www.tojt.com

A puppeteer ensemble that has grown far beyond the days of Punch and Judy, Tears of Joy Theatre, based in Vancouver, Washington, has been delighting kids and adults for years with its mythologically driven dramas, life-size puppets, and wondrous costumes. As well as touring through the U.S., Tears of Joy also performs at the Winningstad Theatre in Portland. A new project from Tears of Joy is a Puppet Camp where children ages seven to twelve get to join the puppeteers in creating their own puppet plays. Kids will build puppets and masks and learn performance skills. These camps, usually during summer, are funded by the city of Vancouver. Tickets for performances are $9 for children and $13 for adults.

Tygres Heart Shakespeare Company
1111 S.W. Broadway
(503) 288–8400
www.tygersheart.org

With the proud pronouncement of offering "all Shakespeare all of the time," Tygres Heart has been winning hearts with its performances in the intimate, 250-seat Dolores Winningstad Theatre, a contemporary version of the Bard's courtyard theater in the round. Known for its vivacious interpretations of Shakespeare's canon, this troupe has gone beyond traditional enactments to stage *Julius Caesar* in a modern-day senate chamber as well as other plays in contemporary costumes and demeanor. The results are reinvigorating the notorious playwright's wondrous words.

Visual Arts

The Art Gym
Marylhurst University, 17600 Pacific Hwy.
(503) 699–6243
www.marylhurst.edu

Unlike many college art museums and galleries that, for better or worse, only reflect work undertaken by faculty and students, The Art Gym at Marylhurst is a consistently exciting venue for contemporary artists in and out of school, often out on the cutting edge. Once the gymnasium for this private school, the 3,000-square-foot gallery is large enough to hold sizeable sculptures and large installations. The Art Gym is open Tuesday through Sunday, noon to 4 P.M.

Augen Gallery
817 S.W. 2nd Ave.
(503) 224–8182
www.augengallery.com

A venerable institution in Portland's art world, the Augen Gallery sustains its reputation for eclectic fine art with a large collection featuring not only local artists but internationally renowned masters such as Stella, Hockney, Motherwell, and Warhol as well. Put this gallery on your itinerary when you begin your sampling of art during your First Thursday stroll.

Blackfish Gallery
420 N.W. 9th Ave.
(503) 224–2634
www.blackfish.com

Look for the sign of the wooden fish to swim with or against the tide of art lovers moving in and out of this popular gallery. Here, the artwork of the nation's oldest artists' cooperative is displayed during monthly exhibits. Examples of this widely varied effort include abstracts, weavings, and sculpture. The gallery is open Tuesday through Saturday, noon to 5 P.M.

Blue Sky Gallery and Nine Gallery
1231 N.W. Hoyt St.
(503) 225–0210
wwwblueskygallery.org

These two galleries are the quintessential Pearl District art scene. Blue Sky, around since 1975, offers a tasty blend of contemporary, international, and historical photographs while its neighbor, a new kid on this block, is a lively venue for a group of local artists who have fun dreaming up the next show. The galleries are open Tuesday through Saturday, noon to 5 P.M.

Columbia Arts Center
400 W. Evergreen Blvd., Vancouver
(360) 693–0350
www.columbiaartscenter.com

Located in a former Presbyterian Church built in 1911, this community center for the performing and visual arts reflects local interest and support of the arts. The center's gallery, with its rotating exhibits of work by local and regional artists is open to the public without charge Monday through Friday from 9 A.M. to 6 P.M. and on Saturdays from 10 A.M. until 2 P.M.

Community Art Share at Red & Black Café
S.E. Division and 22nd Ave.
(503) 234–3662
www.community art.4dw.com

A bimonthly showcase of artwork by painters, sculptors, and photographers is celebrated by musicians jamming with writers reading from their own work. A suggested donation of $5 will keep this innovative collaboration between creative folk happening at one of Southeast Portland's more radical venues.

Insiders' Tip

There are two definitive visual guides to art exhibits: "The First Thursday" brochure and "Art Gallery Guide." The first is a collaborative directory primarily announcing and directing viewers to the top ten galleries downtown and in the Pearl District. The second brochure is produced by ArtMedia, an art supplies shop. It is a more comprehensive listing of forty-two local galleries spread all over town. Both brochures are available at most art galleries listed in one or both helpful directories.

Contemporary Crafts Gallery
3934 S.W. Corbett Ave.
(503) 223-2654

Tucked in the forgotten, but due to surface soon Corbett neighborhood just west of Interstate 5, you'll find the Contemporary Crafts Gallery, founded in 1937 as the oldest nonprofit gallery in the country. Recently renovated to create more space for its permanent collection, this gallery has a handsome sampling of craft and art and is known for its glass and ceramic exhibits. Stop by for one of its artists' receptions and sip and nibble on its back deck, which offers a great view of the city. The gallery is open Tuesday through Saturday, 10 A.M. to 5 P.M. and Sunday, 1 to 5 P.M.

Elizabeth Leach Gallery
207 S.W. Pine St.
(503) 224-0521
www.elizabethleach.com

One of Portland's premier art scenes, Elizabeth Leach Gallery, located in the spacious Hazeltine Building in the heart of Old Town, represents both Northwest and national artists in monthly exhibitions. One recent show, in which emerging artists shared common threads, was titled In Synch. The gallery has also showcased the sculpture of David Eckard, which suggests a post-modern punkish tribalism in leather, steel, and fabric. Hours are Tuesday through Saturday, 10:30 A.M. to 5:30 P.M.

Froelick Gallery
817 S.W. 2nd Ave.
(503) 222-1142

Located next door to the prestigious Augen Gallery, the Froelick Gallery has consistently discovered and exhibited emerging regional artists as well as exciting new international talent. Recent shows featured a collection of snow globes, prints by a visiting Russian printmaker who demonstrated creating his art form, and the haunting photos of Susan Seubert, a fresh, local eye behind the lens. One of the traditions in the works at Froelick is an annual group show of Asian artists.

Gallery Schmallery
2132 S.E. Division
(503) 239-3735

With the exuberant credo "Art for All," this gallery with a funny name is new on the Southeast art scene. Recently they held a group show of local artists and the also have a permanent display of locally created gifts. Most of their open houses for artists on display are highlighted by a festive get-together with beverages and refreshments.

Guardino Gallery
2939 N.E. Alberta St.
(503) 281-9048
www.guardinogallery.com

This epicenter of a vital rebirth of culture along N.E. Alberta Street is making a small tsunami in the Portland art world with high quality exhibits of local painters, printmakers, and sculptors. A recent show, *Paper!*, offered handmade and manipulated paper by eight artists. When you stop by the string of galleries, studios, and shops on Alberta that celebrate Last Thursday, be sure to visit Guardino Gallery. Chat with the Guardinos, who are happy to share their thoughts on the artists on display as well as their own ongoing creative work. Or you can stop by any time on Tuesday through Saturday, 11 A.M. to 5 P.M., or Sunday, 11 to 3 P.M.

Hi-iH Lamps and Lanterns
2927 N.E. Alberta St.
(503) 493-4367

Those strolling Alberta Street Artwalks every Last Thursday stop in their tracks when they get to Hi-iH, a small gallery adorned with one-of-a-kind handmade paper lamps and lanterns, delightfully outlandish sculptures, and a couple of

"The Schnitz," Portland's Historic Concert Hall

"The Schnitz," as Portlanders fondly call the Arlene Schnitzer Concert Hall, is the mothership of four performance sites that comprise the Portland Center for the Performing Arts (PCPA). A recently renovated Italian rococo palace, The Schnitz has a long, lustrous history of showcasing national vaudeville acts and stars of the silver screen.

On March 8, 1828, after a year of construction at the corner of Broadway and Main, the Portland Publix Theatre opened its ticket booth to a crowd eagerly waiting in line beneath a 65-foot marquee pulsing with 7,000 light bulbs and 1,100 feet of neon tubing, to see a first-run comedy, *Feel My Pulse*, a newsreel accompanied by a pipe-organ recital and orchestral music, all for sixty cents a seat.

Once inside, filmgoers gazed at what an advertisement proclaimed as "a magical city in a palace of dreams." Designed by George Rapp of the Chicago/New York Architectural Firm of Rapp & Rapp, this lavishly ornamented hall had vaulted ceilings, mirrored walls, marble columns, and terazzo floors. Decorator Morris Greenberg added paintings, marble statues, and tapestries, and a double-console Wurlitzer organ was installed for $60,000.

It was clear to entertainers and well-traveled Portlanders that the Portland Theater, renamed The Paramount in 1930, was nationally recognized as a magnificent expression of the era of great movie palaces. But a Depression, a World War, and a few hazy decades of dwindling audiences reduced this ornate performance space to an oft-vandalized venue for rock concerts and closed-circuit TV broadcasts of sports events.

In 1971, its owner threatened to replace it with a parking garage, but a public outcry saved the grande dame from destruction. A year later, the city council declared The Paramount a historic landmark, and in 1983 the city of Portland acquired the property. After the passage of a $28 million bond measure aimed at establishing four performance sites, the first step—a $10 million restoration of "The Schnitz"—began with a groundbreaking in September of that year.

An aggressive renovation cleansed away years of dinginess, reduced cramped seating from 3,036 to 2,776, restored gold leaf on ceilings and walls in the lobby, and refurbished chandeliers with Austrian crystal donated by Zell Brothers, a local jewelry shop.

As well as returning the hall to its former opulence, two elevators, a sprinkling system, and a new symphonic acoustic shell were installed. Computerized stage lighting, a sound-mixing booth in the upper balcony, and an infra-red sound system for those with hearing disabilities melded state-of-the-art theatrical technology with the decorative restoration to make this hall a world-class performance space.

To glimpse how it used to be at the "Home of the Big Shows," take a look at a series of old photographs framed along the northern lobby wall. One displays tall drapes and statuary in the old lobby, another shows a sizeable orchestra pit, reflecting the era before talkies when soundtracks were provided by live musicians.

While you're in the lobby, stop by the brass callbox studded with buttons and knobs. Ushers used this charming antique to track down available seating for latecomers in a time when decor and function were lavishly mingled.

Perhaps those were the days, but so are these, thanks to a community that refused to see its finest turned into a parking garage. Now home to the Oregon Symphony and host to traveling and local dramas and musicals, lectures, and other entertainment, the Arlene Schnitzer Concert Hall is a reclaimed gem polished virtually every night by a full house of enthusiastic attendees.

The lamps and sculptures in Quang's shop range from $60 to $400 and he gets $10 to $30 per lampshade panel. After you drop off your lamp in need of a facelift, hike across Alberta to Bernie's Cafe for a bite and a gander at the dried-flower window Quang created for his neighbor. It feels like a page from a nineteenth century book with a pressed flower between its pages and yet, there is a sly hint that Quang likes to play with your head, that he is out there on the rim of what is art and what is debris.

Indian Art Northwest
616 S.W. 11th Ave.
(503) 224–8650

The Indian Art Northwest gallery features work by past and present members of the Indian Art Northwest's artist council.

Katayama Framing and Gallery
2219 N.W. Raleigh St.
(503) 224–3334

Fixtures on the local art scene for more than a decade, Katayama's frequently hosts art fund-raisers and other civic charities. They also showcase nearly all the artists from all the galleries in the region.

Not only that but Katayama is a framing business. Old World craftsmanship and gold laying techniques dating back to the thirteenth century are all in a day's work here. In fact, Katayama's has forged a reputation as one of the highest quality custom-frame designers on the entire West Coast. With more than 250 years of combined picture-framing experience, the Katayama team of thirteen employees includes a gold and sliver gilder, a Japanese and European carving expert, a colorist and frame restorer, and tapestry specialists. With their combined skills and experience, the shop can create replicas of any historical or period frame. Last year the owners moved their business across N.W. Raleigh Street into its new building, doubling their space to 10,000 square feet. Hours are Monday to Friday 9 A.M. to 6 P.M. and Saturday 10 A.M. to 5 P.M.

"Honey, would you close the window?" watercolor by Penelope Gulberston from the "Windows?" show at the Hawthorne Arts Gallery, which recently closed its doors.

walls hung with exotic photography. Half of the space is proprietor and papermaker Lam Quang's eccentric emporium and the other half is his studio where he makes lampshades with handmade paper imprinted with leaves, flowers, and in one case, strands of the artist's own long black hair. A spooky sconce mounted on the east wall of the shop features a dried frog carcass. "Disney Studio borrowed this one for a made-for-TV Halloween movie," Quang says, quietly proud of his inclination to collage natural elements to create his quirky art.

Laura Russo Gallery
805 N.W. 21st Ave.
(503) 226–2754

One of Portland's largest and most prestigious galleries, Laura Russo Gallery offers classical and controversial artwork by the Northwest's finest artists as well as young talent in a setting that is itself a work of serene art. Recent exhibits include painting and sculpture by Otto Fried, whose metal sculptures are genteel yet forceful abstracts, and paintings and prints by Rae Mahaffey that evoke decorative domestic scenes. The gallery is open Tuesday through Friday, 11 A.M. to 5:30 P.M. and Saturday, 11 A.M. to 5 P.M.

Photographic Image Gallery
240 S.W. 1st Ave.
(503) 224–3543
www.photographicimage.com

Located in the historic Old Town District, The Photographic Image Gallery is an exhibition space showing a unique mix of fine photographs, decorative photography, and photographic posters. It is the oldest commercial photo gallery in the Pacific Northwest.

Quintana Galleries
501 S.W. Broadway
(503) 223–1729
www.quintanagalleries.com

A popular stopping spot in downtown Portland since it opened in 1972, Quintana has a bounty of American Indian and Hispanic art. Walking by its windows is a show itself with a sumptuous display of Northwest tribal masks and totems as well as pueblo pottery, fetishes, and other crafts from the Southwest. The gallery also has a good collection of photographs by Edward Curtis as well as collector-quality antiques.

Thurman Street Pottery
2774 N.W. Thurman St.
(503) 228–2477

In the '60s and '70s, a climate of cooperation among artisans engendered collectives with shared workspaces and retail outlets. Nearly all those artistic outfits split up after weak sales and inevitable ego-friction, but not Thurman Street Pottery, a collective of nine successful ceramic artists. Many of the artists live near this shop, which was built circa 1925 and houses a retail space, eight studios, and a kiln room holding personal electric kilns. The backyard is home to two huge gas-fired kilns, each with 30 cubic feet of firing space.

Look for their open-house events and special sales when visitors can tour the studios and buy great gifts for the holidays during a show held through the first week in December. Hours are by appointment.

Insiders' Tip

Here's a real challenge for art fans: A traveling art show called "the donut shop" has been popping up at various locations with quickly mounted displays of relatively unknown local artists. The focus seems to be on video or conceptual installations and kinetic (i.e. moving) sculpture. There is a suggested donation of $5—a modest sum to track down and hang with the cutting-edge gang here in Portland.

Close-up

Portland Taiko Makes Waves
with Ancient Japanese Drumbeats

Portland Taiko, an Asian-American drumming ensemble, made a resounding splash with *Making Waves*, a concert held at the Scottish Rites Center.

Against a backdrop of waves crusted with foam reminiscent of Hokusai's famous watercolor, the group began its first full-length performance with a thundering composition centered on the *odaiko*, or largest drum. Next, the ensemble performed "Return of the Salmon," a robust homage to the miraculous cycle of the Pacific Northwest icon. The drumbeats and spinning *bachi* (drumsticks) rose and fell like thrashing rapids and tranquil pools through which salmon swim to get to their spawning beds.

The stage then quieted down for "Spring Mourning," a tribute to the new life that comes with spring, tinged with a somber reminder that all life ends. This lovely piece featured composer Janice Choy on drum and Zachary Zemke on mournful violin.

The group returned to a high-energy pitch with "Fireworks," a joyous version of a fireworks display. As with most of the show's episodes, the group's body language was precisely choreographed and their syncopated yells and yips brought smiles to a rapt audience.

Next, the mood changed with "Something New Learned from Ancient Knowledge," a remarkably dissonant piece that captured the tensions between generations of Asian Americans and the struggle for cultural identity in America. After this tumultuous piece reached a harmonious resolution, a drum and a flute duet, "Suwako," calmed the waters on stage.

The first half of the performance ended with "Ama no Uzume," a collaboration between Portland Taiko and local dancers led by Chisao Hata. This vividly told story of Amaterasu, the Sun Goddess who has to be coaxed out of hiding, was highlighted by imaginative costumes, painted faces, and lively theatrics.

Other selections in the show included: "Rainstorm," an episode that began with whispering drops and ended with a thunderous storm; tales about mythical dragons; Mongolian folk songs; "Lima," a whimsical piece by Filipina member Rachel Ebora; another visit with the Sun Goddess, and a finale in which four drumheads are played simultaneously.

Established in 1994, Portland Taiko is part of a revival of an ancient Japanese tradition that began as far back as 2,000 years ago. The *taiko* (Japanese for drum) was a utilitarian tool used in villages to scare birds away from crops, call folks together, and inspire local soldiers. Some believe that village boundaries were defined by the distance in which the taiko could be heard.

Taiko was also integral to religious ceremonies and community festivals and as it evolved, became a part of court music and Kabuki and Noh theater. The interest in Kumo daiko, or group performance drumming, emerged in post–World War II Japan as interest in traditional folk arts was renewed. Currently, there are over 5,000 taiko groups in Japan playing various drums, including the huge, barrel-like *odaiko* (traditionally made by hollowing out a log, but now made from an oak wine barrel), bongo-like *shimedaiko*, and the fan-like *uchiwadaiko*. American-style taiko began in the late 1960s and early 1970s when efforts were made to establish ethnic studies on college campuses. Since then, American taiko has grown in popularity and now is performed by one hundred groups throughout North America.

Proud of its multiethnic membership that includes, in addition to Japanese Americans, people of Afro-Asian, Chinese, Korean, Filipino, and European descent, Portland Taiko both celebrates tradition and explores new territory with compositions that borrow from other cultures. In an article in the January 1997 issue of *Sforzando*, Maya Muir said "This kind of collaboration is part of what marks the evolving tradition of taiko in this country. . . . Taiko here is distinguished by its incorporation of influences, including jazz, Latin percussion, and modern dance."

As well as presenting an annual concert, the Portland Taiko plays at community festivals, holds residencies and outreach programs at colleges and schools, and offers workshops open to the public. A popular program is an ongoing taiko class for children seven and up. For more information on this program and Portland Taiko performances, call (503) 295–9709 or write P.O. Box 6795, Portland, OR 97228.

Portland Art Museum
1219 S.W. Park Ave.
(503) 226–2811
wwwportlandartmuseum.org

The Portland Art Museum is architecturally and artistically our city's pride and joy even if we quarrel about what exhibits are inside. The second oldest fine arts museum in the Pacific Northwest, it was established in 1892 when business and cultural leaders created the Portland Art Association and ponied up dough to collect a group of one hundred plaster casts of Greek and Roman sculpture. It was a start. In 1905, the museum found a physical location at S.W. 5th Avenue and Taylor Street and in the 1930s it ended up in its current building designed by the noted architect, Pietro Belluschi. In fall 2000, the museum reopened after an extensive renovation with the Hoffman Wing: three floors devoted to Native American art and new exhibit space for European, regional, contemporary, and graphic art. There is also a new gift shop, outside sculpture garden, and the Whitsell Auditorium used for ceremonies and films. Now one of the twenty-five largest museums in the United States, the Portland Art Museum has a collection with over 32,000 works of art from American Indian artifacts to Monet's *Waterlilies*, to an impressive assembly of Asian art. To display the large collection of Asian paintings, ceramics, prints, and sculptures, three permanent Asian art galleries have been added to the museum's exhibit space. After strolling past a changing gallery that reflects the flavor of the permanent displays, visitors can view art in the Japanese, Chinese, and Korean galleries.

Recently, the museum has staged four huge touring exhibits, Imperial Tombs of China, Splendors of Ancient Egypt, Monet: Late Paintings of Giverny, an important collection of paintings during the artist's final days and Stroganoff: The Palace and Collections of a Russian Noble Family. Another memorable show was the International Print Exhibit, reportedly the largest print presentation in U.S. history. The late Dr. Gordon Gilkey, Curator of Prints and Drawings at the museum organized this stunningly comprehensive display of contemporary prints from seventy-four countries. The museum is not always oblivious to edgy modern art. One of the most popular exhibits in recent years was a show that combined artwork devoted to Marilyn Monroe with pieces focused on Elvis Presley.

The Portland Art Museum is open Tuesday through Saturday 10 A.M. to 5 P.M., Sunday noon to 5 P.M. On Wednesdays and the first Thursday of each month, the museum is open late until 8 P.M. Admission is free to museum members; nonmember prices are $7.50 for adults; $6 for students (sixteen and over) and seniors, and $4 for visitors age five to eighteen. For information on shows and programs, call (503) 226–2811.

Oaks Bottom Wildlife Refuge lets you get away from it all right in the middle of town.
CREDIT: RACHEL DRESBECK

Recreation

Oregonians have their share of skyscrapers, computer chip plants, and Jaguar dealerships, but we also have forests, snow-topped mountains, phenomenal river gorges, a 300-mile coastline, one of the most fertile valleys in the world, a lacy network of creeks and rivers, and an extensive system of parks and wilderness areas. Though the great expanse of our state may be crisscrossed with highways, while even our trails may be crowded with exuberant hikers, there is still a wild, true outback here where a soul can find solitude, clean air to breathe, and a vision of unspoiled land, river, or seacoast.

The Portland area in particular is home to or close to some of our best outdoor attractions. So Portlanders love to get out and about—to bike, hike, paddle, putt, shoot, set the hook, and slide down our slippery snowy slopes. In this chapter we've listed some of our favorite spots, so you can try out your outdoor or indoor recreational skills in our beautiful Portland setting. We've included a few organizations and commercial operations that can help you on your way.

The Nature of Oregon Information Center
800 N.E. Oregon St.
(503) 731–4444

Near the Convention Center and Lloyd Center, this information center is open 10 A.M. to 5 P.M., Monday through Friday. Outdoor recreationists come here to examine books and pamphlets about geology and other natural history features of Oregon. Topographic maps, brochures, and books are also on sale. You can also obtain from them a free publication list from the Oregon Department of Geology.

Biking

Bicycling Magazine has repeatedly proclaimed Portland the most bike-friendly city in the United States. People ride their bikes to work, to school, for fun—no matter how steep the hill or how dreary the weather. Tri-Met provides help for this popular form of transportation with racks on its buses and light rail. Once you purchase a $5 pass and take a quick mounting test, you can store your bike on the front of the bus or train and ride to your neighborhood or out into the country for a recreational spin. There are also many bike repair shops where you can chat with bike mechanics or do the work yourself for a small fee. In short, if you've got skinny or fat tires, a rusty yet beloved Schwinn or a shiny new Yeti, this is a great town for biking.

A fine resource for any Oregon cyclist is *Oregon Cycling Magazine*, which is actually a free newspaper published ten times a year. This informative medium is sponsored by the Eugene-based Center for Appropriate Transport and in it you'll not only find calendars, racing schedules, and lists of bike shops and co-ops, but you'll also find essays devoted to every aspect of cycling. It's widely available at bike shops, or for $12, you can have it delivered to your mailbox for a year. Write them at 455 W. First Avenue, Eugene, OR 97401.

Biking Organizations

Bicycle Transportation Alliance (BTA)
1117 S.W. Washington St.
(503) 226–0676
www.bta4bikes.org

With more than 1,200 members statewide, the mission of the Bicycle Transportation Alliance is to get more people out of cars and on bicycles for the commute to and from work. BTA coordinates its efforts with the Bike Gallery chain and Cycle Oregon to promote cycling as a fun, healthy, and environmentally friendly mode of transport. If you want to work to get more bike lanes and biker-friendly legislation, this is an outfit that will appreciate your help.

Portland United Mountain Pedalers (PUMP)
818 S.W. 3rd Ave., Ste. 228
www.pumpclub.org

Dedicated to active, responsible mountain biking, Portland United Mountain Pedalers arranges rides, maintains trails, puts out a newsletter, and keeps Portland mountain bikers organized. You don't need to be a member to participate in events, which include everything from weekend rides to weeknight clinics; rides may be as "simple" as a night jaunt through Forest Park, or as involved as a bike camping trip in the Cascades. (If you're a nonmember planning to join a ride, you should call first so the group doesn't leave without you.) You can call Sharon Yee at (503) 690–5259 for information about membership or Andrea deRuyter at (360) 263–5097 for more about the calendar. The newsletter, "The Mountain Pedaler," is widely available at bike shops. PUMP doesn't keep an organization phone, but it does have an active Web site with useful information.

Portland Wheelmen Touring Club
(503) 257–7982

The Portland Wheelmen Touring Club, founded in 1971, promotes cycling via a social organization for cyclists with over 1,100 members. The primary focus of the club is recreational riding: It sponsors up to two dozen rides on a weekly basis, including rides every day of the year and many evenings. You don't have to be a member to go on a ride. The outings are listed in their monthly newsletter, "Riders Digest," available at most Portland area bicycle shops and in *The Oregonian's* arts and entertainment section every Friday.

Insiders' Tip

The City of Portland wants you to ride your bike: thus, they sponsor a useful Web site, www.ci.portland.or.us/maps.htm, that offers a collection of bike maps. These maps will show you great trails, family-friendly bike rides, and good commuting routes in the city of Portland and throughout the area. Many are available in PDF format; others you can order online for a small fee to cover printing and mailing costs. Print copies of many bike maps are also widely available at bike shops and bookstores.

Teens on the Trail
740 S.E. 106th Ave.
(503) 823–3450

This group sponsors rides for teens who not only enjoy the outings but also work on the bike trails to improve them for everybody. Good examples of their efforts are the trail improvements along the Springwater Corridor Bike Path between Portland and the tiny town of Boring.

Popular Rides

I–205 Bike Path

Built in the early 1980s, this path is basically a good way to get from point A to point Z with little flair or charm but, hey, there are no four-wheelers to bob and weave around. It starts on the S.E. Evergreen Highway and 120th Avenue in Vancouver, Washington and runs south for 1.5 miles to a mile south of the Clackamas Town Center. Most of the route is along the western side of Interstate 205, a major freeway that skirts east around Portland. Along the way, you can peel off on one of the major arterials and head for your destination. Basically, it's a bike expressway.

Portland Bridge Pedal
Bike Transportation Alliance
(503) 226–0676

For information on this trek, call its sponsors. Held every August, this third-largest urban bike ride in the country brings together a very long string of more than 10,000 participants who bike and hike over bridges crossing the Willamette River. The city closes nine of these spans to auto traffic so that the noncompetitive bikers can claim the bridges as their own. During their 28-mile trek, these pedalers can gaze down at a bustling cityscape, freighters getting loads of wheat at huge grain elevators, and other bikers struggling up the on-ramp. At the end of the ride, a festive get-together celebrates biking with T-shirts, certificates of accomplishment, and vendors selling cold drinks and spicy grub.

Willamette River Greenway

This path is gentle and more scenic than the Interstate 205 route and is accessible from many streets. Try launching your bike at the northern end of Tom McCall Park, a lovely greenway that used to be under a freeway. You can bike from the Fremont Bridge all the way south to Willamette Park. Still a work in progress, this route is part of a plan to have bike paths on both banks of the Willamette. Meanwhile, bikers can meander down by the river, watch the shorebirds, catch a glimpse of an otter, and people-watch, for joggers and strollers share the trail.

Mountain Biking

The controversy over where mountain bikers can take their rugged rigs and still help protect the environment has settled down here in the Portland area. Most local mountain bikers are sensitive enough to stay on marked trails. Maps of those trails are available from the Outdoor Recreation Program at Portland Parks and Recreation, 1120 S.W. 5th Avenue, Room 1302, (503) 823–5132. Portland United Mountain Pedalers (PUMP), (see their individual listing above), is another good resource. Let them know you want to be on their mailing list for a newsletter that publishes information on weekend rides. A third spot to get the lowdown on climbing high into the hills is the Fat Tire Farm, 2714 N.W. Thurman Street, (503) 222–3276. This bike shop not only fixes and rents mountain bikes but also sponsors the annual Fat Tire Cross Crusade, a cyclocross event held in winter that takes mountain bikes along a course that changes from paved road to gravel to mud.

Leif Erikson Drive

Start at the end of N.W. Thurman Road in Northwest Portland. This 6-mile ride takes you along the paved, gravel, and dirt roads that loop along the ridge that defines Forest Park, the largest tree zone

Portland Bike Shops

These shops can help you find a bike, the tools to repair it, all the gear you'll need for soggy commutes, and information about where to ride on the weekend. Some of them will also rent bikes.

Beckwith Bicycles
4235 S.E. Woodstock
(503) 774–3531

Bicycle Repair Collective
S.E. 45th and Belmont
(503) 233–0564

Bike Central Co-op
732 S.W. First Ave.
(503) 227–4439

Bike Gallery (5 stores)
5329 N.E. Sandy Blvd.
(503) 281–9800

1001 S.W. Salmon St.
(503) 222–3821

3645 S.W. Hall Blvd.
Beaverton,
(503) 641–2580

200 B. Ave., Lake Oswego
(503) 636–1600

2332 E. Powell Blvd., Gresham,
(503) 669–5190

Bob's Bicycle Center
10950 S.E. Division
(503) 254–2663

Bridgetown Bicycles
2635 N.E. Broadway
(503) 288–8431

9120 S.W. Hall, Tigard
(503) 620-7544

Citybikes Worker's Cooperative
734 S.E. Ankeny
(503) 239–6951

Fat Tire Farm
2714 N.W. Thurman
(503) 222–3276

Kissler's Cyclery Center
10030 S.W. Beaverton-Hillsdale Hwy.,
Beaverton
(503) 644–5008

Multnomah Bicycle Shop
7429 S.W. Capitol Hwy.
(503) 245–5615

Northwest Bicycles
916 N.W. 21st
(503) 248–9142

R.E.I.
1798 Jantzen Beach Center
(503) 283–0319

7410 S.W. Bridgeport Rd.
Tualatin
(503) 624–9751

River City Bicycles
706 S.E. Martin Luther King Jr. Blvd.
(503) 233–5973

within a U.S. city. It's a wild trek down steep slopes. You may have to dodge boulders and hikers, but once on top you'll get a spectacular view of the city to the east.

Powell Butte Nature Park Trail System

Start in the parking lot of Powell Butte Nature Park at the end of S.E. 162nd Avenue. This network of 9 miles of biking, hiking, and horseback riding trails is perhaps the most popular mountain bike trail in the metro area. This 570-acre park is home to old orchards, meadows, cattle pastures, and lots of hawks, deer, coyotes, and other wildlife.

Boating

A city at the confluence of two major waterways and surrounded by myriad ponds and lakes, Portland has a lot of boats parked in driveways, moored at docks, and afloat as bobbing homesteads. All through summer the Willamette River swarms with nautical traffic, water-skiers zooming the more tranquil waters below Ross Island, and sailboats dipping and bowing to the skyscrapers as they wend between downtown bridges. And during the winter holidays, volunteer boaters decorate their crafts and line up for the Christmas Fleets as they take a week of chilly nights to entertain Portlanders with their imaginative use of lights shining on dark water.

The Willamette's major launch sites, both operated by Portland Parks and Recreation, (503) 823-2223, are at Willamette Park and Sellwood Riverfront Park. Others are RiverPlace, an elegant moorage close to downtown, (503) 241-8283, and Chinook Landing Marine Park, adjacent to Blue Lake Regional Park on Marine Drive, (503) 665-4995. The entrance fee to Blue Lake is $3 per vehicle. Wherever you launch, be sure to put the children in life jackets, as it is required by law. And you'd better put on one yourself, too.

Rentals

Blue Lake Rentals
Blue Lake Park, 20500 N.E. Marine Dr., Fairview
(503) 661-6087

If you want to rent a paddleboat, rowboat, canoe, or kayak at Blue Lake, call Blue Lake Rentals or find them easily at the Blue Lake Dock. From Memorial Day to Labor Day, from 11 A.M. to late afternoon, you can rent a canoe or paddleboat for $5 per hour and a rowboat for $6 per hour. (The same outfit runs River Trails, a shuttle service on the Sandy River that provides transportation, raft, and gear for nonguided white-water jaunts down 16 miles of this lovely stream. To reserve a trip call 503-667-1964 or write to River Trails, 336 E. Historic Columbia Highway, Troutdale, OR 97060.)

Sportcraft Marina
1701 Clackamette Dr., Oregon City
(503) 656-6484

This is a good rental operation for those who want to boat on the Willamette River. Open year-round Tuesday through Saturday from 9 A.M. to 5 P.M., they rent 14-foot aluminum fishing boats complete with motor and life jackets for a $150 deposit, $35 for the first hour and $5 each additional hour. The marina also rents, with a $50 deposit, solo canoes and kayaks for $15 the first hour and $3 each additional hour; tandem canoes go for $20 for the hour and $4 for each additional hour. If you want to rent a craft on Sunday or Monday, call for special arrangements.

Island Sailing Club
515 N.E. Tomahawk Island Dr.
(503) 285–7765

If you're into sailing, you'll want to check out the Island Sailing Club. Here you can rent a 20-foot Santana for $100 for a half day or $140 for a full day, or a 23-foot Santana for $140 for a half day and $175 for a full day on the Columbia. For a more ambitious adventure, the club will rent a charter sailboat for up to a week out of a moorage in DesMoines, Washington, near Seattle. You can choose a 30-foot Catalina for $1,150 for a week or a 36-foot Catalina for $1,650 for a week. You don't have to take one of these large sleek beau- ties out for the whole week. For the uncertain, captains can also be rented—$100 for a half day, twice that for a full day.

Willamette Sailing Club
6336 S.W. Beaver Ave.
(503) 246–5345

If you're going to be here a while, you might consider joining this member-run group dedicated to small sailboats, which moors its craft near Willamette Park. If you're a member you can rent a dinghy here. The club holds meetings and classes and invites members to crew with each other. For more information, check out their Web site: www.willamettesailingclub.com.

Bowling

Grand Central Bowl
808 S.E. Morrison St.
(503) 232–5166

Open 24 hours daily, Grand Central has wheelchair access, a full bar, and recorded dance music. While it's a hangout for seniors during the day and at night, a younger crowd shows up for the Cosmic Bowling parties at 7 P.M. and 9:30 P.M. on Friday and 7 P.M., 9:30 P.M., and midnight on Saturday. First, the lights go down, then black lights come on, revealing glow-in-the-dark pins and bowling balls. A sound system in tune with a laser-light show accompanies the bowling. Cost is $13 per person and the limit is 160 ardent bowlers. The owners invite you to wear white so you'll glow in the dark too!

Valley Lanes
9300 S.W. Beaverton-Hillsdale Hwy., Beaverton
(503) 292–3523

Home of glow-in-the-dark laser lanes, Valley Lanes also offers bumper bowling for kids. It has thirty-two lanes open from 9 A.M. to midnight, seven days a week. Fees are $1.75 per game from 9 A.M. to 5 P.M. Monday through Friday and $3 per game at other times. Shoe rentals are $2 per pair. Valley Lanes also has a full-service restaurant and lounge.

Camping

In a region renowned for a vast menu of camping sites, it's hard to pick just a few to recommend, but here are some nearby sites that are at the top of the list. Note that some state parks require a $3 day-use fee; you can also purchase an annual pass for $25. Camping fees depend on the park, the time of year, and the luxuriousness of the facility. For state park information call (503) 630-7150 or (800) 551-6949. If you want to make a reservation (a good idea), call (800) 452-5687.

McIver State Park
South side of Clackamas River,
off Springwater Rd., 4 miles northwest
of Estacada
(800) 452–5687 (reservations)

This spot is an excellent stop for RVs with its forty-four electrical hookups and four primitive tent sites. Lots of trailheads lead into riverside forests, and plenty of meadows invite roaming about. Open as a park all year, it is available for camping March through November. To get there, take Interstate 205 to Oregon Highway 212. Make a lazy right turn off Oregon Highway 212 onto Oregon Highway 224, which leads to Estacada. From here backtrack down the river on Springwater Road to the Park.

Mount Hood Recreational Area
Mount Hood Information Center
65000 E. U.S. Hwy. 26, Welches,
Oregon 97067
(503) 622–4822, (888) 622–4822
www.mthood.org

or Zigzag Ranger District
70220 U.S. Hwy. 26
(503) 622–3191

You'll find plenty of gorgeous spots in the Mount Hood Wilderness only 60 miles east of Portland. To get there, take Interstate Highway 205 to S.E. Powell Boulevard, which morphs into U.S. Highway 26, the trail up the hill to all the fun.

Backpackers can take one of many trails leading from Timberline Lodge, a National Historic Monument with huge beams and logs for posts and lintels built in 1937. This justly famous hotel offers rustic luxury—if such a thing is possible—in its rooms, but campers might be more interested in the wonderful restaurant.

For those who want to stay down in the trees, there are plenty of campsites and picnic areas. With fifteen sites on the Salmon River Road, Green Canyon is a charming pull off close to a store for stocking up on all that gooey stuff that goes into s'mores.

To get there, take U.S. Highway 26 to Zigzag, then drive 4 miles northeast on the Salmon River Road (2618) to the campground. One of the prettiest campsites in this wilderness area is Tollgate, on the banks of the Zigzag River 1 mile east of the tiny town of Rhododendron. Another good campground, Camp Creek, with thirty sites, lies on Camp Creek Road a short distance beyond the Tollgate turnoff.

One of the largest and most popular campsites in the Mount Hood National Forest is Timothy Lake, acclaimed as one of the ten best camping spots in the West by *Sunset* magazine. This scenic lake with its postcard view of Mount Hood is easily accessible from Portland. Take U.S. Highway 26 beyond the junction with Oregon Highway 35 and turn south on Skyline Road and east on Forest Road 57, both of which are marked with signs to Timothy Lake. Once at this huge lake ringed by fir, hemlock, and pine trees, pick a spot at one of its three main campsites, or simply hike or canoe to a more secluded camp. To make a reservation at Oak Fork, Gone Creek, or Hoodview, call (877) 444–6777, the number for ReserveAmerica. For more information on camping in the Mount Hood Recreational Area, call the Zigzag Ranger District at the number above or write to them at the above address in Zigzag.

Oxbow Regional Park
6 miles east of Gresham on Division St.
(503) 663–4708

Oxbow Regional Park is a close-in site for tent camping that's open all year and operated by Metro, the regional governing body that runs the zoo, Tri-Met, and other public services. Six miles east of Gresham on Division Street, this site has forty-five tent and RV campsites with no hookups.

Canoeing, Kayaking, and Rafting

Paddlers looking for water deep enough for their canoes, kayaks, or rafts can find a launch spot within minutes anywhere in the Portland area. Here, where the Clackamas, Sandy, Willamette, and Columbia Rivers amble together west toward the Pacific Ocean, are stretches of flat calm, cataracts of white fury, and fast water rippling over dappled round boulders. And for those who want to just ease along, there are also a few boat-friendly lakes and ponds. Here's a sampling of aqua-jaunts available close to town:

Blue Lake
8 miles east of Portland in the town of Fairview along I-84

Blue Lake Regional Park, at the low-slung gateway to the Columbia Gorge, is just twenty minutes east of downtown Portland. Although it gets crowded with splashers and fishers, it is worth a visit for its accessibility and amenities. Chinook Landing Marine Park, adjacent to Blue Lake Regional Park, is a sizeable boating facility with a six-lane launch ramp and picnic area. There are also trails through nearby wetlands for opportunities to view wildlife.

Multnomah Channel

Multnomah Channel is a backdoor watercourse that starts at the southeast tip of Sauvie Island and winds northwest through a lazy, lacy wild of sloughs, swamps, and grassy pastures to the little lumbertown of St. Helens and a confluence with the Columbia River. If you want to meander up or down a stretch of the channel, a good spot to launch your canoe or rowboat is the Sauvie Island Boat Ramp at the junction of the Burlington Ferry and Sauvie Island Road, just north of the intersection with Reeder Road. (See our Close-up on Sauvie Island in the Portland's Parks chapter.) You'll find picnic tables, toilets, and plenty of parking nearby.

Ross Island

A loop around Ross Island is a great two-to-three hour canoe or kayak trip that will get those kinks out of your arms and back. The put-in spot is Willamette Park in Portland's southwest side. If you need to rent a craft, try Ebb and Flow, (503) 245-1756, just across the street from the park. Once in the river, cross over to Ross Island, hang a right around its northern tip and go down the Holgate Channel to the entrance to the lagoon. After you visit this tranquil pond and perhaps sight a Swainson's thrush, black-headed grosbeak, or a spotted sandpiper, paddle down the channel, around the southern edge of the island, and back downriver to Willamette Park.

Smith and Bybee Lakes
In North Portland, 2.5 miles west on Marine Dr. off of I-5

Smith and Bybee Lakes are the liquid portions of a 2,000-acre wildlife area across the mouth of the Willamette River from Sauvie Island. Here, at the confluence of the Columbia and Willamette Rivers is a huge intersection of waterfowl flight paths where federal, state, and regional agencies have established refuges for birds wintering or just passing through. Canoeists and kayakers can paddle quietly among thousands of mallards and Canada geese as well as great blue herons nesting along the shoreline. Osprey are common in the summer and bald eagles take over their fishing spots in wintertime. Nesting great horned owls have also been sighted. You can reach these lakes by taking Interstate 5 north of Portland to the Marine Drive West exit. Drive west 2.5 miles to the parking lot on the south side of Marine Drive or continue to the Kelly Point Boat Launch farther west on Marine Drive. From the launch it's a short cruise down a slough to the southwest edge of Bybee Lake. Once you arrive at the lakes, if the sun is cooperating, it will be easy to spot lots of Northwest painted turtles basking on logs.

Tualatin River Paddle Trip
Tualatin Riverkeepers
16340 S.W. Beef Bend Rd., Sherwood
(503) 590–5813

A canoe paddle down the Tualatin River is a terrific family outing on a placid stream that starts near Hillsboro west of Portland and wanders quietly through sixteen hamlets before it joins the Willamette River just south of Oregon City. Tualatin Riverkeepers is a nonprofit group dedicated to protecting this fragile watercourse. Every year the Riverkeepers sponsor Discovery Day, a guided paddle trip for the general public through a seldom-seen stretch of this pristine watercourse.

Rentals and Resources
Alder Creek Kayak & Canoe
250 N.E. Tomahawk Island Dr.
(503) 285–0464

Alder Creek is a good place to rent a canoe or kayak on Tomahawk Island, a close neighbor of Hayden Island where I-5 crosses the Columbia. This full-service outfit offers a complete line of gear for white-water enthusiasts, as well as low-key paddlers.

Ebb & Flow Paddlesports
0604 S.W. Nebraska St.
(503) 245–1756

Located just across Macadam Avenue from Willamette Park's boat launch, this handy shop rents canoes, kayaks, and gear at affordable prices. Operated by Peter and Donna Holman, the outfit also holds classes in sea kayaking, a sport that is growing in popularity.

Portland River Company
315 S.W. Montgomery St.
at Waterfront Park
(503) 229–0551

Portland River Company is another outfit that provides everything you will need to paddle a single or double sea kayak. It also offers guided tours. The Willamette River two and one-half-hour tour costs $35. First-time kayakers and experienced paddlers alike will enjoy this marine view of Portland. The adventure starts at RiverPlace Marina, crosses over to the historic USS *Blueback*, a submarine docked at Oregon's Museum of Science and Industry, and continues up river, circling Ross Island, where you may catch sight of great blue herons, osprey, and bald eagles.

The Columbia River daytrip, with lunch provided, costs $75, and takes you to several national wildlife refuges along

Insiders' Tip

Bike riding can be a great form of exercise for city children. But parents rightly worry about safety: dogs, cars, and other cyclists can make riding hazardous. The Community Cycling Center is an organization dedicated to teaching children about bicycle safety, riding, and repair. They can be contacted at 2407 N.E. Alberta Street, (503) 288-8864, or by e-mail at comcycle@teleport.com.

the lower Columbia River that are ideal for exploring via sea kayak. During the winter months, bald eagles abound along this stretch of the Columbia River, which is one of Oregon's best-kept secrets for sea kayaking. Beginners are welcome on the Columbia River tour, but will probably have more fun if they've been on the Willamette tour first.

REI rents canoes and kayaks, but not what employees call the "software," namely, wetsuits, gloves, and other equipment. The REI store is in the Jantzen Beach Shopping Plaza off Interstate 5.

Climbing

A glance to the east or north will suggest that Portlanders have plenty of mountains and cliffs to climb when they get the urge. At roughly 11,235 feet, Mount Hood or Wy'east, as this gorgeous peak is still known, looms above the Cascade ridges. When spring chases the snow up this glacier (the season lasts from May to July), technical climbers grab ice axes and crampons for various ascents suited for novices to masters. It is a relative easy climb until the last 1,500 feet. Due to cagey weather fronts and unstable snow, this last stretch is far more difficult: rescue units have sometimes been forced to pluck unlucky climbers off the steep slope. Other sites that will challenge the crampon crowd are Horsethief Butte, 2 miles east of The Dalles Bridge on Oregon Highway 14, and Broughton's Bluff at Lewis and Clark State Park east of Troutdale on Interstate Highway 84. Just thirty minutes from town, it offers a number of tough climbs.

ClimbMax
2111 S.E. Division
(503) 797–1991
www.climbmax.net

Routinely noted as one of the best mountaineering stores in the country, Climb-Max carries everything for the serious climber, from crampons, axes, and ropes to get you up the mountain to probes, beacons, and shovels in case it falls down on top of you. They supply gear for the climbing gym too. Clients rave about this store, a must-stop for all Portland climbers. You can also order from them on-line.

Mazamas
909 N.W. 19th Ave.
(503) 227–2345

This 3,000-member mountaineering group is named after Mount Mazama, a huge mountain that blew itself apart to create Crater Lake in southern Oregon. Founded in 1894 when 193 climbers ascended to the summit of Mount Hood, the Mazamas are legendary for all the mountains they've climbed, and the resources they provide for their members. To join, all you have to do is climb a mountain with a living glacier.

Portland Rock Gym
2024 S.E. 6th Ave.
(503) 232–8310

When the weather is keeping you off the rocks, or when you want to fine tune your ascension skills, stop by Portland Rock Gym for some indoor climbing on a 40-foot wall. The Portland Rock Gym has 8,000 square feet of climbing space and offers classes and equipment rentals. The gym is open Monday through Friday from 11 A.M. to 11 P.M., on Saturdays from 9 A.M. to 7 P.M., and Sundays from 11 A.M. to 6 P.M.

Stoneworks Climbing Gym
6775 S.W. 111th Ave., Beaverton
(503) 644–3517

While Stoneworks has the usual features of a rock gym, and they rent gear, hold classes, and sponsor competitions, it is really renowned for its bouldering area, which is more than 2,000 square feet and has drawn national accolades. For $40 per month, you can take advantage of the intriguing overhang bouldering and a large number of different holds. Stoneworks is open Monday through Thursday from noon to 10 P.M., Friday from noon to 9 P.M., and on the weekends from noon to 8 P.M.

Fishing and Fly Fishing

Anglers who live in the Portland area can wet their lines all year long. Spring chinook salmon and summer and winter steelhead spawn up the Clackamas and Sandy Rivers, and rainbow trout can be hooked in those streams as well as the Willamette River and in Blue Lake, a popular fishing hole and recreational site. A good spot to land a steelhead is at the confluence of the Clackamas and Willamette Rivers near Milwaukie. The Oregon Department of Fish and Wildlife (ODFW) keeps a minimum of spawning salmon en route to their upstream beds by issuing quotas in Portland-area water. But as long as the season is open, go for it. To find out where they're biting and where it's legal to hook them call ODFW's twenty-four-hour automated number, (503) 872-5263. Fisherfolk can also catch bass and crappies in the Willamette and sturgeon and shad in the Columbia and Willamette, as well as in sloughs and bays feeding into those streams. ODFW has a free pamphlet, *Guide to Warmwater Fishing in the Portland Metropolitan Area*, which will guide fishers to piers, pilings, and ponds where those lunkers lay about. For information about casting classes, see the Close-up in this chapter on the Rajeff Fly Fishing School.

Sporting Goods Stores and Marinas

Countrysport
126 S.W. 1st Ave.
(503) 221–4545

This shop specializes in fly-fishing tackle, classes, rentals, and guided excursions.

Fisherman's Marine & Outdoor
1120 N. Hayden Meadows Dr.
(503) 283–0044

This huge store has anything you'd ever want, from bait to spinners to outboard motors, and you might be able to coax the location of a hot fishing hole out of the friendly clerk.

Kaufman's Streamborn
8861 S.W. Commercial St., Tigard
(503) 639–7004

Kaufman's provides fly-fishing equipment, workshops, and worldwide bookings for piscatory outings abroad.

Insiders' Tip

Climbers and other recreators on a budget will appreciate Next Adventure, which carries—in addition to new equipment—a wide variety of used, consigned, closed-out, and traded climbing gear, as well as equipment for lots of other recreational activities. The owners are especially helpful in locating the odd piece of equipment you need to finish outfitting yourself. Find them at 426 S.E. Grand Avenue; their phone is (503) 233-0706.

Close-up

The Rajeff Fly Fishing School

Something about fly fishing brings out the philosopher in most of us who undertake it. Perhaps it's because this particular art is done for its own sake—most of the time you let the fish go. Or perhaps it's because the skills required for casting and for reading the water and the fish that live in it demand that you lay aside your ego and concentrate on the world beyond your head, no matter how much you want to catch something really impressive. At its best, fly fishing shakes us out of the routine of our daily lives and connects us to the world beyond ourselves. That's where the Rajeff Fly Fishing School comes in.

Through the Rajeff Fly Fishing School, you can brush up on your casting and fishing skills before you head out to enjoy the great fishing surrounding the Portland area. Tim Rajeff and Katherine Hart, the delightful people who run the Rajeff Fly Fishing School, hold local classes for private clients and groups in both casting and fly fishing. They also hold workshops across the country. The school provides comprehensive insight into this mystical sport; they concentrate on casting, since that's the hardest part of fly fishing, but they also have sessions in which they teach students about fish feeding habits, how to use flies that match fish food, and how to read the water, tie knots, and also make the best use of your equipment. And they give classes for women only.

Both Tim and Katherine have had a lifelong passion for fly fishing. Tim, the school's director, was entering casting tournaments, most notably at the distinguished Golden Gate Angling and Casting Club in San Francisco, by the time he was nine. Tim won the national overall accuracy and distance fly casting title in 1984, and added to his accomplishments when, while competing in Austria, he became the World's Fly Distance Champion with a cast of 205 feet. Though he no longer competes, he still holds the current record for U.S. fly fishing accuracy. Tim is a Master of Casting Instruction, certified by the Federation of Fly Fishers, the only nationally recognized organization to make such certifications, and after passing the Masters level he became one member of the Board of Governors of this National Organization. Not only that, he is an experienced guide, working the rivers of Alaska, Russia, Mongolia, and the Bahamas for many years.

Katherine Hart, his partner and the office manager of the school, is also a phenomenon: she is one of only three women in the nation to have qualified at the Masters' level for fly fishing instruction by the Federation of Fly Fishers. She got her start early—at her family home in the suburbs of Portland, a small lake provided bass and bluegill for her to practice on. And when the family would take trips to central Oregon, she found her metier in the rivers and lakes of that lovely region. Her passion eventually took her to Alaska, where she met Tim, and since then, the two of them have built a successful business based on the sport they love. Katherine is currently developing more women-only programs; women have been underserved by traditional fishing venues, yet they have an intense interest in the sport. So far, the response has been extraordinary.

Katherine and Tim have also recruited Tim's brother Steve Rajeff, the current World Casting Champion, and Hank Rolfs, an expert in the fisheries of both Alaska and Florida, to teach at the school. Steve is also the top rod designer at G. Loomis and, in addition to all of his other virtues, contributes the lowdown on the latest technology. And Hank has run his own school in Florida; his wealth of teaching experience and expertise in various techniques adds a profound dimension to the school. Together, the staff offers decades of experience in fly

Katherine Hart, master fly-fishing instructor. CREDIT: COURTESY OF THE RAJEFF FLY FISHING SCHOOL

fishing, tournament casting, and instruction. They are knowledgeable on both the techniques of fishing and the theories behind them. Moreover, their approach to teaching builds student confidence: they'll analyze your strengths in addition to suggesting what else you might try if you want to fish more effectively.

The Portland area is a great one for fishing—good lakes, streams, and rivers can be found minutes from downtown. There are other resources for fisherfolk in training right in town, too, such as the casting ponds at Westmoreland Park. The Rajeff School makes use of all of these. But they also go beyond the Northwest and travel the world. For five years, Tim and Katherine operated a lodge on the Ponoi River in Russia, where they had the exclusive use of 50 miles of river to fish for Atlantic salmon. (In addition to all of his other skills, Tim is fluent in Russian.)

Lately, they have been fascinated with Mongolia. Their longtime friend, the acclaimed guide Jeff Vermillion, has been developing the fishery there, and the Rajeff school is in the process of exploring it further. It is easy to see why. The desolate, windswept plains of Mongolia sustain beautiful, clear rivers where lenok thrive. And then there are the taimen, which can grow to more than 6 feet long. To see one swimming toward you as you are about to cast your dry fly—well, words can hardly do it justice.

But you don't really need words. You just need the Rajeff Fly Fishing School.

Tim Rajeff, the most accurate fly-fisherman in the United States. CREDIT: COURTESY OF THE RAJEFF FLY FISHING SCHOOL

Here are some of the services that the Rajeff Fly Fishing School offers:

Fly-Fishing Schools

A one-day comprehensive fly-fishing school in the Portland area costs $200 per person, with a four-person minimum. Meals are included. If you want to spend the weekend working on your casting, two-day schools can be arranged. They will also take the "school" just about anywhere and have held classes everywhere from Mongolia to the Bahamas to Oregon's Deschutes River; contact them if you want them to run a workshop in your area.

Fly Casting Lessons

Private lessons in the basic techniques of fly casting for one person run about $100 per hour, with a two-hour minimum. For two to four persons, the cost is $200 per hour. For the one-day casting school, the cost is $250, with a minimum of four persons. They will also develop custom classes just for you or your group. These classes might cover distance, accuracy, salt water fishing, or fishing with two hands.

Travel

All the members of the Rajeff Fly Fishing School suffer from incurable wanderlust and would love to take you with them when they travel to Alaska, the Bahamas, Russia, Mongolia, or wherever else they happen to be searching for fish. Contact them to find out more information about the trips they have planned and how you might join them.

You can reach the Rajeff Fly Fishing School at (360) 695–5114 or rajeffsports@home.com. You may also visit them on-line at www. rajeffflyfishing.com.

Hiking

A visitor to Portland may glance about at all the folks with backpacks, cargo shorts, and bandanas striding about the urban landscape and guess that most of us are heading for a hike. Maybe so—or maybe it's just the fashion here. Either way, an abundance of nearby trails await hikers of all levels, from those wanting a mellow stroll, like the 2-mile nature path through Marquam Park, to those dedicated enthusiasts who might enjoy the 27-mile Wildwood Trail along the crest of Forest Park. Here are a few close-in hikes among this wide range of possibilities.

Columbia Gorge
Rooster Rock State Park, I-84, Exit 25
P.O. Box 100, Corbett, Oregon 97019
(503) 695–2261

Columbia River Gorge National
Scenic Area
902 Wasco Ave., Ste. 200, Hood River
(541) 386–2333

Sweltering Portlanders and Vancouverites have a couple of choices for proximate relief from humid summer days. They either head for the coast or the Columbia Gorge. If they choose the latter, they can stretch their legs on lots of shady trails up and down high, heavily forested basalt promontories. If they decide on a hike to the summit, they get an eye-popping view of one of largest, most scenic river valleys on the planet. This 300,000-acre wilderness encompasses twenty-two state parks and is crisscrossed with 167 miles of well-maintained to rough trails. From fifteen-minute walks to 20-mile days, there are hikes for all ages and abilities.

Hopeful casters practice on local waters. CREDIT: COURTESY OF KATHERINE HART

After forty million years or so of volcanic rock and roll, much of the Pacific Northwest was a 3-mile deep bathtub ring of mud and debris covered with a thick skin of lava that had oozed from fissures as far away as Idaho. As the Ice Cap began to melt (about 15,000 years ago), a 2,000-foot dam of ice and rocky rubbish formed in western Montana, creating a pond roughly half the size of Lake Michigan. This dam broke 3,000 years later, releasing a monster deluge called the Missoula Flood that used tumbling boulders and tree snags the size of small schooners to scour the region for seven millennium. Along its thunderous way toward the Pacific, this Rocky Mountain cataclysm gouged the mammoth canyon we called the Columbia Gorge.

Down from bluffs above, hundreds of creeks now tumble, crystal torrents cataract down steep wooded ridges, waterfalls hide mossy, dark, glistening caves. And alongside the creeks and across bridges in constant mist, are pathways of varying difficulty: Mount Defiance Trail, Wahkeena Loop with Devil's Rest Option, Bridal Veil Falls and Overlook Loop Trail, and Starvation Ridge Trail. To get to all these wondrous strolls, take Interstate Highway 84 (also dubbed the Banfield Freeway), out of Northeast Portland and head east along the Columbia Gorge to the Corbett exit (number 22). From there you take the Columbia River Scenic Highway, which travels along the top of the southern bluff to Vista Point and then down the cliff to a stretch of magic with all of the above hikes and viewpoints easily accessible. Just watch for signs. If you want to plan an excursion to any of these shady glens and sparkling waterfalls, contact the Scenic Area Headquarters, 902 Wasco Avenue, Hood River, Oregon 97031 or call the Gorge Information Service at (800) 222-8611. You can also find out all you need to know by stopping by the Multnomah Falls Information Center in the Multnomah Falls Lodge, a centrally located facility with restrooms, a restaurant, and on-duty rangers. Public spaces in the gorge are overseen by either of the two agencies listed above. There is also further information about the Columbia Gorge in our Daytrips chapter.

La Center Bottoms
25 miles northwest of Portland along La Center Rd. (319th St.), accessed from Exit 16 off I–5

If you get a hankering to cross the River of the West for a hike on the Washington side, try La Center Bottoms, a 200-acre preserve along the Lewis River and near La Center, a hamlet in northwest Clark County. This bottom is flapping with lots of wildfowl, including hawks, herons, ducks, and red-winged blackbirds. To get there from Portland-Vancouver, drive north on Interstate 5 to Exit 16. Take the east exit and travel to 319th Street, which turns into La Center Road. Just after entering town and passing the WELCOME TO LA CENTER sign, turn right and park in front of the blue posts at the trailhead. Then you are out and walking on a 1.5-mile developed trail which becomes a 0.5-mile improved path.

The Marquam Park Trail
S.W. Marquam St. just off S.W. Sam Jackson Rd.
(503) 823–2223

A guide with references to stops along the way is available at a nature shelter at the beginning of the hike. The climb leads through leafy bowers until it arrives at Council Crest Park, the highest point in the city limits, at 1,070 feet above sea level.

Oaks Bottom Wildlife Refuge
(503) 823–5122

This stretch of wild along the east side of the Willamette is a treat for city dwellers who want to get into the woods in a hurry. To get here from downtown Portland, take the Ross Island Bridge to Powell Boulevard. Turn south on Milwaukie Avenue and just after crossing Holgate

Wahkeenah Falls is a shady retreat on summer days. CREDIT: COURTESY OF CHRISTINE FROST

Boulevard, look for the parking lot on the west side of the street in the 5000 block. From this trailhead, you angle down the hill into the refuge. Another approach is the trail that begins at the north end of Sellwood Park at S.W. 7th Avenue. To get to this starting point, you can take the Sellwood Bridge and bear left after crossing the Willamette. Along with beavers and muskrats, this wetland along the river is home to woodpeckers, warblers, orioles, and great blue and green herons. It can be muddy, so wear appropriate footgear.

Overlook Trail
(503) 823-2223

This newly-built, wheelchair-accessible trail is .25-mile of hardened gravel surface connecting the MAX Zoo Station with Hoyt Arboretum. There are also links with the Wildwood Trail (see below). The 10-foot-wide path makes frequent switchbacks as it ascends a gentle grade to the top of the hill and the arboretum's outdoor living museum of trees.

You can catch the beginning of the trail across the street from the MAX station at the north end of the World Forestry Center. If you are driving instead of taking MAX, park at the zoo.

Tryon Creek State Park
11321 S.W. Terwilliger Blvd.
(503) 636-9886

Just south of the Lewis & Clark College campus, Tryon Creek trickles through a deep ravine, the last free-flowing stream in the metro area and one of the few urban streams that still has a steelhead run. Bike paths and wide, paved, woodsy boulevards invite visitors from all over the area to explore the more than 600 acres of woodland. One trail in particular, Trillium Trail, is beautifully and fully wheelchair accessible. At the bottom of the ravine, an interpretive center with nature displays explains the plants, animals, and other features of the park. This site is a happy memory for thousands of kids who've come here on field trips.

The Wildwood Trail
Near Vietnam Veterans Memorial
in Washington Park
(503) 823-2223

Easily accessible from the MAX Zoo Station, this trail goes over hill and woody dale through Forest Park. At 4,700 acres, this is the largest park within a U.S. metropolis. Free maps of the trail are available at the Hoyt Arboretum Visitor Center at 4000 S.W. Fairview Boulevard, which is also on the trail itself.

Ice Skating

The Ice Chalet
953 Lloyd Center
(503) 288-6073

Clackamas Town Center,
12000 S.E. 82nd Ave.
(503) 786-6000

While these shopping-mall ice rinks offer lessons for young Olympics hopefuls, they are also popular with teens and adults, who swoosh about the ice oblivious to shopping spectators. Both rinks provide the gamut of lessons, parties, summer camps, broomball, and other icy activities. Admission is $5.25 for kids under eighteen years of age, and $6.25 for all others. You can rent ice skates for $2.50.

Motorcycling

Rose City Motorcycle Club
P.O. Box 91085, Portland, Oregon 97291
(503) 257-7047
Twn@teleport.com

Tracing its origins back to 1911, Rose City Motorcycle Club is Oregon's oldest AMA Chartered Road Club. Its over 160 members ride a wide variety of motorcycles, including touring, cruising, and sport bikes. In addition to its internal activities, such as monthly Saturday breakfasts and rides, the Club annually hosts the 250-mile Annual Rose City Oregon Tour, which benefits the Oregon Kidney Association. These motorcyclists also join others in a remarkable visit to kids in the Doernbecher Children's Hospital right around Christmas. The sight of all these leather-clad bikers bearing presents and wearing Santa costumes is definitely memorable.

Roller Skating

Oaks Amusement Park
S.E. Spokane St.,
north of Sellwood Bridge
(503) 236–5722

Open year-round as part of a surrounding carnival, this largest roller-skating rink in the Pacific Northwest is vintage Americana, with a huge Wurlitzer pipe organ playing Tuesday through Thursday nights and Sundays. A live DJ is on duty Saturday night. It's a great chance to join everyone as they "skate backwards" to the driving beat of oldies and goldies. Fees are $4 for the 1 to 5 P.M. session and $5 if you skate between 7 and 10:30 P.M. For more information on this site, see our Kidstuff and Attractions chapters.

Running

Runners feel at home in Oregon where Nike was born. Heroes like University of Oregon coach Bill Bowerman, along with Phil Knight of Nike, invented the waffle-soled running shoe, and legendary runner Steve Prefontaine brought thrills to the solitary sport. Now those participating in the Portland Marathon, the Cascade Runoff, the Hood to Coast Run, and other long distance events have resources close at foot. The Portland Marathon's number is (503) 226–1111. Team Oregon, at www.teamoregon.com, has a really useful website that coordinates running resources in the area, providing links to the Portland Marathon and hosting a calendar of area running events and races. It also sponsors marathon clinics and scheduled practice runs, as well as good running coaches; Team Oregon's coaching programs are very reasonably priced. Runners should also visit Running Outfitters, 2337 S.W. 6th, (503) 248–9820, for good gear.

Skiing and Snowboarding

Mount Hood Wilderness

Looming above the valley like a white-robed monarch, 11,239-foot Mount Hood is the state's largest peak. During the winter months, the flanks of the mountain draw thousands to Mount Hood Meadows, Timberline, and other popular resorts for Alpine and Nordic skiing, snowmobiling, and snowshoeing. Also, the area abounds in cross-country ski trails for those who want to get away from it all.

Downhill

Mount Hood Meadows
Forest Rd. 3555, 6 miles north of Jct. OR
Hwy. 35 and U.S. Hwy. 26
(503) 337–2222
This day-ski area is located on the sunny, wind-protected east side of Mount Hood. For thirty years, Mount Hood Meadows has enticed skiers and snowboarders to Oregon's most challenging terrain. Currently, ten chair lifts, including three high-speed quads, provide access to eighty-two trails over 2,150 acres.

Mount Hood SkiBowl
87000 E. U.S. Hwy. 26
at Government Camp
(503) 272–3206, (503) 222–2695 (info line)
This wildly popular ski bowl is the closest action to Portland, 52 miles east of town. It has a top elevation of 5,056 feet, a vertical drop of 1,500 feet, four double chairs and five surface tows, and 960 acres to play upon. Skiers and snowboarders have sixty-five day runs and thirty-four night runs, with the longest run, Skyline Trail, measuring 3 miles. The season generally

lasts from mid-November to mid-April. Snowboarders should note that there is a new park exclusively for snowboarders, which includes a half-pipe, rail slides, and jumps.

Summit Ski and Snow Play Area
U.S. Hwy. 26, at the east end
of Government Camp
(503) 272–0256
This site is best known for its inner-tube cruising down a gentle hill just right for tots and timid skiers. There is also a ski zone and a 400-foot double chairlift. The chairlift is open on weekends and holidays and the tube rentals and slope are open daily.

Timberline Lodge and Ski Area
6 miles north of Government Camp,
off Forest Rd. 50
(503) 231–7979, (503) 222–2211 (ski report)
To get to this spectacularly huge resort built in the '30s, turn north from U.S. Highway 26 at the eastern edge of the town of Government Camp and go 6 miles up Forest Road 50. Boasting the longest ski season in North America, Timberline has over 1,000 acres of snowfields for skiers and snowboarders. Thanks to the new Palmer chairlift, which was upgraded in January 1998, skiers have access to 300 acres situated between 7,500 and 8,500 feet in elevation, not to mention some of the most scenic views in Oregon. Because of its terrain, Timberline is a good choice for beginners and intermediate skiers. Overnight lodging is available, but it fills up fast. To book one of the lodge's fifty-nine rooms, call (800) 622-7979. For information regarding snow conditions, call the lodge's snow phone at (503) 222-2211 or (877) 754-6734.

Cross-Country

Mount Hood Meadows
Forest Rd. 3555, 2 miles north of
OR Hwy. 35
(503) 337–2222
This resort offers a full-service Nordic center and 15 kilometers of trails on Mount Hood.

Oregon Department of
Transportation Ski Areas
(503) 986-4000
There are sixteen sno-parks in the Mount Hood region operated by the Oregon Department of Transportation. Popular spots are Bennett Pass, Glacier View, Snow Bunny, Frog Lake, and Trillium Lake.

Cross-Country Ski Clubs
Bergfreunde Ski Club
10175 S.W. Barbur Blvd.
(503) 245–8543
As the local branch of an international club with over 2,500 members, the Bergfreunde Ski Club organizes activities that go beyond the winter season to

Insiders' Tip

Snow removal on roads leading to ski areas is costly. To help pay for this service, Sno-Park permits ($15 per year, $7 for three days, or $3 for one day) are required to park legally in winter recreation areas from November through April. Sno-Park permits can be purchased at ski areas, outdoor stores, or DMV offices. Don't leave home without one!

Winters at Mount Hood entice throngs of sledders. CREDIT: ZYLPHIA FORD

include year-round entertainment for active adults, including organized rafting, golf, dance, and theatre outings as well as cross-country skiing. Bergfreunde (friends of mountains) is a socially lively club for men and women who are single or married and over twenty-one.

Oregon Nordic Club Portland Chapter (503) 222–9757 (twenty-four-hour hotline) Organized in 1968 by Nordic ski enthusiasts interested in cross-country skiing on public land, the Oregon Nordic Club now has over 400 members. Activities are usu-

ally day and overnight trips, most of which are held on weekends. The Portland chapter of the Oregon Nordic Club also sponsors ski-related special events, including a yearly ski sale, a ski instruction and demonstration day at Teacup Lake, and sanctioned competition. On the first Tuesday of each month, a general membership meeting is held at the Multnomah Art Center, 7688 S.W. Capitol Highway, with potluck beginning at 6:30 P.M. The hotline number above will get you recorded information on the week's events.

Swimming

North Clackamas Aquatic Park
7300 S.E. Harmony Rd., Milwaukie
(503) 650–3483

This splash parlor is perhaps the biggest and most popular swimming hole in the tri-county area. It has three water slides and a 4-foot wave pool. The park is open Monday through Friday from 4 to 8 P.M., and Saturday and Sunday from 11 A.M. to 3 P.M. and 4 to 8 P.M. Admission fees are $4.99 for children ages three to eight; $6.99 for those ages nine to eighteen and seniors sixty-two and older; and $9.99 for all others. Families can get a discount on Sundays and Fridays. Please don't bring in any outside food or drinks.

Tualatin Hills Aquatic Center
Howard M. Terpenning Recreation Complex,
15707 S.W. Walker Rd., Beaverton
(503) 645–7454

This aquatics center is located in the Terpenning Recreation Complex, a sprawling ninety-acre park in the Tualatin Hills southwest of Portland. A close competitor to the North Clackamas Aquatic Park, it draws folks from all over the region on those muggy days when it's great to take the plunge. Call for drop-in hours. Children who live within the boundaries of the Tualatin Hills Parks and Recreation District pay $1.50 with residency cards; nonresident children pay $3. Adult residents pay $2, while nonresident adults pay $4.

YMCA of Columbia-Willamette
Metro Family, 2831 S.W. Barbur Blvd.
(503) 294–3366

Northeast Family, 1630 N.E. 38th Ave.
(503) 284–3377

Southeast Family, 6036 S.E. Foster Rd.
(503) 774–3311

In the great tradition of Ys everywhere, these Portland YMCAs have good-size pools for the general public as well as their membership. After showing identification, nonmembers over eighteen pay $10; those under eighteen pay $5. This is a day-use fee, which also allows for use of other facilities at the Y.

Portland City Pools

Portland Parks and Recreation, (503) 823–8529, has six indoor and six outdoor pools at its various parks and centers throughout the metropolitan area. To find the pool nearest your location, see the list below. The outdoor pools are open only during the summer.

Pool hours vary, but most are open from 6 A.M. to 9 P.M. daily, opening a little later on the weekends. Most of the time, there are lanes devoted to adult lap swim, but these may be taken over during swim team practices or other events. Admission to Portland Parks and Recreation pools varies, but will run about $3 to $4 for adults, $1.75 for those three to seventeen; and free for kids two and younger. For further information, call the number above.

Indoor Facilities

Buckman Swimming Pool
320 S.E. 16th Ave.
(503) 823–3668

Columbia Swimming Pool
7701 N. Chautauqua Blvd.
(503) 823–3669

Dishman Pool
77 N.E. Knott St.
(503) 823–3673

MLC Pool
2033 N.W. Glisan St.
(503) 823–3671

Mt. Scott Swimming Pool
5530 S.E. 72nd Ave.
(503) 823–3813

Southwest Community Center
6820 S.W. 45th Ave.
(503) 823–2840

Outdoor Facilities

Creston Swimming Pool
4454 S.E. Powell Blvd.
(503) 823–3672

Grant Swimming Pool
2300 N.E. 33rd Ave.
(503) 823–3674

Montavilla Swimming Pool
8219 N.E. Glisan St.
(503) 823–3675

Peninsula Swimming Pool
700 N. Portland Blvd.
(503) 823–3679

Pier Swimming Pool
9341 N. St. Johns St.
(503) 823–3678

Sellwood Swimming Pool
7951 S.E. 7th Ave.
(503) 823–3680

Tennis

The Portland Parks and Recreation Department has close to one hundred tennis courts in the metro region. Because most of the courts have no phone, call (503) 823–2525 for directions. Meanwhile, here's a short list of some of the best ones in town:

Creston Park
4454 S.E. Powell Blvd.

These two courts are rarely used so you're almost guaranteed immediate access. Advantages include high metal walls that save errant balls. The downside is that Creston Park is down in a woodsy swale where it might seem gloomy. The courts are not lighted.

Irving Park
Northeast 7th Ave. and Fremont St.

These courts are well-lit and popular with folks on the inner eastside of town.

Laurelhurst Park
S.E. 39th Ave. and Stark St.

With its tranquil duck pond, huge fir and cedar trees, and sloping lawns, Laurelhurst Park is one of the loveliest and most peaceful spots in town. The two tennis courts here are old relics that are often busy, but its worth the wait. Plan on playing during the day, for there is no lighting.

Mount Tabor Park Westside
Entrance near S.E. 62nd Ave. and Main St.

Three courts are tucked against the base of a living volcano and near one of the city's drinking-water reservoirs. They are

Insiders' Tip

If you have special needs or disabilities that have kept you from fully enjoying the great outdoors, try Adventures Without Limits, (503) 681-9471. This outfit sponsors hikes, cross-country ski trips, snowshoeing, indoor rock climbing, and canoe adventures. While fees are charged, scholarships for daytrips and overnighters are available.

Mount Hood is popular all year-round. Here, hikers rest atop Split Rock at Paradise. CREDIT: JANET TOON

also along a trail leading up to the top of Mount Tabor and its terrific view of the downtown skyline. Play a few sets under the lights and then stroll around the reservoir and up to the summit to catch a spectacular view of the glittering city across the river.

Tennis Center
324 N.E. 12th Ave
(503) 823-3189.

These four indoor and eight newly resurfaced outdoor courts make this one of Portland's most popular facilities. To play you need to make a reservation and pay a small fee of $7 each for singles and $4.50 each for doubles before 4 P.M. on weekdays and $7.75 for singles and $5 for doubles after 4 P.M. on weekdays and all day Saturday and Sunday. Hours are 6:30 A.M. to 10 P.M. Monday through Friday, and 7:45 A.M. to 9 P.M. on the weekends. There is plenty of good lighting, lots of easy parking, showers, and restrooms.

Washington Park
400 S.W. Kingston Ave.

This is a popular spot for tennis players who also like to stop and smell the roses at the nearby rose garden. The courts are not in perfect condition, but you'll have the pleasure of playing in a beautiful location close to the zoo, the Japanese Garden, and lots of places for post-game hikes.

Outlying Areas

Lake Oswego Indoor Tennis Center
2900 S.W. Diane Dr., Lake Oswego
(503) 635-5550

This court is convenient for those living south of Portland. The center is open Monday through Friday from 2 to 7 P.M., Saturday from 11 A.M. to 4 P.M., and Sundays 9 A.M. to 2 P.M. This friendly court welcomes everyone for games and private lessons; they offer senior discounts.

Windsurfing

On a bright and windy day in the Gorge, motorists cruising along Interstate 84 on the Oregon side or down-winding Washington Highway 14, are entertained by the multicolored confetti of windsurfer's sails sprinkled on the broad Columbia River. Ask any group of windsurfers and they'll enthusiastically regale you with the wonders of this world-class stretch where the wind blows hard against the sail and boards whip up and down the river. Back in the early '80s when this sport was in its infancy, there were a few pioneers noodling around near Hood River.

Now the town is booming with windsurfing shops, manufacturing plants, and windsurfing schools, as well as cafes, saloons, motels, and other services aimed at the thousands of visitors with those easily recognizable poles and canvas on top of their rigs. Retail shops in Hood River include **Hood River Windsurfing,** 101 Oak Street, (541) 386-5787; **Big Winds,** 503 Cascade, (541) 386-6086 (these two shops also offer windsurfing schools); **Hood River Windsurfing,** 101 Oak Street, (541) 386-5787; **Gorge Animal,** 509A Cascade, (541) 386-5524; and **Windance,** 108 Oregon Highway 35, (541) 386-2131. Check the bulletin boards in these shops for events, classes, and more arcane info appealing to those who scoot around on the water on a surfboat with a sail.

The best spots to launch are the Hook and Event Center at exit 63, off Interstate 84, and the Hatchery and Swell City, a couple of miles west of the Hood River Bridge on the Washington side of Hood River's Sailpark at exit 64.

Children scout the waters at Battleground Park. CREDIT: MARY ALLISON

Portland's Parks

City Parks

State Parks Near Portland

You could just about call Portland "Park Place."

The Portland Metro area offers an amazing amount and variety of park space, from Forest Park, which, at 4,900 acres, is the largest urban forest in the nation, to Mills End Park, which, at 452 square inches, may be the smallest park in the nation. Portlanders like to weave open, green spaces, no matter how tiny, into their urban landscape, so that wherever you go in this city, you are never far from a park. Moreover, the parks here serve diverse functions: many are community gardens, many are educational centers, some are attached to schools and are used for playgrounds, some are golf courses, some are left alone and preserved as wildlife habitats. And some are just old-fashioned parks with benches, swings, and duck ponds.

Whatever their nature, Portland parks really do offer something for everyone, and they are so much a part of Portland life that we probably take them as a given. Through our parks, countless citizens of all ages have learned to swim, dance, knit, speak Spanish, use computers, paint with oils, identify native plants, and climb mountains. Portland Parks and Recreation manages most parks within the city boundaries; their resources are extensive and it is easy to get information from them about their many offerings, the breadth and depth of which are astonishing. They put out a useful catalog each season that gives the details of the tennis lessons, swimming lessons, arts and dance classes, and the innumerable other programs; call (503) 823-7259 to request one. The department also runs a compelling Outdoor Recreation Program whose offerings change seasonally but will include things like sea kayaking, sailing trips to the San Juan Islands, classes in fly fishing, and tours with historical themes. The Outdoor Recreation Program can be reached at (503) 823-5132. For those of you who like your parks raw, the city maintains more than 7,600 acres of space devoted to wildlife, including Smith and Bybee Lakes, Powell Butte, Elk Rock Island, Marquam Nature Park, Oaks Bottom Wildlife Refuge, and Forest Park. In addition, a regional trail system called the 40 Mile Loop, together with the Willamette Greenway Trail links 140 miles of paths throughout the area, forming a circle through and around the city. Maps of this system, which was originally inspired by the Olmsted Brothers, are available from Portland Parks and Recreation for about $2. You can read more about some of these parks and programs in the Attractions, Kidstuff, and Recreation chapters.

The City of Portland is not the only organization that maintains wonderful parks in the area. Metro, our regional government, in addition to establishing growth boundaries, keeping up the zoo, and running the mass transit system, is also responsible for a number of parks and grids of open spaces. You can find out more about Metro's parks by visiting them online at www.metro-region/parks. And the State of Oregon has a fine website that gives a comprehensive look at the parks in the state system: www.oregon-stateparks.org.

City Parks

Southwest Portland

Council Crest Park
S.W. Council Crest Dr.
(503) 823-7529

High in the Southwest Hills—perhaps higher than anywhere else in the city—rests verdant Council Crest Park. This forty-two-acre site used to host an amusement park, but the traces of that history have vanished, and now it's a quiet neighborhood park with a large water tower. You'll also find trails, natural areas, restrooms, and picnic tables. But the major draw is the view.

Gabriel Park
S.W. 45th Ave. and Vermont St.
(503) 823-7529; (503) 823-2840
(Southwest Community Center)

A large, multifaceted park, Gabriel Park draws enthusiasts from all over the city. Within the ninety acres of the park, you'll find tennis courts, picnic tables, trails, community gardens, sports fields, and a dog off-leash area. In addition, the splendid new Southwest Community Center, which has spotless gyms and pristine swimming pools, give it that country-club feel. The community center holds the usual breathtaking array of classes and programs; call them for their latest catalogue.

Hoyt Arboretum
Washington Park,
4000 S.W. Fairview Blvd.
(503) 823-7529, (503) 228-8733

Hoyt Arboretum is a tree garden within the boundaries of Washington Park, a park within a park. Its 214 forested acres offer unsurpassed beauty and it's large enough that you can get into some backwoods areas where you aren't bumping into other hikers every time you round a bend in the trail—though it's popular with trail runners, so be careful when rounding those blind corners. Hoyt Arboretum features a vast collection of conifers, 10 miles of trails, the vestiges of our rural past, and some striking views of the city and the Cascades. This is a grand place to take a sack lunch and hike to your heart's content. We love to take the Fir Trail all the way to Pittock Mansion. It only takes about forty-five minutes and the view is stunning. (See our Attractions chapter for more information.)

Japanese American Historical Plaza
S.W. Naito Ave. near the Burnside Bridge
(503) 823-7529

This poignant site along the Willamette River in Waterfront Park just north of the Burnside Bridge is a memorial to the Japanese-American citizens who were banished to internment camps during the World War II. Cherry trees border the plaza. "Talking stones," sculptures, and other artwork beautifully relate the story of this sad part of our history in the hope that it might not be repeated. There is no admittance fee.

Japanese Gardens
S.W. Kingston Rd. and Washington Park Dr.
(503) 223-1321, (503) 223-9233 (for tours)

The Japanese Gardens comprise five different gardens within five and one-half acres and have received, in their nearly forty years of existence, many accolades for their beauty and fidelity to Japanese traditions. Tours are available. The admission cost is $6 for adults and $3.50 for students older than six; seniors pay $4. See our Attractions chapter for a full account.

Plaza Blocks (Chapman and
Lownsdale Squares)
S.W. 4th Ave. and Main St.
(503) 823-7529

This tiny (1.84 acres) but well-loved park consists of two adjacent city squares and

Rough winds may shake the darling buds at Washington Park, but visitors come anyway. CREDIT: RACHEL DRESBECK

is also known as Lownsdale Park. In 1974, the squares were designated Historic Landmarks; they have been public spaces for about 150 years. Chapman Square, the southern square, was donated to the city by early Portland attorney William Chapman, while Lownsdale Square was contributed by Daniel Lownsdale, who arrived in Portland in 1845. The squares were originally popular sites for public oratory and other gatherings. And they have a quaint history—at one time, the idea was that women would gather at Chapman Square, while the men would have Lownsdale to themselves. Lownsdale Square is the home of a military monument—the Soldiers' Monument, built in 1906, is a granite pillar supporting the likeness of an infantryman. This soldier represents Oregon's contribution to the first major force of American troops dispatched overseas, the Second Oregon United States Volunteer Infantry. And two small cannons at the base of the monument are from Fort Sumter; they honor the northern and southern soldiers killed during the Civil War. A large elk stands alert right in the middle of Main Street, between the two squares, reminding us of the wildlife that used to graze freely there. It's actually a fountain, built in 1900 at the behest of then-mayor David Thompson. It's hard for modern residents to imagine that the fountain, which has a special drinking trough for horses and dogs, was initially regarded as monstrous by some local residents (notably the Exalted Order of Elks). Later residents objected to its placement in the middle of the road, but it appears that, unlike its natural predecessors, the bronze elk is here to stay.

Washington Park
The western end of S.W. Park Place
(503) 823-7529

The crown jewel of the city's park system, 145-acre Washington Park is one of the oldest, best-loved, and well-used parks in Portland, offering beautiful scenery, summer concerts, statuary, playgrounds, water reservoirs, fantastic views of Mount Hood, its foothills, and the Willamette Valley, and some of the region's premiere attractions. This is the home of the famed International Rose Test Garden with more than 400 varieties of roses; the Japanese Gardens; the Children's Museum, and the Oregon Zoo (see our Attractions chapter). Besides these world-renowned sites, and the lush trees, shrubs, flowers, and ferns, the park is a treasure-trove of history and a tribute to prescient urban planning. Washington Park has been a city property since 1871, when forty acres were purchased for the development of a park—at a time when most of the city was still wilderness. Early residents thought the city was crazy.

By the turn of the century, however, Portland was glad to have the park, and never more so when they hired the distinguished Olmsted brothers, the landscape architects who designed New York's Central Park, to advise them on their own park system. The Olmsteds envisioned a series of parks that would be linked together with greenways all across the city. But they also made some specific suggestions for Washington Park, including the preservation of the natural habitat in addition to formal plantings.

While the major attractions of Washington Park are obvious, some of the minor ones are just as interesting. The first public statue of a woman is here—it's the bronze Sacagawea, the intrepid Shoshone who made it possible for Lewis and Clark to navigate the West, and which was commissioned for the Lewis and Clark Exposition in 1905. Women all over the nation contributed money to pay for this statue. The park is also home to an arresting Lewis and Clark Memorial, consisting of a granite shaft with the seals of the States of Oregon, Washington, Montana, and Idaho at its base; the foundation stone for this memorial was laid in 1903 by Theodore Roosevelt himself.

Washington Park's attractions also include the World Forestry Center, the Oregon Vietnam Veterans Living Memorial, and the Hoyt Arboretum with its miles of nature trails. And you will find many facilities for recreators of all ages: an archery range, group picnic facilities, stage, covered picnic areas, a soccer field, and tennis courts are all here. And if you have children, don't miss the fanciful play structure just south of the Rose Gardens. This bright and inventive gem has slides, bridges, swings, sand, musical toys, ropes, and anything else your children never knew a playground ought to have until now.

Waterfront Park (Gov. Tom McCall Waterfront Park)
S.W. Naito Ave. from S.W. Clay St. to N.W. Glisan St.
(503) 823-7529

This thirty-six-acre city park, which stretches into Northwest Portland, showcases the Willamette River and is throbbing with activity on sunny days. Hugging the west bank of the river, Waterfront Park extends from southwest Clay Street to the Steel Bridge, 22 blocks in all; its the site of many Portland events from the Rose Festival to the Brewer's Festival to the Blues Festival (for more information, see our Festivals and Annual Events chapter). It seems as if something is always going on there, but often it's not an organized event, just throngs of joggers, bikers, and those out for leisurely lunchtime strolls along the pleasant waterside pathway. There are basketball courts, fountains, statuary, and opportunities to sightsee, both for people watchers and those more interested in the scenic views of barges and cruise ships passing under the bridges.

You may want to see the Battleship Oregon Memorial, erected in 1956 to honor the original ship. Also, the benches near the Salmon Street Springs are a great place to hang out on a warm day while folks frolic in the refreshing water of a large, beautiful fountain controlled by an underground computer that changes the pattern of the fountain's water jets. If you are an early bird, the morning sunrises as viewed from Waterfront Park are incredibly gorgeous sights, with clear views of majestic Mount Hood and several of the smaller mountains on the Eastside.

Willamette Park
S.W. Macadam Ave. and Nebraska St.
(503) 823–7529

Nestled along the banks of the Willamette River and just a few miles south of downtown, Willamette Park is undoubtedly one of Portland's busiest and most popular parks. This is a fine place for boating, picnicking, watching the Fourth of July fireworks celebrations, or just kicking back. The parking lot fills up fast, especially in the summertime and on weekends, and some areas of the park itself can get a little crowded. But with more than thirty acres, including a boat ramp, soccer field, tennis court, playground, and hiking and bicycling trails, there's room to spread out. If it's raining and you have an outdoor party or barbecue planned, Willamette Park has covered group picnic facilities.

Northwest Portland

Couch Park
N.W. 19th Ave. and Glisan St.
(503) 823–7529

First thing: it's pronounced "cooch." But however you say it, this little neighborhood park, with lovely trees and a playground, is a draw for residents and for the students next door at the Metropolitan Learning Center. And it is a true neighborhood park, even down to its design and execution, which was largely the work of students and neighbors. Its namesake, Captain John Heard Couch, was responsible for the alphabetized street names of this sector of town, which he developed. The park site was originally the estate of one of Captain Couch's daughters and her family.

Forest Park
West Hills, N.W. Skyline Rd. to the City of St. Helens
(503) 823–7529

Forest Park is remarkable for many things, one of which is its size. At 4,900 acres, it is thought to be the largest urban forest in America. The city bought the property at the end of the nineteenth century; they had thought about turning it into a park ever since the Olmsted brothers suggested it would be a good use of the property, and the park, after much debate, was finally established in 1948. Today, Forest Park gives Portland residents more than 60 miles of trails for running, walking, and biking. It is a haven for more than 110 species of birds and more than fifty species of mammals, including the human visitors who love to hike and picnic in its lush forest canopy. You'll find Forest Park on the eastern side of the Northwest Hills, once called the Tualatin Mountains, and when you get there, you'll be hiking along some of the same trails—some of which are now paved—that farmers used as shipping routes. Contact the Portland Park Bureau, (503) 823–7529, for a detailed map of Forest Park. Forest Park is also part of the 40 Mile Loop, the regional trail system that winds through the city.

Wallace Park
N.W. 25th Ave. and Raleigh St.
(503) 823-7529

Wallace Park is constantly busy with community activities, in part because it is right next to Chapman School and in part because of its namesake, Hugh Wallace. He was the city councilman responsible for this park and the buzz of activity within it is a fitting tribute. The four-acre park contains basketball and tennis courts, softball and soccer fields, places to picnic and play horseshoes, and a playground.

Southeast Portland

Creston Park
S.E. 44th Ave. and Powell Blvd.
(503) 823-7529

This green, tree-filled oasis bordering bustling Powell Boulevard is a great place for a tranquil picnic or a quiet afternoon reading a paperback. Less than fifteen acres, it offers an outdoor swimming pool, lighted tennis court, well-equipped playground, group picnic facilities, and restrooms. While the pool gets very crowded on warm days and is a favorite for summertime swimming lessons, the park grounds are usually quiet and serene on weekdays. Weekends are a different story; many reunions and parties are held here.

Crystal Springs Rhododendron Garden
S.E. 28th Ave. and Woodstock St.
(503) 823-7529; (503) 771-8386

The seven acres of Crystal Springs comprise one of the most gorgeous and popular sites on the Eastside. Crystal Springs offers the tranquillity of a peaceful refuge away from the hurried pace of urban living, and in the early spring and summer, its gardens explode in a riot of colors with every size and shade of rhododendron and azalea imaginable. A host of birds and waterfowl also thrive in the sprawling ponds, where children of all ages enjoy feeding the ducks. Crystal Springs also holds annual shows (see our Festivals and Annual Events chapter), at which visitors can see rare and unusual rhododendrons and azaleas not normally found in this area. From Labor Day through February, admission is free. From March through Labor Day, admission is $3 if it's between 10 A.M. and 6 P.M. on Thursday through Monday for those older than twelve. Duck food is sold separately.

Laurelhurst Park
S.E. 39th Ave. between Stark and Burnside
(503) 823-7529

The Olmsted-inspired Laurelhurst is among the most popular parks in the city for picnics, cookouts, or summer fun. Its thirty-four-plus-acres offer a huge variety of trees, shrubs, and flowers as well as a three-acre pond with a small island as a centerpiece and many ducks as residents. A paved path circles the pond and the entire outer edge of the park and is well used by early-morning fitness buffs. Laurelhurst is a terrific location for larger get-togethers; there's something for everyone to do here, including basketball and tennis courts, a large horseshoe pit, and an excellent play structure. The Laurelhurst Studio is here; it's the Eastside conduit for ballet, tap, and other dance programs in the Parks and Recreation system. The park is gorgeously landscaped; it was once judged as the most beautiful park on the West Coast.

Leach Botanical Garden
6704 S.E. 122nd Ave.
(503) 761-9503, (503) 823-7529

The Leaches were a couple devoted to plants: John Leach was a pharmacist and his wife Lilla was a botanist. Together, they collected more than 2,000 species, some of which they discovered. The Leach Botanical Garden was their estate; its nine acres have been given over to preserving and studying plant life and maintaining a seed bank, as well as preserving the legacy of the couple who made this lovely, botanically diverse sanctuary possible. The grounds include the garden, the manor house, and natural areas. Garden and guided tours are free, and special tours are given by appointment. (For more information, see our Attractions chapter.) There's a gift shop and library; classes are offered for adults and children. It's closed on Mondays.

Mt. Scott Park
S.E. 72nd Ave. and Harold St.
(503) 823-7529;
(503) 823-3123 (Community Center)

Harvey W. Scott was the editor of *The Oregonian* from 1865 to 1910 and by all accounts was a force to be reckoned with (you can see him in statue form, pointing west, at the top of Mt. Tabor). Mt. Scott Park is named for him. The park encompasses twelve arboreal acres with a playground, softball field, and tennis courts, as well as picnic benches. The Mt. Scott Community Center, on the grounds of

the park, was recently refurbished and offers one of the nicest pools you'll find anywhere. Did we say one pool? Make that two—a beautiful lap pool and a fun leisure pool with a great water slide, current channel, and imaginative built-in water toys, as well as a separate spa. The facility also has meeting rooms, gyms, classes, an auditorium, and a roller-skating rink. Call for times and fees (which are low—about $3 for adults).

Mt. Tabor Park
S.E. 60th Ave. and Salmon St.
(503) 823-7529

This park affords some of the best views in the city of rugged and stately Mount Hood and Mount St. Helens on the one side, and Portland's West Hills on the other. This park is truly a wonderful place for picnics or for walking on wooded trails. Mt. Tabor has a number of reservoirs for Bull Run water, the city's water source; these are contained in whimsical crenellated tanks that are nonetheless heavily watched. (Don't try to throw anything in!) The reservoirs add a piquant touch to western views. The 196-acre park also offers basketball courts, a stage for theater or music, lighted tennis courts, group picnic facilities, covered picnic areas, volleyball courts, trails, and public restrooms. A new play structure is a big draw for families—they've resituated the play structure to take advantage of the sunshine, though the big fir trees still provide plenty of shelter.

Mt. Tabor sits on top of an extinct volcano; this volcano distinguishes Portland as one of two U.S. cities to have an extinct volcano within city limits (the other city is Bend). Many paths, some paved and some not, wind through the park and offer entirely different vistas. Sometimes you feel as though you're in the woods, but right around the bend you may be reminded of an orchard. The hilly terrain makes the park a favorite with runners, dog walkers, mountain bikers, disc

Crystal Springs showcases rhododendrons, azaleas—and ducks. CREDIT: MARY ALLISON

golfers, go-carters, and just about anyone who likes a good view and a vigorous climb. Birders may be spotted early in the morning. In fact, the birders are on to something—a sunrise at Mt. Tabor is spectacular and worth the struggle out of bed in the morning.

Oaks Bottom Wildlife Refuge
Portland Parks and Recreation
(503) 823–5122

Great blue heron are the star attraction here, but you can also view 139 other species of birds in this 160-acre refuge. The trail is easy and only 1 mile long, and thus it's good for small children. The park is on a floodplain of the Willamette, so the trail can get quite muddy. This park is not wheelchair accessible. See the Recreation chapter for more information.

Powell Butte Nature Park
S.E. 162nd Ave. and Powell Blvd.
(503) 823–7529

We love big Powell Butte Nature Park, the site of a long-ago farm, its vestiges there to remind us of our history. Its entrance is unprepossessing, but a walk along the trails is more than rewarding, for soon you will find large meadows that encourage birds of prey, as well as raccoons, foxes, and coyotes; shady old orchards; ripe blackberries if you're lucky; and amazing views. It's possible to see a number of peaks from this volcanic mound. Powell Butte attracts mountain bikers, joggers, and a lot of equestrian activity over its 9 miles of trails. There's also a .5-mile, wheelchair-friendly trail. You really have to get out and walk or bike around to enjoy this area, which stretches all the way down to Beggar's Tick Wildlife Refuge, a large marshy wetland teeming with birds and wildlife.

Sellwood Park
S.E. 7th Ave. and Miller St.
(503) 823–7529

Tall, well-spaced trees distinguish this pretty park, which is a crowd pleaser for its sports fields, its excellent playground, and its wonderful round swimming pool. The park has both sunny, grassy, open spaces and shady, cool refuges. On the bluff above Oaks Bottom and the Willamette River, you'll get pretty river views as you peer between the trees. Trails link Sellwood Park to Oaks Bottom and Oaks Park. The pool is outdoors, so it's only open during the summer, and it is wildly popular. An abundance of picnic tables encourage large groups—it's a favorite spot for reunions and company parties.

Westmoreland Park
S.E. McLoughlin Blvd. and Bybee St.
(503) 823-7529

Expansive, forty-seven-acre Westmoreland Park brings folks from all over town to play baseball—the fields are lighted, and on summer nights they seem to illuminate the whole neighborhood. But Westmoreland also has casting ponds, soccer fields, tennis courts, and a terrific playground to interest people. In addition, the duck ponds lure many kinds of water fowl and interesting things happen when the water birds mingle with the toddlers.

North/Northeast Portland

Arbor Lodge Park
N. Bryant St. and Delaware Ave.
(503) 823–7529

Portland has many little parks like Arbor Lodge. This small neighborhood park adjoins Chief Joseph School and offers some nice trees, softball and soccer fields, a tennis court and playground, restrooms, a wading pool, and horseshoe pit. On a sunny day this is a wonderful spot to bring a picnic basket and spread a blanket. You can enjoy a paperback while the kids romp on the playground.

Cathedral Park
N. Edison St. and Pittsburgh Ave.
(503) 823–7529

This park—on the banks of the Willamette River and one of Portland's most scenic spots—is named after the tall gothic arches that support the St. John's Bridge, towering above the park and inspiring that sense of awe that you're bound to have in a cathedral. The park, which has a stage, is home to popular summertime concerts; it also includes soccer fields, a boat ramp and docking facilities, and trails. Cathedral Park is also alive with history—not only is it the site of St. John's very first plat, but it is also suspected to be a favorite fishing site for the Native Americans who lived here before.

Chimney Park
9360 N. Columbia Blvd.
(503) 823–7529

We like to recycle things in the Pacific Northwest, and our land is no exception: Chimney Park used to be the city's incinerator. The only thing left of that original building, however, is the chimney; Now you'll find a lovely hiking trail and some nice trees. Best of all, you'll find the City of Portland's Archives Building, which is a fabulous place to do extensive research on the city's origins and colorful early days. The park is a designated off-leash area for dogs, so be alert.

Columbia Park
N. Lombard Ave. and Woolsey St.
(503) 823–7529

Healthy competition is a good thing, and when the old City of Albina saw that Port-

Close-up

Springwater Corridor

Springwater Corridor is a gentle yet invigorating family bike trek along a 16.8-mile rail-to-trail route that begins at S.E. 45th Avenue and Johnson Creek Boulevard in Southeast Portland and ends in Boring, a wide spot on the road to Mount Hood a few miles south of Gresham.

It's an easy, breezy outing through the backyards of outer Portland, alongside old industrial zones and into the country, and makes a straight beeline for farmlands at the base of Mount Hood and its razorback foothills.

Dedicated in 1996 after $2.5 million in improvements such as marked crossings to ensure safe travel, the route is one of northwestern Oregon's most popular stretches for walkers, in-line skaters, and those in wheelchairs, on bikes, and astride horses. It's mostly blacktop or chip-sealed surface, with a thin gravel surface on the last 4 miles. There aren't any steep hills or dangerous dips, so even lasses and lads with training wheels or seniors in need of gentle trails can enjoy this charmingly rural bike path.

One of the trail's delights is a sense of local history that is soon evident as you discover remnants of the old Bellrose rail line and read historical markers that tell how farmers took produce west to Sellwood and their families to nearby Oaks Park for a lively hurrah at the carnival.

Flanking the route are huge clumps of blackberry vines, lots of sweet peas, long-stemmed blue chicory, Queen Anne's lace, 5-foot mullein, spirea with its pink fluffy cones, dark brown Indian tobacco, and magenta poppies. There are rest spots along the trail in the shape of benches with slanted roofs, reminiscent of those train stops along the Bellrose line. There are also a few country stores like Bellrose Station where bikers can stop for a snack and cold drink.

A particular wayside worth a quick loop or a leisurely lunch is Beggars-Tick Wildlife Refuge, a postage-stamp wilderness in the heart of the farm belt. Next, about halfway down the path, a straight-ahead view of Mount Hood is a stunner.

Those looking for a more realistically challenging change-of-pace from the tranquil corridor can try the Powell Butte Nature Trail, an exit off the path that offers 9 miles of single-track trails with steep climbs leading to terrific views.

Back on the corridor and after a meander along a small creek, the trail putters alongside Gresham's city park with its grassy knolls, nature walks, and recreational facilities. Beyond the park, the corridor passes by the Columbia Brickworks, founded in 1906 and still in business as the oldest brick kiln in Oregon. It's fun to try and spot mossy brickstacks hiding in the bushes along the trail.

After the brickworks, the trail fades into a gravel path angling southeast to Boring. Unless you're the sort that insists on completing every trail to say you have done so, turn around here at the beginning of the gravel and head back to Portland.

land was developing Washington Park, they were not going to be outdone. They purchased thirty acres on Lombard Street in 1891. Soon after, however, Albina was annexed to Portland. But it took many years before Columbia Park, which was eventually patterned after a park in Berlin, became the handsome, wooded place it is today. In addition to the grounds, the park offers fields for soccer, baseball, and softball, lighted tennis courts, volleyball courts, and a swimming pool.

Grant Park
N.E. 33rd Ave. and Ulysses S. Grant Pl.
(503) 823-7529

President Grant visited Portland three times, which is remarkable considering he traveled by horse. But this park, named in his honor, is now more famous for its Beverly Cleary Children's Sculpture Garden, in which Ramona Quimby, Henry Huggins, and his pooch Ribsy, all born of Cleary's lively imagination, are fixed in bronze. (Four blocks away is the actual Klikitat Street, where Ramona "lived" and Cleary herself grew up in the neighborhood, attending Grant High School in the 1930s.) The sculptures sit atop a fountain and in the summer children play there all day long. At Grant Park you'll also find nice sports fields, tennis courts, and a swimming pool here.

Kelley Point Park
N. Kelley Point Park Rd. and Marine Dr.
(503) 823-7529

This quiet and out of the way ninety-six-acre park is one of our favorite places in the entire Portland Metro area, offering a large sandy beach, and views of the Willamette and Columbia Rivers as well as Mount Hood and Mount St. Helens. Picnic tables are scattered all over this park—some are even on the beach—and there are a wide variety of conifers and deciduous trees. The park is named for Oregon advocate Hall J. Kelley, who was a great friend to the state. He wanted to found a city at the convergence of the Willamette and the Columbia, but with twenty-twenty historical hindsight, it's a good thing he was overruled. Still, the park named in his honor is a wonderful spot, and it provides the anchor for the 40 Mile Loop—a fine legacy, in any case.

Peninsula Park and Rose Gardens
N. Albina St. and Portland Blvd.
(503) 823-7529

Portland emerged as a city at a historically astute moment from the perspective of a park lover, and Peninsula Park demonstrates why. Its formal design was characteristic of its early twentieth-century era; it is most known for its rose garden, but its striking gazebo bandstand is also

Insiders' Tip

If you're interested in exploring more deeply the city wildernesses of Portland, have a look at *Wild in the City: A Guide to Portland's Natural Areas.* This book is a fine, comprehensive, and detailed guide to the green spaces in our city, published by the Oregon Historical Society and edited by Michael C. Houck and M.J. Cody.

historically important (it's a Portland Historic Landmark and a National Heritage Historical Structure). And its playground, as well as the community center (a city first), made Peninsula Park quite novel when it was finally finished in 1913. (It was also an early example of urban renewal: previously, the site had been a home to a roadhouse and a racetrack.) The rose garden is still important, with two acres of roses—almost 9,000 plantings of them.

The park, in the Piedmont neighborhood, also includes a softball and soccer field, swimming pool, basketball court, tables for picnics, a fountain, and lawn bowling.

Wilshire Park
N.E. 33rd Ave. and Skidmore St.

Acquired by the City of Portland in 1940, pretty Wilshire Park in the Beaumont-Wilshire neighborhood is popular with softball players and families. Besides the ball field, the fifteen-acre community park offers some very nice trees, group picnic facilities, jogging track, a good playground, and ample tables for birthday parties.

Vancouver and Outlying Areas

Blue Lake Regional Park
Off of Marine Dr., Gresham
(503) 797–1850

Sweltering Portlanders are fond of natural Blue Lake, which is maintained as a regional park by Metro, and is just 8 miles east of downtown Portland, making it easily accessible on summer days. The sixty-four-acre lake has 400 feet of swimming beach and—especially fun for the little ones—a special children's play area in the water. But there's lots for everyone here—a fishing dock and boat rentals, basketball and volleyball courts, playgrounds, baseball fields, and picnic shelters. A food concession stand will supplement your picnic. The Lake House provides facilities for events like weddings or retreats. Trails wind their way through the park; these are especially nice for cyclists, and you can rent bikes on-site. The park also hosts numerous programs and events, many of which are geared toward children (see our Kidstuff chapter for more information).

Elk Rock Island
Willamette River, near S.E. 19th Ave. and Sparrow St., Milwaukie

Elk Rock Island is actually part of the Portland Parks system; it's one of the designated natural areas. This big rock, perhaps the oldest in the Portland area, is an excellent spot for bird-watching, and offers some of the most diverse terrain around. Prized spots include herons, hawks, kingfishers, and egrets. This Milwaukie park also includes a hiking trail.

Frenchman's Bar County Park
Lower River Rd., off of Fourth Plain Blvd., Vancouver
(360) 735–8838

This brand new park isn't huge, but it offers a lot on its mile-long stretch of sandy beach along the eastern shore of the Columbia River. Activities you can enjoy here include bird-watching, sunbathing, fishing, boating, picnicking, and watching the huge container ships, tankers, and freighters that sail up the waters of the Pacific Northwest's mightiest river. There are plenty of walking trails too, plus eight sand volleyball courts, a grassy amphitheater, and some playground equipment for the little ones. This spot also affords a terrific view of Mount Hood.

Sauvie Island
U.S. Hwy. 30, about 10 miles west of downtown Portland

Sauvie Island, a beautiful island of fertile alluvial soil northwest of the city at the confluence of the Willamette and Colum-

Sauvie Island lures wildlife hunters. CREDIT: MARY ALLISON

bia Rivers, is not, strictly speaking, a park. It is hardworking farm country. But the roads are so pretty, and the u-pick farms, river beaches, parks, and wildlife areas are so enticing, that the entire island seems like a park to many Portland residents who converge there on Saturday mornings to pick blueberries or ride their bicycles. This is a mixed blessing—it's good, on the one hand, that we can see the farms that grow our food and that the farms are supported by local dollars. On the other hand, its bucolic nature encourages people to visit, thus increasing traffic and busyness, diminishing the bucolic nature of the place.

In an effort to preserve that nature, some of the island has been set aside in wildlife preserves and parks. The Sauvie Island Wildlife Viewing Area, maintained by the Oregon Fish and Wildlife Department, is an excellent spot for bird-watching. There you will see the ubiquitous ducks and Canada geese, but you may also spy swans, bald eagles, sandhill cranes, herons, and rare species of gull. Winter is an especially good time to look for these birds because many species stop here on the way to warmer places, and some reside here all season, but be aware that some parts of the refuge are closed in the winter. You'll need a day permit to park at the wildlife area—these may be obtained at the Cracker Barrel Grocery, at the north end of the Sauvie Island Bridge. (You can't miss it—it's the only building right off the bridge on the island side.) The wildlife area is also north of the bridge. For more information about the wildlife area, you may contact Oregon Fish and Wildlife at (503) 621-3488.

More wildlife, as well as human relationships to it, can be seen at Howell Territorial Park, which is part museum and part natural area (and thus run by both the Oregon Historical Society and Metro). This ninety-three-acre park comprises the James F. Bybee House, the Agricultural Museum, old orchards and pastures, and sizeable natural areas, including a lake and wetlands. You can see an incredible variety of birds and mammals in the natural areas, while the museums permit a glimpse into the days of the early pioneer settlers, with a fine collection of historical artifacts. The Oregon Historical Society is inventive in the way it makes use of the museums, hosting many educational events and programs; one notable such event is the "Wintering-In" festival that takes place the last weekend in September, and includes music, food, demonstration of pioneer handicrafts, museum tours, and other engrossing activities. For information on park events, call the Historical Society at (503) 222-1741. (You may also reserve the park for special events; the number for that service is 503-797-1850.)

Insiders' Tip

If you want to speak like a native, you'll call it "Sauvie's Island" even though it is spelled "Sauvie Island."

The museums are open during the weekends from the first week of June through Labor Day. The hours are noon to 5 P.M. Guided tours are offered on the half-hour. To find the park, take U.S. Highway 30 to the Sauvie Island Bridge. Once you've crossed the bridge, follow Sauvie Island Road north for 1 mile, then

Dogs Gotta Run

Be hereby informed, the law says: leashes are required for all pets in parks—and everywhere else—in the City of Portland, except in designated off-leash areas. So where are these areas?

Gabriel Park, at S.W. 45th Avenue and Vermont Street, is a grassy, mixed-use park with a fenced area for dogs off-leash. The off-leash site does provide disposable scoops and trash cans. You'll be able to find water for Fido, so bring a dish. The off-leash area may close for terrain repair if it gets really soggy during the winter.

West Delta Park, at North Expo and Broadacre Roads, is just north of Portland International Raceway, on the west side of I-5. The off-leash site is a large, guardrail-fenced field. You will need to bring water and poop-disposal apparatus.

Chimney Park, at 9360 N. Columbia Boulevard, is a completely leash-free park, otherwise known as doggie-heaven—except for one thing: it's along a busy road, so dogs should be well trained to voice commands. This off-leash park includes sixteen acres of meadows and trails, but does not have water or scoops.

Wherever you are, please be considerate of other park users (including ducks and squirrels), whether you're in an off-leash area or not. Keep your dogs on a leash going to and coming from off-leash areas or Multnomah County Animal Control officers will issue fines.

turn right on Howell Park Road, where you'll immediately see the parking lot on your left.

Sauvie Island Road, by the way, wraps around the whole island. The island is crisscrossed by other roads that wind through farms, orchards, and fields, and following any of them will eventually lead you to something interesting. The u-pick farms that are all over the island are as big an attraction as the parks, and during harvest season—May through October—you will find many people picking berries, flowers, peaches, pumpkins, corn, and everything else that grows well here. Farm stands sell produce for those folks who'd rather not get dusty. During October, the Pumpkin Patch draws thousands of schoolchildren for hayrides and pumpkin picking; it's a rare Portland child who hasn't chosen a jack-o'-lantern here. You can find this institution by circling under the Sauvie Island Bridge and following the road south.

Whichever direction you drive, be respectful of the residents, the cyclists, the chickens, the school children, and everyone else sharing the road with you: in short, drive carefully!

State Parks Near Portland

General information about all state parks is available at (800) 551-6949. To reserve campsites, call (800) 452-5687.

Bald Peak State Park
9 miles from Newberg along Bald Peak Rd., 5 miles northwest of OR Hwy. 219 N. (Hillsboro-Silverton Hwy.)
(503) 678–1251

If you're the kind of person who hasn't lost interest in Sunday driving, you might like Bald Peak. A pretty state park near Hillsboro, but high above the Willamette Valley, Bald Peak is still close enough to town to be an alluring spot for a spontaneous picnic on a sunny afternoon (no water, though, so pack in yours). Bald Peak offers lovely views of the valley and a number of Cascade peaks in Washington and Oregon, including Mt. Rainier if the visibility is good.

Battle Ground Lake State Park
N.E. 249th St., Battle Ground, Washington
(800) 452–5687

One of the biggest attractions in southwest Washington, Battle Ground Lake State Park tempts recreators from all over the area who are drawn by 280 acres of swimming, fishing, horseback riding, boating, and hiking, as well as fifty campsites. The park is 21 miles northeast of Vancouver; it has a splendid lake in the center of an extinct volcano. The park is open from 6:30 A.M. until dusk from April to September and from 8 A.M. until dusk year-round. Summer camping is a breeze with the available kitchen shelters and showers—but remember, this park fills up fast. Kitchens with electricity may also be rented for large groups (twenty to 150 people); fees depend on the number of people.

Champoeg State Park
Directly off U.S. Hwy. 99 W., 7 miles east of Newberg
(503) 678–1251

Pronounced "shampooey," Champoeg State Park is a place where Portlanders flock for the concerts and other events in the pretty amphitheater, but the park has even more to offer. First, there are the trails that cross the 615 acres; these curl through woods, meadows, and wetlands, and are wonderful for bicycling or hiking. Then there's the historical interest: the park is on the grounds of the first settlers' government, and two museums and many educational programs and tours help to bring that early history alive. The park is regularly visited by school buses full of children eager to learn what life was like during pioneer days. There is a $3 daily day-use fee, but a $25 annual permit grants access to all day-use areas in state parks across Oregon, including this one.

Milo McIver State Park
Springwater Rd., 4 miles west of Estacada
(503) 630–6147

Milo McIver State Park is a quiet park less than an hour's drive from downtown—the perfect place to go camping after work. The Clackamas River shoots through here, so you can use the park as home base for kayaking or rafting days. The park also rents horses; its trails and fields are fine country to explore this way. Another attraction is the disc golf course (eighteen holes). In the summer, a variety of recreational and educational programs are offered, including a Civil War re-enactment. All of these interesting activities are in addition to the sweet, simple pleasures of camping: the park has more than fifty sites of various levels of sophistication. Like many other state parks in Oregon, a $3 daily day-use fee is required (unless you want to spring for the annual pass at $25); overnight camping fees depend on the site.

Tryon Creek State Park
Off Interstate 5 (Exit 297),
Terwilliger Blvd., S.W. Portland
(503) 636–9886

Lucky schoolchildren have fond memories of this pristine state park that's just a few minutes from downtown, the closest state park to the Portland metro area. Actually, it's within the metro area, which is the reason so many field trips are held here—that, and the fact that so much native wildlife can be found here. One of the few streams in the city that steelhead use for spawning is found here, and the native trillium plant grows abundantly. Tryon Creek State Park has shady trails perfect for biking and walking, and lots of signs to tell you about what you're seeing. Much of the park is wheelchair accessible. Day camps are a staple of summer life at Tryon Creek, and guided tours are also available, as well as a gift shop. These last things are run by the Friends of Tryon Creek State Park; call them at (503) 636–4398. There is no fee to use Tryon Creek.

Golf

Golf enthusiasts will be happy to discover that their sport has flourished all around the state of Oregon. From courses situated in fertile valleys below the snowcapped Cascades to the high-desert links with fairways framed by lava rock outcroppings, peppery sagebrush, and twisted junipers, this is a golfer's paradise. Many superior golf courses have sprung up in coastal regions, in southern Oregon, and around Bend, the gateway to central Oregon.

Oregon offers an amazing diversity of golf courses, and the Portland Metro area courses are some of the most interesting, challenging, and attractive golf courses in the state. With dozens of both public and private courses to choose from, you're sure to find the links to suit you, whether you're a seasoned professional or a neophyte.

Professionals and amateurs alike have found Portland a friendly host for tournament play. Portland is home to several major golf tournaments—the LPGA Safeway Classic in September and the Fred Meyer Challenge in August (see Spectator Sports chapter for more information) are regular events. The U.S. Amateur Open has been played in Oregon from time to time, most notably at Pumpkin Ridge in 1996, when Tiger Woods won it.

It's easy to see why the area has an outstanding reputation for golf. In Portland, and in the numerous courses a few minutes just outside the city, the golf courses are beautifully laid out and meticulously cared for. Small lakes and streams do a good job of defending par, and in the summertime, the greens throughout the region are quite fast. While the terrain is impressive, even for well-traveled golfers, and the facilities are superb, golf in Oregon is an affordable luxury. In Portland, greens fees fall mostly in the $20 to $45 range and sometimes lower. Discounts are available for off-season play, and afternoon and twilight rates are also common. Factor in relatively low costs for meals (and accommodations, if necessary), and golf here can be a downright thrifty habit—and a healthy one too. Walking is not only permitted at most of the courses, but here in fitness-oriented Portland, it's also encouraged.

Most Portland-area courses are open year-round, but May to September is prime golfing time. The off-season may be a good time for you to visit a familiar course or to try a new one, because then the courses are quieter and less crowded. In the Portland area alone, about thirty golf courses are open to the public and all rent clubs and carts. The city's four municipal golf courses offer some outstanding golf and lower-than-average greens fees. You can make tee times six days to one hour in advance for the municipal courses—Eastmoreland, Heron Lakes, Red Tail, Rose City, as well as the Metro-run Glendoveer—by phoning one central number, (503) 823-9362. Also, many area courses offer discounted greens fees for juniors, seniors, or both. Senior players may need a discount card—call Portland Parks and Recreation at (503) 823-4328 for more information. But whatever your age or level of play, you are sure to love Oregon golf as much as we do.

Portland Golf Courses

Broadmoor Golf Course
3509 N.E. Columbia Blvd.
(503) 281–1337

This is one of the friendliest, cheapest, and most popular golfing locations in Portland proper. Broadmoor was built in 1931, and since then it has been a favorite of Portland golfers, whatever their ability. The eighteen-hole, par-72 course winds over its 220 acres, dodging water hazards and trees; the billowing fairways flanked by the Broadmoor Lake and Slough add aesthetic interest to the technical challenge of maintaining a low score. In addition, Broadmoor offers a well-equipped golf shop, driving range, and full-service clubhouse. Fees are $26 per eighteen holes on weekends and $22 on weekdays. Carts are optional and cost $12 per nine holes; reservations are recommended thirteen days in advance.

Eastmoreland Golf Course
2425 S.E. Bybee Blvd.
(503) 775–2900, (503) 823–9362 (tee times)

Rated one of the top twenty-five public golf courses in the U.S. by *Golf Digest*, Eastmoreland is Portland's oldest and one of its most beloved greens. Eastmoreland has an endless variety of trees and shrubs on its 6,529 yards, and is bordered by Crystal Springs Lake, the Rhododendron Gardens, and Johnson Creek. The course, which is the site of the annual city championship, also offers a pro shop, restaurant, snack bar, reception and meeting rooms, and a double-deck covered and lighted driving range. The greens fees are among the best values of all the local, private, or public golf courses: fees on weekdays are $11 for nine holes and $21 for eighteen holes. On weekends it costs $20 and $23 respectively. Rates may vary according to the season. Junior and senior rates are available. Carts are optional. Call a week in advance for reservations or to inquire about lessons.

Glendoveer Golf Course
14015 N.E. Glisan St.
(503) 253–7507, (503) 823–9362 (tee times)

This par-73 course is an excellent place to golf and it is usually quite busy. Glendoveer, with thirty-six regulation holes spread out over 280 acres of hills, trees, and water hazards, offers junior and senior rates on the weekdays. This place features a golf shop, driving range, and a great clubhouse with big-screen sports TV and outdoor seating for special events. Regular visitors know this course has a split personality. That's because most of the course swells with hills, except for the front nine holes of the west course, which are as flat as paper. The east course spans 6,296 yards, while the west course runs 5,922 yards. Glendoveer also offers a pro shop, indoor tennis and racquetball courts; the restaurant and lounge, the Ringside, is a Portland steakhouse favorite, and worth a trip even if you're not a golfer. Weekend rates are $25 for eighteen holes and $13 for nine holes, weekday prices are $22 for eighteen holes and $12 for nine holes. Carts rent for $25 for eighteen holes or $13 for nine holes. Reservations should be made a week in advance; lessons are available.

Heron Lakes Golf Course
3500 N. Victory Blvd.
(503) 289–1818, (503) 823–9362 (tee times)

Offering two splendid golf courses designed to try every skill level, Heron Lakes combines a blend of bunkers and water hazards, the latter adding an aesthetic appeal to the technical challenge. The two courses, the Greenback (6,595 yards) and the Great Blue (6,916 yards), which is the flagship of Portland's golf program, were designed by world-renowned golf architect Robert Trent Jones II. Listed by *Golf Digest* as one of America's top seventy-five public golf courses, Heron Lakes has hosted numer-

Golf in Oregon features beautiful views in addition to its beautiful greens. CREDIT: RON THURSTON

ous important golf events. Many birds, including bald eagles, Canada geese, and great blue herons, add to its beauty and make life interesting for golfers. Facilities include a pro shop, snack bar, and natural-turf driving range. Weekend fees are $35 for eighteen holes on the Great Blue. The Green Back charges $21 for eighteen holes and $11 for nine holes on weekdays, $23 and $12 on the weekends. Holiday fees may be higher. Call in your reservations a week in advance—they go fast.

Red Tail Golf Course
8200 S.W. Scholls Ferry Rd.
(503) 646–5166
or (503) 823–9362 (tee times)

The only championship eighteen-hole public golf course in southwest Portland, 7,100-yard Red Tail is a refurbished and redesigned course on the site that was for-

merly known as Progress Downs. While the course needs some time to mature, golfers say that it promises to be one of the best on the Westside. The PGA golf pro, Mark Bolton, has an outstanding reputation for, among other things, cultivating great instructors, which makes this a great course for strengthening your game with professional advice. Red Tail is run by Portland Parks and Recreation, so this beautiful new facility is also reasonably priced: expect to pay about $35 for eighteen holes.

Rose City Golf Course
2200 N.E. 71st Ave.
(503) 253–4744, (503) 823–9362

One of the oldest golf courses in the entire state, Rose City is a challenging course in a beautiful setting. The long par fours and tree-lined, narrow fairways on the eighteen-regulation holes demand concentration and will test your technical skills. With plenty of hills, sand and water hazards, and trees spread over 6,520 yards, this course plays long and affords excellent scenery. Rose City also has two of the hardest finishing holes in all of Portland public golf. Facilities include a pro shop and a full-service snack bar. Rates vary throughout the year, but expect to pay about $20 for nine holes and about $23 for eighteen on the weekends; rates for Mondays through Thursdays are about $10 for nine holes and $21 for eighteen holes. Carts are available at a rate of $12.50 per nine holes. Reservations are recommended and are taken only six days in advance. Lessons can be scheduled with a pro.

Wildwood Golf Course
21881 N.W. St. Helens Rd.
(503) 621–3402

Beautiful Wildwood on the outskirts of Northwest Portland offers eighteen regulation holes on one of the most gorgeous courses in the area. No fewer than three creeks run through the 5,756 yards of hilly greens. You can spend a whole day here, practicing your swing in the driving range, browsing in the pro shop, and celebrating your birdies in the full-bar clubhouse. Weekend rates are about $13 for nine holes and $24 for eighteen holes; on weekdays you'll pay about $11 for nine holes and $20 for eighteen holes. Carts go for $10 for nine holes and $20 for eighteen holes. Lessons are available and reservations should be made a week in advance, but Wildwood can probably squeeze in one or two golfers on short notice.

Vancouver and Outlying Areas

Charbonneau Golf Club
32020 S.W. Charbonneau Dr., Wilsonville
(503) 694–1246

It's no exaggeration to say that this executive course is unique, not only to the area, but to the world. Lakes and trees are abundant on the three finely manicured nine-hole courses, which test the skills of beginners and professionals alike. This lush course is a mix of par fours and long and short par threes. The grass driving range is in a bucolic setting with well-tended turf that makes for great practicing. The practice area is the equal of any PGA Tour site. Weekend rates are $30 for eighteen holes and $18 for nine holes; on weekdays prices drop to $25 and $15. When you call a week in advance for reservations, you may also inquire about the junior and senior rates. Power cars go for $20 or half as much for nine holes, and if you prefer, you may rent a pull cart for $3 or $2 for nine holes.

Forest Hills Golf Course
36260 S.W. Tongue Ln., Cornelius
(503) 357–3347

West of downtown Portland off of U.S. Highway 26, this high-quality facility is equally suitable for the lone golfer or the big tournament. The eighteen-regulation holes are scattered across 6,173 yards of a hilly, well-groomed course that is adorned with magnificent trees and with water hazards that look easier than they play. Forest Hills offers a golf shop with a reputation for outstanding service, as well as a driving range, full-service clubhouse and restaurant, and three practice greens. The prices are $34 for eighteen holes and $17 for nine holes all week long. Carts go for $24 for eighteen holes, and lessons are offered. Make reservations a week in advance.

Lake Oswego Golf Club
17525 S.W. Stafford Rd., Lake Oswego
(503) 636–8228

With an abundance of trees, water, and hills, this splendid eighteen-hole executive course is both challenging and lovely. Local golfers find the topography the perfect place to practice their short game, and though it's an executive course, Lake Oswego Golf Club has the reputation of being a real challenge. The pro shop carries great equipment and the 19th Green Cafe & Grill offers an extensive menu as well. Weekend fees are $14 for eighteen holes and $8 for nine holes, while on weekdays nine holes costs $7 and eighteen holes costs $13. With just 2,693 yards there are no golf carts here, but lessons are available.

Langdon Farms Golf Club
24377 N.E. Airport Rd., Aurora
(503) 678–4653

Just off Interstate 5 about twenty minutes south of Portland, Langdon Farms has only been open a few years but it became immediately popular with Portland golfers. This par-71, eighteen-hole course laid out over 6,935 yards is notable for its unusual contoured terrain. Greens fees, which include cart rental, range throughout the year from $59 to $80 for eighteen holes and from $25 to $64 for nine holes. Rates vary widely—prime-time summer fees are at the high end, but afternoon rates throughout the year offer good value. The club pro offers lessons, and there is a driving range. There are few shade trees, so golfers should wear a hat and apply sunscreen when playing on a hot or sunny day. There are several special rates available at Langdon, among them the one for early birds: about $40 for eighteen holes. Call for more information, and make your reservations two months in advance. The clubhouse resembles a turn-of-the-century farmhouse, reminding golfers that they're playing in some of the most fertile farmland in the nation.

Lewis River Golf Course
3209 Lewis River Rd., Woodland, Washington
(800) 341–9426

Just a half-hour's drive north from Portland, this picturesque public golf course offers gorgeous scenery along the winding Lewis River. The 6,352-yard course is graced with many trees and lakes. Fees are $35 for eighteen holes on the weekends, $26 Monday through Thursday, and $32 on Fridays. Carts are $26 for eighteen holes, and lessons are available. This well-established golf course can handle large groups and tournaments. Besides the driving range and putting green, Lewis River offers a pro shop, restaurant, banquet rooms, and patio dining.

Mountain View
27195 S.E. Kelso Rd., Boring
(503) 663–4869

Exactly one-half of the way between downtown Portland and Mount Hood, this is a dandy place for eighteen regulation holes of golf. Mountain View offers plenty of hazards and hills throughout its 5,926 yards and affords a terrific view of Mount Hood. Be sure to ask about hole number twelve; with an eighteen story drop from the T-box to the green, it is a huge attraction—one of the most unusual holes in the state. Weekend rates are $25 for eighteen holes and $15 for nine holes; on weekdays expect to pay $12 for nine holes and $21 for eighteen holes. Carts are $18 for twenty-four holes and $9 for fourteen holes. Lessons are available. Make reservations seven days in advance.

Persimmon Country Club
500 S.E. Butler Rd., Gresham
(503) 661–1800

There's a lot to like about this sprawling 6,678-yard golf oasis located in the East-side suburbs: gently rolling hills, sculpted, manicured greens and fairways, and a friendly staff that makes you feel at home. Persimmon is a semi-private club, which means that members have first crack at tee times. There's everything you need for a fun day of golf, including a clubhouse, golf shop, driving range, two putting greens, a chipping green, and the Persimmon Grill, which offers an extensive menu. Nonmembers may reserve tee times three days in advance. Lessons are available. Greens fees run about $70 on weekdays, $85 on the weekends; that's with carts.

Pine Crest Golf Course
2415 N.W. 143rd Ave., Vancouver,
Washington
(360) 573–2051

This friendly place is a great spot to practice or to get in nine holes of golf without spending very much money. Greens fees are just $15 on weekends and $13 through the week. Pine Crest isn't big, just 1,206 yards, but it is said to be one of the best par threes around. The course doesn't include any water hazards, but there are plenty of trees and tricky slopes; a ravine cuts through the course for extra challenge. There are no lessons and no driving range, but there is a putting green, golf shop, and snack bar if you are famished. Pull carts are available and the longest hole is 170 yards, and they don't take reservations—so just show up and golf.

Pumpkin Ridge
12930 Old Pumpkin Ridge Rd.,
North Plains
(503) 647–4747, (888) 594–GOLF

Pumpkin Ridge comprises two courses, a public course, Ghost Creek, and a private course, Witch Hollows. Ghost Creek runs through several fairways on the 6,839-yard public side; hence its moniker, Ghost Creek at Pumpkin Ridge. Whatever the name, this is one of the premier golf facilities open to the public on the entire West Coast. Tiger Woods won the U.S. Amateur Open here in 1996.

Witch Hollows is the home of the private Pumpkin Ridge Golf Club. Both courses have bentgrass tees, greens, and fairways. Both are nearly unrivaled in the Pacific Northwest and Witch Hollows is slightly larger with 7,014 yards. Amenities

Insiders' Tip

The Oregon Golf Association, the local liaison to the USGA, will help you establish your handicap, find out about regional tournaments, and answer your questions about golf courses and the environment. Contact them at (503) 981-GOLF.

Portland's courses offer plenty of challenges for golfers. CREDIT: RON THURSTON

include an 18,000-square-foot clubhouse with golf shop, meeting facilities, teaching center, and restaurant. Practice facilities include bunkers, putting and chipping greens, and an expansive driving range. Package deals are available for corporate or tournament outings. Top professional golfers are available for lessons and fees run at about $120 for eighteen holes but change with the season, so inquire when you make your reservations seven days in advance. If you plan to golf at Pumpkin Ridge a lot, take advantage of their Ghost Card, which offers a discounted rate for frequent players.

Quail Valley
12565 N.W. Aerts Rd., Banks
(503) 324–4444

A drive of thirty minutes west on U.S. Highway 26 will take you to the superb Quail Valley Golf Course, which is sur-

prisingly difficult for a course that looks so flat. The difficulty is due to the abundance of water hazards and other environmentally sensitive areas that challenge players in all the right ways. This 6,603-yard course is a favorite for winter play, since it is very well drained. Greens fees run about $30 for eighteen holes on weekdays, and closer to $40 on the weekends.

Reserve Vineyards Golf Club
4805 S.W. 229th Aloha
(503) 649–8191

One of the area's newest golf courses, the Reserve Vineyards offers two eighteen-hole courses, both par 72s: the 7,172-yard Fought Course and the 6,845-yard Cupp Course, as well as a driving range and a pro shop. Greens fees begin at about $35 for off-season weekday twilight play to about $80 for prime-time summer weekends. The mansionlike, 40,000-square-foot clubhouse includes four dining areas and a deli, a pro shop, a wine-tasting area (there are vineyards on and near the course), locker rooms, a trophy room, and a 2,000-square-foot deck. The club is a popular location for corporate and Pro-Am golf tournaments as well as weddings, banquets, and social events, but its claim to national fame is that it's the home of the Fred Meyer Challenge (see Spectator Sports for more information). Make reservations anywhere from a week to thirty days in advance.

Tri Mountain
1701 N.W. 299th, Ridgefield, Washington
(360) 887-3004

Tri Mountain is close to downtown Portland and even closer to downtown Vancouver; its reputation for sogginess has been improved with new drainage systems, and golfers agree that this fun course is well maintained. Sand bunkers are numerous, and eleven lakes that come into play over most of the course's holes keep golfers on their toes. The yardage of this 72-par course is 6,580, and every yard is interesting. Greens fees will set you back more than $30 on the weekends and about $25 for weekday play. Carts are available, as is a full-service clubhouse and an aquatic driving range.

Tualatin Island Greens
20400 S.W. Cipole Rd., Tualatin
(503) 691-8400

Voted "America's Best New Range" in 1995, this public driving range and eighteen-hole putting course is a little out of the way but it is fun practice golf. The focal point of the 315-yard driving range is the island green target, which is reachable from any of the sixty tee stations. After hitting a bucket of balls, you can challenge yourself to a round on the putting course, which consists of eighteen famous holes reduced to scale. In addition to the 6,000-square-foot clubhouse, you'll find a golf shop, grill, and golf simulator. You can tee off on bucket of forty-five golf balls for $4, whack seventy-five balls for $6, or if you really want to smooth out your stroke, you can smack 110 balls for $8. The mini-golf course is $5 for adults and $3 for those sixteen and under.

Insiders' Tip

For the most encyclopedic Internet review of golf in Oregon and southwest Washington, visit the truly excellent Web site www.oregongolf.com. This fine resource gives exhaustive details on each course and links you to the maps to get you there.

Golf Specialty Stores

Looking for some new golf shoes, or perhaps a nice set of new titanium woods? No problem. If golf is your game, you will find plenty of Portland-area shops that carry the latest and best equipment and supplies. Many stores do repair work and offer extensive selections of new and used clubs, bags, putters, and apparel. Here are several specialized stores in the area you may want to visit.

Caplan's Sportsworld
500 S.W. 5th Ave.
(503) 226-6467

The oldest golf shop in the Pacific Northwest, Caplan's has been around since the turn of the last century. This is one-stop shopping for your golf needs—from swing analysis to carts, clubs, balls, and bags. If you're new to town, this place can help you get squared away with equipment as well as information about tournaments and where to get the best lessons. They also have a nice indoor practice range.

Fiddler's Green
91292 U.S. Hwy. 99E, Eugene
(541) 689-8464, (800) 548-5500

All right, so it's not in Portland. Still, Fiddler's Green is worth a visit if you are in the Eugene area—they are the largest golf pro shop in the country. Attached to an eighteen-hole executive course, Fiddler's Green is an ideal place to stock up on gloves, shoes, balls, clothes, and clubs. The driving range provides a good try-out area. This family-run business has numerous fitting experts to help you select the proper clubs. They also will repair your clubs, even regripping them while you wait. Fiddler's Green advertises itself as "the golfer's candy store," and we see no reason to argue. Call them for a catalogue.

Golf Headquarters
10215 S.W. Pkwy.
(503) 297-1808

9515 S.E. 82nd Ave.
(503) 771-4742

Oregon Golf Headquarters carries a full line of golfing equipment and accessories, fitting expertise, and golf apparel. They feature top-quality equipment at discount prices, with expert assistance to help you choose wisely.

Lady Golf Classics
5123 S.W. Macadam Ave.
(503) 223-9100

Lady Golf specializes in golf apparel and equipment, including clubs, shoes, and accessories for women. Their apparel ranges from size two to size twenty-two.

Insiders' Tip

Fiddler's Green, the golf superstore in Eugene, publishes a colorful, free map of all the golf courses in Oregon and Washington. It's widely available at places where tourists are likely to congregate: at the airport, car rental kiosks, and attractions such as The Oregon Zoo.

North Woods Golf
7410 S.W. Macadam Ave.
(503) 245–1910, (800) 666–1910

North Woods Golf focuses on the creation of custom-fit woods and irons made right there in the shop, especially ones that feature graphite shafts. However, they are also distinguished by their experts in repair, and run the largest repair shop in town.

Golf Events

Oregon hosts two regular tournaments, the Fred Meyer Challenge and the Safeway Classic. In addition to these events, roving tournaments of many kinds will alight here, including the U.S. Amateur Open and the U.S.G.A. National Amateur Public Links Championship. Oregon also has its own regiment of local tournaments: the Oregon Golf Association is the best source of information on these. They may be reached at (503) 981-GOLF or on-line at www.orgolf.org.

Fred Meyer Challenge
Peter Jacobsen Productions
(503) 526–9331
www.pjp.com

This event, which is hosted by Portland's premier professional golfer Peter Jacobsen, attracts top golf talent, sports figures, and entertainment celebrities from around the nation. Longtime icons such as Arnold Palmer and Jack Nicklaus usually attend, as well as players such as Tiger Woods, John Daly, David Duval, and Phil Mickelson. For more information about the tournament, see the listing in our Spectator Sports chapter.

Safeway Classic
Tournament Golf
(503) 626–2711,
(503) 287–LPGA (ticket sales)

The LPGA Safeway Classic at the Columbia Edgewater is held the second week in September. Its purse is now at $1 million; it raises millions for children's charities, and is one of the most popular events in Portland golf. Tickets run about $50, but Safeway shoppers can receive significant discounts. See the Spectator Sports chapter for more information on this great golf event.

Spectator Sports

When you can leave Portland and within ninety minutes ski on a glacier, fly fish in a rippling stream deep in a forest, or kayak down a Class IV river, spectator sports are not the only game in town. But on those nights when the Blazers are on a hot finger roll with balls zipping through nothing but net, it's lots of fun to watch our lads smoke the other guys. Now, with games played in the Blazers home court, the Rose Garden, one of the nicest and biggest indoor stadiums in the nation, the team continues to attract fans from all over to sellout games.

In addition to the NBA's Portland Trailblazers, there are lots of other seats to cheer from, including those at minor league baseball games with the Portland Beavers, ice hockey with the Winter Hawks, and soccer matches with our A-League soccer team, the resurrected Portland Timbers. A splendidly refurbished downtown stadium, PGE Park, is the home of the Timbers, as well as our new AAA baseball team, the Beavers, who season young players on behalf of the San Diego Padres. Women's basketball has a loyal following here—we've recently seen the return of professional women's ball via the WNBA Portland Fire. And don't forget the nags hoofing around the far turn at Portland Meadows, and stock cars zipping dusty ovals at Portland Speedway. Here's the lowdown on these athletic showdowns.

Auto Racing

This is the American West, so the national love affair with the internal combustion engine, painted and polished sheet metal, and the excessive consumption of imported fossil fools is in full bloom. What is more American than any type of auto racing? It has everything we love: speed, noise, big and powerful cars, gasoline, beer, fried food, no cops, and no dress codes.

Portland International Raceway
West Delta Park, 1940 N. Victory Blvd.
(503) 823–7223
www.portlandraceway.com

Portland International Raceway is situated in a big park at the north end of the city, with Mount Hood providing an appropriate background to the drama on the field. The racetrack is to the west of I-5 at exit 306-B. This is where sports cars and motorcycles do their stuff. The raceway also hosts bicycle races, motocross, and other less revved competitions. Admission fees and starting times vary according to the event. The season at PIR is July through November, with most races held on weekend nights.

Portland Speedway Auto Racing
9727 N. Martin Luther King Jr. Blvd.
(503) 285–2883
www.portlandspeedway.com

One of the oldest continuously operated racetracks in the nation, this is also the oldest racetrack in Oregon. Six different classes of auto racing, including NASCAR and stock-car racing, happen on this clay-surfaced track. The season at the speedway starts in April and runs through September, with prices and starting times varying with the particular events.

Woodburn Dragstrip
7730 OR Hwy. 219 (I–5 exit 271)
(503) 982–4461
www.woodburndragstrip.com

Less than half an hour's drive south of town, the Woodburn Dragstrip showcases motorcycle, dragster, and Funny Car events from May through September. Admission fees and starting times vary according to the event.

Baseball

The Portland Beavers
PGE Park, 1844 S.W. Morrison St.
(503) 553–5400 (information),
(503) 553–5555 (tickets)
www.pgepark.com

The most recent reincarnation of Portland's long history of successful and popular minor league baseball teams, the Portland Beavers are our new AAA team, and their ballpark has been spruced up to give them a proper welcome. PGE Park, formerly known as Civic Stadium, has been given many modern upgrades for both players and fans, but its wrought-iron fence and friendly appearance convey the old-fashioned atmosphere that fans love about minor league ball. You'll find the stadium just west of downtown, on 18th and Morrison; the MAX line stops right in front. It's within walking distance of many restaurants, hotels, bars, brew-pubs, and coffee shops, and in the park you'll find a brand-new bar and grill run by the Widmer brothers that offers seating right on the edge of the field. The ticket prices are still a good value—bargain tickets are $2.99, single seats about $8.75, and even the "luxury" seats are only about $20. The Beavers play day and night games from mid-June through early September. For you cynics, surprisingly few games are rained out. A word to the wise: it is next to impossible to park near the stadium. Do yourself a favor and take the MAX train. All Beavers tickets enable you to use Tri-Met for free on game day.

Basketball

The Portland Fire
The Rose Garden, One Center Court
(503) 797–WNBA
www.wnba.com/fire

Women's basketball has had a loyal following here—we had a great women's team, the Portland Power, which lasted a couple of years—but since it's an emerging professional sport, it's still working out the kinks. Thus fans of women's ball are happy at the re-emergence of professional women's basketball in the shape of the Portland Fire. With the newly formed WNBA behind it, we're hoping that the infrastructure will allow the Fire to flourish. The Portland Fire has already garnered the devotion of fans, who find the games exciting, intense, and pure fun. (The Fire is also really active in community outreach, particularly in supporting women's health and education.) Ticket prices run from an incredibly reasonable $5 to $75; season tickets are available. See below for more information on the Rose Garden. The season runs from May through August.

The Portland Trailblazers
The Rose Garden, One Center Court
(503) 234–9291,
(503) 321–3211 (events hotline)

For those not inclined to religiously follow the ins and outs of professional sports, the Portland Trailblazers play in the Western Division of the National Basketball Association. The team is owned by Paul Allen, who co-founded Microsoft with Bill Gates.

Before the billionaire bought the bunch, it won the NBA title in 1977 under the stern tutelage of Coach Jack Ramsey who wore plaid pants and striped shirts. That winning team was led by stringbean, carrot-topped Bill Walton.

The still-new Rose Garden, with seats going from $20 (bring your own oxygen) to more than $100, is one of the best places to be a spectator. There's a certain cachet about having season tickets or, even better, a corporate luxury box, but these may be hard to get. However, ordinary tickets are usually available even on game day, depending on the opponent. You can often find refreshments-plus-tickets deals and other promotions too.

While the refreshment prices are steep in this state-of-the-art techno-coliseum, the Rose Garden's thirty-two public restrooms do have piped-in radio for play-by-play updates and there are 700 television monitors so you can watch the game while waiting in line for your garden-burger and local brew.

Tickets are available from the Rose Garden box office and from Ticketmaster, (503) 224–4400, which is also partially owned by Paul Allen. The Blazers' season begins in October; when it ends depends on their skill, luck, opponents, and other play-off-related criteria. It usually ends in May, soon after the end of the regular season.

If you go to a game, don't drive; parking is very expensive. MAX runs to within 100 yards of the Rose Garden and Tri-Met may eventually figure out, as BART did in San Francisco and Oakland, that they should put on extra trains the nights the Blazers play.

Golf

Fred Meyer Challenge
Peter Jacobsen Productions
(503) 526–9331

The Fred Meyer Challenge was established by Oregon native and PGA Tour champ Peter Jacobsen in 1985 as a way to raise money for children's charities in Oregon. It's held in mid-August, on a Sunday, Monday, and Tuesday, and Peter Jacobsen entices famous golfers from Arnold Palmer to Greg Norman to John Daly to take a holiday at the beautiful Reserve Vineyards and Golf Club in Aloha, where they play best-ball golf in twelve two-man teams. The Fred Meyer Challenge (which is actually sponsored by Washington Mutual Bank) also draws its share of nongolf celebrities out of friendship for the affable Jacobsen and out of a desire to compete in the pro-am tournament held on Sunday. And of course it draws many tens of thousands of visitors hoping for glimpses of Tiger Woods, Jack Nicklaus, or Peter Jacobsen himself. Like all golf festivals, there are souvenirs, corporate booths, and promotions galore. Ticket prices range from $40 to $100, unless you bank with Washington Mutual, where you can find discounted tickets for Sundays only. You can read more about this event on the Web at www.pjp.com.

Safeway Classic
Tournament Golf
(503) 626–2711,
(503) 287–LPGA (ticket sales)
www.safewayclassic.org

The Safeway Classic (formerly called the Safeway LPGA Golf Championship) at the Columbia Edgewater is tied for second-oldest event on the LPGA tour. Portland has been hosting it for nearly thirty years, and each year the tournament grows in status, with a purse that is now at $1 million. Even more impressive, the tournament raises millions of dollars for local charities ($6 million in 2000 alone). It is held the second week in September, and draws more than 50,000 people over the week of the tournament. Season tickets are $50, but check for promotional deals, especially if you shop at Safeway.

Greyhound Racing

Multnomah Greyhound Park
944 N.E. 223rd Ave., Wood Village
(503) 667–7700
www.EZ2winmgp.com

Greyhound racing is largely an adult attraction, where visitors can wager on the success of their favorites as they run after the mechanical "rabbit." The Greyhound Park is a huge complex in the midst of a fast-growing residential and retail area on the eastern edges of the city near the Columbia River, off I-84 at Exit 16. Races are run Wednesdays through Sundays from May through October; the starting time is 7 P.M., except on Sunday, when it is at 1 P.M. The Greyhound Park sponsors an adoption program for dogs who are retiring from racing; contact the park for more information.

Hockey

Portland Winter Hawks
Western Hockey League
Portland Memorial Coliseum & Rose Garden
One Center Court
(503) 238–6366

The Hawks, as they are locally known, are another Portland treasure; they've been favorites since they started playing here in 1976. This is a strong, fast-playing team that is a perennial contender for their league's championship. Success on the ice in Portland means a trip to "big show," the NHL, for players. The team consistently draws a good crowd, including many families that really appreciate the players' efforts. And there are lots of special fan events. While there are no $1 million free-throws from center court, at least once a year the Hawks freeze a good load of silver dollars on the surface of the ice and then let a small number of lucky fans scramble, slide and slip (sans skates) as they attempt to gather up the coins and have some good clean fun with only minor abrasions and perhaps some major embarrassment. The Hawks fly over the ice from late September through March; games start at 7 P.M., except on Sundays, when they start at 5 P.M. Tickets to a game range from $11 to $20. Season tickets range from $495 for a season at rinkside to $270 for students or seniors on the third tier.

Horse Racing

Portland Meadows
1001 N. Schmeer Rd. (off I–5 at Exit 306–B)
(503) 285–9144

Probably not in the category of a family entertainment venue, Portland Meadows is one of two major wagering racetracks in the area. This site features horses galloping nose to nose. Racehorses have been bred and raced in Portland for nearly a century, though Portland Meadows has only been around since 1946. There are the usual snack bars and restaurants at the track, but you can also sit in the stands with your binoculars, lucky charms, and wallet to watch your favorite race around the oval.

Neon light aficionados will appreciate the large-scale animated race horses adorning the track's entrance, which are visible from I–5. Admission is free and so is parking; some areas of the park may charge a few bucks for prime viewing. The season is October to April.

Soccer

Portland Timbers
PGE Park, 1844 S.W. Morrison St.
(503) 553–5400 (information),
(503) 553–5555 (tickets)
www.pgepark.com

The sports landscape in Portland has endured some seismic shaking in the past few years, with many teams falling apart, then recollecting themselves. But one thing that never changes is Portland's love for soccer. So we are relieved to have the revived Portland Timbers, our men's A-League team, in their new stadium with their new coach Bobby Howe. Besides being a great player and one of the most respected coaches in the world, Howe is an experienced ambassador to youth soccer—he was the head coach of the Washington State Youth Soccer Association. Since seemingly countless thousands of school-age boys and girls now play soccer, the Timbers are expected to have a big following among Portland's younger set and their parents. Equally importantly, mom or dad can take the kids to see the Timbers without having to take out a home equity loan—the most expensive seats are $18.50. The Timbers games run April through September.

Insiders' Tip

If you're attending a game at PGE Park, your ticket is more valuable than its seat price: it also serves as a Tri-Met pass on the day of the event. You can use it to ride to and from PGE Park on any bus or MAX train. So buy your tickets in advance! And take advantage of this service, because there is no parking near the stadium.

The Timbers mark Portland's return to A-League soccer.

Other Spectator Sports

Most of the area's colleges and universities—Portland State University, University of Portland, Lewis & Clark College, and Reed College, among others—have sports programs that may include football, basketball, soccer, and baseball teams. University of Portland has consistently produced decent men's and women's basketball teams, as well as championship women's soccer teams—in fact, Tiffeny Millbrett, ranked as the best woman soccer player in the world, was a University of Portland star (and a Portland native). The smaller schools, like Reed and Lewis & Clark, may not have men's and women's teams that are contenders in all sports, but they play good college ball, and attract some excellent track and field athletes, rowers, and lacrosse players. And local high school teams are always fun to watch in any sport. There is also a range of amateur teams and leagues playing everything from rugby, soccer, ultimate Frisbee, lacrosse, and, of course, that near-religious experience for aging males, nighttime softball.

Daytrips

No doubt, Portland is a daytripper's delight, but the biggest challenge may be deciding which way to travel. What would you like to see today? Mountains? Ancient forests? The beautiful Oregon beaches? Or perhaps magnificent waterfalls or high desert country? We've listed a few of our favorite daytrips in this chapter, but really, if you have a map and an imagination, you can drive any direction and find that it is impossible to be disappointed. Along your drive you will probably pass numerous parks, campgrounds, and visitor stations with restrooms, maps, free coffee, and brochures to help you along your way.

Whether you're after a real wilderness escape, or simply a pleasant drive in the country, you are in for an exciting adventure. Bring your binoculars, camera, plenty of film, but in your exhilaration, please don't leave common sense behind. Remember, wearing seat belts is a law in Oregon and it is enforced. Watch your speed limit, especially when passing through small towns. Be especially vigilant when driving at night because deer and other smaller animals frequently cross our roads and highways. Carry a good spare tire, because you might find yourself unexpectedly traveling down an old logging road that proved to be irresistible. Bring an extra jacket even in the summertime as the coast and mountains can be surprisingly chilly.

Within just an hour or two's drive west of Portland, you'll find the magnificent Oregon coast with its forests, huge rock formations, and unsullied beaches. An easy hour's drive east leads to the awe-inspiring Multnomah Gorge and its stunning waterfalls, and by another route, the majestic Mount Hood. If you drive south, in an hour you'll reach the largest and one of the loveliest state parks in Oregon, Silver Falls State Park, a hiker's and horseback rider's paradise. If you choose to drive north, you will enter a new world of adventure in our sister state, Washington, which is blessed with a rugged and natural beauty quite similar to our own. You can just about drive off in any direction you choose and arrive at a splendid destination. So pack your picnic basket, a thermos of coffee or tea, a good map—and of course—your Insiders' Guide, and go discover Oregon firsthand.

Silver Falls State Park

Silver Falls State Park
20024 Silver Falls Hwy.,
S.E., Sublimity Park
(503) 873-8681

In the lower elevation of Oregon's Cascade Mountains, just 26 miles east of Salem, lies Silver Falls State Park, which is nestled in the heart of a temperate rain forest. Here, one of the most beautiful trails in Oregon, Canyon Trail (also known as the Trail of 10 Falls) descends to a forest floor covered with ferns, mosses, and wildflowers amidst stands of Douglas-fir, hemlock, and cedar and the rushing, pure waters of Silver Creek.

If you aren't in a hurry, the drive to Silver Falls can be a big part of the fun. Take either Oregon Highway 99 E. or Interstate 205 from Portland to Oregon City. Then just follow 99 E. along the

Willamette River to Woodburn and then turn on to Oregon Highway 214, which cuts through the picturesque towns of Mt. Angel and Silverton on the way to Silver Falls. There are plenty of quaint general stores along the way if you want to stock up on snacks or beverages. If you are squeezed for time, blast down on Interstate 5 South. Just past Salem, jog over to Oregon Highway 22, then hop on Highway 214 and head due east for 25 miles. From Portland the drive takes about an hour and fifteen to twenty minutes.

At the park, all the main attractions are easy to find. The well-maintained Canyon Trail winds along the banks of the north and south forks of Silver Creek leading to no less than eleven majestic water falls, ranging from the grand South Falls (177 feet), to the delicate Drake Falls (27 feet). Four of these falls have an amphitheater-like surrounding, allowing one to walk behind the falls and enjoy the refreshingly cool and misty spray.

Canyon Trail (which does not allow pets and is open to hikers only) joins with the Canyon Rim Trail to complete a 7-mile loop. The trail runs behind several of the taller falls and along the brink of others, providing an exciting excursion for hikers of all ages and levels of endurance.

South Falls, one of the most spectacular sights, is an easy walk from the main parking area and the gorgeous Silver Falls Lodge. The trail descends to the bottom of the canyon and follows the South Fork of Silver Creek 1 mile to Lower South Falls. A quarter mile further, the trail turns east and follows the North Fork of Silver Creek upstream past at least six more waterfalls.

If you want to see some lush scenery and waterfalls, but don't want to walk too far, follow Highway 214 a mile or so past the main entrance and you will come to a trail head that's within a few hundred yards of Winter Falls, North Falls, and Upper North Falls. The distance from South Falls to North Falls is approximately 4.5 miles.

To hike the entire circuit requires a good three to four hours and more if you stop for lunch. For most people who pack a lunch and enjoy the canyon at a leisurely pace, the hike is an all-day adventure. Of course, you need not hike the entire trail. Shorter trips may be made by returning via the Ridge Trail or the Winter Falls Trail. Some hikers prefer leaving a second car at the North Falls parking lot to avoid the 2-mile return hike.

To preserve its primitive nature, there are no shelters, picnic tables, or restrooms along the Silver Creek Canyon Trail, but there are lots of benches and bridges across the many smaller streams that are pleasant spots for a sack lunch picnic. For safety's sake, keep in mind that the bicycle trails are also used by hikers and the horse trails are open to bicycles and hikers alike.

At Silver Falls, you will find RV, cabin, and tent camping in the overnight campground. Additional cabin rentals and complete group accommodations can be found at Silver Falls Conference Center, (503) 873–8681.

There is a $3 day-use fee, or a $25 annual permit buys access to all state park day-use areas for one year.

Insiders' Tip

Be sure to carry your own water and bring along a camera and plenty of film. Silver Falls State Park offers 14 miles of trials for horseback riders, 4 miles of paved bicycle paths, and dozens of miles of hiking trails.

Mount St. Helens

**Mount St. Helens National
Volcanic Monument Headquarters
42218 N.E. Yale Bridge Rd.,
Amboy, Washington 98601
(360) 247–3900,
(360) 247–3903 (24-hour Information)**

One of the most popular daytrip destinations in the entire Pacific Northwest, Mount St. Helens is an easy and very scenic 2.5-hour drive from Portland. Just remember, there is a lot to do and see on this trip, so start early in the morning and pack some ice and refreshments in the cooler. Take Interstate 5 to Exit 49 (the Toutle/Castle Rock Exit), which will lead you onto State Road 504 (Spirit Lake Memorial Highway). The first stop, just 5 miles east, is the Mount St. Helens National Volcanic Monument Visitor Center on the shore of Silver Lake. Don't miss the scaled-down, walk-in replica of the volcano: It really helps kids (and grown-ups, too) understand what's behind all the huffing, puffing, and blasting. A very short and easy trail just outside the center leads to a viewpoint overlooking Silver Lake and Mount St. Helens, which is 35 miles away.

Continue driving east and you'll see plenty of natural beauty on the 46-mile stretch to the new Coldwater Ridge Visitor Center at milepost 43. Washington State Road 504 winds around the north fork of the Toutle River and overlooks along the road offer views of the crater, Castle Lake, Coldwater Lake, and the mountain's northwest lava dome. Food and beverages are available at Coldwater, or if you prefer to picnic, there are plenty of great picnic sites along the way. Hoffstadt Bluffs Rest Area is a good choice that offers a spectacular view of the landslide that preceded the blast. Elk Rock Viewpoint offers another stunning view into the still sediment-choked Toutle River Valley.

Just 5 miles further up the road from Coldwater Ridge, State Road 504 ends at Johnston Ridge Observatory. This wheelchair-accessible site is only 8 miles from the volcano's summit and affords views of the inside of the crater and its dome from near the site of victim David Johnston's camp as it was on the day of the eruption. The center also offers an incredibly high-quality movie about the famous eruption,

Insiders' Tip

If you plan to go spelunking at Ape Cave, bring at least three separate light sources, sturdy shoes, and a warm jacket, as the temperature inside is about forty-two degrees Fahrenheit. And in case you were wondering, there are no apes in the Ape Caves. The cave was first explored in 1946 by the St. Helens Apes—the local Boy Scout troop for which the world-famous attraction is now named.

along with many fascinating, interactive displays and kiosks.

There is so much to do on the mountain, so you'll have some decisions to make. Ask for a map of Mount St. Helens at a visitors center—it will help you understand your options. One great adventure is to circle the entire mountain by following improved Forest Roads. It is possible to do this from June until the first snowfall—usually in November or December.

Other monument highlights include Windy Ridge and Spirit Lake, which rose 70 yards as a result of the blast. Consult with visitor center staff about selecting the best route.

Finally, although it is several hours away (by way of the Woodland Exit and off of Forest Road 83), Ape Cave is worthy of mention. The largest lava tube in the Western Hemisphere, this 12,810-foot tunnel wasn't explored until in 1946. The Ape Caves Information Center is open daily, and guided tours of the caves are available during summer months.

Passes are needed for the visitor centers and many of the recreation areas and vista points. The cost is $8 for adults, $4 for seniors, and free for children. The three visitor centers on the mountain are open year-round and closed only on holidays.

Mount Hood/Columbia Gorge Loop

One of our region's most popular scenic jaunts is the Mount Hood/Columbia Gorge Loop. It's a long, leisurely swoop up into the Cascade Mountains, around the southern edge of Mount Hood, along portions of the Oregon Trail, and then north through the orchards of the Hood River Valley to the town of Hood River, Windsurfing Capital of the Known World. From Hood River it's an incredible cruise along the Columbia River Scenic Highway past spectacular waterfalls and miniature gorges. Hikes up and down the basaltic bluffs of the Columbia Gorge and on into Portland complete your memorable trip. Of course, you can make the loop in reverse, starting up the Gorge and circling Mount Hood from north to east then down the hill to Portland. Depending on your itinerary en route, the journey will be somewhere between 100 and 160 miles and can be made in a day or a couple of days with a camping stop by a lake or stream or lodging at a charming hotel or mountain inn. However you plan it, the loop is a perfect answer to how to spend a sunny day with visiting family or friends. They'll enjoy the outing and so will Portlanders proud to show off a generous portion of local scenery, history, and recreational opportunities.

After flipping a coin, we decided to start a tour of the loop by heading up the gorge, through which thousands of pioneers hung on tight to huge rafts thundering down the Columbia as they made the last link between St, Louis, Missouri, and their new homes in the Willamette Valley.

The best way to travel the gorge is to start with the 22-mile Historic Columbia River Highway Loop. To get there, take Interstate 84 out of Portland and leave the modern freeway at Exit 22 at Corbett, 15 miles from downtown Portland. After meandering alongside the Sandy River, you'll climb up to a remarkable vista called Crown Point. Here, 725 feet above the river, a circular stone Vista House, built in 1917, offers a commanding view of the gorge. It also has restrooms. Then, winding down the bluff to its base, you'll come upon a series of natural wonders all nestled close. Along the 11 miles east of Vista House there's a waterfall every mile to make it the largest concentration of waterfalls in the United States. Some of the prettiest are Latourell Falls, a 249-foot cataract at the end of a paved 150-yard trail; Bridal Veil, a sweet little tumble reached by a third-of-a-mile stroll; and Wahkeena Falls, a 242-foot staircase of thrashing white water ending conveniently at a parking lot.

Close-up

What a Blast!

Mount St. Helens was once known as "the Mt. Fuji of America" because its symmetrical beauty was reminiscent of the famous Japanese volcano, but the graceful cone top and its glistening cap of perennial snow and ice is now almost entirely gone.

On May 18, 1980, after nearly two months of smaller earthquakes and steam eruptions, Mount St. Helens suddenly began a series of massive explosive eruptions when an earthquake cresting at magnitude of 5.1 struck at 8:32 A.M. Within seconds, the volcano's unstable and bulging north flank slid away in the largest landslide in recorded history, triggering a destructive blast of lethal hot gas, steam, and rock debris that swept across the landscape at 1,100 kilometers per hour. Temperatures reached as high as 300 degrees Celsius, melting snow and ice on the volcano and forming torrents of water and rock debris that swept down river valleys leading from the mountain. Within minutes, a massive plume of ash thrust nearly 20 kilometers into the sky, where the wind carried about 490 tons of ash across 57,000 square kilometers of the western United States and, in trace amounts, around the world.

The lateral blast, which lasted only the first few minutes of a nine-hour continuous eruption, devastated 250 square miles of forest and recreation area, killed thousands of animals, and left fifty-seven people dead or missing. The eruptions and huge avalanche removed about 4 billion cubic yards of the mountain, including about 170 million cubic yards of glacial snow and ice. The eruption also caused mudflows so severe that they blocked the shipping channel of the Columbia River 70 river miles away.

Each year tens of thousands of visitors flock to the area surrounding Mount St. Helens to marvel at the effects of the eruption. In 1982, President Reagan set aside 110,000 acres around the volcano as the Mount St. Helens National Volcanic Monument. Since then, many trails, viewpoints, information stations, campgrounds, and picnic areas have been established to accommodate the increasing number of tourists each year.

Visitors can also drive to Windy Ridge, a spectacular vantage point only 4 miles northeast of the crater overlooking Spirit Lake, where they can see the awesome evidence of the volcano's destruction, as well as the remarkable recovery of the forest and wildlife. Mountain climbing to the summit of the volcano has been allowed since 1987.

A trip to Mount St. Helens can be exhilarating, but tiring. If you are running low on petrol, hungry, tired, or want to stock up on supplies, Castle Rock (pop. 2,000), just off of Interstate 5, offers lots of small gift shops, motels, a grocery store, eateries, and gas stations.

But the star of the show is Multnomah Falls, a 620-foot wonder easily gazed upon by folks staring up from an observation zone next to a lodge with restaurant, gift shop and information center. Or you can hike up the cliff to a bridge one-half mile or even further to the top of the falls if you are inspired.

Before you leave the waterfall route, there's a nifty little site called **Oneonta Gorge**. During warmer days, you can wade upstream along bedrock, over boulders and logs, and as the stream narrows and mossy walls get higher, you'll find yourself in a micro-gorge. To plan your visit to the bigger gorge, call the **Gorge Information Service** at (800) 222-8611.

Then, back on I-84, the next tourist stop is **Bonneville Dam,** the oldest Army Corp of Engineers project along the Columbia. To take a tour of this massive, 500-foot-wide plug holding back the mighty River of the West and, in season, watch salmon spawn up a series of fish ladders, call the visitor center at (503) 374-8820. Tucked next to the dam is the **Bonneville Fish Hatchery,** (503) 374-8393, with more than sixty salmon rearing and holding ponds and a recent addition, a viewing pond where you can watch Herman, a 400-pound sturgeon cruising around his lair. The hatchery is open daily from dawn until dusk.

The route you've been traveling is one of America's most remarkable stretches of pavement. After three years of daring road construction, the **Columbia River Historic Highway** was officially dedicated on June 7, 1916, when President Woodrow Wilson touched a button in the White House electrically unfurling "Old Glory" at Vista House on Crown Point. Moments later black sedans started chugging along a 73-mile stretch from Troutdale to The Dalles—the first paved road in the Pacific Northwest, and at the time, the premier scenic highway in the United States.

As more excursionists traveled along this picturesque route through the gorge, roadhouses, auto camps, and gas stations sprang up to peddle fried chicken, overnight accommodations, and petroleum. But the arrival of faster cars too dangerous for a narrow roadbed with a cliff for a curb and the consequent construction of a new freeway in the 1950s sent this famous thoroughfare into an era of neglect and disintegration. Stone railings, bridges, and viewpoints became charmingly archaeological rather than safely functional.

The good news is a portion of the historic highway is under renovation as a scenic route for bicyclists and hikers only. This ambitious highway-to-trail linear parkway from Warrendale to Mosier got its first completed segment in May 1997 when after a year's construction and at a cost of $1.4 million, 1.5-mile stretch of highway-turned-trail launched the project. This link runs west-to-east between Tanner Creek and Eagle Creek, two small streams that can be found tumbling down to the Columbia on either side of Bonneville Dam.

The trail begins at Tanner Creek by exiting 84 at Exit 40 (Bonneville Dam). It's a short drive east to a parking lot. After a few minutes, day hikers and bicyclists reach a quaintly narrow highway with lanes barely wide enough to accommodate a stroller for triplets. This ancient ribbon of asphalt parallels the much newer superslab at a slightly higher elevation and then rises up the bluff to deliver a view of the Bonneville Dam complex. Here, as the curb gets seriously precipitous, you'll see the arched guardrails with tightly set stones that were built by Scottish stone cutters and Italian masons who reportedly sang while they worked. Now this remarkable roadbed, carved out of cliff sides and blasted through small mountains, is getting new railings, bridges, viaducts, and tunnels that are accurate replicas of mossy originals.

A short walk beyond an excellent reproduction of the **Tooth Rock Bridge,** complete with a pair of commemorative plaques, the trail passes below a wall of mud from an ancient flow that is geologically informative and hopefully stationary. Finally, a cement stairway takes a stroller or biker down to a new road leading to the Eagle Creek Fish Hatchery. Here, a trailhead starts hikers up a popular trail with more waterfalls than any other hike in the gorge.

The next site of note on the loop tour is **Cascade Locks,** 8 miles beyond the intersection of the historic highway and I-84. A navigational passage that allowed a by-pass around a series of rapids before it was rendered obsolete when Bonneville Dam was built, Cascade Locks is now a small town, a park, and two museums, one of which is housed in the former home of the lock tender. The Oregon Pony, the first steam locomotive in the Pacific Northwest, is on display at Marine Park. For more information on Cascade Locks, call (541) 374-8619.

If the kids are hungry after a stroll down the highway-to-trail link, a nearby hike, and visits to a half-dozen waterfalls and a couple of museums, take them to **Charburger** in Cascade Locks, just a few miles east at 714 Wa Na Pa Street, (503) 374-8477. Charburger offers mainstream American grub, buffet style, in a folksy atmosphere of pioneer guns and gear on walls, models of stern-wheelers on display tables, and ice cream smothering slices of marionberry pie.

If you are looking for more upscale dining, try the **Columbia Gorge Hotel,** 4000 West Cliff Drive, as you approach the little town of Hood River, (503) 386-5566. Take Exit 62 off I-84 and cross a bridge to the north side of the freeway and follow West Cliff Drive west to what was known in the Roaring Twenties as the "Waldorf of the West." This hotel, voted among the top 500 in the world by *Conde Nast Traveler* magazine, has a dining room with a view up the Columbia River. The prices for the offerings of fish and wild game, including Columbia River salmon, are steep, but well worth the expense. If you're just interested in stretching your legs, amble about the grounds of this sumptuously neo-Moorish palace built by lumber baron Simon Benson. A handsomely landscaped garden ribboned with a little stream crossed by Japanese-style bridges leads to the edge of a cliff where a white wedding bower is poised against the drop of a 200-foot waterfall.

On to Hood River, 64 miles east of Portland on I-84. Once the site of numerous packing plants for apples, pears, and peaches, this little burg of just under 5,000 has reinvented itself as a windsurfers mecca, with thirty-five shops devoted to manufacturing and selling gear to those who travel from all over the globe to cruise upon the nearby broad and windy Columbia. It also has lots of sophisticated restaurants and inns, but if you are just on your way through, grab a quick, affordable grilled meat sandwich at the

Insiders' Tip

Mount St. Helens is 34 miles west of Mount Adams, which is in the eastern part of the Cascade Range. These "sister and brother" volcanic mountains are each about 50 miles from Mount Rainer, the giant of Cascade volcanoes. Mount Hood, the nearest major volcanic peak in Oregon, is about 60 miles southeast of Mount St. Helens.

Purple Rock Art Bar Cafe, 606 Oak Street, (503) 386-6061 or the ginger plum chicken at **Big City Chicks**, 303 13th Avenue, (503) 386-2111. A third spot is the charmingly renovated **Hood River Hotel**, 102 Oak Street, (503) 386-1900. This 1913 vintage hotel has great views of the gorge, an espresso bar, and a cafe with sidewalk tables.

To keep track of all that this region has to offer, contact the **Hood River Valley Visitors Council and Chamber of Commerce** at (800) 366-3530 or (503) 386-2000.

Once you've perused Hood River, follow the main street as it angles southeast on Oregon Highway 35 into the Hood River Valley, a lovely little drainage of the Hood River meandering down the slope of Mount Hood to irrigate thousands of acres of orchards and farms. Two terrific times to visit the Hood River Valley are during the Hood River Blossom Festival, held April 20 through 21, and the Hood River Harvest Festival on October 20 and 21. But at any time, the trip through this pocket of traditional farmland is a journey beyond life in the 'burbs.

After leaving the valley, Highway 35 starts to curve around the eastern slope of the mountain that Native Americans call Wy'East and thousands of Oregonians consider their very own Mount Fujiyama. Soon, you begin to catch close-up glimpses of Mount Hood's glacial cap and if you use your imagination, you can sense the wonder felt by pioneers who opted to take a path around the mountain instead of rafting down the dangerous Columbia. Just before the confluence of Highway 35 and Highway 26, a historical marker announces that you are crossing Barlow Pass, named for Sam Barlow, a trailblazer who found a way down the mountain and set up a tollroad. Barlow charged $5 per wagon and 10 cents per head of cattle for those hearty and brave enough to slide and rope their wagons down the muddy slopes and treacherous canyons that are now traversed by Highway 26. Another historical marker shortly after the Barlow Road marker is a poignant reminder of the cost of this detour. **The Pioneer Woman's Gravesite** is a short distance from the road where you can also view intact wagon ruts near the gravesite.

Once on Highway 26 heading west, there are a number of stopping spots of interest as you cruise down the big hill. One is Trillium Lake, a picnic site and fishing hole stocked with rainbow trout. To get there take Forest Service Road 2656 a couple of miles before reaching Government Camp. If it's ski season, you can zip up to Timberline, Summit Ski area, or Mt. Hood Ski Bowl (see Recreation) for some world-class downhill action. Of if you are simply thirsty and hungry, stop at **Mt. Hood Brewing Company,** (541) 272-3724, at the west end of Government Camp for microbrews and great sandwiches.

After descending from the ski zone, you'll come to Welches, a mountain town with lodging, shopping, dining, and even golf. The **Resort at the Mountains,** (800) 669-7666, not only offers gracious accommodations but the Three Nines golf course. You might also want to stop here at the Mt. Hood Information Center, billed as a "One Stop" visitor center with information on just about everything going on around the mountain. But if the kids have a choice, they'll probably pick the Rainbow Trout Fishing Farm located 7.5 miles east of Sandy on Highway 26 at 52560 East Sylvan Drive. They're open seven days a week from 8 A.M. to dusk with costs depending on the size of the lunker you haul out of the lake. For more info, call (503) 622-5223.

One last site to see is the **Philip Foster Farm and Homestead** at 29912 S.E. Oregon Highway 211, (503) 637-6324. To get there take Oregon Highway 211 at its juncture with Highway 26 in Sandy, and go south for 6 miles to the little hamlet of Eagle Creek. Here you'll find this working farm complete with house, barn, garden, orchard, and blacksmith shop. Visitors are invited to help with chores. There is also a picnic spot and a general store. Hours are Friday through Sunday 11 A.M. to 4 P.M. in June and July and just Saturdays and Sundays during August and September.

The last possible stop on this remarkably scenic parabola up a deep gorge and around a panoramic glacier is its formal conclusion at the **End of the Oregon Trail Interpretive Center** off I-205 at Exit 10 near Oregon City (see Attractions). If you're happy just to be a pioneer fresh off your own version of the Oregon Trail, head back to Portland for a well-deserved rest. If you plan on settling in Portland, you'll probably join many locals who keep making this trek again and again with no complaints that they've run out of places to explore along this wondrous route.

Northern Willamette Valley's Wine Country

Although professional wine making has been a significant enterprise in Oregon for only three decades, a handful of dedicated pioneers have developed a thriving agricultural region that produces internationally renowned wine led by Pinot Noirs that have been winning awards almost from the first uncorked bottle.

Roughly in the same latitude as Burgundy, the great wine-producing province in France, Oregon's northern Willamette Valley has a cool marine climate, rich soil on the southern slopes of rolling hills, and a long, gentle season with ample sunny days. The result is a harvest of grapes that crush into wines, including the prize-winning elegantly brusque Pinot Noirs, crisp Pinot Gris, Riesling, Cabernet Sauvignon, Sauvignon Blanc, and Gewürztraminer. Other favorites include distinctive wines made from Oregon's famous blackberries, raspberries, and boysenberries.

But don't take the judges' or an enthusiastic oenophile's words for it. Taste these remarkable varieties yourself by taking a tour of northwestern Oregon's wine region. It's not only a delightful drive through some of the state's most charmingly bucolic countryside, but a gift to your palate. Most of the wineries are open to visitors; and a few are located near fine restaurants and inns springing up along what is becoming one of the most popular tourist loops on the West Coast.

First, plan for a relaxed jaunt that starts in the morning, loops out into the Wine Country, and back to Portland by evening. Secondly, stop by the **Oregon Winegrowers' Association,** 1200 N.W. Front Avenue, Suite 400, Portland, Oregon 97209, (503) 228-0713, or Portland Visitor and Convention Bureau, 26 S.W. Salmon, (503) 222-2223, and pick up *Discover Oregon Wineries*, a comprehensive guide with maps, addresses, phone numbers, examples of wine labels and descriptions of the sixteen wineries that grace the green hills of Washington and Yamhill Counties. You can either call ahead to make sure the wineries are open or you can take your chances. Either way, most wineries will have tasting rooms open to the public.

If you're in a bit of a hurry and don't mind missing the Ponzi Vineyards, skirt the winery nearest to Portland by taking Highway 99 southwest of Portland. Look for blue-and-white signs directing travelers to tasting rooms, vineyards, and wineries.

If you opt to visit **Ponzi Vineyards,** take I-5 to Highway 217 and on to Highway 210 for 4.5 miles to Vandermost Road. Turn left and head south, following signs to 14665 S.W. Winery Lane. Here, with the exception of January and holidays, visitors are welcome to sample what *The Wine Spectator* lists as one the "Top 100 Wines."

Heading west from Ponzi or Portland, you near Newberg, one of the larger communities in Yamhill County. As you glide down a ridge into Newberg, you'll come upon two wineries across the highway from each other. **Rex Hill Vineyards** north of the highway, has a showcase winery, an elegant tasting room with a fireplace and antiques, and some of the oldest vines in the county. South of the highway, at **Chehalem Winery**, noted wine maker Harry Peterson-Nedry and his crew have collaborated with Patrice Rion, a Burgundian wine maker, to produce excellent Pinot Noir, Pinot Gris, and Chardonnay.

West of Newberg, as Highway 99 breezes through the little 'burg of Dundee and beyond, there is a cluster of wineries and vineyards that will amiably take up most of your day. A worthy stop is **Knudson Erath Winery** up on Worden Hill above Dundee, where pioneering wine maker Dick Erath produces his award-winning Pinot Noir. The tasting room has a terrace that is a great spot for picnicking while gazing across the Willamette Valley.

Right on Highway 99 W in downtown Dundee is **Argyle,** or the **Dundee Wine Company.** One of the top sparkling-wine producers in the U.S., Argyle is housed in a former hazelnut processing plant while its tasting room is in a restored Victorian house.

While in Dundee, stop for lunch at **Tina's,** 760 Highway 99 W., (503) 538-8880. A surprisingly sophisticated eatery this far from the big city, it is a tad spendy, but worth it for its clever use of produce in season, game hen, rabbit, and fresh fish from the Pacific.

Sokol Blosser Winery, a short drive up Sokol Blosser Lane, 3 miles west of Dundee, has a walk-through showcase vineyard—the only one of its kind in Oregon. One of the state's oldest and largest wineries, it has a tasting room open all year long, with picnic grounds, and a gift shop.

Next, take a right turn just beyond Lafayette and head north on Highway 47, past the town of Yamhill to Gaston. Near this tucked-away little town is **Elk Cove Vineyards,** with a tasting room that offers a lovely view of a farm valley that seems to be still lolling in the late nineteenth century. Elk Cove is known for its piquant Pinot Gris.

Just south of Forest Grove is **Montinore Vineyards,** a European-style operation on a 711-acre estate with a Victorian mansion. And lastly, after heading east on Highway 8 and south on 219 at Hillsboro, you'll reach the last site on this tour, **Oak Knoll Winery.** Founded in 1970, it's one of Oregon's oldest and most renowned vineyards. The specialties here are barrel-aged Chardonnay and Pinot Noir. Also popular is a raspberry dessert wine.

From here, travel on Highway 10 through Beaverton and on into Portland. It's been a long drive but worth every drop of gas and sip of vino.

But if you are really adventurous, there is an alternative to driving through the Oregon Wine Country. Vista **Balloon Adventures,** (800) 622-2309, or **Rex Hill Winery,** (503) 538-0666, both in Newberg, and **American Hot Air Lines** of Wilsonville, (503) 224-1179, all offer aerial tours in hot-air balloons for around $175 per hour. If you decide to take what is perhaps the opposite of a plunge and hop in a wicker gondola, you'll soar high above row after row of grapevines ribbing the hills and valleys of Yamhill and Washington Counties like a rolling mantel of green corduroy.

The Oregon Coast

Portlanders need little prompting to pack towels, parkas, shovels, and buckets and head for the Oregon coast. But when it gets hot and humid in late summer, it seems like half the town heads west to feel the breeze again.

There are a number of routes to get to the thundering Pacific. You can cruise on Highway 30 as it curves along the Columbia River to Astoria; you can amble over the Coast Range on Highway 6 and through the dairy farming country to Tillamook and its famous cheese factory; you can motor down Highway 18, slowing to a crawl as traffic thickens near the Spirit Mountain Gambling Casino; or you can take the main route—Highway 26 or the Sunset Highway, as it was named in honor of the Sunset Infantry Company that served in World War II. This straight angle northwest is the fastest way to get to that beach to wiggle your toes in the wet sand.

After zipping through a tunnel that burrows beneath the huge ridge just west of Portland and escaping a spaghetti of expressways that snarls through the suburbs of Washington County, you glide through the farm country of upper northwest Oregon.

If you've packed bikes, how about ambling along an abandoned railroad bed through the Banks-Vernonia Linear State Park? This 20-mile trail is an abandoned train route that roughly parallels Oregon Highway 47 near Banks on Oregon Highway 26 to Vernonia, a quiet little timber town. Six trailheads along 47 provide access to this trail that is Oregon's first linear recreational corridor.

For another treat on your way to the coast, head on to Jewell Junction, turn north on Fishhawk Falls Highway, a romantic label for a modest road, and drive for 9 miles to the hamlet of Jewell. Continue west 1 mile on Oregon Highway 202 to the **Jewell Meadow Wildlife Area**. Here, in the fall before hunting season, you can see Roosevelt elk and blacktail deer. Nearby, at Lee Wooden County Park, is lacey 100-foot Fishhawk Falls.

Back on Highway 26 and about a mile west of Elsie is another roadside attraction: the **Morris' Camp 18 Logging Museum,** (503) 755-2476. If you're curious about the history of logging in the Pacific Northwest, check out this museum's photo and antique equipment exhibits.

One more possible stop before you feel that salty air that is unmistakably marine is **Klootchy Creek Park,** 2 miles before the Seaside-Cannon Beach Junction. This is the site of huge firs and spruce, including the world's largest Sitka Spruce, which is more than 195 feet high and almost 16 feet in diameter.

After any of these previous perambulations or a straight, no-frills shot to the coast, you'll reach the Cannon Beach Junction. By now you're probably ready for lunch. Try **The Crab Broiler,** (502) 738-5313. At the junction where Oregon Highway 26 leaves Highway 101, this roadside diner has a lively menu of crab and cheese dishes.

After short jaunt north on Highway 101, you'll come to **Ecola State Park,** a series of rugged headlands stretching 9 miles north of Cannon Beach. Here are lots of forested hiking trails with beach access and a view of postcard-popular **Tillamook Rock Lighthouse,** a landmark that illuminated the right and wrong ways to navigate up the Oregon coast from 1881 to 1957. A hiking trail over the northernmost point of the park to Tillamook Head is thought to be one of the most scenic portions of the Oregon Coast Trail System.

Insiders' Tip

Mount St. Helens, still a potentially active and dangerous volcano, is known to have produced four major explosive eruptions and dozens of lesser eruptions. One of those, in A.D. 1480, was about five times larger than the May 18, 1980 eruption, and even larger eruptions are known to have occurred during Mount St. Helens' brief but very active 50,000-year lifetime. Following the most recent eruption, on May 18, 1980, there were five smaller explosive eruptions over a period of five months.

Retracing your route south on Oregon Highway 101, you'll reach artsy **Cannon Beach** and its famous **Haystack Rock** (at 235 feet high the third tallest coastal monolith in the world).

Next in a remarkable string of nature's wonders is **Neahkahnie Mountain,** with a trail leading to its summit and a view that is breathtaking for its scope up and down the coast and back into the Nehalem Valley.

South of this scenic marvel, you cruise through the fishing villages of Garibaldi and Bayside and on to Tillamook. Just to the west of this friendly blue collar burg is the **Three Capes Loop,** a 35-mile byway off Highway 101 between Tillamook and Neskowin. As you cruise through gentle, misty dairy country that has a time-out-of-time feel, you'll get far enough west to check out Cape Meares to the north, Cape Lookout midway, and Cape Kiwanda at the end of the loop. This last tan and brawny cape is right next to Pacific City, where dory anglers compete each year in a contest to see who can launch their fishing boat into the surf, row around yet another Haystack Rock, and return with a real fish. While in Pacific City, stop by the **Grateful Bread Bakery** for a filling, tasty lunch featuring homebaked goods.

Just a short ways down the coast is Neskowin, a sweet little town with a pretty beach in the shadow of Cascade Head, a looming monolithic outcrop favored by hikers seeking solace in a genuine rainforest. After hiking or playing on another beach for awhile (who would ever get tired of beachcombing, sifting sand for shiny agates, whirling bull kelp whips, and poking at puckery sea anenomes?) motor a few more miles south to the junction of Highway 101 and Highway 18.

Here, you have a choice of directions. You can continue south along the coast, past Lincoln City on to Newport with its fascinating Oregon Coast Aquarium, Hatfield Marine Science Center, historic Nye Beach, and scenic Yaquina Head with its lighthouse and birdwatching station. It's an easy, if long, journey back to Portland from Newport either by backtracking to Highway 18 or heading east on Highway 20 to Corvallis and then on to I-5 and north. But it will make for a long day so you may want to plan for a stay over in one of the many hotels and motels along Highway 101.

Or you can choose to take Highway 18 and angle back to Portland, stopping for some great grub at the **Otis Cafe** at Otis Junction, 2 miles east of U.S. Highway 101, (541) 994-2813. Try the rhubarb pie, or if it's time for dinner, order the pork chops! Just past Otis you'll enter the Van Duzer Corridor, a stretch of ancient firs that frame the road with their verdant grandeur. Beyond the forest, and past the Spirit Mountain Casino and a broad valley dotted with barns, farmhouses, and roadhouse/galleries, you'll cruise through Yamhill County and on to Portland. Once home, after dumping sand out of your sneakers, you'll start planning another trek to Oregon's wondrous coastline to revisit favorite spots and discover a few more.

Neighborhoods and Real Estate

Portland is repeatedly honored across the nation as being one of the best places to live. Its setting among mountains, farmland, and rivers contributes to its desirability, as does its good economy and unfrenzied style of life. However, these things alone do not define the spirit of the city. That spirit is defined primarily by its neighborhoods: above all, we are a city of neighborhoods. Malu Wilkinson, who works as a planner for the regional Metro government, says that "the fact that this is a city of neighborhoods is a huge attraction for many people who wouldn't want to live in any other kind of city, since it wouldn't have the same community feeling." Government agencies such as Metro, non-profit organizations such as the Coalition for a Liveable Future, neighborhood associations, far-sighted real estate developers, and plain old unaffiliated citizens keep the neighborhood spirit alive and provide a foundation for its strength to grow.

Researchers predict that the Portland Metro area will increase to two and one-half million people in the next fifty years, an increase of about one and one-half percent each year. All these new people will have to live somewhere, but we also need to protect forests to clean the air and water (and the spirit), and farmland to feed all these new residents. That's where Metro comes in. Wilkinson says that the role of the Metro government, which comprises Washington, Clackamas, and Multnomah Counties, is "to coordinate the land use policies across the region so that we grow in the direction that the citizens want." This unusual tri-county government helps to protect open spaces, allow for coordinated transportation management, and stabilize development by encouraging population density instead of suburban sprawl.

Metro and the kind of planning it embodies is not without its critics from both sides of the political spectrum. Some citizens complain in the newspapers' letters to the editor about attempts to expand light rail. Developers rankle under the land-use plans, while environmentalists worry that the urban growth boundary actually encourages growth by requiring a certain amount of urban space to be dedicated to development. The best hope is that the competing interests will work in fertile tension with each other. For example, Metro's encouragement of affordable housing and mass transportation have sparked some of the most innovative developments in the nation. Orenco Station, which was built in Hillsboro specifically to take advantage of the light rail line, has been dubbed as "America's Best Master Planned Community" by the National Association of Home Builders. This assemblage of cottages, craftsman retros, and row houses reverberates with an old village way of life. Similarly, highly accoladed projects such as the Belmont Dairy, Irvington Place, and Albina Corner, which reclaimed underused urban space and now provide attractive, mixed-use facilities and affordable housing for lower- and middle-class residents, might never have happened without the productive constraints of land-use planning.

Once again, however, the neighborhoods are key to these kinds of developments. Wilkinson says that "the city of Portland has used the neighborhoods as the basis for developing comprehensive planning tools, which seems to be working really well." Some, but not all, of the Outlying Areas make use of the neighborhood spirit to encourage smart development. Newer developments may lack the strong identity that the city neighborhoods possess. And they may be less likely to acquire it, since they are often built in a way that does not foster community interaction. However, there are notable exceptions: Fairview Village, to the east of the city, is renowned for its incorporation of public, commercial, and green spaces, in addition to its pretty houses. Fairview Village also has a school and daycare facilities. Similarly, Canyon Creek in Wilsonville, built by former Metro Council member and developer Don Morrisette, is a planned community of 117 houses designed to be within walking distance of the major employers in Wilsonville. Canyon Creek Meadows also incorporates greenways, leaving unbuilt, for example, at least three acres of forested space. These new developments may mark a trend in the creation of neighborhoods, a trend that profits not just the developers, but the souls of the residents who live in them.

Old or new, upscale or downhome, Portland's neighborhoods embody the genius loci of the city. From the friendly, front-porch lifestyles of St. John's to the funky old Victorian houses of eclectic inner Southeast Portland to the stately manors of the elegant Dunthorpe District, Portland is home to a healthy array of diverse and distinct communities. We have ninety-four formally recognized neighborhoods, and this number doesn't even include the Outlying Areas, ranging from little Fairview Village to major cities such as Vancouver, Washington, all of which are considered part of the greater metropolitan area. This chapter is meant to serve as an overview of Portland Metro area neighborhoods, an overview that we hope will encourage you to explore the neighborhoods for yourselves. In the first section of this chapter we try to give you a feel for Portland's four distinct areas—Southwest, Northwest, Southeast, and North/Northeast, and also to introduce you to Vancouver and at least some of the communities outside Portland's formal borders.

After you've had a look at some of our neighborhoods we'll turn to the topic of real estate, and let you know about ways to find your own place in our beautiful metropolitan area.

Portland's Neighborhoods

Southwest Portland

The heart of Southwest Portland is the downtown area. Not only is it the home of many businesses, cultural organizations, government agencies, and remarkable public spaces, it is also the home of many residents, who like the urbane atmosphere and the proximity to work and nightlife. Naturally, downtown is a paradise for shoppers with department stores such as Nordstrom, Meier & Frank, and Saks Fifth Avenue, as well as the Galleria and Pioneer Place all within several blocks. In the heart of this shopper's mecca, Pioneer Courthouse Square is a popular meeting place and offers a wide range of free, live entertainment during the noon hour. But in spite of the tempting stores, the impressive statues, and the well-designed business towers, nothing defines downtown Portland as well as the Willamette River.

In the early 1970s the city underwent a huge renewal project, ripping apart a four-lane highway along the west bank of the Willamette and transforming it into the beloved riparian oasis known as Tom McCall Waterfront Park. It is the site of numerous concerts, festivals, and celebrations, as well as a showplace for community events. Eight blocks west, Park Blocks, a 25-block boulevard of trees, grass, flowers, fountains, and statues, offers another urban refuge for workers, shoppers, and students. Nearby are many of the city's most important cultural and recreational facilities, including the Portland Art

Museum, the Portland Historical Society, the Performing Arts Center, and the Arlene Schnitzer Concert Hall. Just outside the inner city is Washington Park, home to the Metro Washington Park Zoo, the tranquil Japanese Gardens, the World Forestry Center, and Hoyt Arboretum.

Beyond the park's boundaries to the south and west are several of the most established, picturesque, and tree-lined of all the city's neighborhoods. Collectively referred to as the "West Hills," each of these neighborhoods nonetheless has distinctive features. For example, Arlington Heights, one of Portland's most scenic neighborhoods, and just west of downtown, above the city center, gives residents easy access to the spectacular Portland Rose Test Gardens and all of Washington Park. The houses here tend to be older, and the architecture diverse—one house is a miniature replica of Canterbury Castle, in England. Arlington Heights's neighbor, Portland Heights, is also a veritable museum of architectural styles. Ranging from Victorian cottages to the latest contemporary dwellings, these houses are graced by lovely gardens and spectacular views. Nestled amidst the Southwest hills, Council Crest affords extraordinary views of both the city and the western valleys. Further west, on the other side of the hills, you'll find Multnomah Village, named by *Money Magazine* as one of Portland's best neighborhoods. This charming neighborhood offers the grace of older houses and the vitality of the newer ones; but all houses are tempered by a hint of the rural past—it wasn't formally annexed until 1954, and some of the most desirable houses yet repose on unpaved roads. Multnomah Village itself is a notable shopping and business district that offers a congenial center to village life. (See our Shopping chapter.)

Insiders' Tip

If you are buying a house in the metro area, check and make sure that the house is on the sewer lines. If it isn't, be aware that the installation and hook-up fees may easily total $7,000 or $8,000.

More Southwest Neighborhoods
Corbett-Terwilliger and Lair Hill

On a 4-mile-long ribbon of land along the west bank—one of the most scenic segments of the Willamette River—you'll find the Corbett-Terwilliger and Lair Hill neighborhoods, directly south of downtown Portland. Residents here are indirectly responsible for preserving the character of our city: years ago, when urban renewal crept its way to the north end of these older neighborhoods, a backlash resulted in establishment of the South Portland-Lair Hill Historic Conservation District, the first protected historic district in Portland—an appropriate gesture, given that Portland's very first building, a cabin constructed by William Johnson in 1842, was built in what became this neighborhood, near S.W. Gibbs and I-5.

Not all preservation is good, however, and not all renewal bad. A section of the area's riverfront is in the process of converting from heavy industry to residential development.

Hillsdale Neighborhood

Hillsdale is just 3 miles from downtown Portland, but its location atop the Southwest Hills gives it an almost rural feel. Hillsdale's commercial district evolved in the 1940s along old dairy-cow pastures, and after the war, as suburban-style houses were built in the area, the virtues of things such as sidewalks were forgotten. Now Hillsdale residents are guiding developments to foster accessibility and community. Southwest Terwilliger Boulevard, one of Portland's favorite scenic routes for bikers, pedestrians, and cars—and the product of community planning efforts—is a hallmark feature along with Oregon Health Sciences University, one of the major employers in the state.

Hayhurst Neighborhood

A unique feature of the Hayhurst neighborhood area is the Alpenrose Dairy, which continues to operate as a dairy as well as a community center offering sports fields, picnic facilities, entertainment, and bicycle racing. In a sense, Portland's most familiar dairy symbolizes the wholesomeness of this middle-class area, which is made up mostly of single-family houses and is creating ways to accommodate growth while preserving its distinctive neighborhood character and livability. Hayhurst School and its nature learning garden and Pendleton Park with its neighborhood planting projects are some of the community-friendly features of this neighborhood.

Goose Hollow

Goose Hollow's name goes back to the 1870s when women who lived there raised flocks of geese near a depression in the land. Early residents of the district were the barons who guided the destiny of the region from its raw pioneer days through the prosperity of the 1890s and the following war years. But while Portland boomed between 1970 and 1990, Goose Hollow slumbered. However, since 1991, Westside light rail and high density planning have spurred unprecedented developments pumping more than $50 million in improvements into the 3.2-square-mile district. Bordered by downtown, Washington Park, the University District, and Burnside Street, the western end of the district is hilly and residential, while the eastern portion is flat and commercial.

Northwest Portland

Across Burnside Street, Northwest Portland (one of the area's most popular places to live) offers panoramic views of the mountains, the Willamette River, and the city itself. Northwest Portland is a delightful blend of old and new and of classic and Bohemian, and community interaction is extremely high in this area as residents and neighbors strive to create a secure and friendly living environment. Northwest Portlanders and visitors alike enjoy boutique shopping, art galleries, coffee, and culture within easy walking distance. Exceptionally well-built and beautifully reconditioned Victorian houses, huge fir trees, and lush parks and gardens provide an old-world feel. Though many of its three-story Victorian estates have been converted into condominiums, Northwest Portland has retained its elegance and appeal. The numerous shops on Northwest 21st and 23rd Avenues offer unusual and distinctive wares, though chain stores like Pottery Barn and the Gap are slowly encroaching. Still, this is one of the toniest areas of the city—also one of the most densely populated.

Excellent hospital facilities, fine schools, many banks, good grocery stores, and a highly efficient public transit system that includes the new streetcar system add to the desirability of Northwest Portland. Possessing a wide range of socioeconomic diversity, the area supports an impressive variety of employment, volunteer, and recreation opportunities. And it's moments away from Washington and Forest Parks, as well as downtown.

More Northwest Neighborhoods

Pearl District

Money Magazine designated the Pearl District as one of the best places to live in the best city to live in. This comes as a surprise to some old-timers. Not long ago, the area was a grimy, downtown neighborhood that was showing its years. Today it is in transition from an underused industrial warehousing area to one of the most fashionable locations in the close-in city. Extensive renovations and adaptive use of historical and other structures have led to lofts, row houses, new restaurants, theaters, art galleries, and a burst of new retail activity. Also, a flurry of important new urban creative-commerce entrepreneurs, ranging from small Internet service providers to internationally known advertising and multimedia companies, are staking out territory here.

In addition, the Pacific Northwest College of Art, PICA, and other arts organizations chose the Pearl as their home, as well. Well-clad entrepreneurs sip coffee next to spiky-haired students; art supply stores and antique shops vie for attention; cool lofts with cityscape views perch above truck-loading ramps. The atmosphere in the Pearl is a heady brew of past and future productively engaging. Watch for important new retail and residential developments on the site of the old Henry Weinhard brewery (the "Brewery Blocks" development), between Burnside and N.W. Davis, as well as an innovative restoration project by Ecotrust. The latter, the Jean Vollum Natural Capital Center, 907 N.W. Irving, is set to hold a major Patagonia retailer in addition to other shops and offices. This restored brick building is constructed with eco-friendly timber and energy efficient spaces. Its roof is planted with native vegetation that keeps the building cool and filters rainwater.

The Pearl District draws urbanites young and old, but not as many families with children. That may change as developers continue to reclaim industrial areas like the Hoyt Street railyards. But the work in progress here should give hope to cities everywhere.

Linnton

The great documenter of Oregon, Ralph Friedman, writes that the co-founder of Linnton, Peter Burnett, foretold that Linnton would one day "be the great commercial town of the territory." Peter Burnett went on to be elected the first governor of California, which is telling. Linnton was platted in 1843; at the time, its location near forest and river seemed preferable to the flooding swamp of Portland. By the time it incorporated, in 1910, the bustling town had its own train service, two newspapers, and a jail. In 1921, the plywood mills employed more than 1,000 workers, but that prosperity came to a halt during the Depression, and then was killed beyond recovery during the 1940s, when fires burned down the mills. Things got worse as the century crept along, when trucks began to replace railroads as the favored means of transportation, and, in a concomitant development, Linnton's business district was demolished to make way for a larger road.

Today, however, Linnton is being rediscovered and its property is among the newly desirable. New houses are being built on the hillside and younger families are moving in. The neighborhood association is considering a master plan that will guide the proposed developments along the coveted riverfront area.

Old Town-Chinatown Neighborhood

As its name implies, Old Town-Chinatown is one of the pioneer neighborhoods of Portland. Besides serving as the Chinese District, the city's early docks and railroad station were teeming with sailors on shore leave and loggers from the nearby woods, creating colorful—if rowdy—city scenes.

This neighborhood, between the core business district to the south and the sports and convention area east across the river, serves as a gateway to downtown

Portland. Art, music, culture, great ethnic food, unique architecture, small businesses, major corporations, and residents of all income levels thrive here. Numerous social service agencies harmoniously coexist with for-profit businesses. The diversity of the residential population is reflected in the housing, which ranges from single-resident hotels to upper-end apartments and lofts.

The Chinese and Japanese cultural roots of the area are manifested in old buildings as well as new developments, particularly in the Classical Chinese Garden on N.W. 3rd and Everett.

Southeast Portland

The Eastside of Portland has seen a renaissance during the last decade, with expansive renovation, busy commercial activity, and general vigor igniting the return to the city of many former suburbanites and the reclamation of the city by confirmed urbanites who always understood the virtues of established neighborhoods with beautiful parks, good schools, and appealing architecture, especially in the close-in neighborhoods. These neighborhoods offer a reduced commute time and greater access to cultural life than the suburbs. The Hawthorne and nearby Belmont Districts, which are subdivided into many distinctive neighborhoods such as Richmond, Sunnyside, and Buckman, are filled with single-family houses and mixed-use apartment buildings. Bakeries, coffeehouses, boutiques, music and bookstores, micro-pubs, and restaurants are within walking distance of many homes, buses run frequently, and street life is abundant. Historic Sellwood is known for its "Antique Row," composed of more than fifty antique stores tucked into the neighborhood of Victorian houses and turn-of-the-century architecture. Where Sellwood meets the river, you'll find Oaks Bottom, home to the Oaks Bottom Wildlife Sanctuary, a refuge for herons, beavers, ducks, and other marsh animals and birds. Here, the neighborhood floats in houseboats along the river's edge. Sellwood is also renowned for its strong community spirit. Westmoreland is graced with one of the city's most beautiful parks, while Eastmoreland's residential neighborhood, across McLoughlin Avenue, is quiet and tranquil, bordered by the lush Eastmoreland Golf Course, Reed College, Crystal Springs Lake, and the Crystal Springs Rhododendron Gardens.

More Southeast Neighborhoods

Ardenwald-Johnson Creek Neighborhoods

Overlooking the Willamette River and bounded by several creeks, the scenic Ardenwald-Johnson Creek neighborhood lies between Portland and the pioneer river town of Milwaukie, and is a part of Clackamas and Multnomah Counties. The neighborhood sits on a bluff and most houses are modest post–World War II structures, but the area was originally settled on land donation claims in the 1800s.

The Johnson family, among the earliest settlers and the namesake of Johnson Creek, is still active in efforts to maintain the creek, which is known for its untamed rampages in the springtime.

The Springwater Corridor Trail, one of the area's greatest natural amenities, the Tideman Johnson Park, and the Milwaukie riverfront are a few of the noteworthy features that lend character to these neighborhoods. Housing in this area affords a wide range of styles and prices.

Hosford-Abernethy

Also called Ladd's Addition, this neighborhood was settled in the mid-1800s. In the southeast sector, Hosford-Abernethy is one of Portland's oldest neighborhoods. The Ladd tract—one of the nation's first planned communities, with sidewalks, paved streets, electricity, and a streetcar line—began developing early in

Average House Prices by Area

N. Portland	$124,500
N.E. Portland	$169,800
S.E. Portland	$153,900
Gresham/Troutdale	$174,500
Milwaukie/Clackamas	$189,200
Oregon City/Canby	$188,700
Lake Oswego/West Linn	$325,700
West Portland	$293,300
N.W. Washington County	$262,200
Beaverton/Aloha	$182,500
Tigard/Wilsonville	$211,900
Hillsboro/Forest Grove	$172,600

(Figures are from RMLS)

1900. After World War II, many of the residents abandoned the neighborhood in favor of the suburbs and the area declined. In the 1970s and again more recently in the past decade, hundreds of historic houses were restored, bringing back its sense of neighborhood, and now it might be considered an exemplar of good planning. One hundred years later, this neighborhood has some of the most valuable property in the city.

Retail storefronts, schools, parks, churches, community gardens, movie houses, live theater, restaurants, and coffee shops are within easy walking distance, but the centerpiece is still Ladd Circle's beautiful rose garden, which provides the neighborhood with a meeting place and a focus.

Hawthorne Boulevard

Southeast Portland's hip Hawthorne Boulevard supports a thriving district that is throbbing with activity. Here, high-density housing meshes beautifully with retail activity, fashioning one of the city's premier shopping and living districts. Pedestrian-friendly and lined with gift stores, period clothing shops, distinctive restaurants, a musician's treasure chest, and cafes, rental and housing costs have spiked here in recent years. However, this has not stemmed the area's popularity. This district is bordered by the Central Eastside Industrial District, home to the Oregon Museum of Science and Industry and industrial plants that provide 20,000 jobs.

Hawthorne Boulevard ends at the base of Mount Tabor, an extinct volcano and one of the city's most beloved parks. The four Mount Tabor reservoirs hold a large portion of Portland's drinking water, piped straight from the pristine Bull Run Reservoir. The park is blessed with an abundance of picnic tables, trails, bike paths, and stands of old growth Douglas firs and other trees. Its panoramic view of downtown and the West Hills should not be missed, especially at sunset.

Lents

One of the largest of Portland's neighborhoods, Lents is named after Oliver Perry Lents, a stone mason who came to Oregon in the 1850s to farm a 190-acre land claim. In the past two decades the district fell on hard times as properties deteriorated and property crime soared. But positive efforts are now restoring the area's livability. Several businesses have completed storefront renovations and city agencies are providing assistance with economic development strategies to restore the community's vitality. Also, habitat restoration is improving Springwater Corridor and plans are in the works for a one hundred-acre parcel to be developed as an employment center and to provide housing.

The thirty-eight-acre Lents Park recently received a major overhaul, and is now one of the most popular recreation sites in the city. Its amenities include a basketball court, lighted softball, baseball, football and soccer fields, tennis court, picnic facilities, jogging track, playground, stadium, wading pool, and restrooms.

North/Northeast Portland

Many Oregonians regard this section of Portland as an area of tremendous opportunity. Here, Portlanders are rightfully proud of their old, well-established neighborhoods featuring lovely houses and elegant, historic mansions. And that pride has been refreshed, since many intense redevelopment activities are pumping new life and vitality into this section of the city, making it a more exciting and appealing place to live, work, and visit.

Beautiful older houses line the tree-shaded streets in the Northeast neighborhoods of Laurelhurst, Irvington, and Alameda. Some of the houses in the Alameda neighborhood, especially those along the periphery of the ridge, afford breathtaking views of the Willamette River and the downtown skyline.

Attractive shopping areas draw people from around the region, and so does Portland's Convention Center, between the Lloyd District and the river. The MAX train stops outside the center's north entrance and also serves the adjacent Rose Quarter, a forty-three-acre complex featuring the Memorial Coliseum arena, the Rose Garden arena, One Center Court entertainment complex and four parking garages. The Rose Quarter hosts a variety of sports events, including the Portland Trailblazers, the Portland Winter Hawks, college basketball, and indoor soccer. Around Lloyd Center, the Northeast Broadway Business District is blossoming, and just east, the delightful Hollywood District offers a wonderful blend of affordable housing, tasteful retail businesses, and small shops.

Other neighborhoods further north, such as Hayden Island, St. Johns, and Kenton offer their own distinctive charms. These areas, rich in character and history, are blessed with many well-tended parks and green spaces.

More North Portland Neighborhoods
Overlook Neighborhood

Nestled along a high bluff above the Swan Island industrial area and Willamette River Overlook in North Portland, the Overlook neighborhood was once the home of many shipyard workers. Today it has drawn a diverse ethnic population, reflected in an elementary school population, among whom 22 percent study English as a second language.

This historically rich district is home to the historic Kaiser Town Hall, a cherished neighborhood meeting place; popular Overlook Park; Saint Stanislaus Church and Polish Hall, the site of a yearly festival and repository of cultural heritage; the Interstate Firehouse Cultural Center, a recycled firehouse used for a wide variety of community activities; and the Overlook Community Center.

Bridgeton

The first bridges over the Columbia River crossed here, giving Bridgeton its name. Local anglers once moored their boats in little floating shanties that later gentrified into Bridgeton's delightful floating houses. The Columbia River outpost is now rebuilding itself as a dense urban community as houses built in the 1920s along a streetcar line for local meat-packing plant workers are being replaced with townhouses, hotels, condos, and commercial buildings. The old-timers are working together with their new neighbors to create a healthy living environment, and to keep the waterways a refuge for wildlife and native plants as well as people. Bridgeton is working to accommodate higher density development slated for this area, using zoning tools such as design review to maximum advantage.

St. Johns-Cathedral Park Neighborhood

At the tip of the North Portland peninsula near the confluence of the Columbia and Willamette Rivers lies Cathedral Park and adjacent St. Johns, one of Portland's oldest communities. Once an independent village, it still has the feel of a small community, especially in its bustling retail district. The industrial area surrounding St. Johns is a source of employment for residents, but also a point of conflict as the community struggles to protect its livability and adjacent natural resources. The St. Johns Bridge, the prize jewel of Portland's bridges, is the area's most visible landmark and the graceful arches of its base give Cathedral Park its name. The popular park represents a ten-year effort by the locals to preserve some of the riverfront for public use. The area is also home to Smith and Bybee Lakes, both unique natural and recreational resources.

More Northeast Neighborhoods
Central Northeast Neighborhoods

The Central Northeast neighborhoods consist of nine sprawling neighborhoods, three distinct business districts, and the 50,000 people who live and work there. This colorful section of the city boasts a rich history and includes a contrasting blend of semi-rural areas and intensely urban ones, and a diverse and multicultural population.

A few of the highlights include the Southeast Asian Vicariate, the cultural hub of the area's Southeast Asian population; the historic and wonderfully refurbished Hollywood Theater, namesake of its neighborhood and a community restoration project; the Villa de Clara Vista, a housing project for the Latino population; and East Columbia, a farming community on the Columbia River. Also, The Grotto, a religious retreat and a place of quiet beauty and solitude, is one of the city's foremost attractions.

Piedmont Neighborhood

Piedmont, which was originally connected to Portland by the streetcar line, was originally developed as Portland's first suburban community—and a bit of a snooty one at that. Renters were discouraged, and no commercial activity was allowed in the district. Lovely Edwardian houses are a feature of the neighborhood.

Piedmont's character changed during World War II, as Kaiser began to employ shipbuilders, who flocked to the pretty, nearby houses in Piedmont and either bought them or rented them. Although this solid neighborhood was once a popular choice for starter houses, its stability was disrupted by the recession of the 1980s and a wave of crime problems. Thankfully, the area is enjoying an unprecedented rejuvenation as a wide range of community development projects are underway. These include foot patrols, landlord training seminars, concerts in Peninsula Park, a first-time homebuyer's club, and other projects that promote property improvements.

Concordia Neighborhood

A large, northeast Portland neighborhood dating back to the turn of the century, Concordia was once considered a suburb. Though it fell on hard times during the 1970s and 1980s, it is re-emerging as a diverse, healthy, urban neighborhood, and in the past two years, improvement projects have been implemented up and down the avenues. Thanks to the efforts of the neighborhood association and enterprising entrepreneurs, the commercial spine of this area, Alberta Street, is emerging once again as a vital, thriving artery. Concordia University, for which the neighborhood was named, is just 3 miles from downtown and continues to play an important role in the area's positive changes.

A showcase of these positive developments is the old Kennedy School, a neighborhood landmark since 1915. Declared surplus decades ago by the school district, the building slowly deteriorated over the years as competing interests wondered what to do with it. Portland's McMenamin brothers solved the problem by converting it into a huge attraction, complete with two brewpubs, a bed-and-breakfast inn, and a movie house. (See Brewpubs and Bed and Breakfast Inns.) The beneficial effects of the Kennedy School development have helped to revive the real estate market in the area, and have spilled over into nearby neighborhoods.

Sabin Neighborhood

The 1993 Neighborhood USA Neighborhood of the Year, Sabin is another highly diverse residential neighborhood comprised of mostly older houses. In recent years, the nonprofit Sabin Community Development Corp. has developed more than one hundred units of housing for very low-income families in the area.

In other endeavors, Sabin hosted Portland's first multicultural festival and stages an annual Alberta Street Festival on the revitalized Alberta Corridor. There is a new mood in Sabin, and the tree plantings and murals add to the friendliness and attractiveness of the area. Retail activity is starting to take off, and urban pioneers are buying their first houses in this area, where handsome old houses may still be reasonably priced.

Insiders' Tip

Besides lower rent and easier parking, one of the pluses of Eastside apartment living is the easy access to MAX, Portland's light rail system. But the MAX line works for everyone: Portland Realtors say that their East Coast clients want to find houses within walking distance of the MAX line.

Eliot Neighborhood

Formerly the city of Albina, which was established in 1872 and annexed to Portland in 1891, the Eliot neighborhood in inner Northeast Portland started out as a community of European immigrants. Today it is one of the foremost residential and cultural centers of the African-American community.

From 1960 to 1990 the area lost more than half its housing to urban renewal projects, conversion to business and institutional use, and neglect, but the Albina Community Plan is helping it to rebound. The Eliot neighborhood is increasing its density and restoring its population and it also received a commitment from the city to end conversion of housing land to other uses.

Hazelwood/Gateway Neighborhood

Saddled atop the old Barlow Trail, one of the earliest pioneer routes across the Cascade Mountains into Portland, is Hazelwood. This neighborhood stretches throughout east Portland on both sides of Burnside, and most of the area's housing was built during the post–World War II development boom of 1946 to 1960. Some of these developments include high-quality projects such as Cherry Blossom Park. Hazelwood, like most of the outer east area, remained unincorporated until it was annexed to Portland in the 1980s.

This has been a combined blessing and a curse as it allowed the community to acquire new urban services, but also forced it to adapt to a new political system and absorb new development at a fast pace. The old pioneer trails are only a memory, as MAX light rail now cuts a swath through the heart of the district. Other distinctive features include the new East Portland Police Precinct, Midland Branch Library, the Gateway Apartments mixed-use project, Midland Park with plantings by local students, and the blossoming Gateway business area.

Vancouver

In the blink of an eye, Vancouver increased in size from 26 square miles to more than 44 square miles and nearly doubled its population from 68,000 residents to 128,000. At the stroke of midnight on January 1, 1997, with the Eastside annexation, Vancouver, which sits across the Columbia River directly north of Portland, became the fourth largest city in the state of Washington and the second largest city in the Portland metropolitan region.

The seat of Clark County, Vancouver is one of the fastest-growing regions in the United States. This burgeoning high-tech port and city, with a current population of 135,000, was established as a fur-trading center by the Hudson's Bay Company in 1825. The trading post and historic Fort Vancouver, surrounded by a fertile plain, soon became the commercial center for the Pacific Northwest. Although neighboring Portland's superior port facilities made it the leading city of the area, Vancouver's role remained essential to the economy and character of the region. While its suburbs exploded in the early part of the decade, the downtown area declined. More recently, boosted in part by the booming Port of Vancouver, the heart of downtown Vancouver is beginning to revive. In the next two decades, it is expected to be transformed by nearly $1 billion of investment in new housing, offices, retail space, and public amenities.

Outlying Areas

West of Portland

Beaverton

Midway between Mount Hood and the Oregon coast, Beaverton is 7 miles west of downtown Portland in Washington County at the crossroads of U.S. Highway 26 and OR Highway 217. With a population of nearly 68,000, and its status as the largest city in Washington County (total population of almost 400,000), this suburb of Portland is coming into its own as a mini-metropolis.

Spread over 15 square miles, the town features many shopping areas, including Beaverton Mall, Beaverton Town Square, and Washington Square. Tree-lined streets highlight the clean neighborhoods while a 25-mile network of bike paths and trails connect its well-groomed playgrounds and green spaces. Building activity is vigorous.

In the city itself, there are one hundred parks—one within a half mile of every house—encompassing 1,000 acres and offering 30 miles of hiking trails. Beaverton is relatively prosperous and its school district is one of the most esteemed in the state. However, the major traffic artery leading to Beaverton, U.S. Highway 26, or the "Sunset Highway," becomes quite congested, particularly during peak traffic hours.

Hillsboro

Incorporated in 1876, the city of Hillsboro has grown from a tiny farming community into a modern city of 70,000 residents. Originally called Hillsborough, the city was named for David Hill, one of the pioneers who crossed the Oregon Trail and became one of the state's original legislators.

About twenty minutes due west of Portland, Hillsboro is spread out over 19 square miles in the heart of the Tualatin Valley, which is named after the river from the Indian name, "Twality," which means "lazy river." Today, as the seat of Washington County in the heart of one of Oregon's booming high-tech communities, Hillsboro is far from lazy. It lies within the 9,000-acre Sunset Corridor, Oregon's fastest-growing economic development region. Fast becoming the nation's center of parallel processing computer products, a number of impressive facilities have sprung up in Hillsboro, including one of the highest quality corporate parks in the United States: 319-acre Dawson Creek Park, which contains seven lakes with fountains and promenades and more than 5 miles of pedestrian and bicycle trails.

Tigard and Tualatin

Tigard and Tualatin are the southwest outposts of the metro area, both characterized by major new commercial, industrial, high-tech, and residential development. Nearly 40,000 residents live in Tigard; many commute to Portland, but others work in nearby electronics or computer firms. It's a young town—a third of its residents fall in the twenty to forty-four age demographic. Tualatin had 750 residents in 1970. It now has well over 20,000, the great majority of whom arrived between 1990 and 1999, when the city grew by more than 45 percent. Its gazillion new housing developments are big hits with families—there are more children than twenty to forty-four year-old adults here. As with Tigard, many people find work close to home in business services, manufacturing, and other modern forms of employment; there also remains a great deal of agricultural work in the area.

East of Portland

Fairview

Incorporated in 1908, this scenic east county town is just off the Columbia River and near Sandy Boulevard and Interstate 84. Landmarks of this charming village

Portland neighborhoods offer a sweet blend of urban and rural streetscapes. CREDIT: RACHEL DRESBECK

include Fairview Lake and popular Blue Lake State Park (see our Kidstuff chapter for children's activities in the park). The planned housing community of Fairview Village—a showcase of single family houses, row houses, and duplexes—is inside city limits, as is a vintage Grange Hall. The 6,000 residents now have a new grade school and post office to be proud of, a new city hall is currently being built, and a library branch is in the planning stages. Fairview, wedged between the city limits of both Portland and Gresham, has a distinct flavor of its own, accentuated by the river, lakes, and forests.

Gresham

Once a land of berry fields and farmland, Gresham has blossomed into a bustling city of more than 90,000 residents while still retaining its small-town appeal. Now the state's fourth largest city, Gresham sits at the east end of the MAX light rail system, providing its residents with cheap, efficient transportation into downtown Portland. Situated in eastern Multnomah County and encompassing 22.5 square miles, Gresham is the gateway to the Columbia Gorge, and Oregon's year-round playground, Mount Hood National Forest. Its downtown area is particularly appealing and easy to navigate. Colorful, pedestrian-friendly, and well-designed, it offers a wide variety of restaurants, retail shops, and services in a concentrated area. Gresham also maintains an excellent educational system. Every August, Gresham hosts the famous Mt. Hood Festival of Jazz, which has showcased such renowned performers as Ella Fitzgerald, The Manhattan Transfer, and Anita Baker (see our Festivals and Annual Events chapter).

South of Portland

Lake Oswego and West Linn

These two riverside residential cities are pretty and quiet, with reputations for fine schools and well-to-do inhabitants. Lake Oswego, with a population of about 35,000, is known for its older English cottage- and Tudor-style houses built in the first half of the twentieth century, but today, most people live in contemporary houses, many of which are in developments. However, you can find the vestiges of its sleepy rural history evident in the properties that still boast horse pastures and chicken coops. The neighborhood associations are busy and active. Lake Oswego is alluring to many people, but there's only so much of it to go around, so its neighbor West Linn has seen much growth in the past decade. In fact, it's grown about 40 percent since 1970—but its residents still number only about 22,000 people. Both towns are a short commute from downtown Portland, traffic permitting.

Oregon City

This legendary and historic city 10 miles south of Portland was founded in 1844. Oregon City was the first incorporated city west of the Rocky Mountains and when the city of San Francisco was originally platted, its papers had to be filed at the federal courthouse in Oregon City. Because the town awaited at the end of the Oregon Trail, and because Oregon City was the place where pioneers refreshed and restocked before traveling to their new farms south in the Willamette Valley, it became known as "Pioneer City."

For decades, the city thrived as a mill town, but today its economy is becoming much more diversified and its population of 20,000 is swelling rapidly. Housing developments seem to be springing up in its outlying areas almost overnight.

The downtown area, nestled on the banks of the Willamette River, is still a beehive of commercial, retail, and community activity. The Oregon City High School girl's basketball team is legendary for its phenomenal success, having racked up consecutive state championships and national titles in recent years.

Milwaukie-Gladstone

Small-town charm, life on the waterfront, easy access to big city amenities—all of these describe Milwaukie, "the City of Dogwoods." Situated between Oregon City and Portland on Oregon Highways 99 East and 224 in Clackamas County, Milwaukie, a city with more than 20,000 residents, was recently named as one of the fifty best places in the nation to raise a family. Milwaukie and neighboring Gladstone (population 12,000) provide clean environments, thriving job markets, good transportation, excellent schools and health care, and many cultural and recreational opportunities. Many shopping centers, industries, and commercial businesses flourish near this modest to upscale area, which is also the home of the Bomber, an authentic World War II B17G bomber that has been meticulously restored and is one of the best known landmarks in the region.

North of Portland

Camas

Established in 1883 when a mill, surrounded by towering Douglas-fir trees, was built on the banks of the Columbia River, Camas lies just east of Vancouver in Washington. Now better known for its explosive growth than for its reputation as a mill town, this city was named for the Camas Lily, a staple in the diet of the Chinooks, the native inhabitants. Although it remained a small and peaceful river town for a century, the explosive growth of the Portland-Vancouver Metro area is leading Camas and its twenty neighborhood associations to rapid changes.

The city's picturesque past blends interestingly with the high technology developments of recent years. In this pretty river town's downtown area, old landmarks combine with new developments, creating thriving neighborhoods that are adorned by a magnificent view of Mount Hood.

Real Estate

If you are new to Oregon and looking to buy a house in the Portland area, you may be in for sticker shock. People really like living in this area and houses in the Portland Metro area are priced significantly higher than the national average. It is becoming increasingly difficult to find a decent house in the city for less than $150,000.

This trend of high-priced real estate isn't exactly new to Portland. The cost of housing in the metro area increased by 50 percent between 1991 and 1995, and in the past five years the median price (meaning as many houses were sold above that price as below it) of a house in the Portland area increased to $168,000 in 2000, from $97,000 in 1992. Residential real estate sales totaled $4.9 billion in 2000, an increase of $100 million from 1999 and a record-breaking year for real estate dollar volume. The housing market's appreciation rate in 2000 was a slower but healthy 5.3 percent.

The real estate market is gently decelerating. Though the prices of houses have increased, their rate of sale actually slowed a little in 2000, down by 3.1 percent. Also, housing analysts believe that the lower mortgage rates will make more houses affordable to more people. While this is good news for buyers, don't look for the bottom to fall out of Portland's housing market any time soon. All indicators—such as low interest rates, low levels of unemployment, and a generally healthy and diversified economy—point to a strong, stable housing and real estate market. Portland-area housing prices are expected to continue rising in the next few years, though not at the double-digit rate of recent times.

All things considered, Portland's housing picture is a good one, affording shelter in price ranges to accommodate most styles of life. An abundance of small, older houses is on the market, and new house, apartment, and condo construction is underway almost everywhere you look. Mortgage rates are falling, and some houses with motivated owners will always be priced to sell. But you are going to have to look hard or be lucky to find a bargain—the droves of people moving into the area are keeping competition in house hunting very stiff.

The upside is that the market is stable, vibrant, and still affords nice, appreciable profits for house sellers as well as offering good values for savvy buyers.

Like the city of Portland itself, that market is basically broken into quadrants—Northwest, Southwest, Southeast, and Northeast—with additional suburban neighborhoods and Outlying Areas offering many choices and options for housebuyers or investors.

Southwest Portland

With city center as its hub, the Southwest area features every different kind of housing opportunity you could imagine. Downtown has single family residences, duplexes, and triplex housing, and all kinds of condominiums; many having glorious views and all the amenities you could ask for. Prices usually begin at a little less than $200,000 and run into the millions of dollars. Outside of downtown, the inner Southwest area in general, features woodsier settings than the Eastside, with lots that tend to be larger than those found across the river. The Westside is also more expensive—median prices here are about $229,000. Perhaps the most prestigious area is Portland Heights, featuring large, older houses with spectacular views starting at more than $300,000. Council Crest, which borders Portland Heights, is another upscale, established neighborhood with fantastic views.

The Southwest Hills, Raleigh Hills, Bridlemile, Burlingame, and Multnomah Village areas are some of the other Southwest options, each with a wide variety of old and new construction offering an array of choices for home owners. You can find small starter houses for less than $200,000. Goose Hollow, Lair Hill, and the Johns Landing area feature an eclectic mix of older houses with architectural charm, as well as an explosion of condominiums, row houses, and town houses, many with views of the Willamette River. The prices of houses here reflect their architectural diversity.

Other Southwest Portland possibilities include the Corbett-Terwilliger and Lair-Hill neighborhoods, where fine bungalows and smaller Victorian houses sell at prices beginning about $200,000, though sometimes you can find them for less. Or more—some hilltop houses in the southern end of this area afford magnificent views of the Willamette River. Hillsdale and Hayhurst, like much of the area, have many fine houses on big lots starting at about $200,000; these neighborhoods have a slightly suburban feel to them.

Northwest Portland

No area in the city has seen higher appreciating values than the Northwest District. An urban treasure of wonderful older architecture abounds here—including Old Portland, Victorian, Georgian, Colonial, and Bungalow styles—and most of the single-family residences have starting prices at $200,000. There is also a wide choice of condominiums and row houses available, some newly built, as well as older houses radiating charm and character that have been subdivided into smaller units.

The Northwest neighborhoods also include tony Forest Heights and Kings Heights with expensive new houses, most of them in developments with "custom" floor plans and other prepackaged features. In general, the West Hills have most of the seven-digit gated communities. Trees are being felled daily to make room for their mini-mansions, and the forests are toppling like dominos all the way out to the Coast Range. However, the deforestation makes for spectacular views in all directions.

Perhaps the hottest area currently is the Pearl District (see the Neighborhoods section for greater detail), with many older industrial sites converted into residential and combined residential-occupational loft spaces, some quite luxurious.

Insiders' Tip

Want to know more about Portland's neighborhoods? You can get a copy of the Neighborhood Associations Directory from the Portland City Office of Neighborhood Associations at 1220 S.W. 5th Avenue, (503) 823-4519. For a spectacular historical perspective, visit www.ohs.org/cityviews. This splendid site maintained by the Oregon Historical Society provides photos and, in some cases, movies of how your neighborhood appeared one hundred years ago.

Southeast Portland

Southeast Portland features many established neighborhoods with a strong sense of community and median sales prices of $140,000 for the area as a whole. And a lot of people want to live there: the market is busy, with more closed sales in 2000 than any other district in the metro region.

Richmond, Belmont, and Sunnyside are some of the neighborhoods along or near Hawthorne (see Neighborhoods section); the market here is hot, the houses for sale are scarce, and when they do come up for sale, they sell in three hours. But you can still find beautiful houses for less than $200,000—if you pounce. The desirable Mt. Tabor area has a wider variety of houses in price and style, and at its heart is Mt. Tabor Park, which sits on an old dormant volcano and has splendid views of Mount Hood as well as downtown. The architecturally consistent Eastmoreland has, perhaps, the most luxurious houses. Home to a lush golf course, Eastmoreland borders the stately brick and ivy Reed College and showcases older, magnificent houses, many on large lots that are priced in the $300,000 to $500,000 range and up. Its large canopy of trees and distinctive street layout add to its appeal. *Money Magazine* designated Sellwood, the south border of the city, as a top neighborhood in Portland. You will find a mix of housing styles, ranging from modern row houses to pioneer homesteads and stately houses that overlook the river. Prices vary, of course, but you can still find good values, some in the $100,000 to $150,000 range.

The Buckman area, South Tabor, Woodstock, Brooklyn, Montavilla, and Mall 205 neighborhoods feature more modest houses with smaller price tags. These areas are near good schools and plenty of shopping areas and are a great option for those on a budget or seeking starter houses. Also, older houses in the Hosford-Abernethy area tend to be below Portland's overall median price (though its immediately adjacent neighbor Ladd's Addition features houses far beyond the median price). Even lower in price are the houses in Lents (see the Neighborhoods section).

North and Northeast Portland

The Northeast section, where median house prices were $149,000 in 2000, is famous for its older, established neighborhoods of friendly, involved communities. Many lavish and expensive houses preserve the features of days gone by. Alameda, Laurelhurst, and Irvington are all just minutes from downtown and near the flourishing Lloyd Mall Shopping Center; here you will find some of the most beautiful houses in town, with prices that reflect their desirability. Alameda and Irvington not only have some of the best real estate in town, but they also have thriving commercial districts—particularly along the prosperous N.E. Broadway Corridor—that add character to the neighborhood. You can find some of the city's finest shops and restaurants here; the schools tend to be very good, and the residents cosmopolitan (see the listings above for more information on these neighborhoods). Laurelhurst is more residential but bordered by great commercial avenues—Belmont and Hawthorne to the south, N.E. Broadway to the north—and has as its centerpiece lush Laurelhurst Park. Laurelhurst, Alameda, and Irvington tend to be more expensive than other Eastside neighborhoods, but within each area you will find a variety of houses, and there are still deals for those handy with a paint brush and wood stripper.

You can find bargains in many inner Northeast neighborhoods, where small, starter houses stick to the $100,000 range. (The average cost of a house in Northeast Portland is about $170,000, but can range anywhere from $50,000 to $500,000—for more information, see the Neighborhoods section, which discusses some of the community development housing projects.)

Everyone is welcome in the community playhouse at Sherrit Square in Sellwood. CREDIT: RACHEL DRESBECK

You'll most likely find $100,000-range houses in Irvington Heights, the popular Boise and Sabin areas, Beaumont and Wilshire, and Parkrose. Rose City, surrounding one of the area's most popular golf courses, has seen housing costs skyrocket in the last couple of years, but still has reasonable prices for its many charming post-war bungalows. Many great houses in all price ranges surround Glendoveer, another Northeast golf course. We've heard more than a few Realtors say that this area is full of good values.

Eliot has seen significant new housing development, positive new retail ventures, and the refurbishing of its historic older housing stock. In this area it is not unusual to see two or more vintage houses on the same block undergoing a restoration. Realtors are beginning to refer to this neighborhood as "trendy," which translates into "appreciating." But many bargains are available here—it's very popular with first-time owners, and the love they are lavishing on their new houses is paying off. In the far east neighborhood of Hazelwood there is a mix of affordable new and old houses, with prices ranging from $75,000 to $175,000 and new apartment complexes are springing up along the light rail. The Hollywood District is a particularly appealing area characterized by an exceptionally wide range of ethnic restaurants, small businesses, and eclectic housing styles. Hollywood has been the focus of major urban renewal projects in recent years.

North Portland is the most affordable part of Portland—the median sales price in 2000 was $119,000. North Portland is receiving much attention these days as the next neighborhood due for a major renaissance. A number of neighborhoods, such as Overlook and Arbor Lodge, have wonderful older houses at very reasonable prices, and walking-friendly, tree-lined streets. Housing in Bridgeton offers interesting possibilities and is also among the city's most affordable. North Portland is the home of the University of Portland, and the University area is considered the North's prime neighborhood, with elegant houses and panoramic views of the Willamette River and Swan Island. St. John's, long a steadfast, unpretentious working-class neighborhood, has seen a rising popularity, particularly for new house owners. It's still quite possible to get a nice, smaller house for around $100,000.

Vancouver and Outlying Areas

North of Portland, across the Columbia River, Vancouver is reinventing itself for a new century. Vancouver has sixty-four neighborhoods and the housing prices in this oldest city in Washington state are generally lower than in Portland. But the market is booming, with tract houses and mini-mansions bursting forth from the earth seemingly overnight. During noncommute times, Vancouver is about twenty minutes from downtown Portland; Camas, its suburb to the east, just a few minutes more. The whole of Clark County is ripe with big new houses, some with acreage. Your money will definitely go far here, comparatively speaking.

South of Portland are many other livable communities. Dunthorpe is an unincorporated bit of Valhalla along the west bank of the Willamette. The large trees, lovely views, top-rated schools, and fine estates draw some of Oregon's most influential residents, among them former governors, senators, and ball players. The housing prices here belong in the "if you have to ask, you can't afford it" category.

Just to the south, and long considered the home of many of the finer neighborhoods in the entire metro area, Lake Oswego boasts a quick and scenic commute to downtown Portland as well as many lovely and grand houses. A good number of those houses—especially those commanding the highest price tags—are sprawling lakeside mansions or large, elegant houses with lake views. This postcard-like city is clean and quiet and its school district is considered top-notch. In Lake Oswego, median house prices are the most expensive in the metro area, at $260,000; while some properties are available for less than $200,000, the view, lakeside, and country club properties cost millions of dollars. The area also boasts a multitude of condominiums, particularly in the Mountain Park area, with one-bedroom condos going for about $100,000.

Like many of the newly developing "hot spot" communities in and around Portland, West Linn essentially started as an old farming and ranching community and, for a long time, was considered Lake Oswego's poorer cousin. In more recent years, the area has seen an explosion of new construction, taking advantage of the wonderfully lush countryside, and many houses are situated on over-size lots. No longer anyone's poor relation, real estate prices in West Linn have been steadily rising; they are similarly priced to Lake Oswego's, though you can still find houses for around $160,000. Of course these prices go up, depending on the amenities inside the house, location, and lot size.

The largest community outside of Portland's city limits, Beaverton features a wide array of housing, from small houses to lavish mansions, as well as many condominiums. An average house in Beaverton sells for around $182,500. The western edge of Beaverton, as with all the outer Southwest communities, is undergoing a development boom, with thousands of condominiums and single-family dwellings—and the Home Depots, Targets, and Olive Gardens to support them—erected in the blink of an eye where yesterday the horses were pastured and the strawberries grew.

Situated around Intel and the many newer high-tech industrial parks, Aloha and Hillsboro are also booming with new construction, and many older, established neighborhoods in these cities are loaded with cute, affordable houses. In the Hillsboro area, a median-priced house sells for $159,400. Tigard, Tualatin, and Wilsonville are experiencing similar breathtaking development of entire villages of houses with three-car garages.

The median price in these communities is higher, running to about $189,600. Although not far from Portland proper, the commute from all these towns can be a grind, especially if it in anyway involves the Sunset Highway (U.S. Highway 26). Enough development is happening, however, that you might be able to find a job on the Westside and obviate the commute problem.

East of Portland, Gresham is the largest area outside Portland's city limits, and the once working-class and farm neighborhood has—like everywhere—seen an amazing amount of growth, while still retaining some of its wide-open appeal. Gresham provides a good blend of old and newer housing (median price is $160,500), with many affordable houses. Beyond Gresham are the rural and scenic towns of Boring and Sandy, with many houses on big spreads, for those looking to start their own "Bonanza." Many of the newer houses are priced around the $200,000 range, but there's acreage to be had for a good price.

The Clackamas area, home of the still thriving Clackamas Town Center shopping area, is also buzzing with new construction activity, and subdivisions, featuring the typical "three-bedroom, two-bath, double-car garage" family-oriented houses, are sprouting up overnight here as well. Median prices in this area are about $171,000. Nearby Gladstone and Milwaukie have similar markets.

The real estate scene in Oregon City, Canby, and Damascus is affected by the steady growth of the Portland area. These and other surrounding communities are enjoying strong housing markets with new subdivisions popping up wherever the developers can find vacant land. The increase in growth and activity has also made historic houses in towns such as Oregon City a very hot commodity, with prices going up rapidly.

Insiders' Tip

For the most comprehensive picture of Oregon communities, check out the Web site of the Oregon Department of Community and Economic Development, www.econ.state.or.us. This will give you an amazingly detailed breakdown of life in Oregon, community by community, in handy PDF files.

Houses—New or Used?

During the urban flight of the 1970s, many Portland families abandoned city living to flock to new houses in the suburbs. Now a revival is sweeping through the metro area as home owners are rushing back to the older houses in close-in neighborhoods and it isn't unusual to see two or more vintage houses on the same block undergoing restoration.

People want to buy a piece of the past and are getting back to front-porch living and knowing their neighbors, according to Ron Rogers, a Realtor with twenty years experience specializing in older houses on both sides of Portland. "The old houses have real personality and are well crafted. Plus it's great to be close to work and to walk to a movie or cafe." Although the boom started on the Westside, Rogers and other experts say the Eastside, where properties are more available, is now torrid.

But if you are buying a vintage house and gearing up for some major improvements, don't be surprised to find a few problems lurking behind the solid wood siding and hardwood floors. Plumbing and wiring problems scare a lot of people off, but if the house has a good foundation and "solid bones" those things can be fixed. Before jumping in, get to know your house's strengths and weaknesses. (For more information about home improvement resources, see our chapter on Shopping.)

New, mixed-use developments display the creativity of Portland builders and planners. CREDIT: COURTESY OF ORENCO STATION

The competition between house remodeling and new house construction is a pendulum that swings back and forth, but several factors in Portland are tilting the scales in favor of the fixer-uppers. With the spiraling costs of land and building materials, the expense of constructing a new house has doubled in the last decade. The increased focus on achieving higher urban population densities and maintaining the urban growth boundaries are other important factors. "A lot of people who would have bought new houses ten years ago are now buying older houses, remodeling, and building additions," says Tom Kelly, owner of Portland's premiere remodeling companies, Neil Kelly Co. "Portland is extremely eclectic so there are sizes and styles of houses for every taste and budget."

We couldn't agree more. But if you are looking for a fixer-upper, plan on doing some research before making any financial commitments. Check out several neighborhoods and talk to a few different Realtors about promising residential areas. Compare schools, property values, and the quality of the nearby roads. If you like a place in the daytime, go back at night and look around. Problems and noise often come out after respectable people pull their shades. For great inside information, check with longtime residents; they often provide a wealth of information and are good sources because they have no vested interest in a property transaction. Ask lots of questions, never assume anything, and don't be satisfied with a single opinion. The main challenge may be to find a house with no major structural problems, but you'll also want to live in a safe, clean area with decent neighbors. Remember, even if you fall in love with a house, never sign anything binding until the property is checked out by a qualified inspector. For more tips on purchasing an old house, see the Close-up in this chapter.

Older Portland Houses

Older neighborhoods in many of the charming inner-city neighborhoods feature Victorian, English Tudor, bungalow, or old Portland houses along streets lined with one hundred-year-old trees. Below we give a description of these typical Portland houses.

Classical Victorians

These are the "beautiful painted ladies," featuring solid wood trim, hardwood floors, and ornate cedar shingle siding and roofs. The ornate two- or three-story houses, built mostly between 1875 and 1910, are found all around the Portland metro area, especially in the inner Northwest and Southeast neighborhoods. The charming and cozy Victorians can present challenges everywhere from their stone foundations to the hand pattern-cut roofs and complications in these unique houses also frequently arise in plumbing, heating, and electrical upgrades. In addition, many Victorians are framed with 20-foot-long two-by-fours so additional studs and fireblocking must be added.

Craftsman Bungalows

Stone or brick foundations and large porches with battered columns are hallmarks of these houses, which were built from the turn-of-the-century to just before World War II. Low-pitched roofs, wide, overhanging eaves, and exposed roof rafters are distinctive features of these high-quality and sturdy houses. A mix of wood and brick exterior and wood shingle or composition roofs, these structures seldom present serious problems. Still, basement seepage often occurs—it is Oregon, after all—and electrical and plumbing upgrades are commonly required. The more economical post–World War II Bungalows (late 1940s through mid 1950s), built to accommodate the post-war baby boomers, are found in almost every neighborhood in the city. Their main drawback is simply a lack of space.

Portland Four-square

These two-story, one roof-line structures, mostly built between 1910 and 1935, will often retain their original lighting fixtures, molding, and built-in cabinetry. Usually sitting on a hand-poured concrete foundation, these solid houses feature huge front porches. Though crafted with the best timber money can buy, such houses often require major kitchen renovations, insulation, and weatherization. Check to make sure the electric system is up-to-date.

Colonial Revival

Elegance and classic lines define Portland's Colonial Revival houses, built between 1910 to 1955. Concrete foundations, wood frames, and full basements, along with temple entry, stately pillars or columns, and a gabled roof are their hallmarks. These two-story, wood-frame houses—often located in the city's finer neighborhoods—are also rich with moldings and trim, cornices, and elegant, small, paneled windows. Beware of lead plumbing that must be replaced with copper. Also, the Colonial Revival house often needs weatherizing, and because of their symmetry, additions are problematic.

Western Ranch

Footings or slab foundations, all-wood frames, and composition roofs are characteristic of this sprawling one-level house. Of course these popular houses are still being built, but their real heyday was between 1955 to 1970. Overall, the ranch houses present few problems, still, windows and roofs often need repairs, and interestingly, basement conversions are a popular improvement. The most flexible of all housing styles, ranches pose few limitations for vertical or horizontal additions.

Northwest Contemporary

Solid concrete foundations, wood frames, and oversized two- or three-car garages typify these houses, built from the 1960s

Close-up

Buying an Older House

Armed with do-it-yourself zeal and Home Depot charge cards, Portlanders all over town are buying old houses and fixing them up. Old houses can give good value for the money, especially when the sweat equity is factored in. But are they right for you? Michele Frisella, a Realtor with the Hasson Company and a specialist in Portland's vintage houses, advises that you consider the following before purchasing an older house:

Look for as many original features as possible, including doors, windows, moldings, hardware, and floor coverings. These all add value, as well as the intangible asset of ambience.

Look for quality remodeling rather than superficial redos! What is that fresh paint disguising? A house that is fifty to one hundred years old has had many owners who have contributed to its current condition. Determine what can you live with and what will you have to redo.

Check the major systems—electrical, heating, and plumbing—as well as the roof. Get as much information as you can about these systems from the owner and listing agent before you write the offer. When you have the inspection, talk with the inspector in detail about them.

Hire a house inspector that has a lot of knowledge of older houses, and preferably lives in an old house! Expect a list of things that are wrong with the house to come up during the inspection and then talk with your inspector about the seriousness of these problems.

Get to know the known toxins associated with older houses, such as lead paint, asbestos, and buried oil tanks. The helpful staff of the State of Oregon Department of Environmental Quality will help you get comprehensive information on these substances.

Think seriously about what it entails to own an old house. Are you handy enough to do the repairs and remodeling? Which jobs are you able to do and which ones will require the hiring of someone? And will hiring someone for these tasks add too much to the cost for you to enjoy the house? Evaluate whether it is the neighborhood that appeals to you or the house in particular.

Hire a real estate agent who specializes in selling older houses and can identify the potential liabilities and explicit assets of an old house.

to the present. Vaulted ceilings, "great rooms," dramatically pitched roofs, heavy beams and timbers, and lots of glass lend character to these versatile two-story structures some critics refer to as "McMansions." Generally, the Northwest-style houses have fewer complications with electrical and plumbing upgrades, but be on the lookout for shoddy construction and materials, especially when it comes to siding. Windows with "blown seals" are a common headache and inferior craftsmanship and construction materials can result in warped walls, squeaky floors, and worse. Also, most of these houses have little interior architectural detail; that you'll have to do yourself.

New Portland Houses

Whether you are looking to build a new house or remodel an old one, there are plenty of competent and ethical contractors around the Portland metro area. The overwhelming majority of Oregon's 42,000 registered contractors are honest and responsible people, but, as in every industry, there are a few bad apples. Oregon's building explosion is attracting a host of new companies, not all of them desirable. Approximately 20 percent of all new Oregon contractors go out of business within two years and a good number leave behind ugly messes for unlucky home owners to clean up.

A word to the wise—if you feel protected when you are told a contractor is "registered and bonded," don't. Here's why: Almost anyone who pays the fees can get registered because there is no background check or licensing examination in Oregon. The contractors board registers about twenty-five new builders every working day and the whole process takes a couple of hours and costs as little as $500 per person. Also, the state board often does not disclose a contractor's complete claims record over the telephone. Out of a desire to be fair to builders, the agency sometimes doesn't notify callers about complaints it deems unworthy or invalid.

The state's torrid housing market has attracted 20,000 new builders of all skill levels since 1990 as the industry has struggled to meet the insatiable demand for house construction and remodeling projects. As building activity increased by 66 percent in the 1990s, complaints to authorities about homebuilders and remodelers have more than doubled. This deluge of new contractors is making residents and newcomers particularly vulnerable because Oregon is among the weakest of the western states at stopping incompetent builders and protecting consumers. When victimized home owners here seek justice, all too frequently they are on their own. Before stepping down from our soap box, we point out that the other western states have responded to similar problems by raising licensing standards and demanding that builders post higher bonds, but Oregon still has not done so.

As of this writing, there are more than 1,400 firms listed in the Home Builders Association of Metropolitan Portland. There are many other competent, reliable, and ethical homebuilders as well.

To choose your builder carefully, get plenty of information. You can start by calling the Home Builders Association at (503) 684–1880, or visit their really useful and well-linked Web site, www.home buildersportland.com. Talk to your pickiest neighbors and see whom they were happy with. Ask for written bids, get every detail of the project in writing, and have a lawyer take a look at any contract (and keep the original contract!). Don't make large downpayments, and wait until after the inspection to make your final payment. Make sure contracting licenses are up-to-date and contractors are insured. Ask for references, call them, and if possible, have a look at the work itself. And remember, you get what you pay for. Look really carefully at low bids—they might be fine, but they also might reflect a misunderstanding about the work or a lack of experience with your kind of project.

Neil Kelly Co.
804 N. Alberta
(503) 288–7461

This top remodeling firm is worth a special mention because of its ability to combine profitable business practices with good ecological thinking and loyal ties to its North Portland neighborhood. The founder, Neil Kelly, had an eighth grade education and rode the rails during the depression, but he created a true Horatio Alger story with this company in the heart of North Portland. Today, his son, Tom, is carrying on the family legacy. Their business practices are efficient and responsible, and dedicated to accountability. The company is committed to using sustainable woods and other components designed to promote responsible resource consumption. House repair "teams" consisting of a carpenter, sales estimator, and general contractor, run many projects, but may be a single person wearing all hats: with one person handling everything, there is less overhead and no one else to blame for delays, cost overruns, and mistakes. Neil Kelly Co. and its 135 employees have received many awards for community involvement and industry leadership, among them the designation as a "Founder of a New Northwest" by the Sustainable Northwest organization, and the Better Business Bureau's 1998 Business Integrity Award. And its philosophy and high-quality work have paid off: Neil Kelly is one of the most successful contracting companies in the Northwest. Upwards of 80 percent of the company's business comes from repeat business and referrals, and in 1996, they were the only West Coast winner of the National Remodelers' Quality Award. One of the few all-union general contractors in the area, for the past several years Neil Kelley has been named one of the best one hundred companies to work for by *Oregon Business Magazine*. For more information on Neil Kelly Kitchens, see our Shopping chapter.

Street of Dreams
Home Builders Association of
Metropolitan Portland
15555 S.W. Bangy Rd.
(503) 684–1880
www.homebuildersportland.com

Builders showcases have proliferated across the land, but ours was the first! The Street of Dreams started in 1976; each year a new development is built to spotlight the latest, most mouthwatering trends in home design. The popular Street of Dreams is the place where home owners learn that two dishwashers are ever so much more convenient than one, or that granite floors are not just attrac-

Insiders' Tip

Community newspapers are the glue that holds the neighborhoods together. Neighborhood association meetings, traffic plans, discussions with local legislators and officials combine with personal essays, advertisements, and advice columns to provide community spirit and critical information for residents. Look for them locally in stores, coffee shops, and kiosks.

tive but absolutely critical. We're waiting for the houses run entirely by fuel cell, and until then, we'll take the yearly tour with covetous pleasure. And we're not alone—last year, the summertime exhibit drew 80,000 people. Moreover, the Street of Dreams is a fund-raiser for Doern-becher's Children's Hospital. For several years, the particularly generous firm of Wallace Custom Homes has donated time, materials, and labor to create the Miracle House, the proceeds of which benefit the hospital. Who said nothing good ever came from envy?

Condominiums and Row Houses

Portland also offers a wide variety of condominiums and row houses. All over the city—but particularly in Northwest Portland—new and rebuilt condominiums are bursting forth, and for many property owners, developers, and real estate professionals, the outlook is rosy. "There's no rule to it. It's just driven by the market prices," says Windermere Realtor Fred Ross, of the city's condo-craze.

While conventional houses in most desirable locations are going for at least $170,000 to $180,000, many buyers are turning to condominiums, which can be purchased for less. Although condo living isn't for everyone, many people that can't afford their dream house can still get into a very nice condo for between $120,000 to $130,000 and make a great investment. Key assets include what many condo-dwellers call easy living: quick access to city shopping and employment, low maintenance, and no grass to mow, trees to prune, or snow to shovel.

In some aspects, the whole city benefits from the condominium phenomenon, which fits in nicely with the concept of the Urban Growth Boundary and higher population density in the city, particularly along the main transportation corridors. Condos increase the number of owner-occupied houses, which many neighborhoods assume is a big plus because that brings stability, so in the long run, condos can increase property values for all.

Many experts think the rate of condo-conversion in Portland hasn't even peaked yet and predict that it will continue for the next five to ten years. Some condominiums are older, converted apartment complexes, while others are modern, upscale developments featuring recreation facilities and health clubs. Many complexes have professional landscaping reminiscent of wooded estates with hiking trails and babbling brooks.

Interiors of the modern condominiums offer features similar to what you'd find in a single-family house: designer colors, tile floors, fireplaces, and wall-to-wall carpeting. Some feature private terraces and vaulted ceilings. In downtown areas such as Goose Hollow and the Pearl District, many of the old warehouses are being converted into light, airy, and very stylish lofts.

Apartments

The Portland metropolitan area offers a wide variety of apartments in diverse areas, designs, and price range. Residents can choose large apartment complexes offering security and health clubs or tiny efficiency apartments. Finding the right apartment can be challenging, especially if you are on a tight budget, but there truly is something for everyone. Apartment seekers may find downtown or the Northwest area highly competitive. However, if your are able to live in different areas such as St. Johns or outer Southeast, you increase your options immensely. Move-in expenses for a single person, including rent and damage deposits, can easily total $1,000. On the Eastside, a simple studio may range in cost from $400 to $600, and a two-bedroom apartment may cost anywhere from $550 to $1,000. On the Westside, a similar studio ranges from $500 to $700 and a two-bedroom apartment, from $650 to $1,200.

Everything old is new again in the Pearl District. CREDIT: TOM BETHEL

The Sunday Oregonian is a good place to start an apartment search because the information is so current. *Willamette Week,* which is published every Wednesday, also has a very good rental section. *For Rent Magazine* is another resource; it's available for free at many local supermarkets and in little kiosks in urban neighborhoods. Even just thumbing through the pages will help you get a feel for what is available in the Portland area, but be forewarned—most of the listings are really advertisements taken out by developers, so if you rely too heavily on this publication, you will not get a complete picture of the rental scene. Still, it can be useful for comparison purposes, and you may find a perfectly lovely apartment. Check out *For Rent's* Web site at www.aptsforrent.com. If you'd like a copy sent to you, call (800) 845-3337. The best way to find an apartment, however, is to walk around in neighborhoods you'd like to live in and look for FOR RENT signs and moving vans.

Apartment Finding Help

If you don't want to go apartment hunting alone, a few business specialize in helping people find the right match. Some of these places are busy and less than efficient at returning messages; if you call on weekends, you are likely to end up talking to an answering machine. Still, these services help hundreds of people each month, and if you are new in town and without friends or relatives, or if you are trying to find a place from a distance, they can be a godsend.

If you'd rather let your fingers to the walking, several services offer information about apartment housing over the telephone: Accommodations America, (503) 499-6631, the Apartment Blue

Book, (503) 684–8013, and Rental North-west, (503) 296–0068, are all worth a telephone call.

American Property Management
2154 N.E. Broadway
(503) 281–7779

This agency offers free apartment information and has more than 300 complexes to choose from. They cover a wide range of neighborhoods in the metro area and are a good place to start a search.

Apartment Selector
8885 S.W. Canyon Rd., Beaverton
(503) 297–2577, (800) 566–6486
www.relomall.com/relomall/portland.html

If you are looking for housing, from apartments to condos to houses, this nationwide firm can help. Apartment Selector has been in business since 1959 and offers free assistance.

One Corp
34 N.W. 1st Ave., Ste. 105
(503) 827–6886

One Corp specializes in corporate relocation and works directly for you as your rental agent. They'll help you find the right place, whether it's an apartment, condo, duplex, loft-house, or houseboat. A relatively new player in the Portland area, the vibes about this place are great. Shaun Garman's company is racking up rave reviews from high-end clients such as the Portland Trailblazers, Nike, Intel, and Nordstrom.

Rental Relocation
(800) 858–6277
www.rentrelo.com/finders

This agency specializes in matching people with suitable apartments in the Portland-Vancouver area.

Other Kinds of Housing

Alternative Housing

In addition to conventional housing, the Portland scene has several communities of houseboats nestled along the Willamette and Columbia Rivers. These floating houses, for rent and for sale, are ideal for avid water enthusiasts. You can even fish out of, and tie your boat to, your front door. And best of all, you may never have to worry about mowing the lawn again! The metropolitan area also has several spacious mobile home communities with large areas for double- and triple-wide houses. These often feature recreation centers, swimming pools, and tasteful landscaping. Ask any Realtor about alternative housing.

Temporary Housing

Temporary housing facilities vary from elegant suites to family units with kitchens to bed and breakfasts in historic mansions to bare but clean motel rooms.

For those with travel trailers, there are a good number of RV parks surrounding the area available on weekly and monthly rents. For help in locating temporary lodging, call either the Oregon Lodging Association, (503) 255–5135, or the Portland, Oregon Visitors Association at (503) 222–2223. Of course, if you are already in contact with a real estate agent, the firm's relocation department may be able to provide a list of temporary lodging facilities.

Student Housing

The state's largest college, Portland Community College, offers no student housing. Portland State University, the University of Portland, Oregon Health Sciences University, Marylhurst College, Reed College, and Lewis & Clark College all encourage full-time students to take advantage of dormitories. The student housing tends to fill up fast, and if you are planning to attend college in Portland, you should get on the housing list as soon as possible. In most cases, you must register for classes first. The housing, for the most part, is first come, first serve, and the nicer accommodations go fast. There is a tremendous amount of development activity around Portland State University's blossoming University District so more housing is available. Also, many students live in nearby Goose Hollow. Some students who prefer to live off campus team up with their peers and share two- or three-bedroom apartments. Many families or property owners who rent out rooms or efficiency apartment to students advertise on bulletin boards near the student unions or other popular meeting places. Wherever you decide to live, keep in mind that automobile parking is a huge hassle for students, so bicycles, buses, and light rail are popular options.

Lewis & Clark College offers forty-six single-occupancy apartments in the Villa Maria building, which is located in a lush, wooded area. The cost averages around $1,500 per semester and includes meals. To arrange a tour or for more information, call (800) 634-9982.

Oregon Health Sciences University offers its students single-occupancy rooms in the seven-story Residence Hall for around $400 a month, and doubles for around $300. The cost includes many amenities and well-furnished common

Insiders' Tip

If you don't know what your tenant rights are, or if you have questions in general, call the Landlord/Tenant Hotline at (503) 282-1964. They have experts that can help you with advice as well as information and referrals.

areas. For more information call (503) 494-7747.

Portland State University offers a wide range of housing through College Housing Northwest (CHN). Monthly prices range from as low as $230 for sleepers to $620 for nice two-bedroom apartments. CHN offers student housing in eleven buildings on campus and four buildings off campus. To qualify, applicants must be students at PSU or another school in the Oregon State System of Higher Education. For more information, call (503) 725-4333.

Buying a House

Help for First-time Buyers
Portland Housing Center
1605 N.E. 45th Ave.
(503) 282-7744

Buying a house is the biggest, most important investment that most people make in their lives and jumping through all those hoops can be a complicated and frustrating process. If you are a first-time house buyer, you may be eligible for help. Through the combined efforts of the fed-

eral government, Multnomah County, and the City of Portland, the Portland Housing Center is offering counseling and first-time-buyer programs that can help you overcome such barriers as financing and credit problems. This program also offers classes in first-time house-buying, and as many as 600 individuals each year benefit from the services. If you qualify financially, it doesn't matter whether you are new to the area or have lived here all of

If you lived here, you'd be home by now: Orenco Station features condominiums with offices on the bottom and living spaces above. CREDIT: COURTESY OF ORENCO STATION

your life. Give the Portland Housing Center a call. Their well-trained, informed, and courteous staff can often do a preliminary screening over the telephone and they also offer comprehensive information and referral services.

Realtors

For people relocating to a new area, one of the first and most important contacts is their realtor. Most of the larger real estate companies have relocation departments dedicated to making your move easier. These specialists have a good working knowledge of the area, neighborhoods, schools, and commute routes. It is important that you get along with your realtor and establish a good working relation-

ship. Be prepared to answer lots of questions about your lifestyle, the type and size of house you want, and your price range. Armed with the right information, these professional house and apartment finders can start the hunt for you before you arrive and can sometimes be able to help arrange temporary housing. You can also ask them to help you get preapproved financing. For more information on selecting a real estate agent, contact the Portland Board of Realtors at (503) 228-6595. Listed below are some of the area's Realtors; many of them have offices citywide, in addition to the branches we have included here. Most also have good Web sites.

Southwest Portland

Barbara Sue Seal,
Coldwell Banker Properties
Portland Uptown Shopping Mall
at 2275 W. Burnside
(503) 224–7325

Barbara Sue Seal, who built her biz from a cell phone into an empire, has eased herself out of the fray by turning over operations to Coldwell Banker. She is now an advisor to Coldwell Banker's president. Meanwhile, there are sixteen offices in the greater Portland area from Vancouver to Wilsonville that bear her name. You can find a house by using the mouse with this outfit or you can pick up a copy of their "Real Estate Buyer's Guide." Either way, there are lots of tasty looking properties to choose from.

The Hasson Company
10960 S.W. Barnes Rd.
(503) 643–9898
www.hasson.com

The Hasson Company is known for its attention to detail and its outstanding and intelligent service; it is locally owned and one of the top sellers in the area. Hasson's 170 agents operate five offices, big enough to maintain some of the resources of larger agencies, such as corporate relocation, but small enough to remain neighborhood specialists. Their offices are in Lake Oswego, east Portland at Sunnyside, west Portland in the Sunset Corridor, N.W. 23rd and, N.E. Broadway. In 1998, Hasson had the highest average sales volume per agent of any company in the area.

Windermere, Cronin & Caplan Realty
733 N.W. 20th Ave.
(503) 220–1144

Cronin & Caplan sold out to Seattle's Windermere a few years ago to take advantage of their vast resources, but they seem to have retained their solid Portland roots and are still local experts. Windermere has grown from modest beginnings to become the leading real estate firm in the Northwest, with more than 180 offices, all locally owned and independently operated by 4,800 sales associates. A huge operation with offices on both sides of the river, it can help you find a house on the Westside or practically anywhere. Every time a house is sold by a Windermere agent, a portion of the commission goes directly to a foundation helping homeless youth by providing transitional living, emergency facilities, and an outreach program.

Windermere Realty
6443 S.W. Beaverton-Hillsdale Hwy.,
Ste. 100
(800) 758–7578
www.movingtoportland.net

This Windermere office is notable, among other things, for its outstanding website maintained by the firm's Susan Marthens, a relocation expert. This regularly updated site has wise observations about the area, as well as fantastic links to U.S. Census data, job information, architectural history, and anything else you might be interested in. Even if you're not moving to Portland, you should bookmark this site.

Southeast Portland

Century 21, Rickard Realty
12046 S.E. Sunnyside Rd., Clackamas
(503) 698–7653

This particular office is relatively new, but the owners and brokers Rex and Lucianne Rickard have a combined forty years real estate experience. Rickard Realty covers East Portland, Clackamas, Gresham, Milwaukie, Sunnyside, and all of the greater Eastside, also focusing considerable attention on the small, rural communities south of Oregon City. This full-service provider assists those with relocation needs and also provides market analysis through its well-seasoned staff of about twenty real estate professionals. Rickard Realty keeps tabs on the new house construction that is cropping up like gangbusters throughout the outer Southeast Portland Metro area.

Hanna Realty
6432 S.E. Foster Rd.
(503) 774–8893

This family-owned business has been based in the same location for sixty-six years. Don Hanna, the broker for the past four years, is assuming more responsibility from his father, Don Sr., who founded the company. Hanna Realty, and its crack team of four agents, covers all of East County, especially the unincorporated areas that offer many possibilities for people who yearn for wide open spaces. Don Hanna likes running a relatively small company and being able to respond to his client's needs personally. He is proud that 75 percent of his business is either repeat or referral. The firm is updated with the latest computer and Internet resources and is a member of the multiple listing service.

John L. Scott Real Estate
4111 S.E. Woodstock
(503) 775–4699

When other Realtors want an informed opinion about a house in Portland's established Eastside neighborhoods, they often call Ron Rogers at this John L. Scott office. In addition to having a great rapport with his clients, he is also known for his excellent relations with other agents. Ron is an associate broker with John L. Scott Real Estate; he has a keen interest in architecture and a remarkable memory for detail (he constantly amazes friends and clients with his ability to remember contacts from many years ago, what they bought or sold, the price of the property, and other fine points of the transaction). This office provides top-quality services and a level of personal attention that everyone appreciates.

Portland's Alternative Realtors
933 S.E. 31st Ave.
(503) 238–7617
www.climbatree.com

This firm has earned its reputation as the kind of place that will go the extra distance to help out a client; its agents are willing to climb trees (reflected in the company motto) to scope out a backyard,

if necessary. They are friendly, down-to-earth, and easy to work with. The firm is especially good at finding older houses in inner Eastside neighborhoods.

Realty Trust
5015 S.E. Hawthorne Blvd.
(503) 232–4763

This is a very small but dynamic real estate firm that knows the Mt. Tabor and Hawthorne areas inside and out. All seasoned veterans, they know the houses, schools, businesses, and even the history of the neighborhoods. More important, they live in the neighborhoods they sell in, so they have an additional interest in keeping their neighbors happy, since these agents run into them every day. Jan Caplener, the company's head, is an expert in the history of Southeast Portland, and often writes about it for the community papers.

Mt. Tabor Realty
6838 S.E. Belmont
(503) 252–9653

No one knows Portland's scenic Mt. Tabor area better than Mert Allen, the broker of Mt. Tabor Realty since 1965. Allen and his small team of agents have assisted in hundreds of transactions in the area surrounding our inner-city volcano (yes, it is dormant). This full-service realty company is small, but big in service and heart and has acquired a sterling reputation. Mt. Tabor Realty does go out of their neighborhood to assist in the sales of other quality Eastside houses, but their bread and butter is helping people near beautiful Mt. Tabor Park.

Windermere Real Estate, Moreland
6237 S.E. Milwaukie Ave.
(503) 233–7777

Anyway you slice it, Windermere Cronin and Caplan Realty Group, Inc. is one of the biggest, most successful realty companies in the state, and this friendly twenty-one-agent office has access to all the resources of the corporate office through its conveniently located branch in Sellwood. Broker Lynne Murphy has been running the show for the past few years, and the vast majority of the realtors working in the Moreland office live in the Southeast Portland-Sellwood area, so they know the territory well. Windermere Realtors, which specializes in residential sales, has a reputation for strong, professional performance and great customer service.

North/Northeast Portland

Century 21 Realty, Peninsula
8040 N. Lombard
(503) 286-5826

This well-established agency, the first of the Century 21 franchises in Oregon dating back to the 1970s, works exclusively with residential real estate. The agents live and work in the North Portland area, but will go to any section of town to help nail down a transaction. There are still some great deals to be found in many North Portland neighborhoods and Peninsula's team of twenty realtors, led by broker Patricia Hodges, is on top of the action. This office is friendly, experienced, knowledgeable, and highly professional.

ERA Freeman & Associates Realtors
10808 N.E. Halsey
(503) 256-0111

This is one of the top real estate firms working the Eastside. In recent years,

Doug Freeman has replaced Mel Fox as broker, but this firm's integrity and exceptional customer service is still the same. In business since the early 1970s, the firm handles all kinds of real estate transactions, but specializes in residential sales. ERA is open seven days a week, offers free market value reports, house warranty programs, and multiple listing services. The firm's forty or so agents have a reputation for going to extremes to provide client satisfaction.

Farrell & Associates Realtors
4772 N. Lombard
(503) 283-1900

There's a lot to like about this eighteen-year-old, family-owned realty company. Nancy and Larry Farrell are the co-owners, and their son, Mark, is also a broker. This one-office operation is friendly and well organized and the vast majority of its twenty-person team of realtors lives in North Portland and feels the area's pulse. Farrell and Associates handles a wide range of real estate sales and property management, but their main focus is residential real estate, particularly in the St. Johns, Overlook, University, and Cathedral Park areas where there are still some great values to be found. Farrell & Associates is open for business seven days a week.

Insiders' Tip

Who pays the realtor? In Oregon, realtors can represent sellers, buyers, or more infrequently, both parties. The seller almost always pays the commission, which is either 6 or 7 percent. The commission is split 55 percent/45 percent between the listing agent and its broker, and the selling agent and its broker. A buyer-broker contract guarantees that the realtor will get paid if unusual circumstances arise. In the event of a sale by owner, flat fee, or special discount in which the seller does not pay the full commission, the buyer must chip in to cover the difference.

RE/Max—Equity Group
2100 N.E. Broadway
(503) 287–8989
www.equitygroup.com

This was the largest and most successful homegrown real estate firm in Portland—it's still large and successful, but RE/Max purchased it in 2001. The Equity Group does over $1 billion in sales annually through its fifteen branches strategically located around the metro area. The vast majority of the firm's realtors are well seasoned and informed veterans of Portland's dynamic real estate scene. This firm specializes in residential transactions and offers comprehensive relocation services.

Township Properties Inc.
4122 N.E. Broadway
(503) 281–8891

You won't get lost in the shuffle at Township Properties, a twenty-two-year old firm that employs fourteen full-time realtors. Township specializes in all kinds of property transactions on the Eastside but particularly the sales of private houses in the Hollywood, Parkrose, Alameda, Irvington, and Laurelhurst neighborhoods. The firm also has agents assigned to work the sales and leasing of apartments and duplexes. Realtors like to stay at Township Properties, so even their "new" employees have been with the firm for five or six years and they really know their territory.

Vancouver and Outlying Areas

Hildreth & Associates
33465 S.W. Maple, Scapoose
(503) 543–3151

If you want to really get away from it all, why not vamoose to Scapoose? You can find some great buys in the neighboring woods and valley, as well as in this small community on Highway 30 between Portland and Astoria. Led by Jan Hildreth, this team will track down that cedar chalet, farmhouse, ranch-style, or remodel that's just right for someone who is retiring or happy to commute a short way to Portland.

Prudential Northwest Properties
4970 S.W. Griffith Dr., Beaverton
(503) 646–7826

The real estate angle of "The Rock," primarily known for insurance, is a focus on relocation. With a head office in Beaverton, Prudential Northwest Properties has two dozen branch sales offices stretching from Vancouver to Wilsonville. The company uses personal planners, e-mail, and an online database to help companies find new houses for reassigned employees. It also has a huge listing of houses for local folks seeking new houses.

Vernonia Realty
953 Bridge St., Vernonia
(503) 429–6203

Vernonia is a small ex-mill town of 2,425 about 45 miles west of Portland with a commute time of thirty to forty minutes to the high-tech corridor of the Silicon Forest. It's a great place to raise kids and escape the urban hubbub. There are lots of older houses and a few newly constructed houses in the vicinity running from $70,000 to $300,000. Examples include log houses, craftsman-style houses, and country-style houses with big decks. First-time house buyers have been finding affordable housing here since the Oregon American Lumber Mill shut down in 1957.

Why USA/Advance Realty
3350 S.W. 198, Aloha
(503) 591–9366

If listings in the West Hills running around a quarter million are a bit above your budget, try Why USA, an outfit specializing in low-cost houses that calls itself "America's real estate alternative." Advance Realty in Aloha, a local outlet for Why USA, has three-bedroom houses for $145,000, trailers, single-wides, double-wides, and turn-of-the-century farmhouses in need of TLC.

Education

Philosophers tell us that there is no education without growth. Oregonians have seen a lot of growth in the past decade, which has both influenced education and has been an education in itself. The institutions devoted to education have also had to contend with growth. As a result, they are multifaceted and diverse—they include state and private universities, community colleges, and public and private elementary, middle, and high schools. Portland is home to Portland State University, one of seven universities run by the Oregon University System. It is also the site of a commendable list of private colleges, among which are Reed College, Lewis & Clark College, Marylhurst University, and the University of Portland. Portland is also the home of the Oregon Health Sciences University, which is devoted to teaching and training medical professionals and research scientists.

Community colleges play a major role in the area's educational scene. Indeed, Portland Community College has more students than any other college in the state. All the community colleges offer a broad range of programs for a broader range of students, whose reasons for attending are various and idiosyncratic. You will find newly graduated high school students who plan to transfer to a four-year college, students wishing to finish their high school degrees, students returning to college after a number of years or even decades, students who are pursuing some kind of professional training, and students who just want to take a sculpture class or two. Besides Portland Community College, which has satellite campus sites around the area, you will also find Mt. Hood Community College in Gresham, Clackamas Community College, southeast of Portland off Interstate 205, and Clark College in Vancouver.

More than 200 public schools and a robust selection of private institutions complete the picture. In both public and private schools, you may find a selection of special-needs facilities, as well as experimental settings where students are challenged in different ways, from learning other languages to designing business plans. This chapter presents a snapshot of schools and colleges in the area, divided in two major sections, K–12 and Higher Education. The K–12 section is organized alphabetically into elementary, middle, and high schools, and multigrade schools in Portland, with some coverage of Outlying Areas; the Higher Education section begins with universities and colleges and then covers community colleges.

K–12 Education

Ninety percent of area residents send their children to public schools, making Portland Public Schools one of the few remaining intact urban school systems, despite constant budget pressures. Changing demographic information also places pressure on the schools, for even as the area balloons in population, many families moving into the area choose the suburbs, and current projections predict enrollment declines for city schools. Although Portland's population is increasing, many new urban residents are young and childless or retired with grown children. Thus, the State Legislature has pushed Portland Public Schools to cut costs, and Portland Public Schools have suffered budget cuts. These have resulted in fewer teachers, librarians, and counselors, fewer electives, ailing physical plants, and pressure to increase the student-to-teacher ratio.

Ironically, however, Portland schools are sometimes less crowded than suburban schools; anecdotal, unscientific evidence suggests that some families are moving back from the suburbs to the city because the schools are smaller and can make better use of cultural resources. Moreover, many schools have become the nexus for dynamic neighborhood and community development. In 1999, a number of schools in Multnomah County introduced a program called "SUN Schools." "SUN" is an acronym for Schools Uniting Neighborhoods, and the idea behind it is to use the schools, which are natural gathering places for families, to serve their communities even more thoroughly. In this program, buildings open early and stay open late to act as neighborhood centers that provide health clinics, computer labs, entertainment, or other activities for residents.

The SUN Schools Program is just one of the innovative programs designed to solve persistent school-funding and other education-related troubles. Another is the charter school law, passed in 1999. This bill allows Oregon to apply for federal charter school development funds. Charter schools are independently run public schools that are taxpayer-funded. They are free to set their own curricula and rules of operation. If the charter school produces students whose performances don't meet academic standards, the school's charter can be revoked and the school could be closed. While a handful of Oregon charter schools have formed, so far there is only one in the Portland area, McCoy, which serves teenagers who have dropped out of school. The slow start in forming charter schools may indicate that Portland schoolchildren already have many choices.

Portland schools should also benefit from the increased expectations of Oregonians. In 1996, the State Board of Education adopted a new set of demanding educational standards for Oregon children. The standards were developed by parents and teachers across the state, and they call for students to master six academic areas: English, mathematics, science, the social sciences, the arts, and a second language. Students are tested in grades three, five, eight, ten, and twelve. Students who reach the curriculum goals for grade ten receive a Certificate of Initial Mastery (CIM); those who reach the goals for grade twelve will receive the Certificate of Advanced Mastery, the standards for which are currently being drafted. The CIM is not required for graduation, but is intended to serve as an academic benchmark.

These standards are not without controversy, but the hope is that by challenging students to do their best, the students will rise to the occasion. The first CIM test results spurred parents, students, and teachers to work harder to raise scores, and testing scores have been on the rise ever since. These standards may have payoffs in other areas: in 1997, 1998, and 2000, Oregon high school students had the highest combined SAT scores in the nation among states where more than 40 percent of the students take the SAT. (In 1999, they fell to second place, behind Washington state, which beat them by one little point.) In 2000, 54 percent of Oregon's high school students took the SATs. Scores for the ACT test have also been high, ranking in the top five for the past several years.

The number of Portland-area schools is high enough to demand numerous school districts (see listing in this chapter). The largest is Portland Public Schools (School District 1J), a prekindergarten through twelfth grade district with nine preschools, sixty-three elementary schools, seventeen middle schools, ten high schools, and fifty special needs sites. Listed here are a few selected public and private schools in the Portland Metro area. We're highlighting schools with distinctive approaches to education such as arts or science programs or language immersion schools where students speak to each other and their teachers in a foreign language for half of their time at school. We've grouped the schools into elementary, middle, high, and multigrade schools, and sorted them further by whether they're public or private. Since parents may choose to send their children across town, schools are listed alphabetically rather than geographically.

Elementary Schools

Public Elementary School Programs

Portland does have a flexible school choice policy, but unless you live within the boundaries for your chosen school, you'll have to apply for an administrative transfer. You can get the paperwork from the school that you are designated to attend. Special programs within schools may have their own application processes; contact the schools for more information.

Bridger Elementary: Creative Science School
7910 S.E. Market St.
(503) 916–6336

This science-based program for grades K–5 is based on the research of psychologist Jean Piaget. Its curriculum is fashioned to educate through activities such as observation, interaction, experimentation, and theorizing; independent thinking and problem solving are prized very highly here. Subject periods are longer than at most elementary schools; an individual lesson might last an hour, and the particular unit may be incorporated throughout many lessons during the day. Children are encouraged to combine scientific reasoning with play: one example is a yearly float trip down the Willamette River for the kindergarten students during which they determine what floats and what sinks, as well as examining other physical properties of water.

Buckman Elementary School:
Arts Magnet Program
320 S.E. 16th Ave.
(503) 916–6230

Buckman has an award-winning arts program that incorporates dance, drama, visual arts, and music into the regular curriculum. Students are encouraged to use their artistic gifts to devise interdisciplinary approaches to research projects and other academic work. The student body is astonishingly diverse, with about ten different languages heard in the halls. The teachers are also diverse, and make use of the "multiple intelligence" approach to learning. Families are deeply involved in this beloved school. And there's a swimming pool.

Language Immersion Programs
Ainsworth Elementary School:
Spanish Immersion Program
2425 S.W. Vista Ave.
(503) 916–6288

Atkinson Elementary School:
Spanish Immersion Program
5800 S.E. Division St.
(503) 916–6333

Richmond Elementary School:
Japanese Immersion Program
2276 S.E. 41st Ave.
(503) 916–6220

Sunnyside Elementary School:
American Sign Language
3421 S.E. Salmon St.
(503) 916–6226

Woodstock Elementary School:
Mandarin Immersion Program
5601 S.E. 50th Ave.
(503) 916–6380

In a modern world of global awareness, the Portland School System gives its students a chance to learn about cultures through immersion in their languages. Immensely successful, these language immersion elementary schools are taught half in English and half in a foreign language. The special schooling gives students not only second language competency, but a greater cultural understanding and proficiency by grade five. These programs operate as separate schools within the building in which they are housed and students must apply to get into all of them except for Sunnyside where all children attending the school learn American Sign Language.

Requirements and activities may vary in each program: for instance, children who wish to attend the immersion program at Richmond Elementary must start as kindergartners, unless they are from Japan or have lived in Japan up to the time of registration. And to help raise funds to send its graduates on a summer jaunt to Japan, students use their calligraphy skills to create greeting cards, which are sold to fund the program.

Year-round Schools
Edwards Elementary
1715 S.E. 32nd Pl.
(503) 916–6204

Peninsula Elementary
8125 N. Emerald St.
(503) 916–6275

Every autumn, teachers have to spend weeks replacing all the knowledge that children have forgotten over the summer. Not at these two schools, which operate on a year-round calendar, leading to better retention and reinforcement of learning. And the yearlong calendar allows for innovation in the curriculum: at Edwards, for example, the students have built a garden and the teachers have integrated the garden into their science, math, history, language, and culture lessons—lessons that they can sustain beyond spring planting into midsummer harvest and maintenance. The garden also provides an arena for recreation and for service. Both schools are small, close-knit communities with active parent volunteers. An added benefit for families: they can vacation when everyone else is in school; children get the same number of days off as other Portland students, they just take them at different times.

Private Elementary Schools
Belmont Academy
3841 S.E. Belmont St.
(503) 232–8985

This small independent school, accredited by Northwest Schools and Colleges, holds computer training, music, Japanese classes, and dance for preschool through sixth graders. The school's basic philosophy is that children are adept at learning, and they learn especially well when they interact with their environment in an intelligent way, using their bodies as well as their minds. Thus, the school focuses on cognitive, social, and physical development through a variety of activities and in close, nurturing partnerships with adults. Problem-solving and critical thinking are fostered. Work with computers and spe-

Insiders' Tip

If you're moving to Oregon with school-aged children, visit the useful Web site sponsored by the Oregon Department of Education—it features school report cards, information about Oregon's standards, and other helpful data: www.ode.state.or.us/relocation.htm. And even if you live here already, you'll find the parents' page of the Portland Public Schools Web site to be of infinite help, with information on everything from magnet schools to school menus: www.pps.k12.or.us/entry/parents.shtml.

cialized art instruction begins in kindergarten. Japanese is offered to all students. Accelerated learning is encouraged at all levels. This school and day-care center accepts children from infants through grade four.

Cascadia Montessori School
10316 N.E. 14th St., Vancouver
(360) 944–8096

Cascadia School, for elementary school-aged children, bases its philosophy on the Montessori curriculum. The small, close-knit school encourages children to grow, educate, and challenge themselves not only in academic subject matter, but also in cultural awareness. Like all Montessori schools, children's interests are respected and mutually respectful relationships with adults are nurtured.

Cedarwood School
3030 S.W. 2nd
(503) 245–1477
www.cedarwoodschool.org

Cedarwood School, with 125 students, is based on the Waldorf philosophy; they are rather new and are in the process of acquiring full Waldorf accreditation. Each year they are adding a new grade; as of this writing, they educate pre-kindergarten through the third grade, and hope to have a full K-8 school by 2005. The school is just south of downtown, in the Lair Hill neighborhood, making it convenient for commuting parents.

French American School
8500 N.W. Johnson
(503) 292–7776
www.faispdx.org

Since 1979, the French American School has been immersing students in the language of diplomats, and its graduates have gone on to great successes in Portland and far beyond. The school is devoted to academic rigor, a nurturing environment, and small class sizes. Tuition is about $8,500 per year. There are 375 students in the school, but this number includes the Gilkey Middle School (see below). The elementary

school serves pre-kindergarten through fifth grade students.

The International School
025 S.W. Sherman St.
(503) 226–2496

The International School, which teaches 200 children ages three through grade five, offers full-immersion programs that nurture as well as challenge students. The school focuses on traditional academic areas in its small classes (the average student-to-teacher ratio is nine to two). Chinese classes are offered for three- and four-year-olds, Japanese classes for three-year-olds through third graders, and Spanish for children three years through fifth grade.

Whole Child Montessori
5904 S.E. 40th Ave.
(503) 771–6366

One of a number of Montessori schools in the Portland area, Whole Child is distinguished by its excellent teachers and its beautiful children's garden. Whole Child teaches preschoolers through kindergartners; their graduates are remarkably prepared for the first grade. Children are encouraged to follow their intellectual paths on their own, but in an atmosphere of supportive preparation that enables the children to effectively teach themselves. The well-designed garden, with its evergreens, flowers, bridges, paths, and perennials, makes a wonderful place for children to roam safely and freely, reconnecting their modern little minds to their bodies.

Woodhaven School
11265 S.W. Cabot Rd., Beaverton
(503) 520–0807
www.woodhavenschool.org

This school has small classes for students in preschool through kindergarten, with individualized instruction in art, crafts, music, drama, and Spanish. Woodhaven is also known for its focus on environmental awareness and global studies. The approach is to teach mixed ages through projects and themes. A two-year kindergarten is a special feature.

Middle Schools

Public Middle School Programs

da Vinci Arts Middle School
2508 N.E. Everett St.
(503) 916–5356

This public middle school, founded by a group of parents in 1996, serves 300 students who come from the entire metropolitan area. It's an arts magnet and students must apply to get in; classes are a mix of age groups. Besides special instruction in visual arts, dance, music, theater, and writing, the school requires rigorous academic classes infused with aesthetic principles.

Environmental Middle School
at Abernethy
2421 S.E. Orange St.
(503) 916–6490

The Environmental Middle School, or "EMS," as it's known around here, is a special-focus program of Portland Public Schools in which students in mixed-age classes study the traditional subjects but with an emphasis on the natural environment. For example, a basic question throughout many courses is "How does history influence the environment and how does the environment influence history?" The environmental core curriculum, studied by all students at the same time, consists of three-year rotations focusing on rivers, mountains, and forests. EMS is a small program, and its nurturing size and low ratio of students to teachers makes it very desirable. Accelerated math and Spanish are also available; community service is a key component of the curriculum as well.

Harriet Tubman Middle School
2231 N. Flint Ave.
(503) 916–5630

Harriet Tubman Middle School has a special, interdisciplinary focus on the health sciences and biotechnology, and has formed community partnerships with, among others, Legacy Emanuel Hospital, Oregon Health Sciences University, and the American Lung Society. Tubman students can work alongside research scientists and others from these organizations. Many electives, such as marine biology, are not available to middle school students elsewhere in the district.

Whitaker
5700 N.E. 39th Ave.
(503) 916–5620

A science and technology magnet, Whitaker is known for its Ecosystem Research Program, which integrates math, science, and technology throughout the curriculum. Whitaker also has a community partnership with Oregon Health Sciences University. The school has a varied student body.

Private Middle Schools

Gilkey Middle School
8500 N.W. Johnson St.
(503) 292–7776
www.faispdx.org

Part of the French American School, this school provides bilingual education in German, French, and Spanish, but also offers an international track in which no previous foreign language experience is required to attend. Small class size and an academically rigorous program are added features. Tuition is about $8,500 per year. (See the French American School, above, for more information.)

Whole Child Montessori Center encourages children's natural desire to learn, inside and out.

CREDIT: WHOLE CHILD MONTESSORI CENTER

High Schools

Public High School Programs

Lincoln High School
1600 S.W. Salmon
(503) 916–5200

Lincoln's excellent reputation stems in part from its International Baccalaureate program, which focuses on international studies and foreign languages. It is the site of the Spanish Immersion program's high school, allowing students to continue their immersion experiences if they've started them earlier. Lincoln also has very active writing teachers, and sponsors a literary magazine, appropriately named *Polyglot*.

Private High Schools

Central Catholic High School
2401 S.E. Stark St.
(503) 235–3138
www.centralcatholichigh.org

Central Catholic High School, teaching grades nine through twelve, is a college-prep school that emphasizes moral and ethical training in addition to its academically challenging program. Tuition runs from about $5,000 to $6,000 per year; about 800 students attend.

Northwest Academy
1130 S.W. Main
(503) 223–3367

This independent, accredited school for grades eight to twelve takes advantage of its downtown location to integrate the visual arts (painting, printmaking, and photography), the performing arts (jazz, dance, and theater), and media arts (film, video, sound design, and audio engineering) into its curriculum. Of course, all the traditional subjects are taught as well. The school has sixty students, who enjoy small classes (the average number of students is fifteen). Tuition is $10,000.

St. Mary's Academy
1615 S.W. 5th Ave.
(503) 228–8306

Catholic nuns established St. Mary's in 1859 and since then it has educated more than 7,000 young women. Its long history has served it well—three times, it has received the U.S. Department of Education's Blue Ribbon award for schools of excellence, the only school in the region to be so honored. Its curriculum is academically rigorous but also imaginative, flexible, and interesting; graduating from St. Mary's is shorthand in Oregon for being well educated. And don't let the old-fashioned brick façade fool you—it is thoroughly wired, one of the most technologically advanced schools in the city. Enrollment at St. Mary's is about 550, and the average class size is thirteen. Tuition is about $5,500 per academic year.

Saturday Academy
(503) 690–1190
www.ogi.edu/satacad

Saturday Academy is not exactly a school, but it deserves attention from parents and students. Affiliated with the Oregon Graduate Institute (see Higher Education), this innovative pre-college program offers enrichment courses in science, math, and technology, and is especially dedicated to reaching underserved students through its courses. The faculty is made up of science and math professionals from the community, who have shared their labs, specializations, and equipment with the more than 99,000 students and teachers who have participated in this community-based curriculum. Courses emphasize hands-on experimentation and critical thinking. Tuition help is available for those who need it. Saturday Academy has been the recipient of no less than seven National Science Foundation grants, as well as many other distinguished awards and grants. Some courses are available for elementary school-aged children.

Multigrade Schools

Most people like their children's elementary schools; it's what happens afterward that they worry about. Many people feel that public middle schools are just not working, and so quite a number of schools, both public and private, are returning to a multigrade plan. Of course, some multigrade schools have always been that way: Portland has a strong network of Catholic schools such as St. Thomas More in Southwest Portland (503) 222–6105; St. Ignatius, (503) 774–5533, and St. Stephens, (503) 235–7040, both in Southeast Portland; and Cathedral Catholic School (503) 275–9370, in Northwest Portland; all offer solid academic programs and traditional values for grades K-8. But in the private schools that are not religiously affiliated, parents have responded so positively to their children's elementary education that many of the private schools have added grades. A fine example is the Gilkey Middle School (see above), but Waldorf initiative schools such as Cedarwood (see Elementary Schools) are also adding grades. Parents and teachers find that mixing the ages together seems to work better for everyone; not only does it help the students academically, but it fosters a sense of connection and responsibility for all.

Public Multigrade Schools

Portland Public Schools maintains a number of multigrade schools or programs within schools. Here are just a few of the notable ones; for more information, visit the special programs page of the PPS Web site, www.pps.k12.or.us/schools/specprogs.html.

Family Cooperative School at Sunnyside
3421 S.E. Salmon
(503) 916-3250

A special-focus program of Portland Public Schools, the Family Cooperative School features an interdisciplinary curriculum for 160 students in grades K-8. Middle-schoolers learn through many community service projects. Parents are an integral part of the school.

Metropolitan Learning Center
2033 N.W. Glisan St.
(503) 916-5737

Portland Public School District's only K-12 school, the Metropolitan Learning Center provides a noncompetitive atmosphere with written evaluations (instead of letter grades), cooperative learning, cross-age experiences, and off-school activities. A particular focus of the school is a healthy environment, and many lessons are devoted to this. Governor Kitzhaber recognized it as the first "green" school in the state. But the students and teachers at MLC are imaginative enough to understand that the "environment" is the place we live; thus, a major focus of the school is the urban community that surrounds MLC and it's an essential part of the curriculum.

Winterhaven
3830 S.E. 14th Ave.
(503) 916-6200

For 160 students, ages five to thirteen, Winterhaven is a wonderful public school magnet program that makes use of mixed-age classrooms, interdisciplinary intellectual approaches, and positive discipline techniques to foster personal responsibility. Winterhaven has attracted a high number of TAG students who respond well to these approaches, which allow them to bloom in their own way while still being academically challenged, particularly through its focus on math, science, and technology. Like MLC, traditional grades are not given. Also like MLC, community involvement is prized, and families are required to volunteer fifty hours per year.

Private Multigrade Schools

Cascade Valley School
13515-A S.E. Rusk Rd., Milwaukie
(503) 653-8128

Cascade Valley School, whose students range in age from four to nineteen, has

---

Insiders' Tip

If you want instruction in a foreign language to be part of your child's extra-curricular activities, try Kids Like Languages, an excellent organization that will help you set up private language instruction for small groups: (503) 493-8424. Berlitz also offers language instruction; they can be reached at (503) 274-0830.

been inspired by Aristotle's observation that humans are naturally curious: The school seeks to foster that curiosity so that the students become self-directed, responsible, and capable persons whose curiosity survives their formal education. Democratic principles are practiced for students as well as for faculty; when it comes to their education, students are given both a wide range of choices and a wide range of responsibility. This small, interesting school is helpful for many underachieving students who dislike the rigidity of most curricula. The campus is fifteen minutes from downtown Portland on a thirteen-acre site.

The Catlin Gabel School
8825 S.W. Barnes Rd.
(503) 297–1894
www.catlin.edu

This distinguished coeducational school is well known for its dedication to individuality, rigorous academics, and liberal arts training. Courses educate the total person, incorporating academic excellence along with the visual and performing arts, physical education, and a strong sense of community service. Students are encouraged to devote service hours to the school and to the community; in fact, one of the requirements for upper-school students is to dedicate twelve hours of service to local agencies. Catlin Gabel has an enrollment of about 680 students in preschool through grade twelve. The average class size is seventeen. Tuition runs between $12,000 and $15,000. Catlin Gabel is not affiliated.

Franciscan Montessori Earth School & St. Francis Academy
14750 S.E. Clinton St.
(503) 760–8220
www.fmes.org

Parents who send their children to Montessori preschools grow misty-eyed when they later recall the wonderful experiences their children had there. Now they can extend this effective learning atmosphere all the way through high school graduation. This school is the only accredited Catholic Montessori program in the nation for students from their preschool years to grade twelve. About 350 students from the Portland metro area, including Vancouver (it's right off I–205) attend this environmentally and globally focused school. Students grow gardens and are even prepared for travel abroad. If we're lucky, they'll start a graduate school for the rest of us.

Insiders' Tip

Do your children know how far their dinner traveled to get to the table? Do you? The Chefs Collaborative knows, and they would like to shorten that distance. The award-winning Portland chapter of this national network of culinary professionals can adopt your school by setting up a program for professional chefs to teach children about local, sustainable, and seasonable food. The specific elements of the program can be tailored to support the curriculum requirements of individual teachers. Since it is a group made up entirely of volunteers, they have no telephone; contact them through their Web site at www.portlandcc.org.

The Gardner School
16413 N.E. 50th Ave., Vancouver
(360) 574-5752
www.gardnerschool.org/home.html

The Gardner School is dedicated to developing the potential of its one hundred students. Howard Gardner's Multiple Intelligences model serves as a framework for individualized skill development and interdisciplinary, thematic studies. Community partnerships provide students with real-life experiences that help them become productive, responsible, compassionate citizens. Classes are held for preschoolers through grade eight. The average class size is sixteen. Tuition is a yearly $7,200. The school is very new and has been approved by the state of Washington; it's in the process of becoming accredited.

Oregon Episcopal School
6300 S.W. Nicol Rd.
(503) 768-3115
www.oes.edu

Oregon Episcopal School (OES) is a coeducational, independent, college preparatory school where teachers challenge students in small, demanding classes. Active parent involvement is encouraged. OES holds its students to rigorous academic standards, while encouraging a free spirit as part of the joy of learning. A sense of humor and tolerance for eccentricity permeate a charming campus in a wooded glen. The school is staffed by easygoing teachers who work with students individually and in small classes. Modern dormitories staffed by resident-faculty families provide a safe home away from home for students coming from far away rather than commuting every day. One of the highlights of the sports year is the intense rivalry between the OES Aardvarks and the Catlin Gabel Eagles. OES serves 720 students, fifty of whom are boarders. Half of these are international students, mostly from China, Japan, and other Asian countries. Most of the other boarders are from eastern and southern Oregon, California, and Washington. The school-wide student-teacher ratio is seven to one. Tuition runs to more than $12,000 per year.

Portland Lutheran School
740 S.E. 182nd Ave.
(503) 667-3199

Founded in 1905, this school began its life as a training school for Lutheran ministers, but over the years, its focus changed. By 1989, it was a K-12 school, and it's now the fastest-growing parochial school in the east part of the city. It offers prekindergarten through twelth grade. The elementary program is centered on traditional single-grade classrooms through the eighth grade, while the high school's main focus is a college-prep curriculum in both liberal arts and the sciences. Ninety-five percent of its graduates attend college. PLS is owned and operated by the Portland Lutheran Association for Christian Education (PLACE), a pan-Lutheran association of churches dedicated to providing quality Christian education to the young people of the Portland metropolitan area. Enrollment at Portland Lutheran School is 440. Classes usually have twenty-five to twenty-seven students, except for prekindergarten through kindergarten classes, which usually consist of ten to twelve students. Tuition for K-8 students is about $4,000 (about half that for half-day kindergarten). High schoolers pay $8,000 or so.

Portland Waldorf School
109 N.E. 50th Ave.
(503) 234-9660
www.portlandwaldorfschool.org

The Waldorf School ethos is very Portland; in fact, there are other Waldorf-based schools in the area, two of which have started up recently—Cedarbrook (listed above) and Swallowtail in Hillsboro, (503) 846-0336. But the Portland Waldorf School is the original one in the area. Established in 1982, the Portland Waldorf School has more students than any other Waldorf School in the Northwest. Known for fostering creativity by nurturing the "head, heart, and hands" of

The garden at Edwards Elementary School cultivates splendid beings. CREDIT: LINDA COLWELL

the whole child, the Waldorf School challenges its students to develop their intellect and compassion. Kindergarten focuses on storytelling, music, movement, and artistic activity. The academic program is culturally enriched with Spanish and German, needlework, drama, drawing and painting, gardening, folk dancing, orchestra, and woodworking.

Portland Waldorf has an enrollment of about 300 students and a faculty and staff of about fifty persons. The Portland Waldorf School recently added high school grades and now serves students through eleventh grade; grade twelve will be added in 2002. Tuition is $2,000 to about $8,000 per year.

Higher Education

Higher education in Oregon has a long history—longer than anywhere else in the western U.S. The Rev. Jason Lee established the Oregon Institute in his parlor in 1842; that event is now honored as the founding of what would eventually become Willamette University in Salem. Willamette also established the first western medical school, in 1866, and the first western law school, in 1883. Ever since 1842, Oregonians have been creating and nurturing high-quality independent colleges and universities.

Excellent higher education that is also affordable is a struggle for most Americans; here in Oregon we have made some progress in achieving this combination. A number of fine private and public universities, as well as a variety of smaller colleges, inhabit the region. Together, this network allows students access to many academic programs. Because Portland is the state's major population center, several state universities have continuing education programs here, particularly Oregon State University and the University of Oregon, both of which offer certificate programs, for-credit classes, and graduate classes in Portland through satellites and extension programs. The University of Oregon's extension program can be reached at (503) 725-3055; Oregon State's can be found at (503) 725-2000.

Oregon's network of public community colleges stretches across the state, and in the metropolitan area, students may choose among Clackamas Community College in Oregon City, Mt. Hood Community College in Gresham, or the state's largest school, Portland Community College with its campuses in Southwest Portland, Washington County, North Portland, and Southeast Portland. These schools offer an astounding array of educational opportunities, ranging from traditional undergraduate academics to noncredit classes in sailing, kayaking, Chinese cooking, or dog training.

The area also boasts private schools that offer a wide range of vocational and career-oriented training in religious education, the technical sciences, computer skills, and various medical and health programs, in addition to their other degrees.

The diversity of Oregon's people is clearly reflected in its high-caliber institutions, which provide undergraduate liberal arts and sciences curricula, specialized two- and four-year professional and technical training, and a wide range of graduate studies. Enrolling more than 60,000 students in the Oregon University System (OUS) alone, and employing some 11,000 tax-paying Oregonians, these schools add a combined annual budget of more than $500 million to the state's economy. They keep thousands of Oregonians from leaving the state for specialized college experiences elsewhere, and also attract out-of-state students drawn to Oregon for a variety of reasons.

In addition to the OUS institutions, the state's independent institutions of higher education produce thousands of additional graduates each year. While these degrees are not cheap, they are made more affordable by financial aid, and most students at both state institutions and independent colleges depend on a wide array of direct financial assistance to meet their tuition and other costs. Among the sources of this aid are the colleges themselves, private donors, community scholarship funds, churches, foundations, corporations, and state and federal financial-aid programs. Most students at Oregon's colleges and universities receive financial assistance. Many students attend community college, which can be economical, depending on one's style of life, before they go on to finish their degrees at a four-year school.

Whether you are just out of high school, returning to school after a some time off, or looking for a new way of being in the world, Portland's colleges and universities offer excellent choices and opportunities. They also offer good values, and whatever your hopes for your higher education, you are likely to find a program that suits you.

Chef Linda Colwell of the Chefs Collaborative serves a lesson in fish heritage. CREDIT: COURTESY OF LINDA COLWELL

Colleges and Universities

Concordia University
2811 N.E. Holman St.
(503) 288-9371

A Christian liberal arts school and part of the Concordia University System, Concordia University is a small college that draws about 1,100 students from all over the world to its campus in Northeast Portland. Courses of study include psychology, biology, theology, health and fitness management, humanities, and education. Graduate degree programs within the College of Education were established in 1996. Concordia is accredited by the Northwest Association of Schools and Colleges, and it offers small classes and an opportunity to work closely with professors.

George Fox University
414 N. Meridian St., Newberg
(503) 538-8383

Originally founded in 1891 by Quaker pioneers, this liberal arts college has been named one of America's best colleges numerous times by *U.S. News & World Report*. It includes Herbert Hoover among its alumni, though when he attended, the college was known as Friends Pacific Academy. Some things have stayed the same since President Hoover's time: the pretty residential campus is still in the town of Newberg, about a half-an-hour southwest of downtown Portland. It still emphasizes moral and religious as well as intellectual development. But George Fox is in every way a modern college too, with a new mission that includes working adults in its graduate, seminary, and degree-completion programs. Classes for the George Fox MBA program, which are held in Portland, are offered one night a week and occasionally on weekends at the Newberg campus. The students, faculty, and staff number about 2,700 persons.

Lewis & Clark College
615 S.W. Palatine Hill Rd.
(503) 768-7000
www.lclark.edu

Lewis & Clark College, which sits on a lush site overlooking the Willamette River, is distinguished by its nurturing ambience, its fine and accessible faculty, and the demanding academic standards of its undergraduate, graduate, and law schools. Lewis & Clark can trace its history to 1858, when Presbyterian pioneers established Albany Academy; then it was a tiny neighborhood school but it moved to its present location in 1942, changed its name to Lewis & Clark, and now it is the largest independent college in the state, with a total enrollment of around 3,000. (The undergraduate program has about 1,800 students; the Northwest College of Law, about 700; and the other graduate programs, another 500 or so.) In 1965, Northwestern School of Law was merged with Lewis & Clark College and in 1984 graduate programs in education, special education, and counseling psychology were consolidated into the Graduate School of Professional Studies. All programs of the college have excellent national reputations.

Marylhurst University
17600 Pacific Hwy. (OR Hwy. 43)
(503) 636-8141, (800) 634-9982
www.marylhurst.edu

Marylhurst, a Catholic liberal arts university, is nationally noted for being an excellent value, especially considering that no classes have more than fifty students in them. Accredited by the Northwest Association of Schools and Colleges, Marylhurst offers its students a great deal of flexibility, with bachelor's or master's degree programs that can be completed during the weekdays, evenings, or weekends. Many returning students have completed their degrees here. If you're the type of person who never likes to leave the computer screen, Marylhurst's classes, programs, and degrees that use Web-based learning might be for you. There are, of course, regular on-site classes as well. The university also sponsors some absorbing graduate programs, such as a Master's in Art Therapy or in Interdisciplinary Studies. They have very generous life-experience credits. Though it was originally founded by Catholic sisters, Marylhurst is co-educational and accepts persons of all faiths.

National College of Naturopathic Medicine
49 S.W. Porter
(503) 499–4343
www.ncnm.edu

National College of Naturopathic Medicine has been in continual operation since 1956, making it the oldest accredited naturopathic medical school on the continent. This extremely rigorous and competitive medical school offers two postgraduate degree programs, the Doctor of Naturopathic Medicine and the Master of Science in Oriental Medicine. Applicants are expected to have a strong background in science. The ND program is accredited, and the MSOM program is a candidate for accreditation; graduates are eligible to take board exams in their fields. In addition to lab and lecture courses, students are expected to devote 1,500 hours to clinical work. Students come from all over the U.S. and from other countries to study at NCNM, where enrollment has doubled in recent years. Each entering class is kept to 120 students, and currently only one out of every three applicants is accepted. Perhaps that's because academic worth is not the only criterion: NCNM college admissions literature states that "in addition to the educational prerequisites, candidates for admission must demonstrate to the college that they possess outstanding moral character, maturity, academic aptitude, and commitment to naturopathic medicine."

Oregon College of Art and Craft
8245 S.W. Barnes Rd.
(503) 297–5544

Oregon College of Art and Craft was born in 1907 during an international movement to preserve and revive the arts and crafts that humans had practiced for a thousand years. Since then, the Oregon College of Art and Craft has been training students in fiber art, metalworking, ceramics, and the production of many other useful and beautiful objects. Their book arts program is renowned the world over. The college, which rests on the grounds of an old filbert orchard, grants a Bachelor of Fine Arts degree; the training for that includes liberal arts, professional practices, and writing. The college also grants certificates in individual specialties. And there are numerous courses and programs available for those who want to simply take a pottery course or learn how to bind books. See The Arts chapter for more information.

Oregon Executive MBA
18640 Walker Rd., Ste. 1008, Beaverton
(503) 725–2250

Though there are other executive MBA programs in the nation, not one of them has the firepower of Oregon's, and that's because it's the only one made up of a consortium of universities. In 1985, Portland State, the University of Oregon, and Oregon State combined to begin this program for working mid- to senior-level managers. Because students are busy running their companies, the tough academic work is balanced by a task-oriented curriculum. Innovative assignments demonstrate in real-world terms the theory that's being taught. A chief hurdle before graduating, for example, is the completion of a major feasibility study or a business plan. Students report other advantages to this program: the peer support is good, and the chance to network, unparalleled. Classes take place on Fridays and Saturdays over short terms, allowing managers to earn their MBAs in two years.

Oregon Graduate Institute of Science and Technology
20000 N.W. Walker Rd., Beaverton
(503) 690–1121
www.ogi.edu

Oregon Graduate Institute of Science and Technology (OGI) has been, until now, Oregon's only private institution that grants graduate degrees in science and technology, and its faculty members are known the world over for their research prowess. OGI offers Masters of Science programs in biochemistry, molecular biology, environmental science and engineering, computer science and engineering, a special Oregon Master of Software Engineering degree, and other programs. OGI also grants Ph.Ds in biochemistry and molecular biology, and in electrical, computer, and environmental sciences and engineering. But OGI also offers some singular programs in management, at both the Ph.D and master's level, as well as certificate programs in finance and management, enabling students to have a solid foundation for corporate, as well as academic, work. In short, this is an institution with the twenty-first century in mind. In December 2000, OGI announced a merger with Oregon Health Sciences University. This should bolster the research capabilities of both institutions.

Oregon Health Sciences University
3181 S.W. Sam Jackson Park Rd.
(503) 494–8311

Oregon Health Sciences University (OHSU) has roots that reach back to the 1800s, but its modern history began in 1974, when the Oregon State Board of Higher Education combined extant schools of nursing, dentistry, and medicine with the Medical School Hospital, Doernbecher Children's Hospital, and various clinics to form Oregon Health Sciences Center. In 1995, the center, now called OHSU, extracted itself from the Oregon State Board of Higher Education to form a nonprofit public corporation governed by a state-appointed board. The result has been a major expansion of services and an even larger infusion of research grant money. Today, OHSU educates health professionals and biomedical researchers in a variety of fields, and it provides excellent, state-of-the-art health care and research. It also devotes many resources to community service and education, including caring for the neediest patients in Oregon. And finally, it is the largest corporate employer in the city. All

Insiders' Tip

Parents often want to enrich their children's education, and Portland has many resources to extend the lessons of the classroom. Besides Portland Parks and Recreation, which holds every kind of lesson you could imagine, Oregon Ballet Theater (503-227-6890), the Northwest Children's Theater and School (503-222-2190), and the Suzuki Violin School (503-246-9945), all augment basic education with their superb programs. And children adore Mad Science, which teaches science through fun demonstrations. Call them at (503) 230-8040.

things considered, few institutions have such a direct and indirect influence on the life of Portland citizens.

The campus overlooks the city that it serves, poised atop Marquam Hill, with stunning views of the Cascades, the Willamette, and the city. The central campus is a maze of buildings connected by bridges, tunnels, stairs, and skyways, but the relatively compact nature of the hospital complex makes a visitor forget that there is another whole 260-acre campus west of Portland, as well as many other clinics and facilities throughout the city and beyond. OHSU's programs and services extend across the state's entire 96,000 square miles reaching into neighboring states.

The main components of OHSU are the School of Dentistry, the School of Medicine, and the School of Nursing. One of America's first-rate academic health care and medical research centers, top-ranking students from throughout the country vie for the opportunity to attend OHSU. Graduates of the School of Dentistry had a first-time pass rate of 100 percent when they took their licensing exam in 2000. And the School of Medicine has equally impressive numbers; not only do graduates usually maintain a 100 percent first-time pass rate, but the primary care education program ranks among the top 2 percent in the nation. Similar numbers are available for the School of Nursing graduates, whose master's programs also ranked in the top 2 percent. OHSU's research units are also distinguished; they include but are not limited to the Center for Research on Occupational and Environmental Toxicology, the Vollum Institute for Advanced Biomedical Research, and the Oregon Regional Primate Research Center. Soon, the Oregon Graduate Institute (see above) will be adding its initials to the OHSU lineup. Research funding has almost tripled since 1995, and discoveries by OHSU scientists are in the news daily.

Oregon Institute of Technology
7726 S.E. Harmony Rd. and 18640 N.W. Walker Rd., Beaverton
(503) 725–3066

The Oregon Institute of Technology (OIT) offers four-year degrees, degree-completion programs, and a number of workshops and seminars on its campuses in Klamath Falls in southern Oregon, where OIT was founded, and on its campuses in Portland and Beaverton. Its degrees are granted in a broad spectrum of different engineering, science, and technological disciplines, including—but not at all limited to—health technologies, applied sciences of various kinds, communications, and environmental engineering.

Pacific Northwest College of Art
1241 N.W. Johnson
(503) 226–4391

The Pacific Northwest College of Art (PNCA) has been training students in the visual arts since 1909, when it was an arm of the Portland Art Museum, but by 1994, PNCA was a separate institution that granted Bachelor of Fine Arts degrees in addition to its community education classes. Over the years, PNCA grew so much that it had to move from its lovely Pietro Belluschi-designed building next to the museum to a large, visually stunning converted warehouse in the Pearl District. This has allowed the college to add two times the space devoted to photography, as well as providing state-of-the-art computer capability. Public galleries showcase the work of students, and the Swiggert Commons, a large space for exhibitions, installations, lectures, and other events, provides an exciting new hub for aesthetic activity in the already-happening Pearl. Students here receive careful, attentive training in their specialties and are regarded for their imaginative design. They are also trained in useful and practical skills like writing, math, and professional concerns. See The Arts chapter for more information.

Portland State University
1721 S.W. Broadway
(503) 725–3000
www.pdx.edu

One of the eight universities and colleges of the Oregon University System, Portland State (PSU) is Oregon's urban university, responding to the needs and interests of the greater Portland area. PSU offers more than one-hundred undergraduate and graduate degrees in the humanities, sciences, social sciences, and professions, including doctoral degrees in education, electrical and computer engineering, environmental sciences and resources, public administration and policy, social work and social research, systems science, and urban studies and planning. PSU grants more graduate degrees than any other university in the state.

The thirty-six acres of the university, which straddles the southern Park Blocks downtown, are replete with big trees, fountains, ivy-covered buildings, hip students in coffee bars, and other accoutrements of a modern urban campus. Visitors will also find beautiful new buildings that house some of the most prestigious programs (such as the College of Urban and Public Affairs, which is appropriately found at the southern terminus of the new streetcar system). About 15,000 students are enrolled at Portland State, including more than 4,200 graduate students. Continuing education programs add thousands more students to the total numbers. Most students commute, but there are some dormitories and the university can assist students in finding housing, applying for financial aid, acquiring a campus job, and other staples of student life.

Extra-curricular activities at the school are abundant. The PSU Vikings play fifteen intercollegiate varsity sports. Men's intercollegiate sports are football, basketball, baseball, cross-country, golf, soccer, track, and wrestling. Women's sports are cross-country, basketball, soccer, softball, tennis, track, and volleyball. Baseball competes within Division I of the NCAA; all other sports compete within Division II. On the cultural front, PSU regularly sponsors events such as theater, films, guest speakers, art exhibits, and concerts. The Florestan Trio, Friends of Chamber Music, PSU Piano Recital Series, Guitar Series, and Contemporary Dance Season deliver more than 15,000 fans to PSU's Lincoln Performance Hall annually.

Like all decent universities, the programs at PSU extend beyond the tree-lined campus to serve all citizens. PSU is the epicenter of a variety of cutting-edge research and public service programs, including the Center for Black Studies, the Center for Science Education, the Center for Population Research and Census, the Center for Software Quality Research, the Center for Urban Studies, the Institute on Aging, the Institute of Portland Metropolitan Studies, and the Portland Educational Network.

Reed College
3203 S.E. Woodstock Blvd.
(503) 771–1112
www.reed.edu

Reed College looks like the cinematic version of a private college, all ivy and brick, with grassy playing fields and a picturesque stream. However, appearances can deceive: Reed College, founded in 1908, is much less traditional than it looks. One way Reed is different is that conventional letter grades for each course are recorded, but not distributed. As long as you're doing satisfactory work, you don't have to worry about grades. This frees students to actually learn something, a freedom that pays off for everybody. Writer Loren Pope describes it as "the most intellectual college in the nation," one at which faculty are thrilled to teach because the students are genuinely interested in learning. A measure of the success of this approach is the rate at which Reed students win awards like Watson Fellowships and Rhodes Scholarships (thirty Rhodes Scholars at last count, the second-highest tally in the nation).

Reed is a four-year liberal arts school (though the college does offer a Master's degree in liberal studies as well). The standard liberal arts majors are available, but in addition, the college offers a number of interdisciplinary majors in subjects such as theater-dance and biochemistry. Its annual enrollment is about 1,400, small enough to provide an intimate environment for learning, but large enough so that everyone isn't exactly like everyone else. All Reed students take a one-year course in humanities their freshman year, and all write a senior thesis. Many departments hold weekly seminars by faculty, students, and visiting scholars, and frequent lectures and seminars further expand the opportunities for intellectual exchange. Reed's Hauser Library, with its 430,000 volumes and more than 1,500 periodical subscriptions, is worthy of mention. The periodical section is very good for a college of its size. The library, a depository for U.S. government publications, also maintains special collections of rare books, manuscripts, and archival materials.

University of Portland
5000 N. Willamette Blvd.
(503) 943–7911
www.uofport.edu

The University of Portland has been consistently ranked by *U.S. News and World Report* as a top-ten university in its class. Its 2,600 students pursue seventy-five undergraduate and graduate degrees, notably in the liberal arts, business, education, nursing, and engineering. Founded in 1901, the University of Portland is affiliated with the Congregation of Holy Cross, the Catholic order that also runs its sister school, the University of Notre Dame; its dedication is to the heart and spirit as well as the mind. Its reputation increases daily—with a faculty that garners substantial awards and grants (from the National Science Foundation and the National Endowment of the Arts, among others) and a fourteen-to-one student-faculty ratio allowing personal contact, it's no wonder. The University of Portland sits on a dramatic bluff overlooking the Willamette; its 125-acre campus is in a pretty, residential neighborhood of North Portland.

Insiders' Tip

Those schooled at home have many resources available in the Portland area. City parks and recreation programs give supervised instruction in sports and other activities just for homeschoolers. Call them at (503) 823-4000 for more information. And check out the Greater Portland Homeschooler's Support Group at www.expage.com/page/gphomeschoolers. Their information line is (503) 241-5350; you can also write them at P.O. Box 82415, Portland, OR 97283. They'll help you pool resources, sort out regulations, and bolster you with moral support.

Warner Pacific College
2219 S.E. 68th Ave.
(503) 517–1020
www.warnerpacific.edu

A Christian liberal arts college founded in 1937, Warner Pacific College, which serves 650 students, is in Southeast Portland near Mt. Tabor Park. Accredited by the Northwest Association of Schools and Colleges, Warner Pacific has trained students in a Christian-centered curriculum of liberal arts for more than sixty years. Warner Pacific offers a number of education programs, including early childhood education, teacher education, and English as a second language (ESL), in addition to its four-year degrees. Warner Pacific also has an imaginative degree-completion program that is ideal for many returning students who work full time.

Community Colleges

The Portland Metro area is blessed with no less than three top-notch community colleges, and they all offer state-of-the-art facilities and a wide range of academic, technical, and vocational learning opportunities. Besides the savings in tuition, the easy access, excellent instruction, and desirable teacher-to-student ratios make community colleges an attractive option.

Clackamas Community College
19600 S. Molalla Ave., Oregon City
(503) 657–6958
www.clackamas.cc.or.us

Serving about 28,000 students annually, almost 7,000 of them full time, Clackamas Community College (CCC) may have a lot of students, but it feels like a small college. CCC students take advantage of a variety of programs, from basic literacy and study skills to college-prep courses. Popular programs include the two-year Associate of Science degrees or the Certificates of Completion; these are granted in more than thirty areas of study. Students also may pursue the Oregon Transfer degree, an Associate of Arts degree that guarantees junior standing at any

Oregon University System school (and which many non-Oregon University System schools will also honor). Transfer-degree students have more than seventy options for major study.

Because many students lack the basic skills to obtain even a high school degree, CCC also offers personal tutoring and courses that cover fundamental academic and life skills. Some of these programs cover GED preparation and English for nonnative speakers, in addition to courses in career possibilities and parenting. CCC also offers credit and noncredit courses that cover dozens of areas of personal interest at more than one hundred locations.

Mt. Hood Community College
26000 S.E. Stark St., Gresham
(503) 491–6422
www.mhcc.cc.or.us

Mt. Hood Community College (MHCC) enrolls approximately 27,000 students each year at its campuses. MHCC's services cover the spectrum from providing adult literacy classes to preparing students for transfer to a university or entry into highly technical fields such as microelectronics, and the college provides one- and two-year degrees and certificates in more than one hundred professional, technical, and transfer programs. Academic opportunities are, naturally, also available, including the Oregon Transfer Degree, the Honors College, and the MHCC-Portland State University Co-Admission program. In addition, continuing education classes are offered to the community at locations throughout MHCC's district with topics ranging from art to aerobics, cooking to computing, investing to woodworking. Classes are offered at the 200-acre main campus, as well as at satellite campuses throughout the district. MHCC may be best known for its jazz festival—see the Festivals and Annual Events chapter for information on this fine event.

Portland Community College
12000 S.W. 49th Ave.
(503) 244–6111
www.pcc.edu

Portland Community College enrolls more students than any other college in Oregon—97,000 annually, full- or part-time. PCC is a two-year college that offers a staggering array of educational opportunities. Three main campuses provide lower-division college transfer courses, two-year associate degree programs, professional, and technical career-training programs, and adult basic education courses. Several other locations offer workforce training, literacy training, and other training courses in addition to their basic academic services. And an open campus offers programs in a variety of places throughout the district. Moreover, PCC also offers many community outreach services available to students and nonstudents alike. If you do decide to enroll, you may make courses at any of the campuses—it all depends on what is offered at what times. And anyone may attend PCC, even those who haven't yet finished high school.

PCC's Cascade campus sits in an urban area off of North Killingsworth Street, and more than 9,000 students each year attend this city campus. It has become a focal point for rebirth in the neighborhood, for many area residents have turned to the Cascade campus for job training, college transfer, and self-improvement courses. Many community services such as childcare, legal aid, neighborhood associations, and job referral services are found on the campus. Cascade also hosts the Festival of African Films each year, as well as a Mardi Gras celebration; these events draw visitors from all over the area.

About 10,000 students attend the Rock Creek campus, which lies 12 miles west of town and draws many of its students from the Beaverton-Hillsboro. As with all community college campuses, a multiplicity of programs is available here. One draw is the Aviation Technology Hangar, where students can have direct experience working on airplanes and helicopters.

The Sylvania Campus, PCC's administrative center, in Southwest Portland, has the largest campus. More than 26,000 students attend the programs here each year. In addition to its well-regarded basic programs, Sylvania has three specialized programs with admirable reputations: the nursing, dental, and developmental education programs. The new library and theater are focal points of the campus—that is, if you can tear your eyes from the western view, which extends over the valley to the Coast Range Mountains.

All residents of the district covered by PCC receive free catalogs each term, so you can see for yourself the courses offered, from fundamental writing and math courses to home decor and advice for small businesses.

Specialized Schools

Apollo College
2600 S.E. 98th Ave.
(503) 761–6100

The medical field is full of opportunities for people with good technical skills. Apollo College offers an alternative to traditional two-year or four-year colleges. One of six campuses in three western states, Apollo offers associate degrees in Medical Laboratory Technology, Respiratory Therapy, Occupational Therapy Assistance, and Medical Radiography. You can also study in a diploma program here to become a dental or medical assistant, pharmacy technician, medical records technician, or a medical administrative assistant. Some form of financial aid is available to almost all of the approximately 300 students. Job placement services are available on-site.

Heald College
625 S.W. Broadway, Ste. 200
(503) 229-0492

One of twelve campuses in three states, Heald College of Portland, in the heart of downtown, offers associates degrees in Computer Business Administration and Computer Technology, as well as certificates in network technology for Cisco Systems and Microsoft Windows 2000. Accredited by the Western Association of Schools and Colleges, Heald is a non-profit school founded in San Francisco in 1863. Its students get plenty of hands-on computer and technical experience before graduating, and then they receive ongoing job placement services. Training and internships are provided in the days and evening, and many students qualify for financial aid. No student housing is available but counselors work with students to help them find suitable options.

International Air Academy
2901 East Mill Plain Blvd., Vancouver, WA
(360) 295-0722

Got that traveling bug? The International Air Academy has placed 17,000 graduates in airline careers and they can get you started in a travel career through their twenty-week Airline Travel Specialist diploma program. For many students, this is the first step towards becoming a certified travel consultant. Graduates of the program are qualified for a broad range of positions, including travel and tour agent, customer service agent, and for a variety of jobs in transportation, travel, and hospitality marketing. Another diploma program, the ten-week Airline Reservations and Airport Services, provides entry to jobs in reservation sales, ticket agents, and gate and ramp agent positions. Many alumni of International Air Academy are hired by major airlines as flight attendants, in customer service positions, and as schedulers or reservation agents. Founded in 1980, this school

is accredited by the Accrediting Commission of Career Schools and Colleges of Technology. The majority of students qualify for financial aid and dormitory housing is available for out-of-towners.

Western Culinary Institute
1201 S.W. 12th Ave.
(503) 223-2245

Every year some 600 students take their first step toward becoming artists in the kitchen at Western Culinary Institute. The twelve-month course is full time and culminates in a diploma, certification, or both. Significantly, Western Culinary Institute has formed a partnership with Le Cordon Bleu, the renowned French institute of cooking instruction. And not only does WCI offer Le Cordon Bleu certification in the culinary arts, but it recently became the first school in the U.S. to offer Le Cordon Bleu certification in restaurant management—quite a coup for the school. Notable chefs from around the world teach classes Monday through Friday at WCI; the curriculum emphasizes fine dining, hotel and resort cooking, and catering. Students learn hands-on at three on-site restaurants as well as through off-campus internships. Western Culinary offers financial aid to most students and assists with housing needs and part-time employment; the school claims a very high job placement rate.

Western States Chiropractic College
2900 N.E. 132nd Ave.
(503) 256-3180
www.wschiro.edu

Western States Chiropractic College (WSCC) is a private, nonprofit, professional school that educates students in the art, science, and philosophy of chiropractic self-healing, and its graduates are prepared to work within an interdisciplinary medical framework. Its reputation is outstanding: its graduates test very well on their board exams, and the college was the first chiropractic college ever, in 1994, to receive federal research money—nearly $1 million dollars in grant funds from the

Department of Health and Human Services. This grant has been renewed at the same sum. Between 400 and 500 students attend the college; 70 percent of them are from outside the Pacific Northwest. The WSCC student population numbers between 400 and 500 and comes from all parts of the United States and from several foreign countries; about one third of the students have earned a B.A. before they arrive, and many are already working professionals in some other field. Originally founded as the Pacific Chiropractic College, the school was reorganized and became Western States Chiropractic College in 1932. In 1986, the college opened its 9,000-square-foot Outpatient Clinic on campus, making it the largest chiropractic facility in the Northwest.

Portland teachers make lifelong friends. CREDIT: RACHEL DRESBECK

Portland Area School Districts

General information and questions about schools in the following districts can be obtained by calling the following:

Multnomah County

Centennial SD 28J
18135 S.E. Brooklyn
(503) 760–7990

David Douglas SD 40
1500 S.E. 130th Ave.
(503) 252–2900

Gresham Schools
1331 N.W. Eastman Pkwy., Gresham
(503) 618–2450

Multnomah Education Service District
11611 N.E. Ainsworth Cir.
(503) 255–1841

Portland Public Schools
501 N. Dixon St.
(503) 916–2000

Washington County

Beaverton SD 48
16550 S.W. Merlo Rd., Beaverton
(503) 591–8000

Hillsboro SD 1J
215 S.E. 6th Ave.
Hillsboro
(503) 648–1126

Sherwood SD 88J
400 S. Sherwood Blvd., Sherwood
(503) 625–8100

Tigard-Tualatin SD 23J
13137 S.W. Pacific Hwy., Tigard
(503) 431–4000

Clackamas County

Canby SD 86
811 S.W. 5, Canby
(503) 266–786

Clackamas Education Service District
P.O. Box 216, Marylhurst, OR 97036
(503) 675–4000

Estacada SD 108
P.O. Box 519, Estacada
(503) 630–6871

Gladstone SD 115
Gladstone
(503) 655–2777

Lake Oswego SD 7J
2455 S.W. Country Club Rd., Lake Oswego
(503) 636–7691

Molalla River SD 35
412 S. Swiegle Ave., Molalla
(503) 829–2359

West Linn-Wilsonville SD 3J
P.O. Box 35, West Linn, OR 97068
(503) 673–7000

Clark County, Washington

Battle Ground SD 119
11104 N.E. 149th St., Brush Prairie
(360) 885–5300

Camas SD 117
2041 N.E. Ione, Camas
(360) 817–4400

Educational Service District 112
2500 N.E. 65th Ave., Vancouver
(360) 750–7500

Evergreen SD 114
13501 N.E. 28th St., Vancouver
(360) 604–4000

Ridgefield SD 122
2724 S. Hillhurst Rd., Ridgefield
(360) 887–0200

Vancouver SD 37
605 N. Devine Rd., Vancouver
(360) 696–7000

Washougal SD 112-6
2349 B St., Washougal
(360) 835–2191

A child chooses her jack'o lantern. CREDIT: TRACY BROWN

Childcare

Portland's solid sense of community, reinforced by consistently high marks for its quality of life, makes it a fine place to raise a family. Still, childcare can be difficult to find, especially for infants and toddlers. Like everywhere else in the country, parents are often bewildered by the number of choices and flabbergasted by the cost of finding someone reliable to watch over their little ones. But this hasn't lessened demand: according to state statistics, nearly half the population of young Oregonians receive paid childcare of one sort or another. Fortunately, a number of resources are available to help you sort through your options and find the best childcare arrangement for your family. Oregon has organized sixteen state-funded childcare resource and referral agencies that serve most counties, providing direction and consumer education to parents, training and technical assistance to childcare providers, and information on work-family issues to employers. Nonprofit, community-driven programs dedicated to child advocacy are growing in number, and research about the realities of life for children in Oregon is conducted, collected, and reported on a regular basis. Two free publications, *Portland Parent* and *Portland Family*, offer regular updates on childcare facilities in the area. And informal networks through community centers, libraries, religious organizations, and word of mouth can put parents in touch with good caregivers.

Regardless of what option seems to best suit your needs, you should start your search for childcare early. A vast range of care is available, but a lot of other parents are looking for qualified help for their childcare needs, and waiting lists are not unusual. It takes time to find the right person or center for your child and your family.

State Programs and Initiatives

The Oregon Commission for Childcare, an advisory board to the governor, studies the issues concerning the development of accessible, affordable, and high-quality childcare, and makes legislative recommendations based on its findings. The OCCC has become a major player on these issues since its inception in 1985. Its recent work includes attempts to prevent cigarette smoking, implement processes for on-site safety reviews at all regulated childcare facilities in Oregon, research on the work-life practices of employers in Oregon, and requirements for family childcare provider training to include CPR and safe food handling. And, based on its track record, the OCCC is likely to be successful with these initiatives. They are already responsible for the improving state of childcare in Oregon, spearheading campaigns for a parental leave law, registration and insurance requirements for family childcare providers, and tax credits for employers who subsidize childcare.

More visible is the OCCC's creation of a state-funded program for childcare resource and referral, and the Childcare Division of the Oregon Employment Department. This division certifies childcare centers through criminal history checks and inspections of facilities. It also registers family childcare business, though it does not inspect them. (Family childcare providers are still required to undergo criminal background checks and a certain amount of training.) The division sponsors mentoring and training programs for providers, working closely with the Center for Career Development in Childhood Care and Education at Portland State University.

Good childcare includes the whole child. CREDIT: JUANITA PETERS

Childcare Resource and Referral Program

The Childcare Division of the Oregon Employment Department has also developed the Childcare Resource and Referral (CCR&R) agencies. These community-based agencies strive to provide all parents with as much information and as many options for quality childcare as possible. The CCR&R directs parents toward resources for childcare screening, as well as to other community resources, including childcare provider support groups. Although the CCR&R programs are extremely busy, and you must leave a message on a recording, they generally return calls within a reasonable amount of time and are quite helpful. CCR&R staff are knowledgeable and will answer questions about a wide range of topics and dispense information about childcare accreditation, local workshops for providers, and information about scholarships to help cover training and accreditation fees. Your local CCR&R can also meet with you and provide a personal consultation to address concerns about your childcare situation, health and safety matters, child development issues, activities for children, and even technical information regarding business development, taxes, and zoning. CCR&R resources are considerable, including a lending library of videos, books, toys, and equipment, so don't be afraid to ask for help or advice. Referral hours are from 9 A.M. to 3 P.M., Monday through Friday. For statewide referral, contact the Oregon Childcare Resource & Referral Network in Salem, (503) 375-2644 or (800) 342-6712, or contact them online at www.open.org/occrrn/ or at occrrn@opengovt.open.org. In the Portland Metro area, which is served by three offices at one central number, call Metro Childcare Resource & Referral, (503) 253-5000, (800) 695-6988, or TDD: (503) 252-1332.

Other Resources

Children First for Oregon is the child-advocacy conscience of Oregon. Improvements in childcare can only come with extensive research and data, and each year Children First produces a report card for the state on its progress toward meeting the health, education, and well-being benchmarks for children. This independent, nonprofit group collates public data and compiles statistics, analyses, and directives based on their research. Their reports are available for free online, and they cover issues such as high-school dropout rates and infant mortality in addition to their information on childcare. Recent reports indicate that while in theory childcare benchmarks have been met, parents of infants and toddlers still face a struggle to find affordable, high-quality childcare. No worries about grade inflation here: they are not afraid to tell it like it is.

The kind of data produced by Children First is used all over the state to address the needs of children, their parents, and their childcare providers. Portland State University has developed Oregon Childcare Basics (O.C.C.B.), which is a training program for providers designed to promote constructive care and education of children. The training program covers health, safety, nutrition, and the social and emotional development of children. It's a short program, but the benefits have been documented to be long lasting and to encourage further education among providers. You can find them at the Oregon Center for Career Development in Childhood Care and Education, (503) 725-8535 or (800) 547-8887, ext. 8535.

Childcare Providers

Finding someone to care for your child can be remarkably stressful, but surveying the territory will make things a little easier. We've included in this chapter a list of questions to help guide your search; below are the basic kinds of childcare available in the Portland Metro area.

Doulas and Early Care

Childcare begins early for some of us. Many Portland parents find the transition to their new roles goes more smoothly with the help of a doula, a professional family helper who provides nonmedical assistance to new parents at home. Doulas may show anxious parents how to hold, bathe, dress, and feed the new little one; they may take care of the house or older siblings; they may aid with nursing; in general, they help to keep things peaceful and calm. Since hospital stays for post-partum women are notoriously abbreviated, a doula could be just the person to ease you through the surprise of new parenthood. You can find doulas in a variety of places. Your OB-GYN may have some contacts, and midwives are very good sources; often midwifery practices include them on staff. Northwest Doulas, (503) 788-3536, is an agency that specializes in this particular form of care. You can also contact the Care Givers Placement Agency, (503) 244-6370. Some doulas charge by the hour (hourly rates begin at about $15); others charge a flat fee.

Sometimes all you need is the support of other parents. Hospitals and healthcare organizations will often run programs for new parents and their infants. Hosted by nurses or other healthcare professionals, these free or low-cost forums allow you to ask questions about breastfeeding, child development, and other issues. Just hanging out with the other parents is comforting, especially when you find out they all feel the same way that you do. Check with your hospital or HMO to see whether they offer such programs and look in community newspapers (see our Media chapter), where parent support groups are listed. Two such groups are ParentCare, which gives parents the opportunity to discuss and explore their roles in the family and as individuals, and

Mom's Home, which gives support to mothers at home caring for kids. ParentCare meets Wednesdays at 9:30 A.M. in Northeast Portland; call (503) 284-7141 for more information. Mom's Home meets every other Wednesday morning from 9:15 to 11:15 at the Tigard United Methodist Church; call (503) 524-1936. And don't forget the power of the spoken word: most of the people we know found their "moms groups" informally, through friends of friends, story time at the library, the baby swings at the park, the Baby Gap store at the mall, or interesting conversations about baby acne at the local Starbucks. Later, when the babies get bigger, these groups are invaluable resources for setting up casual baby-sitting co-ops.

Nannies

If you read *The New York Times*, you might worry that hiring a nanny will require you to sign away not just your first-born child but your entire inheritance; however, this is still Oregon, and while nannies are expensive, they are still affordable for many families. In fact, nanny care is growing in popularity, for it may be the least disruptive to the family. Nannies can be full- or part-time; they can live in your house or in their own; they can be temporary or long-term. The salary of your nanny can range from $275 to $600 per week for a nanny who lives out, to $300 to $650 per week for one who lives with you. Part-time nannies earn from $8 to $15 per hour. It all depends on what you want them to do: different nannies have widely varying responsibilities and duties, such as housework, meal preparation, and picking the children up from school and driving them to sports or extracurricular functions. You should make it clear what duties the job entails and spell them out in a contract.

Two good sources for nannies are Northwest Nannies and Care Givers Placement Agency. Contact Northwest Nannies at (503) 245-5288 or online at www.nwnanny.com. You can reach Care Givers Placement Agency at (503) 244-6370. Both agencies can find you temporary or permanent, full- or part-time help. Care Givers will also help you find temporary emergency childcare; contact them in advance, if you think you might be subject to emergencies, to see how their system works. While the nannies we have known have been trustworthy, reliable, and resourceful, nannies are unlicensed in Oregon; going through an agency may afford you some protection since the agency screens the applicants and expects them to have some training.

The Milk of Human Kindness

Need help nursing your new little one? These organizations offer advice, equipment, and moral support:

Beaverton Pharmacy and Home Health Care, (503) 644-2101

Beyond Birth Home Lactation, (503) 232-2229

La Leche League, (503) 282-9377

Medela, (503) 658-3708, (800) 669-3708

Nursing Mothers Counsel of Oregon, (503) 293-0661

Westside Breastfeeding Center, (503) 640-2757

Graduation from daycare is bittersweet. CREDIT: CHRISTINE FROST

Daycare Centers and Family Care

Daycare centers, which charge rates anywhere from $300 to $2,200 per month, are open 52 weeks a year, are licensed by the state, and are usually staffed with a number of teachers who are supervised by a director. Caregiver-child ratios are strict, and vary with the age of the child. Daycare centers are becoming increasingly specialized and are more competitive than ever. These centers, which according to state law must provide at least 35 square feet of space per child, can be quite large and usually offer lots of recreational and educational activities to help children acquire new skills as they burn off their seemingly endless supply of energy. There are hundreds of daycare facilities in the area. Many families choose one close to either home or work, but wherever you live and work, you'll have to sort through the facilities to find one that coheres with your outlook on things. As you might expect, the kind of care and theory behind it varies widely; we have pretty much everything here, from Waldorf-based philosophies to Montessori philosophies to Piaget's philosophies, and everything in between. Many daycares incorporate religious themes. Some of the nationally known chains that operate in Portland are the Learning Tree, Kindercare, La Petite Academy, and Children's World, but there are many locally grown centers for you to probe.

In-home, or, as the state refers to it, "family" daycare, is ubiquitous throughout Oregon and involves utilizing temporary or long-term surrogate families for your little ones. It can cost from $300 to $800 per month. The in-home daycare operations must be registered with the state and can provide care for up to ten children at a time. As with daycare centers, strict requirements for ratios of caregivers to children apply. Operators and employees must undergo criminal background checks, and new training requirements demand that they have an overview session, are trained in CPR, maintain a food handler's certification, and are trained to prevent child abuse and neglect. They must also carry household insurance. For a comprehensive list of state regulations, visit the excellent Web site www.americatakingaction.com/childcare, which, in addition to its good childcare resources, is a clearinghouse for information about the nation's schools.

Insiders' Tip

For a comprehensive online listing of Portland Metro childcare providers, try www.portlandchildcare.com.

Extended Care and Summer Programs

Many Portland schools, both public and private, offer extended care programs after and before school for children whose parents have incompatible work schedules, and these programs often run during school breaks as well. The public schools have contracts with eighteen state-certified, nonprofit providers, who run programs right in sixty-two elementary schools. Two additional schools have childcare within a safe walking distance (that is, a distance that could be covered by a child in kindergarten). Your child's school can give you information about these programs, or you can call the Portland Public Schools Childcare coordinator at (503) 916-3230.

In addition to extended care within the schools, you'll find other weekday programs that take care of children until their parents can. Boys and Girls Clubs are helpful in this regard; they have four clubs in the area, and run summer programs in addition to their extended-care programs. Their administrative office in S.E. Portland, at 7119 S.E. Milwaukie, (503) 232-0077, is a well-equipped facility that keeps kids busy with all kinds of wholesome activity, from basketball to photography. The number for the Club is (503) 238-6868. Other locations include the Lents Club, 9330 Harold Street, (503) 775-1549; the Blazers' Boys and Girls Club, 5250 N.E. Martin Luther King Jr. Boulevard, (503) 282-8480; and in Hillsboro, at 560 S.E. 3rd Avenue, (503) 640-4558.

The YMCA of Columbia-Willamette has ten regional centers and a number of in-school programs for childcare, education, and extended care. The YMCA offers flexible and affordable daycare and does a great job of keeping youngsters involved in stimulating and challenging activities. These fully licensed and well-staffed centers are conveniently located on both sides of the river and offer full- or part-time options for busy parents. In addition, the YMCA manages a half-dozen Child Development Centers for six-week old infants up to five-year-old tots. As an added bonus, members of their childcare programs receive a reduction fee from 25 percent up to 75 percent in monthly membership dues at any YMCA Fitness Facility with the joining fee waived. You can reach them at (503) 946-5437 or www.ymca-portland.org.

Portland Parks and Rec and summer camps, both covered in the Kidstuff chapter, can also help you take care of your child. Summer camps are a popular form of "childcare." Devoted to activities like basketball, dance, computer or language training, monitoring baby animals at The Oregon Zoo, or a numbing array of other things, they provide care for the kids and peace of mind for their parents. Portland Family publishes a multipart guide to camp, and camps themselves sponsor a big exhibition, the Summer Camp and

Vacation Show, at the Convention Center in the spring. Tickets to this event, unlike the camp fees themselves, are very inexpensive—$2 for grown-ups, and $1 each for the kids.

Finally, Portland Parks and Recreation sponsors many after-school and school-break programs throughout the city. These offerings change regularly and vary according to the season; they range from acrobatics to Zen flower arrangement. Their number is (503) 823–PLAY; call them and they will send you a nice big catalogue.

Evening Childcare

Grandma's Place
1505 N.E. 16th Ave.
(503) 249–7533

If you work at night, you know how hard it is to find evening childcare. Therefore, Grandma's Place is a godsend for many busy parents. Grandma's Place is a drop-in daycare center that offers part-time and temporary daycare services for young ones from just six weeks up to twelve years of age. Unlike many centers, Grandma's is open seven days a week and it's open until midnight.

Finding Daycare: Asking the Right Questions

Whether you have decided to hire a daycare or family care facility to take care of your little one, you want to make sure that the place is safe, that you feel good about leaving your child there, and that your child will be happy there. Trust your instincts. Watch the caregivers interact with the children. Don't be afraid to show up for a surprise visit. The following questions can help you form a decision about the right place for your child.

Legal Issues:
Is the facility licensed or registered by the State of Oregon? Are there certificates or licenses available for inspection? Are they up-to-date in their registration and training?

Staff Qualifications
Do the staff and director have training in first aid, childhood development, and infant CPR/choking? If it's a family care provider, what is the previous training of the provider? Are there references?

Does the caregiver appear to be in good health? Has the caregiver had a TB test or lung X-ray within the last year? Is there any sign of cigarette smoking around the children?

Center Safety
Is the facility clean and attractive?

Has it been "childproofed" so that potential hazards are eliminated?

Are babies separate from the older children?

Do babies have individual cribs?

Are emergency exits marked and clear? If it's a family care center, what are the procedures in case of a fire or other emergency?

Are emergency numbers posted and obvious?

Care and Attention

Does the facility accept infants? If so, how many caregivers work with the babies? State law mandates four per infant, but the ideal is three.

If you're nursing, will the facility store your breast milk properly and feed it to your child?

Does the staff turn over frequently? (This could be a sign of poor working conditions for the caregivers.)

Do the caregivers appear to like their jobs? Do they appear to like children?

Are babies rocked when they cry? Are they picked up and played with? Do they ever go outside? How often are diapers changed? Is the changing area clean? Will the caregiver take notes on the baby for you?

Extended-care programs in the schools are popular with busy parents and children. CREDIT: RACHEL DRESBECK

Daily Life

What is it like on a normal day? What kind of activities are offered?

What, if any, is the facility's philosophical orientation?

What kind of discipline is used?

Clear Communication

Can you communicate easily with the caregiver?

Are you allowed or expected to participate?

Can you visit whenever you want?

Practicalities

What are the hours and days?

What happens if your child is sick?

What happens if your child needs medication—will they administer it?

Do you need to fill out a form to authorize medical care?

Do they offer to arrange care if the caregiver or the child is sick, or do you take care of that?

What is the cost? Are you charged for late pickup? Are you charged when your child is absent?

Is the facility near your house or workplace? Will its location ever be an inconvenience?

Health and Wellness

Portland's impressive yet people-friendly healing community is at the heart of a state known for exciting advances in health reform, medical research, innovative practice, and cutting-edge legislation.

Such new legislation includes Oregon's 1994 Death with Dignity Act, which allows for physician-assisted suicide, and another law that allows for the use of marijuana for medical use.

A third break-through piece of legislation is the Oregon Health Plan. Initiated through a series of laws enacted from 1989 to 1995, it provides health insurance to low-income residents. Roughly 100,000 Oregonians now have health coverage including the working poor, seniors, people with disabilities, children, and pregnant women.

Another notable trend suggests that Oregon and its major metropolitan center are in the forefront of a worldwide movement to integrate health care modalities: Providence Health Plans and Kaiser Health both offer coverage of visits to chiropractors and acupuncturists, and Providence also works with the Community Selfcare Center located in Nature's Northwest, a local health food and nutrition outlet. At the medical school of Oregon Health Science University (OHSU), students are learning about alternative as well as allopathic medicine.

OHSU is not the only school in Portland teaching healing crafts. The Western States Chiropractic College teaches chiropractic, the Oriental College of Oriental Medicine teaches acupuncture and herbal healing, the National College of Naturopathic Medicine offers degrees in naturopathy, and East-West College of Healing Arts has classes in massage and bodywork.

For those of you who are not headed toward wearing a white smock with a nametag, but simply need medical assistance, there's a major hospital with emergency service nearby anywhere in the Portland area. The big three in the mainstream healing community are the four hospitals of the Legacy Group, the eight hospitals, centers, and clinics of the Providence Health System, and OHSU, an academic health center with a sprawling campus, a medical library, public hospital, children's hospital, and an eye and dental clinic, all clustered atop Pill Hill in Southwestern Portland.

There are also an impressive number of medical professionals, walk-in clinics, and practitioners offering alternative-medicine options if you're seeking acupuncture for pain management, reiki massage for sore muscles, herbal treatment for that chronic cough, or chiropractic relief from that regrettable quick snap of your neck.

PDX also has its share of fitness centers where you can feel the burn as you bike, hike, heft, and stretch toward better health.

If you need emergency assistance, dial 911, but if your medical problems aren't that dire, try the 24-Hour Hotline, (503) 291-6030, which can direct you to the help you need. This hotline can also provide information on finding the right doctor, emergency procedures, women's health issues, nervous disorders, and other ailments. We have also listed other important healthcare phone numbers at the end of this chapter. But before you reach for your phone, first check out our profiles of Portland's Health and Wellness facilities. We begin our look with hospitals; our list is ordered geographically.

Southwest Portland

Oregon Health Sciences University
3181 S.W. Sam Jackson Park Rd.
(503) 494–8311.

Nicknamed "Pill Hill," for its sprawling campus atop a ridge in Portland's Southwest hills, OHSU is an internationally renowned center for research and education as well as a complex of hospitals and clinics tracing its beginning back to the turn of the century. Recently ranked among the best hospitals in the country by *U.S. News & World Report*, OHSU has an operating budget of $675 million and more than 9,400 employees. Its cancer research center, the Oregon Cancer Center, opened in November of 1998 and now hosts 175 scientists, all working on cures and therapies for cancers. One of seven centers on the West Coast funded by the National Cancer Institute, it also receives part of its $50 million budget from foundations.

Since 1887, OHSU has also trained 23,000 medical professionals. Once one of Oregon's universities, it is now an independent public corporation with a student body of 2,700. Not only does Pill Hill train medical students and push the envelope of medical research, it offers medical help to the general public. Along with a remodeled general hospital, OHSU has a new children's hospital, a new school of nursing, a Women's Health Center in its final stages of development, and the recently completed Hatfield Research Center, named after retired Senator Mark Hatfield, who worked tirelessly to expand this world-renowned medical center.

Central to Pill Hill's learning climate and of great service to the general public is OHSU's Biomedical Information Communication Center (BICC) with 227,300 books and magazines as well as brochures. Resources also include an online catalog available to the general public. A popular service is the OHSU Health Information by Mail, (503) 494-8881. By calling this number you can get pamphlets, articles, or overviews on your health question sent by mail free of charge, or you can order customized research packets beginning at $25.

Healthy Talks is a series of Saturday morning talks with OHSU faculty who discuss medical issues at the auditorium free of charge. The talks are also broadcast via Portland Cable Access on Channel 30. For information on these talks, call (503) 494-5046.

The OHSU School of Nursing faculty also hosts live Internet discussions on Sapient Health Network (www.shn.net). The faculty will answer questions about breast cancer, hepatitis C, and other medical conditions.

Not everything happens in the seventy-two buildings up on Pill Hill. OHSU has a number of outreach programs that connect it with the community down the slope. One exciting example is the Indochinese Socialization Center, an innovative operation with a national reputation for its work with refugees from Vietnam, Laos, and Cambodia. This clinic offers counseling, job training, and advocacy with the INS for those who suffer from a post-traumatic stress disorder related to war experiences.

Providence St. Vincent Medical Center

9205 S.W. Barnes Rd.
(503) 216–1234
www.providence.org/oregon

One cold December day in 1856, five Sisters of Providence debarked from a steamer at Ft. Vancouver across the Columbia River from Portland. They came from Montreal to care for the sick and poor, and settled down here to build schools, orphanages, shelters for the mentally ill, and homes for the aged. They also opened Oregon's first hospital, St. Vincent, in 1875. Since those arduous days, the Providence Health System has grown to a regional service that has 1,500 physicians in forty specialties as well as 10,000 other health professionals. In this particular hospital there are 451 beds, 1,600 medical staff, and 3,271 employees. Its specialties include a heart program, a women and children's program, and the Oregon Medical Laser Center where lasers are used in surgery rather than scalpels. Providence St. Vincent Medical Center is also the home of the area's only in-patient mental health facility. For information on another of Providence's hospitals in Portland see the entry for Providence Portland Medical Center in the section on North/Northeast Portland.

Northwest Portland

Legacy Good Samaritan Hospital & Medical Center
1015 N.W. 22nd Ave.
(503) 413-7711

Known fondly as "Good Sam," this hospital was originally constructed in 1873 as a hospital and orphanage. The old wooden structure, which opened with thirty beds, has since been replaced by the current brick structure, which has an average of 280 beds available each year. A Community Health Education Center, (503) 335-3500 or (503) 413-7047 (TDD), is located across the street from the hospital in the administration center. Staff provide information on a variety of health and wellness topics and treatment options. Legacy is also home to the Visiting Nurses Association, (503) 220-1000, and the Breast Health Center, (503) 335-3500, where diagnostic, educational, and support services allow women to get mammograms, receive results quickly, and obtain follow-up tests, counseling, and care.

Overton Place Services for Seniors Under One Roof, 2145 N.W. Overton, (503) 335-3500, provides health and social services to seniors. Among these are the Retired and Senior Volunteer Program (R.S.V.P.), which recruits and places volunteers with a wide variety of non-profit organizations; Store-to-Door, an

Insiders' Tip

Legacy Good Samaritan Community Health Information Center offers a bounty of classes and workshops designed to enhance a healthy life. For a catalog of learning opportunities, call Legacy Referral Services at (503) 335-3500.

organization that delivers groceries, household goods, and prescription medicines to elderly or disabled people; Willamette Columbia Parkinson Society, an information and support organization for Parkinsonians and their families; and the Oregon Stroke Association, an information and support organization for brain-injured persons and their families. And right next door to Overton Place is the Alzheimer's Association office. In addition to housing these volunteer-based, nonprofit organizations, Overton Place is also the symbolic front door to a wide variety of Legacy programs and services offered to seniors and families managing chronic illness.

Southeast Portland

Adventist Medical Center
10123 S.E. Market St.
(503) 257-2500

Located in outer Southeast Portland near Mall 205 is a 302-bed hospital with a medical staff of 500 and 1,600 employees. It is part of Adventist Health, a not-for-profit healthcare system of twenty hospitals throughout the western United States, all open to the general public. The hospitals and clinics are operated by the

OHSU's Physician's Pavillion is home to many doctor's offices. CREDIT: DAVID JOHNSON

Seventh-day Adventist Church with head-quarters in Roseville, California.

Adventist Hospital has a long history in this area. The first hospital in Portland to have all private rooms, it was founded in 1893, by Dr. Louis Belknap as a sanitarium. In 1896 the Seventh-day Adventist Church took full charge of the sanitarium and it began its transformation into a hospital. The Adventist Health System also offers nineteen clinics in the metro area. To make an appointment or find out more about available medical professionals, call the Physicians Referral Line at (503) 256–4000.

Eastmoreland Hospital
2900 S.E. Steele St.
(503) 234–0411

Located near Reed College, this hospital serves the neighborhoods of East and Westmoreland, Sellwood, Woodstock,

and Brooklyn. It's a full-service, community medical center with one hundred beds and 130 physicians on its staff.

North/Northeast Portland
Legacy Emanuel Hospital & Health Center
2801 N. Gantenbein Ave.
(503) 413–2200

During 1902, the hospital's first year, records list just two physicians working for Legacy Emanuel. Today the medical staff is over 2,100. Besides being the largest hospital in the local Legacy Health System, this health center is also the site of one of the two level-one trauma centers in Portland. It is also the home of Legacy Emanuel Children's Hospital staffed by a team of pediatric healthcare professionals who mend bones and treat serious illnesses. To promote safety and health for children, Emanuel also sponsors an annual Healthy Kids' Fair in the spring highlighted with sales of bike helmets and car safety checks. The Children's Hospital has its own Emergency and After Hours Care. After hours, call (503) 313-4684. Call the number above for both information and physician referral.

Providence Portland Medical Center
4805 N.E. Glisan St.
(503) 215–1111
www.providence.org/oregon

The Providence Health System began when Mother Emilie Gamelin of Montreal, Quebec, after the death of her husband and only child, turned to helping the sick and dying. In 1843 she founded the Sisters of Providence. Today her legacy can be seen in a complex system of hospitals, clinics, health plans, long-term care facilities, and educational programs throughout the west from Alaska to California.

Providence Health System offers graduate medical education in the Portland, Oregon, area at Providence Portland Medical Center and Providence St. Vincent Medical Center in two distinct programs. Portland is also home to the Earle A. Chiles Institute, a multidisciplinary center devoted to the research of heart disease, cancer, diabetes, infectious diseases, and heart disease; the Robert W. Franz Cancer Research Center, which focuses on the immune system in treating breast cancer; and the Albert Starr Academic Center for Cardiac Surgery where Dr. Starr, co-inventor of the artificial heart valve, and his colleagues continue to explore the field of cardiac surgery, now including heart transplants.

The campus of the Providence Portland Medical Center is also home to the Child Center at 830 N.E. 47th Avenue, (503) 215-2400. This pediatric outpatient clinic serves children with autism, seizure disorders, and mental health difficulties. The Gamma Knife Center is the newest addition to Providence. The gamma knife is a highly advanced technological tool that uses beams of gamma radiation to treat a variety of brain lesions and disorders. The center opened in March 2001. Providence Resource Lines are (503) 216-6595 or (800) 562-8964. Both lines will help callers select physicians and health education classes and obtain access to various programs. General information on the Providence Health System can be obtained by calling the number given above.

Woodland Park Hospital
10300 N.E. Hancock St.
(503) 257–5500

Along with Eastmoreland Hospital, Woodland Park Hospital is owned and

Insiders' Tip

Want to give those tired dogs a break? How about a half-hour of personalized foot care? Each appointment at one of forty-four Legacy Foot Care sites in the Portland Metro area includes foot evaluation, soaking, cleaning, nail trimming, buffing of corns and calluses, and a massage, all for $19. For a location near you and an appointment call (503) 225-6307.

operated by New American Healthcare Corporation based in Brentwood, Tennessee. This corporation also owns nine other hospitals and medical centers in the United States. The hospital has a physician referral center, which can be reached at (800) 700-3956.

Vancouver

Southwest Washington Medical Center
Medical Center,
400 N.E. Mother Joseph Place
Memorial Health Center,
3400 Main, Vancouver
(503) 972-3000

This center is in fact two medical facilities, both located in Vancouver, and serving Clark County and southwest Washington. Southwest Washington Medical Center—Medical Center, the first hospital in the Pacific Northwest, was established in 1858 by Sister Joseph of the Sacred Heart and was originally called St. Joseph Hospital. It has 360 beds and a level-two trauma center. Clark General Hospital opened in September, 1929, and then changed its name to Vancouver Memorial Hospital in 1945 to honor veterans. In 1977, St. Joseph and Vancouver Memorial Hospitals merged, forming Southwest Washington Hospitals. In 1989, the name was changed to Southwest Washington Medical Center. The latest development at this medical complex is the Family Birth Center with forty-nine beds, many in private rooms with Jacuzzis.

Recently, the main medical campus on Mill Plain Boulevard added a $32 million wing, a $6 million Cancer Center, and a $31 million Physician's Pavilion just west of I-5. All of these new additions combine with earlier facilities to make Southwest Washington Medical Center one of the top one hundred hospitals in the nation.

Specialized Hospitals and Other Medical Facilities

Doernbecher Children's Hospital
3181 Sam Jackson Park Rd.
(503) 418-5700
www.ohsuhealth.com/dch

Child Development and
Rehabilitation Center
(503) 494-8095

Since its founding in 1926, Doernbecher has provided the best available medical care to children in Oregon and southwest Washington, including children from families with limited incomes. Financial assistance, through the Oregon Health Plan or Oregon's Children's Health Insurance Program, assures that services here are available to all of Oregon's youth. About 30,000 children visit Doernbecher every year, some from as far away as northern California, Idaho, Alaska, Hawaii, and Montana.

Today Doernbecher is in a new facility. Thanks to help from tens of thousands of individuals, businesses, and community groups contributing more than $35 million, the new Doernbecher Children's Hospital opened its doors on July 14, 1998. It's a gorgeous building with lots of architectural art aimed at delighting the child in all of us. Also, every family has a private room, complete with its own shower and bathroom. Parents lounges and a research library make stays easier for family members, and large playrooms, courtyards, and an in-house art therapy program help youngsters take their minds off their illnesses.

Doctors here not only do groundbreaking research but also provide a wide range of medical services from bone marrow, stem cell and organ transplants, to treating cancer, cystic fibrosis, and rare bacteriological infections.

VA Hospital on Pill Hill in Southwest Portland is considered one of the best in the nation. CREDIT: DAVID JOHNSON

Pacific Gateway Hospital
1345 S.E. Harney St.
(503) 234–5353, (800) 234–4545

This is Oregon's only freestanding hospital devoted solely to emotional, psychological, and alcohol and drug problems. The sixty-six-bed psychiatric facility, accredited by the Joint Commission on Accreditation of Healthcare Organizations (JCAHO), is divided into three treatment units: an intensive care unit for adults, an adult unit for men and women age eighteen and older, and a unit for adolescents ages twelve to seventeen. Each of these programs is a secure, separate unit within the hospital building. The programs offer an intense seven-days-per-week treatment schedule with programs emphasizing structure and consistency in a safe, supportive, and caring environment for individuals requiring intensive care. Length of stay is individualized to meet the needs of each patient.

U.S. Veterans Hospital
3710 S.W. U.S. Veterans Hospital Rd.
(503) 273–5289
www.portland.med.va.gov

This fairly new and impressively functional VA hospital is good news for regional vets with medical problems. Rather than dodge "Big Nurse," these men and women who served their country receive excellent care from cheerful, nurturing doctors and nurses. They may lose your files once in a while and there's that old "hurry up and wait," but what else is new? One big plus is that this facility is professionally and literally linked to OHSU, its neighbor on Pill Hill. To get from one hospital to the other, patients and staff walk across a Sky Bridge with a terrific view of Portland, the Willamette River, and Mount Hood.

Walk-In and Urgent-Care Clinics

For Portlanders and visitors with urgent health needs, here are a few recommended walk-in clinics and urgent-care facilities. With a few exceptions, like screenings for toxins, you won't need to make an appointment. The listings are arranged geographically. The first one, though, is a handy service provided by Multnomah County Health Department. With one phone call, they'll direct you to the best place for your particular health needs.

Multnomah County Health Department
Health Information and Referral
(503) 248–3816 (voice and TDD)

This is an excellent resource for referrals to urgent-care facilities in your neighborhood or just about any health and wellness facility in the tri-county area. They are open Monday through Friday, 8 A.M. to 5 P.M.

Southwest Portland

Doctors EmergiCenter
9735 S.W. Shady Ln.
(503) 639–2800

This urgent care center's hours are 8 A.M. to 8 P.M. Monday through Friday and 9 A.M. to 6 P.M. Saturday and Sunday.

National College of Naturopathic Medicine
Westside Clinic, 4444 S.W. Corbett St.
(503) 224–8476

The clinic offers walk-in assistance Tuesday to Friday, 8 A.M. to 12 P.M. and a number of free screenings for a variety of conditions held throughout the year. To get a schedule of screenings, call the above number.

Northwest Portland

Legacy Good Samaritan Urgent Care
1015 N.W. 22nd Ave.
(503) 413–8090

Hours for the Good Sam walk-in clinic are 9 A.M. to 9 P.M. Monday through Friday and 10 A.M. to 8 P.M. Saturday and Sunday.

Southeast Portland

Eastmoreland Hospital
2900 S.E. Steele St.
(503) 234–0411

Eastmoreland is not only a hospital but also an urgent-care center operating 24 hours a day.

The National College of
Naturopathic Medicine
Eastside Clinic, 11231 S.E. Market
(503) 255–7355

The clinic offers walk-in assistance Tuesday to Friday, 8 A.M. to midnight. Free screenings for a variety of conditions are held throughout the year. To get a schedule of free screenings call the above number.

NHC Neighborcare Health Clinic
3653 S.E. 34th St.
(503) 288–5995

Neighborhood Health Clinics take care of Portlanders who aren't covered by health insurance or the Oregon Health Plan. An appointment is required. Services include lead screening at a walk-in pediatrics program held from 9 A.M. to 1 P.M. every other Saturday. (This S.E. 34th Street clinic alternates with the NHC Clinic on Martin Luther King Jr. Boulevard to provide this service on all Saturdays.)

Old Town Clinic
219 W. Burnside Ave.
(503) 241–3836

Located in the center of a rehabilitated skid row, this walk-up clinic run by Ecumenical Ministeries offers general and preventative medicine for low-income patients. This care includes physical checkups and information on diseases and treatment for outpatient needs.

North/Northeast Portland

NHC Health Help Clinic
5329 N.E. Martin Luther King, Jr. Blvd.
(503) 288–5995

The NHC Health Help Clinic is another resource for Portlanders not covered by health insurance or the Oregon Health Plan. The clinic holds a lead screening at a walk-in pediatrics program held from 9 A.M. to 1 P.M. on alternate Saturdays. To make an appointment, call the number above.

Insiders' Tip

While shopping at the Boone's Ferry branch of Nature's Fresh Northwest, a gourmet natural food store, stop by the Community Self Care Center for advice on nutrition, information on healthy lifestyles, and an extensive supply of natural healing resources. There is also a naturopath on duty to answer your questions. The address is 17711 S.W. Jean, Lake Oswego; the number is (503) 635-8950.

Hospices

Oregon Hospice Association
812 S.W. 10th Ave.
(503) 228–2104

Hospice is a program of supportive care for anyone with a terminal illness. Hospice focuses on providing a full range of physical, emotional, social, and spiritual comfort to both the patient and his or her family. The Oregon Hospice Association is the primary referral and information source in Oregon for information on hospice care and other options at the end of life. Other resources include: Hospice, 2701 N.W. Vaughn Street, Suite 750, (503) 225-6370, Mt. Hood Hospice, (503) 668-5545, and Providence St. Vincent Hospice, 9340 S.W. Barnes Road, Suite M, (503) 291-2001.

Support Groups for the Mentally Ill

National Alliance for the Mentally Ill
of Multnomah County
619 S.W. 11th Ave., Ste. 219
(503) 228–5692
www.nami.org

This grassroots, self-help and advocacy organization has been in operation since 1979, helping people with mental illness and their families live better lives. Members can attend family education programs, support groups, and general meetings. Membership includes three newsletters.

Sports Medicine Clinics

Rebound
1 Center Ct., Ste. 110
(503) 732–686
www.nwsurgical.com

Located only a limp away from the Rose Garden, home of the Portland Trailblazers, this sports medicine clinic is staffed by physical therapists, a neurosurgeon, and physicians affiliated with Northwest Surgical Specialists and the Portland Orthopedic Clinic. Although professional athletes are its primary patients, Rebound is also open to those who have stretched too hard pruning a tree as well as to point guards whose shooting arms give out in the third quarter. Call the number above for free, twenty-four-hour sports injury information.

Alternative Medicine

With the help of nearly $16 million in federal funds, the Kaiser Center for Health Research, OHSU, the Oregon College of Oriental Medicine, and the National College of Naturopathic Medicine are teaming up to study the effectiveness of alternative medicine. Here are some Portland-based medical alternatives:

Schools and Associated Clinics

East-West College of Healing Arts
4531 S.E. Belmont St.
(503) 231–1500
www.eastwestcollege.com

As well as offering certification in therapeutic massage and bodywork, this college has a continuing education program for licensed massage therapists, massage students, and health-care professionals. It also has a student clinic at which you can get a Swedish massage for $20 and a graduate clinic that also includes shiatsu, deep tissue, and sports massage for $35.

The National College of
Naturopathic Medicine
049 S.W. Porter
(503) 499–4343
www.ncnm.edu

Downtown Clinic,
2220 S.W. 1st Ave.
(503) 499–4343

Eastside Clinic
10226 S.W. Parkway
(503) 255–7355

Westside Clinic
4444 S.W. Corbett St.
(503) 224–8476

The college was founded in 1956 with its first campus in Seattle and a student body of fewer than ten. Now that number has grown to 490 students seeking a four-year doctoral degree in naturopathic medicine or a three-year Master's program in Asian medicine. Classes include anatomy, homeopathy, nutrition, and endocrinology. Along with its academic facility, the college has two teaching clinics in Portland where interns and supervising naturopathic physicians work with patients seeking relief from allergies, colds and flus, sinusitis, arthritis, menopause-related complaints, and many other conditions. For more information see the Walk-In Clinics listed above.

Oregon College of Oriental Medicine
10541 S.E. Cherry Blossom Dr.
(503) 254–3566
www.ocom.edu

This school, founded in 1983 with fourteen students, now has over 150 students working toward a Master's degree in acupuncture and Asian medicine. Courses include traditional Chinese herbal medicine, anatomy, and Western medical pathology. Students come here from China, Korea, Israel, Ecuador, and Mexico as well as Oregon (half the students are from Oregon). There are evening and Saturday appointments at its acupuncture and herbal clinic for the general public.

Insiders' Tip

Want to contribute to the health and wellness of your community by getting some great exercise yourself? Every August, the Providence Health System sponsors the Providence Bridge Pedal, a bicycling jaunt over a series of bridges that arc across the Willamette River from Sellwood to St. Johns. Proceeds from your entrance fee and that of roughly 10,000 other bikesters go toward health and wellness projects.

Western States Chiropractic College
2900 N.E. 132nd Ave.
(503) 255–6771

West Burnside Clinic
134 W. Burnside Ave.
(503) 223–2213

Founded in 1904 with five students, the college now has 500. Ranging from age twenty-four to forty-six, chiropractic interns hail from Belgium, Ireland, Korea, South Africa, and Switzerland. The college has two clinics open to the public: one at the college and another on West Burnside that serves low-income, uninsured patients. If you get a serious kink in your swing you can stop by for a same-day appointment.

General Alternative Care

Hypnosis & Massage Werks
7409 S.W. Capitol Hwy.
(503) 293–9243

Daniel Satchel, a licensed massage therapist, and Jackie Satchel, a clinical hypnotherapist, offer a combination of hypnosis, massage, and body-mind work to decrease stress, chronic pain, and negative habits.

The Macadam Clinic
4650 S.W. Macadam, Ste. 100
(503) 226–2126

Combining allopathic and alternative medicine, this clinic offers a wealth of options, including medical family care, chiropractic care, acupuncture, Chinese medicine, sports medicine, physical rehabilitation, and nutrition.

New Renaissance Bookshop
1338 N.W. 23rd Ave.
(503) 224–4929

This is a good place to find further information about alternative medical practitioners. Located in a Victorian house, the shop is not only the largest metaphysical bookstore in town, it is also a nexus for acupuncturists, massage therapists, aromatherapists, and other holistic healers. The hearty soup in their restaurant side is perhaps all you need to cure what ails you!

Health Spas

Pleiades
1222 S.E. Ankeny St.
(503) 238–8089

Owned and operated by six women, this cooperative spa in an old Victorian house specializes in Ayurvedic-based facials and individually tailored massages ranging from $30 to $80.

Urbaca Salon & Spa
120 N.W. 9th Ave.
(503) 241–5030

This modern facility offers a complete relaxation package from aromatherapeutic massage to manicure/reflexology combinations.

Emergency Numbers and Support Groups

About Face-Portland (for persons with facial disfigurements)	(360) 750–4625
Aging and Disability Services Helpline	(503) 248–3646, (503) 248–3683 (TTY)
Alcohol and Drug Helpline	(503) 232–8108
Alcoholics Anonymous	(503) 223–8569
Alzheimer's Disease Support Groups	(503) 413–7115
(East Portland)	(503) 215–2220
Arthritis Support Group	(503) 222–7246
Brain Injury/Greater Portland:	
Survivor, Family, and Spousal Support Groups	(503) 413–7707
Brain Tumor Support Group	(503) 216–2904
Breast Cancer Education and Support Group	(503) 216–4673
Cancer Support Group	
(East Portland)	(503) 215–6516
(West Portland)	(503) 216–2051
Caregiver Support Group	(503) 215–6048
Domestic Violence Resource Center (24 hours)	(503) 640–1171
Multnomah County Mental Health Crisis (24 hours)	(503) 655–8401
Oregon Poison Center in Portland	(503) 494–8968
Portland Women's Crisis Line	(503) 235–5333
Stroke Support Group	(503) 215–1111, ext. 5264
Urgent Care (Adventist Hospital's 24-hour urgent care)	
(In its Emergency Room)	(503) 251–6155

Athletic Clubs

Loprinzi's Gym
2414 S.E. 41st Ave.
(503) 232–8311

Loprinzi's is one of the oldest and reportedly the friendliest gym in town. There are no initiation fees—just a $40 monthly fee, or $31 if you are fifty-five or older, or a student with an ID, even middle and high school. A couple can use the gym for $32 each. Along with free weights, nautilus, and stairsteps, there's a steam room for men and a sauna for women. There are also free classes in aerobics, Chinese boxing, and yoga. Hours are Monday through Friday from 5 A.M. to 10 P.M., Saturdays 7:30 A.M. to 5 P.M., and Sundays 8 A.M. to 5 P.M.

Nautilus Plus Downtown
614 S.W. 11th Ave.
(503) 222–2639

A social club as well as a workout parlor, Nautilus has an indoor pool, indoor track, state-of-the-art machines, kickboxing classes, whirlpools, saunas, and a steam room. Now this is exercise with style.

Resort to Fitness
2714 N.E. Broadway
(503) 287–0655

This All-Women's fitness club has been around since 1947. Monthly fees are $25 with the first visit free. Rated as the cleanest health club in Portland by *The Oregonian*, Resort to Fitness has thirty-five classes ranging from belly dancing to kickboxing as well as the usual weights and stairsteps. Hours are Monday through Friday 5:15 A.M. to 9:30 P.M. and Saturdays 6:45 A.M. to 6 P.M. It's closed on Sundays.

Veterinary Clinics

Forest Heights Veterinary Clinic
7365 S.W. Barnes Rd., Ste. H
(503) 291–1757

Drop-offs and walk-ins are welcome at this full-service clinic that provides surgery, dentistry, lab work, dog and cat boarding, bathing services, and discounts on healthcare packages for little critters, especially ferrets.

Rose City Veterinary Clinic
809 S.E. Powell Blvd.
(503) 232–3105

This sweet-natured little outfit has a complete medical-dental hospital, doctor-supervised boarding, and custom grooming for your pet. The vets and their staff seem to really like animals and to corroborate this, a couple of resident felines wander about saying hello to visitors.

Sunset Animal Clinic
14740 N.W. Cornell Rd., Ste. 20
(503) 690–8249

A noted aspect of this clinic is that it has a veterinary oncologist on staff to work with animals with cancer. The facility also offers surgery, dentistry, geriatric care, grooming, and parasite control.

Retirement

Portland is a particularly agreeable place for retirement whether you are moving here specifically for that purpose or have lived here your whole life. And that's because public life is still celebrated here. We have a sophisticated, affordable, and reliable mass-transit system that is sympathetic to the needs of seniors, an outstanding public library, world-class healthcare, a fine public parks system, and most of the other amenities that make life worth living. The temperate climate ensures that there usually won't be too many very hot or very cold days. In the interest of full disclosure, however, we should let you know that many seniors in the area spend part of the year in warmer climates like Palm Springs, and save their Portland time for the months from June through October, when the weather is especially good.

Portland seniors will find many different housing options in many different parts of the city. (Currently, Washington County has the fastest-growing senior population.) You will find communities devoted solely to seniors, as well as neighborhoods that have a balance of all ages, whichever you prefer. If you live independently but are ready to give up such tasks as mowing the lawn and maintaining a house, you'll have a wide variety of choices available. And this is also true if you need more help than just having the lawn mowed. One word of caution: Portland is comparatively expensive when it comes to real estate, and most decent houses start at about $150,000. However, if you look hard, you can usually find something less expensive, especially if you're looking for rowhouses or condominiums. Many charming, well-planned, affordable housing communities are being built all across the region; some of these are close to the MAX line. See the Neighborhoods and Real Estate chapter for more information.

Choosing a Retirement Community

Finding the right retirement community is not as simple as it looks. There are so many things to decide! If you've decided it's time to let someone else handle the housework, here are a few tips that may help you find the retirement community that's right for you.

One of the first things to consider is the level of assistance that you'd like. Do you want or need extensive assistance or do you just want to be absolved of mowing the lawn and pruning? And keep in mind that your needs may change over time. Many retirement communities offer graduated levels of care. If the one that you're interested in doesn't, think about whether you'll be willing to pull up roots again in a couple of decades when you need more help.

Another thing to consider is the location. Will you be far from the important features and relationships of your life, like your friends and family, your church, or the nice girl at the neighborhood deli who knows how to make the turkey sandwich just how you like it? What about your favorite activities? Will you be too far from them? You should also find out whether the community provides transportation, is close to mass transit, or both, in case you don't want to drive.

Depending on the extent of its services, you will also want to inspect the level at which they are delivered. Ask if you can see the kitchen and take a look at what they're serving. Check to see whether the furniture is comfortable and the rugs are maintained. Look at the landscaping.

Naturally, the folks in the front office will be pleased to take you around their retirement community, but you should attempt to get the real scoop on the place by talking with residents. You might try visiting during a meal service so you can measure the ambience and take a look at the food. See what kind of activities are offered and find out about pets and visitors. Is there any space for visitors from out of town? Is the community close to a park where you can take the grandchildren?

Don't be too quick to make up your mind, but start your research early—if you need more extensive care, such as that offered by nursing homes, you might find waiting lists. For people older than fifty-five, choices in senior housing are multiplying. From exclusive golf course and tennis court resorts to skilled nursing care communities, there are facilities for every need and desire.

Our retirement communities offer independent apartment, house, or condominium living, along with support services such as weekly housekeeping. Some locations offer one or more meals per day. Many of these places contract with private home health agencies to provide extra assistance to residents, for which there are additional fees. In general, these retirement communities are not licensed as care facilities, but some locations offer floors or sections that are licensed to provide a higher level of care. There is no financial assistance available to help cover the cost of housing in nonlicensed retirement communities.

In the Portland area alone, there are more than one-hundred retirement communities—one for every taste and budget. Some have buy-in fees and long-term leases, some rent apartments by the month. Some have heated swimming pools, health spas, and tennis courts; others focus on providing activities such as bridge clubs, group outings, and community meals. Many offer different levels of care should you ever need them. We've listed a representative sample of housing styles here to get you started, but you can ask your Realtor, the State Office of Senior and Disabled Services, or an online service such as Senior.com for more comprehensive information. Most retirement centers will be delighted to send you a brochure and arrange a guided tour.

While many of the retirement communities listed below are designed for seniors without serious medical problems, many of them do provide continuing care when needed. Some of the following communities are designed to meet the increasing care needs of an aging resident by providing independent apartment living supplemented by

Insiders' Tip

Portland, like other cities, has apartment buildings solely intended for seniors with low or moderate incomes. Rent is defined as affordable, but it is not subsidized as it would be in buildings operated by Housing and Urban Development. Tenants in these buildings live independently, without supervised assistance. For information, call the Housing Authority of Portland, (503) 228-2178.

an on-site healthcare facility, usually licensed by the State of Oregon Senior and Disabled Services office. The residency agreement includes a contract, and tenants pay a large entrance fee (or buy-in) in addition to monthly rates. Before making a decision on any retirement community, check with Senior and Disabled Services at (800) 232-3020. They can tell you about any complaints made against the place you are considering. If you are in the market for Alzheimer's care or other intensive, continuing-care facilities, we suggest you also call the Ombudsman for Long-term Care at (800) 522-2602. This office can provide a list of comprehensive questions appropriate for the level of necessary care and help you find the right care center.

Retirement Centers

Southwest Portland

Cedar Sinai Park
6140 S.W. Boundary St.
(503) 535-4000

Sprawled over seventeen acres, Cedar Sinai Park offers a wide range of residential options in two different groups of facilities. Rose Schnitzer Manor, the independent living units, are large, gracious garden apartments located at the foot of Portland's beautiful West Hills. Robison Jewish Health Center proffers various levels of assisted living in brand-new spacious apartments. These come with a full menu of care options.

Terwilliger Plaza
2545 S.W. Terwilliger
(503) 226-4911

Since 1958, Terwilliger Plaza has existed as one of the only not-for-profit, self-governing, retirement communities in Oregon. Once you move in, you never have to move again; assistance is provided for all needs, including twenty-four-hour-a-day care. Entering Terwilliger Plaza, however, requires physical as well as financial independence. A variety of apartment sizes and styles are available, and Terwilliger's Personal Service Assistance Program— aiding residents with everything from dressing and meals to medication—helps members live independently in their own apartments for many years. If needed, comprehensive medical services such as respiratory therapy, radiology, physical therapy, and laboratory services are available around the clock. On-site amenities

include excellent meals, emergency response systems in each room, library services, hair salon, patio and garden areas, movies, music therapy, and volunteer programs. Weekly activities and field trips are provided. The membership fees are payable under two different plans. Prices vary, but for a one-bedroom deluxe apartment the entry cost will set you back nearly $100,000.

West Hills Senior Living Residence
5711 S.W. Multnomah Blvd.
(503) 245-7621

Right next door to the West Hills Health and Rehabilitation Center, this retirement center offers an array of services, including help with personal care and housekeeping. Some of the charming apartments may accommodate small pets, and the ten acres of wooded grounds are an added bonus.

Southeast Portland

The Altenheim
7901 S.E. Division St.
(503) 775-1583

The German American Society runs The Altenheim, a nonprofit retirement home that offers an old-world atmosphere in its attractive seventy-unit complex. There is no lease to sign, and no buy-in; payments are made monthly. Rates, which are generally less than $1,000, cover three meals a day, linen and maid service, barber or beautician services, and access to common areas and library service. This facility, surrounded by big trees, is near a wide range of transportation, shopping and medical facilities, and other services.

Many churches, temples, and synagogues offer an array of senior programs. CREDIT: COURTESY OF MARY SICILIA

Town Center Village
8709 S.E. Causey St.
(503) 653–1500

This popular community for active and independent-minded seniors offers generation-crossing activity choices and a host of amenities in its seven different housing choices with many optional services and amenities. Located in Clackamas County close to 82nd Avenue and Interstate 205, Town Center provides easy access to shopping and restaurants. It also provides its own services: this really is a village, with a bank and medical clinic on-site as well as a store, a chapel, two restaurants, and a dining room. In addition, the community provides free health club membership. And lest you think this sounds too urban, note that the Town Center has managed to create a feeling of beauty and peace with its lovely walking paths and gardens.

Willamette View Retirement Community
12705 S.E River Rd.
(503) 654–6581, (800) 446–0670

Perched on a bluff near the Willamette River; Willamette View is one of the area's highly regarded retirement communities, and is sprawled across a twenty-seven-acre sanctuary of meadows, lawns, trees, and pools of crystal-clear water. With more than 600 residents, this retirement community offers a variety of housing options and styles in its two private residential apartment buildings, the Manor and Court, for highly independent and active seniors. Entrance fees range from a low of around $40,200 for a studio to a high of $150,000 for a large two-bedroom apartment. Amenities include everything from a Jacuzzi and swimming pool to housekeeping, maid service, and laundry. The apartments are open and sunny, with handsome kitchens, and offer beautiful views. Other goodies include lush walking and jogging paths, an indoor pool and spa, libraries, craft and hobby areas, courtesy transportation, and a wide range of support services. Gardening, woodworking, bird-watching, billiards, tennis, golf-putting and driving (with a net), swimming, and exercise classes are some of the activities that are available to go-getters. They are also in the process of building a new health center with units for those who need more care, including Alzheimer's patients.

North/Northeast Portland

Calaroga Terrace
1400 N.E. 2nd Ave.
(503) 234–8271

Long recognized as one of the area's premier retirement communities, eighteen-story Calaroga Terrace is in the heart of the city and offers studios and one- or two-bedroom apartments with a variety of floor plans. Security is foremost at Calaroga, and the front desk is staffed around the clock. On-site amenities include inside parking and everything from barber, bank, and beauty shop to a dining room, hobby rooms, health center, and outdoor patio gardens. No buy-in fees here; monthly prices range from about $1,000 for a small studio to more than $2,500 for a spacious two-bedroom, two-bath apartment.

Northwest Portland

Bishop Morris Place
2420 N.W. Marshall
(503) 221–2075

You might be ready to give up the hassle of daily cooking and cleaning, but are you ready to give up the charms of urban life? Shopping? Day spas? People-watching? You can keep all those things by arranging to live at Bishop Morris Place, which is right in the heart of the Northwest 23rd neighborhood. Bishop Morris features housekeeping, laundry, and full kitchens in their one- and two-bedroom apartments, or a lovely facility dining room if

you prefer. You will also have access to covered parking and transportation.

Outlying Areas

Beaverton Lodge Retirement Residence
12900 S.W. 9th St., Beaverton
(503) 227–7645

Beaverton Lodge offers rentals of its large one- and two-bedroom apartments for a reasonable price, considering its amenities. Monthly rent ranges from about $1,200 to about $1,800; for those prices, you will have maid service, cable television, kitchens, storage rooms, and decks. Even nicer, you'll have access to the common areas and all they have to offer, from an indoor pool and exercise room to an in-house theater with a big-screen television for movie-watching. Beaverton Lodge is staffed twenty-four hours each day, and they will help you with transportation should you need it. A meal plan is available, and so are tours of the Beaverton Lodge.

Creekside Village Retirement Residence
5450 S.W. Erickson Ave., Beaverton
(503) 643–9735

Creekside Village provides very attractive one- and two-bedroom apartments in a variety of sizes and styles on its four-acre landscaped grounds. The monthly rent, ranging from about $1,350 to about $1,650, includes many popular amenities, such as maid and linen services, transportation, hobby areas, gardens, a library, and many activities. Meals are available. Residents enjoy the outdoor walking and jogging paths as well as the classes and recreational activities. In addition, a senior center, city park, and swimming pool are just a few blocks away. On-site amenities include barber and beauty shops, a bank, a pharmacy, and a little store.

Rose Villa
13505 S.E. River Rd., Milwaukie
(503) 654–3171, (888) 652–7673

Rose Villa, near the Willamette in Milwaukie, offers the best of two worlds: independent living as well as the comfort and security of a retirement community. The substantial acreage (twenty-one of them) is well manicured and attractive. The retirement center is organized around cottage apartments—back as well as front doors and no stairs—that are available in a variety of floor plans and sizes. This is a friendly community that accepts small pets and provides spacious garden areas for residents. Apartments have full kitchens, but Rose Villa also offers flexible meal plans. Moreover, skilled nursing care is available if needed. Rose Villa is a nonprofit retirement community.

Village at Forest Glen
Retirement Community
13775 S.W. Scholls Ferry Rd., Beaverton
(503) 579–6000

The Village at Forest Glen is a lovely independent-living complex that provides dinners Monday through Friday. The rest of the time, you're on your own (kitchens are provided). But that will give you the chance to stroll the immaculate grounds with one of the friendly residents or participate in one of the many activities and outings planned by the staff. The units are privately owned but many of them are rented out for very reasonable prices. It's such a nice place that they're building a facility for assisted living and nursing care next door, so you won't have to leave if you ever need more than weeknight dinners.

Home Ownership in Senior Communities

Home ownership in a senior retirement setting is available in the following communities, which are primarily intended for independent living for persons over fifty-five years of age. Except for the retirement setting, the arrangements are not very different from home ownership in the community at large, and assistance in the home is the responsibility of the resident.

Portland

Claremont Adult Resort Living
15800 N.W. Country Club Dr.
(503) 629–5614

Does the idea of living on the edge of a beautiful golf course sound appealing? Ten miles from Portland's city center, Claremont is one of the most exclusive adult communities in the state, with beautifully built homes selling for between $260,000 and $400,000. While

Insiders' Tip

Need legal help? "Legal Issues for Older Adults," published by the Oregon State Bar Association, is a fine reference guide. It contains 146 pages of legal information ranging from Medicare to age discrimination, and it includes valuable insights on safety, insurance, and landlord-tenant rights. To order, call (800) 452-8260, or check it out on-line at www.osbar.org. If you'd like to speak to a lawyer, call the Multnomah County Legal Aid Society, (503) 224-4086; the Volunteer Lawyers Project, (503) 224-1606; or the Oregon State Bar Referral, (503) 684-3763.

one doesn't have to be retired to live here (it just doesn't allow children younger than eighteen), most residents are fifty-five or older. Many are retired professionals who have active, vigorous lifestyles. The custom-planned houses have fireplaces, private outdoor terraces, spacious island kitchens, big master suites, studies, and oversize garages. There are at least ten distinctive styles of homes to choose from. Claremont's grounds are meticulously maintained; ponds, waterfalls, streams, and fountains are everywhere, and the golf and putting course are excellent. Two elegant and comfortable clubhouses are available only to residents and guests, and a pro shop, two outdoor swimming pools, tennis and croquet courts, lawn bowling, and a fitness center are on-site. The town of Cedar Mills, which offers all the shopping opportunities one could ask for, is just a mile away. Six furnished model homes are open to visitors each day between 9 A.M. and 5 P.M.

Summerplace
2020 N.E. 150th Ave.
(503) 257–0733

This is the biggest and most popular retirement community on the entire Eastside. Summerplace, which has less than 1,000 residents, offers a combination of housing styles and condominiums, with prices ranging from $150,000 to $250,000. There is a wide selection of houses with two bedrooms and two baths. Many seniors here pursue a variety of activities from ballroom dancing to golf, to attending the numerous spaghetti dinners and crab feeds that Summerplace holds. Besides the outdoor swimming pool and billiards room, there are tennis courts and a well-equipped exercise and weight room to help residents stay in shape. Summerplace also offers its residents a variety of fun classes, ranging from woodcarving to flower arranging. Although there isn't a golf course on-site, one of the area's most popular golf clubs, Glendoveer (see our Golf chapter), is only a stone's throw away.

Summerplace is located in a fairly quiet area of outer Northeast Portland off of 148th Avenue, but is close to major arterials such as Marine Drive and Glisan Street. There are numerous medical and shopping facilities and plenty of restaurants in the vicinity.

Outlying Areas

King City
15300 S.W. 116th Ave., King City
(503) 639–4082

King City, which was incorporated as a city in 1966, is widely recognized as one of the most successful adult communities in the Pacific Northwest. Its population of about 2,100 lives in 1,500 homes, apartments, condominiums, and town houses all in a variety of sizes, styles, and prices. Twelve miles south of downtown Portland and just over the hill from the city of Tigard, King City has its own shopping center, which serves its residents and other nearby adult communities as well. The grounds are beautifully manicured and the homes are well maintained. A fine golf course is on-site, as is a modern residential center, which provides comfortable living, dining, and recreation for residents who no longer want to maintain individual homes.

Home Sharing

Shared Housing
1819 N.W. Everett St.
(503) 225–9924

An Ecumenical Ministries of Oregon program, Shared Housing has proven to be invaluable to many seniors, enabling them to stay in their homes in spite of financial or physical limitations. This referral and matching service brings together those who need affordable housing with those who can provide it, and has arranged more than 2,000 home-sharing agreements since 1982. Through the program, housing is provided in exchange for vital services such as cooking, cleaning, and yard work. Agreements can include rent only, services and reduced rent, room and board, and room and board plus salary. Shared Housing staff checks references, arranges initial meetings, and provides periodic follow-ups. There is a one-time placement fee ranging between $25 and $60, depending on the homeowner's income.

Resources for Seniors

Employment

American Association of Retired Persons (AARP)
8440 S.E. Sunnybrook Blvd., Clackamas
(503) 652–8855

AARP Senior Employment Program
4610 S.E. Belmont Ave., Portland
(503) 231–8078

AARP's Senior Employment Program provides temporary work experience for people fifty-five and older who have limited financial resources. The program focuses on giving clients an opportunity to sharpen and develop skills while searching for a permanent job. Clients are placed in nonprofit or public service agency positions for twenty hours per week to receive on-the-job training.

Dislocated Workers Project
4510 N.E. 102nd Ave., Portland
(503) 252–0758

This federally-funded program eliminates the isolation and frustration of looking for a job by offering a wide range of free services, including job search workshops, computer classes, counseling, and a resource room for seniors who are seeking full-time employment.

Life and Career Options Program
Clackamas Community College
19600 S. Molalla Ave., Oregon City
(503) 657–6958, ext. 2526

This free, ten-week class is taught by licensed counselors and helps seniors and others going through life transitions to explore their options, including employment. The classes meet twice weekly and are available during the day and in the evening.

Home Repair and Weatherization

Christmas in April
5000 N. Willamette
(503) 283–7515

12555 S.W. 4th St., Beaverton
(503) 644–4544

This nonprofit agency donates material and labor to do extensive remodeling on homes owned by low-income seniors. They accept referrals in the fall and winter and do the work in the spring.

City of Beaverton Housing Rehabilitation
4755 S.W. Griffith Dr., Beaverton
(503) 526–2533

This program provides grants and loans for roof and other repairs for low-income home owners who live within the Beaverton city limits.

Community Energy Project
422 N.E. Alberta St., Portland
(503) 284–6827

The Community Energy Project helps seniors on a fixed income to enjoy a warmer home and lower utility bills during the winter months. They install vinyl storm windows that roll up and down easily, they weather-strip doors, caulk and eliminate drafts throughout the home, and they save money and energy by insulating water heaters and pipes. Home owners as well as renters are welcome to call and all services and materials are provided free of cost.

Home Access and Repair for the Disabled and Elderly (HARDE)
Washington County Aging Services Dept.,
133 S.E. 2nd Ave., Hillsboro
(503) 640–3489

The HARDE program for low- to moderate-income seniors can provide a $3,000 grant for accessibility improvements such as ramps, wider doorways, grab bars, lower counters, and security devices. Other improvements for home owners may include heating, plumbing or electrical repairs, and roof and siding upkeep. Low-interest loans up to $17,500 are also available for qualifying residents to make needed home improvements. In some cases the repayment may be deferred as long as the senior owns and occupies the home.

Human Solutions Low Income Energy Assistance Program (LIEP)
2900 S.E. 122nd Ave., Portland
(503) 988–5201,
(503) 988–5215,(Gresham area)

This program, similar to the project listed above, helps low-income families and seniors stay cozy while reducing their utility bills during winter months.

Metro Home Safety Repair Program
12000 S.W. 49th Ave., Portland
(503) 977–4582

This free service helps low-income seniors within Portland's city limits stay in their homes as long as possible by providing assistance with minor plumbing and electrical needs, installing railings, and fixing windows, doors, and stairs that may be dangerous.

Portland Community College Senior Job Center
12000 S.W. 49th Ave., Portland
(503) 977–4582

This "hammer and saw" program hooks up handyman seniors with other elderly home owners and provides minor repairs (under $500) as well as some free services depending on the situation. Projects often include installing ramps and grab bars and repairing gutters.

Meals and Grocery Delivery

Loaves and Fishes/Meals on Wheels
6125 S.E. 52nd Ave.
(503) 736–6325

Since 1969, Loaves and Fishes and their army of caring volunteers have carried out their mission: "To enrich the lives of seniors and assist them in maintaining independence by making nutritious food,

Insiders' Tip

What if you're a healthy senior but your spouse needs substantial care? Life can be difficult for those whose family members have chronic and debilitating diseases—but help is close at hand. Expressions, (503) 252-9361, which cares for Alzheimer's patients, recently opened right next door to Summerplace (see Home Ownership in Senior Communities). It's part of a growing trend that places continuing care facilities adjacent to facilities for independent seniors, permitting families to stay together. Adult daycare centers are another way for seniors and their families to find respite and care. Providence ElderPlace is one of a number of interdisciplinary healthcare programs set up to provide comprehensive care for both body and soul to frail seniors who are still living at home. They may be reached at (503) 215-6556. You can also check with your local office of the Agency on Aging or SDSD to find out about similar programs.

social contacts, and other resources easily available." Loaves and Fishes provides more than one million low-cost, nutritious meals to senior citizens in the Portland Metro area each year. In addition, each day Meals on Wheels delivers thousands of hot meals throughout the metro area to homebound seniors who are at least sixty years of age or have a spouse sixty or older. Although the suggested donation for a meal is $2.25, no one is turned away. Besides offering balanced and carefully planned meals and fellowship, Loaves and Fishes sponsors numerous activities and parties throughout the year, especially on the holidays. Loaves and Fishes centers offer a lot more than hot meals—companionship, spiritual fellowship, and ethnic meals and celebrations make the centers a hub of activities for a wide range of elderly clients. (See the gray box for a complete list of Loaves and Fishes centers.)

Store to Door of Oregon
2145 N.W. Overton
(503) 413–8223

This volunteer agency delivers groceries to senior citizens and helps with transportation needs throughout most of Multnomah and Washington Counties.

Senior Citizens Council of
Clackamas County
19241 Beavercreek Rd., Oregon City
(503) 657–1366

The Senior Citizens Council offers a variety of services, including grocery delivery, home care, help with medical equipment and oxygen tanks, and information and referral assistance.

Recreation and Education

Portland Area Senior Centers

Senior centers around the Portland metro area are an oasis of hospitality, compassion, and fun for many senior citizens. Besides offering such wide-ranging activities as ballroom dancing, bingo nights, Bible classes, and knitting and crocheting sessions, they are a place for seniors to meet longtime companions as well as to make new friends and learn about different cultures.

In addition to providing recreational and educational activities, the centers also function as information and referral sites, and periodically provide health and cholesterol screenings, tax and legal assistance, flu shots, and referrals for medical and mental health needs. At many senior centers, volunteers are available to help

Insiders' Tip

The much beloved Multnomah County Library earns the affection of local citizens with programs such as Cyber Seniors, which teaches seniors how to use computers. Volunteers from the library can bring computers to senior centers in order to teach people how to tame the wilds of the Internet, reserve books over the Web, use e-mail, and other useful subjects. For more information, call the Cyber Seniors coordinator at (503) 988-6256. Once you're wired, Cyber Seniors maintains an excellent Web site for you to peruse: www.multnomah.lib.or.us/lib/seniors.

Loaves and Fishes Centers in the Portland Metro Area

Beaverton
5550 S.W. Hall Blvd.
(503) 643–8352

Belmont
4610 S.E. Belmont St.
(503) 988–5566

Cherry Blossom
740 S.E. 106th Ave.
(503) 256–2381

Downtown
601 W. Burnside St.
(503) 226–1906

Fook Lok
4937 S.E. Woodstock St.
(503) 771–3601

Gresham
50 N.E. Elliott St.
(503) 665–7191

Hollywood
4400 N.E. Broadway
(503) 281–8109

Lents
10325 S.E. Holgate St.
(503) 762–8997

Northeast
5325 N.E. Martin Luther King Jr. Blvd.
(503) 248–5211

Northwest
1819 N.W. Everett St.
(503) 223–5069

Sellwood-Moreland
1814 S.E. Bybee Blvd.
(503) 235–0112

Southwest
7688 S.W. Capitol Hwy.
(503) 244–3873

St. Johns
8832 N. Syracuse St.
(503) 286–8156

Tigard
8815 S.W. O'Mara St.
(503) 620–4613

Tualatin-Durham
8513 S.W. Tualatin Rd.
(503) 692–6767

University Park
9009 N. Foss St.
(503) 285–8199

with a variety of in-home services, shopping and transportation, and other needs. See the box in this chapter that gives addresses and phone numbers for many Portland centers.

Senior Leisure Service
Portland Parks and Recreation
426 N.E. 12th Ave.
(503) 823–4328

Activities ranging from piano lessons and ceramics classes to Native American Pow-wows and hikes on Mount Hood are available at low cost through the Portland Parks and Recreation's Senior Leisure Service program. There are also a variety of excursions and daytrips planned throughout all seasons of the year. Some are close, such as jaunts to see the Swan Island dahlias and to ride the Canby Ferry; others are all-day affairs at the Oregon coast or treks up to Silver Star Mountain in Washington. The year-round seniors program provides many great opportunities to meet new friends while staying in good physical condition. Wilderness hikes—to destinations such as Lewis River Falls, Blue Lake, Mount Adams, and Devil Rest Trail in the Columbia Gorge—are offered every weekend during the summer and spring months. The program is progressive, giving novices a chance to build up stamina and strength. Other activities include dances to big band orchestras, visits to area golf courses, art classes, yoga training, and computer classes. Activities are held at park sites throughout the city. The service will also help golfers obtain an identification card for reduced greens fees at City of Portland courses. The cost for the card is $5. Be sure to check out the Portland's Parks chapter for more information on the vast offerings of this wonderful park system.

Portland Parks and Recreation
Community Centers
1120 S.W. 5th Ave.
(503) 823–7529

Portland Park Bureau's community centers offer a variety of programs and a good number of them are designed specifically for senior citizens. Many of the centers have swimming pools; most have fitness centers and basketball and volleyball courts. It would be impossible to list all the courses that Portland Parks offers—even classifying them takes several pages in the seasonal Portland Parks and Recreation catalogue. However, to give you an idea, recent offerings included line dancing, drawing and watercolor painting classes, guitar and piano lessons, birdhouse building, stained glass, sculpting, origami, and flower arranging. Community centers provide more than instruction and classes—they are hubs of social activity. Contact the Parks office to have a complete catalogue sent to you.

Transportation

The senior centers in the Portland metro area provide a wide variety of services, including help with transportation needs in their area. But they can only do so much, so a variety of other agencies and volunteer groups have stepped up to fill the gaps in transportation services for seniors.

American Red Cross
3131 N. Vancouver Ave.
(503) 280–1445

Providing nonemergency transportation to seniors throughout Multnomah and Washington Counties, the American Red Cross will gladly help with almost any request in return for a modest $1.25 donation. This helpful service is available on weekdays from 9 A.M. until 3 P.M., but they stay very busy and it is best to schedule your ride at least four days in advance.

Portland seniors bridge the generation gap. CREDIT: COURTESY OF MARY SICILIA

Portland's Senior Centers

Southwest Portland

Neighborhood House Senior Center, 7688 S.W. Capitol Hwy., (503) 244–5204
Northwest Pilot Project, 1430 S.W. Broadway, (503) 227–5605
Mittleman Jewish Community Center, 6651 S.W. Capitol Hwy., (503) 244–0111

Northwest

Friendly House Senior Center, 1816 N.W. Irving St., (503) 224–2640

Southeast

Fook Lok Woodstock Loaves & Fishes, 4937 S.E. Woodstock Blvd., (503) 771–3601
Portland Impact Senior Center, 4610 S.E. Belmont St., (503) 988–3660
Volunteers of America, 537 S.E. Alder St., (503) 235–8655

North/Northeast

YWCA-St. Johns Branch, 8010 N. Charleston St., (503) 721–6777
Peninsula Senior Center, 7548 N. Hereford St., (503) 289–8208
Hollywood Senior Center, 1820 N.E. 40th Ave., (503) 288–8303
The Salvation Army Rose Center for Seniors, 1785 N.E. Sandy Blvd., (503) 239–1221
Urban League of Portland, 10 N. Russell, (503) 280–2600

Mid-County (Outer East Multnomah County)

YWCA Mid-County District Center, 2900 S.E. 122nd Ave., (503) 248–5480

East County

YWCA East County District Center, 501 N.E. Hood St., Gresham, (503) 306–5680

Washington County

Community Senior Center of Hillsboro, 750 S.E. 8th St., Hillsboro, (503) 648–3823
Tigard Senior Center, 8815 S.W. O'Mara St., Tigard, (503) 620–4613
Elsie Stuhr Adult Leisure Center, 550 S.W. Hall Blvd., Beaverton, (503) 643–9434
Tualatin-Durham Senior Center, 8513 S.W. Tualatin Rd., Tualatin, (503) 692–6767

Clackamas County

Canby Adult Center, 1250 S. Ivy St., Canby, (503) 266–2970
Estacada Community Center, 200 S.W. Clubhouse Dr., Estacada, (503) 630–7454
Gladstone Senior Center, 1950 Portland Ave., Gladstone, (503) 655–7701
Lake Oswego Community Center, 505 G Ave., Lake Oswego, (503) 635–3758
Milwaukie Center, 5440 S.E. Kellogg Creek Dr., Milwaukie, (503) 653–8100
Molalla Senior Center, 315 Kennel St., Molalla, (503) 829–4214
Pioneer Community Center, 615 5th St., Oregon City, (503) 657–8287
Sandy Senior and Community Center, 38438 Pioneer Blvd., Sandy, (503) 668–5569
Wilsonville Senior Center, 7965 S.W. Wilsonville Rd., Wilsonville, (503) 682–3727

The Oregon Senior & Disabled Services Division (SDSD) of the Oregon Department of Human Services is the agency that assists older adults, persons with disabilities, and their caregivers, and they are dedicated to helping people live dignified and independent lives. They serve as a clearinghouse for all kinds of information, from how to find a nursing home to how to find discounts on travel. You can reach the state office of SDSD at 500 Summer Street NE, Salem, OR 97310, (503) 945-5811, (800) 282-8096 (voice/TTY). Their Web site, www.sdsd.hr.state.or.us, is easy to use, comprehensive, and features many links to local, state, and national organizations. Listed below are local branches of SDSD.

Multnomah Area Agency on Aging
421 S.W. 5th, 3rd Floor, B161, Portland
(503) 248-3620

Multnomah District Office
740 S.W. Mohawk St., Tualatin
(503) 691-6587

**Multnomah County Area
Agency on Aging**
2900 S.E. 122nd Ave., B303, Portland
(503) 248-5480

**East Multnomah County Aging
Services Division**
(503) 248-3840, (503) 306-5678 (voice/TTY)

**Portland East Disability Services and Area
Agency on Aging Office**
3552 S.E. 122nd Ave., Portland
(503) 248-3722, (503) 760-7674 (voice/TTY)

**Portland North Disability Services and
Area Agency on Aging Office**
4925 N Albina Ave., Portland
(503) 248-3479

Portland N.E. Area Aging Agency
5325 N.E. Martin Luther King, Jr. Blvd.,
Building 322, Main Floor, Portland
(503) 248-5470

Portland S.E. Area Aging Agency
4610 S.E. Belmont St., 2nd floor, Portland
(503) 248-3660

**Portland S.E. Disability Services Office
and Area Agency on Aging Office**
2446 S.E. Ladd Ave., Portland
(503) 248-3288, (503) 231-0091 (voice/TTY)

Portland West Area Aging Agency
1430 S.W. Broadway, Ste. 100, Portland
(503) 248-5460

**Portland West Disability Services Office
and Area Agency on Aging Office**
1139 S.W. 11th, Portland
(503) 248-3690

**Washington County Dept of Aging and
Veterans' Services**
133 S.E. 2nd Ave., Hillsboro
(503) 640-3489, (503) 640-6167,
(503) 640-6398 (TTY)

Hillsboro Senior Resource Center
133 S.E. 2nd Ave., Hillsboro
(503) 693-0999, (503) 681-2693 (TTY)

Tigard Senior Resource Center
11515 S.W. Durham Rd., Ste. E-5, Tigard
(503) 968-2312, (503) 968-2713 (voice/TTY)

Beaverton SDSD Disability Service Office
4805 S.W. Griffith Dr., Ste. B, Beaverton
(503) 627-0362 (voice/TTY), (503) 626-4996

Clackamas Area Agency on Aging
18600 S.E. McLoughlin Blvd., Oak Grove
(503) 655-8640

Clackamas County Social Services Transportation Reaching People
(503) 655-8208, (800) 422-7741

Through this agency, volunteers provide transportation to medical appointments, barbers and beauty shops, grocery stores, senior centers, and restaurants. The services are restricted to seniors and disabled persons residing in Clackamas County.

Medical Transportation
(503) 802-8700

This agency, which bills services to the Oregon Health Plan or Medicaid, contracts through Tri-Met—the area's public mass transportation agency—and specializes in providing senior citizens with rides to and from medical appointments from 7 A.M. to midnight on as little as thirty minutes notice. They use a variety of private sources, including cab companies.

Neighborhood House Aging Services
7688 S.W. Capitol Hwy., Portland
(503) 244-5204

Neighborhood House helps with transportation needs to medical and dental appointments in southwestern Multnomah County.

Project Linkage
2200 N.E. 24th Ave., Portland
(503) 249-0471

Through its 175 volunteers, this agency assists elderly people living in Northeast Portland with a wide range of transportation needs, as well as yard work, house keeping, minor bookkeeping and bill paying, shopping, and home maintenance.

Tri-Met
4012 S.E. 17th Ave., Portland
(503) 962-2455 (request line),
(503) 802-8000 (lift service)

Tri-Met has a number of senior and disabled services. The transit system runs a request line that operates from 7.30 A.M. to 5.30 P.M. weekdays. But more than that, Tri-Met's lift service will provide door-to

Insiders' Tip

The Ombudsman Program, (503) 823-5269, provides a variety of free services to elderly clients, including information, referral, assistance completing forms, and safety checks.

door transportation for almost any senior citizen in need in the greater Portland area. First, call and apply; it takes about three weeks for an application to be processed.

Volunteer Opportunities

If you have the time, many agencies, services, and hospitals in the Portland Metro area would be grateful for your volunteer services. Here are just a few places to get you started.

Elders in Action
501 S.W. Washington St.
(503) 823-5269

Foster Grandparents Program
Metro Family Services
2200 N.E. 24th Ave.
(503) 284-9322

OASIS Intergenerational Tutoring
621 S.W. 5th Ave.
(503) 321-5022

Oregon State Department of Human Resources Volunteer Services Program
(503) 731-3208

Retired and Senior Volunteer Program of Multnomah County
(503) 413-7787

Worship

Whether you are new to town and looking for a home church or just visiting, Portland has hundreds of places of worship, ranging from Adventist Churches to Zen Buddhist Temples, and every denomination in between. The telephone book is one obvious place to help you find a church, temple, or synagogue, but other resources are also available. *The Oregonian* publishes an extensive religion section each Saturday; there, you may find more information about services. Its calendar lists a wide variety of religious events, including everything from bake sales and concerts to plays, seminars, and lectures. You can also call the Ecumenical Ministries of Oregon at (503) 221-1054. This association comprises sixteen denominations, has a wide range of participating members, and can serve as a good referral source, as well as providing general information.

If you are in town long, you may find that some of your new friends and acquaintances don't attend church. Reports in *The Oregonian* regularly observe that Oregon residents rank lowest nationally in claiming affiliation with organized religions, which is, given Oregon's early religious history, ironic. About 17 percent of Oregonians classify themselves as "nonreligious," compared with a national average of 7 percent. It's not that they don't believe in anything, however. Only about 1 percent of Oregonians claim to be agnostic, and an even smaller percentage claims to be atheist. Apparently, a significant number of Oregonians are following their own spiritual path, even if it's not one that is readily labeled.

Oregonians tend to be a diverse lot when it comes to religion. A profusion of spiritual traditions thrive in Portland and throughout Oregon. In addition to more established churches, Oregon's mountains, plains, and forests shelter many a retreat center devoted to the practices of Native American spirituality, Chi Gong, Western Buddhism, healing arts, and meditation. While the majority of religious persons in the state practice some form of Christianity, with Catholics and the Latter-day Saints having the largest congregations, other faiths are also well represented. Judaism, Islam, and Buddhism all have active populations; in fact, practitioners of Buddhism can claim to have the largest following of any faith besides Christianity. The Unitarian Church and other liberal churches are quite vigorous. We have also made room for less conventional faith practices—the Wiccans and Neo-Pagans, for example, have a visible, if small, presence, and they are representative of the variety of spiritual practices found in the area and the total numbers they attract—especially if you add those 17 percent of Oregonians who are believers in spirituality but don't consider themselves religious.

In addition to their spirit of religious independence, Portlanders also are known for their tolerance and, among churchgoers, for their ecumenical spirit, both of which were strengthened in the early 1990s when a group proposed anti-gay legislation. This event mobilized the area's spiritual community to oppose it, bringing more religious coalitions together (from Catholics and Jews to Mormons and Buddhists) than any other happening in Oregon's modern history. At the forefront of the movement was the Ecumenical Ministries of Oregon, which can trace its history back more than eighty years, and which from 1982 to 1992 grew from being the smallest ecumenical ministry in the nation to being the largest.

Portland's Early Religious Communities

Many of Oregon's earliest eastern settlers were Christian missionaries. Methodist missionaries were particularly drawn to the area, determined to save the souls of the local Indians. At this, they were remarkably unsuccessful, but they did persuade some of the soldiers, trappers, and traders who had preceded them, thus establishing the roots of Protestant Christianity and middle-class American life in the area. Arriving at Fort Vancouver in 1834, Rev. Jason Lee got right to work building churches and schools in various spots throughout the Willamette Valley, notably at Oregon City, the eventual end of the Oregon Trail. Moreover, the Methodist missionaries were very well connected to Washington, D.C., and were able to persuade Congress if not to practice Methodism, then at least to implement some of the economic and political measures that the missionaries believed were expedient.

Catholic missionaries were energetic and organized, as well; having been invited by French Canadian settlers from Fort Vancouver, two priests, the Rev. Father Blanchet and his assistant, the Rev. Father Demers, arrived in 1838. Blanchet was a particularly talented administrator who understood better the native tribes, but the Catholics also had more success with the white settlers when it came to recruitment. And, like Jason Lee and his brethren, they founded schools and parishes, providing a solid foundation for Catholicism in Oregon.

The Methodists and Catholics were soon joined by Congregationalists and Presbyterians, and others followed thereafter. By the middle of the nineteenth century, most of the major Christian denominations were well represented in Portland. Together, the various missionary sects had a significant influence on the social, political, economic, and institutional life of the state. (Other forms of worship, such as Judaism and Buddhism, were also well represented, though their influence on the emerging government was less direct.)

The building of churches was a frequent activity of Portland citizens during the last half of the nineteenth century. By the 1890s, the area's population was served by dozens and dozens of churches—at least one church for every 600 people, according to some sources. Throughout western Oregon, visitors can find examples of pioneer churches and their more elaborate successors. St. Paul's Church in St. Paul was built in 1846 and is the oldest Catholic parish in the state, its brick edifice succeeding a log church built ten years before. In Portland, **Oaks Pioneer Church** (855 S.E. Spokane) at the edge of Oaks Park, was originally built in 1851 and lived most of its life as St. John's Episcopal Church in Milwaukie. It has been moved three times but now rests in Oaks Park as an historic landmark. **St. James Presbyterian** (1315 S.W. Park); **First Presbyterian Church** (1200 S.W. Alder); the **First Congregational Church** (126 S.W. Park); the **First Baptist Church** (909 S.W. 11th); and **St. Patrick's Church** (1639 N.W. 19th); were all completed by the mid-1890s. **"The Old Church,"** which was originally Calvary Presbyterian Church (1422 S.W. 11th), was finished in 1882; this structure is now used for lectures, concerts, and other community events. **Trinity Cathedral** (147 N.W. 19th) was finished in 1906. And the Christians were not the only congregations building houses of worship; three synagogues were built in the area, one of which is **Temple Beth Israel** (1931 Flanders), which was originally founded in 1858. Its present building was completed in 1928 and is a striking example of Byzantine architecture.

All creatures great and small: Trinity Cathedral includes the family pets as it honors St. Francis of Assisi.
CREDIT: COURTESY OF MARY SICILIA

African-American, Buddhist, LDS, and Other Religious Groups

When it comes to ethnic and cultural harmony, Oregon's early history was lamentable. For groups that suffered prejudice, especially African Americans and Chinese workers, their houses of worship provided respite from the danger and tedium of the daily struggle. African-American churches have a long history in the area. The earliest African Methodist Episcopal Church was the People's Church, founded in 1862 on the Westside and later moving to the Eastside, where it became the African Methodist Episcopal Zion Church. Bethel AME was founded in the 1890s, as was Mount Olivet Baptist. **Bethel AME,** 5828 N.E. 8th Ave., and **Mount Olivet,** 8725 N. Chautauqua, are both more vigorous than ever, with many innovative programs for fostering social capital among parishioners and the community. And they are not alone: there are now more than fifty-five African-American churches in North and Northeast Portland.

Like other West Coast cities, Portland had a thriving Chinatown in the nineteenth century. This was in part due to the discovery of gold in the south of the state, partly due to steamship service between San Francisco and Portland, and mostly due to direct trade between Portland and cities in China. Portland's Chinatown was at one time the second largest in the nation. The Chinese, however, endured an unimaginable amount of bigotry from the white settlers in the area, and as a result, tended to live together. Many workers, moreover, regarded their life in Oregon as merely temporary, so they did not build many buildings. Nor did they build temples. Instead, they met on 2nd Avenue at a place called the "Chinese Joss House." Japanese workers, who also believed their stay here to be temporary, did choose to erect a temple. In 1891, even though fewer than one hundred Japanese were then living in Portland, the Methodist Episcopal Church in San Francisco commissioned Portland's Japanese Methodist Church, which is now Epworth United Methodist Church. By 1900, more than 2,500 Japanese, mostly young men, lived in Oregon, and the importance of the church grew. Not all Japanese were Christian, of course; the first Japanese Buddhist Temple in the region is the Oregon Buddhist Church in Southeast Portland, which is nearly one hundred years old. Another major temple, the Buddhist Dhihozan Temple, also in Southeast Portland, was founded in 1940, and during the last ten years, the area has seen a remarkable increase in the number of Buddhist Temples built for Chinese, Korean, Cambodian, Vietnamese, and other Asian congregations. In fact, according to some recent data, it appears that the Buddhist population is slightly larger than the Jewish population in Oregon, the only state in which this may be the case.

The Mormon Church (the Church of Jesus Christ of Latter-day Saints) has a significant presence in the Portland area and around the state, with about 100,000 practicing members and 228 congregations in Oregon, in spite of a rather violent beginning. By 1898, the first LDS branch in Oregon was established in Southeast Portland, but the first chapel wasn't built until 1915 at the corner of Madison Street and Southeast 25th Avenue.

Portland's Jewish Community

With eight synagogues in the metro area, compared with only four in the remainder of the state, the Portland Jewish community is quite active. Congregation Shaarie Torah, 920 N.W. 25th Avenue, is Portland's only traditional synagogue; its home—the third since its founding in 1905—is in Portland's Northwest neighborhood. Its busy, vibrant programs include education and outreach, in addition to traditional services. Congregation Beth Israel is stronger than ever; this reformed congregation, which still inhabits its unusual temple, claims the largest membership in Oregon (about 3,000 people). And of

Insiders' Tip

Several churches in Portland offer free or low-cost concerts. Trinity Episcopal Cathedral, 147 Northwest 19th Avenue, (503) 222-9811, has a first-rate choir and hosts many world-class singers and musicians; on the first Sunday of the month at 5 P.M. from October to May, the church offers a splendid vespers service. St. Phillip Neri Catholic Church, at Southeast 18th Avenue and Division Street, (503) 231-4955, also offers many high-quality concerts.

Portland churches, temples, and synagogues are friendly places. CREDIT: COURTESY OF MARY SICILIA

particular importance to Portland's Jewish community is the **Mittleman Jewish Community Center,** 6651 SW Capitol Highway, an excellent facility that is dedicated to enriching Jewish lives. The MJCC, which has been serving the social, cultural, educational, and recreational needs of the community for more than eighty years, features a tremendous assortment of programs for seniors, infants, and Jewish people of all ages. Activities include arts, crafts, swimming, golf, drama, music, and a variety of daytrips. The center also provides kosher lunches five days a week with special Shabbat meals each Friday. MJCC also provides kosher meals on wheels for all homebound persons over sixty who cannot prepare their own meals due to illness, recent hospitalization, or disability. Call MJCC at (503) 244-0111 for more information.

The Catholic Presence in Portland

The Catholic presence in Oregon has been strong since Father Blanchet arrived in 1838 to teach the Indians about Christianity. The Catholic priests had more success in this endeavor, by all accounts, than the Protestant missionaries. One reason may be that they were less interested in holding claims to property. Another reason may be that they had a more sophisticated understanding of Indian cultures. Many Catholic missionaries learned Indian languages so that they could converse better with those they desired to convert. Moreover, these missionaries tried to explain their faith in terms that would be familiar to the local Indians (the most famous of these is the "sahale stick" or the "Catholic ladder," which depicted essential beliefs of Catholicism). Though eventually the Indians declined to become thoroughly Christian, by the time they decided, Catholicism was well established in the valley. Today, the Archdiocese of Portland is vast; it includes close to 300,000 members in 123 parishes, in addition to its missions, schools, universities, and hospitals. The church in Portland plays an active role in the greater community through a wide range of charitable services. The **St. Vincent de Paul Church and Downtown Chapel,** 601 W. Burnside Street, sponsors a wide variety of activities—including community soup dinners, visitations, and open fellowships—that serve the inner city population. Catholic Charities also has a significant presence. This sixty-five-year-old nonprofit social-service agency organizes services to the poor and needy through Catholic agencies. Programs include Adoption and Crisis Pregnancy, AIDS Ministry, Asian Social Services, Centro de Canby, Immigration Legal Services, Ministry to the Elderly, and the Refugee Resettlement.

Modern Era: Variety as the Spice of Faith

By post–World War II, the railroads, shipbuilding industry, and general growth of commercial activities brought increased racial and religious diversity to the Portland area, and today the area's religious community truly reflects the many different beliefs of its people. This diversity has led to even some of traditional faiths to present new aspects of themselves. For example, **The Bridge,** 527 S.E. Pine, is a nondenominational Christian congregation aimed primarily at young people—especially young people who are alienated and alone. Their ministry consists of acceptance, agape, and a healthy dose of liturgical punk rock. The tattooed and pierced preachers perform their ministry through programs such as a skateboard youth group, in addition to the customary premarital counseling, healing support groups, and so on.

Portland is, however, also the home to many conservative and traditional ministries. Ten different Pentecostal churches, more than twenty-five charismatic churches, and fifteen different branches of Baptist churches minister to area residents. Two of the most

Insiders' Tip

All over Oregon, people are gathering to meditate, chant, align their chi, and breathe. The popular and attractive Breitenbush Hot Springs, (503) 854-3314, south of Portland in the Cascades, is a busy center for different New Age practices. In town, the New Renaissance Bookshop, 1338 N.W. 23rd (at Pettygrove), (503) 224-4929, not only provides an abundance of information about the breadth of spiritual practices in the area, but also offers workshops on everything from Kabbalah to Knitting for the Goddess. Another useful resource is the free publication *Alternatives for Cultural Creativity,* widely available throughout the city, especially at coffeehouses and bookstores.

Youth groups in Portland practice good stewardship. COURTESY: MARY SICILIA

active and dynamic are **New Beginnings Christian Center,** 7600 N.E. Glisan Street, which offers a full range of adult and youth services and support groups; and **New Hope Community Church,** 11731 S.E. Stevens Road. Founded by Dale Galloway twenty years ago, New Hope is one of the largest and most active spiritual communities in the state, and its annual pageants and concerts draw thousands of visitors.

Portland also possesses a small, but growing, number of Muslim faith communities. In 1993, the Muslim Educational Trust was founded in order to educate both its Islamic members and their non-Muslim neighbors about the faith. This organization serves as a central resource for several mosques, community centers, and other Islamic resources in the area, and provides outreach and education programs of its own.

Not surprisingly, Portland is also regarded as a stronghold of liberal religion and some of the most dynamic churches in the Pacific Northwest, including the First Unitarian Church of Portland and the Living Enrichment Center, both of which are led by renowned women ministers, may be found here.

Members of the **First Unitarian Church of Portland,** 1011 S.W. 12th Avenue, boldly express their liberal, progressive beliefs, and are often at the forefront of political and socioeconomic issues. Founded in 1866, First Unitarian is one of the most active Unitarian Universalist congregations in North America. It is now the largest Unitarian Church in the nation, with more than 1,500 members, having doubled its membership in the 1990s. Its present church building was finished in 1924—it's a beautiful example of Georgian-style architecture. Its music ministry features ten choirs, piano and pipe organ music, and bell choirs. Outreach programs include adult education classes and groups that serve the homeless and work for social justice, especially the causes of environmental justice, racial equality, and peace. The Rev. Dr. Marilyn Sewell, the senior Unitarian minister, is an eminent writer, speaker, and spiritual leader who is known throughout the nation.

The Living Enrichment Center, 29500 S.W. Grahams Ferry Road in Wilsonville, is a thriving spiritual community based on the principles of New Thought Christianity. The founder and spiritual leader of Living Enrichment is Mary Manin Morrissey, whose weekly sermons attract people from all over the Oregon and Washington area. In addition to Sunday and Wednesday services, the LEC offers ongoing support groups, small group events, pastoral support and counseling, and ministries devoted to the spiritual concerns of men, women, youth, singles, seniors, and others as well. Moreover, LEC has an effective and well-organized "distance ministry" program, where tapes of Mary Manin Morrissey provide the center for focused discussion groups that meet all across the nation.

Dr. Wayne Dyer, Dr. Joan Borysenko, Gary Zukav, Dr. Barbara Marx Hubbard, John Bradshaw, and Gerald Jampolsky are among the well-known guest speakers the LEC has hosted and many popular musicians, including Kenny Loggins and John Denver, have also performed there. Headquartered in Wilsonville on ninety-five forested acres, the LEC shelters the Namaste Retreat and Conference Center; the whole operation gains in popularity each year, drawing thousands of people to the center each week and even more people beyond.

And new ways of exploring old traditions are evolving all the time. The Center for Spiritual Development, directed by the Reverend Canon Marianne Wells Borg, is one of Portland's new forums for spiritual exploration. Associated with Trinity Episcopal Cathedral, the Center has a five-point program of education and outreach. In addition to long (two to three years) interfaith courses that study issues such as spirituality, justice, and religious tradition, the center also teaches different forms of spiritual practice, sponsors programs in healing, organizes pilgrimages, and hosts public lectures by acclaimed writers and speakers such as Karen Armstrong and Huston Smith.

Insiders' Tip

During the warmer months, Sunday masses are celebrated outside in the parklike setting of the Grotto. The Grotto is at Northeast 85th Avenue and Sandy Boulevard; call (503) 254-7371 for schedules.

Media

Newspapers

Magazines

Television

Radio Stations

The first newspaper published in the Pacific Northwest was the *Oregon Spectator*, printed in 1846 on a Washington handpress at Oregon City just south of Portland. Four years later, *The Oregonian* began with a rotary press shipped north from San Francisco. *The Oregonian* is now the largest daily newspaper in the region. The greater metropolitan area is also home to numerous smaller publications, more than forty radio stations, and nearly a dozen different TV stations, including a fine public television network with a half-dozen channels providing around-the-clock programming. With cable hookup, Portlanders have access to about sixty viewing channels.

The local television and radio scene gives viewers and watchers abundant choices, including community, ethnic, and neighborhood publications. Add to this health and wellness, religious/spiritual, food and wine, and business publications sprouting like mushrooms in the Oregon rain. But major daily and weekly newspapers are not as plentiful. Since *The Oregonian* has been in operation since 1850, it has outpaced seven other local papers and eventually lost its daily competitor, the *Oregon Journal*, back in 1961. Now the recently launched *Portland Tribune*, which hopes to go from twice a week to daily, has posed a challenge to the "BIG O." Since the recent closure of the alternative arts and culture paper, PDXS, there are only two news weeklies in the metro area: the long-entrenched *Willamette Week*, once a radical rag, now a more staid watchdog and *Portland Mercury*, a fresh, new voice enjoying its insolence.

If you'd like to get a quick sampling of the variety of magazines and newspapers in the region, most public libraries offer a fairly comprehensive selection, ranging from *The Skanner* and *The Asian Reporter* to *Our Town* and *The Examiner*.

Starting with the daily newspapers, working through the weeklies, biweeklies, monthlies, and quarterlies, here is our take on Portland (and surrounding-area) publications. Unfortunately there is one that got away. In the early 1900s, the *Pacific Monthly*, a literary magazine, had a circulation of 85,000. That once popular publication moved to Arizona and goes by the masthead: *Sunset Magazine*.

Nowadays you can find the big daily newspapers and *Willamette Week* in just about any market or grocery store, but some of the smaller zines are hard to find. Any county library branch is a good place to check, and many small coffeehouses and pubs are brimming with alternative publications. In the second portion of the chapter, we introduce you to Portland's radio and television scene.

Newspapers

Daily publications

The Columbian
701 W. 8th St. Vancouver
(360) 694–3391
www.columbian.com

By far the biggest daily newspaper in southwestern Washington, *The Columbian* started out as a weekly newspaper in 1890. In 1908, it became a daily, and in 1972, grew to include a Sunday morning paper. Herbert Campbell bought the newspaper in 1921, and it has been owned by the Campbell family ever since. *The Columbian* is one of the few family-owned and -operated dailies left in the nation and is the fourth largest newspaper in Washington, with a current daily circulation of 56,000 and a Sunday circulation of 66,000. An afternoon newspaper, *The Columbian* is published every day of the week except Saturday. It prints TV Times on Thursdays, an entertainment guide titled "Weekend and Beyond" on Fridays, a monthly real estate magazine, "Home Book," and a weekly nonsubscriber product "Cover Story," as well as numerous special sections throughout the year. *The Columbian* is available at all newstands and many library branches. You can also look for it on-line.

The Daily Journal of Commerce
2840 N.W. 35th Ave.
(503) 226–1311
www.djc.com

This tabloid newspaper covers everything from local small businesses to venture capital dealings around the Pacific Northwest. Founded in 1872, the *DJC* is a five-day court and commercial newspaper that is the official publisher for the City of Portland. In addition to general business news, the *DJC* publishes extensive construction industry news and data, mostly for readers in Oregon and Washington. The *DJC*, which was purchased two years ago by Dolan Media Co. of Minneapolis, is no giant—its circulation is about 4,000, but it also publishes monthly news-magazines focusing on a wide range of business topics.

The Daily Vanguard
P.O. Box 347 Portland
(503) 725–5686

Published Tuesday through Monday during school months, *The Vanguard* is PSU's free student newspaper. Besides reporting on campus affairs, it covers a variety of news, culture, sports, and social issues. Started as a weekly in 1946, *The Vanguard* became a daily in 1984, and its readership of 5,000 extends beyond the campus into the nearby downtown area. *The Vanguard* publishes an arts and entertainment guide on Fridays, which is packed full of information about places to go and things to do over the weekend. It also prints about eight to ten special issues each year geared to university-related events such as spring break, career days, and a back-to-school survival guide.

The Oregonian
1320 S.W. Broadway
(503) 221–8327
www.oregonlive.com

Owned by the New York-based giant media conglomerate Advance Publications, *The Oregonian* casts a long shadow—not just extending over Portland but over the entire state and well beyond.

Loved by some, intensely disliked by others, it seems everyone has an opinion about "the Big O." It is charged with being too conservative and pro big-business on one hand, while on the other it is accused of leaning too far to the left. Even its critics would agree, however, that as the only major daily newspaper in Oregon, *The Oregonian*, with the largest daily circulation in the Pacific Northwest (upwards of 350,000), dominates the print media scene not only in Portland but in the entire state.

In recent years, Sandra Mims Rowe, who became editor in 1993, made significant changes in the style and structure of the newspaper by reorganizing the departments into news teams that cover broad areas of interest, such as healthcare; education; and crime, justice, and public safety. Most insiders feel that her approach has lessened the organization's hierarchy and bureaucracy and resulted in better and more effective news coverage.

The Sunday Oregonian (circulation 441,000) is a whale of a newspaper, at least triple the size of the typical daily even after the considerable amount of auto, real estate, and other advertisements are culled out. All the regular sections are expanded and such goodies as "Arts and Books," the comic pages, "TV CLICK," and *Parade Magazine* are included. The Friday *Oregonian* is also noteworthy for the special "Arts and Entertainment Guide," full of fun stuff and information about everything from unique places to go hiking, biking, and bird-watching to classical music performances and public lectures. The guide also features comprehensive coverage of clubs, restaurants, movies, and Portland's live music, and fine arts and literary scene. Also, the listing of American and ethnic restaurants (a special recommendations section is conveniently price coded) and the ten-day planner—an "A&E" special fold-out calendar— are particularly useful.

Semiweeklies

Gresham Outlook
1190 N.E. Division St. Gresham, OR
(503) 665–2181
www.theoutlookonline.com
Published Wednesdays and Saturdays, the *Outlook* reports on all the goings-on in the Gresham area and is particularly noted for its education and sports coverage. Founded in 1911, the *Gresham Outlook* is owned by the Pamplin Corporation, which has also snapped up many community newspapers. In 1996, the *Outlook* boosted its total circulation to more than 12,000 by purchasing a sister publication, *The Sandy Post*, which reports on the city of Sandy, just to the west, and its surrounding area.

Portland Tribune
629 S.W. 5th, Ste. 400
(503) 226–6397
This new biweekly (Tuesday and Thursday) is a traditional newspaper with objective news coverage, features, and columns. Plans call for it to shift into daily publication as soon as it gets its sea legs. If so, the shoulder-bumping of two dailies will take Portland readers back to the pre-dish and cable days of fiercely competitive journalism.

Weeklies

The Asian Reporter
922 N. Killingsworth, Ste. 1-A
(503) 283–4440
www.asianreporter.com
This ethnic newspaper carries a unique blend of local, regional, national, and international news that impacts or is of interest to the area's Asian community. *The Asian Reporter* features at least three regular opinion columns and frequently profiles notable Asian personalities, including local and visiting artists, writers, and political activists. Besides featuring a variety of carefully selected wire

stories, the newspaper provides in-depth coverage of issues related to schools, family, human rights, and culture. The "Arts, Culture, and Entertainment Calendar" lists and describes almost every noteworthy Asian event—be it theater, cultural fair, film festival, or art/photo exhibit—that comes to town.

Beaverton Valley Times
6975 S.W. Sandburg Rd., 2nd Floor, Tigard
(503) 684–0360

Formerly the *Valley Times*, this community newspaper, dating to the early 1950s, has a circulation of approximately 18,000. It covers news, sports, and livability issues affecting Beaverton and its surrounding environs. It is distributed on Thursdays.

The Business Journal of Portland
851 S.W. 6th Ave.
(503) 274–8733
www.bizjournals.com/portland

Part of the nationwide *Business Journal* chain that includes thirty-nine newspapers, the *Business Journal of Portland* was founded in 1984 and is owned by Advance Publications Inc., which also owns *The Oregonian*. The *BJ*, as it is called, underwent huge changes when Mike Consol took the reigns as publisher in 1997. The editorial staff has been completely replaced and the coverage of the paper has broadened to include much more in-depth reporting of nonprofit agencies and environmental and social issues. No longer just concerned with how businesses can improve their bottom line, *The Business Journal's* editorials have taken large corporations to task for relying heavily on local government for tax cuts and has spoken out against other forms of corporate welfare. They have also championed causes unpopular with the business community—particularly startling was their endorsement of a ballot measure banning clear cutting, a measure that was strongly opposed by a good many of their readers and advertisers. This public stance was all but unthinkable a few years ago, and although the

paper took a good deal of heat, the editors did not back down.

Catholic Sentinel
5536 N.E. Hassalo St.
(503) 281–1191
www.sentinel.org

Founded in 1870, the *Catholic Sentinel* is the oldest Catholic publication on the entire West Coast. A tabloid with a circulation of approximately 16,200, it covers the local, regional, and national news of interest to the region's Catholic community. The *Sentinel* is the official publication for the Archdiocese of Portland, which encompasses 29,717 square miles and extends from the summit of the Cascade Mountains in western Oregon to the Pacific Ocean. It's owned and operated by the Oregon Catholic Press of Portland, which is a large publisher of religious books and liturgical materials.

El Hispanic News
2130 S.W. 5th, #5
(503) 228–3139
www.hispnews.com

This well-designed weekly is dedicated to the service of the Hispanic and Spanish speaking communities of the Northwest, as well as relevant national news. The paper has pages dedicated to opinion, religion, education, health, and local news.

The Jewish Review
506 S.W. 6th Ave., Ste. 606
(503) 227–7464
www.jewishreview.org

Serving Oregon and southwest Washington since 1959, this twice-a-month tabloid is published by the Jewish Federation of Portland and features a wide range of national, international, regional, and local news articles and features. *The Review* covers political and sociological issues, features a number of syndicated columns, and regularly reviews adult and children's books. Its calendar provides a good overview of the seminars, concerts, plays, and other events that are of special interest to the Jewish community.

Just Out
P.O. Box 14400 Portland,
OR 97293-0400
(503) 236–1252
www.justout.com

This free, twice-monthly tabloid covers current events and social-political issues affecting the area's gay and lesbian community. The staff regularly reports on the Oregon State Legislature as well as on national issues. The seventeen-year-old publication also features sections containing news briefs gathered from other states and from around the globe. In each issue *Just Out* runs a comprehensive calendar, including everything from theater and chamber music events to gay roller-skating parties and discussion groups.

The Portland Alliance
2807 S.E. Stark St.
(503) 239–4991

Founded in 1981 and published by the Northwest Alliance for Alternative Media and Education, *The Alliance* focuses on social, political, and environmental advocacy and reports on a wide spectrum of human rights issues. This progressive, alternative, local news monthly also features a comprehensive calendar of events ranging from peace rallies to union-organizing sessions. The newspaper's 21,000 copies are distributed throughout the Portland Metro area by the small but hardworking and versatile group of volunteers that make the *Alliance* tick.

Portland Mercury
1524 N.W. 23rd Ave. Ste. #2, Portland
(503) 294–0840
www.portlandmercury.com

A brand new kid on the block, this irreverent weekly hit the deck running in 2000 with a sassy editorial tone that many Portlanders find refreshing. In addition to a sizeable investigatory article in each issue, knowledgeable coverage of the local music scene, CD takes, and pithy film reviews, the paper offers columns by staffers on books, television, restaurants, and the hilarious advice to the love-torn by notorious Dan Savage.

Portland Observer
4747 N.E. Martin Luther King Jr. Blvd.
(503) 288–0033
www.newsatportlandobserver.com

Portland's oldest and largest newspaper serving the African-American community, the *Observer* was founded in 1971, and covers a broad range of issues. Its readership of 30,000 includes part of the Hispanic community, as the *Observer* has been printing a Spanish edition of the paper for the last couple of years. It's distributed on Wednesdays throughout the Portland and Vancouver Metro areas.

Insiders' Tip

The Portland Press Club, according to local journalist Gregory Nokes, was established in 1901, endured Prohibition, and closed in the mid-'50s. It interviewed notable visitors such as Eleanor Roosevelt and Ronald Reagan and featured strippers, including Tempest Storm, to entertain the reporters.

Longtime publisher Joyce Washington has recently passed away, but the family is carrying on the tradition with her son, Chuck Washington, who now guides the newspaper.

The Skanner
415 N. Killingsworth St.
(503) 285-5555
www.theskanner.com

Founded in 1975, *The Skanner* covers the news, politics, and events affecting Portland's African-American community, with a good amount of ink devoted to the family, education, and livability issues of North and Northeast Portlanders. *The Skanner* has won a host of regional and national journalism awards and in 1996 received the Northwest Family Business Award for the small family business of the year. In 1987, The Skanner News Group published its first Seattle edition; today the combined papers have fifteen employees and a readership of approximately 75,000. In addition to its regular publication, *The Skanner* prints a half-dozen special issues each year, including a black history edition in February, a career guide in June, a minority business enterprise edition in October, and a holiday issue in December.

Willamette Week
822 S.W. 10th Ave.
(503) 243-2122
www.wweek.com

Founded in 1974 by Ron Buel as an alternative newspaper, *Willamette Week* (WW) has grown in size to a circulation of 80,000 and is distributed Wednesdays throughout the Portland Metro area (and well beyond) at stores, restaurants, coffee shops, and microbrew pubs. This free weekly tabloid has evolved into an upscale publication geared towards a sophisticated audience.

At times more recognized for its in-depth coverage of the local arts and entertainment scene and its personal ads, *Willamette Week* is—and always has been—a serious newsmagazine, and it takes its role as public watchdog—particularly in coverage of environmental and public utility issues—quite seriously. It was the first newspaper in Oregon to challenge the use of nuclear power and an early *WW* investigative piece about the Oregon Liquor Control Commission resulted in the agency chief's resigning. But even as *WW* was winning national acclaim for its journalism, financially it was floundering. Its 1977 purchase by the *Register-Guard*—Eugene's daily newspaper—helped some, but not enough. Then, in 1983, Richard Meeker and Mark Zusman purchased the publication. Meeker, who became publisher, had worked for the paper as a reporter after completing law school in 1974 and served as editor for several years. Zusman, who earned a Master's degree in journalism at the University of Oregon and apprenticed under Jack Anderson in Washington, D.C., became editor. The two men built up the business end, nearly doubled *WW's* press run, distributed the paper free throughout the Portland area, and in 1995 moved from Old Town into their improved new headquarters across from the central branch of the Multnomah County Library. The good times haven't blunted *WW's* flair for provocative investigative reporting and it continues to nearly sweep the statewide journalism awards although there is some complaint that *WW* has grown out of its radical history to snuggle closer to the middle of the road.

Watch for *WW's* "Best of Portland" issue in July; it covers everything from the best drinking fountain to the best elevator in town—and is a scream. *Willamette Week* also publishes an extensive voter's guide in election years as well as annual guides describing the area's best restaurants and brewpubs, which are lively, well written, and informative.

Office of Willamette Week, *a well-established alternative newspaper to the daily* Oregonian.

Monthlies, Bimonthlies, and Quarterlies

The Bear Deluxe
P.O. Box 10342 Portland, 97296
(503) 242–1047
www.orlo.org/beardeluxe

Formerly known as *The Bear Essential*, the new and improved *Bear Deluxe* is a lively literary and environmental magazine. Printed quarterly by the Orlo Foundation, which uses the arts to explore current environmental issues, this eclectic publication includes a variety of investigative reporting, interviews, essays, poetry, and fiction, and is primarily devoted to nature and conservation issues. The magazine is distributed throughout the western states.

Christian News Northwest
P.O. Box 974, Newberg
(503) 537–9220
www.cnnw.com

This monthly newspaper serves the evangelical Christian community throughout Portland, Salem, Vancouver, Eugene, Bend, and large areas of western and central Oregon and southwest Washington. *Christian News Northwest* has a monthly circulation of 28,000 and is available free at bookstores, coffeeshops, churches, Christian book and supply stores, and other locations throughout the region. Mail subscriptions are $20 per year in the United States and $25 elsewhere. The newspaper is published by Christian News Northwest Ministries Inc., a nonprofit corporation and is a member of the national Christian Newspaper Association.

Community Newspapers

The Hollywood Star
2000 N.E. 42nd Ave.
(503) 282–9392

One of the older and better-established community newspapers in town, *The Hollywood Star* does a solid job of covering the news happenings and people of central Northeast Portland, including the Hollywood, Alameda, Grant Park, Rose City Park, and Madison neighborhoods. The Star, which is printed at the beginning of each month, has changed hands several times over the years, and Mary De Hart, the owner since 1994, has expanded its circulation to 23,000, which is distributed by mail and newsstands. The focus is on community news, new businesses, and neighborhood livability issues.

The Mid-County Memo
4052 N.E. 22nd Ave.
(503) 287–8904

Founded fifteen years ago, this monthly tabloid reports on the news, events, and personalities in outer Northeast Portland, from 82nd Avenue west to 155th Avenue and from Stark Street north to Sandy Boulevard. *The Memo*, with a circulation of about 15,000, focuses on neighborhood concerns and on livability issues like education and crime, and also features profiles of small businesses and people who are making a difference in the Gateway and Parkrose Districts as well as covering several other smaller mid-county neighborhoods.

The Northwest Examiner
2066 N.W. Irving St.
(503) 241–2353

As far as monthly community newspapers go, *The Northwest Examiner*, founded in 1986, is in a class by itself. It tackles controversial issues and isn't afraid of offending advertisers or business interests: Instead of the typical puff pieces about cronies and business supporters, it is full of hard news, unusual feature articles, and offers a well thought-out editorial column that addresses current neighborhood issues. Recently editor Allen Clausen started a new section covering the bustling Pearl District. It also does a nice job of describing the restaurants, pubs, bistros, and other businesses on lively 21st and 23rd Avenues. *The Exam-*

Insiders' Tip

If you hike or bike to the summit of Mt. Tabor at the east end of S.E Hawthorne, you'll encounter a statue of Harvey Scott, editor of *The Oregonian* from 1865 to 1910. Scott, with his arm stretched out and finger pointed accusingly at the objects of his editorial wrath, once said "write so the hod carrier will understand you."

iner's 14,000 circulation is distributed throughout the Northwest District and nearby surrounding areas.

The Southeast Examiner
P.O. Box 14791, Portland, OR
(503) 234–1770
www.southeastexaminer.com

Founded as the *Sunnyside Up News* in 1990 and once a sister publication to *The Northwest Examiner*, this monthly tabloid is now independently owned. *The Examiner* covers news from inner Southeast Portland, including the Industrial District, the booming Hawthorne District, and the emerging Belmont and Division Streets all the way out to 82nd Avenue. With a circulation of 20,000, of which 15,000 are home delivered, its coverage area extends roughly from Burnside Street south to Foster Road. *The Southeast Examiner* reports on a wide range of topics with a focus on neighborhood issues, arts and music, food, and history.

The Sellwood Bee
P.O. Box 82127,
Portland, OR 97282-0217
(503) 232–2326

One of Portland's oldest community newspapers, *The Sellwood Bee* serves the Eastmoreland, Westmoreland, Sellwood, Brooklyn, and Reed neighborhoods in inner Southeast Portland. The focus of

this monthly publication is news coverage of the events and people that impact the local community. The Pamplin Corporation recently acquired the paper.

St. Johns Review
8525 N. Lombard, Ste. 5
(503) 283–5086

Dating to 1904, this biweekly, with a circulation of 3,500, reports on the news, issues, and personalities affecting North Portland and the St. Johns community. The *St. Johns Review* is distributed by mail and is also available at about forty drop sites in local neighborhoods.

Special Publications

Street Roots
1231 S.W. Morrison St.
(503) 228–5657
www.streetroot.org
www.poorpeopleguide.org (resources)

Formerly known as *The Burnside Cadillac*, this small, lively monthly newspaper gives voice to the homeless while addressing issues relating to homelessness, including health and survival. *Street Roots*, which is published the first of every month, contains news stories, columns, and editorials and 14,000 copies are distributed throughout downtown Portland. Recently, they announced that they were taking poetry submissions if poets submitted a blanket with their poems.

Magazines

Cascadia Times
25-6 N.W. 23rd Pl., # 406
(503) 223–9036

Experienced environmental writers Kathie Durbin and Paul Koberstein head up this twenty- to twenty-four-page tabloid that is published ten times a year. Both worked as reporters for *The Oregonian* and now use their investigative reporting skills to provide comprehensive coverage of natural resource and conservation issues. Founded in 1994, *Cascadia Times* is distributed from San Francisco to Alaska (although its primary audience is

in Oregon and Washington) and its circulation varies from 10,000 to 12,000.

NW Palate Magazine
P.O. Box 10860, Portland, OR
(503) 224–6039
www.nwpalate.com

This bimonthly, glossy, consumer magazine focuses on gourmet food, wine, entertainment, and travel in the Pacific Northwest. *N.W. Palate*, which was started as a wine newsletter fifteen years ago by owner/publisher/editor Cameron Nagel, is still independently owned and has now built its circulation to 45,000 with readers in all fifty states and Europe—most concentrated in Washington and Oregon.

Oregon Business Magazine
610 S.W. Broadway, Ste. 200
(503) 223–0304

Founded in 1981, owned by MEDIAmerica Inc., and with a circulation of 20,200, this highly polished publication covers the business scene all over Oregon and southwestern Washington. Longtime editor Kathy Dimond and managing editor Shirleen Holt both left in late 1998, but the publication doesn't seem to have missed a beat under new executive editor Gillian Floren. Issues regularly contain investigative business reporting, small business articles, profiles of unique people and their companies, and section pieces ranging from transportation issues and electronic commerce to education. The continuing focus of the magazine is helping large and small businesses identify and solve problems. Each year *Oregon Business* publishes special editions, which cover the fastest growing companies in Oregon and the one hundred best companies to work for.

Portland Living
P.O. Box 40205, Portland, OR 97240
(503) 522–511
www.portlandmag.com

With a circulation of around 26,000, *Portland Living* (formerly *Portland Food and Home*) writes about the lifestyles of interesting Portlanders, community events, fine dining, food and wine, and travel around the Pacific Northwest. Founded in 1993 by owner, publisher, and editor Susan Stringer, *Portland Living* is distributed ten times a year throughout the Portland and Salem areas in Oregon, and throughout the Vancouver area in Washington.

Senior Lifestyles
10555 S.E. 82nd Ave., Ste. 200
(503) 652–701

Published by 4-D Publishing Inc., *Senior Lifestyles* covers issues and topics of concern to seniors of all walks of life. Besides regular legislative updates, features cover topics such as health insurance, investment advice, health and wellness, and travel. *Senior Lifestyles* offers a blend of local and national articles and also provides information about classes, jobs, and volunteer opportunities that are available to the elderly in the Portland area. The magazine regularly profiles interesting seniors and special issues focus on topics such as gardening and home improvement, retirement guides, and RV vacations and travel tips.

Portland Family Magazine
P.O. Box 33136, Portland, OR 97292
(503) 255–3286

This slender and wholesome-as-apple-pie magazine offers useful information for all concerned parents. Besides tackling serious issues such as education, health and wellness, and child development, *Portland Family* keeps a calendar of events listing and describing events and fun activities that parents and their kids can enjoy together. A handsomely designed monthly with short readable stories and blurbs, *PFM* includes a column, "School Notes," with the latest info on education and "The Spirit of Giving," a guide for families, organizations, and individuals in need. A good resource for families, *PFM* is distributed throughout the Portland and Vancouver areas.

Portland Parent
P.O. Box 80040, Portland, OR 97280
(503) 638–1049

This user-friendly guide for new and/or expectant parents offers a variety of thoughtful articles pertaining to the overall well-being of children. Besides offering an extensive calendar of events, *Portland Parent* regularly features a directory for new parents that includes a wide assortment of support groups and resources for special needs children. "Going Places," the monthly calendar, is jam packed with all kinds of stuff, ranging from children's theater to carnivals, concerts, and special exhibits that are geared towards the whole family.

Puncture Magazine
P.O. Box 14806, Portland, OR 97293
(503) 232–1649
www.puncturemagazine.com

This independently owned and published quarterly consumer magazine covers the national and international alternative rock music scene as well as popular culture issues. Founded in 1982, *Puncture Magazine's* paid circulation now exceeds 11,000. It's available at many bookstores and newsstands.

Television

The Portland Metro area is home to a half-dozen major television affiliates, all competing fiercely for their slice of the demographic pie. To pump up their viewing audience, a couple of stations have plastered their talking heads on MAX trains and Tri-Met buses, but it's still a tight race with no station outdistancing the others in Nielsen ratings. KGW, however, led all Portland TV stations in 1999 Northwest Regional Emmy Awards, with five Emmys. KOIN earned three and KPTV one.

In keeping with a national trend, local stations have increased their news coverage and have begun offering more than the traditional half-hour news reports on Saturday and Sunday evenings. Now you can catch the news morning, noon, and night. This attempt to increase audience size seems to be working. Because of its additional newscasts throughout the day, KGW's Sunday evening newscasts now draw more viewers than any other local newscasts, including weeknight newscasts.

The use of helicopters to report news and traffic conditions during the morning and evening commutes is another national media phenomenon, but here in Portland the stations have expanded the role of these whirlybirds. A good example is KOIN's chopper pilot/reporter Warren Petrie, who is not only a good pilot but also an excellent reporter. During the summer of 1999, he was reporting on a lost hiker in the Columbia Gorge when he actually spotted the stranded adventurer and beamed images of the frantically waving hiker long before the search-and-rescue team even knew he was found. As with many other aspects of modern life, Portland's media seems to be in the forefront, breaking new ground and playing the role of trailblazer.

Speaking of blazers, one pay-to-view TV series that has held its audience through the years is BlazerVision, televised play-by-play, hoop-to-hoop coverage of local basketball games pitting Portland's NBA team against out-of-town guys. Those who are social and want to root for the team with other fans, usually find their way to the many sports bars throughout "Rip City."

Two other television traditions we can always count on here in Portland: weather people hunched over in the rain, snow, or sleet, clad in Gore-Tex and clutching mikes as they report on slick road conditions and river flood potential. The other yearly field duty is cheerfully tackled by TV personalities who chat, converse, admire, and expound as they cover the Rose Festival Parade (the second largest parade in the country).

Major TV Affiliates

KATU-TV Channel 2 (ABC)
2153 N.E. Sandy Blvd.
(503) 231–4222
www.katu.com

This ABC affiliate was the first to get a Web site. Its slogan, "The Power of 2," refers to their number on the dial and to a pair of weather and traffic choppers hovering over the town like two dragonflies. Not only does KATU deliver crisp and clear news reports, it also hosts a Town Hall roughly every quarter where citizens get to sound off about issues making headlines. A new feature at KATU is "The Advisory Council," a feedback loop in which viewers get a chance to talk about programming they love or hate. To participate, call (503) 872–2949, or if out of town, call (800) 777–KATU.

KGW-TV Channel 8 (NBC)
1501 S.W. Jefferson St.
(503) 226–5000
www.kgw.com

This NBC affiliate is one of the first stations in the U.S. to offer 24-hour live news on its website. Perhaps the most flamboyant of all the local stations, it seems to have the biggest news staff. Maff Zaffino, an affable weather guy, is also a ski buff who briefs fellow snow sportsters about conditions up in the Cascade Mountains. Another popular show is KGW's Unit 8, a consumer hotline that sends investigators out to find out who's scamming seniors, adding bogus charges to your phone bill, or charging the government big bucks for sub-standard housing.

KOIN-TV Channel 6 (CBS)
222 S.W. Columbia Dr.
(503) 464–0600
www.koin.com

This pioneer broadcasting operation began as a radio station in 1925, sending out a signal from a single room in the Portland Hotel. By 1930, KOIN was Portland's CBS affiliate and on October 15, 1953, KOIN-TV signed on as Portland's first VHF television station and as an affiliate of the CBS Television Network. KOIN was the first station in Portland to broadcast a one-hour newscast at 5 P.M. Currently, KOIN is in the KOIN Tower, an easily recognizable landmark in downtown Portland.

KOPB-TV Channel 10 (PBS)
7140 S.W. Macadam Ave.
(503) 244–9900
www.opb.org

The Oregon Public Broadcasting station started in 1922 as an engineering professor's fifty-watt transmitter. KOPB now serves the entire state and a portion of

southwest Washington as the affiliate for PBS and a venue for local issue-driven and cultural programs.

KPTV-TV Channel 12 (United Paramount)
211 S.E. Caruthers
(503) 230–1200
www.oregon12.com

This TV station in Portland was launched in 1952. It is the local affiliate for the United Paramount Network and the nation's first laboratory for digital-to-air technology. It's also known for its independent, quirky broadcasting like the popular *Good Day, Oregon,* which might feature taking your dog on a hike through the snow, how to braise chicken legs, or what's the latest hot exhibit for kids at the Oregon Museum of Science and Industry (OMSI). KPTV also gets viewer points for airing the ten o'clock news an hour earlier than most late-night newscasts.

KPDX-TV Channel 49 (FOX)
14975 N.W. Greenbriar Pkwy., Beaverton
(503) 548–4949
www.kpdx.com

The only local programming on KPTV, the local FOX affiliate, is a news program at 10 P.M. But those who watch FOX's "tabloid television" to catch the goofy pratfalls and dangerous dangles by the adventurous network don't seem disappointed at the lack of local shows.

The headquarters of KPTV (Channel 12), the local UPN affiliate and the oldest TV station in Portland.

Radio Stations

Portland is a town brimming with music lovers, querulous sorts who enjoy debating hot issues over the air and commuters keeping an ear on traffic conditions. All of them can find their niche on the local radio dial. Unlike Nashville or Dallas, Portland doesn't lean toward country, but there are plenty of boot-scootin' tunes; and since we've grown beyond Northwest grunge, there is a multiplicity of sounds, from reggae to baroque, from alternative rock to Celtic folk music. We Portlanders also like talk shows but they aren't dominating the regional airwaves. In brief, there is plenty of radio to go around. Here is a quick look at a few of the most popular radio stations in the Portland/Vancouver area. Then we will list a few more on the dial and what ears they're aimed at.

KBOO/90.7 FM
20 S.E. 8th Ave.
(503) 231–8032
www.kboo.org

The call letters KBOO were chosen because the gang organizing the station decided to go for it on Halloween, 1963; they were on the air the following June. The local Pacifica Affiliate, it is dedicated to innovative programming, including classical, rock, and folk. In the early '80s, KBOO broadened its commitment to multicultural programming by adding Spanish, Asian-American, and African-American musical shows.

KINK/102 FM
1501 S.W. Jefferson St.
(503) 241–1020
www.kink102.com

A popular station for thirty years, KINK is home base for local baby boomers who enjoy aging rockers, folksingers, and jazz artists as well as new releases by contemporary popsters. A late-night hit is *Lights Out,* during which mellow instrumentals lull listeners to sleep. The next morning, *The Morning Show* features Les Sarnoff and Mike Rich, a couple of laid-back DJs who describe themselves as pseudo-celebrities. Rich did achieve actual status when he wrote the screenplay for *Finding Forrester,* a box-office hit. The two often invite local and visiting performers to perform their latest hits live from the KINK studio. The station also hosts the KINK Performance Lounge, which holds up to forty listeners of national as well as Portland musicians.

KFXX/910 AM
0700 S.W. Bancroft Rd.
(503) 223–1441
www.kfxx.com

This sports and news station delivers the play-by-play for local prep and college sports and also covers regional and national athletic events.

KUIK/1360 AM
3855 N.E. Cornell Rd., Hillsboro
(503) 640–1360
www.kuik.com

Another notch on the dial where you can catch sports and sports news as well as general news and talk shows twenty-four hours a day.

KBPS/89.9 FM & 1450/AM
515 N.E. 15th Ave.
(503) 916–5828
www.allclassical.org

This is a classical music station with a broad view of what is classical. In *Age of the Organ,* KBPS offers music for organ, trumpet, and English horn; in *Northwest Previews,* the station presents previews of performances by the Oregon Symphony and Portland State University recitals. This station is partially run by Benson Public School students.

KEWS/620 AM
4949 S.W. Macadam Ave.
(503) 802–2620

KEWS is a talk-show station offering a chance to sit in, listen, or lunge for your phone when you can't take it any longer.

The slant is toward the right side of issues.

KKRZ/100 FM
4949 S.W. Macadam Ave.
(503) 226–0100
www.z100portland.com

This station, known as Z-100, has been No. 1 in the local ratings competition for the past few years because of the wide appeal of its contemporary hits format.

KMHD/89.1 FM
26000 S.E. Stark St., Gresham
(503) 661–8900

"The Jazz Station" since its start in 1984, KMHD is operated by Mt. Hood Community College in nearby Gresham. With an extensive library of over 6,000 LPs and CDs, KMHD plays a full spectrum of jazz artists ranging from Ella Fitzgerald to Miles Davis to Horace Silver.

KNRK/94.7 FM
432 N.E. 74th Ave.
(503) 252–0792

Portland's boldest champion of new rock stretches the envelope of alternative music with live broadcasts from local rock venues as well as a steady bill of edgy tunes.

KOPB/91.5 FM
7140 S.W. Macadam Ave.
(503) 293–1905
www.opb.org

The local spot on the dial for National Public Broadcasting, KOPB will connect you to the *Prairie Home Companion*, the Irish show, *Thistle and Shamrock*, and *Alternative Radio*, a controversial news show, as well as local talk shows and a lecture program called *City Club of Portland*.

FM Stations

Adult Contemporary

K103 FM
500 S.W. Macadam Ave.
www.k103.com
(503) 222–5103
www.kio3.com

Classic Rock

KGON/92.3 FM
0700 S.W. Bancroft Rd.
(503) 733–5466
www.kgon.com

Smooth Jazz

KKJZ/106.7 FM
222 S.W. Columbia, Ste. 350
(503) 223–0590
www.kkjz.com

Alternative/Progressive

KRRC/104.1
(Reed College) 3203 S.E. Woodstock Blvd.
(503) 771–2180
www.krrc.com

Album Rock 'n' Roll

KUFO/101 FM
2040 S.W. 1st Ave.
www.kufo.com

Hip-Hop

KXL/95.5 FM
0234 S.W. Bancroft Rd.
(503) 417–9595
www.kxl.com

AM Stations

Urban Contemporary

KBMS/1480 AM
601 Main St., Vancouver
(503) 222–1491
www.kbms.com

Business News

KBNP/1410 AM
811 S.W. Naito Pkwy., Ste. 420
(503) 223–6769
www.kbnp.com

News and Information

KEX/1190 AM
4949 S.W. Macadam Ave.
(503) 225–1190
www.kex.com

Religious

KKSL/1290 AM
4700 S.W. Macadam Ave.
(503) 242–1290
www.kksl.com

Christian Music

KPAM/860 AM
10209 S.E. Division St.
(503) 251–1277

Christian Talk

KKPZ/1330 AM
4700 S.W. Macadam Ave.
(503) 242–1950
www.kkpz.com

Talk Radio

KGUY/1010 AM
6035 S.E. Milwaukie Blvd.
www.guytalk.net
(503) 235–1010

FM & AM Stations

Hard Rock

KISN/97 FM and 910 AM
888 S.W. 5th Ave.
(503) 226–9791
www.kism.com

Country Music

KUPL/98.7 FM and 970 AM
222 S.W. Columbia Dr., Ste. 350
(503) 733–5000
www.kupl.com

New Country

KWJJ/99.5 FM and 1080 AM
2000 S.W. 1st Ave.
(503) 223–2582
www.kwjj.com

Index

Portland International Film Festival, 246

Portland International Performance Festival, 259

Portland International Raceway, 349

Portland Juggling Festival, 249

Portland Living, 482

Portland Lo/Op, 268

Portland Lutheran School, 411

Portland Marathon, 266–67

Portland Meadows, 353

Portland Mercury, 477

Portland Nursery, 174

Portland Observer, 477–78

Portland Opera, 287

Portland Oregon Visitors Association, 246

Portland Parent, 482–83

Portland Parks and Recreation Community Centers, 460

Portland Pendleton Shop, 173

Portland River Company, 305–6

Portland Rock Gym, 306

Portland Rose Festival, 253

Portland's Alternative Realtors, 398

Portland Saturday Market, 230, 247

Portland Scottish Highland Games, 259

Portland Speedway Auto Racing, 349

Portland State University, 419

Portland Steak and Chop House, 91

Portland Taiko, 294

Portland Timbers, 353

Portland Trailblazers, The, 350–51

Portland Travelodge Suites, 75

Portland Tribune, 475

Portland United Mountain Peddlers (PUMP), 298

Portland Vintage Trolley, 202–3

Portland Waldorf School, 411–12

Portland Wheelmen Touring Club, 298

Portland White House, 61

Portland Winter Hawks, 352

Portland Youth Philharmonic, 283

Pottery Paint Box, 238

Powell Butte Nature Park, 330–31

Powell Butte Nature Park Trail System, 301

Powell's City of Books, 168–69, 235, 282

Powell's Travel Store, 169

Preservation Hall, 164

Pride Northwest, 253

private elementary schools, 404–5

private high schools, 407–8

private middle schools, 406

private multigrade schools, 409–12

Produce Row Cafe, 106, 150

Project Linkage, 464

Providence Portland Medical Center, 439

Providence St. Vincent Medical Center, 436–37

Prudential Northwest Properties, 400

public elementary school programs, 403–4

public high school programs, 407

public middle school programs, 406

public multigrade schools, 409

Publisher's Cafe, 118

pubs

    North/Northeast Portland, 150–51

    Southeast Portland, 149–50

    Southwest Portland, 149

    Vancouver, Washington, 151–52

Pumpkin Ridge, 344–45

Puncture Magazine, 483

Q

Quail Valley, 345

Quintana Galleries, 293

R

Raccoon Lodge, 122–23

radio stations, 486–88

Radisson Hotel Portland, 77

rafting, 304–6

Rajeff Fly Fishing School, 308–10

Ram's Head, The, 125

RAW, the Reed Arts Weekend, 246

RD Steeves Imports, 15, 182

Reading Frenzy, 169

real estate

    alternative housing, 394

    apartments, 392–94

    average house prices, 373

    buying new *vs.* used, 386–92

    condominiums, 392

    help for first-time buyers, 395–96

    North/Northeast Portland, 383–85, 399–400

    Northwest Portland, 382

    outlying areas, 385–86, 400

About the Authors

Rachel Dresbeck

Rachel Dresbeck, a writer and editor, has observed and written about Portland for a variety of publications, including *Willamette Week* and citysearch.com. She is also an author of *The Insiders' Guide to the Oregon Coast*. She was educated at Whitman College and the University of Oregon, and taught writing and literature at Portland Community College and the University of Oregon. She lives with her husband and daughters in the Richmond neighborhood of Portland, Oregon, where she studies the ways in which citizens sustain their civility and community spirit against all odds.

Dave Johnson

Dave Johnson, co-author of *The Insiders' Guide to the Oregon Coast*, is a native Oregonian who has worked as a journalist and freelance writer for more than thirty years. His articles have appeared in many Pacific Northwest newspapers and magazines, including *The Oregonian*, *Willamette Week*, *Eugene Weekly*, *Daily Columbian*, *Oregon Coast*, *Oregon Parks*, *Northwest Palate*, *Journeys*, *Northwest Examiner*, *Historic Properties*, and *The Ruralite*. Also, he contributed a chapter on U.S. Highway 26 in *Road Trip USA* and contributed the Eastern Oregon section for *The Oregon Handbook* published by Moon Publications.

While growing up in Oregon, Johnson fished, hiked, camped, and explored much of the Pacific Northwest. This early knowledge of the woods, rivers, lakes, and coastline of the region has contributed to his expertise as a travel and recreation writer. Since his move to Portland in 1993, he has also used his urban know-how while working as the arts and entertainment editor of the *Southeast Examiner*, a monthly newspaper serving neighborhoods in Southeast Portland, and as an arts editor for *The Asian Reporter*, a monthly published for the Asian-American community in the Portland Metro area. He is married to poet Josephine Bridges and lives in a 1912 bungalow in the historic Brooklyn neighborhood of Southeast Portland.